MANPOWER SERVICES COMMISSION

Classification of Occupations and Directory of Occupational Titles

VOLUME 3

Definitions of Production Occupations

LONDON: HER MAJESTY'S STATIONERY OFFICE

HER MAJESTY'S STATIONERY OFFICE

Government Bookshops

49 High Holborn, London WC1V 6HB
13a Castle Street, Edinburgh EH2 3AR
41 The Hayes, Cardiff CF1 1JW
Brazennose Street, Manchester M60 8AS
Southey House, Wine Street, Bristol BS1 2BQ
258 Broad Street, Birmingham B1 2HE
80 Chichester Street, Belfast BT1 4JY
Government publications are also available through booksellers

ISBN 0 11 885306 6*

First published 1972
Fourth impression 1978

This publication is a reprint without any textual amendment of a document previously published under the auspices of the Department of Employment.

CONTENTS

MAJOR GROUP XI

Farming, Fishing and Related Occupations

Workers in this major group cultivate and harvest crops and trees, breed, tend and train animals and catch, gather and breed fish and other aquatic life.

The occupations are arranged in the following minor groups:

50 Farming, Horticultural, Forestry and Related Occupations

51 Fishing and Related Occupations

Minor Group 50 FARMING, HORTICULTURAL, FORESTRY AND RELATED OCCUPATIONS

Workers in this minor group cultivate and harvest field and other crops, breed, tend and train animals, perform forestry work and carry out closely related activities.

The occupations are arranged in the following unit groups:

500 Foremen (Farming, Horticultural, Forestry and Related Occupations)

501 Farm Workers (Arable and Mixed Farming)

502 Animal Tending and Breeding Occupations

503 Horticultural Workers

504 Gardeners and Groundsmen

505 Agricultural Machinery Operators

506 Tree Cultivating and Harvesting Occupations

509 Farming, Horticultural, Forestry and Related Occupations Not Elsewhere Classified

Unit Group 500 Foremen (Farming, Horticultural, Forestry and Related Occupations)

Workers in this unit group directly supervise and co-ordinate the activities of workers in farming, horticultural, forestry and related occupations.

500.10 Foreman (arable crop workers)

Directly supervises and co-ordinates the activities of arable crop workers

Performs appropriate tasks as described under SUPERVISOR/FOREMAN (UNSPECIFIED) (990.00) and in addition implements decisions on behalf of management on matters such as: type and amount of crops to be grown and areas to be planted; the selection and purchase of seeds, fertilisers and other essentials.

May (01) keep cost and production records

(02) drive trucks to transport workers and supplies

(03) plan and schedule ploughing, planting, cultivating and harvesting operations.

Additional factor: number of workers supervised.

500.20 Foreman (mixed farming workers)

Directly supervises and co-ordinates the activities of mixed farming workers

Performs appropriate tasks as described under SUPERVISOR/FOREMAN (UNSPECIFIED) (990.00) and in addition implements decisions on behalf of management on matters such as: pairing livestock for breeding purposes; selecting livestock for sale; buying or selling crops.

May (01) perform tasks such as keeping cost, production and breeding records.

Additional factor: number of workers supervised.

500 .30 Foreman (farm livestock workers)

Directly supervises and co-ordinates the activities of farm livestock workers

Performs appropriate tasks as described under SUPERVISOR/FOREMAN (UNSPECIFIED) (990 .00) and in addition implements decisions on behalf of management on matters such as: milk and egg production; basic and supplementary feed requirements; breeding and rearing livestock; selecting and pairing livestock for breeding purposes; selecting livestock for sale.

May (01) keep cost, production and breeding records
(02) attend shows to display livestock.

Additional factor: number of workers supervised.

Other titles include Poultry foreman.

500 .40 Foreman (animal workers other than farm livestock workers)

Directly supervises and co-ordinates the activities of animal workers other than farm livestock workers

Performs appropriate tasks as described under SUPERVISOR/FOREMAN (UNSPECIFIED) (990 .00) and in addition implements decisions on behalf of management on matters such as: basic and supplementary feed requirements; tending, breeding, training, and exhibiting of birds, pets and other animals except farm livestock; selecting and pairing animals for breeding purposes; preparing animals for exhibitions.

May (01) keep cost and breeding records
(02) attend shows to display animals.

Additional factor: number of workers supervised.

Other titles include Head keeper (zoo), Overseer (zoo).

500 .50 Foreman (horticultural workers)

Directly supervises and co-ordinates the activities of horticultural workers

Performs appropriate tasks as described under SUPERVISOR/FOREMAN (UNSPECIFIED) (990 .00) and in addition implements decisions on behalf of management on matters such as selecting crops for cultivation and the techniques to be used in production.

May (01) keep cost and production records.

Additional factor: number of workers supervised.

500 .60 Foreman (gardeners and groundsmen)

Directly supervises and co-ordinates the activities of gardeners and groundsmen

Performs appropriate tasks as described under SUPERVISOR/FOREMAN (UNSPECIFIED) (990 .00) and in addition implements decisions on behalf of management on matters such as: selecting particular varieties of plants to be cultivated; arranging for the layout and construction of landscape gardens, paths and driveways.

May (01) keep cost and production records
(02) carry out specialised plant breeding and propagation.

Additional factor: number of workers supervised.

Other titles include Head gardener.

500 .70 Foreman (agricultural machinery operators)

Directly supervises and co-ordinates the activities of agricultural machinery operators

Performs appropriate tasks as described under SUPERVISOR/FOREMAN (UNSPECIFIED) (990 .00) and in addition implements decisions on behalf of management on matters such as: type of machine or equipment to be used; arranging for maintenance of machinery and plant; ordering fuels, lubricants and replacement parts.

May (01) repair and/or supervise repair of machinery.

Additional factor: number of workers supervised.

500 .80 Foreman (tree cultivating and harvesting workers)

Directly supervises and co-ordinates the activities of tree cultivating and harvesting workers

Performs appropriate tasks as described under SUPERVISOR/FOREMAN (UNSPECIFIED) (990 .00) and in addition: decides and marks trees to indicate amount of pruning required and selects and marks mature trees for felling; implements decisions on behalf of management on matters such as: the type of trees to to be planted, the siting of trees, fences, roads and drains and the hiring or requisitioning of equipment and machinery.

May (01) measure standing timber and calculate cubic content
(02) grade felled timber according to quality.

Additional factor: number of workers supervised.

Other titles include Foreman (forestry), Forester (Forestry Commission).

500.98 Trainee

Performs, under instruction or guidance, various tasks including training exercises and as appropriate pursues studies in order to acquire the basic skills and knowledge required to perform the tasks of foremen (farming, horticultural, forestry and related occupations).

500.99 Other foremen (farming, horticultural, forestry and related occupations)

Workers in this group directly supervise and co-ordinate the activities of workers in farming, horticultural, forestry and related occupations and are not elsewhere classified, for example:

(01) **Foremen inseminators.**

Additional factor: number of workers supervised.

Unit Group 501 Farm Workers (Arable and Mixed Farming)

Workers in this unit group carry out tasks in the cultivation of arable crops and in the raising of both arable crops and livestock.

501.10 Agricultural worker (general) (arable crops)

Carries out various tasks by machine and hand in the production and harvesting of crops

Drives tractors and operates other machines and equipment for ploughing, harrowing, sowing seed, fertilising, spraying and otherwise cultivating crops; carries out or assists in carrying out such other tasks as are required in the production, handling and storing of crops.

May (01) service tractor and other farm equipment
(02) maintain and repair farm buildings and equipment
(03) drive lorries to transport workers, supplies and produce
(04) prepare and/or pack crops for sale or shipment
(05) supervise seasonal helpers
(06) lay and maintain agricultural drains (869.18)
(07) carry out hedging and ditching (509.50)
(08) construct and repair dry walls.

Excluded are Agricultural workers (hop-gardens) (501.30), Orchard workers (503.40) and Agricultural machinery operators (505.10)

501.20 Agricultural worker (hand) (arable crops)

Carries out various manual tasks in the production and harvesting of crops

Prepares soil and spreads fertiliser; cultivates growing crops by hoeing, spraying and thinning as necessary; harvests and stores crops; carries out or assists in carrying out various other manual tasks in the production of crops.

May (01) maintain and repair farm buildings and equipment
(02) prepare and/or pack crops for sale or shipment
(03) supervise seasonal helpers
(04) lay and maintain agricultural drains (869.18)
(05) carry out hedging and ditching (509.50)
(06) construct and repair dry walls.

501.30 Agricultural worker (hop gardens)

Carries out tasks in planting, cultivation and picking of hop vines and the picking of hops

Prepares soil and spreads fertiliser; erects poles and wire-work and string; prunes vines and takes out diseased shoots (spiking); replaces diseased vines or plants new garden; cultivates growing crops by hoeing, weeding and spraying as necessary; picks and assists in drying hops.

May (01) drive tractor and operate other machines and equipment (505.10).

501.40 Agricultural worker (mixed farming)

Performs tasks in both the production of arable crops and the care of farm livestock (cattle, sheep, pigs or poultry)

Performs tasks as described under AGRICULTURAL WORKER (GENERAL) (ARABLE CROPS) (501.10) and STOCKMAN (MIXED FARM LIVESTOCK) (502.02).

Note: workers on a mixed farm primarily engaged either in cultivating crops or in rearing livestock should be classified 501.10 or 502.02.

501.98 Trainee

Performs, under instruction or guidance, various tasks including training exercises and as appropriate pursues studies in order to acquire the basic skills and knowledge required to perform the tasks of farm workers (arable and mixed farming).

501.99 Other farm workers (arable and mixed farming)

Workers in this group carry out tasks in the cultivation of arable crops and in the raising of both arable crops and livestock and are not elsewhere classified.

Unit Group 502 Animal Tending and Breeding Occuptions

Workers in this unit group carry out tasks in the breeding, rearing, training, protection, upkeep and exhibition of farm livestock (cattle, sheep, pigs, poultry) and all other animals.

502.02 Stockman (mixed farm livestock)

Performs a variety of tasks in and requiring knowledge of the breeding and rearing of more than one kind of farm livestock (cattle, sheep, pigs, poultry)

Implements breeding policy; mates animals and tends them during birth of young; rears calves and maintains records of breeding progress; weighs and mixes feeding stuffs; feeds and waters livestock; selects suitable grazing; cleans yards and/or animals' quarters to keep them in a hygienic condition; marks animals as necessary for identification; prepares livestock for market and/or shows; treats minor ailments and assists veterinary surgeon as required.

May (01) decide breeding policy
(02) assist with general farm work
(03) drive lorry or tractor
(04) repair and maintain fences
(05) assist with artificial insemination
(06) milk cows (502.99).

Other titles include General farm worker (livestock).

502.04 Cowman

Performs a variety of tasks in and requiring knowledge of the breeding and rearing of dairy cattle

Feeds cows and prepares them for milking; checks for any evidence of disease; attaches milking equipment and disconnects the equipment on completion of milking; cleans milking premises and sterilises equipment; treats minor ailments and assists veterinary surgeon as required.

May (01) decide breeding policy
(02) decide feeding policy
(03) assist with general farm work
(04) record milk yields
(05) drive tractor (505.10)
(06) operate bottle or carton filling and sealing machines.

Other titles include Dairy cowman, Stockman (dairy cattle).

See Milkers (502.99)

502.06 Stockman (beef cattle)

Performs a variety of tasks in and requiring knowledge of the breeding and rearing of beef cattle

Performs tasks as described under STOCKMAN (MIXED FARM LIVESTOCK) (502.02) but specialises in beef cattle.

May (01) drive tractor (505.10).

Other titles include Cattleman, Yardman.

502.08 Stockman (sheep)

Performs a variety of tasks in and requiring knowledge of the breeding and rearing of sheep

Performs tasks as described under STOCKMAN (MIXED FARM LIVESTOCK) (502.02) but specialises in sheep; erects lambing pens and arranges for dipping and shearing.

May (01) shear sheep using hand or power operated clippers
(02) attend auctions and advise farmer on condition of sheep up for sale
(03) train sheep dogs.

Other titles include Shepherd.

502.10 Stockman (pigs)

Performs a variety of tasks in and requiring knowledge of the breeding and rearing of pigs

Performs tasks as described under STOCKMAN (MIXED FARM LIVESTOCK) (502.02) but specialises in pigs; weighs and measures pigs to check progress.

Other titles include Pigman.

502.12 Attendant (domestic or working animals except farm livestock and horses)

Performs a variety of tasks in the breeding, care, training and upkeep of domestic or working animals

Cleans, grooms, trims and exercises animals; prepares food, and feeds and waters charges; cleans animals' quarters and renews bedding as necessary; trains animals for special tasks; prepares animals for shows, races or demonstrations; assists with breeding and rearing of young animals; deals with minor ailments and assists veterinary surgeon as required.

May (01) drive lorry or van to transport animals
(02) attend shows and races to parade charges
(03) skin and butcher carcases for hounds' food.

Additional factor: species or breeds of animal in which specialised.

Other titles include Huntsman, Kennelman, Whipper-in.

502.14 Attendant (wild animals)

Performs a variety of tasks in the care, upkeep and security of wild animals

Prepares food, and feeds and waters charges and checks their health; maintains correct temperature of animal houses; tends minor ailments and nurses sick animals; cleans animals' quarters and renews bedding as necessary; moves animals to and from exercise or display enclosures or into boxes for transportation; carries out minor repairs to animals' quarters and to heating and other ancillary equipment; constantly checks security of charges.

May (01) escort visitors round animals' quarters and answer queries
(02) accompany animals on journeys
(03) assist with the breeding of animals
(04) carry out gardening work
(05) specialise in a particular species of animal.

Other titles include Menagerie keeper, Zoo keeper.

502.16 Attendant (horses)

Performs a variety of tasks in the breeding, care, training and upkeep of horses

Feeds, waters, grooms and exercises horses; breaks and trains young horses; rides racehorses and/or jumps steeplechasers in training; cleans and rebeds stables; cleans saddlery and other equipment; assists veterinary surgeon as required; treats minor ailments.

May (01) travel to race-meetings to tend and guard horses and equipment
(02) drive lorry or car towing a horse box
(03) give riding lessons
(04) parade horses in paddock before races
(05) assist with the mating, breeding and foaling of horses and be known as Stud groom
(06) take stallions to other establishments for mating purposes and be known as Travelling stud groom.

Other titles include Groom, Stablehand.

502.18 Gamekeeper

Breeds, rears and protects game animals and birds on estates and preserves

Incubates eggs and rears game birds in a hatchery; patrols estate or preserve to protect game birds such as pheasant, partridge, grouse, woodcock and wild duck and game animals such as hares and deer from predatory animals and birds, using gun, snare, poison or trap; guards game against poachers and trespassers; controls the burning of heather to encourage new growth for feed; during shooting season sites shooting "butts" and organises beaters.

May (01) train gun dogs
(02) perform duties of GILLIE (479.99)
(03) prepare shot game for market.

502.20 Beekeeper

Rears bees for honey, wax and breeding purposes

Rears queen bees and nucleus stocks; feeds bees according to season with sugar syrup, sugar candy or fondant; treats diseases by fumigation; reduces swarming by adding hive extensions (supers or section racks) to increase space in hives; recovers swarms of bees using control methods such as the Snellgrove system or the Demaree method; removes dead bees and parasites from hives; sterilises hives with chemical solution; extracts honey from honeycombs by machine; prepares honey for market in accordance with regulations of British Standards Institute; salvages wax and renders by melting in hot water; moves hives to selected pastures, as necessary.

May (01) breed special strains of bees
(02) assemble and repair hives and frames.

Additional factors: knowledge of a particular type of honey extraction machine such as 50 frame radial extractor; knowledge of diseases such as foul brood, acarine disease, nosema.

Other titles include Apiarist.

502.22 Mink farm assistant

Performs a variety of tasks involved in breeding mink and preparing mink pelts

Under direction of farm proprietor or manager performs some or all of the following tasks: feeds and waters animals to strict annual dietary programme designed to produce pelts of best size and quality; maintains cleanliness and hygiene of breeding quarters and feeding equipment; arranges for mating according to proprietor's fur production plan; maintains records of pedigrees and breeding data; rehouses grown offspring; assists in vaccination; grades and selects animals for breeding and pelting; kills selected animals; skins carcases; blubbers (removes fat) and dries pelts; maintains buildings, paths and fences of breeding establishment; repairs and constructs cages.

May (01) assist farm manager to select animals for killing.

502.24 Inseminator

Inseminates animals by artificial means

Assists foreman or stockman at a breeding centre in the extraction of semen; dilutes semen with chemicals and prepares for storage; according to daily requirements, selects appropriate semen from store; conveys semen to farms or other establishments and confirms strain of semen to be used; injects animal recipient with semen, using syringe, pipette or catheter; issues certificate giving pedigree details and date of insemination.

May (01) accept cash payments and issue receipts
(02) advise clients on improvement of stock.

Additional factor: whether licensed by Ministry of Agriculture, Fisheries and Food (England) or approved by Department of Agriculture and Fisheries for Scotland.

502.50 Poultryman

Performs a variety of tasks in and requiring knowledge of the hatching, breeding and rearing of poultry and game birds

Feeds and waters stock by hand or automatic means; regulates ventilation in poultry houses, incubators, batteries or breeding units; ensures cleanliness and hygienic condition of housing and equipment.

May (01) collect, wash and pack eggs for market or packing station
(02) specialise in rearing chickens for egg or meat production
(03) specialise in various types of poultry such as ducks, geese or turkeys.

Other titles include Stockman (poultry, game).

502.60 Hatchery worker

Performs tasks in the incubation and hatching of eggs

Tests eggs for fertility; controls the hatching process by maintaining correct temperature and humidity of incubators; packs and supplies chicks for meat or egg production or, in the case of game birds, for preserve.

May (01) determine sex of chicks.

502.98 Trainee

Performs, under instruction or guidance, various tasks including training exercises and as appropriate pursues studies in order to acquire the basic skills and knowledge required to perform the tasks of workers in animal tending and breeding occupations

502.99 Other animal tending and breeding workers

Workers in this group carry out tasks in the care, breeding, rearing, training, protection and exhibition of farm livestock (cattle, sheep, pigs, poultry) and all other animals and are not elsewhere classified, for example:

(01) **Chick sexers** (determine sex of chicks); (02) **Dog trimmers**; (03) **Flock fieldsmen** (advise on egg production for breeding purposes); (04) **Milkers** (milk cows by hand or machine and perform other tasks connected with milk production); (05) **Sheep shearers**.

Unit Group 503 Horticultural Workers

Workers in this unit group carry out tasks in the intensive cultivation of vegetables, plants, trees, shrubs, fruit and flowers in glasshouses, nurseries, market gardens and orchards.

503.10 Glasshouse worker

Cultivates food or horticultural crops in glasshouses

Prepares soil and/or composts in beds or pots using machines such as rotary cultivators where necessary; mixes soil fertilisers and/or organic matter; sterilises soil; sows seed and thins and transplants seedlings; propagates vegetatively, for example by taking cuttings and by grafting and budding; waters plants, controls pests and diseases and growth of plants by means of chemicals; regulates temperature and humidity of glasshouses.

May (01) pick, prepare and pack produce for market (509.90)
(02) specialise in growing a particular crop
(03) specialise in growing plants for amenity or commercial purposes.

Other titles include Propagator.

503.20 Nursery worker (excluding glasshouse worker)

Cultivates trees, shrubs or other plants in a nursery

Prepares soil in fields or outdoor beds by hand or machine; mixes soil, composts, fertilisers and/or organic matter; sterilises soil; feeds and waters plants; controls pests and diseases; propagates plants; plants out and transplants by hand or machine and pots plants for sale; prunes trees or shrubs.

May (01) prepare and pack produce for market (509.90)
(02) sell plants
(03) drive tractor (505.10)
(04) specialise in growing particular plants.

503.30 Market garden worker (excluding glasshouse worker)

Carries out tasks in the intensive cultivation of soft fruit, flowers and vegetables in a market garden

Spreads fertiliser and manure; digs, ploughs, harrows and otherwise prepares the soil using machinery and equipment as necessary; cleans and sterilises the soil for seed beds, boxes and cold-frames; sows seed and propagates plants from seed or by vegetative means, for example cuttings; transplants seedlings, prunes trees and bushes and controls weeds; irrigates crops and controls pests and diseases.

May (01) drive tractor (505.10)
(02) pick, grade and pack produce ready for market (509.90)
(03) drive lorry and deliver produce
(04) pot-up bulbs and plants.

Excluded are Agricultural machinery operators (505.10)

503.40 Orchard worker

Performs a variety of tasks in the planting and cultivation of fruit trees and the harvesting of the fruit

Spreads fertiliser and manure using a tractor; plants, buds, grafts and prunes fruit trees; supports trees by staking and wiring; applies weed killer, fungicidal and insecticidal sprays; thins fruit as required; performs tasks in the harvesting and carting of fruit.

May (01) supervise fruit pickers
(02) erect and maintain fences
(03) cut grass using motor mower
(04) pick, grade and pack fruit (509.90)
(05) drive and operate fork-lift truck.

Other titles include Fruit plantation worker, Fruitman.

503.98 Trainee

Performs, under instruction or guidance, various tasks including training exercises and as appropriate pursues studies in order to acquire the basic skills and knowledge required to perform the tasks of horticultural workers.

503.99 Other horticultural workers

Workers in this group carry out tasks in the intensive cultivation of vegetables, plants, trees, shrubs, fruit and flowers in glasshouses, nurseries and market gardens, parks and similar establishments and are not elsewhere classified, for example:

(01) **Bulb growers**; (02) **Mushroom growers**; (03) **Watercress growers.**

Unit Group 504 Gardeners and Groundsmen

Workers in this unit group carry out tasks in the cultivation of flowers, fruit, shrubs, trees and other plants in public or private gardens (excluding market gardens) and in laying, maintaining and landscaping grassed areas.

504.10 Gardener (public gardens)

Cultivates flowers, trees, shrubs and other plants in parks or public gardens

Prepares soil and plants, transplants, prunes, weeds and otherwise tends plant life in the open; conditions soil for greenhouses, plants seeds and nurtures seedlings for transplanting; sprays plants against disease and pests; maintains lawns. Performs these tasks in relation to public gardens.

May (01) maintain paths, tennis courts and swimming pools
(02) carry out landscaping (504.30)
(03) arrange floral displays for municipal or other occasions
04) use and maintain mechanical equipment (505.10)
(05) pick and pack some produce for market (509.90).

504.20 Gardener (private gardens)

Cultivates flowers, trees, shrubs and other plants in private gardens

Performs tasks as described under GARDENER (PUBLIC GARDENS) (504.10) but in relation to private gardens.

May (01) maintain paths, tennis courts or swimming pool
(02) carry out landscaping (504.30)
(03) arrange floral displays for special occasions
(04) pick and pack some produce for market (509.90)
(05) perform household duties such as stoking boilers and rough painting and be known as Gardener-handyman.

504.30 Landscape gardener

Moves soil, plants, flowers and greenery and constructs artificial features to improve the appearance of existing terrain

Working from plans or from own ideas on lay-out, prepares land by levelling or moving soil and changes surface contour of land using mechanical equipment as necessary; installs drainage system as required; prepares soil and plants trees, shrubs and flowers; seeds or turfs lawns; constructs paths, driveways, rockeries, ponds and other features.

May (01) select and purchase equipment and supplies
(02) maintain lawns and undertake nursery and other gardening work
(03 prepare estimates of cost.

504.40 Turf layer

Cuts turf and/or levels ground and lays turf to make lawns, greens and sports playing surfaces

Cuts fresh turf by hand or machine and stacks ready for transport; breaks and levels ground, adding top-soil as required, or cuts and removes existing turf surface; lays drainage system if needed; trims cut turf to specified dimensions using special tool or machine; lays turf using hand mallet to ram down.

May (01) drive lorry, tractor or fork-lift truck and carry out minor running repairs
(02) use dumpy level or automatic level
(03) use boning rods, large spirit levels or other levelling tools
(04) specialise in laying flat and/or "crown" bowling greens and be designated Bowling green layer.

Other titles include Grass court layer, Turf cutter.

504.50 Groundsman

Maintains grassed areas used for sport or recreation

Performs some or all of the following tasks: rolls, mows and waters the grass; seeds, re-turfs or otherwise conditions playing pitches, grass courts, golf-courses, greens or other grassed areas; selects, plants and tends shrubs and flowers; trims hedges and grass along edges of driveways and walks.

May (01) mark out athletic tracks and playing pitches
(02) maintain sports equipment such as goal-posts and tennis nets and be responsible for maintenance of clubhouse or pavilion
(03) carry out landscaping (504.30)
(04) maintain machinery such as mowers and rollers
(05) supervise assistant groundsmen
(06) maintain all-weather tracks and pitches.

Additional factor: experience of sports.

Other titles include Gardener-groundsman, Green-keeper, Groundskeeper.

504.98 Trainee

Performs, under instruction or guidance, various tasks including training exercises and as appropriate pursues studies in order to acquire the basic skills and knowledge required to perform the tasks of gardeners and groundsmen.

504.99 Other gardeners and groundsmen

Workers in this group carry out tasks in the cultivation of flowers, fruit, shrubs, trees and other plants, in public or private gardens (excluding market gardens) and in laying, maintaining and landscaping grassed areas and are not elsewhere classified.

Unit Group 505 Agricultural Machinery Operators

Workers in this unit group drive and operate agricultural tractors, implements and machines.

505.10 Agricultural machinery operator

Drives and operates agricultural tractors, implements or machines for the production of crops and/or for the processing of crops on the holding

Drives tractors; operates trailed, mounted, powered and self-propelled implements and machines, including ploughs, cultivators, drills, planters and distributors, sprayers and dusters, mowers, forage harvesters, hay machinery, balers, combine harvesters, potato diggers, root harvesters, irrigation equipment, elevators, conveyers, hydraulic loaders, crop driers, mechanical feeders, mills, mixers.

May (01) carry out maintenance of machines and equipment
(02) use tractor and trailer as transport vehicle both on and off the holding
(03) carry out mechanical hedge-cutting, ditching or draining.

Other titles include Tractor driver.

505.98 Trainee

Performs, under instruction or guidance, various tasks including training exercises and as appropriate pursues studies in order to acquire the basic skills and knowledge required to perform the tasks of agricultural machinery operators.

Unit Group 506 Tree Cultivating and Harvesting Occupations

Workers in this unit group carry out tasks directly related to the cultivating and harvesting of trees.

Excluded are Orchard workers (503 .40)

506 .10 Forest worker (excluding nursery worker)

Carries out tasks in preparing ground for planting, in cultivating trees and protecting them from hazards and in timber harvesting

Clears ground of unwanted vegetation or woody growth, by hand, machine or chemical means; prepares ground by draining and ploughing, using machines as necessary; erects and maintains fences; clears spaces as fire-breaks; collects seed from trees; plants out young plants; carries out hand and chemical weeding; replaces plants as necessary; thins out growing plantations; prunes trees and clears undergrowth around base of trees; fells mature trees by axe, or power saw; saws felled trees into required lengths and stacks ready for loading.

May (01) strip bark and split poles for fencing rails or stakes

(02) assist in loading timber on to vehicles

(03) drive tractor (505 .10)

(04) patrol forest to guard against fires.

Additional factor: knowledge of fire-fighting and first-aid.

Other titles include Woodman.

506 .50 Tree feller (trimming, felling)

Lops, tops or fells standing trees

Removes tops and lops branches of standing trees and controls fall of branches where necessary by using rope tackle; fells trees, using axe, cross-cut or power saw, controlling direction of fall of tree by inserting wedges; strips branches from felled trees.

May (01) maintain power saws and sharpen other saws and tools such as axes and bill hooks

(02) carry out tasks in tree-planting (506 .10) and land drainage (869 .18)

(03) strip bark and split poles for fencing rails or stakes

(04) cut logs to required sizes.

Other titles include Timber feller, Woodcutter.

506 .98 Trainee

Performs, under instruction or guidance, various tasks including training exercises and as appropriate pursues studies in order to acquire the basic skills and knowledge required to perform the tasks of workers in tree cultivating and harvesting occupations.

506 .99 Other tree cultivating and harvesting occupations

Workers in this group carry out tasks directly related to the cultivating and harvesting of trees and are not elsewhere classified, for example:

(01) Osier growers.

Unit Group 509 Farming, Horticultural, Forestry and Related Occupations Not Elsewhere Classified

Workers in this unit group perform miscellaneous tasks in farming, horticulture, forestry and related occupations and are not elsewhere classified.

509 .10 Classifier and marker (farm livestock)

Sorts and marks farm livestock

Sorts livestock into dockside, market or other pens according to class, brand or owner's mark; makes further identification marks on livestock by ear punching, tattooing or by affixing metal tags to their ears.

May (01) perform tasks of Drover (509 .99).

509 .50 Hedger

Plants and maintains hedges

Banks up earth to form a foundation and plants cuttings or shrubs; maintains hedges by clipping, pruning and replanting where necessary; drives in stakes and weaves cut and trimmed branches to make fences; forms hedges by partly cutting and layering branches and pinning down with stakes.

May (01) pick or lift crops (509 .90)
(02) drive tractor (505 .10) and use special purpose equipment
(03) excavate and maintain ditches and water channels and be known as Hedger and ditcher.

509 .90 Crop harvester

Carries out tasks in the picking or lifting of crops

According to the season, picks soft and hard fruits such as blackcurrants, raspberries, strawberries, apples, pears and plums and places in baskets; picks peas by hand or uses machine to cut plants above ground level; picks, gathers or lifts vegetable crops such as beans, Brussels sprouts, cabbages, onions, potatoes, sugar beet; picks hops from bines or feeds bines into machine pickers; picks or cuts flowers by hand; gathers mushrooms.

May (01) sort, grade or pack produce
(02) assist in the loading of crops on to vehicles

Other titles include Flower picker, Fruit picker, Hop picker, Mushroom picker, Pea puller, Seasonal worker (agriculture, market gardening).

Excluded are Agricultural machine operators (505 .10)

509 .98 Trainee

Performs, under instruction or guidance, various tasks including training exercises and as appropriate pursues studies in order to acquire the basic skills and knowledge required to perform the tasks of workers in farming, horticultural, forestry and related occupations not elsewhere classified.

509 .99 Other farming, horticultural, forestry and related occupations not elsewhere classified

Workers in this group perform miscellaneous tasks in farming, horticulture, forestry and related occupations and are not separately classified, for example:

(01) **Drovers** (drive livestock to or from docksides, markets, etc); (02) **Peat cutters**; (03) **Rabbit catchers,** Warreners.

Minor Group 51 FISHING AND RELATED OCCUPATIONS

Workers in this minor group catch, gather and breed fish and other forms of aquatic life and perform closely related activities.

The occupations are arranged in the following unit groups:

510 Supervisors and Mates (Fishing and Related Occupations)

511 Fishermen

519 Fishing and Related Occupations Not Elsewhere Classified

Unit Group 510 Supervisors and Mates (Fishing and Related Occupations)

Workers in this unit group directly supervise and co-ordinate the activities of workers in fishing and related occupations.

510 .10 Mate (fishing vessel)

Directly supervises and co-ordinates the activities of the crew of fishing vessel and assists and deputises for skipper

Performs appropriate tasks as described under SUPERVISOR/FOREMAN (990 .00) and in addition performs some or all of the following tasks: undertakes watchkeeping, bridge control and navigation duties as directed by skipper; reads charts and navigates using navigational aids such as Decca navigator, direction finder, radiotelephony, radiotelegraphy, radar and automatic steering coupled to gyro compass; assists in fish catching operations; keeps the official and navigation log books; ensures that gear and equipment are properly maintained; organises boat and fire drill, maintains discipline of crew and cleanliness of ship.

Additional factors: class of vessel to which accustomed eg trawler, drifter or line boat; type of fishing to which accustomed, eg seine, drift, ring or trawl; whether accustomed to "inshore" fishing or trawling in distant waters such as Icelandic, White Sea and Greenland; whether in possession of Certificate of Competency as Second Hand (Full), (Limited) or (Special).

Other titles include Fisherman (mate), Fisherman (second hand), Second hand.

Note: *the "Full" certificates are valid for use on all fishing vessels in all waters; "Limited" certificates are only accepted in respect of fishing vessels which do not proceed north of latitude 61°N or south of latitude 48° 30′N or west of longitude 12°W. Holders of the Second Hand (Special) Certificate are entitled to serve as skipper of fishing vessels, not exceeding 50 tons tonnage, which do not proceed beyond the above-mentioned limits of latitude and longitude.*

510.20 Third hand (fishing vessel)

Controls the operation of the fish catching gear and assists and deputises for mate

Performs some or all of the following tasks: shares watches with skipper and mate; checks that correct course is being steered and records landmarks and alterations of course; keeps official, navigation and fishing logs; during fish catching operations, operates mechanism to shoot the trawl net and operates winch to haul it in; supervises and assists crew to maintain and repair nets, lifting gear and other fishing equipment; supervises and assists crew to gut and wash fish; on "factory freezer" trawlers, supervises the processing, freezing and stowing of fish and by-products and maintains necessary records.

Additional factors: whether in possession of Third Hand, Bo'sun or Second Fisherman's Certificate of Competency issued by trawler owners or insurance company; whether in possession of other qualifications such as First Aid and Radar Observer's Certificates.

Other titles include Boatswain, Fisherman (boatswain), Fisherman (third hand).

510.99 Other supervisors and mates (fishing and related occupations)

Workers in this group directly supervise and co-ordinate the activities of workers in fishing and related occupations and are not elsewhere classified.

Unit Group 511 Fishermen

Workers in this unit group catch fish at sea by trawl, net, line or pot.

511.10 Fisherman (deck hand)

Performs allotted tasks in navigation and the catching, storage and unloading of fish

Performs some or all of the following tasks: assists with the shooting and hauling of nets; repairs nets and tackle; guts and sorts fish; extracts oil from fish livers; stows fish on ice or in refrigerated compartments in hold; operates winches and lifting gear; prepares trawl by splicing ropes and wires and attaching netting; lands fish; washes decks; handles hawsers on quayside; steers ship, keeps lookout and calls watches.

May (01) operate radio, echo sounders or radar
(02) operate ship's engine
(03) cook meals (431.25)
(04) bait "small" or "great" lines
(05) assist with general maintenance of vessel whilst in port, eg painting.

Additional factors: whether accustomed to "inshore" or "deep sea" fishing; type of fishing to which accustomed, eg seine, drift, ring or trawl net or line fishing.

Other titles include Deck hand, Spare hand, Trawlerman.

Excluded are Pot fishermen (511.20)

511.20 Pot fisherman

Sets and reclaims pots for catching shellfish in coastal waters

Prepares and lays baited pots attached at intervals along a line; marks each line of pots with a marker-buoy; inspects pots daily and removes catch; rebaits pots; replaces damaged pots and gear; at end of season lifts lines and pots, overhauls, and stows pots and gear.

May (01) operate winch to haul up lines
(02) fish for crab, lobster or whelks, according to season, fishing area or depth of water
(03) cook and prepare shellfish ready for market.

Other titles include Crab fisherman, Lobster fisherman.

511.98 Trainee

Performs, under instruction or guidance, various tasks including training exercises and as appropriate pursues studies in order to acquire the basic skills and knowledge required to perform the tasks of fishermen.

Other titles include Deck hand learner.

511.99 Other fishermen

Workers in this group catch fish at sea by trawl, net, line or pot and are not elsewhere classified.

Unit Group 519 Fishing and Related Occupations Not Elsewhere Classified

Workers in this unit group perform miscellaneous fishing and related tasks, including fish breeding and rearing, shellfish cultivation and mussel and seaweed gathering, and are not elsewhere classified.

519.10 Shellfish cultivator

Cultivates and harvests oysters, mussels or clams on artificial or natural beds

Performs some or all of the following tasks: prepares grounds; marks boundaries; lays stock; controls predators; harvests mature shellfish by raking or dredging; cleans, grades and packs shellfish for market.

Other titles include Oyster bed worker.

519.20 Fish hatcher

Breeds and rears fish in tanks under direction of hydrobiologist

Performs some or all of the following tasks: nets or arranges for the netting of fish from the river and places them in spawning pens; nets fish singly from spawning pens, anaesthetises by spraying gills with solution, strips fish of sperm or eggs and replaces fish in river; maintains constant water temperature in indoor tanks in which young fish are hatched and reared; feeds fish; transfers growing fish of appropriate size into outside fish ponds; nets fish of correct size and age and transfers them to river; assists in carrying out experiments in feeding, water treatment and fish diseases; keeps records, for example amounts of feed, age and mortalities; maintains electric pumps, screens, filters and refrigerators; empties and cleans outdoor tanks and applies anti-fouling paint.

Other titles include Fish hatchery worker.

Excluded are Laboratory Technicians and Similar Scientific Supporting Occupations (254) and Laboratory attendants (991.20)

519.98 Trainee

Performs, under instruction or guidance, various tasks including training exercises and as appropriate pursues studies in order to acquire the basic skills and knowledge required to perform the tasks of workers in fishing and related occupations not elsewhere classified.

519.99 Other fishing and related occupations not elsewhere classified

Workers in this group perform miscellaneous fishing and related tasks and are not separately classified, for example:

(01) **Harpooners (whales)**; (02) **Oyster dredgers**; (03) **Seaweed and mussel gatherers.**

MAJOR GROUP XII

Materials Processing Occupations (excluding metal)

Workers in this major group process and treat hides, skins, pelts, textile fibres, tobacco, foodstuffs, beverages, wood, chemicals and other materials excluding metal, make and finish fabric, tobacco products, paper, paperboard and leatherboard, knit and dye garments and other textile products, slaughter animals, poultry and game, treat products excluding metal in furnaces, kilns and similar equipment and perform closely related tasks.

Included are fusers (vitreous enamelled goods) and stove enamellers.

The occupations are arranged in the following minor groups:

53 Hide, Skin and Pelt Processing Occupations

54 Fibre and Textile Processing and Fabric Making Occupations

55 Tobacco Processing and Products Making Occupations

56 Chemical, Gas and Petroleum Processing Plant Operating Occupations

57 Food and Drink Processing Occupations

58 Wood Processing and Paper, Paperboard and Leatherboard Making Occupations

59 Materials Processing Occupations Not Elsewhere Classified

Minor Group 53 HIDE, SKIN AND PELT PROCESSING OCCUPATIONS

Workers in this minor group treat hides, skins and pelts to prepare them for making up into leather, skin and fur products.

The occupations are arranged in the following unit groups:

530 Foremen (Hide, Skin and Pelt Processing Occupations)

531 Hide, Skin and Pelt Processing Occupations

Excluded are workers colouring leather, skin or fur by brush, spray, pad or curtain coating (81) and Grader-sorters (834.05 and *834.10)*

Unit Group 530 Foremen (Hide, Skin and Pelt Processing Occupations)

Workers in this unit group directly supervise and co-ordinate the activities of workers in hide, skin and pelt processing occupations.

530.10 Foreman (hide, skin and pelt processing occupations)

Directly supervises and co-ordinates the activities of workers in hide, skin and pelt processing occupations

Performs appropriate tasks as described under SUPERVISOR/FOREMAN (UNSPECIFIED) (990.00).

May (01) make minor adjustments to machines

(02) grade and sort hides, skin or leather (834.05) or pelts (834.10)

(03) recommend changes in formulae for chemical solutions

(04) supervise workers employed on particular processes and be known accordingly, for example, Tanning foreman, Finishing section foreman.

Additional factor: number of workers supervised.

530.98 Trainee

Performs, under instruction or guidance, various tasks including training exercises and as appropriate pursues studies in order to acquire the basic skills and knowledge required to perform the tasks of foremen (hide, skin and pelt processing occupations).

Unit Group 531 Hide, Skin and Pelt Processing Occupations

Workers in this unit group treat hides, skins and pelts to prepare them for making up into leather, skin and fur products.

531 .10 Limeyard worker (general), Fellmonger (general)

Performs a number of tasks in the preparation of hides, skins or pelts for tanning or dressing

Performs all or several of the following tasks as directed: cuts and trims hides, skins or pelts; coats hides and skins with a depilatory by hand or machine; unhairs and/or removes flesh from (fleshes) hides and skins by machine or by hand and machine; de-wools pelts by machine; cures, limes, delimes, degreases, pickles or otherwise treats hides, skins or pelts in soaking pits, paddle vats or rotating drums; removes excess moisture from hides and skins by operating pressing or rolling ("sammying") machines or hydro-extractors.

May (01) prepare chemical solutions

(02) check chemical solutions for density or specific gravity

(03) withdraw samples of chemical solutions for laboratory testing

(04) drive fork lift truck to transport hides, skins or pelts

(05) tan hides and skins (531 .60 and 531 .65).

Other titles include Beamhouse worker, Sheepskin dresser, Wet shop operator.

531 .20 Wool puller and sorter (hand)

Removes wool from pelts by hand and sorts and grades the wool removed

Lays pelt, wool uppermost, over shaped work-table; grips pelt firmly and removes wool previously treated with a depilatory, using back of hand or specially shaped knife; repositions pelt and repeats operation until all wool has been removed; examines separated wool and sorts and grades it according to length, colour and quality.

May (01) cut waste pieces from pelts.

531 .30 Splitting machine operator

Operates machine to split hides or skins into two or more layers

Adjusts space between machine rollers to obtain the thickness of layers required; starts machine and feeds hide or skin, with grain side uppermost, between rollers which force its edge against band knife; checks evenness of upper layer as it emerges from cutter, using measuring aid, and adjusts machine as necessary; removes split hide from machine; cleans and oils machine.

May (01) operate fleshing or unhairing machine (531 .50).

Other titles include Hide splitter, Skin splitter.

See Splitting machine operator (leather) (662 .70)

531 .50 Fleshing machine operator, Unhairing machine operator, Scouring machine operator

Operates machine to remove flesh, unwanted hair or other waste matter from hides, skins, or fur- or wool-bearing pelts

(01) Fleshing machine operator, Unhairing machine operator

Starts machine to rotate gripping or nipping rollers and/or cutting cylinder; if fleshing or unhairing hide, skin or large pelt, lays item over feed roller and operates control to bring item into contact with gripping rollers to feed it to cutting cylinder; if unhairing small pelt, feeds pelt to nipping rollers which pull out long hairs or to cutting cylinder; repositions hide, skin, or pelt and repeats operation until all waste tissue and unwanted hair have been removed.

(02) Scouring machine operator

Operates machine similar to fleshing or unhairing machine, but fitted with abrading cylinder in place of cutting cylinder, to remove from hides sediment formed during tanning.

May (03) adjust clearance between feed and gripping rollers to give pressure and depth of cut required

(04) sharpen blades on cutting cylinder using abrading attachment

(05) clean and oil machine

(06) specialise in handling crocodile or other valuable skins.

Other titles include Defleshing machine operator, Puller (fur dressing), Scudding machine operator.

531 .55 Cutter

Cuts hides, skins or chamois leathers into convenient pieces before or immediately after tanning or curing

If cutting hide, positions hide on work-table or sloping bench (beam); examines hide to determine line of cut, by feeling texture and thickness of parts; cuts hide into butt, shoulder and belly pieces using hand knife or mechanical cutting device; folds butt piece in half and cuts it along ridge corresponding to animal's backbone, to form two pieces (bends). If cutting skin or chamois leather, examines item for imperfections and decides on most economical lines of cutting; stretches skin or chamois leather over work-table and cuts into pieces using hand or machine cutting tools; sorts pieces according to size.

May (01) trim hides, skins or chamois leathers before cutting (531 .90)

(02) sharpen cutting tools

(03) specialise in cutting particular kinds of hides or skins.

Other titles include Rounder.

531.60 Tanyard handler

Prepares butt, shoulder and belly pieces of hide for soaking in tanning solutions, and attends row of tanning pits

Pierces corners of hide piece; hooks or ties hide piece to wood or metal pole; lowers hide piece vertically into tanning solution with pole resting across top of pit, or fixes a batch of hides tied to poles on to frame of jib and attaches lifting hook of overhead crane to jig; if manhandling hide pieces, removes from each pit after specified length of time and places in next appropriate pit until tanning process is complete; removes hide pieces from poles after tanning and allows to drain.

May (01) operate mechanisms to rock hides in tanning pits

(02) agitate hide pieces in tanning solution by hand or mechanical paddles

(03) test density or specific gravity of solutions with hydrometer

(04) withdraw samples of solutions for laboratory testing

(05) top up or refill tanning pits with appropriate liquors.

Additional factor: number of pits attended.

Other titles include Suspender man.

531.65 Drum operator

Operates one or more rotary drums to cure, wash, lime, delime, pickle, degrease, tan, dye, fatliquor or otherwise treat hides or skins or fur- or wool-bearing pelts

Examines processing instructions; measures out according to recipe or takes measured quantities of chemical or other solutions; places hides or skins in drum and secures door; opens valves to admit hot or cold water or steam to drum, and/or adds prepared solutions; starts drum rotating and records time; stops drum after specified time, removes bung or drainage cover and drains off liquor; admits clean water, with detergent if specified, and rotates drum for short periods to rinse contents; removes contents on completion of process; cleans and oils equipment.

May (01) take samples of processing liquors for density, acidity or other testing during drumming process

(02) check temperatures during drumming process

(03) operate drum, without adding water, steam or solutions, to soften hides or skins by tumbling and be known as Cager, Dry drummer.

Additional factor: number of drums operated.

Other titles include Curer, Degreaser, Delimer, Dyer, Fatliquorer, Limer, Pickler, Tanner, Washer.

See Tumbler operator (ceramic components) (622.65) and Barrel polishing machine operator (726.60)

531.70 Finisher (machine)

Smoothes, stretches, softens, embosses or otherwise finishes hides, skins or leather by machine

(01) **Finishing machine operator**

As required, adjusts position of machine table and/or regulates space between feed roller and finishing roller(s) or cylinder, or between finishing rollers or machine jaws according to thickness of hide, skin or leather and/or finishing requirements; if embossing patterns on or ironing leather or skin, fixes appropriate roller or plate on machine; positions item to be finished on or over feed table or roller or machine table or between rollers and operates controls to start finishing operation, or starts machine and feeds item between rollers; where appropriate, operates control to release item from machine on completion of operation; repositions item as necessary and repeats operation until required finish has been obtained.

Other titles include Belly roller, Bend roller, Boarding and graining machine operator, Boarding machine operator, Brusher, Brushing machine operator, Embosser, Embossing machine operator, Glazer, Glazing machine operator, Grainer, Ironer, Leather roller, Plater, Plating machine operator, Presser, Printer, Rolling machine operator, Setter-out, Setting machine operator, Shaver, Shaving machine operator, Shoulder roller, Softener, Staker, Staking machine operator, Striker.

(02) **Finisher (belt, wheel)**

Fits felt belt round rollers or fits strip of abrasive or other material to wheel; starts belt or wheel rotating; holds skin or leather against belt or wheel and manipulates as necessary until required finish has been obtained.

Other titles include Plush wheeler, Polisher, Polishing machine operator, Wheeler.

May (03) adjust roller speed or pressure

(04) sharpen cutters of finishing cylinder

(05) clean and oil machine

(06) finish leather using hand tools

(07) perform tasks of PELT DRESSING MACHINE OPERATOR (531.93)

(08) specialise in finishing crocodile or other valuable skins.

Additional factor: finishing operations in which experienced, eg boarding, buffing, embossing, shaving.

Other titles include Buffer, Buffing machine operator, Fluffer, Fluffing machine operator, Sueder, Sueding machine operator.

See Embossing machine operator (excluding wallpaper) (634.55)

531 .90 Trimmer

Trims hides, skins or chamois leathers ready for cutting

Positions hide, skin or chamois leather on work-table or sloping bench (beam); cuts off unwanted parts such as ears, tail and paws, and uneven or hard pieces of skin, using hand knife, cleaver, or hand or mechanical shears or saw; throws waste material into container for disposal.

May (01) remove tufts of hair left on skin using hand or machine cutting tools

(02) sort hides or skins according to size after trimming

(03) assist in cutting operation (531 .55)

(04) specialise in trimming particular hides or skins.

Other titles include Piecer.

531 .91 De-wooling machine operator

Operates machine to remove wool from pelts

Starts machine to rotate driving roller and cutter; places pelt over feed roller; operates control to bring pelt in contact with rotating cutter; allows pelt to travel under blade as far as possible whilst retaining hold on end; operates control to return pelt to original feed position; repositions pelt and repeats operation until all wool has been removed.

May (01) remove shanks and neck of pelt using hand shears.

531 .92 Drying room operative, Conditioning room operative

Prepares hides, skins or pelts for drying or conditioning and/or operates drying or conditioning equipment

Performs one or more of the following tasks: moistens hides or skins with water or damp sawdust, or clips hides or skins to wire lines to absorb moisture from atmosphere (mulling); stretches out hides, skins or pelts and secures them to wood or metal frames by nailing, using clips (toggles) or tying with sisal cord; pastes skins on to sheets of glass or plastic hung from overhead rails or on to metal walls of drying cabinet; positions skins on bed or over feed roller of drying machine or loads skins or pelts into machine; hangs frames of hides, skins or pelts from overhead beams or stands them in drying rooms or tunnels; regulates heat supply and speed of hot air fans or blowers, or starts drying machine; removes hides, skins or pelts from frames, glass or plastic sheets, cabinet walls or drying machine after specified length of time.

May (01) dress hides or skins with selected oils before or after drying

(02) operate hydraulic ram to push frames through drier.

Other titles include Hanger-up, Hydro-extractor operator, Muller, Nailer, Paster, Paster-drier, Sammying machine operator, Saw-duster, Seasoner, Shedman, Stretcher, Toggle drier, Toggle strainer, Toggler, Vacuum drying machine operator.

531 .93 Pelt dressing machine operator

Operates one or more machines to impart a smooth and/or supple finish to fur- or wool-bearing pelts

Performs one or more of the following tasks: positions pelt over padded shoulders of striking machine or on machine table and starts machine to beat pelt with padded striking arm or mechanical beaters; trims wool or fur to an even length using mechanical shears; combs wool by passing pelt between rollers of carding machine; irons wool side of pelt by passing it between heated metal rollers or feeding it to heated rotating cylinder; brushes pelt by machine.

May (01) comb or brush wool by hand.

Other titles include Carder, Carding machine operator, Carrotter, Dresser, Finisher, Fur dressing machine operator, Shearer.

531 .98 Trainee

Performs, under instruction or guidance, various tasks including training exercises and as appropriate pursues studies in order to acquire the basic skills and knowledge required to perform the tasks of workers in hide, skin and pelt processing occupations.

531.99 Other hide, skin and pelt processing occupations

Workers in this group treat hides, skins and pelts to prepare them for making up into leather, skin and fur products and are not elsewhere classified, for example:

(01) **Curriers** (perform various leather dressing tasks by hand); (02) **Degreasing tank operators**; (03) **Dippers,** Limers (pit), Picklers (pit, vat), Vat dyers, Washers (pit) (dip leather into vats of molten grease or immerse hides, skins or leather in pits or vats containing lime, pickling solution, dye or water; (04) **Fleshers (hand),** Unhairers (hand) (remove flesh, unwanted hair or other waste matter from hides or skins using hand tool); (05) **Gatherers,** Pickers (collect hatter's fur after cutting and remove skin adhering to fur); (06) **Hand slickers** (scrape leather using hand tool); (07) **Hand stretchers,** Layers-up (stretch leather by hand using weights or steel blade fixed to stake as necessary); (08) **Hide painters,** Skin painters (apply depilatory to hides or skins); (09) **Oil mill workers** (perform various processing tasks in chamois leather preparation); (10) **Openers and stretchers** (open and stretch fur-bearing pelts by machine); (11) **Pullers (fur dressing) (hand)** (remove top coarse hair from fur-bearing pelts by hand); (12) **Pullers-off** (assist splitting machine operators); (13) **Smearers,** Stuffers (rub oil, grease or salt solution into leather by hand).

Minor Group 54 FIBRE AND TEXTILE PROCESSING AND FABRIC MAKING OCCUPATIONS

Workers in this minor group prepare textile fibres, spin fibres into yarn, weave, knit and otherwise process yarn and fibres into textile piece goods and products, bleach, dye and otherwise treat and finish textiles, and undertake other fibre and textile processing and fabric making tasks.

Included are bristle dressers and feather processors.

The occupations are arranged in the following unit groups:

540 Foremen (Fibre and Textile Processing and Fabric Making Occupations)

541 Fibre Preparing Occupations

542 Textile Spinning, Doubling, Twisting and Winding Occupations

543 Warp Preparing Occupations

544 Textile Weaving Occupations

545 Knitting Occupations

546 Textile Bleaching, Dyeing, Finishing and Other Treating Occupations

547 Textile Repairing Occupations

548 Braid, Plait, Line and Fibre Rope Making Occupations

549 Fibre and Textile Processing and Fabric Making Occupations Not Elsewhere Classified

Excluded are Man-made fibre makers (594 .58) and Sorting and Grading Occupations (834)

Unit Group 540 Foremen (Fibre and Textile Processing and Fabric Making Occupations)

Workers in this unit group directly supervise and co-ordinate the activities of workers in fibre and textile processing and fabric making occupations.

540 .05 Foreman (fibre preparing occupations)

Directly supervises and co-ordinates the activities of workers in fibre preparing occupations

Performs appropriate tasks as described under SUPERVISOR/FOREMAN (UNSPECIFIED) (990 .00).

May (01) set machines

(02) undertake minor repairs to machines

(03) calculate quantities of fibres or rags for blends

(04) regulate amount of oil to be added to fibre or rag blends

(05) check weight of sliver (taking the count)

(06) supervise setter fitter-mechanics, strippers and grinders, woollen fettlers.

Additional factors: type(s) of fibre in which experienced, eg cotton, jute, wool; type(s) of operation supervised, eg carding, combing, drawing, rag grinding; number of workers supervised.

Other titles include Blowing room major, Carding engineer, Under carder, Wool blender.

540 .10 Foreman (textile spinning occupations)

Directly supervises and co-ordinates the activities of workers in textile spinning occupations

Performs appropriate tasks as described under SUPERVISOR/FOREMAN (UNSPECIFIED) (990 .00).

May (01) set machines

(02) undertake minor repairs to machines.

Additional factors: type(s) of fibre in which experienced, eg cotton, jute, worsted; number of workers supervised.

Other titles include Ring frame overlooker.

540 .15 Foreman (textile doubling, twisting, winding occupations)

Directly supervises and co-ordinates the activities of workers in textile doubling, twisting and/or winding occupations

Performs appropriate tasks as described under SUPERVISOR/FOREMAN (UNSPECIFIED) (990 .00).

May (01) set machines

(02) undertake minor repairs to machines.

Additional factors: type(s) of yarn in which experienced, eg cotton, nylon, worsted; type(s) of operation supervised, eg twisting, winding; number of workers supervised.

540 .20 Foreman (warp preparing occupations)

Directly supervises and co-ordinates the activities of workers in warp preparing occupations

Performs appropriate tasks as described under SUPERVISOR/FOREMAN (UNSPECIFIED) (990 .00).

May (01) undertake minor repairs to machines.

Additional factors: type(s) of yarn in which experienced, eg cotton, nylon, worsted; type(s) of operation supervised, eg warping, looming; number of workers supervised.

540 .25 Foreman (textile weaving occupations)

Directly supervises and co-ordinates the activities of workers in textile weaving occupations

Performs appropriate tasks as described under SUPERVISOR/FOREMAN (UNSPECIFIED) (990 .00).

May (01) set machines

(02) undertake minor repairs to machines

(03) set loom clocks to record yardage woven.

Additional factors: type(s) of yarn in which experienced, eg cotton, nylon, worsted; type(s) of operation supervised, eg carpet weaving, lace weaving, fabric weaving; number of workers supervised.

Other titles include Loom overlooker, Loom tenter, Loom tuner.

540 .30 Foreman (knitting occupations)

Directly supervises and co-ordinates the activities of workers in knitting occupations

Performs appropriate tasks as described under SUPERVISOR/FOREMAN (UNSPECIFIED) (990 .00).

May (01) set machines

(02) undertake minor repairs to machines.

Additional factors: type(s) of yarn in which experienced, eg cotton, nylon, wool; number of workers supervised.

540 .35 Foreman (textile bleaching, finishing and other treating occupations) (excluding dyeing)

Directly supervises and co-ordinates the activities of workers in textile bleaching, finishing and other treating occupations (excluding dyeing)

Performs appropriate tasks as described under SUPERVISOR/FOREMAN (UNSPECIFIED) (990 .00).

May (01) calculate amounts of ingredients for solutions

(02) mix solutions

(03) determine duration and temperature of operation

(04) test specific gravity of solutions

(05) test fabric for alkali/acid content

(06) prepare program cards for use on automated equipment

(07) set machines

(08) undertake minor repairs to machines and equipment.

Additional factors: type(s) of operation supervised, eg bleaching, cropping, mercerising, stentering; number of workers supervised.

540 .40 Foreman (textile dyeing occupations)

Directly supervises and co-ordinates the activities of workers in textile dyeing occupations

Performs appropriate tasks as described under SUPERVISOR/FOREMAN (UNSPECIFIED) (990 .00).

May (01) calculate amounts of ingredients for solutions

(02) mix solutions

(03) determine duration and temperature of operation

(04) match colour of dyed material against master card or specimen and determine any variations required in composition of solution.

Additional factor: number of workers supervised.

540 .45 Foreman (textile repairing occupations)

Directly supervises and co-ordinates the activities of workers in textile repairing occupations

Performs appropriate tasks as described under SUPERVISOR/FOREMAN (UNSPECIFIED) (990 .00).

Additional factors: type of textiles in which experienced, eg carpet, woven piece goods, hosiery; number of workers supervised.

540 .50 Foreman (braid, plait, line and fibre rope making occupations)

Directly supervises and co-ordinates the activities of workers in braid, plait, line and fibre rope making occupations

Performs appropriate tasks as described under SUPERVISOR/FOREMAN (UNSPECIFIED) (990 .00).

May (01) decide by which method rope should be made

(02) calculate degree of twist required in rope in relation to its size

(03) set machines

(04) undertake minor repairs to machines.

Additional factors: type(s) of operation supervised, eg braiding, twine twisting, rope making; number of workers supervised.

540 .55 Foreman (pattern card and tape preparing occupations)

Directly supervises and co-ordinates the activities of workers in pattern card and tape preparing occupations

Performs appropriate tasks as described under SUPERVISOR/FOREMAN (UNSPECIFIED) (990 .00).

May (01) undertake minor repairs to machines.

Additional factor: number of workers supervised.

540 .60 Foreman (felt hood making occupations)

Directly supervises and co-ordinates the activities of workers in felt hood making occupations

Performs appropriate tasks as described under SUPERVISOR/FOREMAN (UNSPECIFIED) (990 .00).

Additional factor: number of workers supervised.

540.98 Trainee

Performs, under instruction or guidance, various tasks including training exercises and as appropriate pursues studies in order to acquire the basic skills and knowledge required to perform the tasks of foremen (fibre and textile processing and fabric making occupations).

540.99 Other foremen (fibre and textile processing and fabric making occupations)

Workers in this group directly supervise and co-ordinate the activities of workers in fibre and textile processing and fabric making occupations and are not elsewhere classified, for example:

(01) **Doffing mistresses** (directly supervise and co-ordinate the activities of workers removing (doffing) full packages from spinning frames); (02) **Foremen (hair spinning)**; (03) **Foremen (net making) (hand)**; (04) **Foremen (non-woven fabric manufacture)**; (05) **Foremen (roofing felt manufacture)**; (06) **Foremen (tufted carpet manufacture)**; (07) **Making-up foreman.**

Additional factor: number of workers supervised.

Unit Group 541 Fibre Preparing Occupations

Workers in this unit group prepare natural, man-made and reclaimed fibres for spinning into yarn and making into non-woven fabric, and dress bristles and fibres for use as brush fillings.

Included are rag rippers and cutters and rag grinders.

Excluded are Carbonisers (546.85), Washers (546.86) and Driers (546.89)

541.05 Fibre mixer and blender (machine)

Attends one or more machines which mix textile fibres into uniform blends

Weighs out or takes measured quantities of fibres specified in mixing instructions; sets timer or circuit counter; starts machine; feeds prescribed quantities of fibres into machine hopper or spreads fibres evenly on feed belt; watches operation to ensure that fibres blend evenly and flow properly through machine; clears blockages and unclogs rollers; stops machine after specified time or number of circuits; removes and bundles blended fibres or removes (doffs) containers into which blended fibres have been blown, or routes blended fibres to machines for further processing; cleans machine.

May (01) roughly blend quantities of fibres by hand before feeding into machine

(02) regulate speed of machine

(03) weigh bundles of blended fibres and record weight

(04) specialise in mixing natural and/or man-made fibres.

Other titles include Fibre blender, Fibre blending machine operator, Fibre mixing machine operator.

Excluded are Fur fibre mixers (549.92)

541.10 Fibre separating and aligning machine operator

Operates one or more machines to separate and align raw natural fibres, man-made staple fibres or reclaimed fibres preparatory to drawing, spinning or other processing

Feeds loose fibres manually into machine or regulates automatic feed, or sets input rolls, cans or packages of fibres in position and leads ends from rolls, cans or packages into or through machine or joins to ends in machine; starts machine and watches operation to detect blockages, clogged rollers and where appropriate broken slivers; clears blockages and unclogs rollers; joins broken slivers by rubbing or plaiting ends together or rethreads end through to delivery device; removes loose aligned fibres or output rolls of fibre (laps) from machine, or removes and replaces full output containers or packages; ensures that supply of fibres to machine is adequate; cleans machine.

Other titles include Bristle dresser.

(01) **Hackling machine attendant**

Performs tasks of fibre separating and aligning machine operator on machine which separates and aligns hair and flax and other vegetable fibres and removes short fibres and waste particles.

Other titles include Hackler.

(02) **Carding machine attendant**

Performs tasks of fibre separating and aligning machine operator on machine which separates fibres and aligns them to form lap, sliver or slubbing.

Other titles include Can tenter, Card attendant, Card tenter, Carder, Carding engine attendant, Condenser minder, Sample carding attendant.

(03) **Combing machine attendant**

Performs tasks of fibre separating and aligning machine operator on machine which separates a number of slivers to remove short fibres (noils) and waste particles and re-aligns long fibres into uniform sliver.

Other titles include Comber, Comber tenter.

May (04) assist in setting machine(s)
(05) cut fibres to uniform length before feeding to hackling machine(s)
(06) attend machine(s) which doubles slivers ready for further carding
(07) select appropriate sliver for combing from blending instructions
(08) bundle or bag processed fibres.

Additional factors: type(s) of fibre in which experienced, eg cotton, flax, wool; number of machines operated.

541.15 Drawframe attendant, Speed frame attendant

Attends one or more machines which combine and draw out slivers of short fibres into strands of uniform quality, or attenuate and twist drawn slivers or slubbing or roving

Positions input rolls or cans of sliver behind machine or sets input packages of sliver, slubbing or roving in machine creel; joins ends from input rolls, cans or packages to ends in machine, or threads them through guides and drafting and twisting mechanisms to output rolls, cans or packages; starts machine and watches operation to detect breaks in sliver, slubbing or roving, nearly exhausted input rolls, cans or packages and full output rolls, cans or packages; twists broken ends together; replenishes supply of sliver, slubbing or roving; removes (doffs) full output rolls, cans or packages; cleans machine.

May (01) check weight of sliver, slubbing or roving
(02) make minor adjustments to machines
(03) attend separate machine which doubles laps or slivers for further drawing out.

Additional factors: type(s) of fibre in which experienced, eg cotton, flax, jute; number of frames or spindles attended.

Other titles include Autoleveller machine attendant, Drawer, Drawing frame attendant, Drawing frame tenter, Intermediate tenter, Finisher minder, Rover, Roving frame attendant, Slubbing tenter, Speed frame tenter.

541.20 Gill box attendant, Drawing box attendant

Attends one or more of a series of machines which comb, straighten and draw out long fibres and form slivers (preparing) or combine, attenuate and twist slivers into slubbing and roving (drawing)

Performs a combination of the following tasks: starts preparation gill boxes and feeds in loose fibres or sheets of fibres (laps) by hand; positions input cans of sliver behind preparation or drawing gill boxes, or sets input packages of sliver, slubbing or roving in machine creel; joins ends from cans or packages to ends in machine by twisting, or threads them through guides, drafting mechanisms and combing or twisting devices to output cans, balling spindles or bobbins; starts machine and watches operation to detect breaks in sliver, slubbing or roving, nearly exhausted input laps, cans or packages, output laps ready for removal or full output cans or packages; twists broken ends together; replenishes supply of sliver, slubbing or roving; breaks off output laps or removes (doffs) full output cans or packages; cleans machine.

May (01) check weight of sliver, slubbing or roving
(02) make minor adjustments to machines

continued

(03) attend gill box directly linked to backwash machine.

Additional factor: number of boxes attended.

Other titles include Autoleveller machine attendant, Balling head minder, Can box minder, Can finisher, Dandy rover, Drawer, Drawing box minder, Finisher minder, Finishing box minder, Gill box minder, Punch balling machine attendant, Reducer, Reducing box minder, Rover, Rover minder, Roving box minder, Strong box minder.

See Fibre preparing and spinning set attendant (549 .50)

541 .25 Tow-to-top converter attendant

Attends machine which severs bundles of continuous filaments (tows) and assembles resulting staple fibres to form sliver (top)

Leads ends of tows from input containers over rollers into machine or ties ends to ends in machine; starts machine; watches operation to ensure that tows are cut or broken into staple length required and delivered in sliver form into output cans; replenishes supply of tows; removes (doffs) full output cans; cleans and oils machine.

Other titles include Tow-to-top converter minder.

541 .30 Flagger

Operates machine to split and splay out (flag) ends of hair, bristle or other fibre

Slides back wrapping on fibre bundle (hank) to expose fibre ends; dips exposed fibre ends into soapy solution; secures hank in clamp at top of machine with exposed fibres protruding; operates controls to lower hank on to revolving flagging wheel and rotate clamp; raises clamp and releases fibre hank when flagging has been completed; places flagged hanks into containers and weighs containers when full; cleans flagging wheel.

541 .50 Fibre opening machine attendant

Attends one or more machines which open raw natural fibres, man-made staple fibres or reclaimed fibres preparatory to carding or other processing

Performs a combination of the following tasks: feeds loose fibres into hoppers or spreads them evenly on feed conveyors; feeds ends of lengths of twisted hair or fibre into openings of machine; positions input roll of fibre (lap) on machine and leads end of lap into machine; starts machine; clears blockages and unclogs rollers; removes (doffs) opened fibres from machine or routes them to machines for further processing; removes output laps or packages of fibre from machine or checks that automatic doffing device is working correctly; ensures that supply of fibres to machine is adequate; sprays or operates spraying device to saturate fibres with conditioning lubricant and replenishes supply of lubricant in reservoir as necessary; cleans machine.

May (01) roughly blend fibres by hand before feeding into machine

(02) weigh fibres before or after opening

(03) check alignment of feed belts

(04) set control to produce lap of required thickness

(05) set measuring device to cut or break lap into specified lengths or quantities

(06) bale or bundle opened fibres.

Additional factors: type(s) of fibre in which experienced, eg asbestos, cotton, jute; number of machines attended.

Other titles include Bale opener, Batcher, Blowing room assistant, Breaker, Cotton feeder, Crushing and opening plant attendant, Devil tenter, Fibre breaking machine attendant, Fibre opener, Garnetting machine attendant, Garnetting machine feeder, Jute spreader operative, Lap machine minder, Opening range operative, Rundown tenter, Scutcher attendant, Scutcher tenter, Scutching machine attendant, Shoddy teaser, Softening machine attendant, Softener feeder, Teaser, Teasing machine attendant, Untwister, Waste deviller, Willey machine attendant, Willeyer, Willow feeder, Woolleyer.

541.55 Fibre separating and aligning machine attendant

Feeds and/or doffs one or more machines which separate and align raw natural fibres, man-made staple fibres or reclaimed fibres preparatory to drawing, spinning or other processing

Performs a combination of the following tasks: feeds loose fibres into hoppers or spreads them evenly on feed conveyors; positions input rolls of fibre in roll bank and leads ends of rolls into machine; starts machine; ensures that a continuous supply of fibres is fed to machine; joins ends of new input rolls to ends in machine; removes output rolls of fibre (laps) from machine or removes and replaces full sliver cans; cleans machine.

May (01) perform tasks of WOOLLEN FETTLER (746.60).

Additional factor: number of machines fed and/or doffed.

Other titles include Can dodger, Can taker-out, Card feeder, Card operative, Feeder (cotton waste), Feeder-fettler.

541.60 Fibre cutter

Operates machine to cut fibres such as bass and hair to required length

Adjusts distance between cutting blades or sets cutting guide of guillotine, shearing or clipping machine to cut fibres to specified length; loads hanks of fibre into feed hopper and starts machine, or feeds individual hanks to blades by hand; places cut hanks in container or routes them to flagger.

May (01) bundle cut hanks
(02) operate machine to tighten binding round hanks before cutting and be known as Tightener-trimmer.

Additional factor: type of fibre in which experienced, eg bass, hair, manilla.

Other titles include Bass cutter, Dress cutter, Fibre trimmer, Hair trimmer, Manilla cutter, Rough cutter.

541.65 Rag ripper and cutter

Rips garments into rags and cuts suitable rags into wiping cloths by hand

Examines garments to determine ripping and cutting requirements; rips garments along seams and removes pockets, sleeves and linings, and buttons, fasteners and other unwanted items by holding garment against rotating cutting wheel or by using hand shears or knife; separates usable rags from waste; cuts rags into suitably sized pieces for use as wiping cloths; sharpens hand cutting tools as necessary.

May (01) sort wiping cloths according to quality or size.

Other titles include Cloth stripper, Wiper cutter.

541.70 Waste cutting machine attendant, Waste grinding machine attendant

Attends machine which reduces garments or rags to small pieces or to a fibrous state (flock) or which cuts waste yarn or fabric (thrums) to appropriate length for reprocessing

Performs one or more of the following tasks: starts machine; spreads garments, rags or thrums evenly on feed apron; watches operation to detect clogging of cutters or grinding rollers; stops machine and unclogs cutters; reverses machine and removes obstructions from rollers; removes containers of cut or ground waste, or bags loose waste; cleans machine.

May (01) roughly blend rags by hand before feeding to machine
(02) adjust speed of machine to vary quality of flock produced
(03) attend machine from which cut or ground waste is automatically drawn or blown through ducts to washing, willeying, baling or garnetting machines.

Other titles include Flock grinder, Rag grinder, Rag puller, Rag teaser, Shoddy grinder, Thrum cutter.

541.98 Trainee

Performs, under instruction or guidance, various tasks including training exercises and as appropriate pursues studies in order to acquire the basic skills and knowledge required to perform the tasks of workers in fibre preparing occupations.

541.99 Other fibre preparing occupations

Workers in this group prepare natural, man-made and reclaimed fibres for spinning into yarn and making into non-woven fabric, and dress bristles and fibres for use as brush fillings and are not elsewhere classified, for example:

(01) **Bass dressers,** Drawers (hand), Dressers (hand), Fibre dressers, Hacklers (hand), Jumpers (straighten and clean bass, hair or other fibres and/or draw combed fibres to standard lengths by hand); (02) **Batchers (hand)** (mix raw fibres by hand); (03) **Dust shaker attendants** (attend vibrating conveyors on which dust is shaken from rags); (04) **Rag blenders** (layer sorted rags according to colour, type and quality).

Unit Group 542 Textile Spinning, Doubling, Twisting and Winding Occupations

Workers in this unit group spin fibre into yarn and thread, and double, twist and wind yarn and thread.

Included are twine ballers and spoolers.

Excluded are Warp Preparing Occupations (543), Braid, Plait, Line and Fibre Rope Making Occupations (548), Doffers (549.88) and Man-made fibre makers (594.58)

542.10 Mule spinner

Creels, threads and attends one or more machines which, in separate operations, draw out and twist roving, slubbing or condenser strands into yarn and wind twisted yarn on to paper tubes or other output packages

Sets input packages of roving, slubbing or condenser strands in machine creel; threads ends from input packages through guides and drafting rollers and secures them to output packages; adjusts speed and tension of machine by hand as necessary; starts machine, and patrols work area to detect weak spots in yarn (snarls), broken ends and nearly empty input packages; breaks off lengths of yarn containing snarls; twists broken ends together while machine is in motion; replaces empty input packages; stops machine when output packages are full; removes (doffs) and replaces full output packages; cleans and oils machine; removes and replaces rollers and broken driving belts when instructed.

May (01) use gauge to determine when packages are ready for doffing.

Additional factors: type(s) of fibre in which experienced, eg cotton, silk, wool; number of spindles attended.

Other titles include Head minder, Joiner minder, Mule minder, Side minder.

542.50 Assistant mule spinner

Creels and threads spinning machine and/or joins broken yarn ends, and otherwise assists mule spinner

Performs some or all of the following tasks under the direction or guidance of the mule spinner: sets input packages in machine creel as required; threads ends from input packages through to output packages; pieces broken ends by twisting; removes (doffs) and replaces full output packages; clears waste from machines.

Additional factors: type(s) of fibre in which experienced, eg cotton, silk, wool; number of spindles attended.

Other titles include Assistant spinner, Headstock piecer, Minder assistant, Mule piecener, Mule piecer.

542.55 Frame spinner

Creels, threads and attends one or more machines which simultaneously draw out and twist roving, slubbing or condenser strands into yarn and wind yarn on to bobbins or other output packages

Sets input packages of roving, slubbing or condenser strands in machine creel or positions input cans behind machine frame; threads ends from input packages or cans through guides and drafting rollers and secures them to output packages; starts machine and patrols work area to detect broken ends and nearly empty input packages; joins broken ends by twisting, knotting or rough splicing, or rethreads ends through rollers; replaces empty input packages or cans; where appropriate, stops machine when output packages are full; cleans machine.

May (01) set yardage counter

(02) remove (doff) and replace full output packages (549.88).

Additional factors: type(s) of fibre in which experienced, eg asbestos, cotton, worsted; type(s) of frame on which experienced, eg cap, flyer, ring; number of spindles attended.

Other titles include Cap spinner, Fly side minder, Fly spinner, Gill spinner, Ring spinner, Self doffer minder, Self doffer spinner, Spinning machine tenter.

See Fibre preparing and spinning set attendant (549.50)

542.60 Spinner (metal thread)

Creels, threads and attends machine which spins gold, silver or other metal wire around core of silk, cotton or other textile yarn

Sets input packages of metal wire and of textile yarn in machine creel; passes wire end round grooved metal cone and twisting device, and threads yarn end through guides to output package; adjusts weights and screws to obtain required tension and starts machine; stops machine and removes full output packages; alters twist as necessary by changing pulley wheels.

May (01) clean machine

(02) attend wire flatting machine (729.65).

Additional factor: number of spindles attended.

542.65 Assembly winder

Creels, threads and attends machine which winds two or more yarn strands or filaments together on to packages without twisting

Sets input packages of yarn strands or filaments in machine creel; threads appropriate number of ends from input packages through guides and tensioners to each output package or winder; starts machine and watches operation to detect yarn or filament breaks, nearly empty input packages and full output packages; joins broken ends by hand or mechanical knotting or with adhesive or rethreads ends through machine to appropriate output package; replaces empty input packages.

May (01) remove (doff) and replace full output packages (549.88) or remove coreless packages from winders
(02) use gauge to determine when packages are ready for doffing
(03) weigh and pack full output packages
(04) clean and oil machine.

Additional factors: type(s) of yarn in which experienced, eg glass fibre, silk, worsted; number of spindles attended.

Other titles include Assembler, Assembler winder, Double winder, Doubler, Doubler winder, Folder, Multi-end cheese winder, Roving operator.

542.70 Twister

Creels, threads and attends one or more machines which twist strands of yarn together to increase their strength, smoothness and uniformity or to produce fancy effects, or which insert additional twist into single strands of yarn (uptwisting)

Sets yarn input packages in machine creel; threads appropriate number of ends from input packages through guides and tensioners to each output package; starts machine and patrols work area to detect yarn breaks, nearly empty input packages and full output packages; joins broken ends by hand or mechanical knotting, or rethreads ends through machine to appropriate output package; replaces empty input packages; removes (doffs) full output packages by hand or by operating doffing device; replaces full output packages.

May (01) set yardage counter
(02) use template or gauge to determine when package is ready for doffing
(03) change twisting device on machine
(04) clean and oil machine.

Additional factors: type(s) of yarn in which experienced, eg cotton, nylon, silk, wool; number of spindles attended.

Other titles include Banker, Cap twister, Cop twister, Doubler, Doubling machine attendant, Doubling twister, Fancy twister, Flyer twister, Multi-yarn twister, Ring doubler, Ring spinner, Ring twister, Silk thrower, Single spinner, Throwster, Twiner, Twiner minder, Twist frame attendant, Twister minder, Uptwister.

542.75 Yarn texturer

Creels, threads and attends machine which imparts curl and elasticity to, and increases bulk of yarn produced from, man-made fibres

Sets yarn input packages in machine creel; threads appropriate number of ends from input packages through guides, rollers, heating unit(s) and twisting mechanisms or crimping attachments to each output package, or through guides and over heated knife-edge and roller to output package; starts machine and watches operation for yarn breaks; ties broken ends or wraps loose end round output package; removes (doffs) and replaces full output packages.

May (01) clean and oil machine.

Additional factor: number of spindles attended.

Other titles include Crimp spinner, Edge crimper False twister.

542.80 Winder, Reeler

Creels, threads and attends one or more machines which wind yarn from one package to another to facilitate further processing or for marketing

(01) **Winder**

Places yarn input packages on machine spindles or circular frames (swifts); threads ends from input packages through guides, tensioners, conditioning and clearing devices and secures to output packages; starts machine and watches operation to detect broken or defective yarn, nearly empty input packages and full output packages; joins broken ends by hand or mechanical knotting or with adhesive, or rethreads end through to output package; cuts out lengths of defective yarn; replaces empty input packages; removes (doffs) and replaces full output packages; cleans machine.

Other titles include Bit winder, Bobbin winder, Brass bobbin winder, Cheese winder, Cone winder, Copper, Cop winder, Drum winder, Pirn winder, Quiller, Re-drawer, Rewinder, Slip winder, Spool winder (non-automatic), Unwinder, Weft winder.

(02) **Reeler**

Sets yarn input packages in machine creel; threads ends from input packages through guides and tensioners and secures them to collapsible reels (swifts); starts machine and watches operation to

continued

detect broken or defective yarn and nearly empty input packages; joins broken ends by hand or mechanical knotting; cuts out lengths of defective yarn; replaces empty input packages; cuts yarn when specified amount has been reeled and ties ends of hank together; laces yarn or string through and around hank by hand or machine to prevent tangling; pulls lever to collapse swift or dismantles swift and slides hank off reel.

Other titles include Chenille fur reeler, Hank winder, Reeler and lacer, Reel winder, Skeiner, Swift winder.

May (03) set yardage counter
(04) use hand-operated block and tackle to load yarn on swift
(05) use gauge to determine when packages are ready for doffing
(06) attend machine which automatically doffs full packages and/or replaces input and output packages
(07) replenish conditioning trough
(08) attend machine fitted with automatic knotter
(09) clean machine.

Additional factors: type(s) of yarn in which experienced, eg cotton, jute, silk; number of spindles attended.

Excluded are Ballers (machine) (542.90), Spoolers (machine) (542.90) and Card winders (542.92)

542.90 Baller (machine), Spooler (machine)

Creels, threads and attends one or more machines which automatically wind yarn, thread or twine into balls or on to spools for marketing

Sets input packages of yarn, thread or twine in machine creel; threads ends from input packages through guides, tensioners and knot detectors and secures them to balling pegs or output packages; starts machine and watches operation; replaces empty input packages; where appropriate, watches weight gauge and stops machine when balls or spools reach specified weight; as necessary, cuts yarn, thread or twine and removes (doffs) balls or filled spools; cleans machine.

May (01) manipulate initial windings to form ball centre
(02) regulate speed of machine or of rotation of balling pegs
(03) rejoin broken yarn, thread or twine
(04) assess weight of balls visually
(05) check size or weight of balls or filled spools using hand gauge or weighing device
(06) operate hand press to compress balls of twine
(07) attend machine fitted with automatic doffing mechanism and be known as Self actor spooler.

Additional factor: number of spindles attended.

Other titles include Balling machine attendant, Spool winder (automatic).

542.92 Card winder

Creels, threads and attends machine which winds yarn or thread on to cards for marketing

Sets input packages of yarn or thread in machine creel; places supply of cards on each card holder on machine; threads ends from input packages through guides and tensioners and wraps ends round cards; starts machine which automatically winds measured length of yarn or thread on to each card, cuts off yarn or thread and ejects full cards on to conveyor; watches operation and reports malfunctioning of machine to foreman; replenishes input packages and supplies of cards; cleans machine.

Other titles include Card winding machine attendant.

542.98 Trainee

Performs, under instruction or guidance, various tasks including training exercises and as appropriate pursues studies in order to acquire the basic skills and knowledge required to perform the tasks of workers in textile spinning, doubling, twisting and winding occupations.

542.99 Other textile spinning, doubling, twisting and winding occupations

Workers in this group spin fibre into yarn and thread, and double, twist and wind yarn and thread and are not elsewhere classified, for example:

(01) **Chenille makers,** Chenille workers; (02) **Hand spoolers** (operate hand and foot controls of machine to wind thread on to spools); (03) **Piecers** (repair yarn breakages on doubling, twisting or winding machines); (04) **Yarn curlers** (creel, thread and attend machines which wind yarn on to spools and impart curl to spooled yarn); (05) **Yarn openers** (operate machines to wind hanks of curled yarn on to cones and to separate yarn ends after curl has been set).

Unit Group 543 Warp Preparing Occupations

Workers in this unit group wind warp yarn on to packages and beams, arrange warp threads ready for dyeing, knitting and weaving and perform related tasks.

543 .05 Warp sizer

Operates machine to saturate warp yarn in sheet form with size and wind sized yarn on to weaver's beam

Sets beam(s) of warp yarn in machine creel using lifting equipment; ties ends from warp beams to ends in machine or threads warp ends through rollers in size trough, over drying cylinders or through drying chamber, through spacing devices and on to weaver's beam; fits rods in machine to separate warp ends into layers; operates controls to admit size to trough, to adjust roller pressure and to heat size and drying cylinders or chamber to prescribed temperatures; sets yardage counter; starts machine and regulates speed of warp according to quality of yarn and type and concentration of size; watches temperature and pressure gauges and makes necessary adjustments; watches operation to detect warp breakages and ties or twists broken ends together or joins them with length of similar yarn; ensures that supply of size to trough is adequate; cuts warp threads when required yardage has been wound on to weaver's beam and secures warp ends by knotting.

May (01) calculate concentration of and prepare size solution
(02) adjust width of spacing devices
(03) test yarn by touch to ensure that sizing is proceeding correctly
(04) remove weaver's beam from machine
(05) clean and oil machine.

Additional factor: type(s) of yarn in which experienced, eg cotton, rayon, spun silk, wool.

Other titles include Dresser, Slasher, Slasher sizer, Tape sizer, Taper, Warp sizing machine operator, Yarn dresser, Yarn sizer.

543 .10 Drawer-in (hand)

Draws warp threads through heald eyelets by hand and through reed dents by hand or machine ready for weaving

Ascertains from pattern card the number of heald shafts and size of reed required; ties appropriate number of heald shafts together and secures them in setting-up frame; positions or checks positioning of weaver's beam on frame; pulls warp from beam over framework and ensures that sequence of warp ends corresponds with pattern card; draws each warp thread, offered by reacher-in or reaching machine, by hook through appropriate heald eyelet in correct pattern sequence; secures reed in frame; draws required number of warp threads through each reed dent using a hook or a portable reeding machine; ties ends of warp threads in bunches; re-aligns reed wires and straightens or replaces wire healds as necessary.

May (01) insert lease rods between warp threads
(02) fit droppers on to warp threads by hand
(03) clean or direct cleaning of equipment.

Additional factor: type(s) of yarn in which experienced, eg cotton, jute, silk, wool.

Other titles include Drawer, Enterer, Gear drawer, Healder, Loomer, Reeder, Taker-in Threader-in (warp).

543 .15 Drawing machine setter

Sets up machine to draw warp threads through heald eyelets and reed dents ready for weaving

Selects and places appropriate roller on machine; fixes warp beam and required number of healds and droppers into their respective positions in machine; unrolls warp sheet and secures warp ends using rods and clamps; pushes combs between warp ends to separate them into required layers; selects appropriate reed and positions it on machine; aligns healds, droppers and reed with warp beam to ensure that warp ends are correctly drawn-in; starts machine to check that it has been correctly set up; disconnects gear mechanism when warp has been drawn-in; inserts lease rods through warp, fastens droppers, healds and reed together and wraps drawn-in warp ends around beam; undertakes minor adjustments and repairs to machine.

May (01) draw-in selvedges on either side of warp sheet by hand using threading hook
(02) clean and oil machine.

Additional factor: type(s) of yarn in which experienced, eg cotton, wool, worsted.

543.20 Healding machine operator

Sets up and operates machine to draw warp threads through heald eyelets ready for reeding

Examines healding instructions and plan; selects appropriate punched tape or prepares new tape on punching machine; inserts punched tape in machine; positions heald guides and battery of wire healds in machine; secures beam of warp in warp frame; pulls sheet of warp over frame, brushes and tensions warp ends and clamps them in place; positions warp frame behind healding machine; replaces lease bands separating warp layers with strong cord; tests machine for correct selection of wire healds from battery; starts machine and regulates speed as necessary; watches operation to detect broken threads and to ensure that healding proceeds correctly; ties broken threads together; removes and replaces empty heald batteries; ties loose warp ends in bundles when healding has been completed.

May (01) reed healded threads by hand or using portable reeding machines

(02) operate warp tying machine or twist-in warp by hand (543.25).

Additional factor: type(s) of yarn in which experienced, eg cotton, wool, worsted.

543.25 Warp twister-in

Joins new warp to old warp by hand twisting and/or mechanical knotting

Positions or checks positioning of new warp beam on loom or setting-up frame.

If twisting-in by hand, inserts lease rods in old and new warps; oils tips of warp threads and pulls corresponding ends of old and new warps through holding ring; twists corresponding ends of old and new warps together between forefinger and thumb; joins broken threads.

If twisting-in by machine, positions machine behind loom; combs and tensions old and new warp ends and places them in clamps in correct sequence; inserts lease cord in warps and threads cord ends through machine; starts machine and watches operation to ensure that ends are joined in correct pattern order; hand ties ends missed by machine; removes lease cord; unclamps warps and removes machine.

Turns take-up roller in front of loom to pull joined ends through droppers, healds and reed.

Additional factor: type(s) of yarn in which experienced, eg cotton, nylon, silk.

Other titles include Warp knotter, Warp knotting machine operator, Warp twister-on, Warp twister-up, Warp tying machine operator.

543.30 Warp threader (warp knitting)

Draws warp threads by hand through guides of warp knitting machine ready for knitting

Examines threading chart to ascertain number of guide bars required and sequence of threading; positions guide bars on machine rests; passes individual threads from warp beams through appropriate spaces in reed according to pattern required; cuts tape or paper holding ends of warp threads and draws threads through eyes of guide bars using threading tool; places guide bars in operating position; starts machine; knits sample to check that knitting conforms to specification.

May (01) mount or assist in mounting warp beams on machine

(02) clean guide bars

(03) make minor adjustments to speed of machine.

Other titles include Warp knit threader.

543.50 Warper (machine)

Threads and attends machine which draws warp threads through reed and winds them on to drums, reels or beams preparatory to dyeing or to drawing-in to looms or knitting machines

Examines instructions for length and density of warp required; checks colour and shade identification markings of yarn on input packages or warp beams against specification; positions or checks positioning of input packages or warp beams on machine creel; ties new yarn ends to corresponding old ends, or draws yarn ends through guides, tensioners, reed dents and drop wires and secures to drum, reel or take-up beam; sets yardage counter; starts machine and regulates speed as necessary; watches operation to detect broken, crossed or tangled yarn threads; joins broken yarn by hand or mechanical knotting; breaks crossed yarn threads and joins appropriate ends; brushes out tangles; removes fluff accumulating on machine using hand brush or air hose; cuts warp threads when required yardage has been wound and secures ends on drum, reel or take-up beam by looping, tying or taping; replenishes supply of input packages or beams as required.

Other titles include Ball warper, Cross ball warper, Selvedge winder, Warp dresser.

(01) **Section warper**

Performs tasks of warper on machine which draws warp threads from yarn packages through reed and winds them on to drums or reels to form section of patterned warp.

(02) **Beam warper**

Performs tasks of warper on machine which draws warp threads from a number of drums or reels (warp sections) or yarn packages through reed and winds them on to warp beam.

continued

Other titles include Chain beamer, Creel beamer, Dry beamer, Prebeamer, Scotch beamer.

(03) **Dry taper**

Performs tasks of warper on machine which draws warp threads from a number of warp beams through reed and winds them on to weaver's beam.

May (04) insert lease rods to separate layers of warp threads during winding
(05) adjust width of drum or beam and align spacing devices
(06) remove warp beams from machine using lifting equipment where necessary
(07) perform tasks of BEAMER-OFF (543.99)
(08) oil machine
(09) attend high speed machines fitted with automatic stopping and warning devices
(10) warp short lengths for patterns and ranges and be known as Pattern warper, Range warper
(11) correct warps by rebeaming on to weaver's beam and be known as Rebeamer.

Additional factor: type(s) of yarn in which experienced, eg cotton, jute, silk.

543.55 Drawing machine operator

Operates machine to draw warp threads through heald eyelets and reed dents ready for weaving

Starts set-up machine and regulates speed as necessary; watches operation to detect broken threads and to ensure that warp threads are drawn-in in sequence shown on pattern card; ties broken threads; stops machine when warp has been drawn-in.

May (01) assist drawing machine setter to set-up machine
(02) clean and oil machine.

Additional factor: type(s) of yarn in which experienced, eg cotton, wool, worsted.

Other titles include Looming machine operator.

543.60 Warp pinning machine operator

Operates machine to place droppers (warp stop motion pins) on warp threads

Places beam of warp on pinning frame or positions portable frame over warp in loom; slides lease rods alongside lease cords between warp threads, withdraws lease cords and clamps lease rods in position; lifts machine on to frame rails and loads it with droppers; starts machine and follows its progress across warp sheet to ensure that dropper is placed on each warp thread; replaces faulty droppers; re-inserts lease cords and withdraws lease rods; removes warp beam from frame or portable frame from loom.

May (01) place droppers on warp threads by hand.

Other titles include Dollier, Dropper pin machine operator, Pinner.

543.65 Setter (spool Axminster carpet)

Threads and attends machine which draws pile yarn threads through reed and winds them on to spools in sequence required for spool Axminster carpet weaving

Selects required yarn packages according to appropriate design paper or colour chart and positions them on pegs of setting table or creel in the order specified; draws each yarn thread around or through appropriate guides, tensioners and reed dents and wraps it around spool; starts machine and watches operation to detect broken yarn threads; ties broken threads; lifts filled spool from machine and attaches identification label showing line of pattern to which it relates; replaces and ties in supply packages as required.

May (01) use wire brush to separate yarn threads
(02) clean and oil machine.

Other titles include Spooler, Spool setter.

543.70 Threader (spool Axminster carpet)

Threads yarn ends from prepared spools through tube guides to form rows of pile tufts

Places spools of pile yarn on threading machine; draws ends from spools and secures them over machine frame; slots metal tube frame into threading machine; operates control to insert a row of threading hooks through each tube frame to catch pile ends; checks that each yarn end is on its appropriate threading hook; operates control to withdraw threading hooks and pull yarn threads through tubes; operates cutter to trim row of tufts to required length, where necessary; threads missed pile yarn ends by hand through tubes; replaces broken threading hooks; removes set of spools and tubes from threading machine and fits it in to appropriate position in pattern chain.

543 .90 Reacher-in

Assists drawer-in to draw warp threads through loom harness ready for weaving

Performs some or all of the following tasks: counts and groups healds in shafts; assists in positioning and securing weaver's beam, heald shafts and reed in setting-up frame, and in removing beam and harness from frame on completion of drawing-in operation; pulls warp from beam; assists in inserting lease rods in and withdrawing them from warp; removes lease cords from warp; unties knotted bunches of warp ends; takes individual warp ends in correct sequence and places each end on hook inserted by drawer-in through eyelet of appropriate heald; assists in cleaning and straightening heald and reed wires.

Additional factor: type(s) of yarn in which experienced, eg cotton, flax, wool.

Other titles include Ingiver, Reacher.

543 .98 Trainee

Performs, under instruction or guidance, various tasks including training exercises and as appropriate pursues studies in order to acquire the basic skills and knowledge required to perform the tasks of workers in warp preparing occupations.

543 .99 Other warp preparing occupations

Workers in this group wind warp on to packages and beams, arrange warp threads ready for dyeing, knitting and weaving, and perform related tasks and are not elsewhere classified, for example:

(01) **Beamers-off** (attend machines which wind warp sections on to weavers' beams); (02) **Hand warpers,** Pattern warpers (hand), Stake warpers; (03) **Heald counters** (count out and prepare healds in shafts foı use of drawing machine setters); (04) **Warp leasers** (insert lease bands round warp ends by hand or machine).

Unit Group 544 Textile Weaving Occupations

Workers in this unit group weave yarn of natural and man-made fibres into carpet and fabric.

544 .05 Carpet weaver (power loom)

Operates one or more power driven looms fitted with pile forming mechanism or attachments to weave carpet or rugs

Directs, assists in or checks positioning of pile and warp yarn beams, packages or spools, according to weaving requirements; ties new pile and warp yarn ends to corresponding old ends or draws them through appropriate guides and tensioners; threads shuttles or needles with weft yarn; sets yardage counter or records reading and starts loom; examines carpet for faults in pattern, pile or weave; measures carpet width at intervals and adjusts tensioners to remedy measurement discrepancies; joins broken pile and warp yarn ends and rethreads broken weft yarn; replaces broken weft threads (picks); replaces or directs replacement of faulty and empty pile and warp yarn beams, packages or spools and weft yarn packages; marks or cuts carpet when specified yardage has been woven; reports major weaving and mechanical faults to overlooker or loom tuner; cleans or directs cleaning of loom.

Other titles include Broadloom weaver, Narrow weaver.

(01) **Brussels weaver, Wilton weaver**

Performs tasks of carpet weaver on plain or jacquard loom which weaves carpet over pile forming wires to produce looped pile surface (Brussels weave) or over pile forming and cutting wires to produce cut pile surface (Wilton weave); hooks requisite number of pile forming or forming and cutting wires on to appropriate mechanism; replaces missing wires during weaving operation.

(02) **Gripper Axminster weaver**

Performs tasks of carpet weaver on jacquard loom which draws individual pile tufts from yarn packages, and inserts them between warp threads to produce carpet of limited colour and design variations; sets jacquard cards on pattern cylinder; guides pile yarn ends into yarn carriers and pulls sufficient yarn down from carriers to form individual tufts; trims tufts to uniform length; lifts jacquard attachment and reverses pattern cylinder if grippers miss or reject row of tufts; weaves short plain strip when required yardage has been woven.

(03) **Spool Axminster weaver**

Performs tasks of carpet weaver on loom which draws complete rows of pile tufts from spools carried by endless chains, and inserts them between warp threads to produce carpet of multiple colour and design variations; rethreads missing pile yarn ends through appropriate tubes in tube frames and pulls sufficient yarn down to form tufts; arranges for necessary alteration in length and spacing of spool chain to be made when change in design or measurement o icarpet is required.

continued

(04) **Gripper spool Axminster weaver**

Performs tasks of spool Axminster weaver on spool Axminster loom which inserts complete rows of pile tufts between warp threads by gripper mechanism.

May (05) change pattern cards on jacquard attachment to vary design

(06) repair or replace broken harness cords and jacquard pattern cards

(07) oil loom.

Additional factors: type(s) of loom on which experienced, eg Wilton jacquard narrow, Wilton plain face-to-face, gripper Axminster narrow, spool Axminster broad; number of looms operated.

544.10 Fabric weaver (power loom)

Attends one or more power looms which weave yarn into fabric piece goods

Starts set-up loom and watches weaving operation to detect loose or broken warp threads, defective weft threads (picks) and other weaving faults; varies warp tension as required by adjusting axiliary weights on friction rollers; stops loom when necessary if breakage or other fault occurs; joins piece of yarn to broken end or pulls spare thread from back of loom and threads joined or spare thread through appropriate drop wire, heald eyelet and reed dent using threading hook; reverses loom to, and removes, defective pick; inserts new pick by sliding shuttle through space between separated warp threads (warp shed) or, on shuttleless loom, by restarting loom or blowing yarn across warp shed with an airline; reports multiple warp break (warp smash) to foreman or mechanical fault to foreman or loom tuner; loads and replaces shuttles on non-automatic shuttled loom; replaces empty weft yarn packages in shuttleless loom belting and ties in ends to form continuous yarn feed; cuts off or marks fabric or inserts pick of contrasting colour when requisite yardage has been woven.

Other titles include Broadloom weaver, Narrow fabric weaver.

(01) **Plain weaver**

Performs tasks of fabric weaver on loom which produces fabric of plain weave in sheet or tubular form.

Other titles include Circular weaver, Tappet loom weaver.

(02) **Dobby weaver**

Performs tasks of fabric weaver on loom which produces fabric of simple patterned weave.

(03) **Jacquard weaver**

Performs tasks of fabric weaver on loom which produces fabric of figured or floral design; checks lacing of jacquard cards and ties broken lacing cords; notifies breakage of loom harness to loom tuner.

May (04) attend loom fitted with automatic weft package winding and shuttle changing attachments

(05) repair warp smashes (544.25)

(06) draw-in warp ends (543.10)

(07) tie-in new warps (543.25)

(08) mend threads by splicing or using adhesive

(09) replace faulty heald wires

(10) clean and oil loom.

Additional factors: type(s) of loom on which experienced, eg plain narrow shuttleless, dobby broad, jacquard face-to-face; number of looms attended; type(s) of yarn in which experienced, eg asbestos, cotton, rayon, worsted.

Excluded are Pattern weavers (544.20), Lace weavers (544.30) and Netting weavers (544.50)

544.15 Hand loom weaver (fabric)

Sets up and operates hand loom to weave yarn into fabric

Examines work ticket showing warp, weft and yardage requirements and pattern chart; secures specified beam of warp in position on loom; draws-in warp ends or joins corresponding new and old warp ends together by twisting or knotting; takes up slack warp by adjusting tension weights; inserts yarn package of specified colour and shade into shuttle and threads loose end through shuttle eyelet; presses foot treadle on loom to operate dobby or jacquard mechanism and open (shed) the warp; inserts weft thread (pick) by throwing shuttle across warp shed by hand or by pulling rope to activate shuttle pivot arm; pulls reed carriage forward to beat-up pick; changes package in shuttle when new colour or shade is required; replaces empty packages; examines fabric being woven to check pattern, evenness of warp tension and weave, and to detect broken warp threads or picks; joins broken warp threads using length of yarn; pulls out and replaces broken picks; cuts off or marks fabric when requisite yardage has been woven; straightens or replaces bent wire healds; cleans and oils loom and undertakes minor repairs.

May (01) perform tasks of WINDER (542.80)

(02) perform tasks of WARPER (MACHINE) (543.50)

(03) perform tasks of HARNESS BUILDER (549.04).

Additional factor: type(s) of yarn in which experienced, eg coir, wool, worsted.

Other titles include Coir mat maker.

544.20 Pattern weaver

Sets up and operates hand or power loom to weave sample lengths of fabric under direction of designer

Examines instructions on pattern chart prepared by designer.
If power loom weaving, draws-in warp threads as described under DRAWER-IN (HAND) (543.10) or checks tha warp threads have been correctly drawn-in, or twists-in new warp as described under WARP TWISTER-IN (543.25); places pattern cards on loom as necessary; weaves sample of required length as described under FABRIC WEAVER (POWER LOOM) (544.10).
If hand loom weaving, sets up and operates loom as described under HAND LOOM WEAVER (FABRIC) (544.15).
Passes sample length to designer for inspection; alters arrangement of warp threads, as directed, to vary density of warp or to produce special effects; changes shuttles and yarn packages, reeds and pattern cards, as instructed, to vary colour, design or pattern weave of sample lengths.

May (01) perform tasks of WINDER (542.80)
(02) perform tasks of WARPER (543.50)
(03) perform tasks of HARNESS BUILDER (549.04)
(04) perform tasks of PATTERN CARD CUTTER (549.06).

Other titles include Length weaver, Pattern loom weaver, Range weaver.

544.25 Smash hand

Repairs multiple warp breaks and assists fabric weavers generally in the performance of their tasks

Patrols weaving shed and attends to requests for assistance by individual weavers; untangles broken warp ends in multiple warp breaks; joins a piece of yarn to each broken warp thread and draws it in through appropriate drop wire, heald eyelet and reed dent using threading hook; ensures that threads are drawn-in in correct sequence by reference to weaving pattern or chart; lifts healds and checks arrangement of new warp ends in loom harness; breaks and rejoins threads incorrectly joined or drawn-in and crossed warp threads; draws-in new warp threads or joins corresponding new and old warp ends together by twisting or knotting; slackens tensioners, pulls back fabric and cuts out, or withdraws with needle, faulty weft threads (picks); straightens or replaces defective wire healds and drop wires.

Other titles include Smash tier, Spare weaver, Time weaver.

544.30 Lace weaver

Attends one or more power driven machines which produce plain or patterned lace

Starts set-up machine or threads warp and yarn ends through appropriate guides and tensioners and starts machine; watches operation to detect holes or pattern faults; stops machine when necessary to remedy fault; ties broken yarn ends together; replaces warp beams, yarn spools and bobbins as necessary and ties corresponding new and old warp and yarn ends together; adjusts warp tension and speed of machine as required; cuts off and removes lace when requisite yardage has been produced; reports mechanical faults to foreman or tuner.

May (01) perform tasks of PATTERN CARD LACER (549.93)
(02) fit pattern cards on machine
(03) refill empty bobbins from yarn beams or packages.

Additional factors: type(s) of yarn in which experienced, eg cotton, nylon, terylene; number of machines attended.

Other titles include Lace machine operator, Lace maker, Twist hand.

Excluded are Warp lace makers (545.60)

544.50 Netting weaver

Attends one or more power driven machines on which yarn or twine is intersected and knotted at regular intervals to produce netting

Starts set-up loom, or threads yarn or twine ends from packages and shuttles through guides and tensioners, ties corresponding ends together along needle bar and starts machine; watches operation to detect weaving and knotting faults or broken yarn or twine ends; stops loom when necessary to remedy fault; tightens insecure knots by hand and ties broken yarn or twine ends together; replaces yarn or twine packages and shuttles as necessary and ties corresponding new and old ends together; cuts off and removes netting when requisite yardage has been produced; reports mechanical faults to foreman or loom tuner.

May (01) refill empty shuttles with yarn or twine from beams or packages
(02) specialise in weaving fine or wide mesh netting.

Additional factor: number of looms attended.

Other titles include Net maker, Net weaver.

544 .98 Trainee

Performs, under instruction or guidance, various tasks including training exercises and as appropriate pursues studies in order to acquire the basic skills and knowledge required to perform the tasks of workers in textile weaving occupations.

544 .99 Other textile weaving occupations

Workers in this group weave yarn of natural and man-made fibres into carpet and fabric and are not elsewhere classified, for example:

(01) **Chenille setters,** Chenille setting weavers, Chenille weavers (weave chenille fur into carpet backing on setting looms); (02) **Contour weavers** (weave glass yarn into specified shapes); (03) **Hand loom carpet weavers;** (04) **Hand wiring carpet weavers** (weave Wilton carpet by manually inserting and withdrawing pile wires and cutting pile loops with hand knives).

Unit Group 545 Knitting Occupations

Workers in this unit group knit fabric, garments and other articles from yarn by hand and machine, and undertake closely related tasks in knitting processes.

545 .10 Flat machine knitter (hand)

Operates machine by hand to knit garments or garment parts

(01) **Flat machine knitter (excluding intarsia)**

Places yarn packages on spindles and threads yarn through guides into needle feeders; pushes up required number of needles into position; inserts wire rod attached to weighted bar into needle bed; moves carriage across needle bed by hand to cast specified number of stitches on to wire rod; continues to move carriage by hand backwards and forwards across needle bed until required number of rows has been knitted; fashions article by increasing or decreasing number of needles in use as specified in pattern; casts off stitches and removes articles from machine.

Other titles include Hand flat knitter, Hand flat machinist, Woollen glove machinist.

(02) **Flat machine knitter (intarsia)**

Places yarn packages below machine and threads yarn over clips to needle bed; transfers stitches from knitted welt on to machine needles and attaches weights to welt to pull knitted fabric taut; lays appropriate coloured yarn across machine needles and pushes carriage by hand across needle bed; repeats operation until required number of rows has been knitted; fashions article by increasing or decreasing number of needles in use according to point paper pattern; casts off stitches and removes articles from machine.

Other titles include Intarsia knitter.

May (03) adjust controls to alter tension
(04) replace broken needles
(05) clean and oil machine
(06) make up designs for approval.

545 .20 Flat machine knitter (power)

Attends one or more power-operated machines which produce flat fabric, fully fashioned hose or other fashioned garments or garment parts by weft knitting

Sets machine controls and/or needles to produce article of specified size and pattern, where appropriate; places yarn packages on machine and threads ends from packages through guides and tensioners into needle feeders or ties ends from packages to ends in machine; starts and stops machine as required; watches operation to detect yarn breaks, empty or faulty yarn packages and knitting defects; ties broken yarn ends; replaces empty or faulty yarn packages; reports mechanical faults to foreman or mechanic; cuts or breaks off yarn on completion of knitting and where necessary pulls out draw threads to separate garments or garment parts.

May (01) attend machine fitted with jacquard attachment
(02) perform tasks of PATTERN CARD CUTTER (549 .06)
(03) fit punched card or programmed tape on to machine
(04) position transfer bar containing knitted welts over needle bar of machine
(05) straighten or replace defective needles
(06) clean and oil machine
(07) undertake minor repairs to machine.

Additional factors: number of knitting heads attended; type(s) of goods knitted, eg fabric, hose, outerwear.

Other titles include Frame knitter, Framework knitter, Fully fashioned hose knitter, Straight bar machine knitter.

545 .50 Circular machine knitter

Attends one or more power-operated machines which produce tubular fabric, seamless hose or other seamless garments or garment parts by weft knitting

Starts and stops machine as required; watches operation to detect yarn breaks, empty or faulty yarn packages and knitting defects; ties broken yarn ends; replaces empty or faulty yarn packages and ties ends from new packages to ends in machine or threads new ends through guides and tensioners into needle feeders; reports mechanical faults to foreman or mechanic; ensures that knitted fabric, garment or garment part passes into appropriate container; cuts off tubular fabric when container is full.

May (01) attend machine fitted with jacquard attachment
(02) fit punched card or programmed tape on to machine
(03) straighten or replace defective needles
(04) clean and oil machine
(05) undertake minor adjustments and repairs to machine.

Additional factors: number of knitting heads attended; type(s) of goods knitted, eg fabric, gloves, hose.

Other titles include Circular knitting machinist, Pile fabric knitter, Seamless knitter.

545 .60 Warp knitter

Attends battery of machines which produce fabric piece goods by warp knitting

Starts machines or takes over running machines; guides knitted fabric through tension rollers and on to take-up rollers; patrols knitting area and examines fabric for flaws; ties broken yarn ends and rethreads yarn through guides where necessary; stops machine and notifies foreman or mechanic immediately a mechanical fault is detected; watches automatic counter on each machine and stops machine when required length of fabric has been knitted; cuts fabric close to take-up roller.

May (01) replace broken needles
(02) remove rolls of fabric from machines and insert new take-up rollers
(03) clean machines.

Additional factor: number of machines attended.

Other titles include Warp hand, Warp lace maker Warp loom hand.

545 .70 Bar filler

Runs stitches from knitted welt by hand on to transfer bar to facilitate transfer to framework knitting machine

Secures transfer bar in position on work frame; pulls out draw threads to separate welts where necessary; loops loose stitches of welt over appropriate needles of transfer bar; releases loaded bar from work frame and cuts off or unravels unwanted welt.

Other titles include Runner-on, Topper, Transferrer.

545 .98 Trainee

Performs, under instruction or guidance, various tasks including training exercises and as appropriate pursues studies in order to acquire the basic skills and knowledge required to perform the tasks of workers in knitting occupations.

545 .99 Other knitting occupations

Workers in this group knit fabric, garments and other articles from yarn by hand and machine and undertake closely related tasks in knitting processes and are not elsewhere classified, for example:

(01) **Bar loaders** (operate machines to load bars with stitches from ribbed pieces, and keep knitting machines supplied with yarn); (02) **Crochet workers;** (03) **Frame knitters (hand)** (operate knitting frames by means of hand and foot controls); (04) **Fringers** (form fringes on scarves using knitting points); (05) **Hand knitters;** (06) **Toppers and tailers** (reinforce berets at centres of crowns and add tails, using crochet hooks); (07) **Yarn heald knitters,** Yarn heald makers (operate machines to knit yarn healds).

Unit Group 546 Textile Bleaching, Dyeing, Finishing and Other Treating Occupations

Workers in this unit group bleach, dye, finish and otherwise treat textile fibres, yarn, piece goods, cordage and hosiery, dye garments and other articles made from textile fabric and perform related tasks.

Excluded are Textile Repairing Occupations (547)

546.10 Molten metal dyeing machine operator

Operates machine to dye fabric piece goods to required colour by passing them through dye solution, molten metal and fixing and developing solutions

Performs some or all of the following tasks: prepares dye and fixing salt solutions in separate tanks; prepares and heats developing solution; runs sample of fabric to be dyed through scale model of machine and takes it to foreman for colour matching; varies composition of dye solution as instructed if colour does not conform to specification; sews end of fabric to leader cloth in machine; adjusts panel controls to admit dye and salt solutions from tanks into, and circulate them round, appropriate machine boxes and to heat solutions and metal to prescribed temperatures; starts machine to draw fabric through dye, through molten metal which forces dye into fabric and through fixing and developing solutions; regulates speed of fabric as necessary; watches temperature gauges and adjusts controls as necessary; watches progress of fabric to ensure that dyeing, fixing and developing are proceeding correctly; cleans machine.

546.20 Re-dyer

Re-dyes garments or other articles made from textile materials to customers' requirements

Classifies article according to type of material and to colour required; fills dyeing vessel or machine with cold water; weighs out specified quantities of dyes and other chemicals and adds to vessel or machine; heats solution to prescribed temperature; immerses article in solution in vessel and agitates it by hand or mechanically, or places article in machine, secures feed hatch and starts machine; controls temperature of solution; inspects colour of article after specified period and varies composition of solution as necessary; removes article from vessel or machine when properly dyed.

May (01) wash, rinse and dry articles before and/or after dyeing.

Additional factor: type of equipment used, eg vat, drum, paddle machine, tumbler.

Other titles include Clothes dyer, Garment dyer.

546.50 Backwash attendant

Attends one or more machines which wash, rinse and dry slivers to remove impurities and excess chemicals

Positions balls or cans of slivers at input end of machine; joins ends from balls or cans to ends in machine by twisting, or threads ends through appropriate guides and rollers to delivery end of machine; adjusts controls to admit and circulate washing and rinsing solutions and to regulate temperature of drying chamber; starts machine and watches operation to detect sliver breaks, nearly exhausted sliver balls or input cans and full output cans; twists broken sliver ends together; replenishes supply of sliver; removes (doffs) and replaces full sliver cans; drains and replenishes washing and rinsing solutions as required.

May (01) regulate flow of conditioning liquid on to washed sliver to facilitate further processing

(02) attend backwash machine from which washed sliver is automatically fed into gill box

(03) assist gill box attendant

(04) clean and oil machine

(05) replace worn roller coverings.

Additional factor: number of machines attended.

Other titles include Backwasher.

546.52 Bleacher

Treats fibres, yarn or piece goods with chemical solutions to bleach them

Pours or admits specified quantities of water and chemical solution into bleaching vessel; loads or directs manual loading of items to be bleached into vessel or starts roller or reel to draw in items; operates controls to heat solution and maintain it at prescribed temperature, and to agitate solution or items as required; drains off solution after specified time and rinses items; removes or directs removal of bleached items from vessel.

May (01) mix chemical solutions according to formulae

(02) sew lengths of fabric together by machine before bleaching

(03) winch fabric into and out of bleaching vessel

(04) adjust roller tension

(05) withdraw and test samples of solution during bleaching

(06) perform tasks of WASHER (546.86)

(07) perform tasks of DRIER (546.89)

(08) degum silk before bleaching and be known as Degummer and bleacher

(09) mangle and open out bleached material and be known as Bleaching mangle operator.

Additional factor: type of material bleached, eg cotton linters, silk yarn, rayon piece goods.

Other titles include Bleacher's operative, Bluer, Bowker, Crofthand, Dolly hand, Kier boiler, Kierer, Kierman, Paddle machine operator, Rotary machine operator, Straw plait bleacher, Tinter, Winch hand, Yarn setter.

Excluded are Continuous textile finishing unit operators (546.60)

546.54 Operative dyer

Treats textile fibres, yarn, piece goods, cordage or hosiery with dye solution to give them the required colour

Performs a combination of the following tasks: mixes dye solution according to furmula; admits required quantity of water into dyeing vessel or machine and adds dye solution; heats solution to specified temperature; places items to be dyed in or on to holding device; loads or directs loading of items into vessel or positions items at feed end of machine; sews ends of fabric together to form endless belt; secures end of yarn, cordage or fabric to leader tapes or cloth or to end in machine, or threads end through appropriate guides and tensioners; closes lid or secures feed hatch of vessel or machine; inserts appropriate punched card into control panel of programmed machine; starts machinery to circulate items or solution or to draw items through solutions and/or rollers or to rotate drum or tumbler; adjusts controls to regulate temperature and/or speed of dyeing operation, or checks that preset automatic regulators are functioning correctly; withdraws or cuts off sample of dyed items for colour matching; varies composition of solution as directed; ties broken ends of cordage or yarn; reports mechanical faults to foreman; unloads or directs unloading of dyed items; drains and cleans vessel or machine as directed.

May (01) scour or treat items with softening solution before dyeing

(02) operate equipment to rinse and dry items after dyeing

(03) operate equipment in which reducing agents and/or steam are applied to fabric to fix colours.

Additional factors: type of vessel or machine used, eg vat, drum, paddle machine, tumbler; number of vessels or machines attended; type of goods or item dyed, eg fibres, yarn, fabric, hosiery.

Other titles include Automatic package dyer, Beam dyer, Cheese dyer, Cop dyer, Cordage dyer, Dyehouse operative, Dyer's operative, Hank dyer, Hosiery dyer, Jig dyer, Jiggerman, Padder, Padding machine man, Piece dyer, Range dyer, Star dyer, Top dyer, Tub dyer, Vat dyer, Vessel dyer, Warp dyer, Winch dyer, Yarn dyer.

Excluded are Molten metal dyeing machine operators (546.10) and Re-dyers (546.20)

546 .56 Finishing solution tank operator

Operates equipment to pass yarn, fabric or cordage through starch, size, water-repellent or other chemical solutions to impart required finish

Positions yarn hanks, yarn or cordage packages or fabric on or near equipment, using mechanical aids where necessary; admits solution or checks that solution has been automatically admitted to machine troughs or trays; if mercerising hanks, operates controls to admit hot water to sprays above machine rollers or checks that sprays have been automatically supplied with water; secures ends of yarn or cordage packages or fabric to leader tapes or cloth in equipment, passes end(s) through guides, over or through rollers and round output package or roller or through to folding device, or places yarn hanks on machine rollers; adjusts roller pressure or tension according to type of item to be treated; if hot finishing, operates control to heat solution and drying rollers or chamber to prescribed temperatures; starts finishing operation, and regulates speed of item through equipment as necessary; watches operation to ensure that item is correctly treated and makes necessary adjustments; ties broken yarn ends or joins ends with length of similar yarn; ensures that supply of solution to trough or trays is adequate; removes finished item from equipment.

May (01) prepare solution according to formula

(02) test strength of solution using hydrometer

(03) clean and oil equipment

(04) re-cover rollers.

Additional factor: type(s) of material finished, eg nylon yarn, woollen fabric, carpet.

Other titles include Back filler, Back sizer, Back sizer and drier, Cord waxer, Cordage dresser, Impregnating machine operator, Merceriser, Mercerising machine attendant, Polisher (cordage, fabric, thread), Polishing machine attendant (cordage, fabric), Proofer, Rope sizer, Single end sizer, Sizing machine operator, Starcher, Tarring machine operator, Yarn sizer.

Excluded are Warp sizers (543 .05) and Continuous textile finishing unit operators (546 .60)

546 .58 Miller

Consolidates and shrinks fabric by machine to predetermined width and length

(01) **Dry miller**

Passes end of fabric through guides, rollers and tensioned aperture; sews ends of fabric together to form continuous band; adjusts controls to regulate roller pressure and tension on aperture to obtain specified consolidation and shrinkage; starts machine and regulates speed of fabric as necessary; handles and measures width of fabric periodically and continues milling operation until required consolidation and shrinkage have been obtained; removes milled fabric from machine.

(02) **Solvent miller**

Loads fabric into machine; calculates quantities of water and milling agent required and adds to solvent in machine; starts tumbler mechanism; stops machine periodically and handles and measures width of fabric to ascertain amount of consolidation and shrinkage obtained; starts hydro-extractor when required consolidation and shrinkage have been obtained; removes milled fabric from machine; operates pump and other equipment to reclaim solvent for re-use.

May (03) scour fabric before and/or after milling (546 .86)

(04) prepare and position punched card on machine for automatic milling operation

(05) impregnate fabric with water or liquid soap before milling and be known as Wet miller.

546 .60 Continuous textile finishing unit operator

Operates continuous finishing unit in which fabric is desized, scoured, bleached, dried, starched and stentered

Performs some or all of the following tasks: prepares desizing, bleaching, starch and other solutions according to formulae; regulates flow of solutions into unit; secures ends of fabric to leader tapes or cloth in unit to maintain continuous feed of fabric through unit; sets thermostats to prescribed temperatures; operates controls to start, stop and adjust speed of unit; controls passage of fabric through unit to ensure that required finish is obtained.

546 .62 Singeing machine operator

Burns off protruding fibres from yarn or fabric

(01) **Yarn gasser**

Sets yarn input packages in machine creel; threads ends from input packages through guides and over gas jets and secures to output packages; lights jets; starts machine and watches operation; joins broken ends using mechanical knotter; removes full output packages of yarn.

(02) **Fabric singeing machine operator**

Secures end of fabric to leader tape or to end in machine; adjusts controls to obtain specified roller speed and gas and air pressures; lights gas jets; starts machine and watches operation; monitors gas and air pressure gauges and makes necessary adjustments; removes singed fabric from machine.

May (03) operate equipment in which fabric is desized or steam sprayed after singeing

(04) clean and oil machine.

Additional factor: type(s) of yarn or fabric treated, eg cotton yarn, spun silk, terylene fabric.

Other titles include Fabric gasser, Singer.

546 .64 Stenterer

Operates machine to stretch fabric to, or heat-set fabric at, predetermined width

Performs some or all of the following tasks: positions fabric on or near machine; sews end of fabric to leader cloth or tapes in machine or passes end through tensioning rollers and feed mechanism and fixes first few inches of selvedge to stenter clips or pins; adjusts distance between clip or pin rails according to width required; adjusts controls to heat drying chamber or rollers or drying and setting chambers to prescribed temperature; starts operation and regulates speed of fabric through machine; watches temperature and pressure gauges and makes necessary adjustments; measures stentered fabric periodically to check width.

May (01) dampen fabric before stentering

(02) clean and oil machine

(03) operate machine in which fabric is taken through starch solution before stentering and be known as Wet stenterer.

Additional factor: type(s) of fabric stentered, eg cotton, rayon, pressed woollen felt.

Other titles include Back end man, Dry stenterer, Front end man, Stenter operative, Stenter operator, Stentering machine operator, Stretching machine man, Tenterer, Tentering machine operator.

Excluded are Continuous textile finishing unit operators (546 .60) and Belt stretchers (546 .99)

546 .66 Shrinking machine operator

Operates machine to compress warp of fabric by heat and pressure to shrink material to perdetermined length

Adjusts controls to obtain specified steam and water pressures; sets shrinkage control mechanism according to amount of shrinkage required; passes end of fabric or leader tape attached to fabric over tension rails, through shrinkage unit, round drying cylinder and through folding device; starts operation and regulates speed of fabric through machine; watches temperature and pressure gauges and makes necessary adjustments; measures shrunken fabric periodically to check length.

May (01) clean and oil machine

(02) replace rollers of shrinkage unit and cover of drying cylinder.

Other titles include Sanforizer.

546 .68 Cropper (fabric, carpet)

Shears protruding fibres from surface of fabric, carpet or matting or cuts nap or pile to uniform length by machine

Positions material on or near machine; secures end of material to leader cloth in machine or places end over feed roller; adjusts height of cutter(s) according to thickness of material or depth of pile required; starts machine and watches operation to ensure even cropping; operates controls as required to raise cutter(s) and permit joins in material to pass under blade(s) without being cut; removes cropped material from machine.

May (01) set speed of machine rollers

(02) operate machine in which material is brushed before cropping

(03) clean and oil machine

(04) operate edge or selvedge trimming machine

(05) operate back sizing machine (546 .56) and be known as Cropper and sizer

(06) trim mat edges and cut round pattern or letters on mat using electric shears and be known as Mat shearer and trimmer.

Additional factor: type(s) of material cropped, eg carpet, coir matting, worsted.

Other titles include Clipper, Cutter (woollen, worsted finishing), Cutterman, Shearer, Shearing machine operator.

546.70 Flat presser

Presses fabric in flat-bed machine to impart required finish

Interleaves press papers and heating pads between folds of fabric or fixes roll(s) of fabric on stand in front of machine; transfers prepared fabric to bed of press using lifting equipment and attaches leads to heating pads or sews end(s) of roll to end(s) in machine or passes end of roll between press plates and on to take-up roller(s); operates controls to close press and subject fabric to specified degree of heat and pressure; watches temperature and pressure gauges, and makes necessary adjustments; opens press after specified time; removes fabric from press or take-up roller(s).

May (01) press fabric cold.

Additional factor: type(s) of fabric pressed, eg cotton, rayon, pressed woollen felt.

Other titles include Flat press operator, Hydraulic presser, Hydraulic press operator, Trimmer (knitted fabric pressing).

See Machine presser (garments) (461.10)

Excluded are Automatic press attendants (546.99)

546.72 Raiser

Raises a layer of fibres on surface of fabric by machine brushing, teazling or knife oscillation

(01) Wire raiser, Teazle operator

Sews ends of fabric together or to leader cloth to form continuous band or passes end through nip rollers and secures to take-up roller; adjusts controls to position raising cylinder and to regulate roller and fabric speeds to obtain required finish or adjusts feed position of fabric against raising cylinder(s) to obtain appropriate pressure; starts machine; watches operation and makes necessary adjustments; examines fabric visually and by touch during operation and removes fabric from machine when required finish has been obtained or checks that finish conforms to specification as fabric emerges from delivery end of machine; cleans and oils machine.

Other titles include Brusher (fabric finishing)' Flannelette brusher, Gigger, Teazler.

(02) Knife-raising machine operator

Adjusts height of blade and roller tension on each machine to obtain required finish; starts machines; watches operation and makes necessary adjustments; removes and replaces knives which require regrinding; handles fabric and tests samples in water for absorbency to ensure that finish conforms to specification; cleans and oils machines.

Other titles include Lint raiser, Lint raising machine operator.

May (03) renew brushes or teazle bars

(04) operate machine in which fabric is steamed before raising and be known as Steamer-brusher.

Additional factor: type(s) of fabric raised, eg cotton, nylon, woollen.

Other titles include Blanket raiser, Flannelette raiser, Raising machinist.

546.74 Boarder

Fixes permanent shape of hose or other knitted garments such as berets and gloves before or after dyeing

(01) Boarder (excluding gloves)

Fits garments on to suitably shaped formers or frames; places set of covered formers or frames in drying chamber or on press bed, or operates controls to move set of covered formers into steam chamber; starts drying unit or operates controls to heat press and apply pressure appropriate to type of article being boarded or to lower top of steaming chamber over set of covered formers; strips boarded garments from formers or frames after specified time.

Other titles include Framer, Pressman (hosiery), Trimmer (hosiery boarding), Trimmer and finisher (hosiery).

(02) Glove boarder

Fits gloves over heated hand-shaped metal formers; strips boarded gloves from formers after specified time.

May (03) attend equipment which dyes articles before boarding.

See Glove ironer (461.99)

546.85 Carboniser

Treats raw wool or woollen or worsted rags or fabric with acid solution or fumes to destroy vegetable matter

(01) Wet carboniser

Loads new wool into feed hopper of machine or sews end of fabric to fabric or leader tape in machine; if carbonising fabric, adjusts distance between guides and tensioners according to width of fabric; admits water and acid solution to carbonising tank; adjusts controls to heat solution and drying chamber to prescribed temperatures; starts machine and watches operation to detect clogging of wool fibres or creasing of fabric; unclogs fibres and smoothes out creases; tests density of solution periodically using hydrometer and strengthens or dilutes solution as necessary; stops machine when raw wool or fabric has been carbonised; drains off solution; cleans machine.

Other titles include Piece carboniser, Wool carboniser.

continued

(02) **Dry carboniser**

Loads rags into cylinder in carbonising chamber; secures cylinder hatch and chamber door; regulates supply of heat to chamber; starts machine to rotate cylinder; admits acid to vaporising bowl in chamber when rags are dry; stops machine after specified time and switches on extractor fans to exhaust acid fumes from chamber; removes carbonised rags from cylinder; cleans equipment.

Other titles include Rag carboniser.

May (03) prepare solution according to formula

(04) adjust controls to vary speed of passage of wool or fabric through drying chamber

(05) feed carbonised fabric or rags into crushing or shaking machine to remove charred matter (546.99).

546.86 Washer, Automatic scouring machine attendant

Treats loose fibres, rags, yarn, fabric, feathers or bristles to remove impurities or excess chemicals

(01) **Washer**

Admits water to bowl(s); adjusts controls to heat water to specified temperature; adds prescribed quantities of soap, detergents or other chemicals; feeds items to be washed into equipment by hand or using rollers, conveyors or other mechanical aids and starts washing operation; agitates solution as required; watches temperature gauges and makes necessary adjustments; clears blockages; removes washed items from equipment by hand or using mechanical aids, or regulates their flow to machines for further treatment; drains and cleans bowl(s).

Other titles include Bristle dresser, Cloth scourer, Desizer, Desizing machine attendant, Feather washer, Jig operator, Jigger, Neutraliser, Open soap man, Rag scourer, Rag washer, Scourer, Scouring bowl minder, Scouring machine attendant, Scouring machine operator, Soaper, Soaper finisher, Wash-bowl minder, Washing machine attendant, Wool scourer, Wool washer, Wool washing machine minder.

(02) **Automatic scouring machine attendant**

Loads machine; inserts appropriate program card in instrument panel; ensures that panel switches are set for automatic control; starts scouring process; regulates machine speed and roller pressure as instructed; unloads machine on completion of scouring cycle.

May (03) set controls to regulate machine speed and roller pressure

(04) stitch fabric lengths together or to leader cloths by hand or machine to facilitate passage through equipment

(05) undertake minor repairs to equipment

(06) attend equipment fitted with scutching attachment to open out roped fabric after washing

(07) perform tasks of DRIER (546.89).

Additional factors: type(s) of material washed, eg raw wool, rayon yarn, cotton fabric; type of equipment attended, eg jigs, kiers, paddle washing machines; number of vessels or machines attended.

Excluded are Backwash attendants (546.50) and Continuous textile finishing unit operators (546.60)

546.87 Dipper

Imparts finish to or otherwise treats yarn, fabric, cordage or articles such as sacks, felt hood forms or straw hats by immersion in chemical solutions

Admits solution to or checks that it has been fed into container; adjusts controls to heat solution to and maintain it at prescribed temperature as required; secures items to holding device or packs them in drums where appropriate; immerses items to be treated in solution by hand or using lifting equipment; where appropriate, operates controls to pump solution through items for prescribed period, adds further solution at prescribed intervals and continues pumping operation for stated period, adjusting direction of flow as necessary; transfers treated items to hydro-extractor, vacuum drier or squeezing rollers after specified time or places them on holding device to drain; starts equipment to expel excess moisture; removes items from equipment after prescribed period; where appropriate, transfers items to stove, adjusts temperature controls as necessary and removes items from stove on completion of drying process.

May (01) prepare solution according to formula

(02) load container with items before admitting solution

(03) add fugitive tints to solution to identify yarn lots

(04) weigh textiles before and/or after treatment.

Other titles include Bag dresser, Bag tarrer, Felt hood proofer, Incandescent mantle fabric impregnator, Rot proofer, Sack dresser, Sack tarrer, Silk soaker, Straw hat stiffener, Tanner, Tarring hand, Yarn proofer.

Excluded are Bleachers (546.52) and Operative dyers (546.54)

546.88 Crabber

Sets woollen or worsted fabric in smooth, flat state by machine to prevent uneven shrinkage during subsequent processing

Positions fabric in front of machine; sews leader cloth (wrapper) to each end of fabric; operates controls to admit water to troughs and to heat it to prescribed temperature; starts machine to wind wrappers and fabric on to feed roller; stops machine and passes end of leading wrapper round first crabbing roller (bowl); starts machine to wind wrappers and fabric round bowl and to rotate bowl in trough; after specified time transfers fabric to second and third bowls for further crabbing as required; runs crabbed fabric on to steaming roller; operates controls to obtain and maintain prescribed temperature and pressure; removes fabric from machine after steaming and stacks it for cooling.

May (01) bring pressure rollers into use to remove marks in fabric

(02) transfer fabric to drying frame after crabbing using lifting equipment.

Additional factor: type of fabric treated, ie woollen, worsted.

546.89 Drier, Hydro-extractor operator

Attends equipment in which loose fibres, rags, yarn, piece goods, hosiery or feathers are dried following washing, bleaching, dyeing or other manufacturing process

(01) **Drier**

Adjusts control to heat and regulate temperature of equipment; feeds item(s) into equipment manually or using rollers, conveyors or other mechanical aids; if drying warp yarn or fabric, secures end to leader tape or to fabric in equipment; starts drying operation; watches temperature gauges and reports any marked temperature variations or other malfunctioning to foreman; clears blockages; removes dried item(s) from equipment by hand or using mechanical aids, or routes it to stores or to machines for further processing; cleans equipment.

Other titles include Can drier, Clip drier, Cylinder drier, Drying machine attendant, Feather drier, Felt drier, Hosiery drier, Warp drier.

(02) **Hydro-extractor operator**

Loads hydro-extractor manually or using lifting equipment; distributes items uniformly to balance load and reduce vibration; secures container cover and starts machine; stops non-automatic machine after prescribed period or when water ceases to flow from machine; unloads items.

Other titles include Hydro-extractor attendant, Hydroman.

May (03) set controls to regulate speed of items through equipment

(04) set timing mechanism

(05) check moisture content of items during drying operation

(06) carry out minor repairs to drying equipment

(07) attend drying equipment fitted with attachment to spray dried fibres with conditioning liquids to facilitate further processing.

Additional factors: type of drier attended, eg cylinder drier, hot air drier, hydro-extractor; number of driers attended.

Other titles include Fabric drier, Rag drier, Wool drier, Yarn drier.

See Hydro-extractor operator (461.60)

Excluded are Continuous textile finishing unit operators (546.60)

546.90 Damper

Restores moisture to fabric by machine to prepare it for further finishing operations

Positions fabric in front of machine; sews end of fabric to end or to leader cloth in machine or passes end of fabric through machine rollers; admits water to trough or regulates supply of water to nozzles set in trough; starts machine to rotate rollers in trough or to draw fabric over nozzles of spray or over brush revolving in trough; adjusts speed of rollers or brush or pressure of spray as necessary; removes dampened fabric from machine.

May (01) operate machine fitted with steaming device

(02) clean and oil machine.

Additional factor: type(s) of fabric treated, eg cotton, rayon, woollen.

Other titles include Canroyer, Conditioner, Damping machine operator, Damperman, Dewer, Steam sprayer.

546.91 Calenderer

Operates machine to press fabric or to impart lustre or other type of finish by hot or cold rolling

Positions fabric on or near machine; sews end of fabric to leader cloth in machine or passes end of fabric through machine rollers and secures it to take-up spindle; if hot rolling, heats rollers to prescribed temperature; operates controls to close rollers or raise bed to roller to apply specified degree of pressure to fabric; watches operation, and straightens fabric and regulates roller tension as necessary; removes calendered fabric from machine.

May (01) use lifting equipment to load and/or unload machine

(02) remove dents from roller surface by hot water treatment or smooth rollers using special tool

(03) attend machine fitted with coiling device to wind calendered fabric

(04) clean and oil machine.

Additional factor: type(s) of fabric pressed, eg cotton, rayon, pressed woollen felt.

Other titles include Calender hand, Calender operator, Embosser, Rotary presser, Rotary press operator, Shreinerer.

See Calender hand (461.70)

546.92 Blower

Treats fabric by steaming and suction cooling to impart required finish

Positions fabric on or near machine; places end of fabric between roller and protective wrapper; starts machine to wind fabric and wrapper round perforated blowing cylinder; watches operation to ensure that winding proceeds evenly and adjusts tension as necessary; operates controls to admit steam to cylinder when winding operation has been completed; cuts off steam supply after specified time and operates controls to suck air through cylinder to cool and dry fabric; if necessary, transfers fabric and wrapper to second cylinder and repeats operation; winds wrapper back round roller and runs finished fabric round doffing spindle or through folding device; removes finished fabric from machine.

May (01) replace wrapper periodically

(02) clean and oil machine.

Other titles include Decatiser, Dry blower.

546.93 Clipper (cordage)

Creels, threads and attends one or more preset machines which cut off protruding fibres from rope, cord or twine

Places input packages of rope, cord or twine in machine creel; passes ends from input packages through guides, across knife blades and round output packages; starts machine and watches operation; ties broken ends; removes full output packages from machine; replenishes supply of input packages as necessary.

May (01) clean machine.

Additional factor: number of machines attended.

Other titles include Clipper operator, Cropper.

546.98 Trainee

Performs, under instruction or guidance, various tasks including training exercises and as appropriate pursues studies in order to acquire the basic skills and knowledge required to perform the tasks of workers in textile bleaching, dyeing, finishing and other treating occupations.

546.99 Other textile bleaching, dyeing, finishing and treating occupations

Workers in this group bleach, dye, finish and otherwise treat textile fibres, yarn, piece goods, cordage and hosiery, dye garments and other articles made from textile fabric, perform related tasks and are not elsewhere classified, for example:

(01) **Agers,** Flash agers (operate equipment in which reducing agents and steam are applied to textile fabric to fix colours); (02) **Artificial flower dyers,** Feather bleachers, Feather dyers, Fern bleachers and dyers (bleach and/or dye artificial flowers, feathers or ferns); (03) **Automatic press attendants;** (04) **Bag dressers (mangle),** Bag tarrers (mangle), Sack dressers (mangle), Sack tarrers (mangle) (dip ends of bags or sacks in tar and feed bags or sacks through rollers to spread tar over surface); (05) **Beetlers,** Flat beetlers (operate machines to close up warp and weft and impart lustrous finish to fabric by hammering); (06) **Belt stretchers** (stretch fabric to required width using expanding wheels); (07) **Brushers (hosiery)** (attend machines which raise nap on surfaces of knitted articles or manipulate articles against revolving teazles); (08) **Burr crushers,** Crushers (operate machines to crush vegetable matter destroyed in carbonising and remove it from rags or fabric); (09) **Chalkmen** (attend machines which apply dusting powder to roofing felt); (10) **Cotton wadding sizing machine attendants;** (11) **Circular cutters,**

continued

Cutters (velvet, velveteen, fustian) (operate machines to cut weft threads of fabric such as velvet, velveteen and fustian to produce short pile); (12) **Fibre polishers;** (13) **Frame setters** (stretch lace to required width on adjustable frames); (14) **Heald sizers** (operate machines to size yarn healds); (15) **Lace clippers** (operate machines to clip floating ends from lace); (16) **London shrinkers** (interleave damp wrappers between layers of fabric and suspend dampened fabric in shrinking chamber); (17) **Safety fuse finishers** (operate machines to coat safety fuse to make it waterproof); (18) **Scallop cutters,** Scallopers (cut superfluous material from patterned edge of fabric by hand or machine); (19) **Shoe dyers,** Shoe re-dyers (dye or re-dye fabric uppers and heel coverings of shoes to requirements); (20) **Silk finishers** (operate a variety of silk finishing machines); (21) **Silk glossers,** Silk weighters (soften texture of silk hanks by twisting with polished stick or treat silk with solutions of tin and phosphates to give it weight and body); (22) **Steam box operators,** Steamers, Festoon steamers, Open steam minders, Star steamers, Stovers, Sterilisers, Sterilising plant operators, Feather purifiers (operate equipment in which items such as felt hoods, yarn, hair, fabric, surgical dressings or feathers are steamed to set proof or twist, to fix colours or for the purpose of sterilisation); (23) **Stovemen (bleaching)** (bleach yarn or fabric with burning sulphur in airtight chambers).

Unit Group 547 Textile Repairing Occupations

Workers in this unit group rectify faults in textile goods arising during the course of manufacture and renovate used nets, and repair worn garments and other used articles by invisible mending.

547.10 Mender (woven piece goods)

Repairs faults in woven piece goods by hand weaving

Identifies faults marked by burler or examiner; replaces wrongly coloured, coarse or miswoven threads by weaving appropriate threads into fabric using needle, blending repair with pattern; darns in loose ends; closes holes by hand weaving or by moving warp or weft threads closer together and straightening threads using small bodkin; pulls out or snips off surplus thread.

May (01) smooth down threads after darning using metal comb
(02) remove stains with chemical solutions or hot water and soap
(03) perform tasks of BURLER (547.50)
(04) perform tasks of EXAMINER (833.10)

Other titles include Burler and mender, Darner, Inspector and repairer, Piece mender.

547.20 Invisible mender (repair service)

Repairs tears, holes and other damage in garments or other woven textile articles by invisible mending

Examines damaged article to determine best method of repair; where necessary cuts out damaged part or trims area around defective part to regular shape with scissors; pulls out sufficient number of threads of correct colour(s) or cuts out piece of material of appropriate size from underside of seam, hem or other concealed part of article; repairs tears by weaving matching threads into damaged parts with darning needle; mends holes by sewing patch over hole with matching thread (stoating or rentering) or by placing patch over hole and weaving threads from edge of patching material through fabric of article; replaces patching material cut from article and restitches seams where necessary by hand or machine sewing.

May (01) iron patch by hand.

Other titles include Fine drawer, French drawer, Weaver and patcher.

547.30 Net repairer

Repairs used nets of twine by hand and/or machine and replaces damaged accessories

Examines nets for breaks in mesh and weak parts; cuts away broken twine or weak parts and repairs by intersecting and knotting twine of correct thickness by hand or using flat needle; cuts off surplus twine.
If repairing tennis court nets, removes webbing and machine stitches new webbing to net; punches holes in new webbing and inserts eyelets using hammer and punch; coats repaired nets with preservative.
If repairing fishing nets, checks ropes, floats and weights and replaces where necessary.

May (01) splice additional length of rope to used head or tail rope of fishing net (549.59).

Additional factor: type(s) of net repaired, eg fishing, tennis court, football goal.

Other titles include Beatster, Net mender (used nets)

547.50 Burler (cloth)

Examines woven piece goods and rectifies faults other than by hand weaving

Examines cloth visually and by touch for defects such as knots (burls), excess fluff, loose ends and imperfect threads; pushes knots through surface of cloth to underside using tweezers (burling iron) or needle; removes fluff, grit or other foreign matter with burling iron or whisk; trims loose ends by hand or machine; removes wrongly coloured, coarse, miswoven or surplus threads with needle or scissors; straightens crooked threads using needle or burling iron; marks faults requiring attention of mender with chalk or thread.

May (01) remove stains with chemical solutions or hot water and soap

(02) colour small areas of imperfectly dyed yarn with crayon.

Other titles include Cloth picker, Knotter, Spiler.

547.55 Mender (carpet, rug)

Repairs faults in carpets or rugs by hand

Starts roller to pull article to be mended over inspection and repair table, or spreads article on floor, or observes article during production; examines article for faults marked by inspector, where appropriate, and for other defects; if using table fitted with roller, stops roller when fault is detected; cuts out knots; trims edges of article; replaces badly dyed, incorrectly woven or tufted parts or individual missing tufts with new yarn, using needle or mending gun; on cut pile articles, cuts loops which have been missed or improperly cut by pile cutting knives; removes stains with solvents.
If mending woven articles, repairs broken warp and weft threads by hand sewing.
If mending tufted articles, inserts strips of matching tufted material in bare patches, sticks them to backing with latex or other adhesive and smoothes patches with flat iron; secures loose tufts with adhesive.

May (01) stitch articles together on inspection table and separate them after mending.

(02) brush articles to remove dust

(03) finish ends of articles by hand sewing.

Other titles include Burler, Inspector and mender, Picker, Rectifier.

See Hand sewer (carpet) (657 .65)

547.60 Mender (fibre hose-pipe)

Repairs weaving faults in canvas or man-made fibre hose-pipes by hand

Identifies faults marked by examiner; works pulled threads back into fabric using pick or tweezers and cuts off loose ends; opens weave with pick point and mends holes by weaving appropriate type of thread into hose-pipe using needle; smoothes repair with pick or needle.

Other titlesi nclude Examiner and darner, Picker.

547.65 Mender (hosiery, knitwear)

Repairs faults in hose, knitwear or knitted fabric by hand or machine

Performs some or all of the following tasks: identifies faults marked by examiner; picks up and reknits dropped stitches using mending hook or powered hooked needle and secures last loops by hand sewing; draws pulled threads back into position using needle or by guiding powered mending disc across faulty threads; mends holes and short seaming faults with needle and matching yarn; clips loose ends with scissors.

May (01) press part of article repaired

(02) perform tasks of EXAMINER (GARMENTS, TEXTILE PRODUCTS) (833.35).

Other titles include Darner and mender, Examiner and mender.

547.70 Mender (lace)

Repairs faults in lace by hand and/or machine

Identifies faults marked by examiner or inspects lace for defects; reinserts broken threads into material or replaces them with matching thread by hand or machine stitching; inserts missing stitches and fills in holes with matching thread by hand or machine stitching in appropriate direction; cuts out bad knots and replaces them by hand stitching with matching thread; trims loose ends with scissors.

May (01) clean machine.

Additional factor: whether accustomed to hand and/or machine mending.

Other titles include Darner.

547.75 Net examiner and finisher

Examines and finishes newly made netting of twine

Examines netting for faults such as broken twine, defective knots and irregular weave; repairs breakages or slipped knots using twine and flat needle; tightens loose knots by operating winch to stretch net; cuts out patches of irregular weave and replaces by intersecting and knotting twine using flat needle; snips off surplus twine.

May (01) check size of mesh and shrink netting in steam chest if necessary

(02) knot sections of netting together

(03) cut netting to specific shape and strengthen cut edges with twine

(04) pack finished nets or roll nets by hand or machine.

Additional factor: type(s) of net examined and finished, eg agricultural, fishing, tennis court.

547.98 Trainee

Performs, under instruction or guidance, various tasks including training exercises and as appropriate pursues studies in order to acquire the basic skills and knowledge required to perform the tasks of workers in textile repairing occupations.

547.99 Other textile repairing occupations

Workers in this group rectify faults in textile goods arising during the course of manufacture and renovate used nets, and repair worn garments and other used articles by invisible mending and are not elsewhere classified, for example:

(01) **Examiners (safety fuse)** (examine and check diameter of safety fuse, cut out faulty parts and rejoin ends using metal splices); (02) **Heald examiners** (examine yarn healds and remove and replace faulty ends); (03) **Lookers (felt hood forms),** Examiners (felt hood forms), Pickers (felt hood forms) (examine felt hood forms and rectify defects using tweezers).

Unit Group 548 Braid, Plait, Line and Fibre Rope Making Occupations

Workers in this unit group make braid, plait, line and rope from yarn of natural and man-made fibre.

Excluded are Ballers (542.90), Splicers (549.59), Rope coilers (549.63 and 549.99) and Hankers (549.90 and 549.99)

548.10 Rope maker (rope-walk)

Directs team of workers in the operation of tracked travelling machine and other equipment to twist yarn threads into strands and strands into rope on rope-walk

Calculates numbers of bobbins and strands of yarn required and determines equipment and gearing necessary to produce rope specified; instructs assistants in setting up and operating machinery and equipment necessary for formation of strands; places formed strands in grooved piece of wood (top) to control regularity of lay and fits top on carrier (top-cart); accompanies non-automatic top-cart along rope-walk during rope forming (closing) operation to control compression and twist of rope; inspects rope during formation both visually and by touch, and adjusts or directs adjustments to machine or equipment as necessary.

May (01) perform some of the tasks of ROPEMAKER'S ASSISTANT (548.50)

(02) splice yarn, strands or rope (549.59).

Other titles include Rope layer.

548 .50 Rope maker's assistant

Operates or assists in operating tracked travelling machine and other equipment, under direction of rope maker, to twist yarn threads into strands and strands into rope on rope-walk

Performs one or more of the following tasks: loads frame with yarn packages, runs yarn ends through guides and attaches specified number of ends to hooks on travelling machine; places appropriate gear wheels in travelling machine to control twist; operates travelling machine to draw yarn along rope-walk to required length and twist specified number of threads into strands; cuts strands and attaches one end of each strand to appropriate hook on stationary machine and the other end to central hook of travelling machine; positions rope strands on wood frames (stake heads); starts machines to twist strands together in reverse direction of twist in individual strands; removes stake heads; stops machine when strands have been formed into rope; removes formed rope from machine; replenishes yarn packages and ties on new ends.

May (01) coil rope by hand
(02) oil and grease machine.

Other titles include Assistant rope maker, Bank hand, Fore-end worker, Fore hand, Foregear man, Frame hand, Plate hand, Rope-walk creel attendant, Stake head hand, Traveller hand, Tuber.

548 .55 Line maker, Twine maker

Operates tracked travelling machine and other equipment to twist yarn strands together to form line or twine on handwalk

Separates strands into groups according to size of line or twine required and passes each group over or through holders along walk; attaches each group of strands to appropriate hook of stationary twisting machine; passes strands through guides on lay-cart or travelling machine or places them in grooved piece of wood (fiddle) and secures free ends to hooks on travelling machine; starts machines; controls regularity of lay by pulling lay-cart along walk, by ensuring that strands remain in appropriate guides on travelling machine or by carrying strands in fiddle held overhead; unhooks finished line or twine from twisting machines.

May (01) unwind strands of yarn from packages and cut to required length for twisting
(02) operate coiling machine (549 .63)
(03) polish finished line or twine.

Other titles include Line layer, Twine layer.

548 .60 Rope layer (house machine)

Creels, threads and attends one or more machines which twist strands of yarn into rope and wind rope on to reel

Sets yarn strand packages in machine creel manually or using lifting equipment; fits appropriate die on machine according to rope pattern required; threads strands through twisting devices and die and secures to reel; sets yardage clock; starts machine and checks that rope is being formed correctly; replaces empty yarn strand packages and splices strands from full packages to strands in machine; stops machine and cuts off rope when clock indicates that required length has been formed; ties twine or cord round completed coil of rope; removes reel from machine and slides coil off reel.

May (01) determine by visual inspection amount of rope formed
(02) regulate speeds at which packages and reel rotate
(03) weigh coils of finished rope.

Additional factor: number of machines attended.

Other titles include Closing machinist, House machine operator, Rope maker.

548 .65 Twisting machine operator

Creels, threads and attends one or more machines which twist yarn threads into strands in readiness for rope laying, or which twist yarn threads or strands into finished twine, line or cord

Sets yarn packages in machine creel; threads appropriate number of yarn ends through guides, die and twisting device and secures to each output package; sets length indicator; starts machine and watches operation; replaces empty yarn packages; joins broken yarn ends by knotting or splicing; stops machine and cuts off rope strands, twine, line or cord when output packages are full or when indicator shows that required length has been formed; removes output packages manually or using lifting equipment.

May (01) change lay wheels and fit appropriate die according to pattern required
(02) clean and oil machine.

Additional factor: number of machines attended.

Other titles include Cabling machine operator, Cord spinner, Forming machinist, House machine operator (twine, line, cord), Line maker, Strander, Stranding machine operator, Twine spinner, Twine twister, Twine twisting machine operator, Twister.

See Twister (542 .70)

548.70 Braiding machine attendant

Loads, threads and attends one or more machines which interlace three or more yarn threads or strands to form braid, cord or rope

Positions yarn packages on carrier plate; threads yarn ends through guides, tensioners and braiding or plaiting device; if braiding or plaiting round core, leads end of core material through carrier plate to braiding or plaiting device; sets yardage counter; starts machine and watches operation; replaces empty yarn packages; joins broken yarn by twisting, knotting or splicing, or by binding ends with twine; stops machine and cuts off braid, cord or rope when containers or spools are full or yardage counter indicates that required length has been formed; removes and replaces containers or spools; cleans and oils machine.

May (01) perform preliminary winding operations (542.80)

(02) fix weights to plait to keep it taut

(03) weigh rope.

Additional factors: type of product formed, eg asbestos rope, coir plait, textile smallwares; number of machines attended.

Other titles include Braider, Coir plait maker, Plaiter, Plaiting machine attendant, Square rope machine operator.

548.90 Bullion cord covering machinist

Loads, threads and attends one or more machines which wrap yarn thread(s) round a central core of yarn to form bullion cord or gimp

Positions package(s) of wrapping yarn on carrier plate or on machine spindle; threads yarn end(s) through guide(s) and wrapping device; places package of core yarn on machine and threads end through carrier plate or spindle tube to wrapping device; starts machine and watches operation; ties broken yarn; replaces empty yarn packages; removes and replaces full spools of cord.

Additional factor: number of machines attended.

Other titles include Bullion machine worker, Case cord coverer, Gimp maker, Gimper, Piping machinist.

548.92 Bullion cord maker

Operates tracked travelling machine and other equipment to twist lengths of bullion cord together on handwalk and to twist cords so formed round each other to form single cord

Ties end of bullion cord to fixture at one end of walk; passes cord through hook on travelling machine at other end of walk and back to fixture; repeats operation until number of lengths of cord to be twisted together are in position; starts twisting operation and pushes travelling machine along walk as lengths of cord are twisted together; stops machine at predetermined spot and attached ends of twisted cords to centre hooks of fixture and machine; starts machine to twist cords together in reverse direction of twist in individual cords and pushes machine along walk until cords have been twisted together; cuts finished cord from fixture and winds it by hand on to bobbin; cuts cord free from travelling machine.

548.98 Trainee

Performs, under instruction or guidance, various tasks including training exercises and as appropriate pursues studies in order to acquire the basic skills and knowledge required to perform the tasks of workers in braid, plait, line and fibre rope making occupations

548.99 Other braid, plait, line and fibre rope making occupations

Workers in this group make braid, plait, line and rope from yarn of natural and man-made fibre and are not elsewhere classified, for example:

(01) **Safety fuse spinners** (load, thread and attend machines which form safety fuse from jute and cotton twine).

Unit Group 549 Fibre and Textile Processing and Fabric Making Occupations Not Elsewhere Classified

Workers in this unit group perform miscellaneous textile processing, fabricating and finishing tasks including doubling and splitting warp, preparing pattern cards, tapes, chains and harness for use on textile machines, making non-woven fabric, lapping and winding fabric, hanking and coiling cordage, assisting in operating textile machinery and equipment, repairing textile piece goods, carpet, and hosiery and hosepipes, mixing and purifying fur fibres, forming felt hoods from prepared fur and wool fibres, and hardening, shrinking and stretching felt hoods and are not elsewhere classified.

549.02 Colour matcher

Mixes specimen batches of fibres to match colour samples and prepares specifications for fibre blends to produce yarn of required colour

Examines customer's sample visually or refers to records for weight/colour ratio of appropriate fibre blend; prepares specimen blend by hand or machine; spins blended fibres into specimen yarn length by hand or machine or prepares instructions for spinner; checks yarn specimen against sample; determines alterations necessary in composition of blend to produce yarn of required colour; prepares further specimen blends as necessary until yarn of correct colour is obtained; records details of final specification for production purposes.

May (01) scour and dry blended fibres
(02) prepare instructions for weaving or knitting sample yarn before matching
(03) calculate quantities of fibres required for individual orders
(04) check slubbing and yarn for colour during production.

Other titles include Shader.

549.04 Harness builder

Builds up harness to operate jacquard mechanism from a series of cords and attachments

Examines pattern plan and checks measurements of loom into which harness is to be tied; adjusts building frame according to height of harness to be built; positions dummy bottom board and perforated board (comber board) in frame, using plumb-line and spirit level; forms linen threads into hanks and cuts hanks at both ends to produce threads of specified lengths for use as harness heads and cords; ties number of cords required for each pattern repeat to each head and cuts off loose ends; secures free end of linen head to hook in dummy bottom board; draws cord through appropriate hole in comber board according to plan using small hooked tool (piker); threads cord through loop in wire link (mail), back through same hole in comber board and secures end to cord; repeats until all cords have been threaded and knotted; removes completed harness from frame and ties it into loom, ensuring that heads of harness are hooked on to bottom board of jacquard mechanism in correct sequence; replaces broken and worn cords.

May (01) build harness directly into loom

549.06 Pattern card cutter

Operates machine to punch holes in pattern cards or paper tape used on textile machinery following point paper design diagram or other specification

Positions design diagram or other specification in frame attached to machine; loads machine with blank pattern cards or reels of paper tape; moves control marker to align first row of pattern markings on design diagram or other specification with punch card or paper tape; scans pattern markings point by point and presses appropriate keys on machine keyboard to set up punches in correct sequence; when row is complete operates control to cause set-up punches to pierce punch cards or paper tape; moves control marker to next line and repeats process until each line of markings has been converted into perforations; unloads punched cards or tapes and marks them for subsequent identification; cleans and oils machine.

May (01) operate card repeater machine (549.10)
(02) operate machine which simultaneously produces pattern card and embroidered sample.

Other titles include Card puncher, Card stamper, Jacquard puncher.

See Key-punch operator (alphanumeric keyboard) (333.10)

549.08 Pattern card corrector

Checks pattern cards or paper tape prepared by pattern card cutter and corrects punching errors

Checks punched card or paper tape against point paper design diagram or other specification; checks any major errors against designer's original sketch or pattern; hand punches any missing holes and covers with adhesive paper holes punched in error; checks that punched cards are in correct sequence.

May (01) operate pattern card cutting machine (549.06)
(02) operate peg-holing machine
(03) operate numbering machine (634.55).

549.10 Pattern card repeater operator

Operates machine to produce duplicate sets of punched pattern cards

Examines set of laced pattern cards to be duplicated and unlaces and removes damaged cards; repairs and/or straightens damaged cards and relaces them into appropriate position in set; secures set of blank laced punch cards on to feed drum of machine; positions set of cards to be duplicated around cylinder containing punching mechanism; starts machine to activate punches; checks accuracy of punching and adjusts machine where necessary; cleans and oils machine.

May (01) mark and catalogue duplicated cards
(02) operate pattern card cutting machine (549.06)
(03) operate card lacing machine (549.93).

549.12 Coating machine operator

Operates machine to apply plastic, rubber or bituminous compound to carpet, felt or other textile fabric

Loads or directs loading of material to be coated on machine; passes end of material through machine rollers or attaches end to leader cloth or tape or to end in machine; sets angle and height of spreading blade or adjusts height of coating roller to obtain required thickness of compound; sets controls to obtain required roller speed, tension and pressure; ensures adequate supply of coating compound; operates controls to heat rollers, plates or drying chamber where appropriate; starts machine; watches operation to ensure that coating proceeds evenly and makes necessary adjustments; unloads or directs unloading of coated material from machine; cleans machine.

May (01) mix ingredients to make coating compounds
(02) thread leader cloth or tape through machine
(03) check thickness of coated material using gauge
(04) spread compound on to material by hand
(05) operate machine in which material is stentered or otherwise finished after coating.

Other titles include Calenderer, Feltman, Rubber proofer, Spreader, Spreading machine operator.

549.14 Combining machine operator

Operates machine to combine layers of fabric to make bonded fabric or to bond foam sheeting or paper to carpet or other textile fabric

Loads or directs loading of materials to be combined on machine; passes ends of material through machine rollers or attaches ends to leader cloths or ends in machine; adjusts material alignment devices where necessary; sets controls to obtain required roller speed, tension and pressure; regulates heat of flame or rollers where required; if operating machine which spreads adhesive on material, sets height and angle of spreading blade to obtain correct depth of adhesive; ensures adequate supply of adhesive; sets yardage counter; starts machine; watches operation to ensure that bonding is proceeding correctly and adjusts as necessary; unloads or directs unloading of bonded material.

May (01) mix ingredients to make adhesive
(02) sew ends of rolls of material together to form continuous length before loading on machine
(03) thread leader cloths through machine
(04) spread adhesive in front of blade.

Other titles include Combiner, Fabric bonding machinist, Laminator.

See Combining machine operator (paper, paperboard) (584.20)

Excluded are Combining machine operators (textile printing) (639.99)

549.16 Fuller

Consolidates and shrinks hardened layers of fibre (batts) by mechanical beating to make wool felt sheeting

Folds length of hardened batts into suitably sized laps; ties up lapped length and places it in machine; adjusts hammer weights to obtain specified consolidation and shrinkage; starts machine to pommel hardened batt into felt; handles and measures felt periodically and continues beating until required consolidation and shrinkage have been obtained; removes felt sheet from machine.

Other titles include Miller.

549 .18 Fur felt hood former

Attends machine which matts fur fibres round revolving cone to make felt hood forms

Places skip of hatter's fur at feed end of machine and checks that weight on feed scale is correct for size of form to be made; places elastic belts round base of perforated metal cone to adjust base to obtain size of form required; positions cone in draught chamber of machine and sets draught shutters; starts machine and ensures that fur is correctly fed on to feed apron and blown on to revolving cone; operates control to spray water on to cone to assist matting of fur fibres; stops machine when required amount of fur has been blown on to cone; removes cone from draught chamber and carefully detaches formed hood from cone; cleans and oils machine.

549 .20 Wool felt hood former

Guides fine web of wool fibres round revolving cone by hand to make felt hood forms

Wraps continuous web of wool fibres evenly around rotating former in the shape of two cones joined base to base; cuts round middle of built-up web, using mechanical cutter, to separate formed hoods when former has been covered by required number of fibre layers; breaks fibre web and removes formed hood from each end of former.

549 .50 Fibre preparing and spinning set attendant

Attends set of machines which process fibres into slubbing or roving, and spin slubbing or roving into yarn

Performs tasks of GILL BOX ATTENDANT (541 .20) and FRAME SPINNER (542 .55) as directed.

May (01) perform tasks of FIBRE SEPARATING AND ALIGNING MACHINE OPERATOR (541 .10).

549 .51 Chain maker (loom)

Builds up chains which control the movements of loom weave and pattern mechanisms

Examines work ticket and/or loom card for details of pattern, weaving plan and where appropriate number of shuttles to be used; determines chain sequence and selects chain of appropriate length from stock; rearranges spacing devices on metal link spindles or pegs on wooden boards ('lags') to make chain conform to specification, or assembles pairs of varying shaped links in correct sequence; adds spindles, lags or links to chain as necessary, or removes those surplus to requirements, using hand tools; checks completed chain against specification.

May (01) fix chains on to looms

(02) fit new sections into or repair broken chains.

Other titles include Barrel pegger, Dobby pegger.

549 .52 Chain maker (warp knitting machine)

Builds up chains which control the movement of pattern forming guide bars on warp knitting machines

Selects numbered pattern chain links according to numerical symbols on pattern diagram; places selected links in required pattern sequence; inserts connecting pins through holes in links to form continuous chain.

Other titles include Chain assembler, Pattern assembler.

549 .53 Fibre bonding machine operator

Operates machine to bond fibres together with adhesive or by heat treatment to form non-woven carpet or fabric

Performs a combination of the following tasks: adjusts machine controls to produce carpet or fabric of specified width; positions take-up roller on machine; ensures that supply of adhesive in bath or in feed container of spraying device is adequate; heats rollers and/or drying equipment to prescribed temperature; sets yardage counter and where appropriate automatic cutting device; starts machine; regulates feed of fibrous web to rollers or along conveyor or secures end of web to leader cloth or to end in machine; watches operation to ensure that bonding is proceeding correctly; adjusts tensioners, temperature and speed of rollers, and traverse of spraying device as required; regulates flow of adhesive from spray nozzles; stops machine when specified yardage has been produced and cuts off carpet or fabric; removes or directs removal of lengths or rolls of carpet or fabric; cleans machine and ancillary equipment as directed.

May (01) mix fibres ready for bonding (541 .05)

(02) operate fibre separating and aligning machine (541 .10)

(03) weigh carpet or fabric

(04) oil machine

Additional factor: type of bonding to which accustomed, ie bath, spray, heat treatment.

Other titles include Fibre bonder operator, Spray line operator.

549.54 Tufting machine operator

Operates multi-needle machine which stitches pile yarn threads on to fabric backing to form tufted carpet

Sets or directs setting of pile yarn packages in machine creel, according to creel plan; threads pile yarn ends through appropriate guide tubes, using compressed air gun, and through feed mechanism to needles, or joins ends to ends in machine by knotting or splicing; fixes roll of fabric backing on machine and passes end through guides, tensioners and rollers or secures end to end of roll in machine by hand stitching or with adhesive; starts machine and watches operation to detect broken yarn ends, fabric wrinkles and stitching faults; joins or rethreads broken yarn ends; smoothes fabric and adjusts tensioners where necessary; reports stitching faults to foreman or mechanic; replaces or directs replacement of empty yarn packages and replenishes supply of fabric backing as required; stops machine when required yardage has been tufted; cleans machine.

May (01) set machine to regulate number of tufts per square inch

(02) replace broken or worn needles

(03) replace blunt or damaged pile-cutting knives

(04) feed length of tufted carpet into latexing or rubberising machine to secure tufts

(05) specialise in attending machine which produces loop or cut pile carpet.

Other titles include Tufter.

549.55 Needleloom operator

Operates one or more machines to interlace a sheet (lap) of cotton, wool or other fibre with cotton warp, hessian, paper or other backing material to produce needle-felt or other non-woven fabric

Loads or assists in loading warp beam, hessian or other backing material on to machine; threads backing material round tensioning bars and between needle plates to take-up mechanism; threads fibre lap through loom on to backing material; starts machine; watches operation to ensure that lap is in alignment with backing material and to detect interlacing faults; corrects alignment and interlacing faults where required; cleans and oils machine as directed.

May (01) adjust controls to synchronise speed of machine and action of needle plate

(02) set measuring and cutting devices

(03) join ends of backing material to form continuous feed

(04) replace worn or damaged needles and change needle plates

(05) operate needleloom linked to fibre opening machine.

Other titles include Felt weaver, Interlacer, Needleloom felt machinist, Needler.

549.56 Typewriter ribbon inker

Operates machine to impregnate ribbon with ink to make typewriter ribbon

Fills machine tray(s) with ink(s) of required colour(s); positions roll of ribbon on machine; passes end of ribbon through rollers and secures to core on take-up spindle; adjusts controls to obtain correct density of colour and width of inking; starts machine and watches operation; removes reel of impregnated ribbon from machine.

Other titles include Typewriter ribbon inking machine operator.

549.57 Net maker (hand), Braider

Interlaces and knots cordage to form nets, or braids ends of machine-made netting, by hand

Selects gauge and cordage according to specification; secures foundation line in position or hangs formed netting over pole; winds supply of cordage round holder (needle); knots cordage from needle to end of foundation line or netting; positions gauge against foundation line or netting, loops cordage around gauge and knots it to foundation line or netting, forming half mesh; removes gauge and repeats operation to form row of half meshes; holds gauge against half mesh, pulls cordage around gauge, and knots it on to half mesh to form mesh; repeats operation to form net or to braid formed netting; increases or decreases number of meshes as necessary to shape particular sections; unties foundation line when appropriate and pulls from netting.

May (01) attach ropes or other accessories to nets

(02) make up rope fenders and rope curtains (mantlets).

Additional factor: type(s) of net made, eg agricultural, fishing.

Other titles include Knotter, Netter.

549 .58 Net fixer

Makes up twine nets from netting and attaches ropes and other accessories

Cuts out sections of specified shape and size from sheet of netting; joins sections of netting together to form net, using flat needle and twine; selects ropes and cuts to required lengths; binds ends of ropes to prevent unravelling; secures ropes to net at measured intervals with short lengths of twine (norsels) or sews or binds ropes directly on to net; attaches floats, shackles, weights or lengths of leaded rope, and/or other accessories to net as required; folds completed net for storage or dispatch.

May (01) splice additional lengths of rope on to head or tail ropes of fishing nets (549 .59)
(02) bind outer edge of net with wire ropes
(03) repair used nets and replace damaged accessories (547 .30).

Additional factor: type(s) of net made up, eg inshore fishing, trawl, tennis court.

Other titles include Gabler and corder, Guarder, Net fitter, Net rigger, Norseller, Nosseller, Osseller.

549 .59 Splicer (fibre rope)

Joins, repairs and fits attachments to fibre ropes using a variety of splicing methods

Cuts out damaged sections of rope using hand knife or heat sealing knife according to type of fibre; joins ropes by opening up ends and tucking and interlacing the rope strands to specification to form a joint using spikes, cone shaped wooden tools (fids) and other hand tools; forms end of rope into a loop or eye or fits ends of rope around metal eye or thimble, opens up the end of the rope and tucks and interlaces the rope strands back into the rope.

May (01) bind ends of joint or rope with fine cord
(02) stitch plastic or leather sleeve on to rope to prevent fraying.

See Splicer (wire rope) (general) (774 .35)

549 .60 Felter (mechanical cloth)

Joins ends of cloth together by splicing to form endless belts for use on mechanical equipment

Aligns ends of cloth to be spliced on work-table and secures in position; threads each protruding warp end in turn through needle and weaves it into weft of opposite end of cloth, or ties together ends of corresponding warp threads from each end of cloth, breaks off one thread close to join of material and weaves remaining length of thread through cloth for specified length using needle; cuts off excess thread; repeats on each pair of warp threads, weaving on alternate sides of the join and staggering the length of weave to avoid a ridge.

May (01) withdraw specified number of weft threads from each end of cloth before splicing.

Other titles include Splicer.

549 .61 Felt hood hardening machine operator

Operates machine to shrink and harden felt hood forms by steam and pressure

Positions felt hood form on perforated cone; lowers cloth-covered hardening tool on to top of form; starts machine to oscillate tool and force steam through cone and form; stops machine and raises tool when point of form is sufficiently hardened; removes form from cone and places cloth inlay in form to prevent sides felting together; positions form on bench of machine or in steam heated chest; lowers oscillating hardening tool on to form and starts machine; stops machine after short time, raises tool and removes partially hardened form; repositions form and repeats operation until whole of form has been shrunk and hardened.

Additional factor: whether accustomed to fur felt and/or wool felt forms.

Other titles include Felt hood hardener.

549.62 Felt hood shrinking machine attendant

Attends one or more machines which shrink and consolidate felt hood forms by rolling or beating

(01) **Settling machine attendant, Multi-rolling machine attendant**

Folds hood form; admits water or acid solution to machine trough and feeds form into machine or dips form in hot water or acid solution and feeds form between revolving rubber apron and grooved wooden bed or between grooved rollers; opens and refolds form as necessary and repeats rolling operation in same or similar machine until form has been shrunk to required size.

Other titles include Planker (machine), Settler, Stumper.

(02) **Bumping machine attendant**

Folds hood form, as necessary, and places form in machine trough; admits hot water and acid solution to trough; starts machine to beat form with hammer(s); stops machine after specified time and drains trough; restarts machine, or transfers hood to, and switches on, hydro-extractor to remove surplus moisture.

Other titles include Bumper.

May (03) insert cloth divider in form or wrap one or more forms in cloth before shrinking
(04) prepare acid solution
(05) set control to heat water to prescribed temperature
(06) check measurements of hood after shrinking
(07) pull shrunken hood over wooden block and remove machine marks by hand rubbing
(08) knead (plank) felt hood forms by hand after machine rolling.

549.63 Rope coiler (machine)

Operates machine to form lengths of rope into coils

Positions appropriate cross-piece or plate at each end of spindle according to length and thickness of rope to be coiled; fits connecting metal rods (ribs) into end pieces; places lengths of binding cord along ribs and secures to end pieces; lays end of rope over ribs next to appropriate end piece; starts machine and guides rope round ribs in adjacent and concentric rings; stops machine when length of rope to be coiled has been wound round ribs and secures end with yarn or adhesive tape; binds coil with cord to prevent unwinding; removes cross-piece or plate and slides rope off ribs.

May (01) trim loose ends from rope and bind trimmed end with adhesive tape before coiling
(02) cut out imperfections and join ends with adhesive tape
(03) inspect rope and test for breaking strain (833.55)
(04) weigh coiled rope.

Other titles include Coiler weigher, Plaiting coiler, Rope reeler.

549.64 Warp splitter

Operates machine to separate doubled warp after dyeing or other processing

Separates ends of doubled warp by hand into individual warps; threads ends from each warp through appropriate guides and tensioners, between and round rollers and through to lapping device; starts machine and regulates speed to adjust tension of warp; watches operation to detect entangled or broken warp ends and dyeing faults or other marks on yarn; frees entangled ends; reports other defects to foreman; ensures that separated warps are properly lapped into containers; cleans machine.

May (01) remove marks from yarn using cleaning fluids and brush
(02) pack separated warps.

549.65 Dyer's preparer

Prepares for re-dyeing garments and other articles made from textile material

Checks that articles are suitable for re-dyeing; removes buttons, stiffeners and other items unsuitable for dyeing; unpicks seams where necessary; sorts articles according to colours to be dyed.

May (01) check that article has been properly re-dyed
(02) replace, by hand or machine stitching, items removed before dyeing.

549.85 Hair fibre preparing and spinning machine attendant

Attends one or more machines which prepare hair fibre for spinning, spin prepared fibre into rope and coil formed rope

Starts machine and feeds mixture of hair fibres into hopper or watches automatic feed; threads hair from preparing unit through spinning head and guide and on to reel; stops machine if rope breaks; removes partly filled reel, fits empty reel on machine and threads new end through to reel; cuts rope when reel is full and removes coil; secures coiled rope with twine; ensures that supply of hair fibre to hopper is adequate; cleans machine.

May (01) weigh coils of rope
(02) prepare and affix identification labels to coils of rope
(03) oil machine.

Additional factor: number of machines attended.

Other titles include Hair fibre spinning machine attendant, Hair fibre spinner.

549.86 Fibre batt hardening machine operator

Operates machine to compress one or more layers of fibre (batts) ready for consolidation into wool felt sheeting

Loads batt(s) on to machine; regulates supply of steam to heat plates or metal rollers; sets controls to obtain specified frequency and pressure of plate stroke or required roller tension; starts machine to pass batt(s) between oscillating pressure plates or over heated metal rollers and under oscillating wooden rollers; watches pressure and moisture content gauges and makes or arranges for necessary adjustments to be made; where required guides end of hardened batt(s) round take-up roller; removes hardened batt(s) from machine; reloads batt(s) and passes through machine again if further hardening is required.

May (01) spray warm water on to sheet (bratt) on which batt travels through machine to facilitate hardening
(02) clean and oil machine.

Other titles include Fibre batt hardener.

549.87 Creeler, Battery filler

Positions yarn packages on or in holders ready for warping, weaving, tufting or lace making, or to replace empty packages

Performs a combination of the following tasks: places yarn packages of required colour on creel spindles of warping, weaving, tufting or lace making machines, in specified pattern sequence; loads wound bobbins of correct colour into batteries of automatic looms by hand, or into carriages of lace making machines by hand or machine; places weft yarn packages on spindles of automatic winding attachments on looms; joins new yarn ends to old ends by hand or mechanical knotting, by splicing or using heat-sealing knife; threads yarn ends through eyes of carriages of lace making machines by hand or machine; patrols machines to detect nearly exhausted yarn packages or empty spaces in batteries; replaces yarn packages and bobbins and ties on new ends.

May (01) assist warper or weaver to draw-in new ends
(02) assist warper, weaver or tufting machine operator to join broken ends
(03) redistribute yarn on packages using small winding machine
(04) place wound bobbins in hydraulic or hand press and bake them to compress yarn ready for lace making
(05) clean machines.

Other titles include Alterer (jacquard loom), Assistant beamer, Presser and threader, Spooler, Threader.

549.88 Doffer

Removes full output packages of yarn from spinning or doubling machines and replaces them with empty packages

Lifts full package from take-up spindle; slides empty package on to spindle and wraps yarn round empty package or ensures that yarn is trapped under empty package to facilitate restarting; breaks yarn from full package.

549.89 Warp doubler

Attends machine which combines yarn from two or more ball warps into continuous rope form ready for dyeing or other processing

Sets specified number of ball warps in machine creel; threads warp ends over guides, between tensioners and feed rollers and through to folding (lapping) or coiling device; starts machine and watches operation to ensure that warp is correctly doubled and formed into laps or coils; replenishes supply of warps as necessary and ties ends from new warps to ends in machine; stops machine when required yardage has been doubled; repeats operation as necessary until rope of required thickness is obtained; secures identification tickets to warp ends.

May (01) pack roped warp.

549.90 Lapper (machine), Winder (machine)

Operates or attends machine to fold fabric transversely into measured lengths (laps) or to wind fabric or cordage for further processing or for dispatch

(01) **Lapping machine operator, Winding machine operator**

Positions fabric on or near machine; places take-up roll on machine or core on take-up spindle where appropriate; secures end of fabric to leader cloth or to end in machine, or passes end through guides, tensioners and as necessary creasing attachment to lapping device or round core or take-up spindle; sets revolution or yardage counter; starts machine and watches operation; straightens fabric and adjusts tensioners as required; where necessary stops machine when required amount of fabric has been wound; cuts fabric where necessary and secures end to prevent unwinding; removes lapped or wound fabric from machine manually or using lifting equipment.

Other titles include Beaming machine attendant, Cloth beamer, Creaser, Creaser and lapper, Fabric doubler, Folding and rolling machine attendant, Plaiter, Rolling machine operator, Typewriter ribbon winder.

(02) **Hanking machine operator**

Positions material to be hanked on machine; adjusts distance between rods on hanking reel according to length of hank required; attaches end of material to hanking rod and starts machine to turn hanking reel; adjusts hanking rods to release tension and removes hank; if hanking cordage, binds end of cordage length, where required, and winds and secures end round hank by hand or machine.

Other titles include Hanker, Randed hanker, Randing machine operator.

(03) **Card winding machine attendant**

Positions fabric to be wound on machine; places supply of cards on each card holder on machine; passes end of fabric through guides and tensioners and secures to card; starts machine which automatically winds measured length of fabric on to each card and ejects full cards on to conveyor; replenishes supply of fabric and cards as required.

May (04) stitch pieces or rolls of fabric together to form continuous lengths before winding

(05) cut material into specified lengths before hanking

(06) weigh and/or pack fabric or cordage after lapping or winding

(07) clean machine

(08) wind paper between layers of fabric and be known as Rolling and papering machine operator.

Excluded are Ballers (machine) (542.90), Spoolers (machine) (542.90) and Rope coilers (machine) (549.63)

549.91 Fabric opening machine attendant

Attends machine which opens out fabric to full width after it has been bleached, dyed or otherwise treated in rope form

Secures end of fabric to leader cloth, tape or end in machine or checks automatic feed; starts machine and watches operation to ensure that fabric is fully opened; separates opened fabric from leader cloth or tape where necessary; laps fabric by hand into container.

May (01) sew ends of several lengths of fabric together to form continuous length before opening

(02) attend machine from which opened fabric is automatically lapped into container.

Other titles include Cloth opening machine attendant, Scutcher.

549.92 Fur fibre mixer

Attends machines which separate, blend and clean fur fibres used in making felt hood forms or fur fabric

Feeds fibres of specified colour and type by hand into hopper of opening machine; starts machine to rotate spiked rollers which disentangle matted fibres; feeds opened fibres into hopper of blowing machine; starts machine which forces fibres through chambers containing air blowers and spiked rollers to clean and mix fibres; cleans and oils machine.

Other titles include Fur blower, Fur fibre blender

549.93 Pattern card lacer

Operates machine to lace punched or blank pattern cards together to form a chain

Adjusts position of feed wheels as required to ensure that pattern cards are evenly spaced, using special key; makes necessary adjustments to position of needle heads; checks supply of lacing cord on shuttles and spools and ensures that cord is correctly threaded through guides and tensioners; starts machine and feeds punched pattern cards in numerical sequence or specified number of blank cards on to revolving wheels; replaces empty shuttles and spools as necessary.

May (01) insert wires at intervals in chain

(02) fix laced cards on looms.

549.98 Trainee

Performs, under instruction or guidance, various tasks including training exercises and as appropriate pursues studies in order to acquire the basic skills and knowledge required to perform the tasks of workers in fibre and textile processing and fabric making occupations not elsewhere classified.

549.99 Other fibre and textile processing and fabric making occupations not elsewhere classified

Workers in this group perform miscellaneous fibre and textile processing and fabric making tasks and are not separately classified, for example:

(01) **Back minders,** Back enders (assist ring spinners in creeling and threading machines and replace empty sliver cans, or assist drawframe attendants in replenishing supply of sliver, joining broken ends and doffing full bobbins of roving); (02) **Beam setters,** Beam siders, Dye-house labourers, Slashers' labourers, Tapers' labourers (load and/or unload warping machines, dyeing equipment or warp sizing machines and otherwise assist warpers, dyers or warp sizers as required); (03) **Brass bobbin pressers** (attend equipment to prepare wound brass bobbins for use on lace making machines); (04) **Chain alterers** (adjust spool chains in Axminster looms to take required lengths of pattern); (05) **Chenille cutters** (cut fabric into strips by machine for use in carpet manufacture); (06) **Coilers (hand),** Hankers (hand), Skeiners (hand); (07) **Coners,** Paperers, Repaperers (place bundles of bristles in protective metal cones ready for boiling or wrap bundles of mixed fibre in paper to facilitate flagging or cutting); (08) **Cop strippers,** Pirn strippers, Spool strippers (remove waste yarn from used packages by hand or machine): (09) **Cotton wool rollers and weighers,** Fleecers; (10) **Croziers** (assist felt hood shrinking machine attendants by opening and refolding hood forms); (11) **Edge sealing machine operators** (operate machines to seal edges of typewriter ribbons); (12) **Enders-off** (cut coir mats to required size and finish ends with cord); (13) **Feather curlers,** Feather dusters, Feather mixers (attend machines to curl, extract dust from or mix feathers); (14) **Folders (hand),** Lappers (hand), Plaiters (hand), Plaiters-down (hand); (15) **Gymnasium rope equipment assemblers (non-repetitive)**; (16) **Hank linkers** (link hanks of yarn together by hand to form a continuous chain ready for further processing); (17) **Heald brushers** (clean and separate varnished yarn healds); (18) **Lacing machine operators** (operate machines to thread lacing cords through silk skeins); (19) **Lost end finders** (locate lost ends of glass fibre yarn wound on tubes); (20) **Makers-up** (perform a variety of tasks such as examining, measuring and cutting, rolling and lapping in the final finishing (making-up) of textile piece goods); (21) **Net examiners and finishers' helpers;** (22) **Plankers (hand)** (shrink and consolidate felt hood forms by hand kneading); (23) **Reelermen (roofing felt)** (operate foot controls to reel roofing felt round rollers); (24) **Rollers (hand),** Winders (hand); (25) **Textile machine operators' assistants,** Coating machine operators' assistants, Combining machine operators' assistants, Croppers' assistants, Fibre bonding machine operators' assistants, Fur felt hood forming machine feeders, Hackling machine attendants' assistants, Hopper fillers, Needleloom operators' assistants, Net weavers' helpers, Stenterers' assistants; (26) **Tubers,** Tube sorters (sort and straighten used paper tubes, remove yarn ends, and place empty tubes on spinning machines as required),

Minor Group 55 TOBACCO PROCESSING AND PRODUCTS MAKING OCCUPATIONS

Workers in this minor group process tobacco leaf and make pipe tobacco, cigars, cigarettes and other tobacco products.

The occupations are arranged in the following unit groups:

550 Foremen (Tobacco Processing and Products Making Occupations)

551 Tobacco Processing and Products Making Occupations

Unit Group 550 Foremen (Tobacco Processing and Products Making Occupations)

Workers in this unit group directly supervise and co-ordinate the activities of workers in tobacco processing and products making occupations.

550.10 Foreman (tobacco processing and products making occupations)

Directly supervises and co-ordinates the activities of workers in tobacco processing and products making occupations

Performs appropriate tasks as described under SUPERVISOR/FOREMAN (UNSPECIFIED) (990.00).

May (01) set up and make minor adjustments to machines.

Additional factor: number of workers supervised.

550.98 Trainee

Performs, under instruction or guidance, various tasks including training exercises and as appropriate pursues studies in order to acquire the basic skills and knowledge required to perform the tasks of foremen (tobacco processing and products making occupations).

Unit Group 551 Tobacco Processing and Products Making Occupations

Workers in this unit group process tobacco leaf and make pipe tobacco, cigars, cigarettes and other tobacco products.

551.10 Drier

Operates drying equipment to bring moisture content of cut tobacco to specified level

Sets moisture and heat controls to bring drying machines or pans to required temperature; starts machine and regulates flow of tobacco into machine or over drying pans; assesses moisture content of tobacco by touch or reads moisture meter and adjusts controls as necessary; removes foreign matter observed.
May (01) weigh tobacco before and after drying.

Other titles include Drier and cooler, Drying machine attendant, Machine stover.

551.20 Cigarette making machine operator

Operates machine to make cigarettes

Positions reel(s) of paper, cork or other wrapper on spindles of machine and feeds through rollers and guides; loads hopper with filter tips if necessary; fills ink and gum containers; adjusts automatic printing devices and cut off knife and sharpeners; regulates flow of tobacco to machine; starts machine and watches process; replenishes paper, gum and ink supplies as required; watches automatic weight control indicator; examines samples of completed cigarettes for defects such as faulty cuts, open seams and faulty printing, and adjusts machine settings as necessary; breaks up faulty cigarettes and reclaims tobacco; cleans, oils and greases machine and carries out running repairs; reports faults to foreman.

551.50 Leaf conditioner

Operates machine to moisten or otherwise condition and blend tobacco leaf

Selects quantity and grade of tobacco leaf as specified in blending chart; examines leaf to determine amount of moistening required; calculates weight of water required and sets steam, water and air valves accordingly; loads or directs loading of tobacco leaf into feed hopper manually or using mechanical equipment; operates controls to ensure correct rate of feed of tobacco leaf; watches gauges recording temperature, pressure and moisture content and adjusts valves as necessary; removes leaf from machine for conveyance to next process or to storage containers.

May (01) add acid and aromatic water as required
(02) withdraw samples for laboratory testing
(03) moisten small batches of leaf by spraying with water.

Other titles include Conditioning machine operator, Liquorer.

551.55 Stemmer (hand)

Removes stem from tobacco leaf by hand

Picks up leaves individually and removes stem by hand or using knife or hook to obtain maximum amount of usable leaf; places stem in container; rejects leaf with faults such as holes or tears; separates stripped leaf (lamina) into left hand and right hand sides and places in separate containers or passes for further processing.

May (01) sort leaf according to texture, colour and quality for use in cigar wrapping or binding.

Other titles include Leaf stripper, Stemmer and padder, Wrapper stemmer.

551.60 Cutting machine operator

Operates machine to compress and cut conditioned tobacco leaf, stem or cake to the required form

Positions and secures cutting knives in machine; sets dial or alters gears to vary depth of cut and number of cuts per inch to produce different types of tobacco such as cigarette, loose leaf shag or mixture; starts machine and checks that knives are cutting correctly; regulates flow of tobacco leaf, stem or cake to pressure rollers and cutting knives; inspects cut tobacco at discharge end of machine and removes miscuts; attaches identification details to each tray of cut tobacco; changes knives as necessary and cleans machine.

Other titles include Crossing machine operator.

551.65 Roll spinner

Operates spinning machine to make roll tobacco

Feeds filler and wrapper leaf by hand into machine to produce even roll of specified blend, gauge and length per ounce; watches process and examines quality and finish of roll as it is coiled round drum, wheel or other holder on machine; replaces full drums or wheels with empty ones; records weight of spun, surplus and rejected tobacco.

May (01) oil and make minor adjustments to machine.

551.70 Cigar machinist

Operates machine to make cigars

Checks that hopper is supplied with filler tobacco; places binder and wrapper leaf over vacuum die so as to obtain maximum use of leaf, tearing and patching binder as necessary; starts machine which shapes filler into bunch, rolls, binds and wraps bunch to form cigar and cuts cigar to size; watches process and rejects or repairs faulty leaf or bunch.

May (01) set up machine
(02) inspect finished cigars.

Other titles include Cigar maker, Cigar making machine operator.

551.90 Stemmer (machine), Threshing machine attendant

Operates machine to remove stem from tobacco leaf

(01) **Stemmer**

Unties bunches of tobacco leaf (hands); picks up leaves individually and inserts butt end into stripping machine which cuts out stems with knife; stops machine at intervals and removes stripped leaves (lamina) keeping left hand and right hand sides separate; examines lamina and removes any remaining stem; checks stems and removes by hand any leaf still attached; at end of operation takes lamina for inspection and stems for weighing.

Other titles include Leaf stripper.

(02) **Threshing machine attendant**

Operates controls to regulate flow of tobacco leaf to threshing machine in which stems are cut out by revolving knives; adjusts sieve controls to produce specified size of clean leaf (lamina) and stems; controls air flow to prevent clogging of sieve; examines lamina and removes any remaining stem by hand.

551.91 Machine feeder

Feeds tobacco into machines for processing

Collects or receives tobacco in various forms such as loose leaf, mixture, cake or plug; tips specified amounts of tobacco into feed hopper using mechanical tipper or fills hopper manually; positions trays, containers, retaining bars, etc on machine; operates controls to start, stop and regulate speed of automatic feed; clears blockages.

May (01) assist machine operator to weigh processed tobacco

(02) remove processed tobacco from machine.

Other titles include Cigarette making machine feeder, Cigarette making machine filler, Cutting machine feeder, Cutting machine filler, Hopper filler.

551.92 Press operator

Presses, shapes and bakes tobacco leaf to form cake, plug and bar tobacco or presses and bakes roll tobacco

Fills mould with specified weight of loose tobacco leaf as necessary; operates controls to regulate pressure and produce shape of specified size; places filled mould in oven or places preformed cake and lengths of roll tobacco in steam heated press; operates controls to introduce steam for specified time to bake tobacco; removes processed tobacco from oven or press.

May (01) line mould with wrapper leaf

(02) insert steel plates or battens between moulds and cakes when loading ovens.

Other titles include Cold press worker, Hot press worker, Shaping press filler.

551.98 Trainee

Performs, under instruction or guidance, various tasks including training exercises and as appropriate pursues studies in order to acquire the basic skills and knowledge required to perform the tasks of workers in tobacco processing and products making occupations.

551.99 Other tobacco processing and products making occupations

Workers in this group process tobacco leaf and make pipe tobacco, cigars, cigarettes and other tobacco products and are not elsewhere classified, for example:

(01) **Automatic drying equipment minders;** (02) **Bulkers,** Mixers (mix by hand varieties of tobacco leaf according to formula); (03) **Cigar makers (hand);** (04) **Cigar moulders (hand);** (05) **Cigarette makers (hand);** (06) **Handers,** Pitchers (pass leaves to roll spinners); (07) **Offal mill assistants** (process waste tobacco and stems for re-use, sale or return to Customs and Excise); (08) **Roll makers,** Makers-off (operate machines to cut spun tobacco into manageable lengths); (09) **Snuff makers** (perform a variety of tasks such as chopping, grinding, sieving and mixing in the manufacture of snuff); (10) **Splitters** (operate splitting machine to open waste cigarette and cigar packings and separate tobacco from paper, foil, cellophane, etc); (11) **Stovers (hand)** (tease and spread shredded tobacco on trays prior to drying).

Minor Group 56 CHEMICAL, GAS AND PETROLEUM PROCESSING PLANT OPERATING OCCUPATIONS

Workers in this minor group operate plant to process chemical and related materials.

Included are workers processing non-chemical materials in the manufacture of all products covered by Orders IV and V of the Standard Industrial Classification (Revised 1968) except safety fuse, surgical bandages, dressings, etc (54) and sensitized paper (58). Also included are workers evaporating brine, hardening vegetable and marine oils, distilling whisky, gin and other potable spirits, treating materials chemically to make pulp for paper and board making, and purifying and softening water.

The occupations are arranged in the following unit groups:

560 Supervisors (Chemical, Gas and Petroleum Processing Plant Operating Occupations)

561 Chemical, Gas and Petroleum Processing Plant Operating Occupations

Excluded are Masticating millmen (592.55), workers forming stock material by calendering, extrusion, hydraulic pressing, impregnation or casting (594) and Fillers (cartridges, detonators, fireworks) (699.64)

Unit Group 560 Supervisors (Chemical, Gas and Petroleum Processing Plant Operating Occupations)

Workers in this unit group directly supervise and co-ordinate the activities of workers in chemical, gas and petroleum processing plant operating occupations.

560.10 Supervisor (chemical, gas and petroleum processing plant operating occupations)

Directly supervises and co-ordinates the activities of workers in chemical, gas and petroleum processing plant operating occupations

Performs appropriate tasks as described under SUPERVISOR/FOREMAN (UNSPECIFIED) (990.00).

May (01) analyse information obtained from instrument readings and quality control tests and prepare reports

(02) investigate process irregularities and make recommendations for revision of operating instructions.

Additional factor: number of workers supervised.

560.98 Trainee

Performs, under instruction or guidance, various tasks including training exercises and as appropriate pursues studies in order to acquire the basic skills and knowledge required to perform the tasks of supervisors (chemical, gas and petroleum processing plant operating occupations).

Unit Group 561 Chemical, Gas and Petroleum Processing Plant Operating Occupations

Workers in this unit group operate plant to process chemical and related materials.

561.05 Chief operator

Controls the operation of a plant or group of integrated plants in which a continuous flow of chemical and/or related materials is processed in a sequence of operations, and directs the work of the operating team

Co-ordinates start-up and shut-down of various sections of plant or a group of integrated plants and performs or directs performance of the following tasks: monitors instruments and gauges indicating fluid flow, liquid levels, pressures, temperatures, and other conditions within or affecting the plant(s) and ancillary equipment; adjusts control mechanisms manually or from remote control panel; withdraws or diverts samples for quality control testing.
Maintains operational log and prepares reports as required; ensures the efficient deployment of team members; takes steps to ensure the personal safety of workers and the safe operation of plant(s).

May (01) undertake quality control testing using laboratory or other test equipment

(02) investigate process irregularities and make recommendations for revision of operating instructions

(03) direct manual operation of plant in event of emergency or major breakdown

(04) direct repairs to plant and ancillary equipment

(05) carry out minor running repairs to plant and ancillary equipment.

Additional factors: industry in which experienced, eg oil refining, general chemicals, pharmaceuticals, soaps and detergents, synthetic resins, synthetic rubber; number of plants controlled; certificate(s) held.

Other titles include Group leader operator, Leading operator, Team leader.

561.10 Senior operator

Operates a plant or group of integrated plants in which a continuous flow of chemical and/or related materials is processed in a sequence of operations

Starts up and shuts down plant(s) as directed; monitors instruments and gauges indicating fluid flow, liquid levels, pressures, temperatures and other conditions within or affecting the plant(s) and ancillary equipment; adjusts control mechanisms manually or from remote control panel; reports malfunctioning of plant(s) and ancillary equipment; withdraws or diverts samples for quality control testing; prepares and recovers processing media where appropriate; maintains operational log as required.

May (01) undertake quality control testing using laboratory or other test equipment

(02) carry out minor running repairs to plant and ancillary equipment.

Additional factors: industry in which experienced, eg oil refining, general chemicals, pharmaceuticals, soaps and detergents, synthetic resins, synthetic rubber; number of plants operated; certificate(s) held.

Other titles include Senior process operator.

561.15 Continuous plant operator

Operates a section of a plant in which a continuous flow of chemical and/or related materials is processed in a sequence of operations

Performs appropriate tasks as described under SENIOR OPERATOR (561.10) but in relation to the operation of a section of a plant.

May (01) undertake quality control testing using laboratory or other test equipment

(02) carry out minor running repairs to plant and ancillary equipment

(03) operate a small continuous processing plant under direction of chief operator or senior operator.

Additional factors: section of plant operated, eg cracking, distilling, treating; certificate(s) held.

Other titles include Chemical process operator.

561 .20 Batch plant operator (general)

Operates a variety of plants in which chemical and/or related materials are processed in batches

Ascertains ingredient and processing requirements for batch; loads or directs loading of prescribed quantities of ingredients into plant or regulates flow from conveyors, elevators, hoppers or feed pipes; admits heat, vapour(s), catalyst or other processing agent(s) to plant as required; starts operational cycle; watches operation or monitors instruments and gauges indicating conditions within or affecting the plant; adjusts control mechanisms manually or from remote control panel as required; reports malfunctioning of plant; clears blockages; withdraws or diverts samples for quality control testing; removes or regulates discharge of batch of material on completion of operational cycle or directs performance of these tasks; prepares and recovers processing media where appropriate; cleans plant.

May (01) undertake quality control testing using laboratory or other test equipment

(02) operate ancillary equipment such as mechanical hoists and pumps

(03) carry out minor running repairs to plant and ancillary equipment

(04) perform packaging, labelling and related tasks (84).

Additional factors: types of batch plant operated, eg heat treating, mixing, mechanical separating; number of plants operated; certificate(s) held.

Other titles include Chemical process operator, Pill and tablet maker (general).

561 .50 Batch plant operator (heat treating, chemical reaction)

Operates one or more plants in which chemical and/or related materials are processed in batches by heat treatment and/or chemical reaction

Performs appropriate tasks as described under BATCH PLANT OPERATOR (GENERAL) (561 .20) but in relation to the processing of chemical and/or related materials by heat treatment and/or chemical reaction.

May (01) undertake quality control testing using laboratory or other test equipment

(02) operate ancillary equipment such as mechanical hoists and pumps

(03) carry out minor running repairs to plant and ancillary equipment

(04) perform packaging, labelling and related tasks (84).

Additional factors: type of plant in which experienced eg digesters, evaporators, pot stills, reactors; number of plants operated; certificate(s) held.

Other titles include Autoclave operator, Bleaching plant operator, Burnerman, Calciner, Char house man, Char kiln man, Chemical process operator, Coke oven heater, Converter man, Cooler, Digester man, Digester operator, Distiller, Drier operator, Evaporator operator, Fireman, Furnaceman, Kettle operator, Lofter, Melter, Lumpman, Pearler, Pot stillman, Reaction vessel operator, Retort heater, Treatment plant operator, Vacuum pan operator.

See Heat Treating Occupations (Wood Processing and Paper, Paperboard and Leatherboard Making) (581) and Heat Treating Occupations Not Elsewhere Classified (591)

561 .60 Batch plant operator (crushing, milling, mixing, blending)

Operates one or more plants in which chemical and/or related materials are processed in batches by crushing or milling and/or mixing or blending

Performs appropriate tasks as described under BATCH PLANT OPERATOR (GENERAL) (561 .20) but in relation to the crushing or milling and/or mixing or blending of chemical and/or related materials.

May (01) undertake quality control testing using laboratory or other test equipment

(02) operate ancillary equipment such as mechanical hoists and pumps

(03) carry out minor running repairs to plant and ancillary equipment

(04) perform packaging, labelling and related tasks (84).

Additional factors: type(s) of plant in which experienced, eg ball mills, roller mills, paddle mixers; number of plants operated; certificate(s) held.

Other titles include Batch mixer, Batch blender, Chemical process operator, Compounder, Crusher, Granulator, Grinder, Incorporator, In-line blender, Methylator, Millhand, Ointment maker, Pulveriser.

See Crushing, Milling, Mixing and Blending Occupations (Wood Processing and Paper, Paperboard and Leatherboard Making) (582) and Crushing, Milling, Mixing and Blending Occupations Not Elsewhere Classified (592)

561.70 Batch plant operator (filtering, straining and other mechanical separating)

Operates one or more plants in which chemical and/or related materials are processed in batches by filtering, straining or other mechanical separating

Performs appropriate tasks as described under BATCH PLANT OPERATOR (GENERAL) (561.20) but in relation to the filtering, straining or other mechanical separating of chemical and/or related materials; in addition, positions filter frames or screens or sets angle of separating plates as required.

May (01) coat surface of filter medium with filter-aid to prevent clogging of pores
(02) weigh materials before and/or after separating
(03) undertake quality control testing using laboratory or other test equipment
(04) carry out minor repairs to plant.

Additional factors: type of plant in which experienced, eg centrifuges, filter presses, rotary drum filters, vibratory screens; number of plants operated; certificate(s) held.

Other titles include Centrifuge operator, Chemical process operator, Drug room weigher, Filter press operator, Hydro-extractor operator, Rotary drum filter operator, Screener, Sedimentation plant operator, Siever, Sifter, Strainer.

See Filtering, Straining and Other Separating Occupations (Wood Processing and Paper, Paperboard and Leatherboard Making) (583) and Filtering, Straining and Other Mechanical Separating Occupations Not Elsewhere Classified (593)

561.98 Trainee

Performs, under instruction or guidance, various tasks including training exercises and as appropriate pursues studies in order to acquire the basic skills and knowledge required to perform the tasks of workers in chemical, gas and petroleum processing plant operating occupations.

561.99 Other chemical, gas and petroleum processing plant operating occupations

Workers in this group operate plant to process chemical and related materials and are not separately classified, for example:

(01) **Capsulation operators,** Capsule fillers (operate machines to form and fill capsules or to insert prescribed quantities of material into preformed capsules); (02) **Pill and tablet coaters;** (03) **Pill and tablet compressing machine operators,** Tabletting machine operators; (04) **Plant operators' assistants;** (05) **Water treatment plant operators,** Chlorination plant operators, Filter operators, Water softening plant operators (operate plants to purify and/or soften water).

Minor Group 57 FOOD AND DRINK PROCESSING OCCUPATIONS

Workers in this minor group slaughter animals, poultry and game, and bake, cook, freeze, heat, crush, mix, blend, filter, strain and otherwise process foodstuffs and beverages.

The occupations are arranged in the following unit groups:

570 Foremen (Food and Drink Processing Occupations)

571 Bakers and Flour Confectioners

572 Meat, Fish and Poultry Slaughtering and Preparing Occupations

573 Cooking, Freezing and Other Heat Treating Occupations (Food and Drink Processing)

574 Crushing, Milling, Mixing and Blending Occupations (Food and Drink Processing)

575 Filtering, Straining and Other Separating Occupations (Food and Drink Processing)

576 Plant and Machine Operating Occupations (Food and Drink Processing) Not Elsewhere Classified

579 Food and Drink Processing Occupations Not Elsewhere Classified

Unit Group 570 Foremen (Food and Drink Processing Occupations)

Workers in this unit group directly supervise and co-ordinate the activities of workers in food and drink processing occupations.

570 .10 Foreman (bakers and flour confectioners)

Directly supervises and co-ordinates the activities of bakers and flour confectioners

Performs appropriate tasks as described under SUPERVISOR/FOREMAN (UNSPECIFIED) (990 .00).

May (01) prepare work charts from recipes
(02) set and adjust machinery.

Additional factor: number of workers supervised.

570 .20 Foreman (slaughtermen, butchers and meat cutters)

Directly supervises and co-ordinates the activities of slaughtermen, butchers and meat cutters

Performs appropriate tasks as described under SUPERVISOR/FOREMAN (UNSPECIFIED) (990 .00).

Additional factors: whether in possession of slaughterer's licence; number of workers supervised.

570 .30 Foreman (fish preparers, poultry dressers)

Directly supervises and co-ordinates the activities of fish preparers or poultry dressers

Performs appropriate tasks as described under SUPERVISOR/FOREMAN (UNSPECIFIED) (990 .00).

Additional factor: number of workers supervised.

570 .40 Foreman (cooking, freezing and other heat treating occupations) (food and drink processing)

Directly supervises and co-ordinates the activities of workers in cooking, freezing and other heat treating occupations (food and drink processing)

Performs appropriate tasks as described under SUPERVISOR/FOREMAN (UNSPECIFIED) (990 .00).

May (01) undertake periodic inspections to maintain standards of hygiene.

Additional factor: number of workers supervised.

570.50 Foreman (crushing, milling, mixing and blending occupations) (food and drink processing)

Directly supervises and co-ordinates the activities of workers in crushing, milling, mixing and blending occupations (food and drink processing)

Performs appropriate tasks as described under SUPERVISOR/FOREMAN (UNSPECIFIED) (990.00).

May (01) undertake periodic inspections to maintain standards of hygiene

(02) prepare recipes

(03) test blended wines to determine readiness for casking or bottling.

Additional factor: number of workers supervised.

570.60 Foreman (filtering, straining and other separating occupations) (food and drink processing)

Directly supervises and co-ordinates the activities of workers in filtering, straining and other separating occupations (food and drink processing)

Performs appropriate tasks as described under SUPERVISOR/FOREMAN (UNSPECIFIED) (990.00).

May (01) undertake periodic inspections to maintain standards of hygiene.

Additional factor: number of workers supervised.

570.70 Foreman (plant and machine operating occupations (food and drink processing) not elsewhere classified)

Directly supervises and co-ordinates the activities of workers in plant and machine operating occupations (food and drink processing) not elsewhere classified

Performs appropriate tasks as described under SUPERVISOR/FOREMAN (UNSPECIFIED) (990.00).

May (01) undertake periodic inspections to maintain standards of hygiene

(02) set and adjust machinery.

Additional factor: number of workers supervised.

570.98 Trainee

Performs, under instruction or guidance, various tasks including training exercises and as appropriate pursues studies in order to acquire the basic skills and knowledge required to perform the tasks of foremen (food and drink processing occupations).

570.99 Other foremen (food and drink processing occupations)

Workers in this group directly supervise and co-ordinate the activities of workers in food and drink processing occupations and are not elsewhere classified, for example:

(01) **Foremen sausage makers;** (02) **Racking room foremen (brewery);** (03) **Foremen panel operators (automated brewing plant).**

Additional factor: number of workers supervised.

Unit Group 571 Bakers and Flour Confectioners

Workers in this unit group make bread and flour confectionery and finish flour confectionery products by hand.

Excluded are Ovensmen (573.72), Mixers (574.54) and other Machine operators and attendants (576)

571.05 Bread baker

Prepares and bakes dough to make bread products

Weighs flour, yeast and other ingredients according to recipe and loads into mixing bowl; mixes ingredients and adds specified amount of warm water to obtain the correct consistency; removes dough from bowl and cuts into pieces of required size or weight; kneads, stretches and moulds cut pieces into desired shape by hand or machine; places shaped pieces in tins or on trays or baking sheets; allows pieces to rise; loads tins, trays, etc into ovens at specified temperature; bakes for predetermined time at controlled temperature, checking bread occasionally during baking; unloads tins, trays, etc and allows products to cool.

571.10 Flour confectioner

Mixes ingredients for flour confectionery, shapes and fills pastry and finishes baked products

Weighs flour and other ingredients according to recipe and loads into mixing bowl; mixes ingredients and adds specified amount of liquid to obtain correct consistency; removes mixture from bowl; rolls, cuts and moulds dough or pastry to required shapes and places in tins or on trays or baking sheets; fills pastry shapes as required prior to baking and glazes tops where necessary; measures quantity of mixture for cakes, etc into prepared baking tins; fills, glazes, or decorates baked products as described under HAND DECORATOR (FLOUR CONFECTIONERY) (571.20).

May (01) perform tasks of OVENSMAN (573.72).

Other titles include Pie maker (hand), Scone maker.

571.15 Baker and confectioner

Prepares and bakes dough to make bread products and prepares, bakes and finishes flour confectionery products

Performs tasks as described under BREAD BAKER (571.05), FLOUR CONFECTIONER (571.10) and OVENSMAN (573.72).

571.20 Hand decorator (flour confectionery)

Decorates or finishes cakes or other baked flour confectionery products by hand

Performs a combination of the following tasks: prepares fillings or toppings such as cream, icings or fondants; brushes glazing liquids on baked confectionery products; moulds confectionery pastes such as marzipan on cakes; spreads toppings such as icings, chocolate or cream on products; pipes icing decorations on cakes using icing bag; makes cake decorations from confectionery pastes and places on cakes; sandwiches cakes with fillings such as jam, cream or butter icing; sprinkles sugar or other confections on products; fills products with jam, cream, fruit, etc.

May (01) design cake decorations.

Other titles include Hand finisher.

See Piper (chocolate, sugar confectionery) (579.20)

571.50 Table hand (bakery)

Performs tasks in the preparation of dough, pastry and cake mixtures prior to baking

Performs a combination of the following tasks: cuts dough or pastry into pieces of required size and weight; kneads, stretches or moulds pieces to required shape by hand or machine; places shaped pieces in tins or on trays or baking sheets; measures quantity of mixture for cakes, etc into prepared baking tins; fills pastry shapes as required and glazes tops where necessary; allows dough pieces to rise preparatory to baking.

May (01) prepare baking tins, sheets or trays
(02) clean machines and utensils.

571.98 Trainee

Performs, under instruction or guidance, various tasks including training exercises and as appropriate pursues studies in order to acquire the basic skills and knowledge required to perform the tasks of bakers and flour confectioners.

571.99 Other bakers and flour confectioners

Workers in this group make bread and flour confectionery and finish flour confectionery products by hand and are not elsewhere classified, for example:

(01) Hand decorators (ice cream) (decorate ice cream gateaux).

Unit Group 572 Meat, Fish and Poultry Slaughtering and Preparing Occupations

Workers in this unit group slaughter animals, poultry and game and prepare carcasses and fish for processing and sale.

572 .10 Slaughterman

Slaughters animals or flays and trims the carcasses

Performs a combination of the following tasks: kills or stuns animal using captive bolt pistol, gas or electric current; thrusts knife into jugular vein and drains off blood (sticking); removes skin or hide by hand or machine flaying; dehairs pigs by scalding, hand scraping and singeing, or using a dehairing machine; slits carcass open and removes internal organs; severs feet, tail and head of animal when appropriate; splits carcass into halves by hand or electric sawing or cleaving and washes down carcass meat; examines carcass meat for blemishes or disease; cleans and extracts edible offal from internal organs; sharpens knives and cleans tools and equipment.

May (01) cut up carcass meat into portions for processing or sale
(02) slaughter animals according to Jewish custom and be known as Shocket.

Additional factor: Whether in possession of knacker's licence (which permits holder to slaughter animals unfit for human consumption).

Other titles include Flayer, Knacker, Skinner, Sticker, Stunner.

Note: must hold slaughterer's licence.

572 .20 Butcher

Cuts up carcasses and prepares carcass sections for processing or retail sale

Cuts carcass into sections such as fore quarters, flank, shoulder and rump, using powered or hand saws and cleavers; prepares carcass sections for cooking, curing or other processing or for retail sale as described under MEAT CUTTER (572 .30).

May (01) slaughter animals (572 .10)
(02) make sausages and other meat products
(03) undertake sales tasks in a retail shop (361 .54).

Other titles include Butcher and cutter, Pork butcher, Shopman cutter.

572 .30 Meat cutter

Cuts up and prepares carcass sections for cooking, curing, meat products making or retail sale

Dissects carcass sections into parts such as breast, legs and shoulders using hand and powered saws, cleavers and knives; removes bones, gristle, surplus fat, rind and other waste matter; cuts carcass parts into portions such as joints, steaks and chops suitable for retail sale; cleans tools and equipment; sharpens knives.

Other titles include Bacon cutter, Boner, Featherer, Headman, Spiner, Trimm

572 .50 Poultry dresser

Cleans and prepares poultry carcasses for processing or retail sale

Suspends carcass to drain off blood; removes feathers by scalding and hand plucking or using plucking machine; removes internal organs and extracts edible offal; cuts off head and feet as required; cleans edible offal and places inside carcass.

May (01) stun and stick poultry (572 .99)
(02) cut up carcass into portions for retail sale.

572 .60 Fish preparer (hand)

Cleans, cuts and otherwise prepares fish by hand for processing or retail sale

Performs a combination of the following tasks: scrubs, heads, skins, slits, guts, washes and bones fish; cuts fish into fillets; cuts slits in large fish to facilitate the penetration of salt during curing; places prepared fish, waste matter and damaged or poor quality fish in separate containers; washes work-bench.

May (01) pack fish in boxes, barrels or casks
(02) operate fish preparing machine (572 .90)
(03) assist fish smoker
(04) undertake sales tasks in a retail shop (361 .48).

Other titles include Boner, Filleter, Gutter, Header Nobber, Splitter.

572.90 Fish preparer (machine)

Operates machine to cut and otherwise prepare fish for processing or retail sale

Places fish in position on revolving table of machine according to type of fish and processes to be carried out; starts machine to head, fillet, skin or split fish; places prepared fish, waste matter and damaged or poor quality fish in separate containers; clears simple machine blockages; washes out machine.

May (01) pack fish in boxes, barrels or casks
(02) assist fish smoker.

Other titles include Boner, Filleter, Gutter, Header, Nobber, Splitter.

572.98 Trainee

Performs, under instruction or guidance, various tasks including training exercises and as appropriate pursues studies in order to acquire the basic skills and knowledge required to perform the tasks of workers in meat, fish and poultry slaughtering and preparing occupations.

572.99 Other meat, fish and poultry slaughtering and preparing occupations

Workers in this group slaughter animals, poultry and game and prepare carcasses and fish for processing and sale and are not elsewhere classified, for example:

(01) **Chopping machine operators,** Dicing machine operators, Mincing machine operators (operate machines to chop, cube or mince meat); (02) **Gutmen,** Gut strippers (cut away fat, etc from animal gut); (03) **Pig dehairers** (scald, scrape and shave pig carcasses); (04) **Poultry stickers** (kill poultry); (05) **Sawyers (meat)** (cut meat to sizes suitable for processing).

Unit Group 573 Cooking, Freezing and Other Heat Treating Occupations (Food and Drink Processing)

Workers in this unit group process foodstuffs by cooking, boiling, heating, baking, roasting, smoking, cooling and freezing.

Excluded are Cooks (Catering Services) (431), workers distilling whisky, gin and other potable spirits (561), Bakers and confectioners (571 .15) and Plant and Machine Operating Occupations (Food and Drink Processing) Not Elsewhere Classified (576)

573.05 Sugar boiler (sugar refining)

Operates plant to crystallise sugar liquor by boiling in a vacuum pan

Starts vacuum pumps and opens valves to admit specified quantities of sugar liquor and steam into vacuum pan and water into condenser units; watches boiling process through inspection window; adds powdered sugar to induce crystallisation; withdraws sample from pan and determines whether crystals are forming correctly; controls the growth of crystals by introducing additional sugar liquor; closes steam and liquor feed valves and breaks vacuum when crystallisation is complete; turns valves to discharge crystallised sugar to storage tanks.

Other titles include Pan boiler, Pansman, Vacuum pan boiler.

573.10 Continuous cooker operator (jam)

Operates machine in which fruit pulp mixture and other ingredients are cooked to make jam by continuous process

Programmes machine according to instructions by setting switches, wheels and push-buttons on control panel; sets controls to regulate flow of mixed pulp, syrup, pectin and colouring matter; switches on electronically controlled device which automatically tests acidity of mixture and adds corrective ingredients as necessary; withdraws samples of jam during cooking and tests solids content using refractometer; records meter readings of pumping rate at specified intervals; re-sets controls at finish of production run to empty machine gradually without altering consistency of the jam.

May (01) mix ingredients.

573.15 Refiner (chocolate)

Operates heated rolling equipment to convert coarse liquid chocolate into dry flakes

Loads coarse liquid chocolate into feed hopper; examines consistency of chocolate to determine roller setting and adjusts positions of rollers; checks temperature of each roller; operates controls to regulate flow of water through rollers to obtain required temperature; starts equipment and opens hopper to feed liquid chocolate through rollers; examines refined chocolate and adjusts roller settings or temperature controls as necessary.

573.20 Kilnman maltster

Ripens or dries and cures grain in a kiln ready for malting

Operates equipment to spread grain on floor of kiln or spreads with shovel; sets or operates heat and air controls; manually turns grain on kiln floor, operates mechanical turnover or starts automatic turning equipment; on completion of process empties grain from kiln into storage bins using shovel or mechanical equipment.

May (01) fire and stoke kilns burning solid fuel
(02) test grain for moisture content.

Other titles include Kilnman (malting), Malt fireman.

573.25 Malt roaster

Roasts barley and other grain used in making malt

Fills feed hoppers and operates chutes to route specified quantities of grain to oven; starts oven rotating and switches on heating; roasts contents of oven; withdraws samples, tests for colour and flavour and adjusts heating as necessary; sprays cold water into oven to prevent combustion of grain during or on completion of roasting; unloads oven and spreads grain on floor for further cooling; sends samples of each batch of roasted grain for laboratory analysis; oils and greases bearings of oven and cleans oven and floor.

May (01) bag roasted grain or load on to elevators for removal to storage bins.

Other titles include Barley roaster.

573.50 Drying plant operator

Operates heated equipment to dry and dehydrate foodstuffs

Examines products to determine drying time or ascertains time from job instruction; sets controls of equipment such as heated conveyors, rotating cylinders, kilns, atomisers or rollers to govern temperature and rate of feed of product through drying plant; tests product for moisture content during processing and adjusts controls as necessary; cleans equipment and work area.

Other titles include Dehydration plant man, Draffman (whisky), Drier, Granulator (sugar), Roller plant operator, Spray plant operator.

573.52 Evaporator operator

Operates equipment to evaporate and concentrate liquids used in food processing

Operates controls to pump liquid to evaporator; starts vacuum pump where appropriate; operates controls to admit steam to evaporator, checks temperature and pressure gauges and adjusts controls as necessary; tests density of liquid during process using hydrometer or refractometer; adjusts temperature and pressure to obtain liquid of required concentration; controls discharge of concentrated liquid from evaporator; cleans equipment.

May (01) operate preheating tanks or cooling equipment.

Other titles include Triples operator, Vacuum pan operator, Vacuum oven attendant.

573.54 Cooker (fruit, vegetables, meat, fish)

Cooks fruit, vegetables, meat or fish and other ingredients prior to packaging, bottling, canning or further processing

Loads or regulates loading of specified quantities of fruit, vegetables, meat or fish and other ingredients such as spices, seasoning and preservatives into cooking vessel; operates controls to obtain required temperature or pressure; stirs contents, where necessary, using mechanical or hand paddle; cooks for specified time; withdraws samples at intervals to test progress of cooking; regulates discharge of contents of vessel on completion of cooking.

May (01) prepare and weigh ingredients
(02) feed cooked products through filter presses or pulping machines
(03) soak cooked peel in syrup
(04) send samples to laboratory for testing.

Other titles include Autoclave operator (fruit, vegetables), Boiler (fruit, vegetables), Boiler (meat, fish), Brawn maker, Invalid jelly maker, Jam boiler, Jelly maker, Juiceman (fruit, vegetables), Lemon curd maker, Marmalade boiler, Peel boiler, Pickle boiler, Pie filling maker (meat, fish). Sauce boiler, Tongue boiler.

Excluded are Continuous cooker operators (jam) (573.10) and Potato crisp cookers (573.99 and 576.85)

573.56 Tripe and feet dresser

Cleans and cooks ox and sheep tripe, cow heels, or pigs' and sheep's trotters

Slits open and cleans ox and sheep tripe (stomach) and cleans ox, pigs' and sheep's trotters using hand knives, high pressure water jets and hand scrubbers; immerses tripe and trotters into water which may contain cleansing solutions; raises temperature of water to scalding point; removes tripe and trotters after scalding and scrapes or cuts away any remaining waste matter; dehooves trotters and removes blemishes from tripe or trotters; places tripe and trotters into pans and cooks until tender; removes cooked tripe and trotters from pans and places in tank of cold water or bleaching solution; cuts and trims tripe into pieces suitable for retail sale; cleans equipment.

573.58 Cheese cook (processed cheese manufacture)

Operates equipment to cook blended cheese and other ingredients to make processed cheese

Starts pump to regulate flow of specified amount of cheese from blending tank into heated cooker; adds measured quantities of salt and other ingredients; adjusts heating to cook cheese at specified temperature for predetermined time; withdraws samples for laboratory testing; on completion of cooking regulates flow of cooked cheese to cooling vessel ready for packing.

May (01) clean cooker and work area.

573.60 Sugar boiler (sugar confectionery manufacture)

Operates equipment in which refined sugar, water and other ingredients are mixed and boiled to make toffee or other sugar confectionery

Weighs ingredients such as sugar, water, glucose and fruit juice, and loads into cooking pan; sets thermostat to control temperature; watches boiling process; withdraws sample from pan, determines consistency and adjusts heating if necessary; when process is completed opens discharge valve and starts pump or tilts pan to pour mixture on to cooling slab or into storage tanks.

May (01) add nuts or fruit to toffee mixture
(02) perform tasks of SLAB HAND (579.05).

Other titles include Butterscotch boiler, Caramel and fudge boiler, Creme boiler, Liquorice boiler, Toffee boiler.

573.62 Inversion attendant

Operates equipment to heat liquid sugar and acid solution to make invert sugar

Operates controls to pump specified quantity of liquid sugar into steel vat; adjusts controls to maintain temperature of vat at specified level; pumps measured quantity of sulphuric or hydrochloric acid solution into the vat; withdraws samples for laboratory testing; on completion of process operates pumps to transfer liquid to storage tank.

May (01) add caustic soda to mixture to neutralise the acid.

573.64 Roaster (dextrin)

Operates heated cooking pans to convert acidified starch flour into dextrin

Operates controls to regulate flow of acidified starch flour into cooking pan; sets temperature controls; switches on agitators and cooks contents for predetermined time at specified temperature; withdraws samples during cooking for viscosity, solubility and shade testing; drains resultant dextrin into cooling tanks when tests show that the required quality has been obtained.

Other titles include Calciner, Cooker operator, Pan man.

573.66 Mash room man

Heats and mixes crushed malt and water to produce grain wort used in making alcoholic liquors and beers

Places slotted metal plates in position to form false bottom in mash tun (large mixing vessel) and heats mash tun; opens inlet valve to admit hot water to cover false bottom plates; regulates flow of specified quantities of crushed malt and hot water into mash tun; heats mash for specified time and starts mechanical paddles to mix mash; tests temperature of mash during loading and mixing and adjusts heat as necessary; allows mash to stand for specified time; opens outlet valve in bottom of mash tun and drains strained liquor into coppers or other containers; switches on rotating sprinklers to spray mash with hot water until all the liquor has been extracted; empties spent mash; removes bottom plates and washes out mash tun.

May (01) add cereal liquor when preparing mash for grain whisky.

Other titles include Mash man, Mash tun stage hand, Tun room hand.

573 .68 Copperhead worker

Boils grain wort to produce malt liquor used in brewing beer

Dissolves specified quantity of sugar in water and adds, with specified quantities of hops and/or other ingredients, to grain wort in copper; boils mixture for specified time, adjusting heat and pressure controls as necessary; withdraws samples during boiling process and tests specific gravity and sugar content using hydrometer and saccharometer; drains cooked liquors to settling tanks (hop backs); washes out coppers and feed pipes.

May (01) reduce temperature of boiled wort using cooling equipment.

Other titles include Copper fireman, Copper room man, Copper sidesman.

573 .70 Butter liquefier (margarine manufacture)

Operates equipment to melt and pasteurise butter for use in making margarine

Sets controls to heat chambers of liquefier and pasteuriser to specified temperatures; feeds specified quantity of butter of required quality into liquefier; pumps melted butter from liquefier through pasteuriser to holding tank; flushes out pipes and cleans tanks, equipment and work area.

573 .72 Ovensman (bread, flour confectionery)

Sets and operates ovens to bake bread or flour confectionery products

Arranges sequence of baking to ensure that the most economical use is made of ovens; supervises loading of ovens when correct temperature has been reached; watches baking process and regulates speed or temperature of ovens as necessary; supervises removal of baked products from ovens.

May (01) fire ovens.

Other titles include Biscuit baker.

573 .74 Roaster (nuts, beans, chicory)

Roasts chicory roots, cocoa or coffee beans, nuts, etc

Feeds measured quantity of chicory roots, cocoa or coffee beans, nuts, etc into heated cylindrical roasting vessel; starts vessel rotating and roasts contents; withdraws samples and tests for colour, moisture content and flavour or aroma and regulates heating as necessary; on completion of roasting empties contents from vessel on to cooling trays; cleans equipment.

May (01) operate cooling, grinding, kibbling or winnowing machines.

573 .76 Smoker (foodstuffs)

Controls smoke-house in which foodstuffs are dried and smoked

Loads or assists in the loading of foodstuffs such as bacon, fish or beef into smoke-house; shovels sawdust or wood chips into stove hopper or on to smoke-house floor and sets alight; closes smoke-house doors and controls density of smoke and heat by adjusting ventilators and operating electric blowers; examines foodstuffs during smoking and adjusts heat or smoke as necessary; on completion of process draws off fires, opens ventilators and doors and unloads foodstuffs; cleans smoke-house and equipment.

Other titles include Drier (bacon smoking), Smoker (bacon), Smoker (fish curing), Stoveman (bacon smoking).

573 .78 Retort operator (canned, bottled foodstuffs)

Operates retort in which canned or bottled foodstuffs are cooked, pasteurised or sterilised

Loads retort with filled cans or bottles; closes and secures retort door; opens steam inlet and air exhaust valves; watches readings on thermometers and pressure gauges and adjusts controls to obtain required temperature and pressure; cooks, pasteurises or sterilises contents for specified time; increases retort pressure when reducing temperature to prevent containers bursting; opens retort when cool and unloads contents; cleans equipment.

Other titles include Pasteurising tank attendant (vegetables), Steriliser (canned or bottled foodstuffs excluding milk).

Excluded are Sterilisers (milk, ice cream) (573 .92)

573.80 Cooling equipment operator

Operates equipment to cool substances in the processing of food or drink

Operates controls to regulate flow to cooling equipment of substance to be cooled, for example, wort liquor, condensed or evaporated milk or homogenised ice cream mixture, and to regulate flow of water or chemical refrigerant through cooling coils; sets pressure controls to pump substance through cooling equipment where appropriate; checks temperature of substance during cooling and adjusts controls as necessary; pumps cooled substance to refrigerated or other storage containers or freezing equipment as appropriate; cleans and sterilises equipment.

Other titles include Ammonia cooler attendant (ice cream), Coolerman (brewing, whisky distilling), Paraflow man (brewing).

573.90 Sugar boiler (syrup manufacture)

Boils sugar and water to make syrup for preserves, canned fruits or condensed milk

Operates controls to regulate flow of measured quantities of sugar and water into cooking vessel; adjusts steam pressure or other form of heating to cooking vessel and starts agitator to mix ingredients; watches thermometer reading to ensure that correct cooking temperature is maintained; boils contents for specified time; tests samples of syrup; regulates discharge of boiled syrup from cooking vessel.

May (01) operate heated filter press and feed filtered syrup to storage tanks.

Other titles include Syrup maker.

573.91 Crystalliser attendant (sugar candy manufacture)

Operates equipment to crystallise liquid sugar to make sugar candy

Admits flow of specified quantity of granulated sugar into mixing tank containing specified quantity of liquid sugar; starts agitators to mix granulated and liquid sugar; prepares crystallising tanks by fitting wire frames into grooves in tank interiors; pumps syrup mixture into crystallising tanks and secures lids; regulates heating of tanks and ensures that correct temperature is maintained for specified time; gradually lowers temperature and, when mixture has cooled, runs off remaining liquid to mixing tank; lifts out wire frames and transfers sugar candy to wooden trays; scrapes off crust left in tanks.

May (01) withdraw samples of liquid sugar mixture for laboratory testing.

573.92 Steriliser (milk, ice cream)

Operates equipment in which milk or ice cream mixture is subjected to heat treatment to kill bacteria

(01) **Continuous steriliser operator (bulk milk)**

Operates controls to regulate flow of milk through heating and cooling coils of sterilising equipment and into bottling plant; checks gauges and dials to ensure that required temperature is reached and adjusts controls as necessary; cleans equipment.

(02) **Continuous steriliser operator (bottled milk)**

Watches flow of filled bottles from bottling plant to sterilising equipment; removes damaged bottles; clears blockages; checks temperature and pressure gauges and conveyor speed indicators and adjusts controls as necessary.

(03) **Autoclave operator (bottled milk)**

Loads crates of bottled milk into autoclave; seals door and admits steam to vessel; watches temperature and pressure gauges; adjusts controls to regulate timing sequence for heating and cooling; opens door to release steam and/or water; unloads crates; cleans autoclave.

(04) **Pasteuriser operator (milk, ice cream)**

Operates controls to regulate flow of specified quantity of milk or ice cream mixture into pasteurising plant; adjusts controls of heating and cooling equipment to ensure that temperature is maintained at required level for specified time; regulates flow of milk or ice cream mixture from pasteuriser to storage tanks; cleans equipment.

May (05) withdraw samples for laboratory testing
(06) operate mechanical equipment to load and unload autoclave
(07) spread sodium carbonate on floor of autoclave to prevent galvanised crates from rusting
(08) operate viscoliser or other milk or ice cream processing plant.

Additional factor: whether accustomed to operating a battery of autoclaves.

573.93 Blancher (fruit, vegetables)

Operates equipment to blanch prepared fruit or vegetables

Fills blanching equipment with water or steam; operates controls to adjust temperature and regulate flow of fruit or vegetables through equipment; examines blanched items and removes any which are discoloured; routes blanched fruit or vegetables by conveyor or chute to appropriate processing department; removes skins and other waste matter from equipment.

May (01) operate machines to remove skins and dry blanched items.

Other titles include Nut blancher.

573.94 Freezer operator

Operates equipment to freeze foodstuffs

(01) **Continuous freezer operator (ice cream)**

Operates controls to regulate flow of cooled ice cream mixture from refrigerated storage containers or direct from cooling equipment to freezing equipment; regulates flow of chemical refrigerant through freezing coils; sets pressure controls to pump cooled ice cream mixture through freezing equipment; tests consistency of frozen ice cream and adjusts machine controls as necessary; pumps or extrudes ice cream to cutting, moulding or packing department; cleans and sterilises equipment.

(02) **Plate freezer**

Loads trays of loose or packed foodstuffs such as meat, fish, vegetables, bread or cooked meats on to froster plates in freezer; operates controls to position froster plates and close freezer doors; sets freezing time according to type of foodstuff being processed; after specified time opens freezer doors and unloads foodstuffs.

Other titles include Froster operator.

(03) **Flow freezer**

Feeds prepared foodstuffs on to conveyor of preset freezing equipment; watches flow of foodstuffs through freezing compartment and clears blockages; unloads foodstuffs into bulk containers.

May (04) weigh foodstuffs before freezing

(05) use mechanical handling equipment

(06) spray trays of frozen fish with water to obtain airtight ice glaze

(07) operate associated equipment to package finished product.

573.95 Ice room attendant

Operates equipment to freeze water to make ice blocks

Checks specific gravity of brine solution in freezing tank and adds additional brine as necessary; fills sets of galvanized cans with filtered water; lowers sets of cans into freezing tanks using mechanical handling equipment; where appropriate operates controls to start brine solution circulating in tank and to lower the temperature of the solution; pumps air into cans during freezing process if producing clear ice blocks; when water in cans has frozen lifts cans from freezing tank and lowers into thawing tank for short period to aid release of ice blocks; removes ice blocks from cans and transfers to cold store.

May (01) operate machine to crush ice blocks.

Other titles include Tank room attendant (ice manufacture).

573.99 Trainee

Performs, under instruction or guidance, various tasks including training exercises and as appropriate pursues studies in order to acquire the basic skills and knowledge required to perform the tasks of workers in cooking, freezing and other heat treating occupations (food and drink processing).

573.99 Other cooking, freezing and heat treating occupations (food and drink processing)

Workers in this group process foodstuffs by cooking, boiling, heating, baking, roasting, smoking, cooling and freezing and are not elsewhere classified, for example:

(01) **Brine makers;** (02) **Caramel (burnt sugar) makers;** (03) **Clarification vat attendants (sugar);** (04) **Cookers (potato crisp) (non-automatic equipment);** (05) **Cookers (yeast food);** (06) **Lard makers,** Dripping makers (refine beef or pork fat); (07) **Popcorn machine operators** (roast corn to produce popcorn); (08) **Tempering machine operators (chocolate)** (operate machines to maintain correct temperature and grain of liquid chocolate); (09) **Tunnelmen (ice cream)** (feed blocks of ice cream into hardening plant).

Unit Group 574 Crushing, Milling, Mixing and Blending Occupations (Food and Drink Processing)

Workers in this unit group crush, grind, roll, pulp, mix and blend foodstuffs.

574 .10 Rollerman (flour milling)

Operates bank of rollers to break down grain to make flour

Ascertains from instructions quantities and types of grain to be broken down and/or rolled together; opens feed valves, adjusts position of each set of rollers and starts machine; withdraws samples at intervals during rolling and examines for correct mixture and breakdown of grain; adjusts feed valves or roller settings as necessary; closes feed valves and allows rolling mill to empty before changing over to a different mixture; clears blockages in feed pipes, rollers, outlet chutes or conveyors; maintains correct working level of grain by adjusting feed from screening equipment.

May (01) repair belt drives and replace broken rollers
(02) operate purifying and sifting machines.

574 .50 Rollerman (foodstuffs excluding flour)

Operates rolling plant to break down grain or seed to make food or drink products other than flour

Ascertains from instructions quantities and types of grain or seed to be broken down; opens valves to admit foostuffs such as cooked grain, malted grain, mustard seed or oil seed and adjusts position of rollers; starts machine; withdraws samples at intervals during rolling and examines for correct breakdown; adjusts feed valves or roller setting as necessary; clears blockages in feed pipes, rollers, outlet chutes or conveyors.

May (01) withdraw sample of crushed grain for laboratory testing
(02) operate screening plant
(03) undertake minor repairs to machines.

Other titles include Flaking millman (cereals), Flaking plant machineman (grain), Gristman (brewing), Malt engineman, Malt grinder, Malt miller, Miller (whisky), Millroom man (brewing), Rollerman (mustard milling), Rollerman (oil seed).

574 .52 Grinding machine operator (foodstuffs)

Operates machine to crush or grind foodstuffs other than fruit

Opens valve to admit foodstuffs such as oats, barley, rice, coffee beans, cocoa nibs or blocks, pepper, almonds, granulated sugar or spices into grinding machine; starts machine; withdraws samples at intervals and checks that crushing or grinding is proceeding correctly; adjusts feed valve or machine setting as necessary; clears blockages in feed pipes, grinder, outlet chutes or conveyors.

May (01) weigh and feed crushed or ground grain into sacks
(02) operate other machines such as blenders, polishers and separators.

Other titles include Coffee grinder, Disintegrator (cocoa), Grinder (chocolate), Grinder (cocoa), Grinder (provender milling), Grinderman (grain milling), Grinding machine man (meat preparing), Liquor mill attendant (chocolate), Machineman (provender milling), Miller (sugar manuacfture), Milling machine operator (chocolate), Milling machine operator (cocoa), Millhand (rice milling).

Excluded are Rollermen (flour milling) (574.10) and Rollermen (foodstuffs excluding flour) (574 .50)

574 .54 Mixer (bread and flour confectionery)

Operates machine to mix flour and other ingredients for bread or flour confectionery

Weighs out or collects specified quantities of ingredients such as flour, yeast, salt, wheat germ, lard, sugar and fruit according to instructions; feeds ingredients into mixing machine and starts machine; feeds in specified quantity of water or other liquid as required; examines samples during mixing and stops machine when desired consistency has been obtained; empties bread dough or flour confectionery mixture into containers; cleans machine.

May (01) mix by hand.

Other titles include Batter mixing machine operator, Dough mixer (biscuits), Dough mixer (bread), Paste mixer (pies).

574.56 Mixerman (compound animal food)

Operates machine to mix grain fibres and other ingredients for animal foodstuffs

Feeds measured quantities of ingredients such as maize fibre, molasses, corn dust and limestone flour into hopper of mixing machine; starts machine and operates control to regulate input from hopper; checks that ingredients are mixing correctly and adjusts machine controls as necessary; regulates rate of discharge of mixture to sacks or other containers; clears blockages in machine.

May (01) operate machine to convert mixture into cubes or pellets.

Other titles include Batch mixer, Cuberman.

574.58 Compounder (soft drinks, wines, ciders, liqueurs, spirits)

Operates equipment to dilute or mix wines, spirits, essences and other ingredients in the manufacture of alcoholic or soft drinks

Pumps measured quantities of liquid ingredients such as wine, water, cider or distilled spirits into mixing tank; adds measured quantities of other ingredients such as sugar, malt, fruit essences, colouring and citric acid as required; starts mechanical paddles or operates controls to introduce air and agitate the mixture; checks samples for density, fermentation and taste or passes samples to laboratory for testing; stops mixing when desired blend has been obtained and pumps mixture to storage tanks or to bottling or cask filling department.

May (01) carbonate mixture (576.76)
(02) clean equipment.

Other titles include Blender (wines), Vatman (fruit cordials, etc).

574.60 Butter blender

Operates machine to blend various kinds of butter

Feeds blocks of various kinds of butter into blending machine according to instructions; starts machine to shred the blocks and blend the butter; adds salt as required; tests samples for consistency and stops machine when desired blend is obtained; empties butter into containers; cleans machine.

574.62 Concher (chocolate)

Operates machine to mix and beat refined chocolate to obtain liquid chocolate of fine texture

Loads specified quantity of refined chocolate into conche tank; sets controls to heat tank; starts agitator in conche tank; examines samples during process and adjusts heat as necessary; on completion of process empties chocolate into container; cleans machine.

May (01) add specified quantity of fat or other ingredients to chocolate during the process.

Other titles include Conche man (chocolate).

574.90 Millhand (fruit pulping)

Operates machine to pulp apples or pears used in the manufacture of alcoholic or soft drinks

Operates controls to regulate feed of apples or pears into machine hopper and the flow of fruit from machine hopper into cutting mill; clears blockages in feed pipes or mill; routes pulped fruit to hoppers of pressing plant; cleans equipment.

May (01) operate pressing plant to extract juice from pulp.

Other titles include Apple milling hand (cider), Millman, Pear milling hand (perry).

574.91 Nut processing machine operator

Operates equipment to dehusk and crush roasted nuts

Feeds quantity of roasted nuts into feed hopper of machine; adjusts positions of rough surfaced belts and rollers; starts equipment and opens feed valve of hopper; examines samples of crushed nuts for correct breakdown and adjusts feed valve, belt or roller settings as necessary.

574.92 Mixer (not elsewhere classified)

Operates equipment to mix ingredients in the processing of foodstuffs and is not elsewhere classified

Loads ingredients into equipment; operates controls to start mixing; where appropriate, withdraws samples to check consistency; adjusts controls during mixing as required; unloads mixed ingredients on to conveyors or into containers.

May (01) weigh out ingredients prior to mixing

(02) prepare ingredients for mixing by chopping, sieving, mincing, etc

(03) clean machine.

Additional factor: type of foodstuffs to which accustomed, eg chocolate, sugar confectionery, ice cream, meat products, fruit pulp and pectin, herbs, mincemeat.

Other titles include Melangeur attendant, Mixer (ice cream), Mixer (meat products), Mixer operator (chocolate), Mixer operator (sugar confectionery), Tandem operator (chocolate), Weigher and mixer (chocolate, sugar confectionery).

574.93 Seed tank man (yeast)

Mixes molasses, water and chemicals and adds yeast culture to grow seed yeast

Feeds measured quantities of water, molasses and chemicals into mixing tank according to instructions; mixes ingredients in tank using compressed air or mechanical paddle; adds specified amount of yeast culture to mixture; checks temperature of mixture and operates controls to regulate flow of water through cooling coils; tests acidity of yeast and adds further chemicals as necessary; feeds fermented mixture to separator tanks.

574.94 Viscoliser operator (ice cream), Homogeniser operator (ice cream)

Operates machine to break down fat globules in ice cream mixture

(01) **Viscoliser operator**

Pumps pasteurised ice cream mixture into mixing chamber of machine; starts machine to churn and beat the mixture; pumps mixture to cooling plant on completion of process; cleans equipment.

(02) **Homogeniser operator**

Pumps pasteurised ice cream mixture into homogeniser plant which forces the mixture under pressure through pipes of reducing diameter; pumps homogenised mixture to cooling plant; cleans equipment.

574.98 Trainee

Performs, under instruction or guidance, various tasks including training exercises and as appropriate pursues studies in order to acquire the basic skills and knowledge required to perform the tasks of workers in crushing, milling, mixing and blending occupations (food and drink processing).

574.99 Other crushing, milling, mixing and blending occupations (food and drink processing)

Workers in this group crush, grind, roll, pulp, mix and blend foodstuffs and are not elsewhere classified, for example:

(01) **Flavouring men (cereal manufacture);** (02) **Gelatine preparers** (mix hot water and gelatine powder); (03) **Grinder and roller operators (processed cheese manufacture);** (04) **Homogenisers (milk);** (05) **Mingler machine attendants** (mix raw sugar with sugar syrup); (06) **Mixers (milk foods);** (07) **Mustard blenders;** (08) **Paste makers** (grind and mix ingredients to form confectionery pastes).

Unit Group 575 Filtering, Straining and Other Separating Occupations (Food and Drink Processing)

Workers in this unit group operate equipment to filter, strain and otherwise separate foodstuffs.

575.10 Butter churn operator

Operates equipment to separate cream into butter grains and buttermilk and process the butter grains to make butter

Pumps specified amount of cream into churn and starts churn rotating; checks progress of breakdown of cream into butter grains and buttermilk; stops churn when process is complete; drains off buttermilk; pumps cold water into churn and restarts churn to wash butter grains; stops churn and draws off water; adds specified quantity of salt to butter grains as required, restarts churn and leaves to rotate until butter grains form a solid mass; stops churn and empties butter into container.

May (01) withdraw samples for laboratory testing
(02) feed butter into moulding machine
(03) clean equipment.

Other titles include Butter maker.

575.50 Filter press operator

Operates one or more machines to separate solids from liquids by pumping mixture through filter frames

Positions and seals filter frames in press; sets controls to pump mixture such as sugar solution, fruit pulp, yeast cream, liquid cocoa butter or gluten liquor through filter frames; examines liquid output and adjusts pump controls or stops machine; releases filter frames from press and washes or scrapes off the solidified matter; cleans equipment and replaces filters as necessary.

May (01) coat filters with filtrate paste, eg fuller's earth.

Additional factor: number of machines operated.

Other titles include Filter pressman (foodstuffs), Filterman (foodstuffs).

See Filter press operator (not elsewhere classified) (593.20)

575.55 Rotary drum filter operator

Operates one or more machines to separate solids from liquids by drawing liquids through filters fitted to rotating drum

Sets controls to regulate feed of mixture such as gluten solution or lactose liquor into filter tank; sets rotation speed of filter drum; starts vacuum pump to draw liquid through the filter and positions scraper or mandrel to remove solids adhering to filter; checks that liquids and solids are separating correctly and adjusts controls as necessary; cleans equipment and replaces filters as necessary

May (01) coat filters with filtrate paste.

Additional factor: number of machines operated.

Other titles include Filter attendant, Filter station attendant.

See Rotary drum filter operator (not elsewhere classified) (593.25)

575.60 Centrifuge operator

Operates one or more machines to separate by centrifugal force solids from liquids or liquids of differing specific gravity from each other

Sets feed controls or loads centrifugal container with mixture such as milk, sugar syrup, crushed grain and water, starch liquor or lactose liquor; sets rotation speed of container and machine temperature; positions outlet pipes or containers and starts machine; checks that equipment is operating correctly and adjusts as necessary; stops machine on completion of process and extracts or drains separated substances; cleans equipment.

May (01) operate machines which load, spin, wash and empty foodstuffs automatically
(02) withdraw samples and test for density or pass to laboratory for testing.

Additional factor: number of machines operated.

Other titles include Centrifugal attendant, Spinner, Spinner man.

See Centrifuge operator (not elsewhere classified) (59·330)

575 .65 Sieve operator

Operates one or more machines to separate and/or size foodstuffs by means of gravity separators, vibratory screens or similar equipment

Selects screen with mesh of required size and positions in equipment; sets controls to feed foodstuffs such as grain, rice, cornflour, cocoa beans, sugar or flour into hopper; positions containers at output channels and adjusts hopper controls to regulate flow of foodstuffs on to screens; starts screen vibrating and/or admits flow of air; examines separated or sized foodstuffs and adjusts controls as necessary; clears blockages in feed and output channels.

May (01) operate equipment incorporating a magnetic device to remove metallic particles.

Additional factor: number of machines operated.

Other titles include Cleaner (corn, maize starch), Grader (sugar, cocoa), Presser (cocoa, rice, cornflour), Purifier man (rice, flour milling), Sifter (sugar, cocoa), Silksman (flour, grain, provender milling).

575 .90 Diffuser attendant, Diffusion battery hand

Operates diffusion equipment to extract sugar juice from sliced beet

(01) Diffuser attendant

Sets controls to regulate temperature and flow of water and sliced beet through diffuser sections; watches process at each section of diffuser and adjusts heating, flow or pressure controls as necessary; pumps juice to holding tanks and passes pulp by conveyor to pressing plant; cleans equipment.

(02) Diffusion battery hand

Positions feed pipes to fill each cell of battery with sliced beet and warm water; secures covers on cells and sets controls to heat cells; pumps off sugar liquid on completion of process and empties residue of beet from cells; cleans equipment.

575 .98 Trainee

Performs, under instruction or guidance, various tasks including training exercises and as appropriate pursues studies in order to acquire the basic skills and knowledge required to perform the tasks of workers in filtering, straining and other separating occupations (food and drink processing).

575 .99 Other filtering, straining and separating occupations (food and drink processing)

Workers in this group operate equipment to filter, strain and otherwise separate foodstuffs and are not elsewhere classified, for example:

(01) **Floating room attendants (rice starch)** (mix liquid starch with caustic soda and separate sediment in settling tanks); (02) **Liquormen (char house)** (pass sugar or glucose liquor through char filters); (03) **Press hands (cider, perry)** (fill filter cloths with apple or pear pulp and operate hydraulic presses to squeeze out the juice); (04) **Press operators (cocoa butter)** (operate hydraulic equipment to express cocoa butter from liquefied cocoa in steel pots); (05) **Wet block machine hands (rice starch)** (operate equipment with vacuum device to filter moisture from wet starch in moulds).

Unit Group 576 Plant and Machine Operating Occupations (Food and Drink Processing) Not Elsewhere Classified

Workers in this unit group operate and attend plant, machines and other equipment to perform a variety of tasks in the processing of food and drink and are not elsewhere classified.

576 .05 Ice cream maker

Performs all operations in the manufacture of ice cream

Performs tasks as described under MIXER (ICE CREAM) (574 .92), PASTEURISER OPERATOR (573 .92), VISCOLISER OPERATOR (574 .94), COOLING EQUIPMENT OPERATOR (573 .80) and FREEZER OPERATOR (573 .94).

576 .10 Chocolate maker

Performs all operations in the manufacture of chocolate

Performs tasks as described under GRINDING MACHINE OPERATOR (FOODSTUFFS) (574 .52), MIXER OPERATOR (CHOCOLATE) (574 .92), REFINER (CHOCOLATE) (573 .15) and CONCHER (CHOCOLATE) (574 .62).

Other titles include Millroom hand (chocolate).

576 .15 Utility operator (maize starch, animal food)

Operates a variety of equipment in the manufacture of maize starch or animal foodstuffs

Performs a combination of the tasks as described under STEEP OPERATOR (MAIZE STARCH) (576 .68), WET MILL OPERATOR (MAIZE STARCH) (576 .70), OIL EXTRACTOR (GRAIN GERM, SEED OIL EXTRACTION) (576 .72), CENTRIFUGE OPERATOR (575 .60), FILTER PRESS OPERATOR (575 .50), ROTARY DRUM FILTER OPERATOR (575 .55), EVAPORATOR OPERATOR (573 .52) and DRYING PLANT OPERATOR (573 .50).

576 .20 Cheese maker (excluding processed cheese)

Operates equipment to process milk and other ingredients to make cheese

Performs a combination of the following tasks: operates controls to regulate flow of milk from pasteurisation equipment into heated vat; adds specified quantity of lactic acid (culture); starts agitator in vat to mix culture and milk for specified period and adds rennet to assist coagulation; stops agitator and leaves mixture until curd has formed; maintains temperature at specified level; tests curd for acidity; cuts curd into small pieces using wire cutters or knives; restarts agitator and increases heat for specified period; turns off heat, stops agitator and drains off whey; salts curds as required and feeds into mill to shred curds into small pieces; loads specified quantities of curds into metal moulds lined with linen, calico, cotton gauze or muslin; presses mould to consolidate cheese shape and squeeze out any remaining whey; empties mould and immerses cheese in wax solution; covers cheese with wax paper, wraps in calico binding or sprays with anti-fungus solution; leaves cheese at regulated temperature for specified period.

May (01) weigh and grade cheeses.

576 .25 Macaroni making equipment operator

Operates equipment to produce macaroni or similar products

Selects appropriate dies and cutting knives and positions in equipment; sets temperature and humidity controls; operates controls to feed measured quantities of semolina, water and other ingredients into equipment; starts mixer, worm screw feeder and drier and watches process; checks that dough is of required consistency, that extruded products are of correct length and that drying process is complete; adjusts controls as necessary; cleans equipment and removes and cleans dies as necessary.

May (01) sharpen cutting knives
(02) produce dough in sheet form and shred sheet by machine.

576 .30 Screensman conditioner (grain, seed)

Operates equipment to separate and condition grain or seed for further processing

Sets controls according to type of grain or seed to be processed; starts equipment and feeds grain or seed through screens of separator; routes separated grain or seed through washing, drying or damping equipment according to conditioning required; examines grain or seed and adjusts controls as necessary; clears blockages in feed or output channels; routes conditioned grain or seed to storage silos or to other processing plant.

May (01) examine condition of grain or seed in storage silos.

Other titles include Seed dresser (mustard milling), Tempering bin man (flour, grain, provender milling), Washerman (flour, grain, provender milling).

576 .50 Setter-operator (bakery equipment)

Sets and operates equipment to prepare mixed ingredients for baking or to finish baked products

Sets up equipment parts such as feed magazines, deposit nozzles, dies, die plates, cutters, rollers and conveyors; sets speeds, pressures and temperatures and starts equipment; feeds mixed ingredients or baked products into equipment, checks products and adjusts controls as necessary.

May (01) check weight of finished products.

576 .52 Shredding machine operator (cereals)

Operates machine to shred grain to specified shape and size to make cereal products

Positions machine rollers against cutting knife according to size of shred required; operates controls to regulate feed of grain into shredding machine; withdraws samples, examines shredding and adjusts controls as necessary; clears blockages in machine; regulates discharge of shredded grain to drying equipment.

May (01) replace cutting knives
(02) operate drying equipment (573 .50).

576 .54 Coating equipment operator (confectionery)

Operates equipment to coat confectionery products with chocolate, sugar, syrup or other edible material

Performs a combination of the following tasks: sets equipment controls to regulate temperature of liquid coating, flow of coating material or speed of feed conveyor as required; feeds coating such as chocolate, syrup or sugar into machine hopper; feeds or regulates feeding of centres such as fondants, toffees, nuts, raisins, biscuits, dates or truffles to conveyor or into machine pan; starts machine; checks that products are evenly coated; adjusts machine controls as necessary; separates products which have stuck together; places coated products on trays.

May (01) operate machine which impresses design on coated products

(02) decorate coated products using hand tools.

Other titles include Chocolate pan man, Enrober, Enrobing machine operator, Revolving pan worker (sugar confectionery).

576 .56 Machine moulder (chocolate)

Operates machine to deposit measured quantities of liquid chocolate into moulds to form bars, other solid shapes or shells

Regulates flow of tempered liquid chocolate into machine hopper; sets controls to maintain chocolate and moulds at required temperature, to deposit required amount of chocolate in moulds and to govern speed and vibration of belt conveying moulds through machine; starts machine; examines chocolate products, checks temperatures and adjusts machine controls as necessary.

May (01) manually shake filled moulds to distribute chocolate evenly

(02) check weight of formed products.

Other titles include Shell machine operator, Shell plant operator, Solid machine operator.

576 .58 Acidifier operator (dextrin)

Operates equipment to spray starch with hydrochloric acid or other catalytic agent in the production of dextrin

Fills acid feed container with measured quantity of hydrochloric acid or other catalytic agent; fills acidifier hopper with measured quantity of starch; operates controls to feed starch into acidifier and spray acid or other catalytic agent on to the starch; checks that starch feed and spray nozzle operate correctly and adjusts as necessary; loads starch into container and passes to roaster.

May (01) test acidity of starch before and on completion of process

(02) dilute acid with measured quantity of water.

576 .60 Dairy worker (margarine)

Operates equipment to dilute and pasteurise milk and adds other ingredients for use in making margarine

Regulates flow of specified quantities of liquid or powdered milk and water into heated mixing tank and starts agitators; pumps mixture through pasteurising equipment into ripening tank; adds specified quantity of culture to the mixture to induce souring, heats mixture and allows to coagulate; adds other ingredients such as brine and glucose, according to instructions; when coagulation is complete cooks mixture and pumps to containers; cleans equipment.

May (01) test mixture for acidity or take samples for laboratory testing.

Other titles include Dairyman.

576 .62 Votator operator (edible fat manufacture)

Operates votator equipment to process ingredients to make margarine or other compound edible fats

Operates controls to admit measured quantities of ingredients such as blended oils, milk, vitamins, flavourings and brine into heated mixing tank and starts agitators; sets temperature of cooling equipment and pumps mixture through the equipment; discharges cooled product into storage tanks or pumps through machine which extrudes and cuts the solidified product into blocks of required shape and weight; examines product during processing and adjusts machine controls as necessary; withdraws samples for laboratory analysis; cleans equipment.

576.64 Cube sugar equipment operator

Operates equipment to form granulated sugar into cubes

Adjusts controls to heat drying cabinet to required temperature; checks that there is an adequate supply of granulated sugar in feed hopper of machine; starts equipment; tests cubes before and after drying and adjusts temperature and pressure controls on cube forming drum as necessary; checks that suction plates of cube forming drum are clear and cleans as necessary.

May (01) supervise weighers and packers.

576.66 Barrelman (rice starch)

Operates equipment to convert rice grains into liquid starch

Operates controls to load measured quantity of rice into steel barrel; pumps caustic soda solution into barrel; starts barrel revolving for prescribed time; stops barrel and drains off caustic soda solution; repeats process following a prescribed time cycle; discharges soaked rice into feed hopper of hammer mill; operates mill controls to pulverise the soaked rice and produce liquid starch; pumps liquid starch to holding tanks.

Other titles include Wet miller.

576.68 Steep operator (maize starch)

Operates steep vats to soften maize grains for wet milling

Operates controls to feed measured quantities of maize grain and heated solution of sulphur dioxide and water into steep vats; adjusts controls to maintain temperature of vat at required level; operates pumps to circulate the solution in the vats; allows grain to steep for specified time; controls discharge of mixture through screens; routes steeped grain to wet mill hoppers and steep solution to holding tanks for re-use.

May (01) operate sulphur burning equipment to produce solution of sulphur dioxide and water
(02) withdraw samples of steeped grain for laboratory testing
(03) test acidity of steep water.

Other titles include Steephouseman, Steepman.

576.70 Wet mill operator (maize starch)

Operates equipment to extract oil germs from steeped grains and wash and grind fibre residue

Operates controls to regulate flow of steeped grain through mill; examines crushed grain and adjusts feed rate or mill setting as necessary; operates controls to regulate flow of crushed grain into equipment to extract germ from crushed grain; discharges oil germ to oil house; feeds fibre residue to washing and grinding plant.

Other titles include Germ separating and milling operator, Wet miller.

576.72 Oil extractor (grain germ, seed oil extraction)

Operates cooking vessel and extractor equipment to cook grain germs or crushed seeds and extract the oil

Operates controls to feed and regulate flow of grain germs or crushed seeds into heated cooking vessel; opens steam inlet valves; starts agitators to force grain germs or crushed seed through cooking vessel into extractor equipment; examines crushed germs or seeds and crude oil leaving extractor equipment; adjusts heat supply, feed rate or speed of agitators as necessary; cleans cooking vessel and extractor equipment.

May (01) add solvent to grain prior to cooking.

Other titles include Expellerman, Oil expeller attendant (maize).

576.74 Carbonatation man

Operates equipment to treat sugar liquor with lime and carbon dioxide to remove impurities

Operates controls to feed measured quantities of heated raw sugar liquor and lime into tanks and to pump carbon dioxide gas into the mixture; records specific gravity of the solution using brix gauge; tests acidity and alkalinity of the solution and adjusts flow of sugar, lime or carbon dioxide as necessary; pumps the mixture to filtration equipment.

Other titles include Saturation tank attendant.

576.76 Carbonation and filtration man (ciders, wines)

Filters and carbonates fermented wines, ciders or beer prior to bottling

Operates equipment to pump liquor from fermenting vats through filter presses to remove bacteria; pumps filtered liquor into carbonating vessel; regulates flow of coolant around vessel to keep liquor at fixed temperature; opens pressure valve to admit carbon dioxide and adjusts valve as necessary to maintain constant pressure in carbonating vessel; starts agitator in the vessel; on completion of carbonation process switches off agitator, coolant and carbon dioxide supply and releases pressure; pumps carbonated liquor to bottling department.

May (01) pump carbonated liquor through filter press
(02) dismantle and clean filters.

Other titles include Gasman (cider manufacture).

576.85 Automatic equipment attendant

Attends equipment which automatically prepares, processes, shapes or finishes foodstuffs

Starts equipment when necessary; operates feed controls, checks automatic feed or manually feeds raw or prepared foodstuffs into equipment; watches process and examines foodstuffs; removes faulty items; clears blockages in the equipment; removes finished products as required; reports breakdown of equipment to maintenance staff.

May (01) clean equipment
(02) attend equipment which also wraps finished products.

Other titles include Autolysis man (yeast foods), Bakery equipment attendant, Brushing and glazing machine attendant (rice milling), Compressor attendant (lozenge machine), Divider machine man, Dough baker attendant, Finishing machine attendant (bakery products), Granulating equipment attendant, Machine washer (fish curing), Molasses attendant, Moulding machine attendant (bakery products), Neutraliser attendant (invert sugar, glucose), Ovensman (cereal products), Pie machine attendant, Potato crisp cooker, Poultry plucker (machine), Puffing equipment attendant (cereals), Rennet process worker, Starchless moulding machine attendant (sugar confectionery), Sugar beet washer, Sulphitation man (sugar).

576.86 Sugar beet cutter

Operates machine to slice washed sugar beet ready for processing

Operates controls to regulate flow of beet from washing plant through cutting machine; withdraws samples to check that beet is being sliced correctly; removes cutting blocks as necessary and replaces damaged knives; sharpens blunt knives using grinding machine or hand block; clears blockages in machine; controls flow of sliced beet to diffusion department.

May (01) perform tasks of SUGAR BEET WASHER (576.85).

Other titles include Sugar beet slicer.

576.87 Cutting machine operator (sugar confectionery)

Operates machine to cut or cut and wrap or shape, cut and wrap sugar confectionery

Feeds prepared sugar confectionery mixture into machine; loads wrapping material into machine holders; sets controls to cut, cut and wrap or shape, cut and wrap confectionery; starts machine and examines output; removes misshapen or unwrapped confectionery and adjusts machine controls as necessary; cleans machine.

May (01) dust cut confectionery with sugar or other mixture to prevent adhesion.

Other titles include Cutting and wrapping machine operator (sugar confectionery).

576.88 Mogul operator (sugar confectionery)

Operates machine to make moulds in starch and/or deposit liquid confectionery in the moulds

Fills moulding hopper of machine with starch as necessary and deposit hopper with liquid confectionery such as fondant, marshmallow or jelly; starts machine and feeds trays into machine; checks as appropriate that trays are correctly filled with starch, that impressions are correctly made and that moulds are filled with confectionery; adjusts machine controls to regulate speed and temperature as necessary; removes filled trays from machine.

May (01) check weight of confectionery.

576 .89 Fondant machine operator

Operates equipment to boil, cool and beat sugar mixture to make fondant

Weighs ingredients such as sugar, glucose, syrup and water according to instructions and feeds into cooking pan; sets temperature control and boils for specified time; regulates flow of hot sugar mixture over cooling roller; feeds cooled mixture into beating chamber and starts beating equipment; examines fondant and adjusts controls as necessary; feeds fondant into containers.

Other titles include Base cream machine operator, Base cream maker.

576 .90 Liquorice extruding machine operator

Operates machine to extrude liquorice mixture to make confectionery

Selects suitably shaped die plate and secures in machine; feeds liquorice mixture into machine hopper; starts machine to extrude liquorice through the die plate; cuts extruded liquorice into suitable lengths with hand knife and loads on to trays.

576 .91 Shell separation machine operator (cocoa beans)

Operates machine to break and crush roasted cocoa beans and separate the broken bean nibs from the husks

Operates controls to regulate feed of roasted cocoa beans to machine hopper; starts dual purpose machine to break and crush beans and separate the nibs from husks, dust, etc; examines nibs and husks and adjusts machine controls as necessary; feeds nibs to grinding machine hopper or holding containers and waste materials into sacks; cleans machine.

576 .92 Drying room hand (rice starch)

Scrapes, wraps and stoves blocks of rice starch to make crystallised starch

Feeds blocks of starch through scraping machine to remove stained crust; wraps scraped block in strong brown paper and seals with tape; places the wrapped block into drying stove for prescribed time; withdraws block from stove and allows to cool; removes paper wrapping and places crystallised starch in containers.

May (01) grind starch after stoving (574 .52).

576 .93 Skin filling machine operator (meat products)

Operates machine to extrude meat mixture into skin casings

Loads hopper of machine with prepared meat mixture for products such as sausage, polony and black pudding; selects nozzle of required size, winds on length of skin casing and fixes loaded nozzle in machine or fits preloaded nozzle; starts machine, examines output and adjusts machine as necessary.

May (01) weigh, tie off and link products.

Other titles include Sausage filler, Sausage making machine operator.

576 .98 Trainee

Performs, under instruction or guidance, various tasks including training exercises and as appropriate pursues studies in order to acquire the basic skills and knowledge required to perform the tasks of workers in plant and machine operating occupations (food and drink processing) not elsewhere classified.

576 .99 Other plant and machine operating occupations (food and drink processing) not elsewhere classified

Workers in this group operate and attend plant, machines and other equipment to perform a variety of tasks in the processing of food and drink and are not separately classified, for example:

(01) **Process tank operators (maize starch)** (maintain levels and strengths of liquor and wash water in tanks at various stages in the processing of maize starch, add chemicals or other ingredients as required and control flow to next process); (02) **Remoisteners (dextrin)** (operate humidification equipment to moisten powdered dextrin).

Unit Group 579 Food and Drink Processing Occupations Not Elsewhere Classified

Workers in this unit group control the fermenting of wort, cider or wine, rack beer, coat, decorate and mould sugar and chocolate confectionery by hand, salt foodstuffs and perform other miscellaneous tasks in food and drink processing and are not elsewhere classified.

579.05 Slab hand (sugar confectionery)

Works boiled sugar mixture by hand and machine ready for cutting

Kneads, stretches and rolls boiled sugar mixture by hand and using hand tools such as palette knife, spatula and scraper, or operates kneading, stretching or rolling machines; during process adds flavouring and/or colouring as required; forms mixture into roll or sheet form for hand or machine cutting; dusts mixture with powder to prevent adhesion; cleans equipment.

May (01) insert layers of jam, fruit, etc to form soft-centred confectionery

(02) feed mixture to cutting or cutting and wrapping machine.

Other titles include Slab roller.

579.10 Hand moulder (chocolate, sugar confectionery)

Manually fills moulds with liquid chocolate, fondant or other sugar confectionery

Feeds prepared chocolate, fondant or other sugar confectionery mixture into warming pan; adjusts control to maintain temperature at required level; stirs mixture as necessary; pours liquid chocolate or sugar confectionery into metal, plastic, rubber or starch moulds using ladle, funnel or rod; shakes moulds to ensure that mixture is evenly distributed; places filled moulds on racks and allows mixture to harden.

May (01) add flavouring or colouring to fondant mixture

(02) brush mould with chocolate

(03) join moulded chocolate shapes with liquid chocolate.

Other titles include Centre maker, Cup filler, Funnel hand, Hand dropper.

579.15 Hand dipper (chocolate confectionery)

Coats and decorates confectionery centres with melted chocolate using fingers or hand tool

Feeds chocolate mixture into heated dipping bowl; adjusts control to maintain temperature at required level; stirs chocolate mixture as necessary; dips or drops centres into melted chocolate by hand or using hand tool; removes coated centres and drains off surplus chocolate; makes decorative marks on coated centre using fingers or hand tool; places chocolates on trays to harden.

May (01) add decorations such as nuts to coated centres.

Other titles include Fork dipper, Hand coverer.

579.20 Piper (chocolate, sugar confectionery)

Decorates sugar or chocolate confectionery using piping tools

Inserts nozzle of required shape and size into tip of piping bag; fills bag with decorating material such as liquid chocolate or icing sugar; squeezes decorating material from bag to form required decoration on sugar or chocolate confectionery.

May (01) add cherries, nuts, or novelties to the decorations.

See Hand decorator (flour confectionery) (571.20)

579.25 Fermentation man (brewing, whisky distilling)

Adds yeast to wort liquor and controls fermenting process

Operates controls to regulate flow of cooled wort into fermenting vats and adds measured quantity of yeast to the wort; operates hand or mechanical paddles to stir the fermenting wort; regulates temperature of fermenting wort; pumps fermented wort to holding tanks; cleans vats and pipes.

May (01) draw yeast froth from surface of mixture using suction pipe

(02) control yeast head on wort by spraying with silicone

(03) operate filter press to separate yeast from yeast froth (575.50)

(04) reduce temperature of wort liquor prior to fermentation using cooling equipment.

Other titles include Fermentation attendant.

579.30 Vatman (cider, wine)

Adds ingredients to cider or wine liquor and controls fermenting process

Pumps specified quantity of cider or wine liquor into vat and adds measured quantity of yeast and/or sugar; records temperature and specific gravity of liquor at intervals throughout process; passes readings to laboratory and adds further yeast and/or sugar as instructed until liquor is ready for bottling.

May (01) pump fermented liquor through filter press and carbonating plant (576.76).

Other titles include Cellarman (cider manufacture), Fermenter.

579.35 Briner, Dry salter

Preserves or flavours meat, fish or vegetables with brine or dry salt

If salting meat, performs one or more of the following tasks: injects brine solution into meat such as beef, ham, bacon or pork using hollow steel needle or powered hand gun; rubs in saltpetre by hand; places meat into tank containing brine; after specified time unloads meat and hangs up to drain off excess brine.
If salting fish, places fish on salted floor and turns them over in the salt using a shovel or places fish into barrels or tanks containing brine solution for specified time; unloads from barrels or tanks and places in baskets to drain off excess brine.
If salting vegetables, places vegetables such as onions or beans into barrels or tanks containing brine solution for specified time; draws off brine solution and washes vegetables in water to remove excess brine.

May (01) wash fish prior to salting
(02) immerse herrings in solution of salt and vinegar to produce marinated herrings
(03) saw off hind legs from carcasses
(04) prepare brine solution.

Other titles include Bacon curer, Meat curer, Pickler, Rouser.

579.50 Floorman maltster

Spreads and turns steeped grain on malt room floor to assist germination

Operates valves to discharge grain from steep tanks on to malt room floor or unloads grain from tanks using shovel; spreads steeped grain over floor to required depth and periodically turns the grain using shovel, hand or mechanical plough or turning machine; transfers germinated grain to kiln area.

May (01) load grain into steep tanks
(02) sprinkle grain with water to aid germination
(03) check temperature of grain during germination
(04) operate drying kiln (573.20).

579.55 Racker (brewing)

Performs a number of tasks in the clarification and casking of beer

Performs some or all of the following tasks as directed: cleans and sterilises casks; loads sterilised casks into racking machine; operates controls to fill casks with beer; adds specified quantities of hops, finings or priming syrups; seals casks; marks casks with identification particulars; stacks or palletises casks; cleans and sterilises equipment.

Other titles include Finingsman.

579.60 Preparer (hand) (fruit, vegetables)

Prepares fruit and vegetables by hand for further processing

Tops, tails, peels and slices fruit and vegetables using hand knives; cuts out blemishes, cores, stones, eyes, etc.

May (01) wash fruit and vegetables.

Other titles include Peeler.

See Vegetable preparers (435.99)

579.65 Operative's helper (food, drink processing) (not elsewhere classified)

Performs miscellaneous tasks to directly assist operatives in the processing of food and drink and is not elsewhere classified

Performs one or more of the following tasks: greases equipment such as baking dishes; places prepared ingredients or partly processed products on trays, rods or other holders or in containers prior to feeding into equipment; assists with feeding raw materials, prepared ingredients or partly processed products to ovens, coolers or other processing equipment; assists with removal of finished products from equipment; places finished products on trays or in containers to cool; otherwise assists processing operatives as required.

Other titles include Cooler feeder, Macaroni spreader, Oven feeder, Oven taker-off, Speeter (fish curing), Tenterer (fish curing).

579.98 Trainee

Performs, under instruction or guidance, various tasks including training exercises and as appropriate pursues studies in order to acquire the basic skills and knowledge required to perform the tasks of workers in food and drink processing occupations not elsewhere classified.

579.99 Other food and drink processing occupations not elsewhere classified

Workers in this group perform miscellaneous tasks in food and drink processing and are not separately classified, for example:

(01) **Frame hands (sugar confectionery)** (cut confectionery using hand frames); (02) **Sausage linkers,** Sausage tiers (twist lengths of filled sausage casings at regular intervals to form links and tie them off at required weights); (03) **Sealers (slaughterhouse)** (re-examine slaughtered meat and fix identification seals to Kosher meat); (04) **Washers (hand) (fish curing).**

Minor Group 58 WOOD PROCESSING AND PAPER, PAPERBOARD AND LEATHERBOARD MAKING OCCUPATIONS

Workers in this minor group process and treat wood and perform tasks in the making and finishing of paper, paperboard and leatherboard.

The occupations are arranged in the following unit groups:

580 Foremen (Wood Processing and Paper, Paperboard and Leatherboard Making Occupations)

581 Heat Treating Occupations (Wood Processing and Paper, Paperboard and Leatherboard Making)

582 Crushing, Milling, Mixing and Blending Occupations (Wood Processing and Paper, Paperboard and Leatherboard Making)

583 Filtering, Straining and Other Separating Occupations (Wood Processing and Paper, Paperboard and Leatherboard Making)

584 Plant and Machine Operating Occupations (Wood Processing and Paper, Paperboard and Leatherboard Making) Not Elsewhere Classified

589 Wood Processing and Paper, Paperboard and Leatherboard Making Occupations Not Elsewhere Classified

Excluded are Wood infestation treatment operators (479·65), Bleaching plant operators (561·50) and Digester operators (561·50)

Unit Group 580 Foremen (Wood Processing and Paper, Paperboard and Leatherboard Making Occupations)

Workers in this unit group directly supervise and co-ordinate the activities of workers in wood processing and paper, paperboard and leatherboard making occupations.

580 .10 Foreman (heat treating occupations (wood processing and paper, paperboard and leatherboard making))

Directly supervises and co-ordinates the activities of workers in heat treating occupations (wood processing and paper, paperboard and leatherboard making)

Performs appropriate tasks as described under SUPERVISOR/FOREMAN (UNSPECIFIED) (990 .00).

Additional factor: number of workers supervised.

580 .20 Foreman (crushing, milling, mixing and blending occupations (wood processing and paper, paperboard and leatherboard making))

Directly supervises and co-ordinates the activities of workers in crushing, milling, mixing and blending occupations (wood processing and paper, paperboard and leatherboard making)

Performs appropriate tasks as described under SUPERVISOR/FOREMAN (UNSPECIFIED) (990 .00).

May (01) control operation of large plant from centralised control room.

Additional factor: number of workers supervised.

580 .30 Foreman (filtering, straining and other separating occupations (wood processing and paper, paperboard and leatherboard making))

Directly supervises and co-ordinates the activities of workers in filtering, straining and other separating occupations (wood processing and paper, paperboard and leatherboard making)

Performs appropriate tasks as described under SUPERVISOR/FOREMAN (UNSPECIFIED) (990 .00).

Additional factor: number of workers supervised.

580 .40 Foreman (plant and machine operating occupations (wood processing and paper, paperboard and leatherboard making) not elsewhere classified)

Directly supervises and co-ordinates the activities of workers in plant and machine operating occupations (wood processing and paper, paperboard and leatherboard making) not elsewhere classified

Performs appropriate tasks as described under SUPERVISOR/FOREMAN (UNSPECIFIED) (990 .00).

May (01) direct operation of plant or machinery from centralised control panel

(02) test product for conformance to specification

(03) undertake minor repairs to plant or machinery.

Additional factor: number of workers supervised.

580 .98 Trainee

Performs, under instruction or guidance, various tasks including training exercises and as appropriate pursues studies in order to acquire the basic skills and knowledge required to perform the tasks of foremen (wood processing and paper, paperboard and leatherboard making occupations).

580 .99 Other foremen (wood processing and paper, paperboard and leatherboard making occupations)

Workers in this group directly supervise and co-ordinate the activities of workers in wood processing and paper, paperboard and leatherboard making occupations and are not elsewhere classified, for example:

(01) **Foremen (paper making) (hand).**

Additional factor: number of workers supervised.

Unit Group 581 Heat Treating Occupations (Wood Processing and Paper, Paperboard and Leatherboard Making)

Workers in this unit group operate and attend ovens, kilns and similar equipment in which wood, paper, paperboard and leatherboard are subjected to heat treatment.

Excluded are Benders (679 .50)

581 .10 Kiln drier (wood)

Operates kiln to reduce the moisture content of wood to required level

Directs loading of kiln with wood to be seasoned; selects appropriate kiln schedule or calculates drying time required according to moisture content and type of wood; ensures that kiln door is sealed to prevent loss of heat; admits steam to kiln and starts fan to circulate hot air evenly in kiln; takes temperature and humidity readings and adjusts controls as necessary; withdraws samples from kiln periodically and measures moisture content using meter or weighs samples and calculates loss of moisture; directs unloading of kiln when wood has been correctly seasoned.

May (01) weigh samples before seasoning

(02) set controls for duration of drying cycle

(03) carry out routine inspection and maintenance of kiln and boiler.

Other titles include Drying kiln operator, Kiln operator.

Excluded are Drier operators (581 .50)

581 .50 Drier operator (wood, paper)

Operates oven or similar equipment to dry material such as abrasive coated paper, fibreboard or wood veneers

Lights burners and starts mechanical stoker and fans to heat equipment to required temperature, or sets or adjusts temperature controls as necessary according to type of material to be dried; feeds or directs manual feeding of material on to conveyor or regulates rotation of steel bars (sticks) over which material is looped for drying; checks temperature gauges and speed of material through drier, and makes or arranges for necessary adjustments to be made; ensures that material flows evenly through drier; directs manual discharge of dried material from equipment or ensures that end of material is attached to rereeling spindle.

May (01) thread leader tape over sticks

(02) examine material passing through drier, remove defective sections and join ends using adhesive strip

(03) check moisture content of dried material using moisture meter

(04) operate rereeling machine (584 .80).

Other titles include Drying machine operator, Ovenman (abrasive coated paper, cloth), Takedown operator (abrasive coated paper, cloth), Veneer drier operator.

581 .98 Trainee

Performs, under instruction or guidance, various tasks including training exercises and as appropriate pursues studies in order to acquire the basic skills and knowledge required to perform the tasks of workers in heat treating occupations (wood processing and paper, paperboard and leatherboard making).

581 .99 Other heat treating occupations (wood processing and paper, paperboard and leatherboard making)

Workers in this group operate and attend ovens, kilns and similar equipment in which wood, paper, paperboard and leatherboard are subjected to heat treatment and are not elsewhere classified, for example:

(01) **Leatherboard drier men** (attend equipment in which leatherboard is dried); (02) **Retort firemen (vegetable charcoal)** (load timber into and fire retorts, and remove carbonised timber (charcoal) after specified time); (03) **Stick box men** (attend drying equipment to ensure that material is correctly looped over rotating steel bars (sticks)).

Unit Group 582 Crushing, Milling, Mixing and Blending Occupations (Wood Processing and Paper, Paperboard and Leatherboard Making)

Workers in this unit group crush and mill wood and cork, and operate machines to convert fibrous material into fluid pulp and to prepare pulp for making into paper, paperboard and leatherboard.

582 .10 Beaterman (paper making)

Operates or controls the operation of one or more machines to beat and mix fluid pulps to correct consistency for making into paper or paperboard

Performs or directs performance of the following tasks; opens valves or feed gates or operates pumps to admit specified quantities of fluid pulps (half-stuffs) and water into machine; measures out chemical and other additives according to formula and feeds into machine; adjusts distance between stationary and rotating metal bars of machine to obtain pulp (stuff) of specified degree of fineness; starts machine and watches operation; examines mixture (furnish) for consistency, colour and size of fibres, and makes necessary adjustments; withdraws samples for laboratory testing; opens valves or operates pumps to discharge stuff to storage chest; cleans machine.

May (01) prepare chemical solutions

(02) specialise in preparing stuff for paperboard making and be known as Linerman.

Other titles include Refinerman.

Additional factor: number of machines operated or controlled.

582 .50 Beaterman (leatherboard)

Operates machine to produce stock for making leatherboard

Ascertains ingredient requirements from formula; admits required amount of water into machine; adds prescribed quantities of dry ingredients; starts machine to beat and mix ingredients; measures out chemical solution(s) according to formula and adds to mixture after specified time; checks consistency of mixture at intervals and makes necessary adjustments; pumps prepared mixture (stock) to storage chests; clears blockages and cleans machine as required.

Other titles include Beater operator.

582 .60 Pulper

Operates one or more machines to separate fibres of dried wood pulp or other fibrous material and make fluid pulp ready for beating

Loads dried wood pulp and/or waste paper (broke) or other fibrous material into machine by hand or using mechanical equipment; admits specified quantity of water and where appropriate steam; feeds in chemical and other additives as specified; starts machine to break up (defibre) and mix contents for specified time or until satisfied with consistency; runs off or pumps fluid pulp (half-stuff) to storage chest; carries out minor adjustments and repairs and cleans machine and ancillary equipment, as directed.

May (01) weigh materials and additives before feeding into machine

(02) operate machine to cut waste paper into strips before feeding to pulping machine.

Other titles include Breakerman, Broke pulper man, Hydrapulper, Kollerganger, Potcherman.

582 .90 Wood mill attendant

Attends equipment which crushes or mills wood or cork for industrial use or for further processing

Moves controls or sets automatic controls to start equipment; loads material into feed hopper or on to conveyor by hand or using mechanical aid, or regulates or checks flow along feed pipes or conveyors; clears blockages with hand tools or by reversing machine action; regulates flow or checks automatic discharge of crushed or milled material through screens to storage containers or to machines for further processing; stops plant if fault occurs or feed of material is interrupted and reports to foreman; performs cleaning tasks as directed.

May (01) observe dials and other indicators on control panel to check feed rate and progress of operation

(02) carry out simple adjustments and repairs to equipment

(03) change screens

(04) weigh and/or package discharged material.

Other titles include Chipping and refining machine operative, Cork mill hand, Particle board wood chip maker, Sawdust mill man, Wood mill process operative, Wood wool maker.

582.98 Trainee

Performs, under instruction or guidance, various tasks including training exercises and as appropriate pursues studies in order to acquire the basic skills and knowledge required to perform the tasks of workers in crushing, milling, mixing and blending occupations (wood processing and paper, paperboard and leatherboard making).

582.99 Other crushing, milling, mixing and blending occupations (wood processing and paper, paperboard and leatherboard making)

Workers in this group crush and mill wood and cork, and operate machines to convert fibrous material into pulp and to prepare pulp for making into paper, paperboard and leatherboard and are not elsewhere classified.

Unit Group 583 Filtering, Straining and Other Separating Occupations (Wood Processing and Paper, Paperboard and Leatherboard Making)

Workers in this unit group operate filtering, straining and other separating equipment in wood processing and paper, paperboard and leatherboard making.

583.10 Up-taking machine operator

Operates machine to reduce liquid content of fluid pulp and convert pulp to sheet form ready for further processing

Regulates flow of fluid pulp from storage chest to machine vat; sets machine controls for vacuum pressure and for filter and roller speeds; starts machine to draw pulp on to frame surrounding rotating filter and to extract liquid content; cuts pulp fibre adhering to frame and removes it in sheet form; feeds sheet to rolling and slitting unit; extracts sample sheets of pulp periodically, weighs and dries samples and calculates loss of moisture; adjusts machine controls and/or water supply to storage chest as necessary; ensures that sheeted pulp does not lap round rollers and that automatic slitting device functions correctly; clears or directs clearance of blockages in machine and ancillary equipment.

583.98 Trainee

Performs, under instruction or guidance, various tasks including training exercises and as appropriate pursues studies in order to acquire the basic skills and knowledge required to perform the tasks of workers in filtering, straining and other separating occupations (wood processing and paper, paperboard and leatherboard making).

583.99 Other filtering, straining and separating occupations (wood processing and paper, paperboard and leatherboard making)

Workers in this group operate filtering, straining and other separating equipment in wood processing and paper, paperboard and leatherboard making and are not elsewhere classified, for example:

(01) **Press-pate men,** Concentrator men (operate filtering and screening equipment to remove sediment and excess water from fluid pulp (half-stuff) preparatory to beating).

Unit Group 584 Plant and Machine Operating Occupations (Wood Processing and Paper, Paperboard and Leatherboard Making) Not Elsewhere Classified

Workers in this unit group operate and attend plant and machines used in wood processing and paper, paperboard and leatherboard making and finishing and are not elsewhere classified.

584.05 Paper making machineman, Paperboard making machineman

Operates forming section and directs operation of drying and finishing sections of paper or paperboard making machine

Examines job specifications; sets or directs setting of machine controls according to quality, width and thickness of paper or paperboard required; operates controls to start flow of pulp and water into feed tank of machine; starts machine; regulates flow of fluid pulp on to endless wire mesh belt to form pulp web of required width and thickness, or on to rotating cylinders (moulds) and felt belt to form webs for consolidation into paper or board; ensures that formed web(s) is fed correctly through to drying section of machine; monitors instruments indicating fluid pulp flow, speed and shake of wire mesh belt or rotation speed of moulds, speeds, pressures and temperatures of squeeze rollers and other conditions within or affecting the machine or ancillary equipment; feels pulp web to test texture and examines samples of finished paper or paperboard; adjusts forming section (wet end) controls and/or directs drierman to adjust controls in drying and finishing sections (dry end) as necessary; cleans machine and ancillary equipment and replaces worn or damaged wire mesh belts or moulds, felts and rollers, or directs performance of these tasks.

May (01) position special mesh roll on machine to impress water mark in paper

(02) control operation of hydrapulpers, strainers, beaters and rotary cleaners.

Additional factor: type, size and speed of machine.

584.10 Drierman (paper making machine), Drierman (paperboard making machine)

Operates drying and finishing sections of paper or paperboard making machine under direction of machineman

Examines job specifications; sets dry end controls of machine according to finish required; guides end of paper or paperboard through drying unit, over sizing and calendering rollers to rewinding mechanism; watches passage of paper through machine and adjusts controls to regulate tension of paper or board, and speed, temperature and pressure of rollers to ensure that material is dried and finished to specification; severs paper or paperboard when reel is full and removes filled reel using mechanical aid, or directs performance of these tasks; replaces or directs replacement of reeling mandrel and ensures that end of paper or paperboard is wound or blown around it; deputises for machineman, as required; cleans or directs cleaning of machine and ancillary equipment; carries out minor running repairs.

May (01) control operation of drying and finishing sections of machine from remote-control panel

(02) assist in replacement of worn wire mesh belts or cylinders, felts and rollers

(03) direct operation of slitting, supercalendering and coating machines.

Additional factor: type, size and speed of machine.

Other titles include Back tenter, First assistant machineman.

584.15 Coating machine operator (paper, paperboard), Impregnating machine operator (paper, paperboard)

Operates or controls the operation of machine or section of paper or paperboard making machine to coat or impregnate paper or paperboard with chemical solutions, mineral pigments, abrasive substances or other media

Examines job specifications and sample of material to be treated; sets machine controls according to density of coating or impregnation required, type of medium to be used and width of material to be treated; ensures adequate supply of specified coating or impregnating medium to feed tank, trough or hopper; positions or directs positioning of material to be treated on feed mechanism; joins end of material to end in machine or threads end through coating and drying units and secures to rewinding mechanism, or directs performance of these tasks; starts machine; watches operation and adjusts as necessary to ensure that material is correctly coated or impregnated; examines material for faults and marks defects or recoats faulty area; joins broken ends using repair strip or adhesive or rethreads end through machine, or directs performance of these tasks; removes or directs removal of treated material from machine; cleans or directs cleaning of machine.

May (01) prepare coating or impregnating medium

(02) position printing roller on machine to print data on material being coated

(03) watch and regulate operation of machine from remote-control panel

(04) control workers operating slitting, cutting or rewinding machines

(05) operate or control the operation of machine to make abrasive coated cloth

(06) control machine which crinkles surface of material after impregnating to form crêpe paper and be known as Crêping machine operator.

Other titles include Abrasive coated paper making machine operator, Coater, Coating machineman, Gumming machine operator, Impregnating machineman, Leading hand (abrasive coated paper making), Parchmentiser, Tub sizer, Waxing machine operator.

584 .20 Combining machine operator (paper, paperboard)

Operates or controls the operation of machine or section of machine to combine continuous sheets of paper or paperboard to form laminated material of specified quality and thickness

Examines job specifications; sets controls to regulate machine speed, roller pressure and temperature of rollers and adhesive; positions or directs positioning of reels of specified material on feed mechanism; joins new ends to ends in machine or threads new ends through guides and tensioners, coating or impregnating equipment and combining and drying rollers to cutting or rewinding mechanism, or directs performance of these tasks; starts machine; watches operation and adjusts as necessary to ensure that material is correctly combined; checks alignment of material periodically; ensures adequate supply of coating or impregnating medium; directs removal of cut or reeled pieces of laminated material; cleans or directs cleaning of machine.

May (01) prepare coating or impregnating medium

(02) watch and regulate operation of machine from remote-control panel.

Other titles include Combining machine first hand, Continuous board combiner, Corrugated board maker, Corrugating machine first hand, Double backer, Laminating machineman (continuous sheet), Lining machinist, Pasting machineman, Single facer operator, Vulcanised fibre sheet maker (continuous sheet).

See Combining machine operator (549 .14)

584 .50 Paper making machine assistant, Paperboard making machine assistant

Assists in the operation of paper or paperboard making machine

Performs a combination of the following tasks under the direction of paper or paperboard making machineman and/or drierman: assists in feeding formed web(s) through machine to drying section; assists in feeding paper or paperboard through drying section and over sizing and calendering rollers to rewinding mechanism; examines paper or paperboard for, and marks, flaws; severs paper when reel is full; attaches reel of paper to lifting equipment; operates lifting equipment to remove full reel from machine; replaces reeling mandrel and secures end of paper or paperboard to reel; cleans machine, ancillary equipment and work area; assists in replacement of worn wire mesh belts and cylinders, felts and rollers.

Other titles include Back tenter.

584 .55 Coating machine assistant (paper, paperboard), Impregnating machine assistant (paper, paperboard)

Assists in the operation of machine to coat or impregnate paper or paperboard

Performs a combination of the following tasks under the direction of coating or impregnating machine operator or foreman: loads material to be coated or impregnated on to feed mechanism; joins end of material to be treated to end in machine or leads end through machine and secures to rewinding mechanism; regulates supply of coating or impregnating medium to feed tank, trough or hopper; regulates flow of coating medium on to surface to be coated; removes reel of treated material from machine; cleans machine.

May (01) assist in operation of machine to make abrasive cloth.

Other titles include Abrasive coated paper making machine assistant, Crêping machine assistant, Glue spreader (abrasive coated paper), Grit strewer, Sandhouse man, Sandman, Sizer (abrasive coated paper).

584 .60 Combining machine assistant (paper, paperboard)

Assists in the operation of machine to combine a number of continuous sheets of paper or paperboard to form laminated material

Performs a combination of the following tasks under the direction of combining machine operator: loads reels of material to be combined on to feed mechanism; joins new ends of material to ends in machine or leads ends through guides and tensioners, coating or impregnating equipment, and combining and drying rollers to cutting or rewinding mechanism; prepares coating or impregnating medium; positions cutting and/or slitting devices on machine as directed; replenishes supply of coating or impregnating material as required; removes empty reels from feed mechanism; removes laminated material from machine; cleans machine.

Other titles include Assistant combining machine operator, Assistant pasting machineman, Combining machine second hand, Combining machine third hand, Corrugating machine second hand, Corrugating machine third hand.

584.65 Calender operator

Operates machine to impart glaze or other high quality finish to surface of paper or paperboard by calendering

Sets machine controls to obtain required speed, tension and roller pressure; admits steam to calendering rollers where appropriate; positions or directs positioning of material on feed mechanism; threads end of material through calendering rollers and secures to rewinding mechanism; starts machine; watches operation and makes necessary adjustments; joins broken ends of material using repair strip or adhesive, or rethreads broken end through machine; reports or marks faults in material; removes material from machine and replaces rewinding mandrels or directs performance of these tasks; cleans or directs cleaning of machine.

May (01) oil machine and carry out minor repairs.

Other titles include Friction glazer operator, Supercalender operator.

584.70 Leatherboard making machine operator

Operates machine to make leatherboard

Operates controls to start flow of fluid pulp into feed tank; starts machine and regulates flow of pulp on to endless wire mesh belt or through perforated rollers and along felt belt to forming roller; allows pulp web to build around roller until board of required thickness is formed; cuts across board and removes from machine.

May (01) set machine controls according to thickness of board required

(02) cut formed boards in halves.

584.75 Laminator (power press)

Sets and operates power press to bond two or more precut sheets of materials such as board, paper or wood to form a solid lamination of specified thickness

Builds up required number of adhesive coated sheets in correct order to form pack(s) and loads or directs loading of pack(s) into press, or loads preformed pack(s) into press; sets machine controls according to pressure, temperature and timing cycle requirements; checks alignment of pack(s) in press and squares-up as necessary; operates machine controls to close press and bond layered pack(s) into a solid formation; opens and unloads or directs unloading of press after specified time; checks that sheets have been properly bonded; cleans press.

May (01) repair surface defects in precut sheets

(02) mix adhesive by hand or machine

(03) coat precut sheets with adhesive by hand or machine

(04) specialise in bonding decorative veneers or plastic laminates on to plywood, blockboard or asbestos board.

Other titles include Multi-daylight press operator, Plywood veneerer, Press operator (laminated plastics), Veneer assembler and presser, Veneer press setter-operator.

584.80 Winder operator

Operates machine to wind or rewind paper or paperboard

Positions or directs positioning of material on feed mechanism where necessary; attaches end of material to leader cloth or to end in machine, or threads material through guides and tensioners to reeling core; sets yardage counter where appropriate; starts machine; watches operation and makes necessary adjustments to ensure even winding; examines material for defects and marks reel to indicate defective areas; removes and replaces reeling cores as required or directs performance of these tasks; cleans machine and carries out minor adjustments as required.

May (01) thread leader cloth through machine

(02) cut out faulty parts

(03) secure ends of wound material to prevent unreeling

(04) operate machine fitted with preset expanding roller to cut wound material to form sheets of equal length

(05) operate machine fitted with device to slit wound material into strips of specified width

(06) specialise in operating machine which polishes, dampens or washes material during winding, and be known as Brushing machine operator, Conditioner man, Damperman, Washing machine operator.

Other titles include Humidifying machine operator, Reeler, Reelerman, Rereeler, Reroller, Rewinder.

Excluded are Spoolers (642.92)

584.90 Plant attendant (wood processing and paper, paperboard and leatherboard making) not elsewhere classified, Machine attendant (wood processing and paper, paperboard and leatherboard making) not elsewhere classified

Attends automatic or semi-automatic plant or machine(s) used in wood processing or paper, paperboard or leatherboard making and is not elsewhere classified

Performs a combination of the following tasks: feeds material into plant or machine, checks automatic feed or positions material on feed mechanism; starts plant or machine when appropriate; watches operation and reports malfunctioning to appropriate person; clears blockages; removes material from plant or machine or checks automatic discharge; cleans plant or machine.

May (01) operate mechanical hoist to position material on and/or remove material from machine

(02) build up layers of material for laminating before feeding to press

(03) oil machine.

Other titles include Cork block maker, Press hand (vulcanised fibre), Press operator (vulcanised fibre), Splint impregnating and drying attendant.

584.98 Trainee

Performs, under instruction or guidance, various tasks including training exercises and as appropriate pursues studies in order to acquire the basic skills and knowledge required to perform the tasks of workers in plant and machine operating occupations (wood processing and paper, paperboard and leatherboard making) not elsewhere classified.

584.99 Other plant and machine operating occupations (wood processing and paper, paperboard and leatherboard making) not elsewhere classified

Workers in this group operate and attend plant and machines used in wood processing and paper, paperboard and leatherboard making and finishing and are not separately classified, for example:

(01) **Guillotine operators (leatherboard)** (operate machines to trim edges of formed board); (02) **Leatherboard rolling machine operators** (operate machines to smooth, consolidate and reduce thickness of leatherboard); (03) **Pressmen (wood blocks)** (operate equipment to compress prepared wood blocks to a specified density ready for making into loom shuttles); (04) **Scarfing press operators** (operate presses to strengthen scarfed joints of board); (05) **Vulcanised fibre sheet makers (single sheets)** (operate machines to make single sheets of vulcanised fibre round forming cylinders).

Unit Group 589 Wood Processing and Paper, Paperboard and Leatherboard Making Occupations Not Elsewhere Classified

Workers in this unit group make paper by hand, combine sheets of paper and board by hand, and perform other miscellaneous tasks in wood processing and paper, paperboard and leatherboard making and are not elsewhere classified.

589.10 Paper maker (hand)

Moulds pulp stock by hand to make high quality paper and/or removes newly formed sheets of paper from mould in readiness for layering

Performs some or all of the following tasks: admits pulp stock from holding tank into vat; places frame (deckle) over wire mesh mould; dips mould into stock; raises filled mould and shakes it to remove excess liquid and to mat fibres; removes deckle; turns mould over and deposits newly formed sheet of paper on to felt sheeting ready for layering; checks strength of stock periodically and admits further stock from holding tank or drains off weakened mixture and refills vat; directs layers in the performance of their tasks.

Other titles include Coucher, Vatman.

589.50 Combiner (hand) (paper, paperboard)

Combines and/or mounts backings or facings on sheets of paper or board, by hand, ready for further processing

Performs some or all of the following tasks: feeds sheet of paper or board through rollers of pasting machine; positions pasted sheet on top of unpasted sheet of paper or board and checks squareness of fit; presses and smoothes out surface of pasted sheet by hand to ensure adhesion; stacks combined, backed or faced sheets to dry; ensures adequate supply of paste to machine tank.

Other titles include Mounting machine operator.

589.90 Layer

Lays felt sheets between newly formed sheets of hand-made paper ready for pressing, or presses prepared piles of sheets and separates paper and felt sheets after pressing

Performs a combination of the following tasks under direction of paper maker (hand): lowers felt sheet gently on to sheet of newly formed paper to avoid disturbing its matted fibres; ensures that felt lies flat on paper; repeats operation until pile (post) of paper and felts has been built up to required height; places post on platform of press; operates press to bond paper fibres and remove excess moisture; separates pressed sheets of paper from felts ready for further processing.

589.98 Trainee

Performs, under instruction or guidance, various tasks including training exercises and as appropriate pursues studies in order to acquire the basic skills and knowledge required to perform the tasks of workers in wood processing and paper, paperboard and leatherboard making occupations not elsewhere classified.

589.99 Other wood processing and paper, paperboard and leatherboard making occupations not elsewhere classified

Workers in this group perform miscellaneous tasks in wood processing and paper, paperboard and leatherboard making and are not separately classified, for example:

(01) **Calender machine assistants;** (02) **Creosoters** (attend equipment in which unused timber is impregnated with creosote oil under pressure); (03) **Driers (hand-made paper)** (spread sheets of hand-made paper on canvas in drying loft); (04) **Laminators (hand) (wood)** (glue together boards or planks of wood to make strong beams, stanchions and sections for use in the construction of buildings); (05) **Leatherboard makers (hand)** (mould pulp stock by hand to make leatherboard); (06) **Sheet assemblers (laminated plastics)** (build up sheets of treated paper into packs ready for pressing to form laminated plastics); (07) **Tankhands (vulcanised fibre)** (immerse sheets of vulcanised fibre into tanks of water to remove acid impregnated during manufacture); (08) **Wood veneer builders** (coat and build up wood veneer sheets into packs ready for pressing); (09) **Washing and drying hands (vulcanised fibre)** (wash stained vulcanised fibre sheets by hand or machine and suspend washed sheets in drying chamber).

Minor Group 59 MATERIALS PROCESSING OCCUPATIONS NOT ELSEWHERE CLASSIFIED

Workers in this minor group process and treat materials and products in furnaces, kilns and similar equipment, crush, grind, mix, blend and mechanically separate materials and perform other miscellaneous tasks in materials processing and are not elsewhere classified.

The occupations are arranged in the following unit groups:

590 Foremen (Materials Processing Occupations Not Elsewhere Classified)

591 Heat Treating Occupations Not Elsewhere Classified

592 Crushing, Milling, Mixing and Blending Occupations Not Elsewhere Classified

593 Filtering, Straining and Other Mechanical Separating Occupations Not Elsewhere Classified

594 Plant and Machine Operating Occupations (Materials Processing) Not Elsewhere Classified

599 Other Materials Processing Occupations

Unit Group 590 Foremen (Materials Processing Occupations Not Elsewhere Classified)

Workers in this unit group directly supervise and co-ordinate the activities of workers in materials processing occupations not elsewhere classified.

590.10 Foreman (heat treating occupations not elsewhere classified)

Directly supervises and co-ordinates the activities of workers in heat treating occupations not elsewhere classified

Performs appropriate tasks as described under SUPERVISOR/FOREMAN (UNSPECIFIED) (990.00).

May (01) determine duration and temperature of operation.

Additional factor: number of workers supervised.

590.20 Foreman (crushing, milling, mixing and blending occupations not elsewhere classified)

Directly supervises and co-ordinates the activities of workers in crushing, milling, mixing and blending occupations not elsewhere classified

Performs appropriate tasks as described under SUPERVISOR/FOREMAN (UNSPECIFIED) (990.00).

May (01) direct workers and control the operation of machines from central control panel
(02) set controls of automated plant
(03) calculate ingredient requirements to meet production schedules
(04) check colours against standard or sample colours.

Additional factor: number of workers supervised.

590.30 Foreman (filtering, straining and other mechanical separating occupations not elsewhere classified)

Directly supervises and co-ordinates the activities of workers in filtering, straining and other mechanical separating occupations not elsewhere classified

Performs appropriate tasks as described under SUPERVISOR/FOREMAN (UNSPECIFIED) (990.00).

May (01) test samples for density or specific gravity
(02) undertake minor repairs to equipment.

Additional factor: number of workers supervised.

590.40 Foreman (plant and machine operating occupations (materials processing) not elsewhere classified)

Directly supervises and co-ordinates the activities of workers in plant and machine operating occupations (materials processing) not elsewhere classified

Performs appropriate tasks as described under SUPERVISOR/FOREMAN (UNSPECIFIED) (990.00).

May (01) set plant or machinery
(02) control operation of plant or machinery from central control panel
(03) undertake minor repairs to plant or machinery.

Additional factor: number of workers supervised.

590.98 Trainee

Performs, under instruction or guidance, various tasks including training exercises and as appropriate pursues studies in order to acquire the basic skills and knowledge required to perform the tasks of foremen (materials processing occupations not elsewhere classified).

590.99 Other foremen (materials processing occupations not elsewhere classified)

Workers in this group directly supervise and co-ordinate the activities of workers in materials processing occupations and are not separately classified.

Unit Group 591 Heat Treating Occupations Not Elsewhere Classified

Workers in this unit group operate and attend furnaces, kilns, ovens and other equipment in which materials and products are subjected to heat treatment and are not elsewhere classified.

See Batch plant operator (heat treating, chemical reaction) (561 .50), Cooking, Freezing and Other Heat Treating Occupations (Food and Drink Processing) (573) and Heat Treating Occupations (Wood Processing and Paper, Paperboard and Leatherboard Making) (581)

591 .10 Furnaceman (glass making)

Operates one or more furnaces to melt and fuse ingredients (batch) to make glass

(01) **Tank furnaceman**

Watches control panel or uses dipstick to determine level of molten glass in furnace; regulates batch feed into furnace to maintain required level of glass; watches temperature and pressure gauges and adjusts fuel feed and air flow to maintain prescribed conditions; if operating regenerative furnace, operates control periodically to reverse direction of firing to equalise heat in furnace; replaces burners and cleans or replaces filters as required.

Other titles include Tank teaser, Tank teazer.

(02) **Pot furnaceman**

Operates control to transfer pot into furnace, where necessary; lights burners as required and regulates fuel and air flow to heat furnace to specified temperature; feeds prescribed quantities of ingredients into pot manually; checks temperature recordings and adjusts controls as necessary to maintain prescribed conditions.

If making optical glass, starts automatic stirring device to assist processing as required; withdraws and examines samples (proofs) periodically to determine variations required in temperature and/or periods of agitation or sends proof for laboratory examination and makes necessary adjustments; operates control to lower pot from furnace after specified cooling period.

Other titles include Stoker.

May (03) weigh out and mix ingredients for feeding into pot

(04) check furnace temperature using pyrometer

(05) condition new pots in special furnace (pot-arch)

(06) clear spillage from furnace floor

(07) specialise in making a particular type of glass, eg crystal, optical, plate, sheet.

Additional factor: number of furnaces operated.

Other titles include Founder, Teaser, Teazer.

Excluded are Furnacemen (vitreous silica) (591 .50)

591 .20 Kiln burner (cement)

Operates one or more rotary kilns to produce cement clinker

Regulates heat supply and flow of cement slurry to kiln; operates control to rotate kiln at appropriate speed; watches temperature, feed and other gauges and dials on control panel and checks progress in kiln visually; adjusts controls as necessary to ensure that slurry is properly calcined.

May (01) withdraw samples from kiln for laboratory testing

(02) operate equipment to cool and/or crush cement clinker.

591 .50 Furnaceman (vitreous silica)

Directs operation of one or more furnaces to make vitreous silica

Directs loading of furnace with prescribed quantities and types of ingredients; ensures that graphite rod is correctly positioned in furnace and connected to electrodes; sets timing and temperature controls to produce required fusing of ingredients; if directing operation of rotary furnace, ensures that furnace rotates to coat sides with ingredients by centrifugal force; if directing operation of static furnace, ensures that furnace is in correct working position; switches on current; if directing operation of vacuum furnace, operates control to create vacuum; ensures that fusing is proceeding correctly; removes or directs removal of fusion from furnace using tongs.

May (01) insert graphite core in fusion

(02) draw out fusion to make tubing

(03) position or direct positioning of fusion in mould or press and direct moulding or pressing operation.

Additional factor: number and type of furnaces operated.

Other titles include First man.

591.52 Assistant furnaceman (vitreous silica)

Assists, under the direction of furnaceman, in operating one or more furnaces to make vitreous silica

Performs a combination of the following tasks: loads furnace with prescribed quantities of quartz or silica and other ingredients using lifting equipment where necessary; secures graphite rod in position in centre of furnace; connects rod to electrodes; secures furnace door; operates control to rotate rotary furnace or to turn static furnace to correct working position; withdraws graphite rod at end of fusing period; inserts graphite core in fusion; removes fusion from furnace using tongs; cleans furnace; replaces electrodes as necessary.

May (01) cut and file graphite rod to size for use in furnace
(02) assist in drawing out fusion to make tubing
(03) position fusion in mould or press
(04) operate press
(05) remove billet from press.

Additional factor: number and type of furnaces operated.

Other titles include Second man, Third man.

591.54 Safety glass toughener

Operates equipment to toughen safety glass by controlled heating and cooling

Suspends or directs suspension of glass from frame using clips (tongs); operates control to move frame and carry glass into furnace; watches temperature gauges and adjusts controls to obtain even heating and to ensure prescribed exit temperature of glass; withdraws glass from furnace when prescribed temperature has been reached; operates control to blow cold air on to heated glass for appropriate period; removes toughened glass from tongs.

May (01) test sample from each batch of glass for conformance to British Standards' specification by striking with hammer and counting number of fragments into which glass fractures.

Other titles include Furnace operator.

591.56 Roaster (not elsewhere classified)

Operates one or more furnaces, kilns or ovens to roast solid materials such as minerals or animal charcoal and is not elsewhere classified

Loads or directs loading of equipment manually, or operates controls to regulate flow of material into equipment; lights burners or switches on current as necessary; starts kiln rotating where appropriate; regulates fuel supply or adjusts draught dampers to obtain required temperature, or sets automatic temperature control according to degree of roasting required; monitors temperature and other gauges and/or watches roasting process visually and adjusts controls as necessary; directs manual unloading or operates controls to unload roasted material mechanically, or checks that material is automatically discharged from equipment.

May (01) withdraw samples for testing.

Additional factor: number of furnaces, kilns or ovens operated.

Other titles include Calciner, Calcining charge hand, Kilnman (china clay), Lime burner, Lime kiln attendant.

591.58 Kiln operator (ceramic products)

Operates one or more kilns to fire ceramic products after shaping, glazing or decorating

Checks that products to be fired have been positioned (set) in kiln or loaded on to kiln trucks; places clay rings or pyrometric cones or bars on trucks, where appropriate, for use in checking kiln temperatures; if firing goods on trucks, directs loading of kiln or pushes or operates control to push trucks into kiln at required intervals, or sets device which automatically operates control at regular intervals to push trucks into kiln; ensures that kiln door is sealed to prevent loss of heat; lights fires or burners, switches on current or manupulates dampers to transfer existing fire to chamber of kiln awaiting firing; regulates heat supply as necessary or sets controls which automatically regulate firing temperature; adjusts air supply to kiln as required; takes temperature readings and/or checks progress of firing by observing colour of products or flame, or by watching for melting of pyrometric cones or bars or by withdrawing clay rings and measuring degree of contraction; cuts off heat supply where necessary, after products have been fired.

May (01) operate chambers in which products are dried before being fired
(02) operate kiln through which goods are transported on conveyor
(03) introduce salt into kiln to glaze products
(04) insert measuring rod in kiln and calculate shrinkage of products from measurements obtained
(05) withdraw fired products from kiln
(06) examine fired products for cracks.

Additional factor: number and type of kilns operated.

Other titles include Bottom oven man, Burner (artificial teeth), Enamel kiln fireman, Glost fireman, Hardening-on kiln fireman, Kiln burner, Muffle kiln fireman, Pottery kiln fireman, Pottery oven man, Tile burner, Vitrifier.

591.60 Kiln operator (abrasive, carbon products)

Operates one or more kilns to fire abrasive or carbon products after shaping

Performs appropriate tasks as described under KILN OPERATOR (CERAMIC PRODUCTS) (591.58) but in relation to the firing of abrasive or carbon products.

May (01) place products for firing in fire-clay containers and position containers in kiln

(02) withdraw fired products from kiln.

Additional factor: number and type of kilns operated.

Other titles include Fireman, Furnaceman (pencil lead), Heat treatment operator, Kiln burner.

591.62 Drier and kiln attendant

Attends preset equipment in which bricks are dried and fired after shaping

Ascertains temperature and drying and firing time requirements from schedule sheet; takes temperature readings of drier and kiln at specified intervals; compares readings with information on schedule sheet and reports significant deviations; operates control according to time schedule to move trucks loaded with dried bricks into kiln; pulls trucks of fired bricks from kiln at appropriate intervals; notes fuel consumption readings as required; cleans kiln cars and drying and kiln areas.

591.64 Drier operator (plasterboard)

Operates equipment to dry plasterboard

Checks size and checks or calculates weight of plasterboard to be dried; regulates speed of conveyor which carries plasterboard through drier; sets temperature and humidity controls according to type of plasterboard to be dried; watches gauges recording temperature and humidity, and makes necessary adjustments; ensures that plasterboard moves smoothly through drier; weighs or checks weight of samples of dried plasterboard.

May (01) clean conveyor rollers

(02) clean or change burners.

Other titles include Kiln operator.

591.66 Autoclave operator (mineral products)

Operates one or more autoclaves to bond, cure or otherwise treat mineral products by heat and pressure

Loads autoclave manually with trolleys, crates or other containers of products to be treated, or operates mechanical loading equipment; secures door of autoclave; sets or operates controls to obtain required heat and pressure; watches temperature and pressure gauges and adjusts controls as necessary; operates controls to reduce heat and pressure after specified time; opens door and unloads treated products manually or mechanically when cool.

May (01) load trolleys or other containers with products to be treated.

Additional factor: number of autoclaves operated.

Included are workers treating asbestos composition goods in autoclaves.

591.68 Cooker (not elsewhere classified)

Cooks a variety of ingredients in kettle(s), boiling pan(s) or similar containers to produce materials such as asphalt or linoleum cement and is not elsewhere classified

Positions cooking vessel over burners as necessary; loads ingredients into vessel manually or operates controls to admit specified quantities of ingredients into vessel; lights burners or switches on current and sets thermostat or regulates heat to bring contents of vessel to required temperature; starts mechanical agitator or stirs ingredients by hand as required; watches temperature gauges and/or cooking process and adjusts heat as necessary; adds further ingredients to vessel where specified; removes vessel from heat or discharges or directs discharge of cooked mixture into moulds, tanks or other containers; cleans cooking vessel.

May (01) weigh out ingredients

(02) withdraw samples for testing

(03) test samples for viscosity

(04) operate centrifugal pump or filter press to remove impurities from cooked mixture.

Other titles include Asphalt maker, Asphalt mixer, Kettle operator, Linoleum cement maker, Potman, Smacker hand.

See Potman (asphalt laying) (869.66)

591.70 Belt pressman

Operates one or more presses to vulcanise rubber or plastic belting

Performs some or all of the following tasks: pulls section of belting from feed roll on to press platen; positions stops on press according to width and thickness of belting required; sets press controls for temperature, pressure and vulcanising time required; operates controls to close press and start vulcanising process; watches temperature and pressure dials and adjusts controls as necessary; opens press at end of vulcanising cycle; operates winding mechanism to pull vulcanised section of belting round take-up core; ties up vulcanised rolls of belting and attaches identification data; cleans press.

May (01) operate equipment to stretch belting before vulcanising

(02) fix edging strip or studs to belting with adhesive before vulcanising

(03) lay protective material on edge of belting before vulcanising

(04) position brand plates or rubber stamps on belting before vulcanising

(05) spray releasing agent on press platen to prevent adhesion of belting

(06) operate presses to vulcanise rolls of belting in a continuous process and be known as Rota curer.

Additional factor: number of presses operated.

Other titles include Jobbing pressman, Press curer.

591.90 Annealing equipment attendant (glass, glassware), Toughening equipment attendant (glass)

Attends equipment in which glass or glassware is annealed or toughened by controlled heating and cooling

(01) **Kiln attendant**

Operates control to heat annealing kiln to specified temperature, positions glass in kiln using lifting equipment and secures door, or positions glassware in kiln, secures door and operates control to heat kiln to specified temperature; prepares chart showing prescribed rate of cooling and duration of cooling period and checks temperature periodically against chart, or sets controls to reduce heat gradually after specified period; removes annealed glass or glassware from kiln.

(02) **Lehr attendant**

Observes passage of glass or glassware through annealing oven (lehr); removes broken glass or glassware; watches thermometers to check that temperatures along lehr are within prescribed limits.

(03) **Toughening equipment attendant (safety glass)**

Fixes glass in grooved racks attached to furnace lid and lowers lid over furnace mouth, or places glass on frame, attaches glass to tongs suspended from overhead track and removes frame; sets timer, withdraws glass from furnace after specified time and directs cold air blast on glass for prescribed period, or starts equipment and observes automatic passage of glass through heating and cooling processes.

(04) **Toughening equipment attendant (optical glass)**

Places lens on tray in oven; switches on current and sets timer and oven temperature controls; withdraws lens after specified time and directs cold air blast on glass for prescribed period; operates device to drop metal ball on to lens to test toughness.

May (05) adjust controls to maintain specified temperature in lehr

(06) examine glass or glassware after passage through lehr.

591.92 Heat treatment equipment attendant (not elsewhere classified)

Attends equipment in which materials or products are subjected to heat treatment and is not elsewhere classified

Loads equipment manually with material, products or formers over which material to be shaped has been positioned, operates mechanical loading equipment or checks automatic feed; secures door of equipment to prevent loss of heat where appropriate; lights burners and heats equipment to specified temperature, switches on current or operates controls to admit steam or hot air to equipment as necessary; starts equipment rotating where appropriate; watches temperature and other gauges, notes time or sets timer as appropriate; notifies malfunctioning of equipment to foreman; cuts off heat supply after specified period where necessary; removes treated material or products, operates mechanical unloading equipment or checks automatic discharge.

May (01) operate power-driven truck to convey products to and remove them from equipment

(02) set thermostat

(03) withdraw samples for testing

(04) examine treated material visually or by touch to check moisture content

(05) examine treated articles for cracks

(06) straighten distorted enamelled products after heat treatment using mallet

(07) weigh and pack treated material

(08) clean equipment.

Additional factor: type of equipment attended.

continued

Other titles include Bag curer, Calcining furnaceman (flint), Drier attendant, Fireman (carbon), Flint burner, Frit kilnman, Fritter, Fuser (vitreous enamelled goods), Oven attendant, Spun pipe steamer, Stove enameller, Stover, Vulcaniser, Vulcanising pan attendant.

See 591 .70 for workers who vulcanise rubber or plastic belting.

591 .98 Trainee

Performs, under instruction or guidance, various tasks including training exercises and as appropriate pursues studies in order to acquire the basic skills and knowledge required to perform the tasks of workers in heat treating occupations not elsewhere classified.

591 .99 Other heat treating occupations not elsewhere classified

Workers in this group operate and attend furnaces, kilns, ovens and other equipment in which materials and products are subjected to heat treatment and are not separately classified, for example:

(01) **Burners-off** (operate ovens to blow incandescent mantles into shape, burn off surplus fibres and season mantles); (02) **Clampmen** (fire bricks in clamps); (03) **Fat extractor men,** Digestermen (bones) (cook bones to extract fat content); (04) **Oxide mill operators** (control operation of a number of drums to oxidise lead shot using heat generated by friction); (05) **Pressers (artificial teeth)** (cook artificial tooth mixture in moulds in heated hand presses); (06) **Tallow makers** (cook animal fat in open vessels to make tallow).

Unit Group 592 Crushing, Milling, Mixing and Blending Occupations Not Elsewhere Classified

Workers in this unit group crush, mill, mix and blend materials and perform related tasks and are not else where classified.

See Batch plant operator (crushing, milling, mixing, blending) (561 .60), Crushing, Milling, Mixing and Blending Occupations (Food and Drink Processing) (574) and Crushing, Milling, Mixing and Blending Occupations (Wood Processing and Paper, Paperboard and Leatherboard Making) (582)

592 .05 Colour calculator

Calculates quantities of colouring matter required to dye or print batches of fibres, yarn, fabric or other material and prepares or directs preparation of colouring matter of specified shade and consistency

Ascertains shade and consistency requirements from colour card or specification and where appropriate examines sample of paper or other material supplied; estimates quantity of colouring matter required for batch and calculates ingredient requirements accordingly; performs or directs performance of tasks as described under COLOUR MATCHER (592.10) and MIXING MACHINE OPERATOR (592.75).

May (01) prepare card showing specimen of colouring matter and ingredient requirements
(02) advise machine printer on cylinder pressures necessary to obtain required density of colour.

Other titles include Colour mixer, Colourist, Colourman, Standard maker.

592 .10 Colour matcher

Checks batches of paints or other decorative coatings against standard or sample colours and adjusts or directs adjustments to colour content of batch

Withdraws sample of paint or other decorative coating from batch; sprays, brushes or dabs sample on to metal, wood or other appropriate material; compares colour visually against colour card or sample; selects and measures small quantities of additional colouring matter and stirs them manually or mechanically into batch or into sample withdrawn for matching; rechecks colour at intervals and adds further colouring matter to batch or sample or prolongs stirring until satisfied that required colour match has been obtained; if adjusting sample, directs batch mixer to add specified quantities of colouring matter to batch; withdraws sample from checked and adjusted batch for laboratory testing.

May (01) prepare batches
(02) operate pump to transfer checked batches to container filling department
(03) mix samples to formula or customer's specification.

Other titles include Colour shader, Tinter.

592.15 Liquor man (leather tanning)

Prepares solutions (liquor) according to formula for tanning hides and skins, and ensures that each tanning pit is supplied with liquor of correct strength

Ascertains vegetable extract and/or chemical solution requirements from formula; feeds prescribed amounts of extracts and/or solutions into mixing tank or tanning pit manually or regulates flow from feed pipes; admits specified quantity of water to tank or pit; tests specific gravity of prepared liquor using hydrometer; pumps liquor from mixing tank to appropriate tanning pit as required; drains off liquor from each pit as directed and pumps it to preceding pit in tanning line or strengthens liquor to original specific gravity.

592.20 Dough preparer (artificial teeth)

Prepares and colours dough according to formula for moulding into artificial teeth

Ascertains chemical and/or mineral ingredient requirements from formula; measures out prescribed amounts of powdered ingredients and mixing liquid into mixing machine or vessel; adds colouring matter required to ensure that colour of dough conforms to specification; starts machine or stirs mixture with hand tool until required malleability and colour are obtained.

May (01) grind ingredients before mixing.

Other titles include Dough mixer.

592.25 Slip maker (ceramics), Glaze maker

Controls the operation of one or more machines to make slip or glaze for use in ceramic goods manufacture

Weighs or directs weighing of prescribed quantities of ball and china clay, or of ground frit and other glaze ingredients; feeds or directs feeding of measured ingredients into appropriate machine(s) (blunger(s)) and admits specified amount(s) of water to blunger(s); starts mechanical paddle(s) to mix contents until required consistency is obtained; withdraws sample from each blunger for testing.

If making slip, checks weight and density of samples of liquid ball and china clay (slip) against mixing chart and adjusts appropriate liquid level markings on measuring stick to ensure that correct proportions of slip are fed into mixing vessel (ark); fixes dipstick in ark and admits required quantities of slip and of wet mixtures of flints and stones to ark; starts mechanical agitators to mix contents of ark for specified time.

Pumps prepared slip over sifter(s) and electromagnets or runs off or operates compressed air line to blow glaze to storage vessel; where necessary, starts agitator in storage vessel; cleans or directs cleaning of equipment.

May (01) grind or direct grinding of glaze ingredients
(02) add colouring to slip or glaze
(03) examine slip in storage vessel visually and by touch to check consistency
(04) pump slip from storage vessel to filter press.

Additional factor: number of machines controlled.

592.50 Mineral crushing plant operator

Operates plant to crush lumps of minerals into pieces of required size for industrial use or for milling or other processing

Positions or checks positioning in plant of grading screens of required mesh or ensures that apertures in screen fixtures are set to required size; starts up crushers and ancillary equipment in specified sequence; regulates flow of minerals from conveyors, chutes or feed hoppers; forces large lumps of mineral between crushing jaws and breaks oversized lumps using hand or powered portable tools, or directs performance of these tasks; regulates speed of plant operation to avoid or rectify overloading and ensure uniform flow of crushed material through grading screens; clears or directs clearance of blockages; regulates flow or checks automatic discharge of crushed material to storage containers or to machines for further processing; cleans, oils and greases plant.

May (01) load or direct loading of lumps of minerals into feed hopper
(02) weigh lumps of minerals before feeding into plant
(03) withdraw sample quantities of crushed mineral pieces for testing
(04) undertake minor adjustments and repairs to plant and ancillary equipment
(05) operate mill and be designated Crusher miller or Crushing millman.

Other titles include Mineral crusher operator, Mineral crusherman, Raw materials crusher.

592.55 Masticating millman

Operates one or more machines to masticate raw or reclaimed rubber or rubber or plastic compounds, ready for further processing

Performs some or all of the following tasks: adjusts distance between cutting blades and clearance between masticating rollers according to width and thickness of stock required; sets timing and measuring devices; starts machine and feeds material on to or between rollers, or loads material into and regulates flow from feed hopper; regulates speed, temperature and pressure of rollers as necessary to ensure uniform mastication of material; adds colouring and/or other ingredients as directed; cuts off and folds masticated material adhering to roller and refeeds it between rollers until required plasticity is obtained; cuts material of required plasticity from roller in specified lengths or ensures continuous discharge of material to cooling plant or to machines for further processing; cleans machine.

May (01) weigh raw materials, colouring and other ingredients

(02) break up (crack) raw material by feeding it through corrugated mill rollers before masticating and be known as Breaker millman.

Additional factors: type, size and number of machines operated.

Other titles include Rubber mill operator, Warmer-up millman.

592.60 Miller (not elsewhere classified)

Operates one or more mills to grind or pulverise materials such as minerals, casein or rubber into particles of required size for industrial use or for further processing and is not elsewhere classified

Regulates flow of materials from conveyors, elevators or feed pipes, or loads or directs manual loading of machine; adds further ingredients and/or grinding agents as specified; disconnects feed pipes and secures feed hatches where appropriate; starts machine, watches operation and adjusts speed of machine as necessary to rectify overloading and milling faults; clears blockages with hand tools or by reversing machine action; regulates flow or checks automatic discharge of ground or pulverised materials through screens to storage containers or to machines for further processing; cleans, oils and greases machine.

May (01) select and position appropriately sized screens or set apertures of fixed screens

(02) weigh and/or mix materials before or after milling

(03) withdraw samples of ground or pulverised material for testing

(04) specialise in grinding materials in wet or dry state

(05) undertake minor adjustments and repairs to machine.

Additional factors: types of mill operated, eg ball mill, hammer mill, roller mill; number of mills operated.

Other titles include Ball mill grinder, Dry miller, Grinder, Hammer mill grinder, Millman, Pebble mill grinder, Pellet mill grinder, Potter's millman, Roller mill grinder, Triple mill grinder, Wet miller.

592.65 Beaterman (asbestos-cement)

Operates one or more machines to produce slurry for making asbestos-cement goods

Ascertains ingredient requirements from formula; weighs out prescribed amounts of dry ingredients and feeds into machine by hand or regulates flow from feed hoppers or pipes; admits required quantity of water to machine; starts machine to beat and mix ingredients; where appropriate adds further liquid ingredients in specified order; checks consistency of slurry at intervals and adjusts composition of mixture as necessary; stops machine when required consistency has been obtained; discharges or pumps prepared slurry to storage chest; clears blockages and cleans machine.

May (01) blend ingredients by hand or machine.

Additional factor: number of machines operated.

Other titles include Hollanderman.

592.70 Rubber compounder, Rubber mixer

Operates mixing machine to prepare rubber compound, dough or solution of specified consistency or quality

Ascertains ingredient and mixing requirements; measures out or directs measuring of prescribed quantities of ingredients or checks measured quantities; feeds or directs feeding of ingredients into machine by hand or mechanical ram, or regulates flow from feed conveyors, hoppers or pipes; starts up machine when necessary; mixes ingredients for specified time or until required consistency or quality has been obtained; adds vulcanising reagents, oil and/or other chemical additives to mixture where specified; monitors instruments and adjusts controls to regulate speed and temperature of machine during mixing operation as necessary; carries out prescribed checks and/or withdraws or directs withdrawal of sample for laboratory testing; removes prepared compound, dough or solution by hand, or discharges or directs discharge to storage container(s) or to machine for further processing; cleans or directs cleaning of machine.

continued

May (01) feed hard rubber compound into cracking mill to soften it for further mixing

(02) mix small quantities of reagents and other chemical additives by hand.

Other titles include Dough mixer, Latex mixer, Mixing millman, Open mill mixer, Solution mixer.

592.75 Mixing machine operator (not elsewhere classified), Blending machine operator (not elsewhere classified)

Operates one or more machines to mix or blend materials such as minerals to required consistency or quality and is not elsewhere classified

Ascertains ingredient and mixing requirements; measures out or directs measuring of prescribed quantities of ingredients or takes measured quantities or checks automatic weighing equipment; feeds or directs feeding of ingredients into machine by hand or regulates flow from feed conveyors, hoppers or pipes; adds mixing media as specified; ensures that feed hatches are secured and inlet valves closed where appropriate; operates machine to mix or blend ingredients until required consistency or quality is obtained; adds further ingredients to mixture where specified; monitors instruments and controls temperature of ingredients during mixing or blending as required; carries out prescribed checks and/or withdraws or directs withdrawal of sample for laboratory testing; adjusts machine speed and/or composition of mixture or blend as required; removes prepared mixture or blend by hand or discharges or pumps it to storage containers, packaging machines or to machines for further processing, or directs discharging operation; cleans or directs cleaning of machine.

May (01) couple up or direct coupling of flexible hose-pipes to transfer liquid or solid ingredients and/or mixtures or blends

(02) control operation of automated mixing or blending machines from central control panel

(03) mix materials by hand

(04) grind, sieve, filter and/or dry materials before and/or after mixing or blending.

Additional factors: type of machine operated, eg ball mill mixers, paddle mixers; number of machines operated.

Other titles include Ball mill mixing machine operator, Compounder, Dispersion mill operator, Lime hydrator, Paddle mixer operator, Slip maker (pencil lead), Wash mill operator.

592.90 Crushing plant attendant (not elsewhere classified), Mill attendant (not elsewhere classified)

Attends automatic or semi-automatic plant which crushes or mills materials such as minerals or raw or reclaimed rubber for industrial use or for further processing and is not elsewhere classified

Starts up and shuts down plant as required; loads material into feed hopper by hand or using mechanical aid or regulates or checks flow rate along feed pipes or conveyors; breaks up or removes oversized pieces; watches operation or monitors instruments and gauges; stops plant if fault occurs or feed of material is interrupted and reports to foreman; clears blockages with hand tools or by reversing machine action; regulates flow or checks automatic discharge of material through screens to storage containers or to machines for further processing; cleans plant.

May (01) carry out simple adjustments and repairs to plant

(02) change screens

(03) withdraw samples for testing

(04) weigh and/or package discharged material

(05) attend remote-controlled plant

(06) attend automatic mill in which iron shot is heated before crushing and be known as Shot plant attendant.

Other titles include Ball mill attendant, Bore mill attendant, Cracker unit attendant, Grinding machine attendant, Hammer mill attendant, Milling machine attendant, Pan mill attendant, Pan mill feeder, Pitch and coal feed attendant, Roller mill attendant, Scratcher (linoleum).

592.92 Mixing machine attendant (not elsewhere classified), Blending machine attendant (not elsewhere classified)

Attends one or more automatic or semi-automatic machines in which materials such as minerals are mixed or blended to required consistency or quality, and is not elsewhere classified

Feeds measured amounts of ingredients into machine by hand or checks automatic feed, and/or operates pumps to transfer liquid ingredients or slurry to machine or storage tank; adds mixing media as directed; secures feed hatches, closes inlet valves and starts machine where necessary; discharges or checks automatic discharge of prepared mixture or blend to storage containers or to equipment for further processing; reports malfunctioning of equipment to foreman; cleans machine.

continued

May (01) couple up flexible hose-pipes to transfer liquid ingredients to machine

(02) grind, sieve, filter and/or dry materials before and/or after mixing or blending

(03) withdraw samples for testing.

Additional factor: number of machines attended.

Other titles include Back-end man (cement), Batching plant attendant, Concrete mixer driver, Frit kiln mixer attendant, Pugman.

592.98 Trainee

Performs, under instruction or guidance, various tasks including training exercises and as appropriate pursues studies in order to acquire the basic skills and knowledge required to perform the tasks of workers in crushing, milling, mixing and blending occupations not elsewhere classified.

592.99 Other crushing, milling, mixing and blending occupations not elsewhere classified

Workers in this group crush, mill, mix and blend materials and perform related tasks and are not separately classified, for example:

(01) **Mixers (hand) (not elsewhere classified).**

Unit Group 593 Filtering, Straining and Other Mechanical Separating Occupations Not Elsewhere Classified

Workers in this unit group operate and attend filtering, straining and other mechanical separating equipment to process materials and are not elsewhere classified.

See Batch plant operator (filtering, straining and other mechanical separating) (561.70), Filtering, Straining and other Separating Occupations (Food and Drink Processing) (575) and Filtering, Straining and Other Separating Occupations (Wood Processing and Paper, Paperboard and Leatherboard Making) (583)

593.05 Flotation plant operator

Operates equipment to separate constituents of a mixture of solids by froth flotation

Regulates flow of mixture, flotation agents and water to tanks (cells) or to duct leading to flotation channel; starts agitators in cells or channel to cause frothing; watches separation process to ensure that froth containing particles of one of the solid constituents is scooped into trays or into waste drainway at top of channel and that other solid particles sink to bottom of equipment, and makes necessary adjustments; where appropriate checks that solid particles are washed off from bottom of equipment into containers and drains off surplus water from containers when particles have settled at bottom; ensures adequate supply of flotation agents to equipment; withdraws and filters samples periodically in readiness for laboratory testing, or personally tests samples for density using hydrometer; cleans equipment.

May (01) mix flotation agents according to formula

(02) set device to tip flotation agents into duct automatically at prescribed intervals

(03) operate plant in which separated materials are automatically filtered and dried.

Other titles include Coal washery operator, Froth plant operator.

593.10 Heavy media plant operator

Operates equipment to separate impurities from solid materials using heavy media solution

Tests or directs testing of solution in bath for specific gravity using hydrometer or special scales; adds media such as sand or shale as necessary to bring solution to required specific gravity; starts equipment and regulates flow of material into bath; watches process to ensure that lighter constituent(s) of impure material remains in suspension whilst heavier constituent(s) sinks to bottom of bath; checks that material from which impurities have been removed is forced by compressed air or paddle wheel on to screen(s), and that screened material and impurities are discharged to appropriate chutes or conveyors; adjusts equipment as necessary and maintains specific gravity of solution at prescribed level to ensure satisfactory separation; cleans equipment.

May (01) operate equipment incorporating magnetic device to remove metallic particles.

Other titles include Coal washery operator.

593.15 Magnetic separator operator

Operates machine to separate constituents of a mixture of solids by magnetism

Sets magnet strength and feed rate controls according to instructions; positions empty containers at machine outlet points as necessary; starts machine; watches process, checks dial readings to ensure that constituents are separating satisfactorily and makes necessary adjustments; checks that magnetic and non-magnetic materials are discharged through appropriate machine outlets; ensures adequate supply of mixture to machine.

May (01) operate equipment to dry mixture before separation
(02) withdraw samples for laboratory testing
(03) weigh out and pack specified amounts of separated constituents.

Other titles include Ore separator.

593.20 Filter press operator (not elsewhere classified)

Operates one or more machines to separate solids from liquids by pumping mixture through filter frames and is not elsewhere classified

Positions and seals filter frames in press; sets controls to pump mixture through filter frames; watches filtering process to ensure clarity of liquid output and makes necessary adjustments; stops pump when filtering cycle is complete; releases filter frames from press and removes or directs removal of solid material using water or compressed air where necessary; cleans equipment and replaces filters as required.

May (01) add filter-aids to mixture before filtering
(02) coat filters with filter-aids
(03) withdraw samples for testing
(04) test samples for specific gravity using hydrometer.

Additional factor: number of machines operated.

Other titles include Filter press emptier, Filter pressman.

593.25 Rotary drum filter operator (not elsewhere classified)

Operates one or more machines to separate solids from liquids by drawing mixture through filters fitted to a rotating drum and is not elsewhere classified

Regulates or checks flow of mixture to filter tank; adjusts controls to regulate speed of filter drum; operates controls to apply vacuum to draw mixture through filter and positions scraper or chain to remove solids adhering to filter; switches on discharge conveyor where appropriate; watches filtering operation and checks dials and gauges to ensure that solids and liquids are separating satisfactorily and makes necessary adjustments; cleans equipment and replaces filters as required.

May (01) withdraw samples for laboratory testing
(02) attend equipment in which solids are dried after separation
(03) repack pump glands.

Additional factor: number of machines operated.

593.30 Centrifuge operator (not elsewhere classified)

Operates one or more machines to separate by centrifugal force solids from liquids or liquids of different specific gravity from each other and is not elsewhere classified

Operates feed controls or loads centrifugal container manually with material for separation; starts machine and regulates rotation speed of container as necessary to ensure satisfactory separation; stops machine when process is complete and extracts or drains separated material; cleans equipment.

May (01) fix filtering media in machine
(02) operate machine fitted with heating attachment.

Additional factor: number of machines operated.

593 .35 Siever (not elsewhere classified)

Separates and/or sizes solid chemicals or minerals using gravity separators, vibratory screens or similar equipment

Positions screens with mesh of required size in equipment or sets angle of separating plates where necessary; places empty containers at machine outlet points as required; loads hoppers manually or using mechanical aids and adjusts hopper controls to regulate feed of material to screens, or checks or regulates flow of material for separating or sizing along feed pipes or conveyors; starts equipment vibrating and/or admits flow of air; regulates flow from water jets on to vibratory equipment, where appropriate; watches process to ensure even flow of material through equipment and makes necessary adjustments; clears blockages and replaces damaged screens; removes filled containers from machine outlet points or regulates or checks discharge of separated or sized material to appropriate chutes or conveyors; cleans equipment.

May (01) sift small quantities of material using hand sieve or mobile electric sieve

(02) operate equipment incorporating magnetic device to remove metallic particles

(03) weigh materials before or after separating or sizing

(04) withdraw samples for laboratory testing

(05) examine separated or sized material and remove extraneous matter manually

(06) discharge material into road or rail wagons.

Additional factor: type of equipment operated.

Other titles include Bone picker, Coal dry cleaning plant operator, Grading and screening operator, Screener, Seed cleaning machinist, Sifter, Slime dresser tableman, Strainer, Straining machine attendant.

593 .40 Sedimentation plant operator (not elsewhere classified)

Operates equipment to separate solids from liquids by gravity and is not elsewhere classified

Regulates flow of mixture to settling or desanding tank or to tray-type separating equipment (thickener); starts agitators where appropriate; watches separating process to ensure that solid particles sink and settle at base of tank or thickener and that liquid is drawn to outlet tubes or into collecting troughs; regulates discharge of solid particles from equipment.

May (01) withdraw samples for testing

(02) test samples for specific gravity using hydrometer

(03) regulate flow of separated liquor to storage tanks or to plant for further processing.

Other titles include China clay refiner.

593 .45 Sewage works attendant

Attends plant in which sewage is treated by screening, sedimentation and filtration

Performs some or all of the following tasks: regulates flow of raw sewage into screening plant; cleans out screen compartment manually or using mechanical shovel; releases screened sewage into detritus channels in which sand and grit are removed; inspects and empties detritus pits as required; adjusts valves to control flow of sewage through settling tanks in which sludge is separated from sewage water by sedimentation; removes sludge from sedimentation tanks manually or using mechanical scraper; pumps sewage water from sedimentation tanks to filtration beds; cleans out filtration beds.

May (01) attend unit in which raw sewage is macerated before screening

(02) check that flowmeter readings are within prescribed limits

(03) drive tractor to plough furrows to within sludge is pumped

(04) maintain grounds surrounding sewage works

(05) prepare compost by mixing straw and lime with sludge.

Other titles include Sewage plant attendant, Sewage plant operator.

593 .98 Trainee

Performs, under instruction or guidance, various tasks including training exercises and as appropriate pursues studies in order to acquire the basic skills and knowledge required to perform the tasks of workers in filtering, straining and other mechanical separating occupations not elsewhere classified.

593.99 Other filtering, straining and mechanical separating occupations not elsewhere classified

Workers in this group operate and attend filtering, straining and other mechanical separating equipment to process materials and are not separately classified, for example:

(01) **Coal washery attendants,** Coal wash-box operators (attend coal washing plants under direction of foreman or washery operator); (02) **Filtermen (rubber reclamation),** Washers (rubber reclamation) (attend equipment in which devulcanised rubber is screened and pressed); (03) **Grit washers** (attend plant in which grit is washed and dried); (04) **Hydraulic press operators (slurry)** (operate hydraulic presses to remove moisture from slurry); (05) **Lime plant attendants** (attend equipment in which lime is slaked and strained for use in sugar manufacture); (06) **Rotary sieve operators** (operate equipment to sieve slurry to required degree of fineness); (07) **Rubber strainers** (operate or attend machines to refine raw or reclaimed rubber by forcing it through wire mesh screens).

Unit Group 594 Plant and Machine Operating Occupations (Materials Processing) Not Elsewhere Classified

Workers in this unit group operate and attend plant and machinery to process materials and are not elsewhere classified.

594.10 Machine man (flat asbestos-cement sheet making)

Operates or controls the operation of one or more machines to make flat asbestos-cement sheets from prepared slurry (stuff)

Sets machine controls, directs positioning of reeling drum and starts machine, or takes over and checks performance of running machine; watches operation to ensure that stuff is picked up by revolving cylinders, deposited on endless belt and built up correctly on reeling drum; operates mechanical cutter or directs operation of hand cutter to cut asbestos-cement of required thickness from drum or checks automatic cutting operation; regulates flow of stuff to machine, and adjusts speed of machine and thickness gauge setting as necessary; directs removal of formed sheets and trimming and/or cutting of sheets to required dimensions; cleans and oils machine or directs performance of these tasks.

Additional factor: number of machines controlled or operated.

Other titles include Machine driver.

594.20 Machine man (asbestos-cement pipe making)

Operates or controls the operation of machine to make asbestos-cement pipes from prepared slurry (stuff)

Sets machine controls; positions or directs positioning of forming mandrel on machine; where appropriate, secures end stop plates and couples vacuum pipe to perforated mandrel or directs performance of these tasks; starts machine and regulates flow of stuff through spreading mechanism and on to endless belt and rotating mandrel, or directs feed of stuff from flexible hose-pipe along surface of perforated mandrel and starts machine and vacuum pump to rotate mandrel and extract excess moisture; watches operation to ensure that pipe is correctly formed round mandrel and adjusts machine controls and/or evens out deposit of stuff around mandrel using hand tools as necessary; stops machine when pipe is formed and checks dimensions; directs removal of pipe and mandrel from machine and extraction of mandrel from pipe.

May (01) operate machine from control panel
(02) position or direct positioning of shaped mandrel on machine to make pipes with collar ends.

Other titles include Machine driver, Machine moulder.

594.50 Machine man (corrugated asbestos-cement sheet making)

Attends automatic machine which makes corrugated asbestos-cement sheets from prepared slurry (stuff)

Starts machine or takes over and checks performance of running machine; watches formation and automatic cutting to size of corrugated sheeting and makes necessary adjustments to machine operation from control panel; directs removal of cut sheets and stamping of identification details on sheets; directs cleaning and oiling of machine.

May (01) set up machine by adjusting panel controls.

Other titles include Machine driver.

594.52 Corrugator (asbestos-cement sheet)

Operates machine or press to corrugate flat uncured asbestos-cement sheets

Positions flat asbestos-cement sheet of required size on corrugated moulding tray manually and places tray in corrugating machine or operates controls to regulate movement of flat sheets along conveyors and on to corrugated die in press; moves controls to operate corrugating machine or press; removes and stacks corrugated sheets manually or using mechanical equipment.

May (01) operate equipment which cuts and trims flat asbestos-cement sheets to required size before corrugating

(02) cut corrugated sheets to size using hand saw or portable mechanical cutter.

594.54 Assistant machine man (asbestos-cement sheet, pipe making)

Assists, under the direction of machine man, in the operation of a machine to make asbestos-cement sheet or pipe

Performs a combination of the following tasks: positions reeling drum or forming mandrel on machine; wraps cloth round forming mandrel; couples and uncouples vacuum feed pipe as required; opens valve to admit liquid stuff into feed trough or feeds liquid stuff from flexible hose-pipe on to surface of forming mandrel; cuts off sheet of material formed around reeling drum using hand knife or cutting cord; guides cut sheet on to conveyor; wraps sheet round roller and transfers to pallet; unrolls sheet on pallet; trims edges of formed sheet and/or cuts sheet to specified size using hand or mechanical tools; removes formed sheet or pipe by hand or by operating lifting equipment; operates equipment to withdraw forming mandrel from formed pipe; stacks sheets or mounts pipes over support cores for drying; removes cloth from the inside of formed pipe and rinses it in water ready for re-use; cleans and oils machine.

Other titles include Back tenter, Stringer, Taker-off.

594.56 Plasterboard making machine operator

Operates machine to make plasterboard

Performs some or all of the following tasks: sets machine controls according to board specification; checks that reels of backing paper have been positioned on feed mechanism; regulates flow of slurry on to bottom backing paper and ensures even spread of slurry; watches operation to check that bottom backing paper is correctly scored and folded and that top paper is automatically glued to edge of bottom backing paper; adjusts machine controls as necessary to ensure that board is formed to specification; examines or directs examination of paper backing for defects such as ripples or tears; adjusts tensioners to remedy rippling; repairs or directs repair of tears; ensures that supplies of paper and glue are adequate; adjusts depth and angle of scoring knives as required; cleans or directs cleaning of machine.

Other titles include Edgeman, Plasterboard making machine controller.

594.58 Man-made fibre maker

Attends plant in which fibre-forming solution (polymer) is extruded and wound into packages of continuous filament or cut into short lengths (staple fibre)

Performs a combination of the following tasks: feeds polymer chips into hopper of melting unit or regulates flow of liquid polymer from storage tank into feed pipe; starts pump to force polymer through holes in jet heads (spinnerets) into coagulating bath or evaporating or cooling chamber; gathers extruded filaments into a specified number of strands; feeds strands through guides and over rollers and through appropriate treatment units to winding or cutting equipment; patrols plant to watch operation; joins ends of broken filaments; lubricates and/or replaces spinnerets as required; removes wound packages of continuous filament and replaces winding cores or reeling boxes, or removes and replaces or directs removal and replacement of staple fibre containers; checks and replenishes supplies of feedstock and treating solutions as required; cleans plant.

May (01) set temperature of rollers used to stretch and impart strength to filaments

(02) strip spinnerets and replace defective filters and washers

(03) specialise in wet or dry spinning process.

Other titles include Continuous filament maker, Jet spin operative, Nylon spinner, Rayon spinner.

594 .60 Calender operator (rubber, plastics)

Operates machine to make rubber or plastic sheeting or to combine continuous sheets to form laminated material by calendering

Performs some or all of the following tasks: sets machine controls and admits heat and/or coolant to calender rollers; positions roll of lining fabric on feed mechanism and threads leading end through machine to take-up mandrel; feeds masticated rubber or softened plastics material to forming rollers by hand, positions conveyor to direct feed from warming mill or mixing machine or positions rolls of rubber or plastic sheeting on feed mechanism and threads leading ends through guides, tensioners and coating equipment to combining rollers; starts machine and watches operation; guides formed sheeting or laminated material through calender rollers and/or cooling equipment to take-up mandrel or cutting unit; checks dimensions of sheeting or laminated material, examines surface and marks defects; adjusts guides, tensioners, trimming cutters, and speed, temperature, and pressure of calendering rollers, as necessary, to ensure that sheeting or laminated material is formed to specification; removes or directs removal of sheeting or laminated material from machine; cleans or directs cleaning of machine.

May (01) mix and/or warm up plastics material in readiness for calendering
(02) operate mechanical equipment to load and unload machine
(03) position and replace reeling mandrels
(04) oil machine and carry out minor running repairs
(05) direct operating team and be known as Leading calenderhand.

Other titles include Calenderhand, Calenderman.

594 .62 Extruding machine operator (rubber, plastics)

Operates one or more machines to extrude compounded rubber or plastics materials to form stock of specified shape and size

Positions appropriate die on machine; sets machine and temperature controls when required; loads or directs loading of compounded material into feed hopper or warming unit or pours material into feed container; starts machine; watches operation and examines extruded stock for faults such as bubbles, splits or wrinkles; checks dimensions of extruded stock; adjusts machine speed and temperature controls, as necessary, to ensure that stock is formed to specification.

May (01) immerse compounded rubber in hot water to give it plasticity before extrusion process
(02) operate continuous process machine in which stock is vulcanised after extrusion
(03) cut extruded stock into specified lengths by hand or machine
(04) coil and tie lengths of stock
(05) clean machine and carry out minor adjustments
(06) specialise in extruding stock in tube, rod, strip or sheet form.

Additional factor: number of machines operated.

Other titles include Extruder, Forcer, Seamless latex tubing machine operator.

See 681 .58 for operators of extrusion machines covering cables or wire with rubber or plastics.

594 .64 Coating machine operator (film, recording tape)

Operates machine to coat film or recording tape base materials with sensitising solutions

Ensures adequate supply of liquid graphite or other sensitising solution to coating machine; positions base material on machine and guides leading end(s) through coating and drying units to rewinding equipment or checks that machine is ready for operation; checks temperature and thickness gauges, where appropriate, records readings and reports variations to foreman; watches operation to detect defects in coating or base material.

May (01) set and adjust machine controls
(02) remove reel(s) of coated base material from rewinding equipment.

Other titles include Emulsion coater (photographic film), Graphite coating operator (recording tape).

594 .90 Calenderer (asbestos composition)

Attends machine which makes asbestos composition sheeting by calendering

Spreads quantity of plasticised composition (dough) on take-in roller; starts machine and watches operation to ensure that dough builds up evenly around heated calender roller; adds further dough as necessary, and hardeners when appropriate; stops machine after specified time and cuts across calendered dough; restarts machine and peels off formed sheet; reports malfunctioning of machine to foreman; cleans machine.

May (01) set machine controls
(02) admit coolant to take-in rollers and heat to calender rollers
(03) mix ingredients to form dough for calendering
(04) incorporate reinforcing material in sheeting
(05) operate guillotine to cut formed sheeting into pieces of specified size.

Other titles include Calenderman.

594.92 Materials processing plant attendant (not elsewhere classified), Materials processing machine attendant (not elsewhere classified)

Attends automatic or semi-automatic plant or machinery in which materials are mechanically processed and is not elsewhere classified

Performs a combination of the following tasks: loads material to be processed into machine or into feed hoppers by hand or using mechanical aid, or regulates or checks flow of material from conveyors, elevators or feed pipes; positions lengths of material on intake mechanism or machine bed; operates controls to start and stop plant or machinery as required; admits heat to plant or machinery; watches operation and reports faults in processed material and malfunctioning of equipment to foreman; replenishes supplies of material and/or processing media as necessary; removes processed stock by hand or using mechanical aid, or regulates or checks its passage to equipment for further processing.

May (01) position on machine cores round which pipes are formed
(02) change dies on machine to vary size of stock pellets formed
(03) cut formed stock into standard lengths by hand or machine.

Other titles include Asbestos composition pipe maker, Asbestos composition slab machine attendant, Briquetting machine man, Calender hand (linoleum), Extruder, Extruding press attendant, Gut seeking machine attendant, Gut splitting machine attendant, Hydraulic press man, Impregnating machine attendant, Micanite sheet builder, Micanite tube roller, Paste slugger, Pelleting machine attendant, Pressman, Sectional pipe maker (asbestos composition).

See 681.94 for attendants of extrusion machines covering wire or metal goods with rubber or plastics materials.

594.98 Trainee

Performs, under instruction or guidance, various tasks including training exercises and as appropriate pursues studies in order to acquire the basic skills and knowledge required to perform the tasks of workers in plant and machine operating occupations (materials processing) not elsewhere classified.

594.99 Other plant and machine operating occupations (materials processing) not elsewhere classified

Workers in this group operate and attend plant and machinery to process materials and are not separately classified, for example:

(01) **Bundling machine operatives (plasterboard),** Magazine attendants (plasterboard) (attend machines which grind edges of plasterboards square and bundle boards); (02) **Casting machine operators (film),** Dry threaders (film), Wet threaders (film) (operate machines to produce transparent wrapping material from prepared chemical solution); (03) **Coal washery operators (coal washing and mixing plants),** Coal washing and mixing plant controllers (control the operation of automated coal cleaning and mixing plants from master control panel); (04) **Coating machine operators (electric cables)** (operate machines to coat electric cables with lacquer or wax); (05) **Cutters (materials processing) (not elsewhere classified)** (operate or set and attend machines to cut materials into pieces for processing or to trim or cut processed material to stock size and are not elsewhere classified); (06) **Foilers** (set and operate machines to apply foil or plastic sheeting to plasterboard to provide thermal insulating qualities); (07) **Gut polishers** (set and operate machines to polish gut); (08) **Gut seekers (machine),** Gut spinners (machine), Gut twisters (machine) (clean, spin or twist gut using hand-operated machines); (09) **Kiln feed men (plasterboard)** (attend machinery which automatically cuts formed plasterboard to standard lengths and conveys cut boards to drying ovens); (10) **Reelers (not elsewhere classified)** (operate machines to reel sheets of material after processing and are not elsewhere classified); (11) **Rubber curers (cold process)** (operate machines to treat continuous lengths of rubber with vulcanising solution; (12) **Taking-down machine operators (floor covering)** (operate machines to wind dried floor covering on to reels).

Unit Group 599 Other Materials Processing Occupations

Workers in this unit group position articles ready for heat treating, mould and build up materials by hand to form stock and perform other miscellaneous tasks in materials processing and are not elsewhere classified.

599 .10 Kiln placer

Positions formed, glazed or decorated articles of domestic and ornamental pottery ready for firing

Carries out some or all of the following tasks: arranges fire-clay slabs to form a base on kiln floor or truck using short props to enable heat to circulate under first layer of articles; positions formed articles on base according to shape and size, bedding them in alumina or sand where necessary to prevent distortion and ensure even contraction; builds up piles of formed articles on bench to required height using fire-clay shapes (cranks) and alumina or sand, and transfers piles (bungs) to kiln truck; spreads layers of sand in fire-clay containers (saggars), positions formed articles in sand and transfers packed saggars to kiln or truck; places glazed or decorated articles on truck, using cranks and/or other kiln furniture to ensure that articles do not fuse together; forms additional shelves as necessary in kiln or on truck using fire-clay coated supports and positions articles on shelves; ensures that articles are positioned to make best use of space available; checks loaded truck with profile gauge to ensure that it will enter kiln.

May (01) operate control to push truck into kiln
(02) fire kiln (591 .58)
(03) withdraw trucks from kiln on completion of firing
(04) unload fired articles from kiln or truck.

Other titles include Biscuit placer, Glost placer.

599 .50 Kiln setter

Positions carbon products or mineral products other than domestic or ornamental pottery ready for firing

Carries out a combination of the following tasks: transfers or directs transfer of products to be fired to kiln; arranges products of varying shapes and sizes on kiln racks or shelves or on kiln trucks; smoothes kiln floor using straight-edge; builds up stacks of regular shaped products on trucks or pallets or on floor of kiln chamber; positions products on slabs or other kiln furniture to provide adequate support and/or to ensure that they do not fuse together; packs products in fire-clay containers (saggars) using dust or other packing material; positions packed saggars in kiln; sets loaded pallets in kiln; builds products into special close formations (clamps) on layers of fuel or rough breeze; ensures that all products are positioned to allow for shrinkage and to provide uniform heat distribution during firing.

May (01) operate lift, hoist or other mechanical aid to transfer products to kiln
(02) seal kiln in readiness for firing products
(03) inspect fired products and segregate faulty items for breaking-up, reglazing or refiring
(04) unload products on completion of firing and be known as Kiln setter drawer.

Other titles include Crowder, Kiln loader.

599 .60 Hand moulder (not elsewhere classified)

Moulds materials such as asbestos-cement or micanite to form stock of specified shape and size and is not elsewhere classified

Selects appropriate mould; places material for moulding over or in mould or opens chute to admit material into mould; works material to shape of mould by hand or using hand tools; removes moulded stock or transfers mould to press for consolidation of contents.

May (01) warm material in readiness for moulding
(02) trim sheets to shape using hand tools before and/or after moulding
(03) operate fly press to consolidate contents of mould.

Other titles include Hand corrugator (asbestos-cement sheet), Micanite moulder.

See Hand moulder (asbestos-cement products) (623 .06)

599 .70 Mica splitter (hand)

Splits pieces of mica into layers (splittings) of specified thickness by hand

Holds piece of mica in position on work-table; where necessary scrapes edge of mica with knife to locate cleavages; inserts cutting tool gently into cleavages to split mica into layers; checks thickness of splittings using gauge; takes further cuttings, as necessary, to reduce splittings to thickness specified.

May (01) check mica pieces for flaws and faults
(02) set gauge
(03) bundle splittings ready for further processing.

599.90 Impregnator (immersion) (not elsewhere classified)

Immerses stock material or components in impregnating solutions and is not elsewhere classified

Prepares prescribed quantity of impregnating solution or takes prepared solution; pours or admits solution into impregnating vessel; places or lowers material or components into impregnating vessel by hand or using mechanical aid; watches process when appropriate; reports faults to foremen; removes impregnated material or components from vessel after specified time.

May (01) dry and/or cool impregnated material

(02) operate hydraulic ram to remove surplus solution from impregnated material

(03) operate equipment to reclaim impregnating solution

(04) check temperature and specific gravity of impregnating solution using thermometer and hydrometer

(05) clean vessel.

Other titles include Armature impregnator, Impregnator (asbestos composition goods), Pencil lead preparer, Vatman (battery cells).

599.98 Trainee

Performs, under instruction or guidance, various tasks including training exercises and as appropriate pursues studies in order to acquire the basic skills and knowledge required to perform the tasks of workers in other materials processing occupations.

599.99 Other materials processing occupations not elsewhere classified

Workers in this group perform miscellaneous tasks in materials processing and are not separately classified, for example:

(01) **Bedmen (asphalt),** Fillers (asphalt), Floormen (asphalt), Moulders (asphalt) (assemble moulds and fill them with liquid asphalt to form asphalt blocks); (02) **Bifocal fusers** (place assembled bifocal lenses on conveyor feed belts ready for fusing in furnaces); (03) **Blunger chargers,** Sliphouse men (charge blungers, regulate flow of slip to mixing ark or ensure that slip flows smoothly over sifters); (04) **Carriers-in (kiln, lehr),** Lehr loaders, Takers-in (feed glass articles to annealing or firing kilns or lehrs); (05) **Festooners (linoleum),** Stovemen (linoleum) (festoon lengths of linoleum on rollers in preheated chambers to mature and harden); (06) **Fusers' mates** (remove dust from vitreous enamelled items prior to fusing and assist fusers (vitreous enamelled goods) in loading and unloading furnaces); (07) **Grog mill workers** (assist in the operation of machines in grog mill); (08) **Gut cutters (hand),** Gut enders (hand), Gut splitters (hand) (cut, separate or split lengths of gut by hand); (09) **Gypsum dressers** (sort uncalcined gypsum according to quality and remove adhering marl using axes or pneumatic chisels); (10) **Herbal extract makers** (prepare herbal extracts from ingredients such as leaves, roots and bark); (11) **Hoverkiln attendants** (feed pottery and other ceramic articles to be fired into, and remove them from kilns through which they pass on a cushion of air); (12) **Materials processing machine operators' assistants (not elsewhere classified),** Beatermen's assistants (asbestos-cement), Blending machine operators' assistants (not elsewhere classified), Coating machine operators' assistants (film, recording tape), Hopper fillers (materials processing) (not elsewhere classified), Laminating machine feeders (plasterboard), Micanite building machine operators' assistants, Mixing machine operators' assistants (not elsewhere classified); (13) **Micanite sheet builders (hand),** Micanite tube rollers (hand) (build up micanite sheets of specified thickness by hand, using paper, shellac and mica splittings or build up micanite tubes by hand round forming mandrels); (14) **Papermen (plasterboard),** Supplymen (plasterboard) (load rolls of paper on to plasterboard making machines and replenish supply of paper as required); (15) **Saggar packers** (pack products in saggars ready for kiln setting); (16) **Skimmers** (skim impurities off surface of molten glass in furnaces); (17) **Slippers (asbestos-cement)** (position formers for use on corrugating machines and remove formers from between corrugated sheets, or remove corrugated sheets from machine); (18) **Sponge cutters,** Sponge dressers (wash, bleach, cut and/or trim natural sponge); (19) **Stone breakers** (break up large pieces of stone or mineral using sledge hammers or pneumatic air breakers); (20) **Takers-off (plasterboard)** (check that finished boards are automatically discharged from machines on to loading platforms and remove faulty boards, or remove boards from machines and stack ready for removal).

MAJOR GROUP XIII

Making and Repairing Occupations (Excluding Metal and Electrical)

Workers in this major group perform making and repairing tasks, other than painting and repetitive assembling, in the production of glass, glassware and ceramics and of goods and products of concrete, abrasive stone, paper, textile materials, fur, leather, wood, rubber, plastics and other miscellaneous materials, except metal and electrical and perform printing tasks.

Included are photographic processing occupations.

The occupations are arranged in the following minor groups:

61 Glass Working Occupations

62 Clay and Stone Working Occupations

63 Printing, Photographic Processing and Related Occupations

64 Bookbinding, Paper Working and Paperboard Products Making Occupations

65 Textile Materials Working Occupations

66 Leather Working Occupations

67 Woodworking Occupations

68 Rubber and Plastics Working Occupations

69 Making and Repairing Occupations Not Elsewhere Classified

Minor Group 61 GLASS WORKING OCCUPATIONS

Workers in this minor group shape and form glassware, finish and decorate glassware, other than by painting, and shape and finish optical glass products.

The occupations are arranged in the following unit groups:

610 Foremen (Glass Working Occupations)

611 Glass Shaping and Forming Occupations (Hand) (Excluding Optical Glass)

612 Glass Shaping and Forming Occupations (Machine) (Excluding Optical Glass)

613 Optical Glass Shaping, Forming and Finishing Occupations

614 Glass Finishing Occupations (Excluding Optical Glass and Painting)

619 Glass Working Occupations Not Elsewhere Classified

Unit Group 610 Foremen (Glass Working Occupations)

Workers in this unit group directly supervise and co-ordinate the activities of workers in glass working occupations.

610 .10 Foreman (glass shaping and forming occupations (hand) (excluding optical glass))

Directly supervises and co-ordinates the activities of workers shaping and forming glass, other than optical glass, by hand

Performs appropriate tasks as described under SUPERVISOR/FOREMAN (UNSPECIFIED) (990 .00).

Additional factor: number of workers supervised.

610 .20 Foreman (glass shaping and forming occupations (machine) (excluding optical glass))

Directly supervises and co-ordinates the activities of workers shaping and forming glass, other than optical glass, by machine

Performs appropriate tasks as described under SUPERVISOR/FOREMAN (UNSPECIFIED) (990 .00).

Additional factor: number of workers supervised.

610 .30 Foreman (optical glass shaping, forming and finishing occupations)

Directly supervises and co-ordinates the activities of workers in optical glass shaping, forming and finishing occupations

Performs appropriate tasks as described under SUPERVISOR/FOREMAN (UNSPECIFIED) (990 .00).

May (01) set machines
(02) decide whether defective glass should be scrapped or reprocessed
(03) specialise in supervising workers in a particular process, eg glazing or surfacing.

Additional factor: number of workers supervised.

Other titles include Prescription manager.

610 .40 Foreman (glass finishing occupations) (excluding optical glass and painting)

Directly supervises and co-ordinates the activities of workers in glass finishing occupations other than optical glass and painting

Performs appropriate tasks as described under SUPERVISOR/FOREMAN (UNSPECIFIED) (990 .00).

Additional factor: number of workers supervised.

610.98 Trainee

Performs, under instruction or guidance, various tasks including training exercises and as appropriate pursues studies in order to acquire the basic skills and knowledge required to perform the tasks of foremen (glass working occupations).

610.99 Other foremen (glass working occupations)

Workers in this group directly supervise and co-ordinate the activities of workers in glass working occupations and are not elsewhere classified

Unit Group 611 Glass Shaping and Forming Occupations (Hand) (Excluding Optical Glass)

Workers in this unit group form glassware by mouth and mould blowing and shape glassware, other than optical glass, by heating and working with hand tools.

611.05 Chairman, Servitor

Shapes and finishes glassware partly formed by footmaker

Places blowpipe, with partly formed article attached, across the arms of glass maker's iron chair; rotates pipe along the arms of the chair and shapes article with tongs, formers and other shaping tools; for attachments such as handles or decorations, shears off requisite amount of molten glass from gatherer's rod on to glass article and shapes with tongs, formers, or other tools; reheats article in small furnace (glory hole) as required during shaping.

Other titles include Gaffer, Workman.

611.10 Glass blower (mould)

Forms glassware by blowing into molten glass in a mould

Gathers a quantity of molten glass from tank or pot on to blowpipe as required; blows gently down pipe to form an envelope; swings pipe back and forth to elongate envelope and control distribution of the glass; inserts end of pipe with glass attached in neck of open mould on floor; operates pedal to close mould; blows through pipe to force glass to the shape of mould, spinning pipe to ensure even distribution of the glass; opens mould, withdraws formed article still attached to pipe and passes to knocker-off for removal of article from pipe.

611.15 Crown glass maker

Blows and spins molten glass to form discs

Gathers a quantity of molten glass from tank or pot on to blowpipe; blows through pipe to form a bulb; holds pipe while a small amount of glass on gathering rod is attached to bulb by gatherer; cuts bulb from pipe with shears leaving it attached to gathering rod; rests gathering rod across iron table (marver) with end projecting, rotates rod between hands until bulb opens out into a flat disc and continues rotating rod until the disc is the required size and thickness.

611.20 Glass tube maker (hand drawing), Glass rod maker (hand drawing)

Blows and draws out molten glass to form glass tubes or rods

Gathers a quantity of molten glass from tank or pot on to blowpipe; blows through pipe to form a bulb; rolls glass on iron table (marver) to shape bulb into a cylinder; gathers further quantity of molten glass and repeats process to build up cylinder to required size; sets pipe in a clamp support and blows to form start of tube or rod; holds pipe, while an assistant inserts metal bar into cylinder and pulls glass out to form tube or rod; if making tubing, continues to blow through pipe to maintain air cavity; cuts drawn tube or rod to length with cold file; places waste glass in cullet bin.

611.25 Glass tube bender (neon signs)

Heats and bends glass tubes to form letters or shapes for neon signs

Positions glass tube over actual size drawing of letter or shape and cuts off length required; marks position of bend on tube; holds tube over gas burner at point of bend, rotating the tube to ensure even distribution of heat; stops one end of tube and blows into other end to prevent glass from collapsing; bends tube, checking against drawing to ensure accuracy of shape; continues heating and bending until letter or shape is formed; positions and fuses electrodes in each end of tube.

May (01) perform tasks of NEON SIGN PUMPER (699.78)

(02) colour tubes by coating interior with luminescent powder.

611.30 Glass bench worker

Forms scientific and/or industrial glassware and components from tubing by heating, blowing and shaping at work bench

Heats glass tubing over flame until pliable turning glass to ensure even distribution of heat; blows tubing into required form; bends and shapes blown tubing with hand tools; fuses sections of tubing together to form articles or components; checks dimensions of finished work with callipers, verniers and micrometers.

May (01) perform tasks of GLASS LATHE WORKER (612.50)
(02) if forming thermometers, expel air from tube and draw in thermometer filling such as mercury.

Other titles include Lamp blower, Lamp worker, Quartz manipulator, Scientific glass blower, Tooler.

611.50 Footmaker

Partly forms glassware by blowing ready for further shaping and finishing by servitor and/or chairman

Gathers a quantity of molten glass from tank or pot on to blowpipe; rolls glass on iron table (marver) to form rough shape; inserts end of blowpipe with glass attached in neck of open mould on floor; operates pedal to close mould; blows through pipe to force glass to the shape of mould, spinning the pipe to ensure even distribution of the glass; opens mould, withdraws partly formed article from mould and passes to servitor or chairman for further shaping and finishing.

May (01) partly form article by mouth blowing.

Other titles include Footblower.

611.60 Glass bender

Bends flat glass by heating and moulding

Sets temperature controls of furnace; positions sheets of flat glass on prepared moulds; transfers moulds and glass to furnace; if working on large items, supports each end of glass sheet with angle iron and removes supports just before glass is ready to drop over mould; removes from furnace when glass has assumed the shape of moulds; transfers shaped glass to annealing kiln or deposits on conveyor belt to cool.

May (01) make moulds.

Other titles include Bent glass maker.

611.70 Piece opener

Forms lips and edges on glassware such as jugs and beakers

Heats mouth of glass article over flame turning the article to ensure even distribution of heat; reshapes and expands mouth of article using wooden prong and metal spatula; forms lip by pressing and levering the rim with a metal knife.

Other titles include Lipper.

611.98 Trainee

Performs, under instruction or guidance, various tasks including training exercises and as appropriate pursues studies in order to acquire the basic skills and knowledge required to perform the tasks of workers in glass shaping and forming occupations (hand) (excluding optical glass).

611.99 Other glass shaping and forming occupations (hand) (excluding optical glass)

Workers in this group form glassware by mouth and mould blowing and shape glassware, other than optical glass, by heating and working with hand tools and are not elsewhere classified.

Unit Group 612 Glass Shaping and Forming Occupations (Machine) (Excluding Optical Glass)

Workers in this unit group mould, cut, drill and otherwise form and shape glassware, other than optical glass, by machine.

612.10 Glass presser

Forms glassware by pressing molten glass in manually operated or automatic moulding presses

If working on manually operated press, positions plunging mechanism in press; lights gas jets to heat moulds; shears off correct amount of molten glass from gatherer's rod or ladle into mould; operates pedal or lever to lower plunger into mould; withdraws plunger when article has been formed and passes mould to knocker-out.

If working on semi-automatic press, shears off molten glass into mould; starts machine which presses the glassware automatically.

If working on fully automatic press, set valves to co-ordinate timing of plunger with rotation of turntable and regulates the flow of molten glass into the moulds; starts machine which presses the glassware automatically.

May (01) inspect pressed glassware for defects.

Other titles include Pressing machine operator.

612.20 Cut-off man (sheet glass)

Operates automatic machinery to cut to length a continuous sheet of vertically drawn glass

Sets cutters to score cutting line at specified intervals as glass passes from vertical drawing kiln or lehr; checks glass as it emerges from lehr for faults such as distortions, foreign bodies or cracks; notifies balcony man or tank operator of faults to be rectified; fixes mechanically operated suckers against glass; pulls glass away from machine breaking it along scored cutting line; transfers glass to breaking table for trimming; keeps record of quantity of glass passing through department.

May (01) direct carriers to remove glass from the machine and break off spoiled edges.

612.30 Glass tube maker (machine), Glass rod maker (machine)

Operates a machine to make glass tubes or rods

If operating horizontal drawing machine, operates drawing mechanism manually until glass drawn by muffleman from furnace over mandrel passes through into cutting mechanism; switches on power drive; adjusts drawing speed and checks that cutting mechanism and electronic inspection device are working correctly; checks dimensions of drawn tubes or rods and notifies muffleman if any adjustments are required to flow of glass or air.

If operating vertical drawing machine, tends machine which is in continuous operation; ensures that drawing proceeds correctly and adjusts controls as necessary to alter diameter of tubes; oils machine.

Other titles include Glass rod making machine operator, Glass tube making machine operator.

612.50 Glass lathe worker

Operates glass working lathe to shape and join glass components or articles

Positions glass components or article to be worked on lathe; adjusts flame on burner; starts motor and regulates rotation speed; turns handwheels to bring workpiece(s) into contact with flame; shapes, joins or smoothes the heated glass with hand tools and blowpipe attached to lathe; reduces heat gradually to anneal the workpiece; stops motor and removes finished workpiece from lathe.

612.55 Balcony man (vertical lehr)

Inspects sheet glass during vertical drawing process and rectifies faults

Checks sheet of glass passing through vertical annealing oven (lehr); notifies tank operator on floor below if adjustments are required to glass flow, mix or speed of rollers; rectifies faults such as cracks before they extend down to tank.

May (01) control rollers which grip edges of glass as it travels up through lehr.

612.60 Glass tube cutter

Cuts glass tubes or rods to length

Sets adjustable stop in cutting frame or grooved bench at the required distance from cutting wheel or file; positions length of tube or rod on frame or bench with one end against the gauge and the point to be cut opposite or over the cutting tool; if using electric cutter, sets wheel in motion; moves tube or rod against rotating wheel or backwards and forwards over file until glass is cut.

May (01) cut a number of tubes or rods simultaneously.

612.65 Glass driller

Drills holes in glassware or sheet or plate glass

Fixes appropriate drill bit(s) on machine; positions and secures glass or glassware on machine; starts machine to drill holes, drilling halfway through from each side as necessary; removes drilled glass and checks diameter of hole.

612.70 Automatic bottle making machine operator

Operates automatic machine to make bottles and other glass containers by blowing and/or pressing

Adjusts valves to control flow of molten glass to moulds; lubricates moulds periodically to prevent adhesion of glass; removes any damaged containers; makes a random selection of completed containers, checks weight and dimensions against specifications and adjusts machine controls as necessary; assists in changing dies and moulds.

612.75 Tank operator (flat glass)

Controls flow of molten glass from tank to drawing or rolling mechanism or float bath

Adjusts controls to regulate flow of glass and speed or tension of rollers to maintain desired width and thickness of glass; undertakes day-to-day maintenance of machinery.

Other titles include Cathedral maker, Cathedral operator, Drawer (sheet glass).

612.98 Trainee

Performs, under instruction or guidance, various tasks including training exercises and as appropriate pursues studies in order to acquire the basic skills and knowledge required to perform the tasks of glass shaping and forming occupations (machine) (excluding optical glass).

612.99 Other glass shaping and forming occupations (machine) (excluding optical glass)

Workers in this group mould, cut, drill and otherwise form and shape glassware, other than optical glass, by machine, and are not elsewhere classified, for example:

(01) **Bath operators (float glass)** (record and observe all changes in bath temperatures and atmospheric flow, making adjustments where necessary); (02) **Bottle making machine operators (semi-automatic);** (03) **Edge roller attendants (float glass)** (check flow of glass through edge rolling machines and make adjustments to remove foreign bodies from edges of glass); (04) **Flange making machine operators (electric lamp making)** (operate machines to form flanges on end of glass tubes); (05) **Mufflemen (glass tube making)** (control flow of molten glass from furnace over forming mandrel and attach start of glass tubing to drawing mechanism); (06) **Sealers (float glass)** (ensure bath is completely sealed to prevent any ingress of oxygen); (07) **Vitreous silica tube drawers,** Quartz tube drawers (redraw heated hollow silica or quartz billets to form tubing of required diameter).

Unit Group 613 Optical Glass Shaping, Forming and Finishing Occupations

Workers in this unit group mould, cut, grind and finish lenses, prisms and other optical glass products.

Excluded are Optical silverers (715.50) and Vacuum metallisation plant operators (715.55)

613.05 Moulder

Shapes optical glass lumps into rectangular slabs, prism blocks or lens blanks by heating, hand moulding and pressing

Clamps appropriately shaped mould on hydraulic press; lights furnace; adjusts furnace temperature to heat glass to desired state of plasticity and inserts piece of glass in furnace using tongs; shapes glass to approximate contour of mould using rod; transfers glass to press mould and operates press to mould glass to required shape and size; re-opens press and removes slab, prism block or lens blank from mould.

May (01) attend annealing furnace (591.90).

613.10 Optical slab grinder and polisher

Attends machines which grind, smooth and polish surfaces of annealed optical glass slabs

Sets glass slabs in circular bed of plaster of Paris; positions bed on grinding machine; starts machine to bring revolving grinding disc in contact with glass surface; stops grinding machine when all ridges have been removed from glass; removes or arranges removal of glass slab to smoothing machine by fork-lift truck; mixes abrasive paste for application to smoothing disc; starts smoothing machine; stops machine when surface of glass is smooth; removes or arranges removal of glass to polishing machine by fork-lift truck; dresses polishing disc with fine abrasive powder; starts polishing machine and observes glass periodically; stops machine when required finish has been obtained; turns slab over and re-sets in plaster of Paris bed; repeats grinding, smoothing and polishing operations on other surface.

613.15 Optical element worker (hand)

Grinds, smoothes and polishes optical lens or prism blanks to fine tolerances by manipulation against stationary or rotating tool

Selects appropriately shaped tool (lap) and places it in tool holder or machine head; dresses lens or prism blank or tool with abrasive as required; starts tool rotating, where necessary; manipulates blank against stationary or rotating tool; dresses blank or tool periodically with finer grade abrasive and continues grinding and smoothing until approximate curvature of lens or dimensions and angles of prism are obtained; finishes lens or prism in similar manner to measurements required, using rouge or other polishing agent; measures curvature with proof plate or spherometer, and prism faces and angles with micrometer and vernier during grinding, smoothing and polishing operations to ensure accuracy of both shape and dimensions of finished element.

May (01) test finished elements using equipment such as interferometers, goniometers or collimators.

Additional factor: finest limits to which accustomed

Other titles include Hand grinder and polisher.

613.20 Optical element smoother and polisher (machine)

Operates machine to smooth and polish blocked optical lenses, flats or prisms to proof plate standard

Selects appropriately shaped iron tool; positions tool and blocked elements in machine; sets controls to obtain degree of curvature or angles required; dresses surface of each optical element with coarse abrasive; starts machine to rotate block and oscillate tool over surfaces of elements; stops machine periodically to dress elements with finer grade abrasive and continues smoothing until approximate curvature or angles are obtained; washes smoothed elements in water; faces tool with felt pad or other polishing material and in similar manner finishes elements to measurements required, using rouge or other polishing agent; measures curvature with spherometer and angles with micrometer during smoothing and polishing operations to ensure accuracy of both shape and dimensions of finished elements; tests finished elements with interferometer.

May (01) block elements (619.99) before smoothing
(02) face smoothing tool with ceramic pieces embedded in beeswax or pitch to obtain shape required
(03) clean and oil machine.

613.25 Lens surfacing machine operator

Operates machines to grind, smooth and polish lens blanks to final finish according to ophthalmic prescription

Selects and fixes appropriately shaped tool on grinding machine; positions and secures blocked lens on tool; starts machine to rotate tool and grind lens, and directs flow of coolant; finishes grinding by oscillating lens over tool by hand; washes lens; fixes appropriate tool on smoothing machine; positions ground lens in holder and secures it on machine; lowers lens on tool; sets time switch and starts machine to rotate tool, oscillate lens over tool and feed tool with abrasive, or starts machine, applies abrasive to tool and oscillates lens over rotating tool using hand pressure; removes and washes lens when smoothing is complete; fixes appropriate tool on polishing machine; secures smoothed lens on machine; starts machine which automatically polishes lens using rouge as polishing agent; stops machine after specified time; removes and washes lens; examines lens visually for flaws;

continued

measures thickness and curvature of lens periodically during processes using optical callipers or gauge and spherometer.

May (01) cut lens to rough size before grinding, using trepanning machine
(02) grind blanks by hand
(03) set and operate glass milling machine (613.60)
(04) specialise in surfacing spherical or cylindrical lenses.

Other titles include Surfacer.

613.30 Smoother (ophthalmic prescription)

Operates one or more machines to smooth ground lens blanks according to ophthalmic prescription

Fixes smoothing tool, positions and secures lens, operates smoothing machine and examines and measures lens as described under LENS SURFACING MACHINE OPERATOR (613.25).

May (01) polish smoothed lenses (613.70)
(02) specialise in smoothing spherical or cylindrical lenses.

613.35 Hand glazer

Cuts ophthalmic stock lenses to required size and shape using hand cutter or hand-operated lens cutting machine

Places former or spectacle frame over lens, or fixes template of shape specified in prescription in machine; draws outline of former or inner rim frame on lens, or places lens in clamp on machine and aligns centre and axis markings of lens with those on clamp; cuts round drawn outline using hand cutter or hand operates machine to cut lens; trims off surplus glass using hand tool.

May (01) make metal former (772.99)
(02) perform hand edging tasks (613.40)
(03) perform lens fixing tasks (699.08)
(04) toughen lenses (591.90).

Other titles include Cutter (ophthalmic prescription), Edger glazer.

613.40 Hand edger

Levels and smoothes edges of ophthalmic lenses by manipulation against revolving wheel

Checks measurement of lens against prescription using optical ruler; manipulates edge against diamond impregnated, carborundum or gritstone wheel rotating in water until edge is ground to specifications; measures and inspects lens frequently during edging operation.

May (01) fix lens in metal-rimmed frame
(02) cut groove round sides and lower edge of lens to hold nylon cord.

613.50 Selector

Breaks up large lumps of optical glass and trims pieces to sizes suitable for moulding

Breaks up large lamp of optical glass with hammer, utilising existing cracks where possible; rubs hammer face along rough edges of glass to smooth off protrusions; trims pieces to sizes suitable for moulding using small hammer; chips out and discards defective parts.

May (01) weigh individual pieces of glass.

Other titles include Cutter (optical lumps).

613.55 Optical glass lump grinder

Grinds surfaces of optical glass lumps by manipulation against revolving wheel to expose defects

Presses each face of optical glass lump in turn against revolving carborundum grinding wheel until all surface flaws are readily visible; washes and examines surface frequently during grinding operation.

613.60 Glass milling machine setter-operator

Sets and operates machine to grind lens blanks to approximate curvature and thickness or blanks of prisms or flats to approximate size

Positions blocked blank(s) in machine holder; adjusts controls to obtain specified curvature and/or dimensions; starts flow of coolant; selects appropriate speed sequence and switches on machine which carries out grinding operation automatically; removes ground blank(s) from machine; checks curvature and/or dimensions of ground blank(s) as required using spherometer, gauges or micrometer.

May (01) block blank(s) before grinding (619.99)
(02) set and operate milling machine adapted to rough grind mirror edges
(03) specialise in grinding a particular type of lens, eg spherical or cylindrical.

Other titles include Generating machine setter-operator, Optical element rougher.

613.65 Smoother (ophthalmic stock)

Operates machines to smooth ground lens blanks to standard for ophthalmic stock

Places blocked ground lens blanks on spindles of smoothing machines; lowers tools on to lenses and starts machines; stops machines after specified time and removes and washes lenses.

613.70 Polisher (ophthalmic lenses)

Operates machines to polish smoothed ophthalmic lenses

Washes blocked smoothed lenses as necessary; places lenses on spindles of polishing machines; positions appropriately shaped polishing tools in machine holders; dresses lens surfaces with abrasive and starts machines or starts machines to rotate spindles and direct abrasive on to lenses; where appropriate, sprays water on to lenses after specified time and continues polishing action; removes lenses from machines after specified time; washes polished lenses.

May (01) examine surfaces of polished lenses using magnifying glass.

613.75 Centerer and edger (optical element)

Determines optical centre of optical lens and grinds edges at required radius from optical centre

Positions holder coated with hot wax or pitch on centring fixture and places lens on holder; adjusts position of lens until reflections of overhead light from both surfaces of lens remain stationary as holder is rotated on centring fixture; allows wax or pitch to set to retain lens in position; places holder containing centred lens in machine chuck and brings lens edge in contact with diamond impregnated grinding wheel; sets gauge for amount of glass to be removed; starts machine to rotate lens against revolving wheel(s) and directs flow of lubricant; stops machine when requisite amount of glass has been removed; checks lens diameter with micrometer or vernier callipers.

May (01) chamfer edge after grinding by holding shaped tool against edge of revolving lens.

613.80 Machine glazer and edger

Sets and attends several machines which automatically cut ophthalmic stock lenses to required shape and size and bevel edges

Positions lens in clamp and fixes clamp on machine; fits former of required shape and size on machine; sets machine dial according to size of former; starts machine which automatically stops when cutting and bevelling is completed; removes and wipes lens.

Additional factor: number of machines attended.

Other titles include Auto-edging machine operator.

613.90 Remoulder

Shapes optical glass squares into lens blanks by heating and remoulding in press

Passes glass squares through a series of thermostatically controlled heaters, using tongs to convey glass between heaters; flicks glass from final heater with rod and transfers it by tongs to press mould; lowers ram of press to mould glass to desired shape and size; removes lens blank from mould with tongs.

613.91 Optical slab cutter

Cuts optical glass slabs by hand into specified shapes and sizes

Positions templates on optical glass slab avoiding imperfections marked by inspector; positions T-square where cut is to be made; rubs rag moistened with paraffin along line of cut; scores glass with hand wheel cutter; places small object, such as handle of cutter, under the scored line and presses gently on either side of score to break glass along scored line.

613.92 Optical glass cutter

Cuts optical glass into slices of required dimensions or thickness for optical element making using diamond impregnated saw

Clamps optical glass in position over edge of work-table, or attaches optical glass with pitch or beeswax to metal plate or plate glass sheet fixed to metal plate; places plate on magnetic chuck of cutting machine; operates controls to rotate saw wheel and bring optical glass and saw together to cut glass according to markings.

May (01) mark cutting line.

Other titles include Slitter.

613.93 Rougher (hand)

Grinds lens blanks to approximate curvature and thickness or blanks of prisms or flats to approximate size by manipulation against revolving tool

Places appropriately shaped grinding tool (lap) in holder and fits holder on to machine spindle; starts spindle revolving; dresses lap with abrasive, where necessary; manipulates blank against revolving lap; stops spindle when approximate size and/or curvature has been obtained; washes ground blank; examines ground blank visually for imperfections and checks measurements with gauges, callipers or micrometer.

613.94 Roughing machine attendant

Attends one or more preset machines which grind lens blanks to approximate curvature and thickness or blanks of prisms or flats to approximate size

Positions blank in holder and mounts holder on machine spindle; moves control until surface of blank is in contact with grinding tool; starts flow of coolant; switches on machine which automatically carries out grinding operation; stops machine after prescribed time, where necessary; removes ground blank from machine spindle and rinses in water; test checks measurements of ground blanks periodically, using preset callipers or lens gauge, and reports inaccuracies to foreman.

May (01) specialise in grinding particular type of lens, eg spherical or cylindrical.

Additional factor: number of machines and spindles attended.

Other titles include Generating machine attendant, Optical element rougher.

613.95 Optical element smoother (machine)

Operates battery of machines to smooth blocked optical lenses, flats or prisms ready for polishing

Ascertains amount of glass to be removed from optical elements using gauge or micrometer and adjusts machine settings accordingly; positions block on machine; adjusts pressure of pads on block; starts machine to rotate block in pan of abrasive liquid and oscillate smoothing pads over surface of elements; stops machine after specified time and removes block; washes block to remove abrasive and checks elements with template; replaces block on machine and continues smoothing if required standard has not been reached; prepares abrasive liquid and refills pan as necessary.

May (01) block elements before smoothing (619.99)
(02) polish elements (613.96).

Additional factor: number of machines operated.

613.96 Optical element polisher (machine)

Operates battery of machines to polish blocked optical lenses, flats or prisms to proof plate standard

Positions block of optical elements on machine; adjusts pressure of polishing pads on block; positions pan of rouge in which block rotates; starts machine to rotate block and oscillate pads over surface of elements; stops machine after specified time and removes block; washes block to remove rouge; refills pan with rouge and water and replaces pads as necessary.

May (01) test polished elements with proof plate or interferometer
(02) adjust machine settings.

Additional factor: number of machines operated.

613.98 Trainee

Performs, under instruction or guidance, various tasks including training exercises and as appropriate pursues studies in order to acquire the basic skills and knowledge required to perform the tasks of workers in optical glass shaping, forming and finishing occupations.

613.99 Other optical glass shaping, forming and finishing occupations

Workers in this group mould, cut, grind and finish lenses, prisms and other optical glass products and are not elsewhere classified, for example:

(01) **Centring and edging machine operators (optical elements)** (operate one or more machines to centre optical lenses by mechanical pressure and to grind edges at required radius from centre); (02) **Optical glass trimmers** (trim rejected glass to size suitable for remoulding).

Unit Group 614 Glass Finishing Occupations (Excluding Optical Glass and Painting)

Workers in this unit group remove surplus glass from glassware, finish glassware by grinding and polishing edges and surfaces, mark out guide lines for decorative cutting of glassware and decorate glassware by cutting, acid etching and sandblasting.

614.05 Decorative cutter (manual)

Cuts freehand or marked patterns on glassware by manipulation against rotating wheels

Ascertains design to be cut from master pattern, drawing, sample or instructions; selects appropriate cutting wheel of aloxite, carborundum, copper or other material of required width and diameter; mounts wheel on machine, starts machine and regulates speed of wheel; holds and manipulates workpiece against edge of rotating wheel to cut pattern freehand or following markings; continues until desired pattern is complete; changes wheels to make cuts of different depths and lengths; uses sling balance to hold workpiece when cutting patterns on large articles.

May (01) mark out patterns on glassware
(02) polish cut glass using wooden or felt wheels and pumice powder or rouge
(03) mould clay to inside of workpiece to prevent shattering during cutting.

Other titles include Glass engraver.

Excluded are Cutters (hand wheel) (glass decorating) (614.60)

614.10 Acid embosser (glass decorating)

Traces and cuts pattern on coating on glass surface and etches exposed glass with acid

Ensures that glass surface to be treated is clean; coats or covers surface using material such as acid resistant black paint, wax or lead foil; traces pattern on covered surface; cuts round tracing outline with knife to expose on glass surface the pattern to be etched; either forms wall of wax or tallow around sides of prepared glass surface and pours acid solution over the surface of the glass or immerses prepared glass in bath of acid solution; leaves for period to etch exposed glass then pours off acid or removes glass from bath; rinses etched glass in cold water to remove all trace of acid; removes protective coating from glass surface.

May (01) trace and cut pattern on masking tape on glass surface ready for sandblasting (614.15)
(02) colour designs by hand or using spray gun.

Other titles include Acid etcher.

614.15 Abrasive etcher (glass decorating)

Traces and cuts pattern on masking tape on glass surface and etches exposed glass with abrasive powder

Ensures that glass surface to be treated is clean; covers surface with masking tape; traces pattern on covered surface; cuts round traced outline with knife and exposes on glass surface the pattern for blasting; positions glass and manipulates compressed air gun to direct jet of abrasive powder against exposed glass surface to cut pattern; removes masking tape and cleans glass.

614.20 Edge finisher (flat glass)

Shapes and smoothes the edges of flat glass by manipulation against grinding and polishing wheels

Selects and mounts appropriate wheel of sandstone, carborundum, steel, wood, felt or other material according to finish required, for example, rough grind, bevel, polish; where appropriate dresses wheel with abrasive compound for grinding or with powder for polishing; starts wheel and holds and turns edge of glass against revolving wheel until the required shape and finish are obtained.

May (01) drill holes in glass (612.65).

614.25 Surface polisher (flat glass)

Polishes surface of flat glass by machine

Places glass on felt covered table of polishing machine; turns on compressed air to hold glass in position by suction; covers glass with liquid or powdered rouge; starts machine to lower felt polishing heads on to glass and polish the surface; examines polished glass for defects.

May (01) apply pressure to polishing head by hand.

Other titles include Scratch polisher.

614.50 Badger (glass decorating)

Takes design impressions from copper plates and transfers and etches on to glassware or etches designs by applying rubber stamp bearing acid medium

If using plate with design engraved in relief, spreads acid resistant ink over plate; scrapes ink off design area leaving it only in background of plate; positions transfer paper on plate and presses between rollers to take impression from plate; presses transfer on to glassware and peels off paper leaving ink impression as acid resistant stencil; extends acid resistant area by painting round transfer with bitumen paint; brushes viscous acid solution over glassware and leaves on for specified time; cleans off acid, acid resistant ink and bitumen paint.
If using plate with design cut into it, applies acid medium to plate; wipes acid off surface of plate, leaving it only in design area; takes impression of design on transfer paper; presses transfer on to glassware and peels off paper leaving coating of acid in design area; washes off acid after specified time.
If using rubber stamp of design, presses stamp on acid pad; applies stamp to glassware; washes off acid after specified time.

614.55 Marker-out (glass decorating)

Marks out straight cutting or dividing guide lines for design to be cut on glassware

Examines drawing or sample of pattern to determine number of cuts to be made; marks horizontal cutting or dividing lines by revolving article against a fixed crayon or wax pencil, or by calculating position with dividers and marking freehand; marks vertical or angled cutting or dividing lines by marking dots in paint at appropriate intervals round top or base of articles and joining dots using straight-edge as guide.

614.60 Cutter (hand wheel) (glass decorating)

Cuts simple curved and straight line patterns on glassware with powered hand wheel cutter

Studies sample pattern; holds glass article in one hand and with the other manipulates powered cutting tool so that the rotating aloxite wheel cuts lines on the surface to match sample; places decorated article in container.

614.65 Hand grinder

Manipulates glassware against rotating wheels and/or continuous belts to smooth, polish, or grind to size

Selects and mounts appropriate wheel or belt of steel, carborundum or other material; where appropriate dresses wheel or belt with abrasive compound or spreads compound or polishing powder on surface of glass; starts motor and holds and turns the edge or surface of the glass against the wheel or belt until the required finish is obtained or the specified amount of glass has been ground away.

May (01) check work during grinding using gauge.

614.70 Machine grinder

Grinds glassware to shape and size by machine

Positions glassware to be ground on machine; applies appropriate abrasive compound to grinding tool on machine or to article; starts machine to bring tool into contact with the article and grind glass from surface; checks size of article visually and with gauges to ensure that the finished article conforms to specifications.

May (01) set up machine.

614.75 Acid polisher (glass)

Immerses glassware in acid to impart a polish

Fills acid and water tanks; turns on steam or electricity to heat both tanks; loads glassware into metal baskets and immerses in acid for specified time; removes baskets and immerses in water tank to rinse off acid.

May (01) prepare acid solution according to instructions.

614.80 Burner-off, Cracker-off

Removes surplus glass from glassware by burning or breaking off

(01) **Burner-off**
Positions and secures glass article(s) in chuck(s) of machine; ignites burners and adjusts flame to maintain required temperature; starts machine to rotate rim of article in flame and burn off (melt) the surplus glass; removes finished article from machine and leaves to cool.

(02) **Cracker-off**
Positions glass article in machine; sets and operates cutters to score a cutting line inside or outside the article; applies heat to the cutting line and breaks off the surplus glass.

May (03) split blown globe to form two articles.

614.90 Pattern cutting machine operator (glass decorating)

Operates a preset machine to cut a pattern on glassware

Positions glassware in rubber chuck on machine and secures by depressing pedal; starts machine to cut pattern on glass article; when cutting is complete releases article from chuck; examines patterned article and places in appropriate container.

614.91 Sandblasting machine operator (glass decorating)

Operates sandblasting equipment to frost, make holes or stencil marks in glassware surfaces

Loads blasting cabinet with glassware for frosting or hole making; depresses pedal to start jet of abrasive powder; manipulates each article in abrasive jet until frosting process is complete or holes have been made; releases pedal to stop jet flow; unloads and examines processed glassware; if frosting is not to specification, repeats process until required finish is obtained.
If stencilling glassware, places article in position behind appropriate stencil in machine; depresses pedal and directs jet of abrasive powder on to stencil to cut glass surface.
Replenishes abrasive powder as necessary; cleans equipment and work area.

See Sandblaster (pottery) (622.20) and Shot blaster (metal) (726.92)

614.92 Acid bath attendant (glass frosting)

Immerses glassware in acid to produce a frosted finish

Ensures that bath contains sufficient acid; secures glassware on holding trays and loads trays to capacity; positions and secures trays so that the glassware is immersed in acid bath to required depth; removes trays when frosting process is complete; directs water jet on to frosted glassware to remove surplus acid; places articles on conveyor.

May (01) weigh, measure and mix chemicals and dilute acids according to formula

(02) assist in packing the finished product.

614.93 Fire polisher (glassware), Melter (glassware)

Imparts a smooth finish to the surface and edges of glassware by heating

Positions glassware on wheel, conveyor or asbestos tray; starts wheel or conveyor which carries glassware between jets of flame or places tray in small furnace (glory hole) to melt glass slightly and form a smooth glazed surface or edge; removes glassware for inspection and annealing.

614.98 Trainee

Performs, under instruction or guidance, various tasks including training exercises and as appropriate pursues studies in order to acquire the basic skills and knowledge required to perform the tasks of workers in glass finishing occupations (excluding optical glass and painting).

614.99 Other glass finishing occupations (excluding optical glass and painting)

Workers in this group remove surplus glass from glassware, finish glassware by grinding and polishing edges and surfaces, mark out guidelines for decorative cutting of glassware and decorate glassware by cutting, acid etching and sandblasting and are not elsewhere classified.

Unit Group 619 Glass Working Occupations Not Elsewhere Classified

Workers in this unit group perform miscellaneous tasks in the working of glass including locating and marking centres and axes on ophthalmic lenses, gathering molten glass for blowing and pressing and performing tasks in the manufacture of glass fibre tissue, wool and filament and are not elsewhere classified.

619 .10 Lens marker-up (ophthalmic prescription)

Locates and marks optical centres and axes on ground ophthalmic lenses to guide workers in cutting, edging and fixing

Studies prescription for lens specification; selects suitable lens and checks for surface defects; positions lens in holding fixture of focimeter, sets focimeter according to requirements of prescription and adjusts position of lens until target appears in focus; checks lens power reading on instrument against prescription; operates attachment to focimeter to mark dots on lens indicating optical centre and axis; transfers lens to protractor meter; aligns lens markings with appropriate gradation on meter scale according to prescription; presses attachment to mark line on lens surface to indicate positioning of lens in frame; removes lens from meter.

May (01) specialise on particular type of lens, eg spherical or toric.

Other titles include Centerer (ophthalmic lens), Lens setter, Optical mechanic.

619 .20 Rimless driller and fitter (spectacles)

Drills lenses and assembles rimless spectacles

Positions bridge mount over lenses and marks position of joins with ink; marks inked points slightly with diamond drill and checks position against mount; drills holes at marked points, drilling halfway through from each side of lens; enlarges holes with hand tools; makes similar holes at outer corner of lenses for attachment of side pieces; screws mount on to lenses; attaches frame arms to mount or screws directly on to lenses.

619 .30 Glass cutter (flat glass)

Cuts flat glass to size and shape

Places glass to be cut on padded table; positions template on glass or measures and marks glass for cutting to required size and shape, avoiding flaws; scores glass with a hand wheel cutter or diamond cutting tool, using template or markings and straight-edge as guide; breaks away scored glass by hand or with pliers; places waste glass in cullet bin.

May (01) operate machine which cuts glass to shape automatically.

619 .50 Gatherer (glass making)

Gathers molten glass from furnace preparatory to blowing or pressing

Gathers molten glass from furnace or tank on blow-pipe or gathering rod or in ladle; deposits glass on partly formed articles as instructed by chairman or servitor or places in mould for blowing or pressing.

May (01) partly form articles by rolling to rough shape on iron table (marver) and/or blowing

(02) form hollow glass balls by blowing and shaping in wooden moulds.

Other titles include Ball gatherer, Ball maker, Ladler, Punty sticker.

619 .55 Laminated glass worker

Performs various tasks in the manufacture of laminated glass sheets or blocks

Performs one or more of the following tasks: cleans surface of glass sheet with acetate solution or in washing machine; feeds vinal interlay material through washing plant to reduce pliability; cuts vinal or other interlay material to required size; places interlay on sheet of glass and positions matching sheet of glass on top; expels air from glass and interlay assembly and presses it together by vacuum method or by feeding through rollers; places laminated sheets on conveyor to carry them through oven or heated tunnel where they are plasticised and made transparent; builds up alternate layers of glass and interlay to form blocks which are bound together by heat and pressure in autoclave; trims off excess interlay from edges of sheets or blocks; sprays edges of laminated blocks with aluminium paint and polishes surfaces.

Other titles include Glass washing machine operator, Laminator, Process worker, Trimmer, Vinal washing plant operator.

619 .60 Plant operator (glass fibre tissue)

Operates plant to form glass fibre tissue from molten glass

Tends furnace in which raw ingredients (frit) or broken glass (cullet) are melted; adjusts controls to set temperature of bushings from which molten glass is extruded; adjusts steam jets which break up extruded fibres as they fall into forming hood; adjusts spray to spray binder liquid on fibres which fall on collecting belt to form a fine tissue; ensures that an adequate supply of binder liquid is maintained in storage tank; alters width of tissue mat as required by adjusting sides of forming hood.

May (01) operate plant in which tissue mat is cured.

619 .65 Sprayman operator (glass fibre wool plant)

Operates plant to form glass fibre wool from molten glass

Adjusts temperature of electric coil which heats base of rotating perforated metal dish from which molten glass is thrown by centrifugal force to form fibres; operates valves to feed appropriate binder liquid to spray nozzles according to rigidity of fibre required; controls distribution of fibres forming wool mat on conveyor belt by adjusting distributor air jets; alters width of wool mat by adjusting sides of forming hood; periodically checks diameter of fibres by weighing and measuring resistance to air pressure.

619 .70 Plant operator (continuous glass fibre filament)

Operates plant to form continuous glass fibre filament from molten glass

Carries out a combination of the following tasks: tends furnace in which raw ingredients (frit), broken glass (cullet) or glass marbles are melted; gathers filaments of molten glass extruded from bushings at base of furnace with rod to form strands of required thickness; pulls strands downwards to pass over a roller fed with emulsion and guides through pull rolls; winds strands on to paperboard cylinder on winding machine; breaks strand when required weight has been wound and removes cylinder from winder; fits empty cylinder on winder; clears obstructions from bushing tips.

619 .75 Plant operator (chopped glass fibre mat)

Operates plant to form matting from glass fibre filament

Operates valves to feed binder liquid from mixing tank to feeder tank and from feeder tank to sprays; adjusts pressure of binder liquid spray outlets; loads cakes of glass fibre filament on plant and feeds ends into choppers; starts plant to take strands through choppers and binder spray to form matting and through curing ovens and cooling rollers; adjusts speed of conveyors as necessary.

619 .90 Knocker-off (lens)

Removes lens blanks from metal or wooden blocks after grinding and polishing

Immerses tray of metal blocks in heated chemical solution to melt block, or prises blanks from wooden blocks with hand tools; washes lenses in water to clean off chemical solution or removes any wax or pitch sticking to lenses; keeps records of number and type of lenses removed from blocks.

May (01) remove lens blanks from pitch block by cooling in refrigerating tank and breaking up block.

619 .92 Breaker-off (sheet glass)

Breaks off spoiled edges from glass sheets

Positions sheet of glass on breaking board; aligns cutting line made by glass cutting machine with straight-edge of board; applies hand pressure to break off edges; places waste edges in pit of breaking board for reprocessing.

619 .98 Trainee

Performs, under instruction or guidance, various tasks including training exercises and as appropriate pursues studies in order to acquire the basic skills and knowledge required to perform the tasks of workers in glass working occupations not elsewhere classified.

619 .99 Other glass working occupations not elsewhere classified

Workers in this group perform miscellaneous tasks in the working of glass and are not separately classified, for example:

(01) **Artificial eye makers (glass);** (02) **Glass bulb/valve coating machine attendants** (tend automatic equipment to coat glass bulbs or valves with chemical solution, paint or lacquer to impart or improve reflective qualities); (03) **Knockers-off (glass blowing)** (remove completed glassware from blowpipes); (04) **Knockers-out** (remove pressed glassware from moulds); (05) **Lens blockers,** Optical element blockers (mount lenses, prisms, etc on block holders preparatory to grinding, smoothing and polishing); (06) **Liners (lenses)** (join dots marked on lenses by lens markers-up); (07) **Mosaic cutters** (cut or break up glass mosaic materials into small squares or other shapes and fix shapes on sheets of adhesive paper to form mosaic squares); (08) **Notchers** (form lugs on glassware by machine moulding); (09) **Pitchers and malletters** (cover lenses with pitch before blocking); (10) **Post boys** (assist glass tube makers (hand drawing)); (11) **Sealers (double glazing units);** (12) **Sealers (valves, lamps) (non-automatic)** (operate non-automatic machines to seal valve or lamp assemblies into bulbs); (13) **Takers-out (automatic bottle-making machines)** (remove formed bottles from machine moulds); (14) **Welders (double glazing units)** (fuse sheets of glass together in furnace); (15) **Wire boys** (place rolls of wire netting on trays which feed wire into plate or sheet glass as it is rolled).

Minor Group 62 CLAY AND STONE WORKING OCCUPATIONS

Workers in this minor group form and finish ceramic goods, other than by glazing and decorating, form and finish concrete, asbestos-cement, abrasive stone and related products, cut, shape and polish natural stone for building and similar purposes and perform related tasks.

The occupations are arranged in the following unit groups:

620 Foremen (Clay and Stone Working Occupations)

621 Ceramic Goods Forming Occupations

622 Ceramic Goods Finishing Occupations (Excluding Glazers and Decorators)

623 Concrete, Asbestos-Cement, Abrasive Stone and Related Products Making Occupations

624 Stone Cutting, Shaping and Polishing Occupations

629 Clay and Stone Working Occupations Not Elsewhere Classified

Excluded are kiln operators, mixers and workers making asbestos-cement sheets and pipes (59)

Unit Group 620 Foremen (Clay and Stone Working Occupations)

Workers in this unit group directly supervise and co-ordinate the activities of workers in clay and stone working occupations.

620.10 Foreman (ceramic goods forming occupations)

Directly supervises and co-ordinates the activities of workers forming ceramic goods

Performs appropriate tasks as described under SUPERVISOR/FOREMAN (UNSPECIFIED) (990.00).

Additional factors: number of workers supervised; type of product to which accustomed, eg bricks and tiles, refractory goods, sanitary ware, electrical porcelain, domestic pottery.

620.20 Foreman (ceramic goods finishing occupations (excluding glazers and decorators))

Directly supervises and co-ordinates the activities of workers finishing ceramic goods, other than glazers and decorators

Performs appropriate tasks as described under SUPERVISOR/FOREMAN (UNSPECIFIED) (990.00).

May (01) keep stock record of pottery in warehouse

(02) inspect and price articles for the calculation of piecework earnings

(03) supervise the packing and dispatch of pottery goods.

Additional factor: number of workers supervised.

Other titles include Biscuit warehouseman (pottery), Enamel warehouseman (pottery), Glost warehouseman (pottery).

620 .30 Foreman (concrete, asbestos-cement, abrasive stone and related products making occupations)

Directly supervises and co-ordinates the activities of workers engaged in making concrete, asbestos-cement, abrasive stone and related products

Performs appropriate tasks as described under SUPERVISOR/FOREMAN (UNSPECIFIED) (990 .00).

May (01) supervise workers making wooden moulds for concrete products.

Additional factor: number of workers supervised.

620 .40 Foreman (stone cutting, shaping and polishing occupations)

Directly supervises and co-ordinates the activities of workers cutting, shaping and polishing stone

Performs appropriate tasks as described under SUPERVISOR/FOREMAN (UNSPECIFIED) (990 .00).

May (01) advise customers on designs for memorial stones

(02) prepare templates for monumental masons or stone carvers.

Additional factor: number of workers supervised.

620 .98 Trainee

Performs, under instruction or guidance, various tasks including training exercises and as appropriate pursues studies in order to acquire the basic skills and knowledge required to perform the tasks of foremen (clay and stone working occupations).

620 .99 Other foremen (clay and stone working occupations)

Workers in this group directly supervise and co-ordinate the activities of workers in clay and stone working occupations and are not elsewhere classified.

Unit Group 621 Ceramic Goods Forming Occupations

Workers in this unit group form pottery, earthenware, refractory goods, clay bricks and tiles and similar products by casting, moulding, pressing, extruding, cutting and shaping.

621 .02 Modeller (pottery, porcelain)

Makes models of pottery or porcelain articles to specifications for use in preparing moulds

Ascertains job requirements from photographs, drawings and/or other specifications; makes freehand trial model using block of moulding clay or plaster of Paris; forms model by hand, using sculpting, measuring and other special purpose tools, potter's wheel and lathe; checks model for symmetrical accuracy using callipers or other measuring aids; marks lines on model for guidance of plaster mould maker.

May (01) create designs

(02) prepare detailed drawings of article to be moulded

(03) specialise in modelling a particular type of product.

621.04 Plaster mould maker

Makes plaster of Paris moulds for use in the casting of pottery and other ceramic goods

Receives model marked with lines to indicate sections in which article is to be cast; covers all but one section of model with clay coating; supports model in framework of linoleum or clay-covered plaster sheets; paints uncovered section of model with sizing solution, makes a thin mix of plaster of Paris and water and pours over model to fill framework; when plaster has set dismantles framework and removes casting; changes position of model and repeats process in turn for each section of model to complete casting of block mould sections; coats block mould sections with size and prepares castings framework to form case mould sections; fits sections of case mould together to form replica of model and adds interlock location guides; dismantles case mould into sections, coats each section with size and repeats casting as described above to produce sections of working mould; trims and fettles exterior of each section of working mould; prepares additional working moulds from case mould as necessary.

May (01) use framework of preformed metal sleeve when making case moulds
(02) check dimensions of mould with gauge
(03) fit metal reinforcements to moulds to be incorporated in castings.

Excluded are Moulders and coremakers (plaster cast process) (foundry) (713.54)

621.06 Thrower (pottery, porcelain)

Forms clay into hollow ware pottery or porcelain goods by hand on thrower's wheel

Starts thrower's wheel (horizontal disc) rotating; throws ball of clay on to wheel; manipulates clay by hand to form squat cylindrical shape or positions on wheel clay piece roughly shaped by thrower's assistant; presses thumbs into centre of rotating clay shape to hollow interior and to raise wall; gradually shapes article and thins wall by hand and finger manipulation; where appropriate inserts hand reamer to shape inside of article; checks size and symmetrical accuracy of formed piece using callipers, template or other measuring aids; smoothes surface of shaped piece using scraper and wet sponge; moistens hands as required and controls rotation speed of wheel during forming process; pulls or directs pulling of bow wire across surface of wheel to separate formed article from wheel.

May (01) knead raw clay, adding water as necessary, to produce clay of required consistency and plasticity
(02) set pointers beside wheel to indicate diameter, curvature and height of finished article.

621.08 Hand turner (pottery, stoneware)

Manipulates cutting tools against rotating workpiece to shape, trim and polish unfired pieces of cast or moulded pottery or stoneware to specifications

Ascertains job requirements from photographs, drawings and/or other specifications; sets up lathe with chuck or jigger head and secures workpiece on machine; starts machine and manipulates edge of cutting tool against revolving workpiece; changes cutting tools and varies speed of lathe as required; checks accuracy of work using callipers, templates or other measuring aids.

May (01) sharpen cutting tools
(02) use thrower's wheel for vertical turning
(03) mould pottery pieces ready for turning
(04) specialise in turning porcelain for insulators or switchgear.

621.10 Jollier, Jiggerer

Manipulates profile tool against clay in or on mould to form pottery, porcelain or stoneware goods

Selects plaster mould of article to be formed and profile tool; positions mould on turn-table (jigger head) and secures profile tool to jolley arm.
If forming hollow ware such as jugs, cups or vases, places ball or disc of clay inside mould and presses clay to shape external surface of article; starts rotation of jigger head and brings profile tool in contact with clay in rotating mould; regulates rotation speed of jigger head and manipulates profile tool against clay to shape interior of article.
If forming flat ware such as dishes, plates or saucers, presses clay on inverted mould, starts rotation of jigger head and manipulates profile tool on clay to produce required shape.
Removes surplus clay from rim of article using knife or similar hand tool; applies damp sponge to surface of article, as necessary, to assist shaping of clay; removes formed article with mould from jigger head.

May (01) shape or cut discs from balls of clay using separate jigger head or from rolls of clay using guillotine cutter
(02) change profile tools to form flanges or cut grooves in surface of article
(03) check thickness of article and accuracy of forming using instruments such as callipers and ruler, or adjust stop on jolley arm to specified thickness.

Other titles include Bowl maker, Flat jiggerer, Jar maker.

621.12 Glasshouse pot maker

Forms clay by hand into fireclay pots for use in the melting of glass

Rolls prepared clay and presses on base-board by hand to form base of pot of specified thickness; allows base to dry naturally for specified period; builds up wall of pot on base by stages, manipulating clay to shape and thickness specified; smoothes surfaces of part-formed pot using pallette knife and rubber pad; allows wall to dry naturally; manually forms crown or dome on wall closing in upper area of pot and adding clay layer by layer to required thickness; cuts mouth aperture in crown and builds up mouth to specified shape by hand; smoothes surface and edges of formed pot; directs removal of pot to drying room and examines maturing of pot at intervals during drying period.

May (01) soak, mill or otherwise prepare clay
(02) use former to assist in shaping wall or crown
(03) cover base or wall with polythene sheet during drying periods to ensure slow drying
(04) form hood or cap for pot in wooden mould and fit to pot
(05) stencil identification marks on formed pot
(06) make ancillary kiln equipment such as pot doors or collars
(07) instal pot in furnace.

621.14 Saggar maker (hand)

Builds up unfired formed or part-formed fireclay components by hand to make saggars

Places unfired saggar bottom on turn-table and positions wall former centrally on saggar bottom; positions side strip with canvas backing around former on saggar bottom; removes canvas backing from side strip; joins ends of strip and joins edge of strip to saggar bottom, kneading clay with wet fingers and wooden tools, while saggar rotates on turn-table; removes former and examines quality of jointing; smoothes surfaces of saggar with damp sponge and checks height of sides with depth gauge.

May (01) perform tasks of BOTTOM KNOCKER (621.99)
(02) perform tasks of FRAME FILLER (621.99).

621.16 Hand presser (pottery), Hand moulder (stoneware, refractory goods)

Presses plasticised clay in or over mould by hand to form pottery, stoneware or refractory goods

Selects plaster, metal, wood or metal-lined wooden mould according to type of article to be formed; wipes mould surface with damp or oil-impregnated cloth, or dusts mould surface with French chalk or sand; where appropriate fits inserts to mould; cuts clay piece from block and kneads to malleable consistency or beats to sheet of required thickness; places clay in or over mould; presses clay to conform to contours of mould, ensuring that no air remains in clay or between clay and mould; trims excess clay from mould with knife or bow wire; inverts mould after specified drying time and removes article and any mould inserts.

May (01) use pneumatic hammer to compress clay in mould
(02) form hollow ware in sectionalised mould, progressively building up component parts in mould sections and joining parts by hand to form complete article
(03) smooth exposed surface of article with rubber pad or wet sponge prior to or during drying out
(04) dress surface of article with knife before firing.

Other titles include Faience moulder, Odd stuff maker (refractory goods), Presser (stoneware).

Excluded are Hand moulders (bricks, roofing tiles) (621.56)

621.18 Caster (pottery, refractory)

Pours liquid clay into moulds to form pottery and refractory goods or components

Examines sections of mould for cleanliness and assembles to form complete mould; fills mould with liquid clay (slip) from feed hose or container, agitating mould as necessary to ensure that slip settles; pours excess slip into recovery drain after specified drying period or when article or component has formed to thickness required; allows casting to dry for further period, dismantles mould and removes casting; trims surface imperfections from casting with fettling knife and smoothes surface with damp sponge or rubber pad.

May (01) dust mould with powder, for example chalk dust or powdered burned clay, before casting
(02) punch or cut holes in partially dry castings.

Other titles include Handle caster, Slip caster, Spout caster.

621.20 Caster (plaster)

Pours plaster into moulds to form figures, souvenirs, novelties or similar goods

Selects suitable plastic or wooden mould; if using sectionalised mould assembles sections and secures assembly with clamps; fills mould with plaster mix using trowel and agitates mould to eliminate air and compact mix; smoothes surface of mix with pallette knife; after specified drying period removes article from mould, dismantling mould sections as necessary; cleans mould and tools.

May (01) prepare plaster mix.

Excluded are Assemblers and casters (plaster cast process) (foundry) (713.56)

621.22 Crucible maker (machine)

Operates machine to form crucibles from fireclay, plumbago or other refractory mix

Secures tapered pan (cup) to machine turn-table and fits appropriate former to machine; sets stops or template to control movement of former; lubricates inside surfaces of mould sections, or lines mould sections with cloth; assembles and secures mould sections on cup and shovels specified quantity of refractory mix into mould, or encloses mix on board with mould sections, secures filled mould and lifts or assists with lifting filled mould into position on cup; starts turn-table rotating and operates controls to lower former into mould to press mix to required shape against interior of mould; periodically checks internal dimensions of formed crucible with measuring rods; cuts excess mix from lip of mould; stops turn-table when shaping is complete; dismantles mould to release formed crucible.

May (01) preheat mould by immersion in hot water
(02) smooth surface of formed crucible with scraping knife and/or wet sponge
(03) paint dried crucible with glazing liquid
(04) set glazed crucible in firing kiln.

621.24 Brick maker (machine)

Sets and operates automatic or semi-automatic wire-cut brick making machine

Sets spacing of cutting wires according to size of bricks; sets water feed regulator to produce clay mix of specified consistency; fits suitable die to extrusion press; checks positioning of take-off rollers or conveyor; operates switches to start machine and release flow of water; watches operation and assumes manual control if fault develops.

May (01) replace cutter wires, extrusion dies or conveyor parts as necessary.

621.26 Sanitary mason

Fits and assembles standard sanitary furnishings to form a single unit ready for wall fixing

Measures and marks each item of unit according to specifications; positions and secures item on bed of machine-saw; sets and operates saw to cut item to size; positions sawn items on fitting bench in correct sequence to build up unit; drills fixing holes using portable power drill; checks assembly for accuracy of fit and overall measurement; removes any unevenness from sides or bottom of unit using hammer and chisel and smoothes surface using powered grinding tool; numbers each item according to position in unit to facilitate erection on site; dismantles assembly ready for packing.

May (01) operate power hoist to move heavy items.

621.28 Furnace moulder

Makes moulds of dry loose plaster on floor of glass furnace for use in bending glass

Makes mound of dry burned plaster on floor of furnace; moulds plaster to shape to which glass is to be bent, using template and trowel; positions metal reinforcements within plaster as necessary; positions steel bars to frame and support plaster, and anchors frame with weights; uses float to smooth surface of plaster; dismantles mould after completion of glass bending and recovers plaster and accessories for re-use.

621.50 Ornamenter (pottery, porcelain)

Forms by hand flowers and similar ornamental accessories for pottery and porcelain articles

Kneads and rolls clay until pliable; flattens small quantities of clay on work-bench and presses it by hand into required thickness; cuts out required shape with small knife and forms each part with fingers and modelling tool; assembles parts to form flower or other decoration, pressing joints with fingers or modelling tool; trims off surplus clay with knife and allows decoration to dry naturally or in drying cabinet.

May (01) shape flower leaves in small hand mould
(02) dress palms and fingers with vegetable oil to prevent adhesion of clay.

Other titles include Figure maker, Flower maker.

621.52 Turning machine minder (pottery, earthenware)

Attends lathe to shape pottery or earthenware articles to requirements

Clamps workpiece in chuck, slides hollow blank on mandrel or operates vacuum device to hold article by suction to plate of horizontal or vertical lathe; starts machine to rotate chuck, mandrel or plate and to bring profile tool(s) into contact with rotating workpiece; removes article from lathe when shaping is complete.

May (01) change and/or sharpen shaping tools
(02) smooth surface of turned article using abrasive paper.

Additional factor: whether accustomed to single or double-headed lathe.

621.54 Jolley machine minder, Jigger machine minder

Attends semi-automatic or automatic machine which moulds pottery articles such as cups, saucers or plates

If attending semi-automatic machine, throws ball or disc of clay into or on mould and places mould on turn-table (jigger head) of machine; starts machine to rotate jigger head and to bring profile tool or shaped roller into contact with clay; removes mould with formed article attached; repeats operation for each article to be shaped; stops machine on completion of batch or if fault occurs.
If attending automatic machine, places empty moulds in carrier (mould holding ring) of machine; starts machine and watches operation; removes formed and dried article from mould, positions it on chuck of sponging mechanism and starts mechanism; removes smoothed article from chuck after specified time.

May (01) attend machine to spread or press charge of clay into disc shape
(02) load and unload preset sponging machine
(03) fit preset forming tool or roller to machine

Other titles include Automatic cup making machine attendant, Cup maker (semi-automatic machine), Semi-automatic flat jiggerer.

621.56 Hand moulder (bricks, roofing tiles)

Presses clay in moulding frame by hand to form bricks or flat roofing tiles

Cuts clay lump into flat slabs (bats) with cutting wire, selects prepared bat or cuts suitably sized clay piece from lump; positions wooden or metal moulding frame on flat metal plate or wooden board (stock); dusts frame and stock with sand and throws bat or clay piece into frame; presses clay by hand or beats with mallet to ensure that frame is completely filled; removes surplus clay from frame with knife or cutting wire and smoothes surface of clay in frame with wet brush or wooden tool; if moulding tiles manipulates device to press nail holes in and form nibs on tile; removes frame and where appropriate dusts surface of shaped brick or tile with sand; slides tile from stock to drying rack or inverts stock to deposit brick on drying board.

May (01) add colouring agent to dusting sand
(02) perform tasks of CHEQUERER (621.62)
(03) check moulding frame periodically for distortion.

621.58 Press operator (ceramics)

Operates hand or semi-automatic power press to form pottery, porcelain, fireclay or similar ceramic goods

Fills container adjacent to press by hand or from feed hopper with powdered, granulated, moistened, shredded or balled clay; checks that correct upper and lower dies are fitted in press; fills lower die with required quantity of clay; operates controls to lower upper die and compact clay; raises die and removes formed article; examines surface for defects arising from worn or faulty dies; cleans and oils surfaces of dies.

May (01) fit dies and/or adjust clearance between dies to vary thickness of article
(02) press article preformed to rough shape
(03) operate press with heated dies and be known as Hot press operator.

Other titles include Crank maker, Faience block presser, Tile press operator.

621.60 Extruding press operator (clay)

Operates machine to extrude clay mix through nozzle in specified shape

Feeds powdered or moistened plastic clay into feed hopper of machine; starts machine and watches process; cuts or breaks extruded clay into specified lengths; refills feed hopper and changes nozzles and plates as necessary.

May (01) admit water or clay dust to feed hopper to vary consistency of mix
(02) adjust extrusion pressure
(03) operate controls to compress clay in feed hopper.

Other titles include Dod box attendant, Lute mill attendant.

621.62 Chequerer (clay building tiles)

Beats flat, unfired clay tiles by hand to camber, curve or form angle in tile

Selects wooden forming rack (horse) with slats shaped to required curvature or angle and positions partially dried tile(s) securely on horse; beats tile(s) with hardwood bat with flat surface (batter) or hollow surface (biddle) until tile(s) conform(s) to curve or angle of horse; removes tile(s) for completion of drying.

621.90 Automatic press minder (ceramics)

Attends preset automatic press which forms articles, other than bricks, from clay

Fills, or checks filling of, feed hopper with powdered clay or moist clay mix; starts machine and ensures even flow of clay from feed hopper, agitating hopper feed as necessary to assist flow; removes formed article and examines surface for defects.

May (01) make random checks of weight of formed article
(02) specialise in making a particular type of article, eg ceramic tiles, electrical porcelain ware.

Other titles include Press attendant.

621.92 Machine attendant (brick, tile making)

Tends automatic or semi-automatic machine in the making of clay roofing or drainage tiles or bricks

Performs one or some of the following tasks: selects and fits extrusion die in machine; loads machine with moulding trays (pallets); checks sanding of moulds; starts machine, watches feed of clay or slurry mix and clears stoppages; operates wire cutter to cut extruded clay into blocks or tiles of specified length; watches passage of pallets or moulds under filling and pressing mechanism; removes formed bricks or tiles from machine; stacks bricks or tiles on racks or trolley to dry; makes up and fits replacement cutting wires to frame as necessary; cleans and oils machine.

May (01) load machine reservoir with oil to be sprayed in pallets of moulding machine
(02) fill and operate clay or slurry mixing machine
(03) operate machine to cut extruded clay tubing into lengths for earthenware drain-pipes
(04) operate portable hot-air drying equipment to dry bricks or tiles.

Other titles include Brick cutter, Brick press operator, Table man (brick making machine), Taker-off (brick making machine), Tile maker.

621.98 Trainee

Performs, under instruction or guidance, various tasks including training exercises and as appropriate pursues studies in order to acquire the basic skills and knowledge required to perform the tasks of workers in ceramic goods forming occupations.

621.99 Other ceramic goods forming occupations

Workers in this group form pottery, earthenware, refractory goods, clay bricks and tiles and similar goods by casting, moulding, pressing, extruding, cutting and shaping and are not elsewhere classified, for example:

(01) **Bat makers,** Batters-out, Bumpers-on (form discs or circular cakes of clay by machine ready for jolleying or jiggering); (02) **Bottom knockers** (mould bottoms for saggars by hand); (03) **Casting belt attendants** (fill moulds with clay slip in readiness for casters); (04) **Frame fillers** (prepare canvas-backed fireclay strip by hand to form sides of saggars); (05) **Handle makers** (mould handles for cups, teapots, ornaments, etc from clay strip); (06) **Ring cutters** (cut extruded unfired clay pipes into rings with bow-wire for setting pottery in kiln); (07) **Saggar makers (machine)** (operate machines to mould saggars from refractory compound); (08) **Stilt cutters** (operate machines to cut extruded clay strip into specified lengths); (09) **Stopper makers** (make fireclay stoppers for hot metal ladles); (10) **Throwers' assistants** (weigh, roll and work clay into rough shape for use by throwers and remove formed articles from throwers' wheels).

Unit Group 622 Ceramic Goods Finishing Occupations (Excluding Glazers and Decorators)

Workers in this unit group smooth, trim and otherwise finish (other than by glazing and decorating) china, earthenware, sanitary ware, stoneware, refractory goods and other ceramic goods.

622.05 Fettler (ceramic goods)

Trims and smoothes surfaces of unfired pottery articles by hand

Examines article for flaws; fills in surface cracks with clay slip or plasticised clay using sponge or hand tool; trims off surplus clay and removes rough spots, sharp edges and mould-joint ridges using fettling knife or other hand tools and abrasive paper; cuts indentations evenly round rim of article with scolloping knife; smoothes surfaces of article using fine abrasive paper, pad of tow or wet sponge.

May (01) apply slip of wet clay and grit (glazing underbody) to smoothed article.

Other titles include Crucible finisher, Scolloper (pottery), Sponger, Tower (pottery).

622.10 Grinder (pottery, porcelain), Polisher (pottery, porcelain)

Operates grinding and/or buffing equipment to smooth and polish surface of fired pottery and porcelain articles

Examines articles for surface defects such as dust specks, burns or colour or glaze blemishes if not already marked; manipulates article against grinding or sanding tool to remove defect, taking care not to grind excessively in depth or area; holds dressed article against buffing wheel or mop to impart polish; rinses article to remove any residual dust and gives final polish with soft cloth.

May (01) level bases of pedestals and sanitary furnishings by pressing article down on to revolving disc dressed with water and sand

(02) fill and/or glaze small surface areas after grinding

(03) enlarge inlet or outlet holes in article using ball-shaped grinding stone

(04) grind article to specified dimensions

(05) specialise in grinding articles which have become distorted during firing and be known as Crook grinder

(06) specialise in grinding articles which need refiring and be known as Refire grinder.

622.15 Scourer (pottery)

Removes faults in decoration or glazing and/or polishes the surface of fired pottery articles by hand

Dips damp sponge or pad in silver sand and lightly rubs surface of article, taking care to avoid scoring glaze; removes specks or splashes of colouring from surface by rubbing stain with pencil-shaped tool dipped in mix of fine sand and hydrofluoric acid; removes scouring dust from surface of article with cloth or air hose; gives final polish to surface with soft cloth.

May (01) pick out ouline of gilt pattern using agate or bloodstone tipped tool.

Other titles include Acid worker, Burnisher.

622.20 Sandblaster (pottery)

Operates sandblasting equipment to remove blemishes from fired pottery articles

Places article on platform in blasting cabinet, closes cabinet and starts air compressor; places arms through openings in cabinet; operates pedal control to regulate flow of sand; directs jet of sand on to area of article to be cleaned, turning article round as necessary; watches operation through observation panel; removes article and examines visually; marks cracks, holes, chips or sharp edges requiring filling or smoothing; replenishes sand in machine as required.

May (01) sort and mark articles for sandblasting.

See Sandblasting machine operator (glass decorating) (614.91) and Shot blaster (metal) (726.92)

622.50 Etcher (pottery)

Immerses pottery articles in acid bath to etch design on surface by acid erosion

Operates pump to fill bath with solution of hydrofluoric acid from storage tank; positions prepared pottery article in metal basket and lowers basket into acid bath to immerse article and to etch exposed design; lifts basket from bath after prescribed immersion period and removes etched article; rinses article in water to remove all traces of acid; at end of work period drains acid in bath into storage tank.

May (01) perform tasks of ETCHER'S ASSISTANT (622.55).

622.55 Etcher's assistant (pottery)

Prepares pottery articles for etching or cleans articles after etching

Performs one or more of the following tasks: applies to article paper transfer on which design to be etched is cut in acid-resistant coating; paints acid-resistant coating (pitch or tar solution) to mask surface of article other than area covered by transfer; peels away backing of transfer to expose design to be etched and touches-up masking coat as necessary using fine brush; washes and scrubs etched article to remove acid-resistant coating and clean out etched lines.

Other titles include Blacker, Transfer placer, Transfer remover, Washer.

622.60 Filler (pottery)

Repairs cracks, pin-holes, chips and similar surface defects in fired pottery articles by hand

Applies semi-liquid clay (slip) to crack, chip or pin-hole with pallette knife or fills defect with chemical paste using small wooden spatula; levels filling with surface of article; smoothes repair and wipes off excess filling with damp sponge or cloth.

May (01) mix slip

(02) touch up repair with glaze (819.60).

Other titles include Biscuit stopper, Glaze stopper, Stopper.

622.65 Tumbler operator (ceramic components)

Operates machines with rotating barrels to clean and smooth small ceramic components

Feeds components into tumbler barrel; adds abrasive material such as carborundum or pumice powder and fills barrel with water; secures feed hatch and starts barrel rotating; stops machine periodically to remove scum and replenish abrasive material and water; repeats operation for specified time according to nature and size of components; unloads components on completion of process and rinses in water; dips components in degreasing solution and places in dryer; when dry transfers components to storage boxes.

May (01) polish ceramic components using mechanical polishing mop.

Additional factor: number of machines attended.

Other titles include Rumbler.

See Drum operator (hides, skins, pelts) (531.65) and Barrel polishing machine operator (metal) (726.60).

622.98 Trainee

Performs, under instruction or guidance, various tasks including training exercises and as appropriate pursues studies in order to acquire the basic skills and knowledge required to perform the tasks of workers in ceramic goods finishing occupations (excluding glazers and decorators).

622.99 Other ceramic goods finishing occupations (excluding glazers and decorators)

Workers in this group pierce holes in made up pottery and smooth, trim and otherwise finish ceramic goods and are not elsewhere classified, for example:

(01) **Brushers (machine)** (hold articles of fired pottery against mechanically driven brushes to remove dust particles); (02) **Drilling machine minders (pottery, porcelain)**, Tapping machine minders (pottery, porcelain) (attend preset machines to drill or tap holes in fired or unfired pottery and porcelain articles or component parts); (03) **Finishers (plaster castings)** (scrape, sand, trim and otherwise finish plaster castings by hand or machine); (04) **Pottery chippers,** Pottery knockers (remove marks caused by firing, or fused fragments of kiln furniture from pottery); (05) **Towing and fettling machine attendants** (load or unload semi-automatic machines which finish unfired flat pottery articles).

Unit Group 623 Concrete, Asbestos-Cement, Abrasive Stone and Related Products Making Occupations

Workers in this unit group form and finish concrete, asbestos-cement, abrasive stone and related products by moulding, pressing, casting, extruding, cutting and shaping and perform closely related tasks.

Excluded are workers making asbestos-cement sheets and pipes (594 and 599)

623.02 Mould maker (asbestos-cement)

Makes asbestos-cement moulds by hand using wooden master moulds

Brushes surface of master mould with oil; spreads sheet of uncured asbestos-cement over master mould and presses sheet with gloved hands to conform to master mould; trims surplus from edge of asbestos-cement with knife; smoothes edge and surface of asbestos-cement with gloved hands; removes formed asbestos-cement mould from master mould after specified time; rubs surface of asbestos-cement mould with oil to impart polished finish; throughout moulding dresses rubber gloves with lubricant as required.

May (01) perform tasks of HAND MOULDER (623.06).

623.04 Moulder's cutter (asbestos-cement)

Cuts uncured asbestos-cement sheets into specified shapes, by hand, ready for moulding

Lays sheet(s) of uncured asbestos-cement on bench and places template on sheet(s); scribes round outline of template with pointed wooden tool; removes template and cuts out scribed shape using special chisel and mallet; passes asbestos-cement shapes to moulder.

623.06 Hand moulder (asbestos-cement products)

Presses uncured asbestos-cement sheets or shapes in or over moulds, by hand, to shape products

Selects mould and separates sections as necessary; coats mould surface with oil or water; unrolls uncured asbestos-cement sheet, cuts to size and where necessary chamfers edges to facilitate joining; positions sheet or shape in or over mould and presses it by hand or with wooden tool to conform to contours of mould; if moulding hollow product closes mould sections and works with fingers and hand tools in mould to knit edges together at joints and to smooth inside surface of product; removes formed product in mould to drying rack.

May (01) wrap asbestos-cement sheet round wooden or metal mandrel before inserting in mould and rotate former to assist internal shaping

(02) trim excess material from mould using saw

(03) perform tasks of MOULDER'S CUTTER (623.04).

623.08 Moulder (abrasive products)

Operates press to mould products such as blocks, slabs or wheels from abrasive mix

If operating manually operated press, selects steel mould, wipes interior with oil impregnated cloth and mounts mould on bed of press or on turn-table; weighs and feeds specified quantity of abrasive mix into mould; spreads and levels mix with straight-edge or operates control to distribute mix evenly by rotating turn-table; positions press plunger and steel packing plates on top of mix; transfers mould from turn-table to press bed as necessary; operates controls to compress mix, watching pressure gauge during pressing operation as necessary; releases pressure and withdraws mould from press; removes packing plates, plunger and formed product from mould.
If operating semi-automatic press, loads feed hopper with abrasive mix and positions mould on press bed; operates controls to fill mould with specified quantity of abrasive mix from hopper and to lower press head on mould; removes mould from press when pressure is automatically released and removes formed product from mould.

May (01) calculate weight of mix required to form product of specified dimensions

(02) embed steel reinforcing ring in mix

(03) check dimensions of products using gauges.

Other titles include Moulder (grindstone block), Presser (abrasive wheel), Press operator.

623.10 Moulder (concrete, cast stone)

Performs various tasks in the casting of concrete or cast stone products in moulds

Performs some or all of the following tasks: selects mould or assembles sectional mould; sprays or brushes inside of mould with oil or lines mould with paper; inserts divider plates into mould and positions core; positions reinforcing rods or mesh in mould and tensions as necessary; lines mould with crushed stone mix or washed stones; part fills mould with concrete mix manually or from chute or feed spout; operates controls to vibrate mould or inserts vibrator into mould and operates vibrator to compact mix; completes filling of mould and repeats vibration process; smoothes surface of concrete mix with trowel or shovel; dismantles mould after specified time and removes or assists in removing product; dresses surface of product with wet cement mix using trowel or wooden float; cleans and dismantles divider plates; cleans mould.

May (01) operate lifting equipment to move moulds, reinforcing pieces or formed products

(02) cut reinforcing rods using oxy-acetylene torch

(03) operate mixing machine to prepare crushed stone mix

(04) use electric or pneumatic hammer to ram and compact mix in mould

(05) embed stones by hand in surface of partially-dry concrete product

(06) perform tasks of CONCRETE FINISHER (623.18).

Other titles include Battery hand (concrete casting)' Casting hand.

623.12 Press moulding machine operator (concrete)

Operates machine to mould products, other than pipes, from concrete mix

Selects and secures mould to movable bed of machine; lines mould with greased paper or sprays mould with oil; sets controls to regulate pressure and quantity of concrete mix released from hopper to mould; operates controls to fill mould with specified quantity of mix and position mould under press head; lowers press head to compress mix in mould; raises press head after specified time, returns mould to filling position and operates controls to remove product from mould.

623.14 Moulding machine operator (concrete pipes)

Operates machine to mould concrete pipes

Operates controls to secure mould in position on fixed base of machine and to raise and start revolving or vibrating core mould; operates controls to fill mould with concrete mix from hopper or conveyor, or shovels mix into mould; operates controls to lower former on to mix and rotate former to shape end of pipe; withdraws former, lowers core and releases mould from machine base.

May (01) smooth internal surface of pipe with liquid cement using grouting device attached to mould core.

Other titles include Pipe moulder.

623.16 Spinner (concrete)

Operates machine to form hollow cylindrical concrete products by spinning mould containing concrete mix

Applies oil by spray, brush or impregnated cloth to internal surface of cylindrical mould; positions wire reinforcing rods or cage in mould as required; assembles sectional mould and fits end-forming plate to mould; positions mould on machine using hoist and starts machine to rotate mould; shovels or operates controls to feed concrete mix into mould; spins mould to compact mix and shape product; stops machine and removes slurry discharge from mix with long-handled brush or trowel; feeds additional concrete into mould as necessary and repeats spinning of mould, at increased speed, for specified time; stops machine and smoothes interior of formed product with long-handled float.

May (01) stamp size, quality or other identification mark on formed, uncured product

(02) remove formed product in mould to steam curing chamber.

623.18 Concrete finisher

Finishes surfaces of concrete products or structural units in workshop or on site

Performs a combination of the following tasks: removes projections and rough surfaces using abrasive block; removes areas of defective concrete using chipping tools; cleans out cracks and holes, fills with fresh concrete and smoothes surface; washes off surface with water or acid to expose aggregate and bring up colour of the stones; applies slurry to surface and operates powered sander or buffing wheel to produce smooth finish; finishes off irregularly shaped faces with powered grinder; produces textured finishes using hand or power tools with chisel and punch attachments.

623 .20 Tile caster (terrazzo, mosaic), Slab caster (terrazzo, mosaic)

Operates press to mould terrazzo or mosaic tiles or slabs

Selects mould and covers bottom with rubber sheet; spreads layer of terrazzo mix of fine marble chippings and coloured cement or arranges irregularly shaped marble pieces on rubber sheet; spreads coloured cement mix over marble pieces using trowel and operates vibrating mechanism to ensure that cement mix fills spaces between marble; fills remainder of mould with concrete mix using trowel or shovel; operates controls to compress mix in mould; removes mould from press and removes and stacks tile or slab.
OR
Positions mould on press bed and fills mould with concrete mix using trowel or shovel; spreads terrazzo chippings over concrete with trowel and covers with waxed paper, or lays on concrete marble pieces set in pattern on adhesive paper; operates press to embed chippings or marble mosaic in concrete and to compress mix in mould; removes mould from press and discards waxed or adhesive covering paper; removes tile or slab from mould.

May (01) prepare terrazzo mix of sand, cement, marble chippings and colourant

(02) operate machine to grind and polish terrazzo or mosaic castings (863 .70).

623 .22 Hone maker

Operates machine to shape clay and abrasive mix in the making of hones

Fits extrusion nozzle of specified size to machine; fills feed hopper of machine with clay and powdered abrasive mix; starts machine and watches extrusion of mix in strip form; stops machine and cuts strip into lengths with hand knife; transfers cut piece to drying board; checks length of cut piece with gauge and trims off excess with hand knife; returns excess to feed hopper. OR
Passes large uncured slabs of clay and abrasive mix through multi-bladed cutting machine to reduce slab to slices of specified dimension, each slice forming a hone; removes slices to drying board.

May (01) weigh and mix clay and powdered abrasive

623 .24 Turner (asbestos-cement)

Manipulates hand tools against rotating asbestos-cement pipe, pipe fitting, bush or similar workpiece to shape workpiece and/or finish surface

Mounts workpiece in lathe chuck; starts workpiece rotating; applies hand tool to rotating workpiece to pare surface to required shape and/or applies hand file or abrasive cloth to surface to impart a smooth finish; stops machine and removes and stacks article.

See Centre lathe turner (722 .04) for workers who set and operate lathes in accordance with engineering techniques to turn asbestos-cement products.

623 .26 Sawyer (asbestos-cement)

Operates sawing equipment to cut cured asbestos-cement products to specified size

Sets cutting edge or guide according to size of finished article; secures workpiece on cutting table where necessary; operates controls to start cutting wheels or band-saws; starts automatic equipment or advances cutting table manually to workpiece and manipulates workpiece against cutting edge; stops machine, stacks finished product and salvages off-cuts; changes cutting wheels as necessary.

May (01) stack asbestos-cement sheets on cutting table and cut several sheets simultaneously.

Other titles include Stone saw operator.

623 .28 Trimmer (abrasive wheels)

Sets and operates machine to cut moulded abrasive wheels to specified shape

Positions moulded abrasive wheel on lathe or on grinding machine; sets stops and secures diamond-tipped cutting tool, dressing tool or rotary grinding head in machine; starts machine and manipulates controls to cut face or edge of wheel to dimensions specified; trues-up parallel faces of wheel, squares or otherwise shapes edge of wheel, grinds centre hole to dimension specified and to ensure concentricity with rim, and grinds face(s) of abrasive wheel to finished state; stops machine and removes wheel.

May (01) operate lifting equipment to move heavy abrasive wheels

(02) apply cutting tool to rotating abrasive wheel by hand

(03) perform tasks of STEEL SHOT SURFACER (623 .30)

(04) specialise in shaping or finishing edges of abrasive wheels and be known as Conical edger, Edge grinder.

Other titles include Shaver, Turner.

623.30 Steel shot surfacer (abrasive wheel)

Operates machine to reduce thickness of abrasive wheels and/or bring wheel surfaces to required finish by steel shot blasting

Secures moulded abrasive wheel on turn-table of machine; fills machine hopper with steel shot; if operating semi-automatic machine sets control to regulate quantity of steel shot released from hopper; starts machine to rotate turn-table; feeds steel shot on to machine plate by hand or operates control to release shot from hopper; stops machine when surface of wheel has been sufficiently treated; repeats process on reverse side as necessary; removes wheel from machine.

May (01) operate lifting equipment to move heavy abrasive wheels
(02) check thickness of finished article using gauge
(03) perform tasks of TRIMMER (623.28)
(04) perform tasks of LEAD BUSHER (713.90).

623.32 Balancer (abrasive wheel)

Checks true running of abrasive wheels and corrects any imbalance

Mounts abrasive wheel on mandrel and positions mandrel on parallel bars or between pivots; spins wheel by hand and checks true running and balance by visual examination, or tests balance by attaching weights to points on perimeter of wheel; corrects any imbalance by one or more of the following methods: drills or chips holes in underweight area of wheel and fills holes with lead or molten metal; injects abrasive grain into porous structure of wheel in underweight area using compressed air equipment; impregnates underweight area of wheel with heated wax; adjusts position of movable weight incorporated in back-plate of wheel; inserts screws into threaded holes in wheel flange plate.

May (01) check dimensions of wheel with measuring instruments
(02) revolve wheel at high speed on electrical testing machine to check for conformity to specifications
(03) examine wheel for faulty material or poor workmanship (833.30).

623.50 Plant attendant (concrete tile making)

Attends automatic or semi-automatic plant which makes concrete tiles by extrusion and moulding

Performs a combination of the following tasks: positions empty moulds (pallets) on conveyor of tile making plant or checks automatic positioning of pallets; fills reservoir with oil or oil and creosote mix and controls drip feed into pallets; watches the extrusion of concrete mix in strip form into pallets and the cutting of concrete strip into lengths to form tiles; separates or watches separation of each filled pallet; operates controls to fill reservoir with tile dye and to drip feed or brush dye on to tile surface; operates roasting plant in which sand is burned, cooled and sieved; watches automatic dressing of formed tiles with slurry, burnt sand or granulated stone and refills feed hoppers as necessary; mixes acid solution and watches automatic spraying of tiles; removes formed tiles on pallets to or from steam bay; removes tiles from pallets by hand and stacks for disposal; recovers excess concrete, granulated stone or burnt sand; cleans plant as required.

May (01) mix silicate of soda and/or colouring matter with burnt sand.

Other titles include Pallet feeder, Pallet puller, Sand burner, Sand face feeder, Taker-off, Tile depalleter.

623.98 Trainee

Performs, under instruction or guidance, various tasks including training exercises and as appropriate pursues studies in order to acquire the basic skills and knowledge required to perform the tasks of workers in concrete, asbestos-cement, abrasive stone and related products making occupations.

623.99 Other concrete, asbestos-cement, abrasive stone and related products making occupations

Workers in this group form and finish asbestos-cement, abrasive stone and related products by moulding, pressing, casting, extruding, cutting and shaping and perform closely related tasks and are not elsewhere classified, for example:

(01) **Cleaners (asbestos-cement, cast stone)**, Fettlers (asbestos-cement, cast stone), Finishers (asbestos-cement, cast stone) (clean, smooth and otherwise finish asbestos-cement or cast stone products by hand and/or machine); (02) **Concrete tile makers (hand)** (fill moulds with concrete mix by hand to form concrete roofing tiles); (03) **Drillers (asbestos-cement)** (operate single or multi-spindle drilling machines to pierce holes in asbestos-cement products); (04) **Press cutting machine operators (asbestos-cement sheet)** (operate power presses to cut or trim uncured asbestos-cement sheets to size and shape); (05) **Slab makers (terrazzo, mosaic)**, Tile makers (terrazzo, mosaic) (fill moulding frames with terrazzo mix or marble pieces and concrete to form terrazzo or mosaic tiles or slabs).

Unit Group 624 Stone Cutting, Shaping and Polishing Occupations

Workers in this unit group cut, shape and polish granite, marble, slate and other stone for building, ornamental, monumental and similar purposes.

624.02 Block cutter (stone, slate)

Splits quarried stone or slate into blocks with hand tools

Examines quarried block to determine best cleavage line; marks line with chalk or scribes line with chisel edge; if cutting slate hammers chisels and wedges along cleavage line to split block; if cutting stone drills series of holes along cleavage line with pneumatic drill or with hammer and circular chisel, inserts into drilled hole steel pieces (feathers) to form tube and hammers plug into tube, or hammers chisel into centre hole, to split stone; repeats splitting process until block has been reduced to required size.

May (01) operate lifting equipment to move blocks
(02) specialise in cutting blocks to size for roofing slates
(03) perform tasks of STONE DRESSER (624.99)
(04) perform tasks of DRILLER (871.50) or SHOTFIRER (871.20).

624.04 Banker mason

Marks out and cuts prepared stone blocks to specified shape using powered chisels and/or hand tools

Marks squared-off outline on stone block using set square, straight-edge, marking tool and pencil or chalk, or places template on rough stone block and marks round template; cuts stone to shape following marked outline, using hammers, mallet and hand or pneumatic chisels.

May (01) check angles of cut stone with metal square or angle gauges
(02) cut groove in sides of stone for grouting
(03) number each cut stone to assist subsequent assembly
(04) perform tasks of STONE DRESSER (624.99).

624.06 Monumental mason

Shapes stone slabs and cuts designs on slabs to make tombstones and similar memorial monuments

Ascertains job requirements from photograph, sketch or scale drawing, or uses template; marks shape and design on slab surface, using drawing instruments, or positions template on slab and marks round template with pencil or scriber; cuts stone to required shape and cuts design on face using power-operated hand tool fitted with cutting or grinding head, or using hand chisels and mallet; checks dimensions and angles with rule, square and gauges, ensuring that head-stones, base stones and side stones fit together accurately; sharpens tools as required.

May (01) erect monument on site
(02) perform tasks of STONE CARVER (624.08)
(03) perform tasks of LETTER CUTTER (624.10 and 624.12)
(04) perform tasks of STONE SAWYER (624.14)
(05) perform tasks of STONE POLISHER (624.55 and 624.60).

624.08 Stone carver

Carves figures and designs to specifications in stone such as granite, marble, limestone or alabaster

Ascertains job requirements from drawings, photograph or written specifications, or uses prepared template of design; plans layout of carving; pencils design on rough-shaped stone, traces design on to stone through special carbon paper or traces round templates to mark design; carves out marked design using power-operated hand tool fitted with cutting or abrasive head, or steel chisels and hammer or mallet; changes cutting and abrasive heads and sharpens tools as required.

May (01) smooth carved surfaces with metal scrapers or carborundum paper
(02) make templates
(03) perform tasks of LETTER CUTTER (HAND) (624.10).

624.10 Letter cutter (hand)

Sets out and cuts lettering by hand on prepared stone

Ascertains job requirements from written specifications; measures stone and calculates spacing of letters; draws guide line on stone using square, rule and pencil or marking awl; draws freehand or with aid of stencil between guide lines, letters in style required; cuts out pencilled outline with power-operated hand tool or with chisel and mallet to incise lettering, or cuts away stone to expose lettering in relief; smoothes incisions with slip stone or carborundum paper.
Applies finish to lettering by one of the following methods: coats cut letters with size and applies gold leaf to sized letters with soft brush; paints cut letters with black paint; drills small holes in base of each cut, beats lead into drilled holes until level with stone surface, trims lead to shape of letter with hand chisel and removes excess lead filling with file or carborundum stone; pours composition into cuts, allows composition to dry and set, and levels composition with stone surface using file or carborundum block.
Sharpens tools as required.

May (01) if working on very hard stone drill holes in pencilled letter outlines, beat lead to fill drilled holes and to lie upon surface of stone, and cut out letters in relief in the lead, using hammer and chisel.

624.12 Letter cutter (machine)

Operates machine to cut lettering on prepared stone

Ascertains job requirements from written specifications or drawings; sticks sheet of rubber or thick paper over surface of stone and draws guide lines on sheet using square and rule; calculates spacing of letters and draws freehand, or with aid of stencil, between guide lines, letters in style required; cuts lettering from rubber or paper sheet with sharp knife; positions stone in cabinet of sandblasting machine, starts machine and guides nozzle by hand to direct blast of abrasive sand or carborundum dust on exposed stone; stops sandblasting when lettering is eroded to sufficient depth; removes stone from machine and uses knife or scraper to remove remaining rubber or paper covering. OR
Positions stone on bed of machine; selects metal letters and arranges them to form wording required; secures letters with adjustable cramp to form rigid template and clamps template beneath tracing point; starts machine and guides tracing point round template, causing pneumatic cutter to cut stone to conform to tracing; stops machine, releases cramp and returns letters to storage; removes cut stone from machine.

624.14 Stone working machine operator

Operates stone working machine to bore, drill, plane, saw or turn stone or slate block to specifications

Positions and secures cutting tools in machine; secures stone on machine; adjusts machine controls as required; operates machine by manual control to bring cutting tool into contact with stone and watches cutting process; removes finished stone from machine.

May (01) check shaping of stone using template or measuring instruments.

Other titles include Saw machine operator, Slate sawing machine operator, Stone planer, Stone sawyer, Stone turner.

624.16 Grindstone maker (natural stone)

Cuts natural stone to form grindstone wheel using hand tools and machine

Ascertains job requirements from specifications; selects rough-cut stone slab, marks approximate centre of slab and scribes circumference of wheel using masonry compass, or places template of required size on slab and chalks round outline to mark out wheel; chips centre hole through stone with pick or operates machine to drill centre hole of specified size; cuts round marked circumference using mallet and chisel or positions slab on bed of cutting machine, adjusts machine cutters according to diameter of wheel, starts machine and operates controls to cut out circular stone; mounts roughly cut wheel on spindle of turning machine, starts machine and applies dressing tool to edge of stone to reduce stone to correct size and to smooth edge; similarly dresses flat surfaces of grindstone, or presses each side of grindstone on oscillating pan of steel shot to smooth sides and reduce grindstone to specified thickness.

May (01) wash grindstone under running water during smoothing operation
(02) check thickness of finished grindstone using gauge.

624.18 Slate cutter

Slits prepared slate blocks and/or trims edges of roughly shaped roofing slates using hand tools

(01) **Slate splitter**

Receives slate block with one face cut to approximate size of roofing slate; rests block against knee; studies grain of block and taps wide-bladed chisel with hammer or mallet into edge of block, following grain, to split block in half; repeats bisecting process until block has been reduced to rough roofing slates of specified thickness.

(02) **Slate dresser (hand)**

Positions roughly shaped roofing slate on floor-mounted blade (break) and presses long knife (whittle) firmly on slate, slightly to one side of breaking line to snap off excess slate and to trim to required size; grades and stacks dressed slates according to size, quality and colour.

624.50 Slate dresser (machine)

Operates cutting machine to trim roughly shaped slates to required size

Sets guide for size of slate required; feeds roughly shaped slate into machine to shave under surface and straighten one edge of slate; turns slate so that straight edge rests against guide and again feeds slate into machine to trim second edge; repeats operation on third and fourth sides, re-setting guide as necessary; examines dressed slates for imperfections and grades and stacks slates of required quality according to size, thickness and colour; cleans machine.

May (01) perform tasks of SLATE SPLITTER (624.18).

624.55 Stone polisher (hand)

Smoothes and polishes blocks of marble, granite or other stone by rubbing with abrasives or using powered hand tools

Positions and secures block of stone on work-bench; rubs surface of stone with blocks of carborundum or sandstone by hand, or fits graded abrasive disc to powered hand tool and guides tool over surface of stone; rubs stone with felt pad to impart final polish.

May (01) wet surface of stone, during smoothing, with damp sponge or brush.

See Terrazzo polisher (hand) (863.60)

624.60 Stone polisher (machine)

Operates machine to smooth and polish blocks of granite, marble or other stone

Positions and secures block of stone on bed of machine; selects abrasive wheel or disc of required grade and fits it to machine head; sets water jets to play on stone surface and starts flow of water; starts machine head rotating; manipulates rotating machine head over surface of stone; stops machine and flow of water; fits wool or felt mop to machine head; starts mop rotating and guides mop over stone to polish surface.

May (01) apply polishing paste to mop.

Other titles include Slate buffer, Slate polisher.

See Terrazzo polisher (machine) (863.70)

624.65 Polisher (machine) (terrazzo or mosaic tiles or slabs)

Operates machine to smooth and polish terrazzo or mosaic tiles or slabs

Clamps tile or slab on bed of machine and secures coarsely-graded grindstone to spindle of machine; starts grindstone rotating and turns on flow of water to workpiece; operates control to lower grindstone on workpiece and manipulates grinding head over tile or slab to grind surface to smooth finish; fills any pitting of surface with cement grouting mix of appropriate colour, using trowel, and allows to set; repeats grinding process using successively finer graded grindstones and buffing stones; removes tile or slab from machine.

May (01) operate multiple-bed machine on which several tiles or slabs are smoothed and polished.

Other titles include Grinder.

See Terrazzo polisher (machine) (863.70)

624.98 Trainee

Performs, under instruction or guidance, various tasks including training exercises and as appropriate pursues studies in order to acquire the basic skills and knowledge required to perform the tasks of workers in stone cutting, shaping and polishing occupations.

624.99 Other stone cutting, shaping and polishing occupations

Workers in this group cut, shape and polish stone for building, ornamental, monumental and similar purposes and are not elsewhere classified, for example:

(01) **Stone dressers** (smooth or bring to uniformly rough finish, surfaces of kerb-stones and other cut stones using hammer and chisel or punch); (02) **Stone splitting machine operators** (operate hydraulic guillotine machines to cut stone into blocks).

Unit Group 629 Clay and Stone Working Occupations Not Elsewhere Classified

Workers in this unit group build industrial insulators, join vitrified clay pipes, mould sealing bands to vitrified clay pipes and perform other tasks in clay and stone working and are not elsewhere classified.

629.10 Industrial insulator builder

Prepares and joins porcelain or earthenware components to build industrial electrical insulators

Ascertains job requirements from drawing and/or other specifications; positions bottom component (base shed) of insulator on turn-table (fettling whirler) base uppermost and starts whirler rotating; levels surface of base and trims flanges to specified dimensions with hand fettling tools and wet sponge; checks levelness of base with T-square and levelling rod, and dimensions of flanges with callipers and measuring rod; reverses base shed on building whirler and fettles and levels upper surface of shed in similar manner; prepares bottom of second shed as described above; applies liquid clay (slip) to upper surface of base shed and lower surface of second shed; positions second shed on base shed with assistance, as necessary; covers top of second shed with plaster batt and strikes batt with mallet to expel air from and assist adhesion of sheds; rotates building whirler and smoothes joint with metal tool and wet sponge; adds further sheds as necessary to build insulator to specified height; checks dimensions and alignment using measuring instruments and plumb-line; directs removal of insulator from building whirler to drying area.

629.20 Junction sticker (vitrified clay goods)

Cuts and joins semi-dry, unfired stoneware pipes, to form junctions, gullies, traps, etc

Positions junction pipe on bench; places template on pipe indicating angle and location of cut and cuts pipe with wire held taut in frame; positions template on main pipe indicating location of junction and cuts aperture with curved knife or wire following outline of template; dampens and scores surfaces to be joined; positions main pipe on bench or in cradling block and fits junction pipe to it; checks accuracy of angle and fit and seals joint with moistened clay strip; trims and smoothes joint using trimming tool and wet sponge or rubber pad; removes product for drying.

May (01) work from drawings or prepare paper patterns for template maker
(02) use metal plug to restore shape of open pipe ends after forming junction
(03) chamfer or score pipe ends
(04) mark product with identification particulars using metal stamp.

629.50 Pipe jointing operative (vitrified clay pipes)

Performs tasks to mould sealing bands on the ends of vitrified clay pipes

Performs a combination of the following tasks: chips away glazed surface on inside of flanged end of pipe (socket) and outside of pipe at other end (spigot) to form a key for sealing band, or coats ends of pipe with an adhesive solution; stands spigot of pipe in mould or fixes hinged hoop round spigot to form mould, and fits mould in socket end of pipe, or fixes moulds to both ends of suspended pipe; pours liquid sealer into cavity between mould and wall of pipe and allows sealer to harden; removes moulds from ends of pipe and trims off excess sealer; checks sealing bands for air bubbles, evenness of surface and adhesion of pipe-wall; stacks pipes for removal to storage; cleans moulds.

May (01) mix sealing solution
(02) clamp moulds to pipe ends using compressed air tool.

629.90 Crucible maker's assistant

Assists under direction of crucible maker (machine) in forming crucibles

Performs a combination of the following tasks under direction of crucible maker (machine): assembles and clamps together mould sections; lubricates interior surface of mould or lines mould with cloth; collects and inserts into mould specified quantity of refractory mix; assists in positioning mould on, and removing mould from, machine turn-table; fits and removes forming tool; removes formed crucible to drying room.

May (01) paint dried crucible with glazing fluid
(02) assist in setting crucible in, and removing crucible from, firing kiln.

629 .92 Mason's labourer (workshop, yard)

Assists stone working craftsman in the performance of his tasks

Assists craftsman to position stone during cutting, shaping and polishing operations; rough finishes stone by hand or using powered hand tool; in addition performs some or all of the following tasks: unloads and stores rough cut stone using lifting equipment; moves stone from stores to craftsman's work area; loads finished stone on vehicle for delivery; keeps workshop or yard clean and tidy; carries out other tasks as directed by craftsman.
If assisting monumental mason with erection of gravestone or similar monument, performs tasks such as mixing concrete, mortar or grouting materials and digging and concreting foundations; assists mason to erect and fix headstone; cleans erected stonework.

May (01) hammer lead into cut lettering.

Other titles include Mason's mate.

629 .98 Trainee

Performs, under instruction or guidance, various tasks including training exercises and as appropriate pursues studies in order to acquire the basic skills and knowledge required to perform the tasks of workers in clay and stone working occupations not elsewhere classified.

629 .99 Other clay and stone working occupations not elsewhere classified

Workers in this group perform miscellaneous tasks in clay and stone working and are not separately classified, for example:

(01) **Mould runners** (remove formed products from moulds, clean moulds and otherwise assist jiggerers, jolliers and pressers); (02) **Moulders' assistants (abrasive products)** (prepare and strip down moulds and otherwise assist moulders (abrasive products)); (03) **Strippers (concrete moulding)** (dismantle and remove sectional moulds from formed concrete products).

Minor Group 63 PRINTING, PHOTOGRAPHIC PROCESSING AND RELATED OCCUPATIONS

Workers in this minor group compose and assemble type and printing blocks, prepare printing plates and cylinders by moulding and photographic process, set and operate printing machines, print by screen and block method, process and print photographic film and perform closely related tasks.

The occupations are arranged in the following unit groups:

630 Foremen (Printing, Photographic Processing and Related Occupations)

631 Printers (General)

632 Composing and Typesetting Occupations

633 Printing Plate and Cylinder Preparing Occupations (Excluding Metal Engraving)

634 Printing Machine Operators (Excluding Screen and Block Printing)

635 Screen and Block Printing Occupations

636 Photographic Processing and Related Occupations

639 Printing, Photographic Processing and Related Occupations Not Elsewhere Classified

Unit Group 630 Foremen (Printing, Photographic Processing and Related Occupations)

Workers in this unit group directly supervise and co-ordinate the activities of workers in printing, photographic processing and related occupations.

630.10 Foreman (composing and typesetting occupations)

Directly supervises and co-ordinates the activities of workers in composing and typesetting occupations

Performs appropriate tasks as described under SUPERVISOR/FOREMAN (UNSPECIFIED) (990.00).

Additional factor: number of workers supervised.

Other titles include Clicker.

630.20 Foreman (printing plate and cylinder preparing occupations) (excluding metal engraving)

Directly supervises and co-ordinates the activities of workers in printing plate, roller and block preparing occupations (excluding engraving)

Performs appropriate tasks as described under SUPERVISOR/FOREMAN (UNSPECIFIED) (990.00).

Additional factor: number of workers supervised.

630.30 Foreman (printing machine operators (excluding screen and block printing))

Directly supervises and co-ordinates the activities of workers operating printing (excluding screen and block printing), die stamping and embossing machines

Performs appropriate tasks as described under SUPERVISOR/FOREMAN (UNSPECIFIED) (990.00).

Additional factor: number of workers supervised.

630.40 Foreman (screen and block printing occupations)

Directly supervises and co-ordinates the activities of workers in screen and block printing occupations

Performs appropriate tasks as described under SUPERVISOR/FOREMAN (UNSPECIFIED) (990.00).

Additional factor: number of workers supervised.

630.50 Foreman (photographic processing and related occupations)

Directly supervises and co-ordinates the activities of workers in photographic processing and related occupations

Performs appropriate tasks as described under SUPERVISOR/FOREMAN (UNSPECIFIED) (990.00).

Additional factor: number of workers supervised.

630.98 Trainee

Performs, under instruction or guidance, various tasks including training exercises and as appropriate pursues studies in order to acquire the basic skills and knowledge required to perform the tasks of foremen (printing, photographic processing and related occupations).

630.99 Other foremen (printing, photographic processing and related occupations)

Workers in this group directly supervise and co-ordinate the activities of workers in printing, photographic processing and related occupations and are not elsewhere classified.

Unit Group 631 Printers (general)

Workers in this unit group compose and assemble type and printing blocks, prepare printing plates and operate printing presses.

631.10 Printer (general)

Composes and assembles type and printing blocks, prepares printing plates and operates a printing press

Determines from customer's requirements layout and kind and size of type to be used; prepares type-forme (blocks of composed type) or printing plate according to type of press to be used; positions forme or plate on machine, sets press and prints proof copies; corrects proof copies, alters forme or plate and adjusts press as necessary; starts, or directs starting of, printing run and ensures that printing proceeds correctly.

May (01) operate a die-stamping press to emboss lettering or decorative designs on stationery (634.30).

Additional factors: method of typesetting to which accustomed, eg hand setting of metal type, machine typesetting, filmsetting; type of printing press to which accustomed, eg flatbed, letterpress, rotary letterpress, small offset lithographic press.

631.98 Trainee

Performs, under instruction or guidance, various tasks including training exercises and as appropriate pursues studies in order to acquire the basic skills and knowledge required to perform the tasks of printers (general).

Unit Group 632 Composing and Typesetting Occupations

Workers in this unit group prepare printing layouts and specifications, compose type and assemble composed metal type and illustration blocks or filmset material into required format for printing and for the preparation of moulds used in the manufacture of rubber stamps.

632.05 Layout man

Prepares layout and specifies typography of printed matter

Discusses layout and design with customer; prepares layout incorporating such items as kind and size of type, width of margin and spacing; sketches designs for covers and title pages and ornaments for chapters; when proposed layout has been approved by customer provides compositor with instructions regarding layout and type to be used.

May (01) design special type-faces
(02) produce finished artwork.

Other titles include Typographer, Typographical designer.

632.10 Compositor (hand)

Assembles type by hand into required order for printing or for the preparation of moulds used in the manufacture of rubber stamps

Determines from specifications or layouts the kind and size of type to be used; adjusts type holder (composing stick) for length of line (measure) required; reading from typescript or manuscript (copy) selects appropriate type and arranges it in composing stick; inserts spacing material between words and lines as necessary; transfers lines of type to larger type holder (galley) when composing stick is full or setting is completed; secures composed type with page-cord; passes composed type to prover for proof printing or prints (pulls) proof copies himself: examines corrected proof copy and makes any necessary alterations to the type; replaces type in appropriate compartments in type cases (distributes type) after printing is completed.

May (01) plan layout and specify typography of printed matter (632.05)
(02) make up pages from composed type and illustration blocks (632.40)
(03) arrange (impose) and secure made-up pages of type in a metal frame (chase) ready for printing (632.15).

Other titles include Case hand, Ludlow compositor

632.15 Compositor (imposition)

Arranges and secures pages of composed type and illustrations in metal frame ready for printing

Places made-up pages of type matter on steel-topped bench (stone) in positions appropriate to the folding sequence to be used; inserts spacing material around pages of type to provide balanced margins; checks alignment of pages and measures and adjusts spacing material; places metal frame (chase) round assembled pages of type; locks type in chase by means of adjustable metal blocks (quoins); places wooden block over type and taps with mallet to obtain level printing surface (planes type); checks that completed assembly (forme) is secure and solid and arranges for proof printing; examines corrected proof and makes necessary alterations to type.

May (01) print and correct proof (634.25).

Other titles include Imposition hand, Stone hand.

632.20 Keyboard operator (typesetting)

Operates keyboard of a perforating machine, computer, composing typewriter or filmsetting machine used in typesetting

(01) **Perforator keyboard operator**

Operates keyboard to convert typescript or manuscript copy and printing specifications into justified or unjustified punched tape to control the operation of a typecasting or filmsetting machine, or as input for a computer.

Other titles include Monotype keyboard operator, Teletypesetting operator.

(02) **Computer keyboard operator**

Operates keyboard to feed typescript or manuscript copy and details of printing specifications directly into computer which produces tape to control the operation of a typecasting or filmsetting machine.

(03) **Typewriter keyboard operator**

Operates keyboard of composing typewriter to produce a camera-ready master copy of printing matter or a data tape to be used as input to a unit producing camera-ready copy or to a computer.

Other titles include IBM composer operator, Justowriter operator, Vari-typer operator.

(04) **Filmsetter keyboard operator**

Operates keyboard to feed typescript or manuscript copy and details of printing specifications directly into filmsetting machine to reproduce type characters on film or sensitised paper.

May (05) arrange filmset material to make up pages (632.40).

See Data typist (322.60)

632.25 Monotype caster operator

Sets and operates typecasting machine in which the casting and composition of type is controlled by perforated paper tape

Ascertains from printing instructions the kind and size of type required; selects appropriate frame of type-moulds (matrix-case) and space wedges and fits on machine; arranges and re-arranges matrices in matrix case as required; sets machine to produce lines of correct length; adjusts machine speed controls; fits on machine roll of perforated tape prepared by Monotype keyboard operator; checks water cooling system and supply of molten metal; starts machine which automatically casts type characters in correct sequence and cools the type before delivering on to type holder (galley); replenishes supply of metal to machine as required; removes composed type and arranges for printing of proof copies (proofing).

May (01) maintain machine
(02) cast founts of type for use by compositor (hand)
(03) melt down type on completion of printing.

Additional factor: number of machines operated.

Other titles include Compositor (Monotype casting).

632.30 Compositor (linecasting machine)

Operates machine to compose, cast and trim complete lines of type

Ascertains from printing instructions the kind and size of type required; fits magazines containing matrices of the appropriate types on machine; sets marginal stops and gauges to regulate length and thickness of lines to be cast; reading from copy, operates keyboard to select required matrices and spacebands and assemble them in correct sequence to form a line; inserts matrices for special characters by hand; operates lever to position the assembled line for casting, to pump molten metal into the matrices, to trim the resulting bar of type (slug) and eject it from machine; checks that slugs are being correctly cast and trimmed; replenishes supply of metal as required.

May (01) maintain machine
(02) control the operation of linecaster by feeding in punched tape produced by perforating machine or computer
(03) melt down type on completion of printing.

Other titles include Intertype operator, Linotype operator, Stringer machine operator, Typograph operator.

632.35 Filmsetting machine operator

Operates tape-controlled filmsetting machine to reproduce type characters or images on film or sensitised paper

Loads film or sensitised paper on machine; feeds in data tape produced on perforating machine or computer; operates machine to reproduce the copy photographically.

May (01) develop exposed film or paper

(02) operate keyboard to produce data tape to control filmsetting machine (632.20)

(03) arrange filmset material to make up pages (632.40)

(04) position and adjust appropriate lens arrangement.

632.40 Make-up hand

Arranges composed metal type of filmset material and illustration blocks to make up pages

(01) **Make-up hand (metal type)**

Arranges hand or machine composed type according to page lay-out specifications; positions illustration blocks and places spacing material between type and blocks and between columns; obtains correct width and length of pages and balances layout of text and illustrations by adding, removing or dividing lines of type and adjusting spacing; secures page with page-cord ready for imposition.

(02) **Make-up hand (filmset material)**

Positions filmset type and illustrations on backing sheet which may be marked out according to page lay-out; fixes material in place; rules in column lines, borders, etc.

May (03) arrange and secure made-up pages in a metal frame (chase) ready for printing (632.15)

(04) p int proof copies of the pages (634.25).

632.98 Trainee

Performs, under instruction or guidance, various tasks including training exercises and as appropriate pursues studies in order to acquire the basic skills and knowledge required to perform the tasks of workers in composing and typesetting occupations.

632.99 Other composing and typesetting occupations

Workers in this group prepare printing layouts and specifications, compose type and assemble composed material into required format for printing and are not elsewhere classified, for example:

(01) **Poster hands** (set up by hand large wooden or metal type for poster or newsbill printing).

Unit Group 633 Printing Plate and Cylinder Preparing Occupations (Excluding Metal Engraving)

Workers in this unit group make printing plates from moulds of composed type, lay out printing copy to be photographed, set out photographed material for printing on plates or cylinders and transfer film images to printing plates or cylinders by photographic process.

Note: engravers of metal printing plates and rollers are classified in unit group 792.

633.02 Stereotyper

Makes moulds from formes of type and illustration blocks, and casts or moulds stereotype letterpress printing plates

Ensures that block of composed type (type forme) is clean and surface is level; places layer of special pulp board (flong) on forme and passes under hydraulic press or rolling machine to form a mould (matrix); positions matrix in casting box or moulding machine; pours in molten metal or operates machine controls to admit rubber or plastic material to form printing plate; removes plate, trims to size and finishes back and sides with planing machine; removes surplus metal from surface of metal plate with routing machine or by hand with a chisel.

May (01) plate face of stereotype with nickel after coating with copper by electro-deposition

(02) perform tasks of electrotyper (633.04).

633.04 Electrotyper

Makes moulds from formes of type and illustration blocks, and makes letterpress printing plates by electroplating moulds of type formes and filling shells with molten metal

Ensures that block of composed type (type forme) is clean and surface is level; lays sheet of specially prepared wax, rubber or plastic on forme and passes under hydraulic press to form a mould; trims edges of mould; coats mould with electro-conductive substance and immerses in electrolytic bath until metal shell of desired thickness is formed on mould; separates metal shell from mould and fills shell with molten metal to form plate; mounts finished plates on wood or metal blocks for flatbed presses or curves finished plates for rotary presses.

May (01) make sheets of plastic or rubber for mould making by heating synthetic compounds in oven

(02) plate face of electrotypes with chromium.

633.06 Printer on metal (process engraving)

Prepares process engraving printing plates by transferring image from negative film of printing copy to plates by photographic process

Scrubs metal plate with a mechanical brush and pumice powder to remove all traces of grease; coats plate with a light-sensitive solution in a coating machine (whirler); lays film negative of the copy on the sensitised plate and places in a vacuum frame; operates vacuum mechanism to obtain perfect contact between the negative and plate; exposes frame to light to print image on the coated plate; after exposure, washes plate in chemical solution to dissolve the coating on the non-image areas; paints back of plate with acid resist as required; fixes the image by immersing the plate in an acid bath; heats plate to burn in the image.

May (01) superimpose shading on line plates (ie plates with no gradation of tone) by further exposure under a negative bearing the required pattern (tint-laying).

633.08 Printer down (photo-lithography)

Prepares lithographic printing plates by transferring image from negatives or positives of printing copy to plates by photographic process

Selects suitable sensitised surface plate or coats deep-etch plate with light-sensitive solution in a coating machine (whirler); lays film negative (for surface plates) or positive (for deep-etch plates) of the copy on the sensitised plate and places both in a vacuum frame; operates vacuum mechanism to obtain perfect contact between the film and plate; exposes frame to light.

If preparing surface plates, covers the exposed plate with black litho ink which adheres to printed image area; develops plate in water.

If preparing deep-etch plates, develops exposed plate in chemical solution; applies etchant to image area; cleans off etchant and applies lacquer to etched area; scrubs coating off non-image area and applies a desensitising solution.

May (01) use "step and repeat" machine to duplicate image where multiple copies are printed from one plate (eg postage stamps, labels).

633 .10 Carbon printer (photogravure)

Prepares photogravure printing cylinders or plates by transferring image from positive film of printing copy to cylinders or plates by photographic process

Positions light-sensitive carbon tissue (pigment paper coated with bichromated gelatine) and a special screen in vacuum frame; operates vacuum mechanism to obtain perfect contact between the tissue and screen; exposes frame to light; replaces screen with film positive; again exposes frame to print image on the screened tissue; wets surface of cylinder or plate; places carbon tissue on cylinder or plate with gelatine surface in contact with the metal and applies pressure to ensure complete and even adhesion; transfers cylinder or plate to a hot water tank and peels off paper backing from carbon tissue; washes off unexposed gelatine, leaving gelatine image on the cylinder or plate ready for etching.

633 .12 Planner (photogravure, photo-lithography)

Arranges film positives or negatives in final layout in readiness for printing on photogravure cylinders or lithographic plates

(01) **Planner (photogravure)**

Examines dummy layout (paste-up) of printing copy arranged in correct order and in sequence of pages prepared by editorial department and alters as necessary; makes outline tracing of the copy, marking dimensions of each page and indicating limits of type-matter and illustrations; passes copy and tracing to camera operator with instructions regarding size of film positives of copy required; on receipt of positives, positions sheet of clear plastic foil on illuminated glass table; fixes the positives in the correct order and in colour sequence on the foil with paste or special adhesive tape using the paste-up as a guide.

(02) **Planner (photo-lithography)**

Arranges negatives or positives of printing copy on plastic foil on illuminated table, using sketch of layout or paste-up as a guide; fixes negatives or positives with paste or special adhesive tape; assembles colour negatives or positives in correct sequence for the printing of colour plates.

May (03) prepare the paste-up

(04) use special projector to reduce or enlarge image of copy to required size for tracing.

Other titles include Assembler (photo-lithography)
Stripper (photo-lithography).

633 .14 Lithographic assistant

Arranges and pastes printing material on paper ready for photographing

On receipt of sketch of projected layout and material to be printed (typematter, photographs, drawings), examines typematter to ensure that all items are of the required standard; where necessary, arranges to have a further copy made; rules off page size on sheet of paper; arranges typematter on the paper using the sketch as a guide; sets the photographs and drawings in the appropriate spaces, trimming them to fit if necessary; pastes all material to the paper and passes the completed layout (paste-up) to the camera operator.

Other titles include Lithographic preparer.

633 .98 Trainee

Performs, under instruction or guidance, various tasks including training exercises and as appropriate pursues studies in order to acquire the basic skills and knowledge required to perform the tasks of workers in printing plate and cylinder preparing occupations (excluding metal engraving).

633 .99 Other printing plate and cylinder preparing occupations (excluding metal engraving)

Workers in this group make printing plates from moulds of composed type, lay out printing copy to be photographed, set out photographed material for printing on plates or cylinders and transfer film images to printing plates or cylinders by photographic process and are not elsewhere classified, for example:

(01) **Collotype plate makers** (prepare collotype printing plates by photographic process).

Unit Group 634 Printing Machine Operators (Excluding Screen and Block Printing)

Workers in this unit group set and operate printing, die stamping and embossing machines.

634.05 Letterpress machine minder (platen press, cylinder press)

Makes ready and operates a platen or flatbed cylinder printing press

Positions and fixes block of composed type (forme) on type-bed of press and ensures that surface of type is level; sets ink supply controls and fills ink ducts; packs surface of platen or impression cylinder with layers of paper so that all parts of work receive correct pressure; loads or directs loading of press with paper and sets and adjusts controls of feeding mechanism; adjusts mechanism which sprays printed material to prevent smudging; runs off proof copies; examines proof and makes adjustments to bring print to required standard; starts printing run and ensures that printing proceeds correctly; ensures that supplies of ink and paper are replenished.

May (01) feed or direct feeding of paper into machine by hand
(02) operate machine with additional equipment to obtain thermographic finish (raised printing surface obtained by dusting printed matter with powder and fusing in heating unit)
(03) clean inking rollers between runs of different colours.

Other titles include Letterpress machine manager (cylinder), Printing pressman (letterpress) (cylinder), Printing pressman (letterpress) (platen).

634.10 Letterpress machine minder (rotary press)

Makes ready and operates a rotary letterpress printing press

Positions and fixes printing plates round printing cylinders; sets ink supply controls and fills ink ducts or tanks as required; packs (dresses) surface of impression cylinders with layers of paper or rubber blanket so that all parts of work receive correct pressure; supervises loading of press with roll of paper (web), supply of paper sheets or other material to be printed and sets and adjusts feeding and counting mechanism; makes trial run; examines proof and makes adjustments to bring print to required standard; starts printing run and ensures that printing, cutting and folding proceed correctly; ensures that supplies of ink and other materials are replenished.

May (01) operate machine with additional equipment to obtain thermographic finish (raised printing surface obtained by dusting printed matter with powder and fusing in heating unit).

Other titles include Letterpress machine manager, Printing pressman.

634.15 Lithographic machine minder

Makes ready and operates a lithographic printing press

Positions and fixes printing plates round printing cylinder; sets controls for supplies of ink and moisture to rollers; adjusts rollers; fills ink ducts; packs impression cylinder so that all parts of plate receive correct pressure and adjusts space between cylinders; loads or directs loading of press with paper or other materials to be printed, and sets and adjusts controls of feeding mechanism; adjusts mechanism which sprays printed material to prevent smudging; makes trial run; examines proof and makes adjustments to bring print to required standard; starts printing run and ensures that printing proceeds correctly; ensures that supplies of ink and other materials are replenished.

(01) **Metal printer**

Specialises in the operation of a lithographic press to print text or designs on metal; controls the operation of drying oven.

May (02) operate a flatbed lithographic press which prints from a flat plate
(03) on web-fed press, control the operation of a drying oven, folder and slitter
(04) operate machine with additional equipment to obtain thermographic finish (raised printing surface obtained by dusting printed matter with powder and fusing in heating unit).

Other titles include Lithographic machine manager, Printing pressman.

634.20 Photogravure machine minder

Makes ready and operates a photogravure printing press

Installs printing cylinders in press; sets and adjusts doctor blades to remove excess ink and mechanism and controls to regulate ink supply and superimposition of colours; fills ink trough as required; supervises the loading of press with paper or other materials to be printed and sets and adjusts feeding mechanism; makes trial run; examines proof and makes adjustments to bring print to required standard; starts printing run and ensures that printing proceeds correctly; ensures that supplies of ink and other materials are replenished.

May (01) on web-fed press, control the operation of a drying oven, folder and slitter.

Other titles include Printing pressman.

634.25 Prover

Operates hand or semi-automatic press to print proof copies to check the accuracy and quality of printing type, illustration blocks and plates

Positions block of composed type (forme or galley) or printing plate on type-bed of press, inks forme, galley or plate by hand or operates semi-automatic inking mechanism; places paper on press in position for printing; operates press to print proofs; for colour work changes plate, superimposes next colour in sequence and repeats till full colour proofs are obtained; passes proofs and formes, galleys or plates to composing, reproduction or proof reading departments for checking and revision as required.

Other titles include Colour prover.

634.30 Die stamper

Sets and operates a die stamping machine to emboss lettering or decorative designs on stationery

Fixes die in machine; stamps impression of die on pad of cardboard (force); cuts around impression, sticks piece of rubber or rubber-coated cloth on top and replaces in machine to act as cushion during stamping; if colour work is being done fills ink ducts, adjusts position of inking roller and sets ink supply controls; loads or directs loading of stationery materials on machine; positions sheet of stationery on machine and stamps proof copy; examines proof and makes any necessary adjustments to bring impression to required standard; starts stamping run and ensures that stamping proceeds correctly; ensures that supplies of stationery materials are replenished.

Other titles include Relief stamper.

634.35 Machine printer (textiles)

Sets and operates a machine to print designs on textiles using engraved rollers

Fits fabric padding round main pressure cylinder of machine and positions endless blanket taut round cylinder and rollers to provide a resilient surface; clamps printing rollers in position in sequence according to pattern to be printed; threads backing cloth (back grey) through machine to prevent colour staining blanket on pressure cylinder; supervises the loading of fabric on machine and threads fabric through rollers over back grey; sets doctor blades to remove excess colour and any lint and fluff from the printing rollers; mounts colour boxes on machine and fills with appropriate dyestuffs; starts machine and makes trial run; examines printed sample and makes any necessary adjustments to machine; starts printing run; ensures that printing proceeds correctly and that colours are replenished as required.

634.40 Machine printer (wallpaper)

Sets and operates a machine to print designs on wallpaper using rollers

Installs printing rollers in machine in sequence according to pattern to be printed; supervises the loading of roll of wallpaper on machine; threads wallpaper through rollers and adjusts feed guides and tension bars; sets edge trimming blades; adjusts controls to regulate running speed of machine and temperature of drying unit; fills paint boxes with appropriate water or oil colours; starts machine and makes trial run; examines printed sample and makes any necessary adjustments to machine; starts printing run; inspects paper at regular intervals to ensure that printing and trimming are proceeding correctly; ensures that supplies of colours and paper are replenished.

May (01) operate a duplex machine which combines two reels of paper and embosses and prints a design.

Other titles include Surface printer.

634.50 Embossing machine operator (wallpaper)

Sets and operates a machine to emboss designs on wallpaper using engraved rollers

Installs embossing rollers in machine; supervises the loading of roll of wallpaper on machine; threads wallpaper through rollers and adjusts feed guides and tension bars; adjusts pressure of rollers; sets edge trimming blades; for colour work, fills paint troughs with appropriate water or oil colours; starts machine and makes trial run; examines embossed sample and makes any necessary adjustments to machine; starts embossing run; ensures that embossing and trimming proceed correctly.

May (01) specialise in operating a particular type of machine, eg vinyl embossing machine, combination duplex embossing machine.

634.55 Embossing machine operator (excluding wallpaper)

Operates a machine to emboss or imprint trademarks or other symbols or identifying information on paper, cloth, leather, wood or plastic materials or articles by stamping

Positions metal stamp or type in holder of machine; if applying gold, silver or other metal foil, positions spool of foil on spindle and feeds through guides and rollers; places material or article on machine bed and starts machine; pulls lever or depresses pedal to emboss or print the material or article; removes material or article and examines for faults.

May (01) make and/or use a template to ensure that article is correctly positioned in machine.

Other titles include Gold blocker, Stamping machine operator.

See Embossing machine operator (leather, skin) (531.70)

634.60 Offset duplicating machine operator

Operates offset duplicating machine to reproduce printed, typewritten, handwritten or drawn matter from prepared paper, plastic or metal master plate

Positions on machine paper, plastic or metal master plate of matter to be reproduced; loads supply of paper on machine; adjusts controls to regulate flow of ink to ink rollers and flow of water to damping rollers; sets controls to adjust feed and speed of machine; starts machine to reproduce required number of copies; cleans machine as necessary between runs.

May (01) prepare master plate.

Additional factors: type of machine to which accustomed; whether accustomed to trade printing or to work in printing department of business or industrial firm (in-plant printing).

Other titles include Small-offset press operator.

634.65 Upper marker (footwear)

Operates machine to mark position of stitch lines, punch holes and decorative features on footwear uppers

Places hardboard pattern guide on machine bed and positions upper on hardboard guide; inserts marker board in frame at head of machine; feeds ink to or brushes ink on inking pad; operates pedal to ink metal strips or pins on board and to lower inked markerboard on upper, imprinting stitch lines, positions of punch holes and other features; changes pattern guide and marker board in machine for each size and style of footwear.

Other titles include Stitch marking machinist.

Excluded are workers marking stitching lines by perforating machine(662.60)

634.98 Trainee

Performs, under instruction or guidance, various tasks including training exercises and as appropriate pursues studies in order to acquire the basic skills and knowledge required to perform the tasks of printing machine operators (excluding screen and block printing).

634.99 Other printing press machine operators

Workers in this group set and operate printing, die-stamping and embossing machines and are not elsewhere classified, for example:

(01) **Carpet printers;** (02) **Collotype machine minders,** Collotype machine managers; (03) **Dial printers (watches and clocks)** (operate machines to print markings on watch and clock dials by means of gelatine transfer heads); (04) **Impression takers (roller engraving)** (take off trial colour impressions from engraved rollers); (05) **Machine rulers** (rule lines on accounts books, ledgers, statistical forms, etc); (06) **Printers (pottery)** (print impressions for pottery decoration on tissue paper from engraved rollers); (07) **Printers (technical ceramics)** (operate hand printing presses to print working instructions on capacitors, condensers, etc).

Unit Group 635 Screen and Block Printing Occupations

Workers in this unit group print lettering and designs on fabric and other materials by screen and block method.

635.05 Screen printer (machine) (excluding fabric)

Sets and operates a screen printing machine to print lettering and designs on materials such as metal, plastics, paper or glass

Clamps prepared screen in position on machine; makes guide marks on machine table as required to ensure that each item to be printed is correctly positioned; fixes in position rubber squeegee which presses the colour through the screen; positions item on machine table against guide marks or fixes item in stand or holder; pours colour into machine trough or directly on to screen; starts machine to position screen over item or item under screen and move squeegee across screen; removes printed item as required and continues process until required number is printed; for additional colours repeats process, using a separate screen for each colour.

May (01) cut and mount stencils (639.60)
(02) prepare screens by photographic process (639.05)
(03) mix colours.

635.10 Screen printer (hand) (excluding fabric)

Prints lettering and designs on materials such as metal, plastics, paper or glass by hand using a prepared screen and squeegee

Fixes prepared screen in printing frame; makes guide marks on printing table to ensure that each item to be printed is correctly positioned; positions item on table against guide marks and lowers screen over table; pours colours on screen and manipulates squeegee to press colour through; removes printed item and continues process until required number of items is printed; for additional colours repeats process using a separate screen for each colour.

May (01) cut and mount stencils (639.60)
(02) prepare screens by photographic process (639.05)
(03) mix colours.

635.15 Block printer (fabric)

Prints designs on fabric by hand using engraved wooden or metal printing blocks

Spreads gum evenly over surface of printing table; unrolls length of fabric to be printed on to backing cloth, smoothes it out and marks it to indicate the positioning of printing blocks; checks that colour has been prepared and that blocks are clean; presses block on pad impregnated with colour (sieve); places block carefully on fabric according to the markings; taps block with mallet (maul) to imprint design firmly; repeats process on same length of fabric ensuring the correct positioning of each subsequent block and using correct colour sequence until length of fabric has been printed according to instructions; continues until specified amount of material has been printed; transfers each completed length to drying frame.

May (01) print sample (fent) first and pass to colourist for checking
(02) superimpose colours on design already printed on fabric.

635.20 Block printer (wallpaper)

Prints design on wallpaper by hand using engraved wooden printing blocks

Dips wooden pattern block into colour tray; positions block between guide marks on blank or partially patterned wallpaper, laying different colours adjacent to or on top of others to form the required pattern; ensures correct matching of pattern by constant visual checks with original pattern.

635.50 Screen printer (machine) (fabric)

Sets and operates a screen printing machine to print designs on fabric

Sorts prepared screens into correct sequence for printing; clamps screens in position on machine; loads or directs the loading of fabric to be printed on to machine; threads fabric through rollers and ensures that fabric is correctly gummed to table surface or backing cloth; adjusts mechanism to ensure that the print from each screen will be superimposed accurately on previous prints; fixes in position the rubber squeegees or metal rollers which press the colour through the screens on to the fabric; pours or operates controls to pour colour into the troughs formed by the squeegee blades or directly on to the screens; starts machine to lower the screens on to the fabric and move the squeegees or rollers across the screens; examines screens during run and makes any necessary adjustments; replenishes colour as required; if backing cloth is used, checks that fabric and backing cloth are separating cleanly at delivery end of machine and that drying unit is functioning correctly; transfers printed fabric to steam chamber to fix colour as required.

May (01) cut and mount stencils (639.60)
(02) prepare screens by photographic process (639.05)
(03) mix colours.

635.60 Screen printer (hand) (fabric)

Prints designs on fabric by hand using a prepared screen and squeegee

Straightens fabric to be printed with heated iron and gums on to backing cloth on printing table; mounts first screen across fabric, setting runners of frame into guide rails along the edge of the table; sets stops in the guide rails which line up the screens for printing; pours colour on screen and manipulates squeegee to press colour through screen on to fabric; moves screen to next preselected stop and repeats; continues until the whole length of fabric has been printed; repeats process for other colours of the design using a separate screen for each colour.

May (01) cut and mount stencils (639.60)
(02) prepare screen by photographic process (639.05)
(03) mix colours.

635.98 Trainee

Performs, under instruction or guidance, various tasks including training exercises and as appropriate pursues studies in order to acquire the basic skills and knowledge required to perform the tasks of workers in screen and block printing occupations.

635.99 Other screen and block printing occupations

Workers in this group print lettering and designs on fabric and other materials by screen and block method and are not elsewhere classified.

Unit Group 636 Photographic Processing and Related Occupations

Workers in this unit group perform tasks in processing, printing and finishing still and cine film.

636.02 Film processor (cine)

Operates a machine to develop negative or positive cine film

Fills tanks of developing machine with prepared chemical solutions; mounts reel of exposed film or magazine containing film on machine; threads end of film through machine and attaches to rereeling mechanism in drying chamber; sets machine controls to regulate speed, timing cycle, temperature of solution in tanks and temperature of drying chamber; starts machine, checks progress during developing and adjusts controls as necessary; changes or replenishes solutions as required; keeps records of films processed; cleans machine.

Other titles include Film developer.

636.04 Film printer (cine)

Prints positive cine film using printing machine

Mounts reels of processed negative and unexposed positive films on printing machine; threads films through machine; adjusts controls to set the printing exposure according to specifications set out by grader; starts machine which prints the positive, separates the negative and positive films after printing and winds them on reels; places positive film in can and passes to developing section.

May (01) operate film printing machine to produce positive film of reduced size from original negative and be known as Reduction printer.

636.06 Sensitometric control assistant

Determines time and temperature of film development to obtain desired degree of gradation in film or sound track

Exposes photographic material to light in a sensitometer; determines correct developing speeds for various films being processed; plots graphs for base density and contrast; determines photographic density (resistance to passage of light) corresponding to each intensity of exposure using a densitometer; calculates required characteristics of film and processing solutions from data so obtained.

636.08 Grader (cine film)

Examines cine film negative to determine and record best exposure times for printing positives of each scene

Examines negative over a light box; judges density of each scene and decides light intensity required for printing, grading black and white film for density changes and colour film for colour correction and density; cuts notches on edge of negative to indicate where changes in degree of exposure are required; records data and passes information to printer; projects printed positive on to screen, examines clarity of scene and makes amendments to printing instructions as required.

May (01) use an electronic cueing system in which the light change positions are marked by removable patches of metal foil.

636 .10 Cutting and assembly worker (cine film processing)

Arranges, cuts and/or joins negative film to correspond with edited positive film and/or matches sound and action film

(01) **Negative cutter's assistant**

Arranges negative film in correct sequence for cutting according to edited positive film and/or written instructions; records sequence data on cutting sheets.

(02) **Negative cutter**

Cuts negative film to correspond with edited positive film; matches sound and action film using synchroniser.

(03) **Film joiner, Negative assembler**

Joins ends of cut negative or positive film by applying cement and pressing in a joining machine; winds film on to reel and examines for defects.

Other titles include Positive assembly worker.

(04) **Rushes synchroniser**

Synchronises rushes of sound and action film for viewing in studio.

636 .12 Regenerative machine operator (cine film)

Operates machines which clean and recondition old, worn and scratched films

Threads film on cleaning machine; sets controls and starts machine to remove dirt, wax and grease from the film; removes cleaned film and attaches reel to regenerative machine; threads film through machine and starts machine to apply chemicals to the film, causing the coating to expand and fill in scratches; removes treated film from the machine.

May (01) clean 16mm film by hand.

636 .14 Retoucher (graphic reproduction)

Modifies colouring and shading of film negatives and positives used for making printing plates

Places negative or positive on special table with translucent top illuminated from below; compares photographic image with original copy and for 'half tone' work examines dot formation for contrast and definition; applies various paints, stains, opaques, washes, acids and other chemicals with hand or air brush to improve photographic qualities of film; covers holes and blemishes with opaque paint.

May (01) use special equipment to produce colour separations, eg electronic scanning machine.

Other titles include Spotter.

636 .16 Retoucher (photographic)

Retouches photographic negatives and finished prints to remove defects or add detail

Examines negatives or prints to determine the features which require to be accented or minimised; removes unwanted detail from the negative or print, using retouching knife; shades negative with pencil to modify tonal gradations; fills in white spots or adds detail to the finished print using paint or dye and spotting brush.

May (01) mount and trim finished prints.

636 .50 Still film processor (manual)

Treats exposed photographic still film or plate with chemicals to develop negative image

Unwinds exposed film or removes exposed plate from lightproof box in darkroom; mixes developing and fixing solutions according to formulae; fills developing, rinsing, fixing and washing baths; determines time and temperature required for immersion of film or plate; immerses film or plate in developing, rinsing, fixing and washing baths in required sequence to develop negative image; dries developed negatives.

May (01) make prints from developed negatives (636 .55)

(02) undertake projection printing (636 .70).

Additional factor: whether accustomed to black and white or colour work.

Other titles include Still film developer.

636 .55 Still film printer (manual)

Prepares contact prints from photographic negatives

Positions negative and sensitised paper in printing frame; closes frame ensuring the negative and paper are in close contact; exposes frame to light for timed period; develops, rinses, fixes and washes the exposed print for set periods in a series of chemical and water baths; dries and trims finished prints.

May (01) undertake projection printing (636 .70)

(02) glaze prints.

Additional factor: whether accustomed to black and white or colour work.

Other titles include Contact printer.

636.60 Photographic processing machine operator (still)

Operates machine to treat exposed photographic still film or sensitised paper with chemicals to develop negative or positive image

Mixes developing and fixing solutions according to formulae; fills tanks of processing machine with appropriate solutions or water; if processing film unrolls films, attaches to metal rods in batches and loads into machine; if processing paper attaches end of roll to leader strip and feeds through machine; sets machine controls to regulate speed and timing cycle, and temperature of solutions and water in tanks; starts machine to develop film or paper; removes developed negatives, transparencies or prints.

May (01) operate printing machine (636.65)
(02) glaze developed prints
(03) cut roll of developed paper into separate prints.

Additional factors: whether accustomed to processing film or paper; whether accustomed to black and white or colour work.

Other titles include Developing machine operator, Film processing machine operator, Paper processing machine operator.

636.65 Photographic printing machine operator (still)

Operates machine to print images from negatives on to sensitised paper

Loads reel of sensitised paper on printing machine; threads roll of negatives through holder on machine; sets machine controls to regulate exposure, colour correction, etc; fits appropriate filters for colour work; starts machine to project light through the negatives and print the images on the sensitised paper.

May (01) operate paper processing machine (636.60)
(02) operate equipment to print standard size enlargements ('en' prints).

Additional factor: whether accustomed to black and white or colour work.

636.70 Projection printer

Prints photographs larger or smaller than original negatives

Determines size and composition of print required and adjusts position of projection printer accordingly; places negative in holder; fits appropriate filters for colour work; adjusts focus of projector until image projected on baseboard or easel is satisfactorily defined; places sheet of sensitised paper on baseboard or easel; exposes for required time to print image from negative on to paper; develops, rinses, fixes and washes print for set periods in a series of chemical and water baths; dries and trims finished prints.

Other titles include Enlarger.

636.75 Photographic finisher

Performs one or more of the tasks in finishing photographic prints

Performs one or more of the following tasks: trims prints with knife or on guillotine; positions piece of dry mounting tissue on back of print; applies heated iron at various points to make the tissue adhere to the print; trims print and tissue; positions print and tissue on mount of paper, cardboard or fabric, places in a heated dry mounting press and operates press to fix print to mount; cuts lengths of transparencies into single slides and mounts slides.

May (01) check prints for faults.

Other titles include Mounter, Print trimmer.

636.98 Trainee

Performs, under instruction or guidance, various tasks including training exercises and as appropriate pursues studies in order to acquire the basic skills and knowledge required to perform the tasks of workers in photographic processing and related occupations.

636.99 Other photographic processing and related occupations

Workers in this group perform tasks in processing, printing and finishing still and cine film and are not elsewhere classified, for example:

(01) **Colourists** (tint or colour photographic prints using brush or air brush); (02) **Driers and glazers** (dry and glaze photographic prints manually); (03) **Exposers** (expose negatives and sensitised paper to light); (04) **Film driers** (tend drying chamber of cine film developing machines); (05) **Film loaders** (load cine film in special magazine for processing in developing machine); (06) **Fixers** (fix prints in chemical solution); (07) **Washers** (wash developed prints).

Unit Group 639 Printing, Photographic Processing and Related Occupations Not Elsewhere Classified

Workers in this unit group perform miscellaneous tasks in printing, photographic processing and related occupations and are not elsewhere classified.

639.05 Screenmaker (screen printing)

Makes up printing screens and reproduces designs photographically on screens in readiness for printing

Marks out and cuts metal or fabric screening mesh to size; for cylindrical screens forms metal mesh into cylinder or covers gauze cylinder with fabric mesh; stretches cylinder or cut mesh in stretching machine; for flat screens, positions a wood or metal frame against mesh in stretching machine and secures mesh to frame; trims off surplus material; prepares photographic emulsion, applies one or more coats to screen and dries screen; positions positive or negative film or colour separation of required design on screen; exposes print or colour separation to light to print design on screen; washes off surplus emulsion and dries screen; prepares separate screens for each colour in design.

May (01) apply coating of lacquer to surface of design
(02) use a "step and repeat" photocopying machine to print repetitive designs on screen
(03) repair damaged screens.

639.10 Screenmaker's assistant (screen printing)

Assists screenmaker in the preparation of screens for screen printing

Cuts length of cloth from roll and sews it to fit stretching machine; fits screen cylinder on to supports on screenmaker's table; inserts portable inspection light in cylinder or beneath flat screen and examines for flaws on surface of lacquered design; retouches by hand any uncovered places on lacquered screen; keeps tools, benches and work areas tidy; otherwise assists screenmaker as required.

639.15 Machine assistant (die stamping)

Assists die stamper in operating a die stamping machine

Feeds single sheets of paper into machine ensuring that die will strike in the correct position; removes stamped paper and lays on drier or on moving belt which carries the paper under a drier; otherwise assists die stamper as required.

Other titles include Feeder.

639.50 Letterpress machine assistant

Assists machine minder in operating a rotary, cylinder or platen letterpress printing press

Fills ink ducts; loads roll of paper (web) on press or stacks paper on feedboard; starts press as directed by minder; keeps press supplied with paper and ink; removes and stacks printed matter; cleans and oils press; otherwise assists machine minder as required.

May (01) check and control tension of paper during run under direction of machine minder.

Other titles include Feeder, Fly hand (rotary press), Layer-on, Reel hand (rotary press).

639.52 Lithographic machine assistant

Assists machine minder in operating a lithographic printing press

Fills ink ducts and water tank; loads paper or other material to be printed on press; keeps press supplied with ink and paper or other material being printed; removes and stacks printed matter; cleans and oils press; re-covers damping rollers with materials such as velmolle or lithonette; otherwise assists machine minder as required.

Other titles include Feeder, Layer-on, Racker-up.

639.54 Photogravure machine assistant

Assists machine minder in operating a photogravure printing press

Adjusts valve to control level of ink in ducts; loads paper or other material to be printed on press; keeps press supplied with ink and paper or other material being printed; removes and stacks printed matter cleans and oils press; otherwise assists machine minder as required.

Other titles include Feeder, Fly hand, Reel hand.

639.56 Textile printer's assistant

Assists machine printer (textiles) in operating a machine to print designs on textiles using engraved rollers

Places roll of backing material (back grey) around endless blanket on cylinder to prevent staining; places roll of textile to be printed on rack; adjusts width guides and tension devices; threads both rolls through machine guides and rollers; places colour boxes in position and maintains supply of colours during printing; washes print rollers after use; assists in changing print rollers; renews lapping and endless blanket around cylinder as required; otherwise assists printer as required.

(01) **Back tenter**

Assists printer on rear side of machine.

(02) **Lurrier**

Assists printer on front side of machine.

639.58 Machine printer's assistant (wallpaper)

Assists machine printer (wallpaper) in operating a machine to print designs on wallpaper using rollers

Assists in changing printing rollers and loading wallpaper on machine; threads wallpaper through machine; draws water or oil colours from colour tank and pours into colour trays of machine; maintains supply of colours during printing process; repairs tears in wallpaper with adhesive paper; cleans rollers and oils machine; otherwise assists printer as required.

Other titles include Back tenter.

639.60 Stencil cutter (screen printing)

Cuts stencil by hand for use in screen printing

Positions transparent gelatinous film on thin backing paper over the design or lettering to be reproduced; using knife cuts outline of design through film leaving the backing intact; eases cut out pieces off backing paper with tip of knife.

May (01) mount prepared stencil on screen.

639.62 Roller changer

Changes or assists in changing printing rollers on textile printing machines

Inserts end of mandrel into hollow centre of printing roller and positions on hydraulic jack using hoist; starts jack machinery to press mandrel into centre of roller to form a solid roller; removes used rollers from printing machine and lifts new ones into position according to pattern to be printed; transports used rollers to warehouse for removal of mandrel, cleaning and storage.

639.64 Stamper (pottery)

Stamps pottery with trade mark, manufacturer's name, badge or decorative design

Pours ready mixed colour into reservoir of machine or spreads over hand stamping pad; positions supply of ware in holding device on machine or on work bench if hand stamping; starts machine to stamp ware automatically or stamps by hand with rubber or sponge stamp; adjusts consistency of colour as necessary.

Other titles include Back stamper, Gold stamping machine attendant.

639.90 Tierer (textile printing)

Assists block printer by performing service tasks as directed

Lays printing blocks on table in colour group sequence for printer to check; helps to wash down table and spread adhesive over its surface in readiness for laying down fabric; collects prepared roll of fabric from stock and assists printer to position and smooth fabric over gummed table; stacks colour cases with sieves and brushes in correct order for colour printing; washes and changes sieves and brushes; helps to loosen printed fabric from table and wind it on drying frame.

639.98 Trainee

Performs, under instruction or guidance, various tasks including training exercises and as appropriate pursues studies in order to acquire the basic skills and knowledge required to perform the tasks of workers in printing, photographic processing and related occupations not elsewhere classified.

639 .99 Other printing, photographic processing and related occupations not elsewhere classified

Workers in this group perform miscellaneous tasks in printing, photographic processing and related occupations and are not separately classified, for example:

(01) **Branders,** Markers, Stampers (print trade marks or other identifiying information on articles by hand stamps or branding machines); (02) **Collotype machine assistants;** (03) **Combining machine operators** (operate machines to gum backing to fabric prior to printing); (04) **Dis hands** (replace type in appropriate compartments in type case after printing is completed); (05) **Machine rulers' assistants** (assist machine rulers to rule lines on accounts books, etc); (06) **Numberers (printed matter)** (print numbers on stationery forms by hand stamp, treadle or automatic machine); (07) **Printers (floor-cloth)** (operate machines to print basic materials on one or both sides of floor-cloth); (08) **Printers' assistants** (assist still film printers (manual)); (09) **Servicers (screen printing)** (assist screen printers (machine).

Minor Group 64 BOOKBINDING, PAPER WORKING AND PAPERBOARD PRODUCTS MAKING OCCUPATIONS

Workers in this minor group bind books and make products from paper, paperboard and abrasive cloth and paper and perform closely related tasks.

The occupations are arranged in the following unit groups:

640 Foremen (Bookbinding, Paper Working and Paperboard Products Making Occupations)

641 Bookbinding Occupations

642 Paper Working and Paperboard Products Making Occupations

Unit Group 640 Foremen (Bookbinding, Paper Working and Paperboard Products Making Occupations)

Workers in this unit group directly supervise and co-ordinate the activities of workers in bookbinding, paper working and paperboard products making occupations.

640 .10 Foreman (bookbinding)

Directly supervises and co-ordinates the activities of workers in bookbinding occupations

Performs appropriate tasks as described under SUPERVISOR/FOREMAN (UNSPECIFIED) (990 .00).

Additional factor: number of workers supervised.

640 .20 Foreman (paper working and paperboard products making occupations)

Directly supervises and co-ordinates the activities of workers in paper working and paperboard products making occupations

Performs appropriate tasks as described under SUPERVISOR/FOREMAN (UNSPECIFIED) (990 .00).

Additional factor: number of workers supervised.

640 .98 Trainee

Performs, under instruction or guidance, various tasks including training exercises and as appropriate pursues studies in order to acquire the basic skills and knowledge required to perform the tasks of foremen (bookbinding, paper working and paperboard products making occupations).

Unit Group 641 Bookbinding Occupations

Workers in this unit group perform tasks in binding books and are not elsewhere classified.

See Embossing machine operators (excluding wallpaper) (634.55) and Loose-leaf binding machine operators (642.52)

641.10 Bookbinder (general)

Performs all tasks in binding books or stationery subsequent to sewing

Compresses sewn book in nipping machine to exclude air and reduce swelling caused by sewing; glues the spine (back) of book; trims head, tail and fore-edge of book using trimming machine; gilds or marbles edges of pages as necessary (edge gilding, marbling); shapes spine of book (rounding and backing); glues a length of scrim (mull) on spine as a first lining and glues on a further lining of brown paper (lining-up); cuts boards for front and back of case and cloth to cover boards and spine and fixes cloth to boards to form case (case making); embosses lettering or decoration on case by hand (finishing) or machine (blocking); fixes case to book (casing-in).

May (01) set and operate a folding machine to fold printed sheets into sections ready for gathering (641.30).

641.20 Bookbinder (sub-divisional)

Specialises in one or more of the operations in binding books or stationery subsequent to sewing and is not elsewhere classified

Performs one or more of the tasks as described under BOOKBINDER (GENERAL) (641.10) and is usually known according to main specialisation, for example, Nipping machine operator, Rounding and backing machine operator, Case maker, Finisher.

May (01) operate machine to cover paper-backed books and be known as Perfect binding machine operator.

Other titles include Board and cloth cutting machine operator, Casing-in machine operator, Lining-up machine operator, Three-knife machine operator.

641.30 Bindery assistant

Performs, by hand or machine, folding, gathering, collating and/or sewing tasks in binding books, periodicals or stationery and assists bookbinders

Performs one or more of the following tasks: folds printed sheets into sections; pastes end papers to first and last sections of book and illustration plates to appropriate sections; gathers sections to make up complete set; if gathered by hand, checks that sections are in correct sequence; sews or wire stitches sections together; otherwise assists bookbinders as required.

Other titles include Bench hand, Checker, Collator, Gatherer, Sewer, Table hand.

641.98 Trainee

Performs, under instruction or guidance, various tasks including training exercises and as appropriate pursues studies in order to acquire the basic skills and knowledge required to perform the tasks of workers in bookbinding occupations.

641.99 Other bookbinding occupations

Workers in this group perform miscellaneous tasks in binding books and are not separately classified, for example:

(01) **Automatic bookbinding machine attendants** (attend machines which perform a number of bookbinding operations automatically); (02) **Folders (rag books)** (fold and gather together pages of rag books).

Unit Group 642 Paper Working and Paperboard Products Making Occupations

Workers in this unit group make products from paper, paperboard and abrasive cloth and paper, wind paper strip and photographic film into rolls and perform closely related tasks.

See Repetitive assembler (paper, paperboard products (821 .10))

Note: titles in this area can be misleading (see Introduction Volume 1 page 13).

642 .05 Machine manager

Sets machines, for operation by other workers, to perform two or more operations in the making of paper or paperboard products

Performs a combination of the following tasks: positions guides, stops and punch heads in machine using hand tools or positions and secures cutting or creasing plate and die; regulates platen, punch or cutting pressure; installs printing die in machine; fills glue and/or ink reservoirs and sets feed controls; loads or directs loading of paper or paperboard on to machine; threads paper from roll through machine guides and rollers or positions sheet(s) of paper or paperboard on machine; adjusts tensioning or clamping devices and counting mechanism; makes trial run, examines product and adjusts settings as necessary.

May (01) regulate temperature of forming device

(02) regulate flow of moisture to paper or paperboard

(03) supervise machine minders.

Other titles include Doily machine manager, Envelope machine adjuster, Machine setter, Serviette machine manager.

642 .10 Machine setter-operator

Sets and operates multi-purpose machine to perform two or more operations in the making of paper or paperboard products

Sets and adjusts machine as described under MACHINE MANAGER (642 .05) and in addition: starts machine to bend, crease, score, cut, punch, emboss, fold, glue, perforate, print, impregnate, roll or wind paper or paperboard; watches operations and adjusts settings as necessary; removes and examines product.

May (01) regulate temperature of forming device

(02) regulate flow of moisture to paper or paperboard

(03) clean and/or service machine.

Other titles include Machine setter-operator (paperboard box), Machine setter-operator (paper sack).

642 .15 Sample maker

Makes up by hand samples of paper or paperboard products such as bags or cartons

Ascertains job requirements from drawings or other specifications or works from measurements of product to be packaged; selects appropriate paper or paperboard; cuts, creases, slots and folds paper or paperboard using hand tools and measuring instruments to form parts of container; assembles and joins parts as necessary to make sample.

642 .20 Spiral-tube winder

Operates machine to wind continuous strips of paper or paperboard around forming mandrels to make tubes of specified dimensions

Ascertains job requirements from written or other specifications; positions appropriate mandrel and winding belt on machine; sets machine controls to obtain required tension, roller pressure, angle of spiral and where appropriate to bring adhesive to required temperature; positions or directs positioning of reels of material on feed mechanism; threads ends of material through guides and rollers, and secures round mandrel; starts machine and watches winding operation; checks dimensions of tubes and adjusts machine as necessary; replenishes supply of adhesive as necessary; removes or directs removal of formed tubes; cleans or directs cleaning of machine.

May (01) insert metallic strips into tubes at measured intervals during winding operation

(02) operate machine fitted with device to coat, line or impregnate material during winding operation

(03) operate machine which bakes coated or impregnated material during winding operation.

642 .25 Paper pattern copier

Reproduces master pattern of garments, soft furnishings and similar articles in paperboard for use as working copy

Arranges pieces of master pattern in most economical layout on paperboard and draws rough outline of each piece; places outlined pattern on additional sheets of paperboard according to number of working copies required and cuts out rough shape of each pattern piece with hand shears; staples copies of each part together; draws precise outline of master pattern on rough cutout; cuts round detailed outline using band-saw machine; cuts slits in pattern to indicate pocket openings and buttonholes using press cutting machine; smoothes edges of pattern pieces with sand-paper; removes staples and separates layers; stamps or marks each pattern piece with size and type of fitting.

May (01) punch holes using hand punch to mark items of detail on pattern.

642 .30 Pattern grader (footwear)

Operates machine to reproduce master patterns of footwear in selected sizes

Secures metal master pattern to top carrier of machine; sets gauges of machine according to size of pattern to be reproduced; clamps sheet of millboard, plastic laminate or other material on bottom carrier of machine; lowers top carrier to contact guide pin and to lower punch cutter on to material on bottom carrier; starts cutter and manually guides edge of master pattern round stationary guide pin causing cutter to punch outline in selected size corresponding to outline of master pattern.

May (01) punch securing screw holes in metal master pattern

(02) perform tasks of PATTERN BINDER (729 .99).

See Garment pattern grader (machine) (729 .94)

642 .50 Machine operator

Operates machine to perform a single operation, other than cutting, slitting or winding, in the making of paper or paperboard products

Performs a combination of the following tasks: positions and secures dies, master plate or former, space guides and stops in machine using hand tools; where appropriate, fills glue reservoirs or loads machine with tape or reinforcing material; threads roll (web) of paper or paperboard through feed-in rollers or positions sheet paper, paperboard, paper patterns or cards on bed of machine; operates machine controls; replenishes supplies of materials as necessary; removes and examines product.

May (01) clean and oil machine.

Other titles include Creasing machine operator, Crimping machine operator, Folding machine operator, Paper pattern driller, Paper pattern puncher, Perforating machine operator, Peg holing machinist (loom card), Taping machine operator.

642 .52 Machine minder

Tends preset multi-purpose machine to perform two or more operations in the making of paper or paperboard products

Threads roll (web) of paper or paperboard through feed-in rollers or places sheet paper or paperboard on bed of machine; aligns stacked sheets; starts machine and watches operation; removes and examines finished product; clears waste paper or paperboard from machine.

May (01) fill machine reservoirs with glue or ink

(02) fill hoppers or feed-reels with metal strip, metallic lustre, tinsel or similar material

(03) clear blockages

(04) make minor adjustments to machine.

Other titles include Bender and slotter (paperboard), Box machinist (paper goods), Carrier bag machine minder, Carton folding and gluing machine minder, Envelope making machine minder, Loose-leaf binding machine operator, Matchbox making machine minder, Paper tray maker, Toilet roll machine minder.

642 .54 Cutting machine operator

Operates machine to cut paper, abrasive paper, paperboard or abrasive cloth into specified length or shape

(01) **Guillotine operator, Guillotineman**

Sets and adjusts edge guides, stops and cutting blade; positions sheets of paper, etc on bed of machine and secures batches of sheets with clamping device; starts machine and watches operation to detect irregular cutting; removes product and clears waste material from machine.

(02) **Press cutter**

Places sheets of paper, etc on feed tray or on table of machine; secures cutting die in machine, positions cutting die on top of batch of paper, etc or adjusts cutting knives; starts machine and watches operation to detect irregular cutting; removes product.

Other titles include Cutterman.

(03) **Rotary cutter**

Stacks sheet paper, etc on feed platform or in hopper of machine or mounts roll of paper on machine; if

continued

cutting paper roll, threads end of paper through feed rollers and between cutting blades and starts machine; if cutting sheet paper, etc starts machine and feeds in sheets as required; watches machine operation to detect irregular cutting and removes cut paper.

Other titles include Cutterman

May (04) replace worn cutting blades
(05) clear blockages in machine
(06) perform tasks of BURSTER OPERATOR (339.99).

Other titles include Envelope cutter, Punching machine operator.

See Guillotine cutter (leather goods) (662.70)

Excluded are Paper pattern cutting machine operators (642.60)

642.56 Slitting machine operator

Operates machine to slit paper, photographic film or similar material into strips of specified width

Secures circular cutting blades and spacers on cutting mandrel of machine according to width of strips to be slit; mounts roll(s) of paper or other material on machine.

(01) **Slitter (photographic film, paper)**

Feeds length of fabric between cutting blades and roller; slits fabric into strips and attaches each strip to spool on reeling mandrel; joins roll of photographic film or paper to end of fabric strip with adhesive tape.

(02) **Slitterman (paper, paperboard or similar material)**

Threads paper or other material through guide rollers and attaches end of roll to centre cores on reeling mandrel with glue or adhesive tape; removes faulty parts of roll as necessary and joins ends.

Other titles include Slitting machine driver.

(03) **Tube cutting machine operator**

Inserts metal rod of appropriate size into paperboard tube and positions rod in machine.

Starts machine and watches operation to detect irregular cutting or winding.

May (04) cut strips of paper, paperboard or film to length
(05) sharpen or change cutting blades
(06) use metering device to measure yardage.

642.58 Tape fixer (paper patterns)

Prepares copy of garment pattern for use in printing paper patterns by screen process

Arranges original pattern in the most economical layout on treated tracing paper; outlines each pattern piece on tracing paper with narrow adhesive tape (beading); measures seam allowances on original pattern pieces and marks stitching lines on outlined pattern, using pen and ruler; superimposes short lengths of a narrower adhesive beading on marked lines; cuts transfers of numerals, names of pattern pieces, size, cutting and making up instructions from printed sheet; sticks transfers to appropriate pieces of outlined pattern on tracing paper; sends completed pattern on tracing paper to screen printer.

642.60 Paper pattern cutting machine operator

Operates machine to cut out bulk quantities of paper patterns from master copy

Selects pack with required number of sheets of tissue paper (batch); clamps master copy in position on top of batch, places on bed of cutting machine (band-saw or reciprocating knife) and starts machine; manipulates batch to cut round outline of master copy; stops machine, removes batch and extracts master copy; clips cut-out patterns together in alignment.

May (01) cut small quantities of patterns using hand operated power cutters
(02) drill guide holes in patterns using power punch or drill
(03) sharpen or change cutting blade
(04) check that pieces make up a complete pattern.

642.62 Measurer (paper patterns)

Prepares diagram to show method of layout of paper pattern on material and yardage of material required

Positions pattern pieces on bench marked in calibrated squares (yardage table) in most economical layout; prepares scale drawing of layout using drawing instruments; arranges for scale drawing to be photographed; positions pattern pieces on yardage table to conform to photograph to check correctness of scale drawing; records yardage requirements on measurement chart.

Other titles include Yardage hand.

642.64 Roll mounting machine operator (stencils)

Sets up and operates a machine to print, back and slot rolls of coated stencil paper and cut rolls into single sheets

Positions and fixes printing plate round printing roller; fills ink ducts and adjusts flow to inking rollers; fills glue container; adjusts feeding, folding and gluing points; adjusts slotting and trimming knives according to specifications; loads machine with coated stencil paper, varnished backing paper and interleaf paper and adjusts guides and tension bars; starts machine and inspects stencils at regular intervals to ensure that operation proceeds correctly; replenishes ink and glue supplies.

642.90 Machine assistant

Assists machine manager or machine setter-operator to prepare or operate machine in the making of paper or paperboard products

Performs one or more of the following tasks: loads machine with paper or paperboard; fills ink and/or glue reservoirs; fills feed hoppers with metallic lustre, tinsel or similar material; feeds in sheet paper or paperboard; removes and stacks finished product; otherwise assists manager or setter-operator as required.

May (01) clean machine and work area.

Other titles include Machine feeder, machine taker-off.

642.92 Spooler (paper tape, film)

Operates machine to wind specified lengths of paper tape or photographic film into rolls or on to spools

Positions material on feed mechanism of machine; places spool on take-up spindle where appropriate; threads material through guides, tensioners and measuring device and secures end to spool or take-up spindle; sets yardage counter; starts machine and watches winding; if breakage occurs, stops machine and joins broken ends or removes partially filled spool; when specified length has been wound stops machine and cuts material; secures end of material and removes roll or spool from machine.

May (01) examine material during winding for surface faults

(02) pack spools of photographic film into special containers and seal containers to exclude light.

Additional factor: whether accustomed to working in darkroom.

Other titles include Cartridge cassette loader (photographic film), Rewinder operator (paper strip), Roll winder (paper).

642.98 Trainee

Performs, under instruction or guidance, various tasks including training exercises and as appropriate pursues studies in order to acquire the basic skills and knowledge required to perform the tasks of workers in paper working and paperboard products making occupations.

642.99 Other paper working and paperboard products making occupations

Workers in this group make products from paper, paperboard and abrasive cloth and paper, wind paper strip and photographic film into rolls and perform closely related tasks and are not elsewhere classified, for example:

(01) **Abrasive paper goods makers,** Naumkeag cap makers (mount abrasive paper or cloth on stiffening material and/or press abrasive discs to impart dome shape); (02) **Box makers** (make throughout and decorate paperboard boxes by hand); (03) **Cutters (hand) (paper, paperboard products)** (cut paper or paperboard by hand into specified lengths); (04) **Strippers (hand)** (strip waste material by hand from partially cut blanks in sheets of paperboard); (05) **Valvers (hand) (paper sacks)** (tuck in corners of sacks by hand to fashion a self-closing aperture).

Minor Group 65 TEXTILE MATERIALS WORKING OCCUPATIONS

Workers in this minor group make and perform tasks in the making of garments, soft furnishings andother articles of textile fabric, upholster furniture and vehicle and aircraft seating, lay carpets and perform closely related tasks.

The occupations are arranged in the following unit groups:

650 Foremen (Textile Materials Working Occupations)

651 Tailors

652 Dressmakers and Makers Throughout of Other Light Clothing

653 Upholsterers, Mattress Makers and Related Occupations

654 Milliners

655 Fur Garment Cutting and Shaping Occupations

656 Pattern Makers, Markers and Cutters (Garments, Upholstery and Related Products)

657 Sewing and Embroidering Occupations (Hand) (Garments, Upholstery and Related Products)

658 Sewing and Embroidering Occupations (Machine) (Garments, Upholstery and Related Products)

659 Textile Materials Working Occupations Not Elsewhere Classified

Excluded are workers in pressing occupations (461)

Unit Group 650 Foremen (Textile Materials Working Occupations)

Workers in this unit group directly supervise and co-ordinate the activities of workers in textile materials working occupations.

650 .05 Foreman (tailors)

Directly supervises and co-ordinates the activities of tailors

Performs appropriate tasks as described under SUPERVISOR/FOREMAN (UNSPECIFIED) (990 .00).

May (01) supervise sewers, pressers and finishers.

Additional factor: number of workers supervised.

650 .10 Foreman (dressmakers and makers throughout of other light clothing)

Directly supervises and co-ordinates the activities of dressmakers and makers throughout of other light clothing

Performs appropriate tasks as described under SUPERVISOR/FOREMAN (UNSPECIFIED) (990 .00).

Additional factor: number of workers supervised.

650.15 Foreman (upholsterers, mattress makers and related occupations)

Directly supervises and co-ordinates the activities of upholsterers, mattress makers and workers in related occupations

Performs appropriate tasks as described under SUPERVISOR/FOREMAN (UNSPECIFIED) (990.00).

Additional factor: number of workers supervised.

650.20 Foreman (milliners)

Directly supervises and co-ordinates the activities of milliners

Performs appropriate tasks as described under SUPERVISOR/FOREMAN (UNSPECIFIED) (990.00).

Additional factor: number of workers supervised.

650.25 Foreman (fur garment cutting and shaping occupations)

Directly supervises and co-ordinates the activities of workers in fur garment cutting and shaping occupations

Performs appropriate tasks as described under SUPERVISOR/FOREMAN (UNSPECIFIED) (990.00).

May (01) advise customers on the remodelling of fur garments

(02) sort and grade pelts (834.10).

Additional factor: number of workers supervised.

650.30 Foreman (pattern makers, markers and cutters) (garments, upholstery and related products)

Directly supervises and co-ordinates the activities of pattern makers, markers and cutters (garments, upholstery and related products)

Performs appropriate tasks as described under SUPERVISOR/FOREMAN (UNSPECIFIED) (990.00).

May (01) supervise sewers.

Additional factor: number of workers supervised.

650.35 Foreman (sewing and embroidering occupations) (hand) (garments, upholstery and related products)

Directly supervises and co-ordinates the activities of workers in hand sewing and embroidering occupations (garments, upholstery and related products)

Performs appropriate tasks as described under SUPERVISOR/FOREMAN (UNSPECIFIED) (990.00).

Additional factor: number of workers supervised.

650.40 Foreman (sewing and embroidering occupations) (machine) (garments, upholstery and related products)

Directly supervises and co-ordinates the activities of workers in machine sewing and embroidering occupations (garments, upholstery and related products)

Performs appropriate tasks as described under SUPERVISOR/FOREMAN (UNSPECIFIED) (990.00).

May (01) fit pattern cards (jacquard cards) on automatic embroidery machines

(02) undertake minor repairs to machines.

Additional factor: number of workers supervised.

650.45 Foreman (hat shaping and finishing occupations)

Directly supervises and co-ordinates the activities of workers in hat shaping and finishing occupations

Performs appropriate tasks as described under SUPERVISOR/FOREMAN (UNSPECIFIED) (990.00).

Additional factor: number of workers supervised.

650.98 Trainee

Performs, under instruction or guidance, various tasks including training exercises and as appropriate pursues studies in order to acquire the basic skills and knowledge required to perform the tasks of foremen (textile materials working occupations).

650.99 Other foremen (textile materials working occupations)

Workers in this group directly supervise and co-ordinate the activities of workers in textile materials working occupations and are not elsewhere classified, for example:

(01) **Foremen sailmakers.**

Additional factor: number of workers supervised.

Unit Group 651 Tailors

Workers in this unit group make tailored garments throughout, make up and assist in making up tailored garments from cut parts, and fit and alter tailored garments.

Excluded are Fabric garment finishers (657.50) and sewing machinists (658)

651.10 Tailor (retail bespoke garments)

Makes bespoke tailored garments throughout or directs and personally performs some of the tasks in the making up of bespoke tailored garments

If making throughout, discusses with customer style of garment and type of material desired; takes and records customer's measurements; prepares individual or adapts stock pattern; arranges pattern pieces on correct grain of fabric in most economical layout ensuring that fabric pattern matches where required; marks round pattern pieces and draws guide lines indicating position of pocket openings, buttonholes, lapel creases, darts, vents and similar design features using chalk; cuts out garment parts with shears; cuts out linings and interlinings; marks chalked guide lines with thread by hand or machine sewing; shapes (works up) interlinings using heavy iron; sews interlinings to garment parts by hand, shaping as required; bastes garment parts together and sews in padding; fits basted garment on customer and marks garment to indicate alterations required; makes necessary alterations and sews garment parts together permanently by hand or machine; makes up and sews in lining; fixes shape of garment by pressing seams as work progresses; makes buttonholes and sews on buttons; presses finished garment.
If not making throughout, performs some or all of the following tasks: cuts out parts such as facings, collar and pocket flaps; works up lapel and collar interlinings as described above; sews interlinings to lapels and collar, shaping as required; sets sleeves in armholes; bastes parts such as collar, lapels and sleeves in position; makes necessary alterations after fitting; carries out final stitching of collar and lapels; directs and examines work of assistants.

May (01) perform tasks of ALTERATION HAND (651.60)
(02) repair tailored garments.

Additional factor: type(s) of garments made.

Other titles include Breeches maker, Coat maker, Skirt maker, Trouser maker, Vest maker.

Excluded are Kilt makers (651.40), Gown makers (651.99) and Robe makers (651.99)

651.20 Tailor (wholesale bespoke, ready-made garments)

Fits together and bastes by hand parts of wholesale bespoke or ready-made tailored garments ready for machining

Performs one or more of the following tasks: hand bastes interlinings or other reinforcements to parts such as lapels and collar, shaping as required; fits and hand bastes facings to jacket fronts; fits and hand bastes collars to coats; sets sleeves in position and hand bastes; fits linings in position in garment and hand bastes, allowing fullness where required.

May (01) trim armholes and tops of sleeves to shape
(02) trim coat lapels (656.18).

Other titles include Baster, Baster-under, Canvas baster, Corner baster and tacker, Lining baster, Over-baster, Under-baster.

651.30 Tailor's assistant

Assists tailor in the making up of retail bespoke garments

Performs some or all of the following tasks: marks chalked guide lines with thread by hand or machine to indicate position of pockets, buttonholes, lapel creases, darts, vents and similar design features; sews padding to interlinings by hand or machine; bastes plain seams; sews in interlinings and linings; cuts and hand sews buttonholes; assists in final stitching of garment by hand or machine; presses garment during or on completion of making up; otherwise assists tailor as required.

May (01) perform tasks of ALTERATION HAND (651.60).

Other titles include Tailoress.

Excluded are Fabric garment finishers (657.50) and Sewing machinists (heavy clothing) (658.50)

651.40 Kilt maker

Pleats and sews tartan fabric to make kilts

Lays out tartan fabric on work-table; marks off with chalk part to remain unpleated (apron) at each end of fabric; calculates number of pleats required for given waist measurement; forms and pins pleats ensuring that tartan pattern is continuous and that correct waist measurement is obtained; sews down each pleat for several inches from waist; bastes round and presses pleats; cuts off excess material at top of pleats to avoid bulk at waist; sews canvas to inside waist to cover top of pleating; sews top band of fabric to kilt or passes kilt to machinist to attach band; removes basting thread; sews facing to aprons and pulls out threads from ends of aprons to form fringe; tears off strip of lining fabric and sews it in kilt across stitched part of pleats, slightly pleating lining; makes holes for and sews on straps and buckles; presses or arranges for pressing of kilt.

May (01) use template to assist in spacing pleats.

651.50 Alteration fitter

Fits tailored garments on customers and arranges for necessary alterations to be made

Checks fit of garment on customer and determines alterations required; marks garment to show nature and extent of alterations or records alteration requirements on docket; passes garment with necessary instructions to alteration hand.

May (01) take customers' measurements for bespoke garments
(02) calculate and record cost of alterations
(03) supervise alteration hands
(04) perform tasks of ALTERATION HAND (651.60).

Other titles include Fitter.

651.60 Alteration hand

Alters tailored garments to fit customers

Examines garment and/or instructions docket to ascertain alterations required; removes stitching where necessary, using scissors or razor blade; makes alterations such as shortening or lengthening sleeves, raising or lowering waist or hem lines, re-setting sleeves or collar, taking in or letting out seams, darts, etc; recuts parts as necessary, and resews garment by hand or machine or marks or bastes garment for guidance of sewing machinist.

May (01) press garments after alterations (461)
(02) repair tailored garments.

Other titles include Adjustment tailor.

651.98 Trainee

Performs, under instruction or guidance, various tasks including training exercises and as appropriate pursues studies in order to acquire the basic skills and knowledge required to perform the tasks of tailors.

651.99 Other tailors

Workers in this group make tailored garments throughout, make up and assist in making up tailored garments from cut parts and fit and alter tailored garments and are not elsewhere classified, for example:

(01) **Gown makers,** Robe makers (make academic, clerical and law robes throughout or make up robes from cut parts); (02) **Pleat makers** (form and baste pleats ensuring that fabric pattern matches where required).

Unit Group 652 Dressmakers and Makers Throughout of Other Light Clothing

Workers in this unit group make throughout and make up from cut parts dresses and other articles of light clothing, and fit and alter light clothing.

Excluded are Fabric garment finishers (657.50) and Sewing machinists (light clothing) (658.55)

652 .10 Dressmaker

Makes dresses or other articles of light clothing throughout or makes up light clothing from cut parts

If making garment throughout, discusses with customer style of garment and type of fabric desired; takes and records customer's measurements; prepares individual or adapts stock pattern; arranges pattern pieces on correct grain of fabric in most economical layout ensuring that fabric pattern matches where required; marks round pattern pieces or pins pieces to fabric; chalk marks or otherwise indicates position of pockets, buttonholes, pleats, darts and other design features; cuts along marked outlines or round pattern pieces with shears; cuts out linings and interlinings, where required; bastes or pins garment parts together; fits garment on customer or on dummy model and adjusts as necessary to ensure good fit; sews garment parts together by hand or machine incorporating interlinings where required; makes up and sews in lining and hems garment as required; fixes shape of garment by pressing seams, pleats, etc as work progresses; makes buttonholes, sews on buttons, fasteners and trimmings and embroiders article as required; presses finished garment.

If making up garment from cut parts, examines making up instructions; bastes or pins parts together, fits garment on dummy model as necessary; adjusts, sews, finishes and presses garment as described above.

Additional factor: type(s) of garment made.

Other titles include Blouse hand, Gown hand, Lingerie hand, Skirt hand, Theatrical dressmaker.

Excluded are Corset makers (652 .20)

652 .20 Corset maker

Makes bespoke corsets and foundation garments throughout

Ascertains from work instructions type and measurements of garment required; marks out garment parts on appropriate fabric from measurements; cuts along marked outlines with scissors; marks parts to show position of stiffeners, straps, buckles or other attachments; sews garment parts together by machine; as necessary inserts stiffeners in encasing strips of fabric on garment and closes ends of strips by hand sewing or by attaching binding by machine; sews on buckles, straps or other attachments as necessary by hand or machine.

May (01) prepare paper pattern from measurements to assist in cutting out garment parts
(02) perform tasks of SURGICAL CORSET FITTER (659 .25)
(03) perform tasks of FOUNDATION GARMENT FITTER (659 .54).

Additional factor: whether experienced in surgical corset making.

Other titles include Corsetiere, Surgical corset maker.

652 .30 Alteration fitter

Fits dresses or other articles of light clothing on customers and arranges for necessary alterations to be made

Performs appropriate tasks as described under ALTERATION FITTER (651 .50) but in relation to the alteration of dresses and other articles of light clothing.

May (01) calculate and record cost of alterations
(02) supervise alteration hands
(03) perform tasks of ALTERATION HAND (652 .40)
(04) in retail establishments, fit and arrange alteration of tailored garments.

652 .40 Alteration hand

Alters dresses and other articles of light clothing to fit customers

Performs tasks as described under ALTERATION HAND (651 .60) but in relation to the alteration of dresses or other articles of light clothing.

May (01) press garments after alteration (461)
(02) in retail establishments, alter tailored garments
(03) repair light clothing.

652 .98 Trainee

Performs, under instruction or guidance, various tasks including training exercises and as appropriate pursues studies in order to acquire the basic skills and knowledge required to perform the tasks of dressmakers and makers throughout of other light clothing.

652 .99 Other dressmakers and makers throughout of light clothing

Workers in this group make throughout and make up from cut parts articles of light clothing, and fit and alter light clothing and are not elsewhere classified.

Unit Group 653 Upholsterers, Mattress Makers and Related Occupations

Workers in this unit group upholster vehicle and aircraft seating and furniture, fix trimmings to the interiors of vehicles and aircraft, make mattresses, curtains and other soft furnishings and perform related tasks.

Excluded are cutters (656), hand sewers (657) and sewing machinists (658)

653 .05 Coach trimmer

Upholsters seats for vehicles or aircraft or fixes panel coverings and other trimmings to interiors of vehicles or aircraft

Performs a combination of the following tasks: measures seat frame to be upholstered or examines drawings or other specifications; marks out covering material from measurements or positions and marks round template ensuring most economical use of material and where appropriate matching fabric pattern; cuts out cover sections with shears or knife; cements or staples cover sections together ready for sewing; tacks, staples or otherwise secures webbing or other base to seat frame using hammer or powered hand tool; sews springs into position on webbing; covers springs with padding and secures padding in position by hand stitching, stapling or cementing with adhesive; positions rubber or plastic foam on webbing; tacks, staples or otherwise fixes stitched cover to padded frame; marks out and cuts insulating material and sews, sticks or otherwise fixes it in position in vehicle or aircraft; cuts and lays carpet or other floor covering and secures in position with adhesive, fixing strip or fasteners; marks out and cuts panel covering or roof lining material; sticks, tacks or otherwise fixes panel covering or roof lining material in position; fixes hand straps, ash trays, light shades and other small fittings using hand tools; removes and replaces worn or defective upholstery or trimmings.

May (01) perform tasks of SEWING MACHINIST (658 .65)
(02) make up and fit curtains or blinds
(03) modify seats for invalids or other persons requiring special seats.

653 .10 Upholsterer (furniture)

Fixes springing to and pads and covers furniture frames

Tacks or staples webbing to furniture frame where appropriate, using hammer or powered hand tool, interlacing and tensioning webbing as necessary; sews springs or spring unit in position on webbing or nails or staples unit to frame where required; pads springs and secures padding by stitching, stapling, tacking or cementing with adhesive, or positions rubber or plastic foam or other padding on webbing or frame; fits lining and covering materials to frame and tacks, staples or otherwise secures in position; trims off waste material; tacks or staples hessian or canvas to base of furniture to conceal springs, and fits castors where required; sews braid or other trimmings on to cover or pins them in position for hand sewer.

May (01) prepare patterns or templates
(02) cut lining and covering materials from measurements or using patterns or templates
(03) repair furniture upholstery
(04) strip upholstery from and re-upholster furniture frames
(05) make soft furnishings (653 .15).

653 .15 Upholsterer (soft furnishings)

Cuts out and makes up soft furnishings

Rolls out fabric on work-table or drapes fabric over chairs, settees, etc on customer's premises; marks out fabric from measurements, positions and marks round template(s) on fabric or marks out shapes required on draped fabric, ensuring most economical use of fabric and where appropriate matching fabric pattern; cuts fabric with scissors; pins sections of furnishings together and joins by machine sewing, inserting piping as required; hems edges of furnishings by hand or machine; cuts out buckram or other foundation for pelmets and sticks fabric to foundation; attaches linings, tape, braid and other trimmings, as required, by hand or machine sewing; presses furnishings as necessary.

May (01) advise on soft furnishings and take measurements on customers' premises
(02) cut out templates from paperboard or plastic
(03) fit soft furnishings on customers' premises
(04) sew up seams of furniture upholstery by hand.

653 .20 Mattress maker

Covers spring assemblies or inserts spring assemblies and/or other filling in prepared covers to make mattresses

If making spring interior mattress, pins sections of cover in position on padded spring assembly, or spreads padding in partly sewn mattress cover, positions spring assembly on padding and inserts further padding as necessary; joins sections of cover together or completes closing of mattress cover by hand sewing, forming roll edge as required.
If making unsprung mattress, fills mattress cover with hair, fibre or other filling, distributing filling evenly throughout cover as necessary; closes open end of cover by hand sewing.
Sews or otherwise secures handles to and/or inserts eyelets or perforated ventilation discs in sides of mattress as required.

May (01) staple or tack webbing and spring assemblies to divan frames

(02) cover divan springs with padding, hessian, canvas and furnishing fabric using stapling machine or hammer and tacks

(03) affix tufts, buttons, etc to mattresses by hand or machine to prevent displacement of filling

(04) cut and bind holes in covers of insulating mattresses

(05) attach hooks to covers of insulating mattresses for securing mattresses in position.

653 .50 Hood and apron maker

Cuts out and makes up hoods and aprons for carriages such as perambulators and wheel chairs

Measures frame to be covered where necessary; marks out covering and where required lining fabric from measurements, or positions and marks round templates on fabric; cuts out cover and where appropriate lining sections with hand shears or powered hand cutter; sews cover sections together by machine, inserting piping as required; where appropriate joins sections of lining together and attaches to cover by machine sewing; stretches and smoothes cover on frame and stitches cover to frame by hand where appropriate; inserts eyelets in cover as required, using punch and dies; sews corner shields, fastening clips, etc to cover by hand.

May (01) sew braid or elasticated webbing to edges of covers by machine.

653 .60 Mattress filling machine operator

Operates machine to compress padded spring assemblies and insert assemblies into mattress covers

Adjusts machine mouth according to size of mattress; pulls mattress cover over machine mouth; loads padding and spring assembly (filling) on to machine tray; lowers compressing device on to filling; operates machine to compress filling and force filling into mattress cover; packs corners of mattress cover with padding by hand; pins together edges of open end of cover ready for sewing.

653 .98 Trainee

Performs, under instruction or guidance, various tasks including training exercises and as appropriate pursues studies in order to acquire the basic skills and knowledge required to perform the tasks of upholsterers, mattress makers and workers in related occupations.

653 .99 Other upholsterers, mattress makers and related occupations

Workers in this group upholster vehicle and aircraft seating and furniture, fix trimmings to the interiors of vehicles and aircraft, make mattresses, curtains and other soft furnishings and perform related tasks and are not elsewhere classified, for example:

(01) **Fillers (hand)** (**cushions, quilts, etc**) (insert feathers, kapok or other filling in covers or cases of cushions, quilts, pillows, bolsters, etc by hand, and close open ends by hand or machine sewing); (02) **Soft toy stuffers** (insert stuffing in soft toys by hand or machine); (03) **Upholstery tufters** (affix tufts, buttons, etc to mattresses, divans or furniture upholstery by hand or machine using twine, tape or plastic strip).

Unit Group 654 Milliners

Workers in this unit group make women's, girls' and children's hats throughout.

654.10 Milliner

Makes women's, girls' or children's hats throughout

Examines photograph or designer's sketch or model, or ascertains customer's requirements; stretches, presses and moulds material such as muslin, canvas or plastic mesh on shaped wooden block to form hat foundation, arranges covering material over foundation and secures by hand sewing or with adhesive, or steams, stretches and moulds felt or straw hood to shape on wooden block or frame; removes hat from block or frame; sews in stiffener by hand where required; inserts lining and headband by hand and/or machine sewing; makes up and sews on trimmings by hand.

May (01) press finished hats.

Other titles include Millinery copyist.

654.98 Trainee

Performs, under instruction or guidance, various tasks including training exercises and as appropriate pursues studies in order to acquire the basic skills and knowledge required to perform the tasks of milliners.

Unit Group 655 Fur Garment Cutting and Shaping Occupations

Workers in this unit group cut out and stretch parts of fur garments to shape and size required and perform related tasks.

655.10 Fur garment cutter

Cuts skins for making up into fur garments

Selects required number of skins; examines skins to ascertain colour, length and texture of fur and to detect blemishes; brushes and combs fur and estimates stretch of skin; where appropriate, cuts skins into strips or makes incisions in skins to assist stretching, using hand knife; cuts out blemishes in skins; arranges skins on pattern, positioning finest skins to form prominent parts of garment and ensuring that parts to be joined match in quality and colour; cuts skins to shape with hand knife; marks skins and strips for guidance of fur machinist; checks that skins and strips have been correctly joined by machinist.

May (01) adapt stock patterns to individual requirements

(02) trim garment parts after nailing

(03) check fit of finished garments on customers.

655.20 Nailer

Stretches fur garment parts to pattern shape

Moistens skin side of garment part; places pattern of garment part on work-table (nailing board), chalks round pattern and marks in seam lines; lays out moistened part on nailing board to conform as nearly as possible to chalk outline; drives nails into part along centre line, seams and edges, stretching part to pattern shape by hand or using pliers; allows part to dry naturally on board or places nailed part in drying oven; removes nails when part is completely dry; lays paper pattern on skin side of part and draws round outline; trims part to correct shape with knife or passes to cutter for trimming.

May (01) brush solutions on skins to produce striped effect

(02) stiffen skins by applying starch or similar solution

(03) press garment parts with heavy iron to flatten seams.

655.98 Trainee

Performs, under instruction or guidance, various tasks including training exercises and as appropriate pursues studies in order to acquire the basic skills and knowledge required to perform the tasks of workers in fur garment cutting and shaping occupations.

655.99 Other fur garment cutting and shaping occupations

Workers in this group cut out and stretch parts of fur garments and perform related tasks and are not elsewhere classified.

Unit Group 656 Pattern Makers, Markers and Cutters (Garments, Upholstery and Related Products)

Workers in this unit group make patterns and mark and cut out material including leather, for the manufacture of garments, upholstery and the making up of soft furnishings and other articles of textile fabric.

Included are carpet planners.

Excluded are Fur garment cutters (655 .10)

656 .02 Modeller

Prepares master patterns of garments from designers' sketches or by adapting existing designs

Examines designer's sketch or selects existing design suitable for adaptation; prepares sketches showing the various pattern pieces required for garment and the location of darts, gussets and other design features; discusses sketches with management and makes alterations as necessary; positions basic pattern on tracing paper; pencils round basic pattern, adjusting outline as necessary; marks position of darts, gussets, etc and of punch holes to indicate seams; cuts holes to mark seam lines and cutting line using punch; cuts out pattern pieces with scissors and notches edges as guide in making up garment; allocates serial number to style; records style number and size on pattern and numbers each pattern piece; cuts out garment parts from fabric using paper pattern; checks fit of made-up model garment (toile) on dummy model where required; discusses toile with management and makes required alterations.

May (01) perform tasks of PATTERN GRADER (HAND) (656 .06)

(02) perform tasks of MEASURER (PAPER PATTERNS) (642 .62).

Other titles include Design cutter, Paper pattern modeller.

656 .04 Fur garment pattern maker and fitter

Prepares patterns and canvas models (toiles) of bespoke fur garments and fits toiles and fur garments on customers

Discusses with customer style of garment and type of fur desired; takes and records customer's measurements; draws pattern on paper according to measurements and style required and cuts out paper pattern; lays paper pattern pieces on canvas and cuts out canvas pattern; sews sections of canvas together to form toile; fits toile on customer and marks necessary alterations; prepares further paper patterns and toiles, as necessary, until correct fit is obtained; passes paper pattern to cutter; checks fit of fur garment on customer.

Other titles include Fitter-designer, Pattern cutter, Pattern maker.

656 .06 Pattern grader (hand)

Draws and cuts out by hand patterns for garment parts in various sizes, increasing or decreasing dimensions (grading) of master pattern

Positions master pattern of garment part on paper or paperboard and draws round pattern; determines, by reference to size chart where appropriate, modifications of dimensions of master pattern necessary to produce graded pattern of required size; plots and marks outline of graded pattern on paper or paperboard using drawing instruments; marks outlined graded pattern with symbols for guidance in making up garment, using punch or pen; cuts out graded pattern with hand shears or powered hand cutter; records style number and size on graded pattern and numbers each pattern piece.

May (01) fit graded pattern on dummy model.

656.08 Marker maker

Prepares layout of garment pattern pieces as guide in cutting fabric to best advantage

(01) **Marker maker (hand)**

Positions paper or paperboard on which layout is to be prepared and where necessary carbon paper on work-table; arranges pattern pieces on paper or paperboard in most economical layout; marks round pattern pieces with crayon, pencil or stylus or affixes pattern pieces to paper with adhesive; removes pattern pieces and carbon paper where appropriate; records identification data on layout.

(02) **Marker maker (machine)**

Positions sensitised paper on work-table and arranges pattern pieces as described above; covers pattern pieces with transparent plastic sheet to hold them in position; switches on ultra-violet lights on machine and sets speed control; operates controls to move machine slowly over layout to subject to ultra-violet light the sensitised paper not covered by pattern pieces; removes plastic sheet and pattern pieces.

(03) **Miniature lay maker**

Performs tasks as described under GARMENT PATTERN GRADER (MACHINE) (729.94) to produce miniature copies of pattern pieces; positions miniature pattern pieces in most economical layout on special work-table marked out to scale; operates camera to photograph layout; develops and prints photograph.

May (04) use photograph or instruction sheet as guide in positioning pattern pieces

(05) operate photocopying machine (334.10) or duplicating machine (334.20) to make copies of layout

(06) perforate outline of pattern pieces using powered punching tool and be known as Perforated lay maker.

See Measurer (paper patterns) (642.62)

656.10 Marker (bespoke tailoring)

Marks out parts of tailored garments to individual requirements ready for cutting

Prepares paper pattern from measurements or selects stock pattern in size nearest to customer's measurements; positions pattern pieces on correct grain of fabric in most economical layout ensuring that fabric pattern matches where required; marks round pattern pieces with chalk, adjusting outlines to customer's measurements as necessary; chalks position of buttonholes, pocket openings, lapel creases, darts, vents, etc and of notches for guidance in making up; bundles marked fabric and appropriate lining material.

656.12 Cutter (bespoke tailoring)

Marks out and cuts parts of tailored garments to individual requirements

Performs appropriate tasks as described under MARKER (BESPOKE TAILORING) (656.10) and CHOPPER (656.52); as necessary, recuts garment parts after trial fitting of basted garment on customer.

Other titles include Cutter and fitter, Measure cutter, Special cutter.

(01) **Alteration cutter**

Examines alteration instructions; measures parts requiring alteration and marks parts with chalk to indicate recutting necessary to obtain correct fit; recuts parts.

May (02) take customer's measurements

(03) advise customer on style of garment and selection of fabric

(04) fit basted garment on customer

(05) cut linings, interlinings and facings to rough shape.

656.14 Cutter (made-to-measure light clothing)

Marks out and cuts parts of dresses, corsets, foundation garments or other light clothing to individual requirements

Performs appropriate tasks as described under MARKER (BESPOKE TAILORING) (656.10) and CHOPPER (656.52) but in relation to the marking and cutting out of dresses or other light clothing; in addition, if marking out parts of surgical corsets, marks position of stiffeners, straps and other attachments as guide in making up.

May (01) take customer's measurements

(02) advise customer on style of garment and selection of fabric

(03) mark out fabric from customer's measurements

(04) fit garment on customer or dummy model.

Other titles include Cutter and fitter.

656.16 Lay cutter (garments)

Builds up layers of fabric to form multiple lay and cuts out garment parts from lay, or cuts out parts from prepared lay

As required, builds up lay, marks out or affixes pattern to top layer of lay and dissects lay as described under LAY CUTTER'S ASSISTANT (656.50); switches on hand cutter or band knife; guides hand cutter round each pattern piece or along outline marked on lay or manipulates lay against blade of band knife to cut out garment parts; as necessary cuts notches in edges of garment parts for guidance in making up.

May (01) separate cut parts and sort them into bundles for making up
(02) cut neck and other openings in knitwear (656.60)
(03) cut hat parts with shears from single lay of fabric
(04) sharpen cutters.

Other titles include Band knife cutter, Electric hand cutter (excluding linings), Shaper-cutter (millinery), Stock cutter (excluding linings).

Excluded are Trimmings cutters (656.56) and Press cutters (garments) (656.58)

656.18 Shaper

Trims lapels and collars of tailored garments to specified size and shape by hand

Examines instructions to ascertain required shape and size of collar and lapels; positions suitable pattern on roughly shaped collar ensuring that fabric pattern matches that on jacket body; marks round pattern with chalk, adjusting outline to customer's measurements as necessary; cuts round marked outline with hand shears; marks out and cuts under-collar to shape and size required; cuts notches in collar and under-collar for guidance in making up; places suitable lapel pattern in correct position on coat; marks round lapel pattern adjusting outline as necessary and trims lapel to marked shape with hand shears; compares lapels and trims as necessary; trims collar and lapel interlinings to corresponding shape and size.

May (01) dampen collar and press to shape with iron.

656.20 Cutter (leather, skin garments), Fur cutter (gloves)

Cuts leather or sheepskin garment parts, or cuts fur for use in making or trimming gloves, by hand

Examines leather or skin for flaws, quality and colour and where appropriate for pattern of grain or lie of fur; stretches leather or skin on cutting table and determines most economical usage; positions appropriate pattern piece(s) on leather or skin in most economical layout ensuring that colour and quality of garment parts match where required; chalks or otherwise marks round pattern piece(s) where necessary; cuts along marked outline(s) or holds pattern piece(s) and cuts round edge(s) using shears or hand knife; sorts parts into bundles for making up.

May (01) moisten leather or skin to assist stretching
(02) scrape leather or skin with knife to smooth surface
(03) adapt stock patterns to individual requirements
(04) mark parts for guidance in making up
(05) sharpen or replace blades in cutting knives.

Other titles include Sheepskin garment cutter, Table cutter.

656.22 Marker cutter (excluding garments)

Marks out parts of articles other than garments and cuts from single lay of fabric

Marks out fabric from measurements or positions appropriate template(s) on correct grain of fabric in most economical layout, ensuring that fabric pattern matches where required, and marks round template(s) with chalk or pencil; cuts along marked outline(s) with hand shears, scissors or knife; marks parts as required for guidance in making up; marks with chalk or pencil the position of eyelets and attachments as necessary; sorts parts into bundles for making up.

May (01) take measurements on customers' premises
(02) drape and mark out fabric on customers' premises
(03) sketch articles
(04) cut fabric with heated hand cutter which seals edges
(05) fold over edges to be hemmed or joined and crease fold with back of knife
(06) trim edge of articles with knife or scissors after stitching
(07) fit made-up articles on customers' premises.

Other titles include Canvas goods cutter (single lay), Flag cutter (single lay), Sail cutter, Soft furnishings cutter (single lay), Tarpaulin cutter, Upholstery cutter (single lay).

656.24 Lay cutter (excluding garments)

Builds up layers of fabric to form multiple lay and cuts out from lay parts of articles other than garments, or cuts out parts from prepared lay

As required, builds up and marks lay as described under LAY CUTTER'S ASSISTANT (656.50); cuts along marked outline or around edge of pattern or template with hand knife, shears or powered hand cutter.

May (01) prepare template from hardboard using hand saw
(02) mark out from measurements
(03) mark parts for guidance in making up
(04) cut parts from single lay of fabric
(05) separate parts and sort into bundles for making up
(06) cut latex or plastic foam to required shape and size for use in upholstering
(07) sharpen cutters.

Other titles include Canvas goods cutter (multiple lay), Flag cutter (multiple lay), Linings cutter (leather goods), Soft furnishings cutter (multiple lay), Umbrella cloth cutter, Upholstery cutter (multiple lay).

656.26 Carpet planner

Prepares layout of carpet for specified area

Measures floor area to be covered; advises customer on choice of carpet and underlay as required; prepares sketch of floor area; determines best arrangement of carpet, ensuring matching of carpet pattern where appropriate and indicates layout on sketch; calculates amount of carpet and underlay required; requisitions carpet, underlay, binding, etc from stock.

May (01) prepare estimates of cost for customers
(02) cut carpet, underlay and binding required from stock
(03) sew carpet strips together by hand (657.65) or machine (658.75)
(04) lay carpet (659.40) or supervise carpet layers
(05) prepare layout of linoleum or other similar floor covering.

656.50 Lay cutter's assistant

Prepares lay and/or assists in the cutting of parts of garments or other articles from multiple layers of fabric

Performs one or more of the following tasks: cuts fabric into uniform lengths and builds up required number of layers of fabric on work-table by hand, or operates laying device to form multiple lay of specified length, ensuring that each layer is smooth and positioned exactly over lower layer; positions pattern pieces on correct grain of top layer of fabric in most economical layout, ensuring that fabric pattern matches where required; chalks round pattern pieces or dusts powdered chalk through pattern perforations to mark outlines on lay or affixes pattern pieces to lay; dissects lay into sections corresponding roughly to shape of each pattern piece using powered hand knife, and clips layers of each section together ready for cutting with band knife; cuts notches in edges of garment parts for guidance in making up; marks position of darts, buttonholes, etc on parts by hand or using powered hand drill.

May (01) separate parts and sort them into bundles for making up.

Other titles include Dissector, Layer-up, Layer-up and marker, Under cutter.

656.52 Chopper

Cuts out parts of bespoke tailored garments marked out on fabric

Unrolls marked fabric and smoothes it out on cutting table; cuts along chalked outlines with hand shears; notches edges of garment parts where indicated by chalk marks; sorts parts into bundles for making up.

656.54 Trimmer (bespoke tailoring)

Cuts out or trims facings and/or linings, interlinings and other trimmings for bespoke tailored garments

Performs a combination of the following tasks: cuts lengths of fabric by hand for garment linings or interlinings; positions garment parts or pattern pieces on appropriate lining fabric and cuts round parts or pattern pieces with hand shears or trims cut linings to size; cuts out interlinings with shears or selects cut interlinings from stock and trims as necessary; cuts out from measurements facings, pocket linings and trimmings such as welts and pocket flaps; selects matching thread and buttons; bundles items for making up.

May (01) chalk mark fabric or marked chalk guide lines with thread for guidance in making up
(02) pin interlining to relevant garment part.

Other titles include Canvas fixer, Fitter-up, Lining cutter.

656.56 Trimmings cutter

Cuts out stock linings or interlining for use in garment manufacture

Performs appropriate tasks as described under LAY CUTTER (GARMENTS) (656.16) but in relation to the cutting of linings or interlinings for ready-made garments or for trimming to size for bespoke garments.

May (01) sharpen cutters
(02) bundle cut parts.

Other titles include Band knife cutter (garment linings), Canvas cutter, Stock linings cutter (garments).

Excluded are Press cutters (garments) (656.58)

656.58 Press cutter (garments)

Operates power press to cut out garment parts or linings

Places material on press bed and positions appropriate cutting die on material to best advantage, or fits die in press bed and positions material on die; where appropriate moves press bed into position beneath press head or moves press head into position above bed; operates control to bring down press head to force die through material; operates control to raise press head where necessary and removes die and cut parts.

May (01) adjust pressure or depth of drop of press head
(02) cut lengths of material for building up into multiple lay
(03) operate mechanical device to build up multiple lay
(04) sort parts into bundles for making up.

Other titles include Block cutter, Cutting press operator, Glove lining cutter, Puncher (gloves), Webber.

656.60 Trimmer (knitwear)

Cuts neck, front and other openings in knitted garments or garment parts by hand

Marks shape of neck opening from measurements or positions and marks round appropriate template or pattern on garment or garment part; cuts along marked outline with shears; makes front openings of cardigans by cutting along guide marks stitched in fabric; forms pocket openings by cutting double-knitted section of garment or garment part.

May (01) mark garment for guidance of linking machinist
(02) cut garment linings using hand shears.

656.62 Brim rounder

Cuts brims of felt hats to required width

Secures hat in position on block of appropriate size on cutting table or inserts edge of brim in cutting machine; where appropriate sets cutter according to size of hat and width of brim required; positions cutter on brim and rotates cutting table manually or operates control to rotate table, or starts machine and guides brim under cutter to remove excess felt.

May (01) round brim with shears or hand knife and gauge.

Other titles include Brim cutter.

656.64 Press cutter (excluding garments)

Operates power press to cut out parts of textile articles other than garments

Performs appropriate tasks as described under PRESS CUTTER (GARMENTS) (656.58) but in relation to the cutting of parts of textile articles other than garments.

May (01) adjust pressure or depth of drop of press head
(02) mark material to assist in positioning cutting die.

Other titles include Press cutter (soft toys), Punching machine operator.

656.66 Slitter

Cuts fabric into pieces of specified width

(01) **Slitting machine operator**

Loads or directs loading of roll of fabric on machine, or folds fabric into laps on machine table; where appropriate sets and secures cutter(s) and spacers on machine according to width of pieces required; if operating bias cutting machine, sets control to obtain correct cutting angle; operates control to heat cutters to required temperature where appropriate; secures end of fabric to leader cloth where required; passes end of fabric or leader cloth through tensioners and where appropriate beneath cutter(s), and secures to take-up roller or leads end to take-off table or conveyor; starts machine; watches operation to detect irregular cutting, holds knife against fabric at cutting line required, or, if cutting fabric on the bias, operates control to move cutter(s) diagonally across fabric; unloads or directs unloading of cut fabric from machine.

Other titles include Bias cutter, Frame hand cutting machine operator, Length cutter, Multiple slitting machine operator, Slitting and winding machine operator.

(02) **Roll cutter**

Positions roll of fabric on cutting table; adjusts guide according to width of strip required; starts rotation of circular knife and feeds roll to knife to slice fabric into rolls of specified width.

Other titles include Bandage cutter.

May (03) operate machine to wind lapped fabric into rolls ready for slitting
(04) set speed of machine
(05) sharpen cutters.

656.68 Pattern marker

Marks out embroidery designs on textile fabric

Places fabric to be marked on work-table and where appropriate positions perforated pattern or stencil on fabric, or secures cloth template bearing embossed design to work-table and clips fabric on template; outlines design on fabric in chalk or pencil from measurements or using stencil, or applies powdered chalk, wax solution, etc by hand to fabric through perforations in pattern, or rubs wax over fabric to transfer embossed design to fabric.

May (01) perforate design outline on paper pattern using powered hand pricking tool
(02) chalk mark fabric to indicate gaps in stitching required for insertion of down or other filling
(03) paint over chalk markings with oil colour, using fine brush.

Other titles include Preparer, Quilt marker, Stenciller, Tracer.

656.90 Cross cutter

Cuts fabric into pieces of specified length

(01) **Hand cutter**

Draws marked fabric on to cutting table or measures off length required and marks fabric by nicking edge or by pulling out appropriate weft thread, or adjusts stop on table according to length of fabric required and positions end of fabric against stop; cuts across fabric with scissors or powered shears or pushes powered cutter across fabric.

Other titles include Coir matting cutter, Household linen cutter.

(02) **Guillotine operator**

Sets stop according to length of fabric required; places roll of fabric on spindle and pulls end of roll up to stop or secures fabric on machine bed; operates hand or foot controls or starts machine to lower blade to cut fabric.

Other titles include Guillotine machinist.

(03) **Cutting machine operator**

Sets speed of machine rollers and cutter where required; leads end of fabric into machine; starts machine to draw fabric to cutter and cut fabric into specified lengths.

May (04) cross cut several thicknesses of fabric simultaneously
(05) tear off lengths of fabric required
(06) sharpen cutters
(07) operate machine which folds lengths after cutting.

Other titles include Sack cutter.

656.98 Trainee

Performs, under instruction or guidance, various tasks including training exercises and as appropriate pursues studies in order to acquire the basic skills and knowledge required to perform the tasks of pattern makers, markers and cutters (garments, upholstery and related products).

656.99 Other pattern makers, markers and cutters (garments, upholstery and related products)

Workers in this group make patterns and mark and cut out material including leather for the manufacture of garments, upholstery and the making up of soft furnishings and other articles of textile fabric, and are not elsewhere classified, for example:

(01) **Bottom parers,** Lining parers (trim coat linings to required length with hand shears); (02) **Button markers** (mark fabric by hand to show position of buttons on garments); (03) **Buttonhole markers**; (04) **Edge shavers** (shave wool from edges of sheepskin garment parts with electric clippers to facilitate stitching); (05) **Fabric cutters (excluding garments) (not elsewhere classified)** (cut shapes marked out on single lay of fabric for making up into articles other than garments); (06) **Glove trimmers** (trim seams, wrist apertures, etc of gloves with scissors or hand knife); (07) **Lace taggers and cutters** (operate machines to measure, tag, cut and count laces); (08) **Spray markers** (position pattern pieces on fabric and operate machines to spray marking solution over lay); (09) **Stamp markers** (mark fabric for cutting, using rubber stamp).

Unit Group 657 Sewing and Embroidering Occupations (Hand) (Garments, Upholstery and Related Products)

Workers in this unit group sew and embroider by hand garments and other products made from textile fabric, fur and skin.

Excluded are Basters (651.20), Stitchers (hand) (footwear) (665.20) and Stitchers (hand) (leather goods excluding footwear) (665.30)

657.10 Hand sewer (fur garments)

Performs hand sewing tasks in the making up or finishing of fur garments

Performs some or all of the following tasks: joins skins together by hand sewing; hems garment edges; sews binding to garment edges; sews padding, interlinings and linings in position; sews buttons, hooks or other fastenings on garments.

May (01) cut parts for interlinings and/or linings with scissors or hand shears
(02) make up linings by machine sewing
(03) press linings (461).

Other titles include Fur garment finisher, Fur sewer, Liner and finisher.

657.20 Hand embroideress

Works decorative designs on, or secures beads, sequins or similar trimmings to, textile fabric by hand stitching

Examines sketch, sample or other specification; selects appropriate needles or tambour hooks, embroidery silks, cottons, etc and where required sequins, beads or other trimmings; where appropriate sets up fabric to be embroidered on embroidery frame; as necessary attaches padding, stiffening, etc to area to be embroidered, by hand sewing or with adhesive; embroiders design by hand varying type of stitch as required, or attaches sequins, beads, etc by hand stitching using tambour hook where appropriate; makes up and affixes tassels and fringes as required.

May (01) mark outline of design on fabric (656.68)
(02) paste design on fabric to be embroidered
(03) cut padding or stiffening to required shape
(04) cut holes in fabric with mallet and punch
(05) iron self-adhesive material to back of embroidered badges
(06) try out and prepare working instructions for new embroidery designs.

Other titles include Tambour beader.

See Embroidery mender (659.68)

657 .50 Fabric garment finisher

Performs hand sewing tasks in the finishing of fabric garments

Performs one or more of the following tasks: hems garment edges; sews padding, stiffening material and linings in position; cuts and sews buttonholes; sews in loose ends and closes seams of knitted garments; sews headbands in, or peaks or chin straps on, hats or helmets; sews buttons, press studs, hooks and eyes or other fastenings on garments; sews loops, pocket flaps, bows, ribbons or other trimmings on garments.

May (01) pick up stitches and close holes in knitted garments

(02) mark position of trimmings or fastenings using measure or template

(03) press seams (461)

(04) perform tasks of SEWING MACHINIST (658 .50) or (658 .55).

Other titles include Buttonhole maker, Button sewer, Dress finisher, Felling hand, Hand buttoner, Hand buttonholer, Hand finisher, Hand trimmer, Woollen glove finisher.

See Repairer (garments, linen, etc) (659 .66)

Excluded are tailors' assistants (651 .30)

657 .55 Hand sewer (leather, sheepskin garments)

Performs hand sewing tasks in the making up or finishing of leather or sheepskin garments

Performs one or more of the following tasks: joins leather pieces together to form garments; sews binding to garment edges; sews buttonholes; decorates garments by hand stitching (pointing) using template as necessary; sews buttons, hooks and eyes, press studs or other fastenings on garments; sews loops, labels or other trimmings on garments; tacks gloves together in pairs.

May (01) rivet buttons or studs to gloves

(02) attach self-adhesive name or size labels to insides of gloves

(03) pack finished garments (841 .35).

Other titles include Hand pointer, Leather glove decorator, Leather glove finisher, Leather glove maker, Leather glove sewer.

657 .60 Hand sewer (upholstery)

Performs hand sewing tasks in the finishing of furniture upholstery and loose cushions

Closes seams of covers fitted to chairs, divans, settees, etc using curved needle and waxed thread; inserts cushions or plastic or latex foam mouldings into cushion covers and sews up open parts of cover seams; attaches braid, fringes or other trimmings to upholstery by hand sewing where required.

May (01) cover buttons with fabric

(02) make up cushion covers by machine sewing

(03) insert or remove cushion fillings using pneumatic equipment.

Other titles include Slipper, Slip stitcher.

657 .65 Hand sewer (carpet)

Performs hand sewing tasks in the making up and repair of carpets

Performs some or all of the following tasks: sews along raw edges of carpet sections to be joined to prevent fraying; sews carpet sections together ensuring matching of carpet pattern where appropriate; hems carpet edge or binds edge with tape by hand sewing; sews fringe to carpet edge; removes worn or damaged parts of carpet and cuts and sews into position replacement pieces, or sews wool tufts of appropriate colour(s) into defective areas affixing canvas patches to carpet backing by hand sewing or with adhesive where necessary.

May (01) seal seam edges by applying adhesive solution

(02) reinforce seams by affixing adhesive tape

(03) flatten seams with hammer or heavy iron

(04) sew pieces of carpet underfelt together by hand

(05) sew long seams by machine (658 .75).

Other titles include Carpet seamstress, Carpet sewer and repairer.

See Mender (carpet, rug) (547 .55)

657.70 Mat binder

Sews plait round coir mat by hand to bind edges

Straightens or squares up edges of mat as necessary by pulling out surplus tufts with hand tool; cuts length of coir plait binding from coil; positions binding against edge of mat and sews to edge with twine, using metal-reinforced hand strap (sewing palm) to push needle through mat; sews ends of plait binding together; flattens binding round edge of mat using mallet.

May (01) sew plait binding on small mats by machine (658.75).

Other titles include Matting binder.

657.75 Umbrella finisher

Sews umbrella covers to frames by hand

Sews round opening at top of umbrella cover; positions waterproof cap at top of frame and pulls umbrella cover over cap; lines up seams of cover with frame ribs and sews edge of cover to ribs through holes at tip of ribs; tacks cover seams to ribs above and below rib joints; opens umbrella and steams cover to set shape.

May (01) hand sew small pieces of fabric or plastic to rib joints to protect cover from joints

(02) cut small rosette from covering fabric and hand sew to top of cover where tip of frame protrudes

(03) hand sew fastening band to cover.

Other titles include Umbrella tipper.

657.98 Trainee

Performs, under instruction or guidance, various tasks including training exercises and as appropriate pursues studies in order to acquire the basic skills and knowledge required to perform the tasks of workers in sewing and embroidering occupations (hand) (garments, upholstery and related products).

657.99 Other sewing and embroidering occupations (hand) (garments, upholstery and related products)

Workers in this group sew and embroider by hand garments and other products made from textile fabric, fur and skin and are not elsewhere classified, for example:

(01) **Hood coverers** (attach hoods to frames by hand sewing in the manufacture of perambulators, invalid carriages and other light vehicles); (02) **Incandescent mantle sewers** (draw ends of mantle fabric together with needle and thread); (03) **Soft toy finishers** (hand sew and otherwise finish soft toys)

Unit Group 658 Sewing and Embroidering Occupations (Machine) (Garments, Upholstery and Related Products)

Workers in this unit group sew and embroider by machine garments and other products made from textile fabric, fur and skin.

Excluded are Sewing machinists (footwear) (665.40) and Sewing machinists (leather goods excluding footwear) (665.50)

658.10 Sewing machinist (general)

Operates standard and specialised machines to sew heavy and light fabric in the making, altering or repairing of a variety of textile products

Secures suitable needle(s) in machine as necessary; loads bobbins or spools of thread or yarn of required colour(s) on machine; passes end(s) of thread or yarn from bobbin(s) or spool(s) through guides, tensioners and eye(s) of needle(s); adjusts machine and as necessary fits attachments to regulate tension of thread or yarn and type, depth and size of stitch according to sewing requirements; where appropriate places together fabric parts to be joined; positions fabric to be sewn under or opposite needle(s) using guide as necessary; starts machine and guides fabric under or past needle regulating sewing speed as required; removes fabric from machine on completion of sewing and where necessary cuts thread or yarn; replaces empty bobbins or spools and damaged needle(s) as required.

May (01) clean and oil machine.

See Repairer (garments, linen, etc) (659.66)

658.20 Fur machinist

Operates twin cup machine to sew fur or sheepskin

Secures suitable needle in machine; loads, threads and adjusts machine as described under SEWING MACHINIST (GENERAL) (658.10); operates control to open feed cups of machine and aligns edges of skins or garment parts to be joined between cups; operates control to close cups to grip skins or garment parts; starts machine to rotate cups and feed edges to needle, holding fur or wool away from needle with hand tool; regulates speed of machine as required; cuts thread on completion of sewing, opens feed cups and removes joined skins or garment parts; replaces empty bobbins and damaged needles as necessary.

May (01) clean and oil machine.

658.30 Embroidery machinist

Operates or sets and attends machine to decorate textile fabric with ornamental stitching

(01) **Cornelly machinist, Irish embroidery machinist**

Examines sketch or sample of embroidered design; loads machine with bobbin(s) of thread of required colour and passes end of thread from bobbin through guides, tensioners and eye of needle; where appropriate clamps in frame fabric on which embroidery design has been marked; positions fabric on machine bed under needle; starts machine, and operates controls to regulate stitching speed and movement of fabric under needle or guides fabric under needle and operates controls to regulate stitching speed and width of stitch; stops machine and rethreads with thread of different colour as required; removes embroidered fabric from machine.

(02) **Pantograph embroidery machinist**

Secures or directs securing of fabric on machine rollers and operates control to stretch fabric between rollers; fixes enlarged diagram of design on pantograph board; loads bobbins of thread of required colour(s) on machine and passes ends of thread from bobbins through guides, tensioners and eyes of needles, or secures threaded needles in machine, or directs performance of these tasks; starts machine and guides pointer on pantograph arm, stitch by stitch, over enlarged diagram, depressing foot pedal or cause machine needles to produce design of required size on fabric; removes or directs removal of embroidered fabric from machine.

(03) **Automatic embroidery machinist**

Secures or directs securing of fabric on machine rollers and operates control to stretch fabric between rollers; loads or directs loading of bobbins of thread of required colour(s) on machine; secures needles in stitching heads and passes or directs passing of ends from bobbins through guides, tensioners and eyes of needles; fits punched pattern card (jacquard card) on machine, as required; starts machine and watches operation to detect broken threads or damaged needles; ties broken threads and replaces damaged needles; rethreads machine with thread of different colour as required; removes embroidered fabric from machine.

May (04) repair embroidery.

See Embroidery mender (659.68)

658 .50 Sewing machinist (heavy clothing)

Operates standard or specialised machine to sew fabric or leather in the making, altering or repairing of heavy clothing

Performs appropriate tasks as described under SEWING MACHINIST (GENERAL) (658 .10) but in relation to the sewing of heavy clothing such as coats, suits and uniforms.

May (01) load binding, tape, webbing or other reeled material on machine

(02) cut pocket openings or buttonholes

(03) mark stitching position on fabric from measurements or using guide

(04) trim excess material from seams

(05) clean and oil machine.

Additional factor: type(s) of machine to which accustomed.

Other titles include Bartack machinist, Basting machinist, Binding machinist, Buttonhole machinist, Buttoning machinist, Chainstitch machinist, Coat machinist, Felling machinist, Jumper-baster, Overlock machinist, Padding machinist, Serging machinist, Skirt machinist, Sleeve machinist, Special machinist, Trouser machinist, Vest machinist, Welt machinist, Zigzag machinist.

See Repairer (garments, linen, etc) (659 .66)
Excluded are Lining making machinists (658 .55)

658 .55 Sewing machinist (light clothing)

Operates standard or specialised machine to sew fabric or leather in the making, altering or repairing of light clothing or garment linings

Performs appropriate tasks as described under SEWING MACHINIST (GENERAL) (658 .10) but in relation to the sewing of light clothing such as blouses, dresses, lingerie or shirts or garment linings.

May (01) load binding, lace trimming, tape or other reeled material on machine

(02) mark stitching position on fabric using guide as necessary

(03) clean and oil machine.

Additional factor: type(s) of machine to which accustomed.

Other titles include Bartack machinist, Belt machinist, Binding machinist, Blouse machinist, Busker, Buttonhole machinist, Buttoning machinist, Collar machinist, Corner stopper, Corset stitcher, Dress machinist, Elasticator machinist, Felling machinist, Flatlock machinist, Gown machinist, Hemstitch machinist, Lining making machinist, Lockstitch machinist, Machine pointer, Millinery machinist, Overall machinist, Overlock machinist, Post machinist, Seamer, Skirt machinist, Sleeve machinist, Special machinist, Strapper, Straw hat machinist, Suspender maker, Tie machinist, Welter.

See Repairer (garments, linen, etc) (659 .66)
Excluded are Linking machinists (658 .60)

658 .60 Linking machinist

Operates machine to close openings in toes of seamless hose or join edges of knitted garment parts loop by loop

Loads cone of yarn of required colour on machine; threads end of yarn from cone through guides, tensioners and eye of needle; places loops of one side or edge to be joined on points of circular linking mechanism so that each point holds one loop; places loops of other side or edge on points holding corresponding loops of first side or edge; starts machine to rotate linking mechanism and link sides or edges, loop by loop; if linking raw edges, cuts off excess fabric at seam with hand knife or sets machine to trim excess automatically during linking operation.

Other titles include Linker, Looper (hosiery).

658 .65 Sewing machinist (heavy fabric) (excluding clothing)

Operates standard or specialised machine to sew heavy fabric other than in the making, altering or repairing of clothing

Performs appropriate tasks as described under SEWING MACHINIST (GENERAL) (658 .10) but in relation to the sewing of heavy fabric in preparation for further processing, for upholstery or in the making, altering or repairing of articles such as sacks, sails and tarpaulins.

May (01) load binding, piping, tape or other reeled material on machine

(02) cut patching material to suitable shapes

(03) clean and oil machine.

Additional factors: type(s) of machine to which accustomed; type(s) of articles made, altered or repaired.

Other titles include Bag mender, Blanket binder, Blanket whipper, Canvas goods machinist, Grey room sewer, Grey room stitcher, Hood and apron machinist, Sack machinist, Sack repairer, Tape edge machinist, Upholstery machinist.

Excluded are Sewing machinists (carpeting, matting, rugs) (658 .75)

658 .70 Sewing machinist (light fabric) (excluding clothing)

Operates standard or specialised machine to sew light fabric other than in the making, altering or repairing of clothing

Performs appropriate tasks as described under SEWING MACHINIST (GENERAL) (658 .10) but in relation to the sewing of light fabric in preparation for further processing or in the making, altering or repairing of articles such as flags, handkerchiefs and household linen.

May (01) load binding, piping, tape or other reeled material on machine

(02) clean and oil machine.

Additional factors: type(s) of machine to which accustomed; type(s) of article made, altered or repaired.

Other titles include Blanket binder, Blanket whipper, Flag machinist, Grey room sewer, Grey room stitcher, Household linen machinist, Lace machinist, Rag book machinist, Soft toy machinist, Umbrella cover machinist.

See Repairer (garments, linen, etc) (659 .66)

658 .75 Sewing machinist (carpeting, matting, rugs)

Operates machine to sew carpeting, matting or rugs

Loads bobbins or spools of thread of required colour on machine; passes end(s) of thread or yarn from bobbins or spools through guides, tensioners and eye(s) of needle(s); positions carpeting, matting or rug on sliding bed of machine or clamps carpet pieces together on machine bed or secures carpet pieces in clamps suspended from rail; starts machine and guides carpeting, matting or rug under needle or moves travelling stitching head or portable machine along edges to be joined; replaces empty bobbins or spools as necessary.

May (01) shave edge of carpeting before sewing using portable machine

(02) load tape or other reeled material on machine

(03) seal raw carpet edges with adhesive

(04) clean and oil machine.

Other titles include Matting binder.

658 .80 Automatic sewing machine attendant

Attends one or more automatic machines to sew textile material

Performs a combination of the following tasks: loads bobbins or spools of thread, yarn or twine on machine; passes end(s) of thread, etc from bobbin(s) or spool(s) through guides, tensioners and eye(s) of needle(s); secures device on machine to guide sewing head; starts machine and brings material to be sewn to needle(s) or places material on conveyor for automatic guiding to needle(s) or secures material on frame, positions frame beneath sewing head and starts machine; watches operation to detect thread breakages; removes material on completion of sewing; replaces damaged needles and rethreads needles as necessary.

Additional factor: number of machines attended.

Other titles include Automatic hemming machinist, Automatic looping machinist (sanitary towels), Automatic quilting machinist, Automatic tufting machinist.

Excluded are Automatic embroidery machinists (658 .30)

658 .98 Trainee

Performs, under instruction or guidance, various tasks including training exercises and as appropriate pursues studies in order to acquire the basic skills and knowledge required to perform the tasks of workers in sewing and embroidering occupations (machine) (garments, upholstery and related products).

658 .99 Other sewing and embroidering occupations (machine) (garments, upholstery and related products)

Workers in this group sew and embroider by machine garments and other products made from textile fabric, fur and skin and are not elsewhere classified.

Unit Group 659 Textile Materials Working Occupations Not Elsewhere Classified

Workers in this unit group block hats and helmets, make articles such as sails, powder puffs and mounts for wigs and hair pieces, lay carpets, finish felt hats and canvas goods and perform other miscellaneous tasks in textile materials working and are not elsewhere classified.

659.05 Felt hat shaping and finishing journeyman

Shapes and finishes felt hats

As required performs appropriate tasks as described under HAT BLOCKER (HAND) (659.10), HAT BLOCKER (MACHINE) (659.15) and FELT HAT FINISHER (659.52).

May (01) examine finished hats for defects.

659.10 Hat blocker (hand)

Shapes hoods to make hats

Softens hood in steam cabinet or over steam jet to facilitate shaping; pulls hood over block of appropriate size and shape, manipulating hood to required shape; where appropriate, ties cord round base of crown to form inside edge of brim and applies further steam to hood; removes creases and marks and where appropriate smoothes brim of felt hood by hand or using hand tool or glazes straw hood by pressing with iron; allows hood to dry naturally on block or places blocked hood in drying cabinet; removes block and cord from hat after drying.

May (01) expand hood on stretching device before blocking
(02) position and secure pieces of cane on hood to form indentations
(03) press hat with iron after drying
(04) check width of hat brim with rule
(05) press edge of brim of straw hat against heated metal block to seal ends of straw plait
(06) perform tasks of HAT BLOCKER (MACHINE) (659.15).

Other titles include Coner, Hat steamer.

659.15 Hat blocker (machine), Fibre helmet blocker

Operates one or machines to shape hoods or fabric into hats or give final shape to hats or fibre helmets

Fits upper and lower sections of block of required size and shape on blocking machine or positions appropriate mould in press bed; softens fabric or article by steaming, soaking or warming over heated metal block to facilitate shaping; positions article to be shaped over lower section of block on blocking machine securing it with cord or wire where necessary or in mould in press bed; operates controls to force lower section of block into upper section, or to lower press head containing rubber bag on to mould and to inflate bag to press article to shape of mould; as required operates controls to pass steam through block sections or to heat blocks; operates controls to release pressure when shaping is complete; removes shaped hat or helmet from blocking machine or press.

Additional factor: number of machines operated.

Other titles include Hat presser, Hat steamer.

659.20 Rainproof garment bonder

Joins rubberised fabric garment parts with adhesive and tapes garment seams and hems

Sorts parts required for garment where appropriate; applies adhesive with finger along edges of garment parts to be joined and overlaps edges, or applies adhesive with finger along edges of stitched seams; presses down edges and consolidates bond using hand roller; affixes adhesive waterproof tape on inside of garment to cover seams and hems; removes surplus adhesive with brush or sponge.

May (01) remove layer of cotton material from edge of fabric before bonding or to facilitate machining
(02) insert eyelets and studs in garment using hand tools or riveting machine.

659 .25 Surgical corset fitter

Measures customers or patients for surgical corsets and fits completed garments on customers

Ascertains from medical prescription type of garment required; takes customer's or patient's measurements; records measurements and particulars of material, stiffeners, straps and other attachments required; checks fit of completed garment on customer or patient and arranges for any necessary alterations to be made.

Other titles include Corsetiere.

659 .30 Sailmaker

Makes and repairs sails, boat covers and similar articles

Ascertains job requirements from drawing or other specification; spreads canvas, nylon or other fabric of required weight and colour on floor; marks out sail or other article from measurements or positions and marks round pattern on fabric; cuts along marked outline with knife or shears; joins sections of fabric together by machine sewing; turns in and machine sews edge of article; cuts reinforcing pieces of fabric and sews in position on article by hand or machine; repairs worn or damaged articles by hand or machine sewing.

May (01) take measurements for sails or other articles required

(02) perform tasks of FINISHER (CANVAS GOODS, FLAGS, ETC) (659 .62)

(03) brush waterproofing solution on to finished article.

659 .35 Wig mount maker

Shapes and sews fabric to form mounts for wigs or hair pieces

Takes measurements of customer's head where required; selects head-shaped block of suitable size and where necessary adapts block to individual requirements by fixing padding in appropriate position(s); fits paper to block and cuts paper to make pattern; cuts out pieces of mount from fabric using paper pattern; pins pieces to block, pleating and tucking fabric as required to ensure correct shape of mount; joins pieces together and secures pleats and tucks in place by hand sewing; sews elasticated ribbon or stiffening material round edge of mount at nape of neck, temples or other specified position; binds edge of mount with silk tape or fabric strip by hand sewing.

May (01) sew tape to mount to mark parting.

659 .40 Carpet layer

Lays carpet on customers' premises

Examines layout prepared by carpet planner; lays hardboard or cement to level floor as necessary and lays required underlay; positions carpet pieces on floor in accordance with layout ensuring matching of carpet pattern where appropriate; joins pieces by hand sewing or with self-adhesive tape, and sews or otherwise affixes binding to edge of carpet where required, or directs performance of these tasks; affixes self-adhesive tape over seams on back of carpet where required; turns in carpet edge and tacks to floor or nails spiked wooden strip or screws hooks along edge of floor and secures carpet to strip or floor hooks, stretching carpet taut with straining tool; nails metal or wooden strip or glues tape over carpet edge in doorway; planes bottom edge of door where necessary to enable door to open over carpet; if laying stair carpet, folds carpet on top and/or bottom stair to allow for repositioning after wear.

May (01) cut carpet, underlay and binding required from stock

(02) lay carpet without securing to floor

(03) lay linoleum or other similar floor coverings (869 .12)

(04) trim carpet to size after period of wear.

Other titles include Carpet fitter.

659 .50 Brim shaper

Curls or otherwise sets shape of hat brims by hand or machine

(01) **Brim shaper (hand)**

Steams or otherwise softens brim to facilitate shaping where necessary; shapes brim by hand using hot iron and curling tools or presses brim to shape on or over frame, template or shaping board using heated bag or pan of sand or warm iron or secures brim on frame with cord and applies further steam to set shape; pares brim where necessary using hatter's plane or knives.

(02) **Brim shaper (machine)**

Sets machine according to shape and depth of curl required; positions hat on machine and starts machine to impart required curl to hat brim.

May (03) fit mould (brow) into hat before shaping brim

(04) check width of brim or curl using slide gauge.

Other titles include Hat brim curler, Hat brim setter, Hat flanger.

659 .52 Felt hat finisher

Imparts required finish to felt hats by hand or machine

Positions hat on turn-table or on arm of finishing machine; operates controls to rotate turn-table and where appropriate to heat wax or starts machine; applies abrasive paper or cloth or molten wax to rotating hat, or operates control to bring hat in contact with revolving finishing attachment and manipulates hat as necessary to ensure finishing of entire surface; as required brushes hat to remove dust or to impart polish or polishes hat with warm pad.

May (01) fit appropriate finishing attachment to machine
(02) operate beating machine to soften hat prior to finishing or to remove dust from felt
(03) operate dust extraction equipment to remove dust from felt.

Other titles include Felt hat polisher, Felt hat shaver, Lurer, Pouncer, Swabber, Velourer.

659 .54 Foundation garment fitter

Advises customers on choice of foundation garments and measures and fits completed garments on customers

Discusses with customer style of garment and type of material desired; takes customer's measurements, using special fitting garment where appropriate; records measurements and particulars of style and material required; checks fit of completed garment on customer and advises customer on adjustment and care of garment.

May (01) advise customers on choice of other light clothing such as brassieres or swim suits
(02) take measurements for and check fit of other light clothing such as brassieres or swim suits
(03) receive payment for garments
(04) give talks on choice and care of foundation garments.

Other titles include Corsetiere.

Excluded are Surgical corset fitters (659 .25)

659 .56 Wire stitching machinist

Operates machine to insert wire staples in palms or backs or round edges of industrial gloves

Secures spool of appropriate type of wire in position on machine spindle; threads end of wire through guides and stitching mechanism; positions glove under stitching mechanism; starts machine and manipulates glove as necessary to ensure that staples are correctly positioned.

659 .58 Sack worker (general hand)

Performs a variety of tasks in the manufacture of fabric bags and sacks

Performs a combination of the following tasks: cuts fabric to size required with shears or powered hand cutter; folds or otherwise arranges cut pieces ready for machine sewing; joins pieces and hems edges of article by machine sewing; attends machine which prints lettering or other identifying information on article; attends machine which turns article right side out; ties sacks in bundles by hand or machine.

May (01) repair bags and sacks by machine sewing.

Excluded are Spreaders (bag, sack) (659 .99)

659 .60 Powder puff maker

Performs a variety of tasks in the making of powder puffs

Performs some or all of the following tasks: positions template on fabric and cuts round template with shears or operates press cutting machine; joins cut parts by gluing or machine sewing or by pressing together in heated press; attaches ribbons, bows, handles or other trimmings to puff by hand or machine sewing or with adhesive; operates machine to emboss lettering on puff; brushes lambs-wool or swansdown surfaces; trims off cotton ends.

659 .62 Finisher (canvas goods, flags, etc)

Performs a variety of tasks in the finishing of canvas sheets, tarpaulins, tents, flags and similar articles

Performs a combination of the following tasks: cuts eyelet-holes in fabric using punch and mallet or operates press cutting machine; hand stitches edges of eyelet-holes with twine or inserts metal eyelets in holes using punch, die and mallet; passes ends of ropes through eyelets and secures by splicing; sews ropes to fabric by hand or machine; passes ends of ropes through hooks and round toggles and secures by splicing; threads rope through hem on side of flag and secures flag to rope with clips or by hand sewing; inserts rod through hem on side of flag and tacks flag to rod; trims off loose threads with scissors

May (01) apply waterproofing solution to articles using brush or spray
(02) stencil identification marks on articles
(03) fold articles for dispatch.

659 .64 Embroidery machine operator's assistant

Assists in setting and/or operating embroidery machine

Performs a combination of the following tasks: secures fabric on rollers of embroidery machine; loads bobbins of thread of required colour(s) on embroidery machine and passes ends of thread from bobbins through guides, tensioners and eyes of needles; operates needle-threading machine; secures threaded needles in embroidery machine; watches embroidering operation to detect broken threads or needles or empty bobbins; replaces broken needles or empty bobbins; rethreads needles as necessary; removes embroidered fabric from machine.

May (01) cut and/or affix pieces of material to fabric (appliqué)
(02) cut out badges or other articles from length of fabric on which they have been embroidered
(03) remove ends of thread from bobbins using hand tool.

Other titles include Back boy, Back girl, Back shuttler, Front boy, Front girl, Pantograph machine minder, Threader.

659 .66 Repairer (garments, linen, etc)

Repairs garments, household linen and other textile articles by hand and machine sewing

Examines article to ascertain repairs required and to determine best method of repair, or ascertains repairs required from work instructions; repairs minor damage or reinforces worn area by hand or machine darning; repairs major area of damage or wear by patching; repairs buttonholes and replaces buttons and other fastenings by hand or machine sewing; resews edges or seams of article as required; presses repaired article.

May (01) replace garment pockets
(02) undertake minor alterations
(03) hand sew identification marks on articles or operate marking machine.

Other titles include Darner, Mender (laundry, dry cleaners, institution), Seamstress.

See Invisible mender (repair service) (547 .20), Garment finisher (657 .50) and sewing machinists (658)

659 .68 Embroidery mender

Examines machine embroidery and repairs faults

Examines machine embroidery for missing threads and imperfect stitching or design; removes broken or unwanted threads with scissors or other hand tool; inserts missing stitches and rectifies other stitching faults and flaws in design by hand or machine sewing with appropriate thread.

May (01) cut out articles from length of fabric on which they have been embroidered
(02) cut out pieces of fabric and affix to back of embroidered articles with adhesive
(03) iron self-adhesive backing on to embroidered articles.

Other titles include Embroidery finisher mender, Embroidery repairer.

See Hand embroideress (657 .20) and Embroidery machinist (658 .30)

659 .90 Felt hood tip stretcher

Operates machine to stretch and round tips of felt hoods

Softens felt hood in steam cabinet or over steam jet to facilitate shaping; secures softened hood over conical frame in machine; starts machine to apply steam to hood and to rotate hood on frame against vibratory stretching and shaping device; removes hood from machine after set time.

Other titles include Starrer.

659 .98 Trainee

Performs, under instruction or guidance, various tasks including training exercises and as appropriate pursues studies in order to acquire the basic skills and knowledge required to perform the tasks of workers in textile materials working occupations not elsewhere classified.

659 .99 Other textile materials working occupations not elsewhere classified

Workers in this group perform miscellaneous tasks in textile materials working and are not separately classified, for example:

(01) **Baste pullers,** Draw threaders, Embroidery clearers, Garment cleaners-off, Unravellers (remove basting stitches, loose threads or other unwanted thread or yarn from garments or other textile articles by hand); (02) **Button makers,** Buttoners (operate machines to cover buttons with fabric and/or to secure covered buttons to cap crowns); (03) **Cap gaugers** (check size of cap headbands and as necessary stretch headbands to correct size using stretching device); (04) **Cotton tiers,** End tiers (pass ends of threads to insides of gloves and tie and trim ends); (05) **Embroidery makers-up** (make up and/or mount or otherwise finish embroidered articles); (06) **Eyeletters** (punch eyelet-holes in garments and rivet eyelets in punched holes by hand or machine); (07) **Layers-down** (place ends of lengths of fabric together ready for sewing stock material prior to bleaching or other finishing); (08) **Masonic regalia table hands** (make up regalia by hand and machine sewing and/or sew or otherwise affix emblems, badges, tassels, etc to regalia); (09) **Millinery trimmings sorters** (select from stock and as required cut to length suitable lining, ribbons and other trimmings for millinery); (10) **Outdoor matchers** (select and purchase appropriate thread and trimmings for use in making up and finishing light clothing); (11) **Pullboys** (assist hat blockers in pulling hoods or hats over blocks and securing them with cord or wire or pull cloth cap covers into position over foundation material); (12) **Sanitary dressing machine attendants** (attend machines which cover cotton wool with gauze to make sanitary towels, surgical dressings, etc); (13) **Sheepskin coat makers** (make sheepskin coats throughout); (14) **Silk hat body makers,** Silk hat finishers (form foundations of silk hats on blocks from pieces of gossamer and muslin, or attach covering material to varnished foundations by ironing and polish hats with warm cloth pads); (15) **Sprayers** (operate spray guns to line rubber gloves with flock or to apply adhesive and/or flock to fabric in the making of foundation garments); (16) **Spreaders (bag, sack)** (fold or otherwise arrange sections of fabric bags or sacks ready for sewing and feed bags or sacks to automatic turning and/or printing machines); (17) **Turners** (turn garment parts, garments or other textile articles right side out by hand or machine); (18) **Wool patchers** (stick patches of skin on wool side of sheepskin garment parts to cover damaged areas)

Minor Group 66 LEATHER WORKING OCCUPATIONS

Workers in this minor group cut out, shape, sew, make up and repair leather goods, other than leather garments, and perform related tasks.

The occupations are arranged in the following unit groups:

660 Foremen (Leather Working Occupations)

661 Boot and Shoe Making (Bespoke and Surgical) Occupations

662 Leather Cutting Occupations

663 Lasting Occupations (Footwear)

664 Leather Goods Makers and Repairers (Excluding Boots and Shoes)

665 Leather Sewing and Stitching Occupations

666 Boot and Shoe Repairers

669 Leather Working Occupations Not Elsewhere Classified

See unit groups 656, 657 and 658 for workers making leather garments.

Excluded are Repetitive assemblers (821·20) engaged in the batch or mass production of leather goods.

Unit Group 660 Foremen (Leather Working Occupations)

Workers in this unit group directly supervise and co-ordinate the activities of workers in leather working occupations, other than the making of leather garments.

660 .10 Foreman (boot and shoe making (bespoke and surgical) occupations)

Directly supervises and co-ordinates the activities of workers in boot and shoe making (bespoke and surgical) occupations

Performs appropriate tasks as described under SUPERVISOR/FOREMAN (UNSPECIFIED) (990 .00).

May (01) build up footwear lasts (669 .08)
(02) supervise workers repairing bespoke or surgical footwear.

Additional factor: number of workers supervised.

660 .20 Foreman (leather cutting occupations)

Directly supervises and co-ordinates the activities of workers in leather cutting occupations

Performs appropriate tasks as described under SUPERVISOR/FOREMAN (UNSPECIFIED) (990 .00).

Additional factor: number of workers supervised.

660.30 Foreman (lasting occupations (footwear))

Directly supervises and co-ordinates the activities of workers lasting footwear

Performs appropriate tasks as described under SUPERVISOR/FOREMAN (UNSPECIFIED) (990.00).

May (01) estimate cost of labour and materials
(02) make footwear lasts (673.35)
(03) supervise workers engaged in finishing and packing footwear.

Additional factor: number of workers supervised.

660.40 Foreman (leather goods makers and repairers (excluding boots and shoes))

Directly supervises and co-ordinates the activities of makers and repairers of leather goods other than boots and shoes

Performs appropriate tasks as described under SUPERVISOR/FOREMAN (UNSPECIFIED) (990.00).

Additional factor: number of workers supervised.

660.50 Foreman (leather sewing and stitching occupations)

Directly supervises and co-ordinates the activities of workers in sewing and stitching leather other than for leather garments

Performs appropriate tasks as described under SUPERVISOR/FOREMAN (UNSPECIFIED) (990.00).

Additional factor: number of workers supervised.

660.60 Foreman (boot and shoe repairers)

Directly supervises and co-ordinates the activities of boot and shoe repairers

Performs appropriate tasks as described under SUPERVISOR/FOREMAN (UNSPECIFIED) (990.00).

Additional factor: number of workers supervised.

660.98 Trainee

Performs, under instruction or guidance, various tasks including training exercises and as appropriate pursues studies in order to acquire the basic skills and knowledge required to perform the tasks of foremen (leather working occupations).

660.99 Other foremen (leather working occupations)

Workers in this group directly supervise and co-ordinate the activities of workers in leather working occupations and are not elsewhere classified, for example:

(01) **Foremen (boot and shoe finishing occupations);**

(02) **Foremen (boot and shoe pattern cutting occupations).**

Additional factor: number of workers supervised.

Unit Group 661 Boot and Shoe Making (Bespoke and Surgical) Occupations

Workers in this unit group make up bespoke and surgical footwear and make cork elevations for surgical footwear.

661.05 Boot and shoe maker (bespoke)

Makes up footwear to individual measurements using prepared upper

Ascertains job requirements from instructions; using prepared last and upper performs tasks as described under HAND LASTER (663.10), STITCHER (HAND) (FOOTWEAR) (665.20), BOTTOM FILLER (669.58), HEELER (BESPOKE FOOTWEAR) (661.30), LEATHER CUTTER (MACHINE) (NOT ELSEWHERE CLASSIFIED (662.70) and FINISHER (661.45); if making welted shoe, cuts welt or shapes precut welt strip using hand knife and positions welt round junction of upper and insole.

May (01) cut outsole using hand knife
(02) soak insoles or outsoles in water and beat with hand tool to improve pliability
(03) make up and assemble parts of surgical footwear.

661 .10 Surgical footwear maker

Makes up surgical footwear according to orthopaedic prescription

Performs a combination of the tasks as described under UPPER MAKER (661 .15), SURGICAL FOOTWEAR BOTTOMER (661 .20), CORK MAKER (SURGICAL FOOTWEAR) (661 .25), HEELER (SURGICAL FOOTWEAR) (661 .35) and HAND LASTER (663 .10) to make up surgical boots or shoes.

May (01) measure feet and take note of abnormalities
(02) make footwear lasts (669 .08)
(03) repair surgical footwear.

661 .15 Upper maker (bespoke, surgical footwear)

Cuts out and assembles parts of uppers for bespoke or surgical footwear

Positions footwear pattern on leather in most economical layout and cuts round outline with knife; cuts linings from soft leather or fabric; pares edges of upper lining pieces using knife or skiving machine; applies adhesive along top edge of upper and lining, turns in edges and hammers fold flat; using template or working freehand, makes decorative punching on upper, if required, with hand punch and hammer; cuts back stay or back strap, stiffening leathers to reinforce toe (toe-cap) and anklet (counter) using knife or press cutter; sews back stay and stiffeners in position and sews upper parts together by hand or machine; trims off surplus leather and hammers seams flat; glues any padding to inside of upper and glues linings to uppers; machine stitches linings to uppers in specified places; marks eyelet holes; punches holes and inserts eyelets using hand tools; cuts out and sews in tongue.

May (01) cut straps for securing leg irons and sew straps to uppers.

661 .20 Surgical footwear bottomer

Joins lasted footwear uppers to outer soles building in metal supports and cork elevations according to orthopaedic prescription

Positions last on bench with upper and insole attached; trims and feathers edge of upper at junction with insole using knife and hammers seam flat; as necessary tacks preformed metal or wood support (shank) in position at waist of insole or cements preformed support pads of foam rubber or cork to insole; cuts shaped piece (filler) from thin sheet cork and cements over insole; cuts and shapes cork elevation according to prescription or cements prepared cork elevation to filler; cuts and affixes a second insole to elevation; pulls flap of upper (cover) over filler, elevation and second (false) insole; hand sews leather strip (welt) to the cover and false insole; cuts outsole to shape and scores stitch channel parallel to edge or uses prepared outsole; tacks or cements outsole in position on filler or false insole; sews outsole to welt by hand or machine and hammers lip of stitch channel to cover stitching.

May (01) bevel or feather edges of leather joints using skiving machine (662 .70)
(02) fill insoles with mastic cork compound
(03) stamp out rough shapes for soles using hand operated press cutter.

661 .25 Cork maker (surgical footwear)

Makes cork elevations for surgical footwear to orthopaedic prescription

Ascertains type and measurements of elevation from written instructions.
If making inside elevation, moulds sock of mellowed (dampened) thin leather or linen scrim to conform to sole of last; when dry cements to bottom of last; as required cements cork blocks together to build up block of required thickness; cuts, scours or otherwise pares surface of block to form recess to fit last sole and cements to sock on last, or cements thin layers of cork to sock on last bottom to build elevation of specified depth; shapes sides and bottom of cork to measurements and smoothes with sandpaper.
If making outside elevation, cuts and shapes cork block as described above but fits to part-built shoe; inserts wooden dowels to reinforce elevation where necessary.

May (01) make paper patterns for elevations of unusual shape
(02) make foot support of sheet metal or cement cork facings to metal supports
(03) sew or cement cloth or thin leather to cork elevation
(04) make cork or leather foot supports.

661 .30 Heeler (bespoke footwear)

Cuts, shapes and builds up heels on or attaches prepared heel to bespoke footwear

Measures heel and cuts layer of stout leather to rough shape; hollows layer with knife to follow curvature of sole of foot to form seat piece; hand sews seat piece to upper and trims to shape; cuts leather strip and bevels one edge; positions bevelled strip (split lift) round perimeter of seat piece to form level heel surface; cuts additional leather pieces (lifts) roughly to shape of seat piece and nails lift through split lift to seat piece; nails further lifts layer by layer until heel is of required height; trims heel to shape with knife; if fitting wooden or block heel, recesses seat piece, cements block in position and secures to insole with screw or nails.

May (01) cement cover of soft leather or fabric to wooden or block heel
(02) nail wooden heel in position using nailing device
(03) fit rubber or steel tips to heel.

661 .35 Heeler (surgical footwear)

Cuts out heel components and builds up heels on surgical footwear to orthopaedic prescription

Draws round seat of lasted footwear on paperboard and cuts out paperboard to make pattern of heel seat; cuts seat piece from selected leather with knife using paperboard pattern; places seat piece on heel seat of lasted footwear and sews or tacks in position; trims seat piece with knife to exact shape; cuts out and tacks in position further layers (lifts) as required to form heel; checks built up heel against prescription and trims to size or shape as necessary.

May (01) fit seat piece and lifts which extend into waist of footwear to support arch of foot
(02) shape, cover and fit cork lifts or heel elevations or fit prepared cork lifts
(03) build up recessed lifts to form hollow heel
(04) build sockets into heel for leg irons
(05) smooth completed heel by sandpapering.

661 .40 Fitter

Fixes together component parts of uppers for bespoke or surgical footwear ready for stitching

Checks that quarters are correct size and shape; folds vamp through centre line to check regularity of shape; performs by hand tasks as described under BEADER (669 .54) and STIFFENER INSERTER (821 .20); cements tape over back seam of quarters and reinforcing fabric or leather to component part where eyelets are to be made; marks edge of quarters to guide positioning of vamp and joins front of quarters with adhesive tape; cements tongue in position and cements quarters to vamp following guide marks.

May (01) cement linings in boots
(02) cement loop or back strap to back of upper.

661 .45 Finisher

Performs various tasks by hand and machine to finish bespoke or surgical footwear

Trims edge of sole as necessary using hand knife or machine; starts finishing machine and presses edges of sole and heel against paring wheel to trim and neaten; smoothes edges of sole and heel against graded abrasive wheels of finishing machine; burnishes edges with hot iron; applies waxed stain to edges with brush, pad or sponge and allows to dry; runs toothed wheel (fudge wheel) round welt or upper edge of sole and round edge of sole surface, or makes fudge decoration by machine to mask stitches and/or stitch channel; applies wax polish to footwear, including surface of sole and heel, and buffs and polishes by holding footwear against appropriate wheels of finishing machine.

May (01) close stitch channel and press with heated iron
(02) cut in-sock from thin leather and fix in boot or shoe with adhesive
(03) thread laces through eyelets.

661 .98 Trainee

Performs, under instruction or guidance, various tasks including training exercises and as appropriate pursues studies in order to acquire the basic skills and knowledge required to perform the tasks of workers in boot and shoe making (bespoke and surgical) occupations.

661 .99 Other boot and shoe making (bespoke and surgical) occupations

Workers in this group make up bespoke and surgical footwear and make cork elevations for surgical footwear and are not elsewhere classified.

Unit Group 662 Leather Cutting Occupations

Workers in this unit group cut out leather component parts for the manufacture of leather goods other than leather garments and perform related tasks such as trimming, piercing and punching.

662.05 Hand cutter (footwear)

Cuts out footwear component parts with hand knife

Selects leather in accordance with work instructions; sharpens knife as necessary; positions pattern pieces or template making optimum use of leather ensuring that stretch is running in correct direction and that colour and grain match; cuts round pattern pieces or templates with knife; refers sample components to foreman for approval or bundles stock components together and attaches work instructions.

May (01) mark parts with size and pattern number
(02) prick parts with awl to indicate position of eyelets, buckles, straps or stitching
(03) cut out component parts by machine.

Other titles include Board cutter, Hand clicker, Hand die cutter (rubber footwear), Sample cutter.

662.10 Hand cutter (leather goods excluding footwear)

Cuts out by hand leather component parts for the manufacture or repair of leather goods other then footwear

Selects leather of specified thickness and colour; determines direction of stretch and run of grain of leather, examines for soft parts and marks flaws; spreads leather on cutting board; selects appropriate templates for articles such as boxing gloves, footballs, golf bags, wallets, handbags, brief cases and saddlery and positions on leather, avoiding flaws; places a weight on each template and cuts round edge of template with knife; pricks through holes in pattern using awl to mark stitching line on leather.

May (01) bundle related items and mark with identification details
(02) cut out component parts by machine.

Other titles include Cutter (saddlery, harness).

662.15 Grading machine operator

Operates machine to shave leather component parts to uniform thickness

Sets machine gauge to specified thickness; starts machine and manually feeds leather component part through rollers to cutter and thickness gauge; watches gauge to check that thickness is within specified tolerance; removes shaved component part; cleans and oils machine.

May (01) operate machine which records number of items treated
(02) set metal stamp in machine to mark thickness on component
(03) change or sharpen cutting blade
(04) check random sample of shaved component parts using hand gauge
(05) sort and stack component parts according to thickness.

662.20 Welt maker

Sets and operates machine to bevel or groove leather strips for use as welts

Sharpens knives of machine as necessary and secures in machine; adjusts controls to regulate angle of bevelling of strip and depth of stitch groove along length of strip, or, if making mock welt, to regulate the dimension of rebate channel to be cut down centre of strip; starts machine and feeds strip to machine; if making mock welt, feeds strip to second knife to slit strip down centre of rebate channel; leads end of strip to powered take-off reel.

May (01) apply adhesive to mock welting by machine.

662.50 Press cutter (footwear)

Sets and operates press to cut out footwear parts

Checks materials and cutting die(s) against work instructions; examines leather and marks flaws to be avoided; as required pulls leather to determine direction of stretch; places material in single or multiple lay on bed of press; sets controls to regulate pressure and depth of cut; positions cutting die(s) to make optimum use of material; brings press head over die(s) or slides bed of machine into position below press head; operates machine control to lower press head and force die(s) through material to cut out required parts; bundles component parts together and attaches work instructions.

May (01) renew fabric covering of machine bed

(02) operate machine which cuts out and press welds rubber or plastic foam to material.

Other titles include Fabric cutter, Machine clicker, Outsole cutter, Pressman (rough stuff).

662.55 Press cutter (leather goods excluding footwear)

Sets and operates press to cut out leather component parts for the manufacture of leather goods other than footwear

Examines leather and marks flaws; positions leather in single or multiple lay on machine bed; sets stops on machine bed and regulates cutting pressure; selects cutting die(s) for articles such as purses, wallets, watch straps, handbags, cases and oil seals and positions die(s) making optimum use of leather; operates controls to position press head over die(s) or to move machine bed into position below press head; starts machine to lower press head and force die(s) through leather to cut out required part(s); removes and stacks component parts.

May (01) measure thickness of leather using hand gauge

(02) trim irregular cuts using hand knife.

Other titles include Clicking press operator.

662.60 Perforating machinist

Operates machine to punch holes in, or stitching guide lines on, leather component parts

If perforating component parts, fits punch or die tool and template or jig on machine as required; positions sheet of fibre or paperboard or reel of impression paper on machine where appropriate to cushion punch action; adjusts machine controls to set spacing of perforations and pressure of punch stroke as required; positions component part on fixed machine bed under punch head or on template or jig on movable machine bed and positions machine bed under punch head; operates machine to punch holes in leather.
If marking stitching guide lines on component part, selects and fits appropriate punch in machine and sets inking device; operates machine to mark lines on leather.

May (01) operate machine which presses eyelets into punched holes

(02) operate lacing device on machine to thread string through eyelet holes on footwear uppers

(03) fit special die or punch to cut flaps or fringes in footwear uppers

(04) clean and oil machine.

Additional factor: type of machine to which accustomed.

Other titles include Die puncher, Eyeletter.

662.65 Trimmer (hydraulic, mechanical leather goods)

Operates special purpose lathe to trim hydraulic and mechanical leather goods such as air or oil seals, leather cups or pump packings

Fits leather cup to shaped block of appropriate size and secures block in chuck or fixes other leather component to lathe; starts machine and advances twin-knifed cutter to meet component and trim inner and outer edges of component, or starts machine and manipulates double-edged knife against component to trim edges to specification.

May (01) remove wax from interior of leather cups using hand knife or chisel

(02) manipulate component against buffing or polishing disc to impart finish

(03) perform other tasks in the manufacture of mechanical and hydraulic leather goods such as splitting leather or moulding leather cups.

662.70 Leather cutter (machine) (not elsewhere classified)

Operates machine to cut leather or leather components to size and/or shape or to trim, split, level or reduce thickness of leather, leather components or articles and is not elsewhere classified

Adjusts guides or stops or sets machine controls to regulate length, width, depth, position and/or angle of cut or thickness of layers to be cut; secures template(s) on machine as required; positions leather or item to be cut on machine bed or on or between templates and operates machine to cut to requirements or starts machine and feeds leather or item to, or manipulates against, cutter(s) or grinding wheel; if cutting leather into strips, attaches ends of cut strips to take-off mandrel; adjusts speed of cutters as required; removes cut leather or item from machine.

May (01) fit cutter(s) or grinding wheel on machine
(02) sharpen cutters
(03) clean and oil machine
(04) guide cutter round template by hand
(05) adjust valves of pneumatic machine to regulate air pressure
(06) operate machine which also tacks welt ends to insole ready for bottoming.

Additional factor: type of machine to which accustomed.

Other titles include Edge trimmer, Flap splitter, Flap trimmer, Flash trimmer, Guillotine cutter, Heel breaster, Heel parer, Inseam trimmer, Insole rounder, Insole seat beveller, Outsole rounder, Pretrimmer, Profile cutter (rubber footwear), Rough rounder, Skiver, Slitting machine operator, Sole channeller, Sole flap splitter, Sole micro-profile machine operator, Sole reducer, Sole rounder, Splicing machine operator, Splitting machine operator, Stripping machine operator, Toe-puff and lining trimmer, Trimmer, Upper trimmer, Welt butter and tacker, Welt cleaner.

See Guillotine operator (paper, paperboard) (642.54)

662.98 Trainee

Performs, under instruction or guidance, various tasks including training exercises and as appropriate pursues studies in order to acquire the basic skills and knowledge required to perform the tasks of workers in leather cutting occupations.

662.99 Other leather cutting occupations

Workers in this group cut out leather component parts for the manufacture of leather goods other than leather garments and perform related tasks and are not elsewhere classified, for example:

(01) **Insole punchers** (punch holes in heel sections of insoles to assist attachment to mould of backforming machine); (02) **Roller press cutters** (pass leather with cutting die in position between pressure rollers); (03) **Shank recess cutters** (operate machines to cut recesses for support shanks in waists of soles or insoles); (04) **Shearers** (cut or trim leather using hand or powered shears).

Unit Group 663 Lasting Occupations (Footwear)

Workers in this unit group position leather and rubber footwear component parts on lasts, shape and join uppers to insoles in readiness for stitching and soling and join uppers to soles in readiness for vulcanising.

663 .10 Hand laster

Prepares and attaches insole to prepared footwear upper on last in readiness for stitching

Places last on insole leather and scribes round last to mark out insole; cuts out insole with hand knife and tacks lightly to last; pulls stitched upper over lasted insole using lasting pincers; aligns toe and heel and shapes upper accurately to last; tacks upper to rim of insole as described under JOINTER (663 .90) leaving heads of tacks protruding to facilitate their removal after final assembly.

May (01) skive edge of insole before tacking to last

(02) cement or sew toe cap (puff) and heel stiffener (counters) to inside of upper before lasting

(03) cut sewing channel on insole after lasting

(04) sew upper to insole

(05) cut and/or sew welt to lasted footwear.

663 .50 Machine laster

Sets and operates machine to attach footwear upper to insole by stapling, tacking or cementing

(01) **Stapling machinist, Tacking machinist**

(*a*) Places last, with insole and upper tacked in position on machine; pulls edge of upper to overlap insole using lasting pincers; checks alignment of upper with last; holds last to stapling or tacking head of machine; operates controls to drive staple or tack through overlap into rim of insole; repositions last and repeats stapling or tacking round rim of insole at intervals.

OR

(*b*) Sets base plate, gripping tools (wiper blades), heel rest and stapling or tacking head of machine according to size and style of footwear; regulates pressure of wiper blades and temperature of heat cabinet, and adjusts controls to determine size of staple or tack; warms upper and insole on last in heat cabinet to promote pliability of leather and assist with removal of creases; pulls edge of upper to overlap insole; positions lasted upper against heel rest on machine; starts wiper blades to fold overlap and hold in position; checks alignment of upper with last and if necessary operates wiper blades to adjust position of upper; operates controls to drive staples or tacks through overlap into rim of insole; removes and examines assembly; replaces faulty staples or tacks.

(02) **Cementing machinist**

Performs tasks as described at (*b*) above but in relation to machine with heated base plate and wiper blades which cements upper to rim of insole.

May (03) check depth of upper after overlap has been made using measuring device

(04) remove tacks inserted by back tacker or insole tacker

(05) replenish supplies of staples, tacks, stapling wire or adhesive on machine

(06) clear stoppages of tacking or stapling machine

(07) operate machine in which precemented component parts are joined

(08) clean and oil machine.

Other titles include Bed laster, Forepart laster, Microlaster, Puller-over, Seat laster, Side laster, Thermolaster, Toe laster, Waist laster.

663 .55 Bench hand (rubber footwear)

Prepares component parts of rubber footwear for assembly and builds up component parts in last

Performs a combination of the following tasks: applies solution by brush to fabric linings and rubber component parts for footwear uppers; cements linings to rubber component parts using hand roller; solutions cut or moulded soles and heels or sole and heel units; cements parts of vamp and counter together to form upper using template as guide; positions insole and assembled upper on last and cements upper to insole; where appropriate forms leg on last and cements leg to upper; cements filler to insole, and beading, toe-cap and other reinforcing pieces to upper or leg; cements presolutioned outsole and heel or sole and heel unit to lasted footwear using hand roller; positions lasted footwear in hand press and operates press to secure bond of outsole and heel to bottom of footwear; cements rubber strip round join of upper with sole; applies stitcher roller by hand to edges of rubber strip and to other seams to simulate stitching.

OR

Assembles component parts cut from processed fabric and shapes on last; clips or cements parts together in readiness for machine stitching or treating with latex solution, and vulcanising.

May (01) operate clamping device to tighten upper on last

(02) hand dip partly made-up footwear in latex solution before attaching sole and heel

(03) operate moulding machine (681 .60)

(04) operate vulcanising machine (591 .92).

Excluded are workers who assemble material for footwear components (821 .20 and 821 .30)

663 .60 Veldtschoen toe former

Sets and operates machine to shape upper of veldtschoen footwear over last and bond upper to insole

Fits toe and press plates to machine according to style of shoe; positions and secures precemented insole on toe plate; adjusts gripping mechanism; positions precemented upper on last; regulates heating of toe and press plates; operates gripping mechanism to adjust position of upper on last and ensure correct shaping; operates control to lower heated press plate, mould upper to last and press edge of upper on insole, bonding upper and insole together; removes assembly from machine.

663 .65 Insole tacker

Operates machine to tack or staple insole to last to provide anchorage for footwear bottom

Checks that lasts and insoles are of size and style specified; loads machine hopper with staples, stapling wire or tacks of specified type; holding last, sole uppermost, positions insole on sole of last; holds insole on last below nozzle of tacking machine; operates control to drive staple or tack through insole into last; drives additional staples or tacks from toe to heel at intervals as required; removes faulty tacks or staples using tack knife.

May (01) trim outline of insole to conform to outline of last sole
(02) adjust machine to regulate length of staple
(03) apply grease or non-stick solution to toe of last to prevent adhesion of upper to last
(04) tack to last insoles cemented to uppers.

Other titles include Tacker-on.

663 .70 Back tacker

Positions footwear upper on last and tacks back seam to insole in readiness for joining upper to bottom

Fixes last with insole attached in holding device; pulls upper over last allowing heel portion of upper to overlap heel of last; clamps toe of upper to toe of last and ensures that heel of upper is correctly positioned on last; folds overlap of upper at heel down on insole; hammers tack through edge of upper and insole into last; releases toe clamp and removes last from holding device.

May (01) insert stiffeners in upper at heel (821 .20) and be known as Back tacker and stiffener
(02) insert tissue or greaseproof paper between last and upper to facilitate removal of last.

Other titles include Tacker-up.

663 .90 Jointer

Attaches prepared footwear upper to prepared insole by tacking or cementing by hand

Positions last with prepared insole and upper on metal stand, insole uppermost; holding last firmly pulls upper over last, using lasting pincers, so that edge of upper overlaps insole; checks that upper is correctly aligned with last and manually smoothes out wrinkles in upper; at specified area hammers tacks through overlap of upper and rim of sole into last or hammers overlap of precemented components to activate cement and effect bond; removes last from stand and examines joint.

May (01) specialise in joining a particular part of upper to insole and be known accordingly, eg Seat jointer, Waist jointer.

663 .92 Examiner

Checks that lasted footwear uppers and insoles conform to specification, examines quality of work and rectifies minor faults

Checks that lasted uppers and insoles conform to work instructions for size, fitting and style; inspects each upper for marks or wrinkles and pounds out wrinkles using hammer; checks that overlap of upper on insole is adequate; checks that joints are strong and inserts tacks or applies adhesive to rectify weak joints; checks heel depth or other specified dimensions using tape measure; takes lasted uppers and insoles in twos and checks pairing; reports major faults to foreman.

663 .98 Trainee

Performs, under instruction or guidance, various tasks including training exercises and as appropriate pursues studies in order to acquire the basic skills and knowledge required to perform the tasks of workers in lasting occupations (footwear).

663 .99 Other lasting occupations (footwear)

Workers in this group position leather and rubber footwear component parts on lasts, shape and join uppers to insoles in readiness for stitching and soling and join uppers to soles in readiness for vulcanising and are not elsewhere classified.

Unit Group 664 Leather Goods Makers and Repairers (Excluding Boots and Shoes)

Workers in this unit group make and repair leather goods, other than footwear and garments.

664.05 Saddler

Makes and repairs saddles from leather and other materials

Selects wood and metal framework (saddle tree) of appropriate fitting and type; cuts and fixes pre-stretched webbing to saddle tree; cuts and prepares leather, sheepskin or pigskin component parts and cuts lining or interlining components from hessian or serge; covers saddle tree with hessian or serge and positions cushioning materials such as wool or foam rubber; joins edges of leather component parts by hand or machine sewing and fits cover on saddle tree, securing in position with cement or tacks and by hand or machine sewing; makes up and fits pockets, girth straps and accessories to saddle by riveting, screwing or sewing; applies dressing and polish to saddle and buffs to impart glossy finish; decorates and cuts lettering into surface of leather, as required, using stamps or punches; undertakes repair work as described under REPAIRER (664.35) but in relation to saddles.

May (01) measure horse for fitting of saddle
(02) make and repair whips
(03) undertake sales tasks
(04) repair leather goods such as handbags and travelling cases
(05) specialise in making paddings for saddle and be known as Pannel maker.

664.10 Harness maker

Makes and repairs horses' harnesses

Ascertains job requirements from written specifications or customer's instructions; cuts harness parts from leather using hand knives and shears; joins component parts by hand or machine sewing; attaches buckles, rings and other metal parts by riveting or sewing; pierces buckle holes in harness with awl or punch; finishes edges using creasing irons and edging tools; cuts decorative design, as required, using punch; applies dressing and polish, and buffs to impart a glossy finish; undertakes repair work as described under REPAIRER (664.35) but in relation to horse harness.

May (01) make or repair other items of horse furniture and clothing
(02) undertake sales tasks.

Other titles include Bridle maker, Girthmaker.

Excluded are Horse collar makers (664.15)

664.15 Horse collar maker

Makes up leather collars for draught horses

Ascertains job requirements from written specifications or uses prepared pattern; cuts component parts using hand knife and shears; skives edges of leather component parts, as necessary, using hand knife; forms tube and joins long edges by hand stitching to make body of collar; fills body with straw and shapes by hand; hand stitches smaller leather tube (forewale); fills forewale with straw and bends by hand to correspond to shape of collar body; makes up hindmost part of collar (afterwale) from leather and collar cloth; hand stitches forewale and afterwale to body of collar; rams additional straw into body of collar using hand tool; strikes collar against shaped block to consolidate straw packing; hand stitches leather cap to apex of collar to cover open ends of body and forewale; hammers finished collar with heavy mallet or hammer to ensure even distribution of packing and remove irregularities in shape; attaches buckles, metal rings and similar fittings by hand stitching; stains edges of leather, applies dressing and polishes finished collar by hand.

664.20 Picker maker, Buffer maker

Makes up hollow leather blocks (pickers) or leather buffers

(01) **Picker maker**

Ascertains job requirements from written instructions; selects leather strip and skives one end of strip using hand tool; applies cement to both faces of strip; positions metal former on leather strip and coils strip round former to make a block; flattens skived end of strip; inserts block in clamp until adhesive has set; positions and secures moulding dies in press and places leather block and former between dies; operates press to mould block to shape and compress leather; removes block from press and extracts former; cleans and oils press.

(02) **Buffer maker**

Assembles leather component parts of buffer and fastens together with leather lacing; compresses assembly as described above; operates hand punching machine to punch holes for buffer springs.

May (03) roughen strip to assist adhesion
(04) weigh strip before assembly to produce picker of specified weight
(05) operate machine to rivet cemented block
(06) repeat press operation after block is riveted.

Other titles include Loom buffer maker, Loom picker maker.

664 .25 Machinery belt maker

Makes up leather belting for machinery by hand and machine

Selects leather and cuts into manageable widths using hand knife; operates cutting machine to straighten edge of leather and cut strips of specified width; squares ends of strips by hand or machine; reduces strips to specified thickness on splitting machine and feathers each end of strip; lays out strips with ends overlapping and checks total length; applies adhesive to roughened ends of each strip and places ends to be joined together under screw press for prescribed time to bond joins.

May (01) stretch leather on machine to prevent belting from stretching during use

(02) round-off edges of strips on splitting machine before assembling

(03) check density of glue or similar adhesive.

Other titles include Leather belting maker.

664 .30 Blocker (hydraulic, mechanical leathers)

Operates press to mould leather blanks into hydraulic and mechanical leathers such as air and oil seals and pump packings

Soaks leather blank in warm water or heats on metal plate until pliable; positions blank on metal mould with former (plug) on top; positions mould with blank and plug on bed of press and lowers press head on to plug forcing leather into mould to form required shape; raises press after specified time and removes shaped leather and plug; trims off surplus leather using hand knife and repeats press operation; removes moulded item from press and places in drying oven for specified time; coats product with wax.

May (01) wax pump packings before pressing

(02) operate machines to split, cut or trim leather (662)

(03) polish product on buffing wheel.

664 .35 Repairer

Repairs or remakes leather goods other than footwear and garments

Unstitches or otherwise dismantles faulty or damaged part of leather article such as handbag or case; cuts out suitably matching replacement part by hand or machine; removes broken fittings; makes up patches or replacement parts and fixes to article by sewing, stapling or riveting or with adhesive, using hand tools or machines; restitches seams and cleans and polishes article.

May (01) estimate cost of repair

(02) remodel leather goods.

664 .50 Strap maker

Makes leather belts, straps or similar articles by hand and machine

Operates stripping machine to cut leather into strips of specified width; operates machine to punch rivet and eyelet holes in strip and press eyelets into position; trims strap ends to shape; brushes wax stain into edges of strap and polishes strap by hand; affixes buckle to end of strap using riveting machine.

May (01) affix paperboard reinforcement to peaks of headgear

(02) decorate straps with metal studs using riveting machine

(03) machine sew backing material to leather strap.

Other titles include Belt maker.

Excluded are Machinery belt makers (664 .25)

664 .60 Blocker (leather products excluding hydraulic, mechanical leathers)

Operates machine press to block or mould and shape leather products other than footwear and hydraulic and mechanical leathers

Selects upper and lower dies according to specification and secures dies in press, or adjusts dies located in press; positions leather blank on lower die and starts machine to press upper die on lower die; operates control where necessary to separate dies after specified interval and removes blocked product.

May (01) adjust stroke of press according to thickness of material

(02) operate press to cut leather blanks (662 .55)

(03) soften leather blanks in water before pressing

(04) operate press in which dies are automatically heated

(05) trim blocked article with hand knife

(06) operate press to emboss design on blocked article

(07) stain edges of product using brush and dye.

Other titles include Blocker (cycle saddle), Rim through and trim operator.

664.70 Beltman

Adjusts, repairs and replaces belting used to drive machinery or convey materials

Checks tension of belting of material such as canvas, leather, rubber or terylene and adjusts pulley positions as necessary; examines belting for splits or other defects; cuts out defective sections using hand knife or removes complete belt; selects length of appropriate belting material and cuts to required size; joins belting by hand or machine sewing, clamping with metal fasteners, or bonding with adhesives; refits belting round pulleys and shafts.

May (01) make up belting from strip material
(02) oil pulleys and transmission shafts
(03) fit replacement pulleys
(04) fit metal reinforcing rods into belting
(05) patrol stretch of conveyor system and clear blockages (949.99).

Additional factor: knowledge of appropriate safety regulations.

Other titles include Belting fitter.

664.98 Trainee

Performs, under instruction or guidance, various tasks including training exercises and as appropriate pursues studies in order to acquire the basic skills and knowledge required to perform the tasks of leather goods makers and repairers (excluding boots and shoes).

664.99 Other leather goods makers and repairers (excluding boots and shoes)

Workers in this group make and repair leather goods other than footwear and garments and are not elsewhere classified, for example:

(01) **Whip makers** (make up riding or training whips).

Unit Group 665 Leather Sewing and Stitching Occupations

Workers in this unit group sew and stitch leather in the making up and decoration of footwear and leather goods other than garments.

665.10 Sewer

Sews component parts of leather goods together by hand and machine

Performs appropriate tasks as described under STITCHER (HAND) (FOOTWEAR) (665.20), STITCHER (HAND) (LEATHER GOODS EXCLUDING FOOTWEAR) (665.30), SEWING MACHINIST (FOOTWEAR) (665.40) and SEWING MACHINIST (LEATHER GOODS EXCLUDING FOOTWEAR) (665.50).

665.20 Stitcher (hand) (footwear)

Stitches footwear component parts together by hand

Positions component parts of footwear in clamp or on bench or holds lasted shoe between knees; teases lengths of hemp to make thread and attaches to natural or nylon bristle or threads needle; waxes bristle and thread by hand; pierces holes in leather using awl; passes thread through holes using plain, locked or tied stitch and pulls thread to obtain required tension.

May (01) cut or skive leather component parts by hand (662).

Other titles include Sole stitcher, Welter, Welt sewer.

665.30 Stitcher (hand) (leather goods excluding footwear)

Stitches component parts together by hand in the manufacture and/or repair of leather goods other than footwear and garments

Secures leather component parts of article in clamps or vice, or grips leather between knees; prepares lengths of hemp and rolls in beeswax to form thread or waxes prepared linen thread; threads needle or fixes bristle to end of thread; pierces holes in leather along seam line using awl or pricking iron; stitches parts together and pulls thread to obtain required tension.

May (01) soften leather in water before stitching.

Other titles include Closer, Turner and closer.

665.40 Sewing machinist (footwear)

Operates standard or special purpose sewing machine to join, decorate or repair footwear component parts

Sets stitch gauge, tension control and sewing guide on machine as appropriate; if sewing heavy leather, sets piercing needle (awl); fits thread of required type and colour on machine; where appropriate, leads binding tape of required type and colour through machine; positions component parts under needle and lowers machine foot or pressure wheel; starts machine and manipulates parts under needle, against guide or along markings as appropriate; stops machine, cuts thread and examines stitching.

May (01) soften leather parts in water before stitching
(02) operate machine incorporating a trimming knife
(03) warm thread in oven to assist pliability or operate control to heat wax bath through which thread passes
(04) operate machine to flatten, smooth or affix adhesive tape over seams
(05) close down stitch channel by hand after sewing
(06) sharpen awl or needle with hand file
(07) clean and oil machine.

Other titles include Bagging machinist, Closing machinist, Fair stitcher, Ornament stitcher, Post machinist, Post trimmer, Sock whipper, Trimming machinist, Veldtschoen stitcher, Welting machine operator, Zigzag machinist.

665.50 Sewing machinist (leather goods excluding footwear)

Operates machine to join, hem or decorate leather component parts in the manufacture of leather goods other than footwear and garments

Performs appropriate tasks as described under SEWING MACHINIST (FOOTWEAR) (665.40) but in respect of leather goods, other than footwear and garments, such as purses, handbags, suitcases and watch straps.

May (01) set awl in machine to pierce hole for needle
(02) soap or wax thread
(03) secure ends of machine stitched seams with one or two hand stitches.

Other titles include Machine closer.

665.98 Trainee

Performs, under instruction or guidance, various tasks including training exercises and as appropriate pursues studies in order to acquire the basic skills and knowledge required to perform the tasks of workers in leather sewing and stitching occupations.

665.99 Other leather sewing and stitching occupations

Workers in this group sew and stitch leather in the making up and decoration of footwear and leather goods other than garments and are not elsewhere classified.

Unit Group 666 Boot and Shoe Repairers

Workers in this unit group repair worn and damaged footwear.

Excluded are Rectifiers (footwear manufacture) (669 .70)

666 .10 Boot and shoe repairer

Repairs worn or damaged footwear

Performs some or all of the following tasks: strips off heel top piece and worn lifts; dismantles entire heel or removes block heel; strips off full or part sole; cuts replacement full or part sole to shape using hand knife or machine or selects precut sole and cuts stitch channel in sole; trims waist of new sole or bevels waist end of part sole; sews sole to footwear bottom by hand or machine and nails half sole along junction with original waist, or fixes half or part sole in position by riveting or with adhesive; rebuilds heel lifts or renews block heel as described under HEELER (BESPOKE FOOTWEAR) (661 .30); removes and replaces worn linings, straps, buckles, eyelets, or other fittings; resews faulty seams and sews patches to uppers by hand or machine; rivets rubber or steel tips or inserts to sole or heel; stains or dyes whole or parts of shoe; trims, smoothes and finishes repairs as described under FINISHER (661 .45).

May (01) press rubber or leather sole to footwear using powered machine if securing with adhesive

(02) undertake minor repairs to surgical footwear or miscellaneous leather goods such as handbags or brief cases

(03) sell footwear accessories such as in-socks, laces and polishes.

666 .98 Trainee

Performs, under instruction or guidance, various tasks including training exercises and as appropriate pursues studies in order to acquire the basic skills and knowledge required to perform the tasks of boot and shoe repairers.

Unit Group 669 Leather Working Occupations Not Elsewhere Classified

Workers in this unit group cut patterns for footwear and leather goods, perform a variety of preparing and finishing tasks in the manufacture of mass produced footwear and miscellaneous tasks in making up leather products and are not elsewhere classified.

669 .02 Pattern cutter (footwear)

Prepares paper or paperboard master patterns of component parts of footwear from designs

Ascertains job requirements from design specifications; moulds plastic sheet round last using vacuum moulding machine or fits paper sections on last, shaping paper by hand to follow precisely the contours of the last; cuts moulded paper or plastic into component parts as required by design; slits shaped parts to enable pattern to be reduced to flat form, positions flattened parts on paper or paperboard and traces round outlines; cuts round outline tracings after making allowances for seams and other joins; pricks or otherwise marks master pattern to show fold lines and position of decorative features.

May (01) mark master pattern parts with identification details

(02) cut footwear component parts from pattern as described under HAND CUTTER (662 .05)

(03) prepare designs from rough sketches or photographs and be known as Pattern cutter-designer.

669 .04 Pattern cutter (leather goods excluding footwear)

Prepares paper or paperboard master patterns of component parts of leather goods, other than footwear and garments, from designs

Ascertains job requirements from designer's sketch and/or other specifications; draws component parts of article such as brief-case, handbag, purse or travel case on paper or paperboard, using drawing and measuring instruments; cuts round outline of pattern and traces each part on millboard or fibreboard, making allowances for seams and folds; cuts out millboard or fibreboard pattern using hand knives; marks pattern to show position of features such as rivets, clasps and fittings.

May (01) prepare making up instructions

(02) make up prototype article in paperboard

(03) cut working pattern from sheet metal using paper pattern as guide.

669.06 Die planner (footwear)

Prepares detailed patterns of footwear component parts from footwear patterns for the production of cutting dies

Ascertains job requirements from paper pattern of footwear and sketch of style; calculates area of throat of footwear upper and determines from this the size of die required; plots punch holes on pattern using compasses and drawing instruments; calculates the position of each hole and marks positions in pencil; checks drawn plan against footwear sketch and adjusts pencil marks to correct inaccuracies; pricks each pencilled spot to make permanent mark.

May (01) adapt an existing die pattern if style requires only minor modifications.

669.08 Last builder-up

Modifies stock lasts by hand and machine to make patterns for surgical or bespoke footwear

Receives footwear specifications showing measurements, style and drawn outline of foot; selects stock last of appropriate size; cements or otherwise secures leather or cork to last to build up features and/or deformities of foot and to shape last to conform to drawn outline; measures last to check that girth, heel pitch, instep, toe height and other features correspond to specifications; fits additional pieces of leather or cork to last or pares down last as necessary.

May (01) shape basic last from wood block (673.35).

669.10 Clog maker

Makes clogs by hand, using prepared upper

Positions beechwood sole of appropriate size on last and secures metal sole and heel plates to wooden sole with nails; selects upper of leather, rubber, treated canvas or similar material and positions in rebate on wooden sole; pricks nail holes through edge of upper and nails upper to back of sole; inserts last and pulls upper over last using pincers; nails toe of upper to sole; pulls upper to shape of last by hand and secures upper to sole by hammering nails round edge; trims off surplus material from upper with knife; nails leather welt or copper strip over joint between sole and upper; removes clog from last; removes any protruding nails with pincers; fits steel toe-caps into safety clogs; fixes clasps to front of uppers if required; nails, screws or glues rubber soles to wooden soles, as required; fixes rubber or asbestos strips or spark-free studs or plates across sole of safety clogs.

May (01) cut leather welt using machine.

669.12 Passer (footwear closing)

Examines made-up footwear uppers and remedies minor defects

Checks number and size of article against work instructions; visually examines each article for defects such as poor matching of colours, bad or soiled leather, poor machine stitching and poor shaping; pushes in stitching using awl and hammers seams flat; trims ends of thread and edges of inner counter with scissors; checks that each component is correctly made up; checks article for finish and appearance; rejects items with major faults; consults quality control engineer or foreman, as necessary, for guidance; records number of articles passed and rejected, with reasons for rejections.

Other titles include Checker, Examiner.

669.14 Examiner (footwear finishing)

Examines made-up footwear and remedies minor defects

Visually examines completed footwear for faults in material or workmanship; checks that sock of correct type and size has been inserted and that brand and size have been accurately stamped; trims ends of thread with scissors; cleans footwear with damp cloth or, if badly soiled, returns it to footwear cleaner; returns faulty footwear to making-up department or footwear rectifier with particulars of repair required; passes other footwear to stock.

Other titles include Crowner.

669.16 Bench hand (leather goods excluding footwear)

Performs a variety of tasks in preparing and joining component parts in the manufacture of leather goods other than footwear and garments

Performs some or all of the following tasks: selects leather component parts of matching colour and skives edges by hand; creases leather parts using flat bone where necessary to form required shape; cuts holes for fittings using clicking knife or hand punch; roughens back of leather with sandpaper or rasp to assist adhesion and applies adhesive; joins solutioned parts, fitting in linings, stiffeners and padding as necessary; forms and/or fits piping; attaches metal fittings, decorative or protective studs or domes to article; trims off surplus material using hand knife; marks stitch line using pricking iron; covers frame by hand or machine; stains edges of material.

May (01) cut material using guillotine machine (662.70)

continued

(02) join component parts or attach fittings using riveting machine

(03) make up metal or wooden frames for articles such as brief-cases or travel cases using hand or machine tools

(04) perform hand stitching tasks (665 .30).

Excluded are Repetitive assemblers (leather goods) (821 .20)

669 .18 Orthopaedic appliance maker (specialised)

Makes and repairs leather parts of artificial limbs, body supports and other orthopaedic appliances

Ascertain job requirements from prescription, plaster cast or other specifications; selects sheet of suitable leather and marks out with guide lines using rules, templates, scribers and pencils; cuts out leather parts using hand knife; assembles prepared leather parts or covers prepared metal or wooden parts with padding and leather and secures by hand or machine sewing or riveting; punches eyelet holes, inserts eyelets and laces and attaches buckles and straps as necessary; repairs or adjusts appliances as required.

May (01) soak leather and mould to required shape.

See Orthopaedic appliance maker (general) (692 .10)

669 .20 Roller coverer (textile machine) (general)

Covers rollers for textile machines with leather cork or synthetic material and/or repairs worn roller surfaces

Cuts cloth or felt under-covering by hand to specified size; covers roller (boss) with adhesive and winds cloth or felt round boss; when adhesive is dry mounts boss on ending machine, starts machine and holds wooden tool against end of boss to smooth down edges of covering; cuts leather or cork top covering to size and skives joining edges by hand or machine; applies adhesive to edges of leather or cork, joins edges to form sleeve, presses joint in hand press (piecing) and operates machine to fit sleeve on roller (pulling on), or covers roller and inside of covering with adhesive, fits cover round roller and clips or pins cover to roller until adhesive is dry; repeats operation on ending machine as described above to press down and seal ends of top covering; operates machine to grind and buff cover to bring roller to specified size and to impart a polished finish; checks diameter of covered roller with micrometer and/or rotates roller against straight-edge to test alignment; if repairing roller, strips off worn material and re-covers as described above, or regrinds and re-buffs worn parts of surface.

May (01) apply varnish to covered roller.

669 .50 Roller coverer (textile machine) (specialised)

Specialises in one or more of the operations in covering rollers for textile machines

Performs one or more of the tasks described under ROLLER COVERER (TEXTILE MACHINE) (GENERAL) (669 .20) and is usually known according to specialisation, for example Ender, Piecer.

Other titles include Grinder, Puller-on, Stripper.

Excluded are Cutters and Trimmers (662)

669 .52 Blocker (footwear)

Operates machine to mould component parts of footwear to required shape in readiness for making up

Selects moulds or adjusts machine according to size and style of component part to be moulded or compressed; secures moulds in machine; if moulding upper, operates controls to clamp upper in position on mould; if moulding soles or insoles, softens leather with water or heats materials other than leather in oven; starts machine to close moulds and press component part to required shape; removes component part after specified time in moulding machine.

May (01) dust component part with French chalk to prevent adhesion to mould

(02) wrap component part in leather sheet to prevent scorching

(03) perform tasks of STIFFENER INSERTER (821 .20)

(04) perform tasks of BACK TACKER (663 .70).

Other titles include Heel compressor, Insole conformer, Sole conformer, Sole moulder, Upper blocker.

669 .54 Beader, Turn-over binder

Folds in top edge of footwear upper or binding stitched to upper

(01) **Beader**

Adjusts controls to regulate width of turn-in; where appropriate, loads machine with reel of tape and fills adhesive reservoir; positions upper on machine against guide with skived top edge beneath creasing foot; where appropriate operates controls to apply adhesive to top edge of upper and feed in reinforcing tape; manipulates edge of upper beneath creasing foot to fold in specified width; hammers fold to effect bond; where appropriate operates machine to pleat or notch turn-in at curves; clips reinforcing tape with scissors.
OR
Turns in skived edge of precemented upper by hand to specified width and hammers to flatten and bond fold.

(02) **Turn-over binder**

Performs tasks as described above to turn in binding stitched to top edge of footwear upper.

May (03) set thermostat of heating device to liquefy adhesive

(04) clean and oil machine.

Other titles include Folder, Knocker-over, Turn binder.

669 .56 Pounder (footwear)

Operates machine to flatten and smooth the margin of footwear upper which overlaps insole

Starts machine and holds bottom of lasted footwear against hammer rollers to beat flat the margin of upper which overlaps insole; manipulates bottom of lasted footwear against abrasive wheel or rotary cutter to smooth upper overlap; manipulates upper against warmed metal plates or steel wheel, or warms upper and hammers by hand to remove wrinkles formed during lasting.

May (01) manipulate footwear against revolving blade to remove tacks holding insole or upper to last

(02) renew hammer rollers on machine

(03) carry out routine maintenance of machine.

669 .58 Bottom filler (footwear)

Fills insole depression of lasted footwear with compound to level surface ready for attachment of outsole

Adjusts controls of machine to set feed pressure and extrusion timing; sets and adjusts toe supporting plate (toe plate); replenishes supply of filling compound (cork paste) in machine as required; switches on thermoplastic heater; positions lasted upper in machine; starts machine to extrude measured quantity of cork paste on to insole; stops machine and removes footwear; spreads cork paste evenly over insole forepart and removes surplus paste using hot spatula; fills heel seat with cold cork paste; cleans and oils machine as required.
OR
Holds shoe beneath nozzle of cementing machine and starts machine to fill insole depression with cement; spreads cement by hand and positions felt filler on cemented area.
OR
Spreads cork paste on insole by hand; places footwear beneath heated pad of press; operates control to lower pad and flatten paste; withdraws footwear and removes surplus filling by hand.
OR
Spreads special compound by hand on area of insole to be filled.

May (01) perform tasks of SHANKER (821 .20).

669 .60 Scourer (footwear)

Operates grinding machine to scour footwear parts to a smooth finish

Starts machine and holds part to be scoured against sanding belt, emery dome or abrasive reel; manipulates footwear part to obtain required finish.
OR
Adjusts machine to scour to required degree; starts machine and places soles on roller feed to sanding belt; watches operation.
Fits new abrasive cloth to grinding machine as required.

May (01) use compressed air jet or hold scoured surface to rotating brush to remove dust or grindings

(02) apply dye to scoured surface with brush.

Other titles include Bottom scourer, Heel scourer, Insole scourer, Naumkeager, Surface scourer.

669 .62 Edge setter

Operates machine to iron wax into edge of sole to seal and impart polished finish

Selects iron according to thickness of sole and distance of stitch channel from edge of sole; secures iron in machine; manually applies heated wax round edge of sole; starts machine and manipulates edge of sole against heated vibrating or oscillating iron, or clamps lasted footwear on machine and operates controls to press heated iron against edge of sole.

May (01) use blend of wax and ink to colour sole edges.

Other titles include Top ironer (footwear finishing).

669 .64 Finisher (mass produced footwear)

Performs finishing tasks by hand and/or machine to prepare mass produced footwear for final examination

Performs one or more of the following tasks: removes protruding nails from insole with hand pliers; grinds protrusions using abrasive wheel; drives staples through insole into heel, using stapling machine, to reinforce the joint of heels cemented to uppers; guides serrated or patterned wheel by hand or manipulates footwear against heated toothed wheel to mark footwear with decorative lines or to mask stitching; applies liquid filler to footwear upper, using brush, sponge or cloth pad, to fill grain of leather, or applies plastic compound by hand to fill small holes in edges of soles and heels; operates machine to form slippers or re-form other footwear to specified shape; applies hot air to uppers by air gun to remove creases; touches up staining with hand brush; polishes soles and uppers by hand.

May (01) spray footwear with polishing or varnishing solutions

(02) perform tasks of FOOTWEAR CLEANER (669 .66)

(03) perform tasks of LAST SLIPPER (669 .99).

Other titles include Bunker, Hot blaster, Insole clearer, Polisher (hand), Stitch separator, Welt wheeler, Wheeler (hand), Wheel bunker.

See Repetitive assembler (leather goods) (821 .20) for workers who affix decorative trimmings to footwear.

669 .66 Footwear cleaner

Cleans made-up footwear by hand to remove blemishes arising during manufacture

Removes excess solution from sole edges or seams of uppers using solvent, scraping knife and dry cloth; cleans linings and removes chalk markings with fine abrasive cloth and/or damp cloth; cleans leather uppers with cloth damped in soapy water, methylated spirit, benzine or special solution; raises pile of suede leather with sponge.

Other titles include Upper cleaner.

669 .68 Repair preparation hand (footwear manufacture)

Prepares faulty footwear for repair by other workers

Ascertains job requirements from written instructions; cuts seams using knife or breaks cementing and removes tacks or nails using pincers; removes defective section of footwear where necessary; collects replacement component parts from stock and associates with defective boot or shoe; sends defective footwear to making-up department or to rectifier for repair.

May (01) apply cement to parts to be re-assembled

(02) perform some of the tasks of RECTIFIER (FOOTWEAR MANUFACTURE) (669 .70).

669 .70 Rectifier (footwear manufacture)

Remedies minor manufacturing faults in mass produced footwear

Performs a combination of the following tasks: removes faulty stitching, breaks cemented joints or extracts nails and tacks; removes defective component parts and repairs damaged welt, where practicable, by hand sewing; affixes replacement parts by cementing, nailing or hand or machine sewing; rubs scuffed or bruised areas of leather with fine abrasive to remove marking and smoothes wax of matching colour over fault, using heated blade of knife.

May (01) spray dressing solution on footwear upper to assist colour matching

(02) cut replacement parts as described under HAND CUTTER (662 .05).

Other titles include Upper and alteration hand.

669.90 Waist marker

Marks off by hand or machine area at waist of insole to be roughened for joining to upper

Sets stop of machine according to size of sole; positions insole on machine table against stop; operates control to ink marking arm and mark insole.
OR
Selects template and places on shoe using heel line as guide; scribes round template by hand to mark limit of area to be roughened.

669.91 Rougher (footwear)

Roughens surface of sole or of bottom edge of lasted upper to assist adhesion

Selects roughing tool and secures on machine spindle; positions pressure roller according to width of sole and area to be roughened and adjusts pressure; starts rotation of roughing tool and roller; places sole on roller and starts machine; manipulates sole until entire surface of sole is roughened.
OR
Starts rotation of abrasive wheel or wire brush; manipulates sole or bottom edge of lasted upper against wheel or brush to roughen required area.

May (01) sharpen wire brush
(02) renew emery cloth on abrasive wheel.

Other titles include Rougher (rubber footwear), Sole rougher, Upper rougher.

669.92 Welt beater

Sets and operates machine to flatten and stretch stitched-in welts

Adjusts space between hammer head and anvil plate according to thickness and type of welt; starts machine and manipulates footwear between hammer head and anvil plate; ensures that entire welt passes under hammer head; examines beaten welt.

May (01) brush water on over-dry welts.

669.93 Leveller (footwear)

Sets and operates roller machine to flatten and level soles of lasted footwear

Ascertains job requirements from written instructions; sets roller pressure, and where appropriate roller angle, and adjusts height of footwear holder; clamps footwear, sole uppermost, on holder; starts machine to press sole against roller or to rotate roller across surface of sole; removes footwear from holder.

May (01) rub sole with shaped wooden bar to reclose stitch channel opened by action of roller
(02) clean and oil machine
(03) perform tasks of CHANNEL SOLUTIONER (821.99)
(04) perform tasks of CHANNEL CLOSER (821.20).

669.94 Polisher (footwear)

Operates machine to polish made-up footwear

Starts powered machine; applies wax to revolving pad, mop or brush (waxing wheel) by hand or by drip feed; holds area of footwear to be polished to waxing wheel and ensures that it is completely and evenly waxed; transfers footwear to revolving mop or brush (buffing wheel) and manipulates waxed area against buffing wheel to impart a high polish; cleans and oils machine.

May (01) clean footwear by manipulation against fibre wheel
(02) apply stain by hand to footwear before polishing
(03) apply polishing paste by hand to waxed surface of leather
(04) change waxing or buffing wheels for different colours of footwear.

Other titles include Bottom polisher, Heel burnisher.

669.98 Trainee

Performs, under instruction or guidance, various tasks including training exercises and as appropriate pursues studies in order to acquire the basic skills and knowledge required to perform the tasks of workers in leather working occupations not elsewhere classified.

669.99 Other leather working occupations not elsewhere classified

Workers in this group perform a variety of preparing and finishing tasks in the manufacture of mass produced footwear and miscellaneous tasks in making up leather goods and are not separately classified, for example:

(01) **Bellows makers (pipe organ)**; (02) **Channel openers** (operate machines to open precut stitch channels in footwear soles); (03) **Edge setters (hand)** (iron wax into edges of soles by hand); (04) **Last slippers** (operate machines to remove footwear from lasts); (05) **Seat beaters** (press heel portion of insoles by machine to shape heel seats); (06) **Seat tackers** (affix heel seats temporarily to insoles by tacking or cementing); (07) **Slipper turners** (turn slippers right side out); (08) **Tape markers** (affix adhesive tape by hand to footwear uppers to guide positioning of decorative rand); (09) **Upper burnishers** (operate machines to feed skived edges of footwear uppers to hot irons to curl, fold in and seal edges).

Minor Group 67 WOODWORKING OCCUPATIONS

Workers in this minor group construct, erect, install and repair wooden structures and fittings, build and repair small wooden craft, make furniture, models, templates and other articles from wood, set and operate woodworking machines, carve wood, make patterns for use in making moulds for metal castings and perform related woodworking tasks.

The occupations are arranged in the following unit groups:

670 Foremen (Woodworking Occupations)

671 Carpenters, and Carpenters and Joiners (Structural Woodworking)

672 Cabinet Makers

673 Wood Fitting and Joinery Occupations (Excluding Structural Woodworking and Cabinet Makers)

674 Wood Sawing and Veneer Cutting Occupations

675 Setters and Setter-Operators (Woodworking Machines)

676 Operators and Minders (Woodworking Machines)

677 Pattern Makers (Moulds)

679 Woodworking Occupations Not Elsewhere Classified

Unit Group 670 Foremen (Woodworking Occupations)

Workers in this unit group directly supervise and co-ordinate the activities of workers in woodworking occupations.

670.10 Foreman (carpenters, and carpenters and joiners)

Directly supervises and co-ordinates the activities of carpenters, and carpenters and joiners (structural woodworking)

Performs appropriate tasks as described under SUPERVISOR/FOREMAN (UNSPECIFIED) (990.00) and in addition: ensures that materials and fittings are delivered to site according to construction programme; plans work in conjunction with other construction trades' foremen.

May (01) mark out wood for woodcutting machinists

(02) reproduce drawings to full scale

(03) estimate time and cost of work.

Additional factor: number of workers supervised.

670.20 Foreman cabinet maker

Directly supervises and co-ordinates the activities of cabinet makers

Performs appropriate tasks as described under SUPERVISOR/FOREMAN (UNSPECIFIED) (990.00).

May (01) set completion times and calculate bonus or piece rates

(02) estimate costs of materials.

Additional factor: number of workers supervised.

670.30 Foreman (wood fitting and joinery occupations (excluding structural woodworking and cabinet makers))

Directly supervises and co-ordinates the activities of workers in wood fitting and joinery occupations (excluding structural woodworking and cabinet makers)

Performs appropriate tasks as described under SUPERVISOR/FOREMAN (UNSPECIFIED) (990.00).

May (01) mark off wood for joiners (bench)
(02) reproduce drawings to full scale.

Additional factor: number of workers supervised.

670.40 Foreman (wood sawing and veneer cutting occupations)

Directly supervises and co-ordinates the activities of workers in wood sawing and veneer cutting occupations

Performs appropriate tasks as described under SUPERVISOR/FOREMAN (UNSPECIFIED) (990.00).

May (01) measure timber consignment
(02) mark timber and advise workers of most economical way of sawing.

Additional factor: number of workers supervised.

670.50 Foreman (woodworking machine workers)

Directly supervises and co-ordinates the activities of setters, setter-operators, operators and minders of woodworking machines

Performs appropriate tasks as described under SUPERVISOR/FOREMAN (UNSPECIFIED) (990.00).

May (01) prepare cutting lists and templates
(02) advise workers of best cutting methods.

Additional factor: number of workers supervised.

670.60 Foreman (pattern makers) (moulds)

Directly supervises and co-ordinates the activities of pattern makers (moulds)

Performs appropriate tasks as described under SUPERVISOR/FOREMAN (UNSPECIFIED) (990.00).

May (01) consult draughtsman on aspects of design and method of constructing pattern
(02) design and make rough model of new patterns
(03) plan work in conjunction with foundry foreman.

Additional factor: number of workers supervised.

670.98 Trainee

Performs, under instruction or guidance, various tasks including training exercises and as appropriate pursues studies in order to acquire the basic skills and knowledge required to perform the tasks of foremen (woodworking occupations)

670.99 Other foremen (woodworking occupations)

Workers in this group directly supervise and co-ordinate the activities of workers in woodworking occupations and are not elsewhere classified.

Unit Group 671 Carpenters, and Carpenters and Joiners (Structural Woodworking)

Workers in this unit group construct, erect, install and repair wooden structures and fittings on site and on board ship, build and repair small wooden craft and prepare launchways.

671.05 Carpenter and joiner

Cuts, shapes and fits wood to form structures and fittings, and installs fittings on site

Ascertains job requirements from drawings and written specifications; selects appropriate hard or soft woods, cuts to size and shapes and cuts joints using hand saws, chisels, planes, powered hand tools or woodcutting machines, or uses wood prepared by woodcutting machinists; assembles prepared wood and fixes by methods such as nailing, screwing, dowelling and gluing to form structures and fittings such as staircases, door and window frames, shop fronts, counter units, doors and panelling; erects and installs structures and fittings on site as described under CARPENTER (CONSTRUCTION) (671.10); checks accuracy of work with square, rule and spirit level; sharpens tools.

May (01) construct and erect shuttering (671.15)
(02) work with plastic laminates
(03) fix sheets of plasterboard
(04) work with perspex
(05) work with metal
(06) specialise in repair work and be known as Jobbing carpenter.

Other titles include Colliery carpenter.

671.10 Carpenter (construction)

Constructs, erects and installs wooden structures for roofing and flooring, and erects and installs prefabricated wooden components on site

Ascertains job requirements from drawings and written instructions; selects and marks out appropriate hard or soft woods; cuts wood to size using saws, planes, chisels and powered hand tools to form joists and roof rafters; positions and fixes with nails and screws rafters, joists, prefabricated staircases and window and door frames, and lays flooring (first fixing); hangs doors, cuts and fixes skirting boards and picture rails, and positions and fixes prefabricated cupboards (second fixing); checks accuracy of work with square, rule and spirit level; sharpens tools.

May (01) specialise on roofing
(02) specialise on first fixing
(03) specialise on second fixing
(04) construct and erect shuttering (671.15)
(05) construct and erect temporary wooden structures to support newly laid brickwork
(06) work with plastic laminates
(07) fix cladding to walls and roofs
(08) fix sheets of plasterboard or insulation panels to walls and ceilings
(09) supervise the erection of wooden fabricated units
(10) fix double glazing units.

Note: in the North of England and in Scotland this occupation may be known as Joiner.

671.15 Carpenter (formwork)

Constructs and erects temporary wooden formwork used in the casting of concrete structures on site

Ascertains job requirements from drawings and other specifications; selects, measures, cuts and drills timber or plywood facing to specifications, or selects stock parts; replaces damaged parts on stock panels; positions or directs crane driver to lift and position formwork parts; checks dimensions and alignment of formwork parts using rule, level and plumb-line and secures with nails, bolts, wire, clamps and wedges; fixes adjustable stays and props to completed formwork to prevent movement during concrete pouring; dismantles formwork when concrete has set.

May (01) apply oil or other releasing agent to face of formwork
(02) lay timber guide rails for road or kerb laying
(03) erect metal panels
(04) erect glass reinforced fibre panels
(05) perform tasks of CARPENTER (CONSTRUCTION) (671.10).

Other titles include Concrete shutterer, Shuttering joiner.

671.20 Ship's carpenter

Examines and repairs ship's woodwork and fittings as member of ship's crew

Checks functioning of watertight doors, hatches, deadlights, ports, ventilators and deck gear, and oils, greases, repairs or replaces defective parts; repairs cabins, compartments, davits, decking, deck spars, winches and other equipment using saws, planes, chisels, etc; builds wooden structure over damaged section of hull and inserts concrete between hull and structure to make a watertight seal and serve as temporary repair; takes soundings of fresh and bilge water in ship's tanks using sounding rod and line; keeps daily record of fresh water consumed and depth of bilge water; drives capstan as required; operates mechanism to lower and raise anchor.

May (01) maintain fire-fighting equipment, sprinklers, fire alarms and fireproof doors
(02) repair pipes and water fittings.

671.25 Stage carpenter

Makes, alters and repairs scenery and other stage properties for theatrical, film and television productions

Ascertains job requirements from drawings and written instructions; selects appropriate hard or soft wood and cuts to shape using saws, chisels and planes; assembles prepared parts and fixes by methods such as nailing, screwing, dowelling and gluing; covers wooden framework with canvas or plywood and fixes by gluing or nailing; fits metal plates or hinges to enable scenery to be easily dismantled; alters or repairs scenery as necessary; sharpens tools.

May (01) make scale models of sets (673.20)
(02) fix scenery in position on set or stage.

Other titles include Studio carpenter.

671.30 Fitter (shop, office, exhibition stand)

Constructs and installs wooden fittings or installs prefabricated wooden fittings to form shop fronts, shop or office interiors or exhibition stands

Ascertains job requirements from drawings and written instructions; selects appropriate hard or soft woods, cuts to size, and shapes and cuts joints using hand saws, chisels, planes, powered hand tools or woodcutting machines, or selects wood prepared by woodcutting machinists; assembles prepared wood and fixes by methods such as nailing, screwing, dowelling and gluing to form fittings such as shop fronts, counter units and stands or selects suitable prefabricated fittings; positions and fixes fittings in shops, offices or exhibition areas with nails, screws and dowels, using saws, hammers, chisels, planes and screwdrivers; checks accuracy of work with square, rule and spirit level; dismantles exhibition fittings; sharpens tools.

May (01) work with plastic laminates
(02) work with perspex
(03) work with metals.

671.35 Ship joiner

Constructs, erects and installs wooden fittings in ships under construction or repair

Ascertains job requirements from drawings and written instructions; selects appropriate hard or soft woods, cuts to size and shapes and cuts joints using hand saws, planes and chisels, or measures and marks wood for woodcutting machinists; assembles prepared wood and fixes by methods such as nailing, screwing, dowelling and gluing for bulkheads, cabins and ship's fittings such as deckhouses, bunks, racks, doors and ship's furniture; fits hinges, locks, handles etc; positions fittings and furniture on board ship and fixes using saws, hammers, chisels and screwdrivers; checks accuracy of work with square, rule and spirit level; sharpens tools.

May (01) work with plastic laminates
(02) work with sheet metal
(03) repair fittings on board ship or in workshop
(04) prepare and install insulation materials such as boarding, glass fibre, etc.

671.40 Boat builder

Constructs small wooden craft such as pleasure boats, barges and pontoons

Ascertains job instructions from drawings and other specifications; cuts timber using prepared wooden patterns or templates, and bends and shapes to form keel using steam press or clamps; builds rib and frame members on to keel, cutting and shaping as required; cuts planks to size using portable saw and nails to framework to form hull; trims deck planking to size, nails or screws to frame and caulks seams; builds in completed fittings such as seats, bunks, tables and cupboards making minor adjustments to ensure good fit; secures mast in position using clamps and wedges; bolts fittings for rigging, boom, and lifelines in position on deck; constructs and fits rudder.

May (01) repair small wooden craft
(02) fit wooden parts to glass reinforced fibre hulls
(03) rivet thin protective covering of copper or aluminium sheet to wooden hull
(04) align propellor shaft, install glands, bearings and engine mounts and affix propeller
(05) work with plastic laminates.

Other titles include Barge builder, Yacht builder.

671.45 Shipwright (wood)

Erects temporary structures to support ship under construction or repair, makes and fits wooden parts of ship and prepares launchways

Directs crane driver to lay keel blocks; aligns blocks with wooden wedges and secures in place; positions hydraulic jacks between keel blocks; builds wooden cradle to support shell of ship using hand woodworking tools; places timber supports between deck levels; cuts, lays and bolts deck planks in position; caulks deck planks by inserting oakum and pitch or rubber compound in the seams; makes and fits wooden hatch covers, cargo battens, wooden framing, guard rails and similar heavy wooden fittings; erects and greases launchway; operates hydraulic jacks, removes temporary structures and prepares ship for launching.

May (01) erect staging (774.30)
(02) perform tasks of LOFTSMAN (MOULD LOFT) (673.15).

Other titles include Outfit shipwright.

671.98 Trainee

Performs, under instruction or guidance, various tasks including training exercises and as appropriate pursues studies in order to acquire the basic skills and knowledge required to perform the tasks of carpenters, and carpenters and joiners (structural woodworking).

671.99 Other carpenters, and carpenters and joiners (structural woodworking)

Workers in this group construct, erect, install and repair wooden structures and fittings on site and on board ship, construct and repair small wooden craft and prepare launchways and are not elsewhere classified.

Unit Group 672 Cabinet Makers

Workers in this unit group make and repair wooden furniture and piano and cabinet cases.

Excluded are Repetitive assemblers (wood products) (821.25)

672.10 Cabinet maker

Makes throughout or repairs wooden furniture other than chairs and/or fits and assembles prepared wooden parts to make furniture

Ascertains job requirements from drawings and other specifications; selects wood and/or prepared parts in accordance with specifications; marks out, cuts and shapes wood using saws, chisels, planes, powered hand tools and woodworking machines; trims and glues joints; fits parts together to form sections of cabinets, tables and drawers; places in hand or pneumatic clamps and applies pressure; reinforces joints with nails, dowels or screws; removes sections from clamps and assembles and fixes to form complete article; fits locks, catches, hinges, drawers and shelves as appropriate; if undertaking repair work, removes damaged part and renews as described above.

May (01) smooth surface of article using scrapers and abrasive paper
(02) make adjustments to or repair minor damage to finished article
(03) stain, dye or polish finished article (815)
(04) make jigs or templates for production runs (673.05)
(05) specialise in making prototypes for production runs
(06) specialise in making reproductions of antique furniture.

Other titles include Coffin maker.

672.20 Chair maker (wood)

Makes throughout or repairs wooden chairs or chair frames and/or fits and assembles prepared wooden parts to make chairs or chair frames

Performs appropriate tasks as described under CABINET MAKER (672.10) but in relation to the manufacture or repair of wooden chairs or chair frames.

May (01) drill holes using hand or machine tools
(02) smooth surface of chair using scrapers, abrasive paper or sanding machine
(03) make adjustments to or repair minor damage to chair
(04) stain, dye or polish finished chair (815)
(05) staple upholstery material to chair seats
(06) rivet safety straps or harness to nursery chairs
(07) make jigs or templates for production runs (673.05)
(08) specialise in making prototypes for production runs
(09) specialise in making reproductions of antique chairs.

672.30 Piano case fitter

Adjusts and fits together prepared parts to make piano cases

Receives standard wooden piano case parts such as ends, cheeks or sides, toes or feet, bottom board, plinth or base, key bottom, top and bottom doors, fall and hollow, and front and back half tops; trims parts using hand planes and chisels, electric drills, electric planes and sanders; fits case parts to strung frame using screws and glue; tacks baize cloth to back of piano; glues and screws mouldings, embellishments and music stands to case; cuts recesses and drills holes for and fits hinges, catches, castors and other metal fittings.

May (01) prepare surface and glue veneer to piano case parts.

Other titles include Fitter up (piano), Fly finisher (piano).

672.98 Trainee

Performs, under instruction or guidance, various tasks including training exercises and as appropriate pursues studies in order to acquire the basic skils and knowledge required to perform the tasks of abinet makers.

672.99 Other cabinet makers

Workers in this group make and repair wooden furniture and piano and cabinet cases and are not elsewhere classified, for example:

(01) **Antique restorers** (restore antique furniture); (02) **Cabinet case makers** (make wooden cases for articles such as clocks, cutlery, jewellery and instruments).

Unit Group 673 Wood Fitting and Joinery Occupations (Excluding Structural Woodworking and Cabinet Makers)

Workers in this unit group cut, shape, fit and assemble wood to make patterns, templates, jigs, models, fittings and other articles and parts of articles, other than furniture, and mark out ships' lines.

Excluded are Pattern makers (moulds) (677)

673.05 Template maker

Makes wooden templates used for marking out wooden articles and metal plates, sheets and tubes

Ascertains job requirements from drawings and other specifications; prepares full-scale drawings using squares, rule, protractors, etc; selects strips of wood or plywood sheets according to type of template required; marks out design and cutting lines on the wood using scriber, pencil and measuring instruments; cuts and shapes wood to required dimensions using hand tools and woodworking machines; assembles parts to form template and fixes with glue, nails or screws; checks dimensions of template with original drawings; marks identifying information and working instructions on templates for guidance of production workers; repairs or rebuilds worn or damaged templates.

May (01) strengthen template with metal brackets or tubes.

Additional factors: knowledge of hard and soft woods; knowledge of engineering and metal working practice.

673.10 Pattern maker (plastics products)

Makes wooden patterns, templates or jigs for use in producing plastics articles such as boats, building units, tanks, vehicle body parts and moulds excluding foundry moulds

Ascertains job requirements from drawings and other specifications; prepares full-scale drawings using squares, rule and protractor; selects wood and marks out using square, scriber and rule; cuts and shapes wood to form pattern parts using hand tools and woodworking machines; fits parts together to form pattern and fixes with glue, screws or dowels; smoothes surface of finished pattern with fine sandpaper to produce high polish; performs tasks as described under TEMPLATE MAKER (673.05) but in relation to template for plastic moulds and articles.

May (01) cover pattern with plastic impregnated fabric or glass fibre to make plastic former or mould.

Additional factor: knowledge of hard and soft woods, metal, plastics materials.

673.15 Loftsman (mould loft)

Draws full scale ship's lines on loft floor and makes wooden templates for use as patterns for structural parts of ship

Ascertains job requirements from drawings and other specifications; draws lines of ship to full scale on loft floor using chalk and measuring instruments; marks sections of hull shape on scrieve boards laid on loft floor or on bench; makes wooden templates as described under TEMPLATE MAKER (673.05); ensures that the construction of ship keeps to planned measurements.

May (01) mark positions of deck fittings on structural work of ship

(02) mark positions for plimsoll and draught lines on ship's bow and stern

(03) prepare data for production of tape used in tape-controlled plate cutting machine.

See Loftsman (scale drawing) (253.40)

673.20 Scale model maker

Constructs precision models of aircraft, buildings, locomotives, motor vehicles, ships, etc to scale for instructional, experimental and other purposes from wood or a combination of wood and other materials

Ascertains job requirements from drawings, sketches, photographs and other specifications; prepares drawings to required scale using squares, rule, protractor, etc; selects materials such as plywood, balsa wood, hardwood, hardboard, metal and plastic; marks out material using scriber, pencil, rule; cuts and shapes material to size using hand tools such as saws, chisels, knives and powered hand tools; fits and fastens parts together using nails, glue and dowels; checks measurements of model as work progresses; makes and fits doors and windows from metal and plastic using hand and powered tools.

May (01) make wooden base or support for model

(02) paint or varnish model (812.70)

(03) make perspex or glass cover for exhibition or display model

(04) install electric lighting in model

(05) visit location and verify background features if making model of building.

Other titles include Architectural model maker.

Excluded are Styling modellers (motor vehicles) (699.18)

673.25 Wood worker (aircraft)

Makes wooden internal fittings for aircraft and models, moulds and jigs for use in aircraft production

Ascertains job requirements from drawings and other instructions; selects wood such as mahogany, spruce, plywood, plastic reinforced hardwood and other materials such as plastic laminate or perspex; marks material to specifications using template, rule, scriber and pencil; cuts and shapes wood or other material using handsaws, planes, spokeshaves, chisels and gouges and powered hand tools; screws, bolts or glues pieces of wood or plastic laminate together to form rough shape; removes surplus material with hand tools and smoothes to final shape using files and sandpaper; checks accuracy of work against template; cuts and assembles plastic laminate parts to form doors, panels and cabinets using hand tools and fits and installs in aircraft.

May (01) cover wood with sheet metal alloy.

Additional factor: knowledge of hard and soft woods.

Other titles include Aircraft joiner.

673.30 Joiner (bench)

Cuts, shapes and fits wooden parts in workshop to form structures and fittings ready for installation on site

Ascertains job requirements from drawings and written instructions; selects appropriate hard or soft woods, cuts to size and shapes and cuts joints using hand saws, chisels, planes, woodcutting machines or powered hand tools, or uses wood prepared by woodcutting machinists; assembles prepared wood and fixes by methods such as nailing, screwing, dowelling and gluing to form structures and fittings such as staircases, door and window frames, shop fronts, counter units, doors and panelling; checks accuracy of work with square, rule and spirit level; sharpens tools.

May (01) repair existing fittings at site or in workshop

(02) work with plastic laminates

(03) work with perspex

(04) work with metals

(05) fit aluminium window frames

(06) glaze windows of units for sectional timber buildings.

Additional factor: knowledge of hard and soft woods.

673 .35 Maker (wooden articles excluding furniture, barrels, crates and packing cases)

Cuts, shapes and fits together wooden parts to make articles such as ladders, picture frames, wheels, textile shuttles and formers

Ascertains job requirements from written instructions or other specifications; measures and/or marks out wood to be machined; sets and operates woodworking machines to shape component parts by sawing, planing, cutting, turning, drilling and sanding; fastens parts together with bolts, screws, nails, pins or similar fasteners and/or by applying adhesive and clamping together; trims parts as necessary with hand tools to ensure good fit; attaches metal fittings such as hinges, guides and brackets with screws or rivets, and fits reinforcing corners, cables or wires; checks accuracy of completed assembly with measure, callipers or gauge; smoothes surface by hand or with portable sanding machine.

May (01) fit rope pulleys to extension ladders

(02) apply coat of varnish, paint or creosote to finished product

(03) make metal fittings.

Other titles include Block maker (caps, hats, wigs), Bobbin maker (textile), Cleft fence maker, Handcart maker, Hurdle maker, Ladder maker, Last model maker, Mast maker, Oar maker, Picture frame maker, Rustic furniture maker, Scull maker, Shuttle maker (textile), Sley maker, Spar maker, Timber fence maker, Trestle maker, Wheelwright, Wooden mould maker.

Excluded are Repetitive assemblers (wood products) (821 .25)

673 .40 Packing case maker, Crate maker

Cuts and assembles wood to make packing cases, crates or similar articles

Ascertains job requirements from written instructions; measures, marks and cuts boards to specified lengths using hand and power saws; places lengths of board on bench or table and fixes to cross pieces to form base or core and sides of container by bolting, nailing, or using clipping or stapling machine; assembles and fixes base or core and sides to form container and trims edges using portable saw; where appropriate makes up and attaches lid; fits metal strips, corner pieces or wire to strengthen container; cuts and fits wedges and packing blocks.

May (01) repair containers

(02) line containers with materials such as waterproof paper, rubber or plastic

(03) build container round large or heavy items such as machinery, secure contents and complete packing

(04) mark identification details on container using branding machine (639 .99) or hand stencils.

Other titles include Box maker, Cable drum maker, Pallet maker.

673 .45 Cooper

Makes throughout, repairs or assembles prepared parts to make wooden barrels or casks

Ascertains job requirements from specifications; selects wood and cuts, shapes, smoothes and tapers boards to form staves using saws, planes and chisels, or uses prepared wooden parts; assembles staves into rough shape inside temporary hoop using hammer and chisel; applies hot water or steam to make wood pliable; cuts, bends and rivets metal or wooden strip to form hoop using hammer and chisel, and fits hoop in permanent position round barrel or cask drawing staves tightly together; removes temporary hoop; fits additional hoops as necessary; draws end of staves together using trussing machine and secures in position with temporary hoops; cuts groove on inside rim of stave ends using sharp metal tool (croze); makes up base and lid (heads) for barrel or cask, or selects prepared heads and fits head into grooves; replaces temporary hoops with permanent hoops as described above; smoothes interior and exterior surfaces of barrel using hand tools such as planes, spokeshaves and adze; if undertaking repair work removes damaged staves and replaces as described above.

May (01) check barrel for leaks and seal by inserting rushes between staves

(02) drill and countersink bung holes.

Additional factor: knowledge of hard and soft woods.

673 .50 Fitter-assembler (sports equipment)

Cuts, shapes and fits together wooden parts to make sports equipment

Ascertains job requirements from drawings or written instructions; selects wood or prepared wooden parts from stock; marks out component parts on wood using template; cuts wood to shape using hand-saws, planes, chisels and woodworking machines and trims as necessary to ensure good fit; glues strips of wood to build up laminated part or glues prepared parts together using former to maintain shape and places in clamps or press to dry and set; drills holes for metal attachments; cuts grooves for rubber or gut inserts; attaches metal fittings such as sole plates or brackets, with screws, bolts or rivets; checks accuracy of assembly with rule, callipers or gauge and checks weight and balance; smoothes surface using scraper or sandpaper; binds handle with thread, fine string or other material.

May (01) attach to handle or frame leather or plastic strip

(02) varnish completed article

(03) insert lead weight in golf club head or tennis racket handle (679 .99)

(04) install gymnasium apparatus on site.

Other titles include Badminton racket maker, Cricket bat maker, Fishing rod maker, Golf club maker, Hockey stick maker, Tennis racket maker.

673 .55 Orthopaedic appliance maker (specialised)

Makes and repairs wooden parts of artificial limbs and other orthopaedic appliances

Ascertains job requirements from prescription, plaster cast or other specifications; selects suitable wood sheet or block and marks out with guide lines, using rules, templates, scribers and pencils; cuts, shapes and smoothes wood using hand tools and wood-working machines; assembles prepared wooden parts and secures by bolting, dowelling or gluing; repairs or adjusts appliances as required.

See Orthopaedic appliance maker (general) (692 .10)

673 .60 Stocker (bespoke guns)

Cuts and shapes wooden stocks and foreparts for bespoke guns using hand tools and assembles wood and metal parts ready for testing

Ascertains job requirements from written instructions; marks position of metal parts on roughly shaped stock blank and forepart; cuts cavities, grooves and inlets in stock blank and forepart as appropriate, using hand tools such as draw knives, chisels, gouges, spokeshaves and rasps; secures metal action parts to stock by screwing and fits barrel(s) and forepart; checks accuracy of work using jig and measuring instruments; scores stock and forepart with chequering tool to produce decorative gripping surface.

May (01) drill cavity in stock and insert weights

(02) perform tasks of FINISHER (BESPOKE GUNS) (733 .40).

673 .98 Trainee

Performs, under instruction or guidance, various tasks including training exercises and as appropriate pursues studies in order to acquire the basic skills and knowledge required to perform the tasks of workers in wood fitting and joinery occupations (excluding structural woodworking and cabinet makers).

673 .99 Other wood fitting and joinery occupations (excluding structural woodworking and cabinet makers)

Workers in this group cut, shape, fit and assemble wood to make patterns, templates, jigs, models, fittings and other articles and parts of articles, other than furniture, and are not elsewhere classified, for example:

(01) **Bellymen (piano)** (cut and assemble wood to form sound board of piano); (02) **Markers-off (piano)** (fit wooden sound board to iron frame of piano); (03) **Neck fitters (stringed instruments)** (attach wooden necks and fingerboards to bodies of stringed musical instruments).

Unit Group 674 Wood Sawing and Veneer Cutting Occupations

Workers in this unit group saw timber into planks and boards and cut veneers from logs and baulks.

See Veneer trimmers (676.60)

674.10 Wood sawyer (primary reduction)

Operates sawing equipment to reduce logs or timber baulks to rough planks or boards

Works to cutting list or other instructions; positions log or baulk on saw carriage, using lifting equipment where necessary, and secures with steel dogs or fits in clamp; adjusts setting and tension of saw to cut to specified thickness; operates controls to start saw and bring timber against cutting blades or to guide timber along rollers to saw blades; retracts carriage or clamp after cutting; turns logs or baulks and repeats cutting operation; off-loads or directs off-loading of cut planks and boards; examines planks and boards for defects and segregates faulty pieces; adjusts blade and tensions as necessary; determines when saw blades need replacing.

May (01) sharpen and re-set teeth of saw blades or fit new blades
(02) carry out routine maintenance of sawing equipment
(03) debark logs by sawing or using hand tools
(04) saw logs to convenient size using chain saw.

Additional factor: knowledge of hard and soft woods.

Other titles include Band mill sawyer, Chain cross-cut sawyer, Circular sawyer, Frame sawyer.

674.20 Wood sawyer (excluding primary reduction)

Operates sawing equipment to cut rough planks or boards to specified sizes and shapes

Works to cutting list and/or other instructions; sets cutting blades, machine tables, guide fences, feed rollers and stops according to specifications; regulates tension and speed of cutting blade; operates controls to start equipment; feeds wood along guides or feed rollers to cutting blade; guides saw through markings on wood or manipulates wood against saw edge, following markings; checks measurements of cut wood and adjusts settings as necessary; cuts away defects in wood using hand tools; removes or directs removal of cut wood from machine.

May (0 1) sharpen and re-set teeth of saw blades or fit new blades
(02) use jigs or templates as cutting aid
(03) carry out routine maintenance of sawing equipment
(04) specialise in operating band saws
(05) specialise in operating circular saws.

Additional factor: knowledge of hard and soft woods.

Other titles include Band mill sawyer, Band sawyer, Circular sawyer, Cross-cut sawyer, Fret sawyer.

674.30 Peeling machine operator, Veneer slicer

Sets and operates machine to peel or slice veneers from logs or baulks

Places log or baulk of wood on machine using hoist and clamps in position; sets cutting blade and pressure bar to cut veneer of specified thickness; operates controls to start machine and rotate log against cutting blade to peel continuous sheet of veneer or starts machine to cut slice of veneer from top or side of baulk; checks thickness of veneer using micrometer, rule and callipers and adjusts cutting blade as necessary; throughout peeling or slicing operation checks log or baulk visually for knots; stops machine to cut out knots or faulty wood with chisel or axe; stops machine when log has been reduced to unworkable size; removes sliced veneer manually from machine.

May (01) replace cutting blades
(02) cut slices vertically from end of block of laminated wood
(03) oil and grease machine
(04) supervise assistant(s) rolling peeled veneer on to mandrel.

Other titles include Slicer operator, Veneer rotary peeler setter-operator.

674.50 Automatic sawmill attendant

Attends automatic sawmill which reduces logs or timber baulks to rough planks or boards

Positions and fixes log or baulk on machine carriage using lifting equipment as necessary; starts machine to cut log or baulk to rough boards or planks of specified length and/or thickness; turns logs for further cutting as necessary; transfers sawn boards or planks to conveyors; cleans and oils equipment.

May (01) debark logs using sawing or peeling equipment.

See Automatic woodworking machine attendant (676.50)

674.98 Trainee

Performs, under instruction or guidance, various tasks including training exercises and as appropriate pursues studies in order to acquire the basic skills and knowledge required to perform the tasks of workers in wood sawing and veneer cutting occupations.

674.99 Other wood sawing and veneer cutting occupations

Workers in this group saw timber into planks and boards and cut veneers from logs and baulks and are not elsewhere classified.

Unit Group 675 Setters and Setter-Operators (Woodworking Machines)

Workers in this unit group set or set and operate woodworking machines to cut, turn and otherwise shape wood to specifications and debark logs.

See Metal working and woodworking machines setter-operator (799.06)
Excluded are Wood sawyers (674)

675.05 Woodcutting machine setter

Sets woodcutting machines to cut or otherwise shape wood to specifications

Ascertains job requirements from drawings and other specifications; selects and fixes jigs, templates and appropriate cutting tools in machines; sets guides and stops as necessary; sets machine controls for rotation and feed speed; operates machine to produce a specimen of finished product; compares specimen with drawing and adjusts machine settings as necessary.

May (01) make and grind tools.

Additional factor: knowledge of hard and soft woods.

675.10 Woodcutting machine setter-operator (general)

Sets and operates two or more types of woodcutting machine to cut wood to specifications

Sets machines as described under WOODCUTTING MACHINE SETTER (675.05); starts machine and operates control to feed wood to cutting tool or manually positions wood on machine table and operates control to move cutting tool against wood or holds cutting tools against wood; checks accuracy of machining using measuring instruments or templates; repositions wood or re-sets machine as necessary.

May (01) grind cutters to required shape
(02) clean and oil machine.

Additional factor: knowledge of hard and soft woods.

675.15 Woodcutting machine setter-operator (specialised)

Sets and operates a particular type of woodcutting machine to cut wood to specifications

Sets machine as described under WOODCUTTING MACHINE SETTER (675.05) but in relation to a particular type of woodcutting machine.

(01) **Boring machine setter-operator**

Positions wood under cutter of boring machine to cut circular holes.

(02) **Dovetailing machine setter-operator**

Positions wood against cutters of dovetailing machine to cut dovetail joints.

(03) **Mortising machine setter-operator**

Positions wood under chain or chisel cutter or oscillating bit of mortising machine to cut mortise joints.

(04) **Multiple cutting machine setter-operator**

Feeds wood to cutters of four, five, six or eight cutter or similar machine to cut, groove, bevel or shape wood to specifications in one operation.
Other titles include Four cutter machinist, Six cutter machinist.

(05) **Planing machine setter-operator**

Feeds wood to cutter of planing machine to smooth wood and square edges.

(06) **Routing machine setter-operator**

Positions wood under cutter of routing machine to cut holes, slots, recesses or shapes.

(07) **Tenoning machine setter-operator**

Positions wood against cutter of tenoning machine to cut tenon joints.

(08) **Thicknessing machine setter-operator**

Feeds wood to cutter of thicknessing machine to cut wood to required thickness.

May (09) grind cutters to required shape
(10) clean and oil machine.

Additional factor: knowledge of hard and soft woods.

Excluded are Spindle woodcutting machine setter-operators (675.20), Wood turning lathe setter-operators (675.25) and Debarking machine setter-operators (675.50)

675.20 Spindle woodcutting machine setter-operator

Manipulates wooden stock against rotating powered cutter to shape wood to specifications

Ascertains job requirements from drawings and other specifications; selects cutter according to job requirements; grinds cutter if necessary to specified shape with aid of template, allowing for correct cutting angle; positions and fixes cutter on vertical spindle in centre of machine bed; positions safety guard and guide fence; sets spindle speed and starts machine; feeds length of wood along guide fence and against rotating cutters, or manipulates wood by hand against cutters to produce a curved surface, using jig if necessary.

May (01) clean and oil machine.

Additional factor: knowledge of hard and soft woods.

Other titles include Spindle hand, Spindle moulding machinist.

675.25 Wood turning lathe setter-operator

Manipulates hand tools against rotating wooden stock to shape wood to specifications

Ascertains job requirements from drawings and other specifications; selects length of wood of square section; marks centre point on each end of wood and positions and secures wood between headstock and tailstock of lathe; fixes tool rest in position; starts lathe and regulates rotation speed; selects hand cutting tool and holds against surface of rotating wood to reduce wood to a rough cylinder shape; marks cutting lines on the wood using pencil and rule or scribing baton; selects tool and cuts wood to shape; verifies dimensions of shaped wood using callipers and rule; removes finished product from lathe.

May (01) grind cutting tools
(02) smooth surface by holding sandpaper against rotating wood.

Additional factor: knowledge of hard and soft woods.

Other titles include Wood turner.

675.50 Debarking machine setter-operator

Sets and operates machine to cut bark from logs

Sets cutting knives to correct angle and tension for spiral cutting action using preset jig; starts machine and moves log from feed platform towards feed trough using hooked shaft or levers as necessary; feeds log through machine which removes bark and discharges stripped log to conveyor; checks visually that entire log is debarked.

May (01) replace dull or defective cutting blades.

675.98 Trainee

Performs, under instruction or guidance, various tasks including training exercises and as appropriate pursues studies in order to acquire the basic skills and knowledge required to perform the tasks of setters and setter-operators (woodworking machines).

675.99 Other setters and setter-operators (woodworking machines)

Workers in this group set or set and operate woodworking machines to cut, turn and otherwise shape wood to specifications and debark logs and are not elsewhere classified.

Unit Group 676 Operators and Minders (Woodworking Machines)

Workers in this unit group operate and attend previously set up woodworking machines which cut, shape and smooth wood and cut veneer sheets to specifications.

Excluded are Automatic sawmill attendants (674.50)

676.10 Woodcutting machine operator (general)

Operates two or more types of previously set up woodcutting machines to cut and shape wood to specifications

Starts machine and checks that machine is working correctly; operates control to feed wood to cutting tool or manually positions wood against cutting tool or cutting tool against wood, using jigs or templates as necessary; removes shaped product from machine. Performs these tasks in relation to the operation of two or more types of woodcutting machine.

May (01) clean and oil machine.

Additional factor: knowledge of hard and soft woods.

676.20 Woodcutting machine operator (specialised)

Operates a particular type of previously set up woodcutting machine to cut and shape wood to specifications

Operates machine as described under WOODCUTTING MACHINE OPERATOR (GENERAL) (676.10) but specialises in operating a particular type of machine.

(01) **Dovetailing machine operator**

Positions wood against cutters of dovetailing machine to cut dovetail joints.

(02) **Drilling machine operator**

Positions wood under drill of drilling machine to cut circular holes of specified depth and diameter.

(03) **Mortising machine operator**

Positions wood under chain or chisel cutter or oscillating bit of mortising machine to cut mortise joints.

(04) **Multiple cutting machine operator**

Feeds wood to cutters of four, five, six or eight cutter or similar machine to cut, groove, bevel or shape wood to specifications in one operation.

Other titles include Groover (pencil).

(05) **Planing machine operator**

Feeds wood to cutter of planing machine to smooth wood and square edges.

Other titles include Panel planer.

(06) **Routing machine operator**

Positions wood under cutter of routing machine to cut holes, slots, recesses or shapes.

Other titles include Clog sole machinist.

(07) **Spindle machine operator**

Feeds wood along guide fence or manipulates wood by hand against cutters to cut mouldings and shapes.

(08) **Tenoning machine operator**

Positions wood against cutters of tenoning machine to cut tenon joints.

(09) **Thicknessing machine operator**

Feeds wood to cutter of thicknessing machine to cut wood to required thickness.

(10) **Turning lathe operator**

Positions wood between headstock and tailstock of lathe and moves cutters to rotating wood to taper or shape wood.

Other titles include Bobbin turning machine operator, Frazer (tobacco pipe), Turner (tobacco pipe).

May (11) sand wooden products (676.30)
(12) polish wooden products (679.94)
(13) varnish wooden products (812.70)
(14) clean and oil machine.

Additional factor: knowledge of hard and soft woods.

676.30 Sanding machine operator

Smoothes flat or shaped surfaces of wood to specifications by manipulation against revolving abrasive surface

Selects and fits appropriate abrasive belt, ribbon, sleeve, drum or disc to machine; starts machine; manipulates wooden article by hand against revolving abrasive equipment and applies pressure as necessary or mounts wooden article on adjustable table and manipulates revolving abrasive belt against surface of wood using flat or moulded pad; checks accuracy of finish visually and by touch and continues process until required finish is obtained; stacks finished product.

May (01) replace abrasive belts, sleeves, etc
(02) clean equipment.

Other titles include Belt sander, Bobbin sander, Drum sander, Horizontal sander, Pneumatic sander, Ribbon sander, Vertical sander.

676.50 Automatic woodworking machine attendant

Attends automatic woodworking machine which cuts or shapes wood or smoothes flat or shaped surfaces of wood to specifications

Positions wood on machine table or in hopper at input end of machine; starts machine which automatically feeds wood to cutters or abrasive equipment; checks that machine is operating correctly and examines finished product.

May (01) clean equipment
(02) replace abrasive belts, drums, sleeves, etc.

Other titles include Automatic lathe attendant, Automatic planer, Automatic sander.

See Automatic sawmill attendant (674.50)

676.60 Veneer trimmer

Operates powered shear to cut veneer sheets to specifications

Ascertains job requirements from cutting instructions; examines sheets for defects; positions sheet(s) under drop knife and operates controls to obtain sheet(s) of specified size without defects; unloads and stacks cut sheets.

Other titles include Veneer clipper operator.

676.98 Trainee

Performs, under instruction or guidance, various tasks including training exercises and as appropriate pursues studies in order to acquire the basic skills and knowledge required to perform the tasks of operators and minders (woodworking machines).

676.99 Other operators and minders (woodworking machines)

Workers in this group operate and attend previously set up woodworking machines which cut, shape and smooth wood and cut veneer sheets to specifications and are not elsewhere classified.

Unit Group 677 Pattern Makers (Moulds)

Workers in this unit group make patterns from wood, metal, plaster and plastics or a combination of these materials for use in making moulds for metal castings.

677.10 Pattern maker (general)

Makes patterns from wood, metal, plaster or plastics as required or any combination of these materials for use in making moulds for metal castings

Performs appropriate tasks as described under PATTERN MAKER (WOOD) (677.20), PATTERN MAKER (METAL) (677.30) and PATTERN MAKER (PLASTICS) (677.40).

May (01) make profiled boards (strickles) for shaping circular moulds without patterns
(02) make templates (673.05)
(03) paint or varnish patterns (812.70)
(04) repair or rebuild worn or damaged patterns
(05) instruct foundry workers on correct assembly of pattern and location of core.

Additional factors: knowledge of characteristics of wood, metals, plastics; knowledge of foundry practice.

677.20 Pattern maker (wood)

Makes patterns or pattern parts from wood for use in making moulds for metal castings

Ascertains job requirements from drawings and other specifications; prepares as necessary full-scale drawings using squares, rule, protractor, etc; selects wood according to type of mould required; marks out wood using measuring devices such as square, scriber and contraction rule; cuts and shapes wood to form pattern parts using woodworking machines and hand tools; fits and fastens parts together to form complete pattern or section of pattern using glue, screws and dowels; checks dimensions of patterns using vernier, micrometer, callipers, contraction rule and protractor; trims to required limits using hand tools and smoothes with sandpaper.

May (01) make profiled boards (strickles) for shaping circular moulds without pattern
(02) make templates (673.05)
(03) make patterns from metal, plastics or plaster
(04) paint or varnish patterns (812.70)
(05) repair or rebuild worn or damaged patterns
(06) instruct foundry workers on correct assembly of pattern and location of core.

Additional factors: knowledge of characteristics of wood, metals, plastics; knowledge of foundry practice.

See Styling modeller (motor vehicles) (699.18)

677.30 Pattern maker (metal)

Machines and fits metal castings and/or metal parts to form patterns for use in making moulds for metal castings

Ascertains job requirements from drawings and/or other specifications; receives metal pattern cast in aluminium, brass or iron or selects metal parts; compares dimensions with original drawing using rule, callipers, vernier, micrometer and protractor; marks out casting or metal parts using scriber and contraction rule; removes rough edges using hand file or portable grinding machine; shapes casting or metal parts to size using metal-working machines; checks dimensions after each machining operation; joins parts of casting or metal parts together using nuts and bolts, or by soldering, to form pattern; smoothes surface of pattern using portable grinder and/or emery cloth.

May (01) make patterns from resin, plastics or plaster.

Additional factors: knowledge of characteristics of wood, metals, plastics; knowledge of foundry practice.

677.40 Pattern maker (plastics)

Makes patterns from epoxy resin or glass reinforced fibre for use in making moulds for metal castings

Ascertains job requirements from drawings and/or other specifications; places master wooden pattern in wooden box and pours plaster of Paris round pattern; allows plaster to set; removes wooden pattern from plaster mould and lines mould with a releasing agent; pours epoxy resin into mould and leaves to dry, or places layers of resin and glass fibre in mould to build up a hard shell; removes resin or glass fibre pattern from mould and compares dimensions with original drawings using contraction rule, callipers, vernier, micrometer, and protractor; removes surplus material from pattern using hand file or portable grinding machine and smoothes surface using sandpaper or emery cloth.

May (01) perform tasks of PATTERN MAKER (WOOD) (677.20)

(02) fill shell of glass fibre with plaster mixture to strengthen pattern

(03) make full scale models of articles such as motor car roofs and wings for use in profile machining of sheet metal forming tools and be known as Model maker.

Additional factors: knowledge of characteristics of wood, metal, plastics; knowledge of foundry practice.

677.98 Trainee

Performs, under instruction or guidance, various tasks including training exercises and as appropriate pursues studies in order to acquire the basic skills and knowledge required to perform the tasks of pattern makers (moulds).

677.99 Other pattern makers (moulds)

Workers in this group make patterns from wood, metal, plaster and plastics or a combination of these materials for use in making moulds for metal castings and are not elsewhere classified, for example:

(01) **Pattern makers (polystyrene)** (cut and shape expanded polystyrene to make patterns for metal castings).

Unit Group 679 Woodworking Occupations Not Elsewhere Classified

Workers in this unit group carve and bend wood, lay hardwood strip and wood block floors, match, join and repair veneers, directly assist woodworking craftsmen and machinists in the performance of their tasks and perform miscellaneous woodworking tasks and are not elsewhere classified.

679.05 Wood carver

Carves designs in wood for furniture, panelling and other decorative purposes using hand tools and woodworking machines

Ascertains job requirements from drawing, model or other specifications; prepares detailed drawing of design, where necessary, and traces it on to wood of suitable size; where design is to be repeated, marks out length of wood using dividers or pointers; fixes cutting tool in routing machine, adjusts depths of cut and removes surplus wood to produce rough outline of design; clamps wood in jig or, for intricate designs, holds wood in hand and carves the required pattern by hand using tools such as gouges, paring knife, chisels and mallet according to the intricacy of the design or lettering; smoothes all edges with chisel or sandpaper.

May (01) use wood cut to rough shape and size by joiner or carpenter
(02) make (673.05) and use template to simplify batch work
(03) copy design from original article
(04) prepare sketch or make plywood model (673.20) for customer's approval
(05) make special purpose chisels
(06) undertake restoration of woodwork in churches and historic buildings.

679.10 Floor layer (hardwood strips)

Lays hardwood strips for constructional or overlay flooring

If laying constructional flooring, measures tongued and grooved hardwood strip against joist, marks and cuts to size with portable electric saw; lines up first strip in corner of floor at right angles to joists, leaving a narrow margin between strip and wall; nails strip to joist through tongue; continues to lay further strips, nailing through tongue of strip and slotting grooves and tongues until floor area is covered, apart from narrow margin round perimeter.
If laying overlay flooring, nails supporting equidistant wooden fillets to floor surface; nails hardwood strip to wooden fillets as described above.
Places cork strip in space left between hardwood flooring and wall; sands completed floor by machine or using powered hand tools; oils and polishes floor by hand or machine.

679.15 Floor layer (wood blocks, parquet)

Lays wood blocks or parquet panels on solid or wooden flooring

Measures area to be covered and marks into working sections using rule, marking knife or pencil; spreads flooring with cold bitumastic adhesive using a trowel, or dips underside of wood block into hot pitch holding block with tongs; places block or panel in position and presses to floor; lays blocks along the length of the longest wall if forming basket pattern, or works from centre of floor if forming herringbone pattern or laying parquet panels; cuts blocks or panels to fit at corners, edges, etc using hand or portable electric saw or chisel; leaves narrow margin between blocks or panels and wall and places cork strip in the space; sands wood blocks or parquet panels by machine or using powered hand tool; oils and polishes floor by hand or machine.

May (01) lay plastic tiles
(02) nail hardboard or plywood sheets to a wooden floor before laying blocks or panels.

679.20 Veneer planner

Matches veneers and marks out ready for cutting

Ascertains job requirements from drawings or other specifications; examines veneer sheets for defects, sorts according to size, colour, grain and porosity and selects sheets most suitable for product; plans layout making optimum use of veneer sheets and ensuring that grains match; measures veneer and marks out cutting lines; numbers cut sheets as guide to veneer edge jointer.

May (01) cut veneer sheet with hand knife or guillotine machine
(02) operate veneer edge jointing machine (679.60).

679.25 Veneer repairer, Plywood repairer

Examines jointed veneer or plywood sheets and repairs defects by hand

Examines surface for defects such as faulty jointing, chips, splits and knots, and determines method of repair; fills small defects or cracks with compound and levels off with knife; affixes adhesive tape to faulty jointing or splits in sheet; cuts out blemishes with hand knife and replaces with a veneer patch taking care to match timber type, colour and grain; inlays replacement patch and secures with adhesive tape, or applies fixative solution and presses into place using heated hand press; cleans surplus solution from surface of sheet and smoothes with sandpaper.

679.50 Bender

Bends wooden component parts to shape by hand and/or machine

If bending thick gauge wood selects lengths of wood of appropriate grade; places wood in steaming machine, tank of boiling water, moist sawdust or moist sand; operates valves of machine or regulates temperature of water to control input of steam; removes wood after specified period and bends to shape around mould, jig or template using hand operated steel straps or levers, or pneumatically operated clamps; secures in required shape with clamps or pegs set in floor or bench and leaves to dry and set.
If bending thin gauge wood bends wood to shape around mould and clamps in position; bends strip of metal by hand or using pneumatic bending machine for use as frame; clamps frame in position round wood; places wood, mould and frame in steaming oven; checks and controls temperature and leaves wood to set for specified period; removes wood from oven; releases clamps and mould and leaves wooden shape to dry.
If bending laminated wood selects length of laminated wood with glue still moist; bends wood around mould and clamps ends together; bends and secures metal strip former round wood; wipes off surplus glue with damp cloth; places wood, mould and former into heat chamber to dry for specified period; removes shaped laminated wood from heat chamber and releases clamps and fixtures.

May (01) make own jigs and templates.

Additional factor: knowledge of hard and soft woods.

679.60 Veneer edge jointer

Operates machine to joint the edges of matched veneer sheets

Positions veneer sheets against guide on machine table following matching instructions prepared by veneer planner and ensures that grains match; adjusts gripping mechanism according to thickness of veneer; fills glue reservoir on moistening tray or loads machine with reel of adhesive tape, where appropriate; starts machine and watches gluing or taping process; stacks jointed sheets.

May (01) examine jointed veneer sheets
(02) repair defects by hand using adhesive tape or filler compound.

Other titles include Jointer operator, Tapeless jointer, Veneer splicer.

679.90 Woodworking craftsman's mate

Directly assists woodworking craftsman in the performance of his tasks

Performs some or all of the following tasks: carries tools, nails, screws and other fittings to work area; conveys logs, planks, boards, sawn or machined wood to work area using trucks, conveyors, hoists or lifting gear as necessary and stacks in position for craftsman's use; conveys finished or partly finished articles to store; places supports in position for shuttering woodwork on building site; shores up boat or ship under construction or repair; assists in building launchways and coats launchways with grease; cleans equipment and work area; performs other tasks as directed by craftsman.

Other titles include Boat builder's labourer, Cabinet maker's labourer, Carpenter's mate, Cooper's labourer, Joiner's labourer, Shipwright's labourer.

679.92 Woodworking machine operator's assistant

Assists woodworking machine operator in the performance of his tasks

Performs some or all of the following tasks: carries logs, planks and baulks of wood from stock yard; assists sawyer or machinist to place wood on saw or machine carriage using lifting equipment as necessary; pushes wood up to saw blade or machine cutters; pulls out wood through machine and removes from machine; stacks logs, planks, boards and sawn or machined wood; loads wood on to truck or conveyor; carries tools to or from store and machine; cleans workshop.

Other titles include Assistant sawyer, Backer-up, Puller-off.

679 .94 Polisher (small wooden articles)

Manipulates small wooden articles against rotating wheels or mops to polish surface

Selects appropriate felt wheel or mop and impregnates with wax or abrasive material; operates controls to rotate polishing head; manipulates wooden article against revolving polishing head to obtain required finish; applies further abrasive or wax material during polishing as required.

May (01) stamp wooden lasts with identification details.

679 .98 Trainee

Performs, under instruction or guidance, various tasks including training exercises and as appropriate pursues studies in order to acquire the basic skills and knowledge required to perform the tasks of workers in woodworking occupations not elsewhere classified.

679 .99 Other woodworking occupations not elsewhere classified

Workers in this group perform miscellaneous woodworking tasks and are not separately classified, for example:

(01) **Last hingers** (cut wooden lasts in two and fit hinges); (02) **Marquetry cutters;** (03) **Pelmet erectors** (install wooden pelmets and made-up curtains at customers' premises); (04) **Repairers (tobacco pipes);** (05) **Weighters** (drill holes and insert weights into wooden golf club heads, racket handles, etc).

Minor Group 68 RUBBER AND PLASTICS WORKING OCCUPATIONS

Workers in this minor group make and repair articles of rubber and plastic materials, including glass fibre reinforced plastics, sheathe cables and wires with rubber and plastic, line and cover industrial plant, equipment and products with rubber and plastic and perform related tasks.

The occupations are arranged in the following unit groups:

680 Foremen (Rubber and Plastics Working Occupations)

681 Rubber and Plastics Working Occupations

Excluded are Bench hands (rubber footwear) (663.55)

Unit Group 680 Foremen (Rubber and Plastics Working Occupations)

Workers in this unit group directly supervise and co-ordinate the activities of workers in rubber and plastics working occupations.

680.10 Foreman (rubber and plastics working occupations)

Directly supervises and co-ordinates the activities of workers in rubber and plastics working occupations

Performs appropriate tasks as described under SUPERVISOR/FOREMAN (UNSPECIFIED) (990.00).

May (01) set up or direct the setting up of machines.

Additional factor: number of workers supervised.

680.20 Foreman (rubber working occupations)

Directly supervises and co-ordinates the activities of workers in rubber working occupations

Performs appropriate tasks as described under SUPERVISOR/FOREMAN (UNSPECIFIED) (990.00).

Additional factor: number of workers supervised.

680.30 Foreman (plastics working occupations)

Directly supervises and co-ordinates the activities of workers in plastics working occupations

Performs appropriate tasks as described under SUPERVISOR/FOREMAN (UNSPECIFIED) (990.00) and in addition sets up or directs the setting up of machines.

Additional factor: number of workers supervised.

680.98 Trainee

Performs, under instruction or guidance, various tasks including training exercises and as appropriate pursues studies in order to acquire the basic skills and knowledge required to perform the tasks of foremen (rubber and plastics working occupations).

Unit Group 681 Rubber and Plastics Working Occupations

Workers in this unit group make and repair articles of rubber and plastic materials, including glass fibre reinforced plastics, sheathe cables and wires with rubber and plastic, line and cover industrial plant, equipment and products with rubber and plastic and perform related tasks.

681.02 Liner (rubber), Coverer (rubber)

Affixes lining or covering of sheet rubber to preformed metal products by hand

Checks that surfaces to be covered have been prepared; cuts rubber sheet to required shape with hand knife; applies solution to surfaces to be covered or wipes surfaces with solvent-soaked cloth.

If lining tanks or covering moulds, paddles, blades or similar products presses covering in position by hand on to solutioned surface and rolls with hand roller to consolidate bonding; trims lining with hand knife; where required repeats process to build up covering of required thickness.

If lining pipes, fits sheet rubber round inflatable former to form tube (sleeve); wipes edges of sleeve with solvent-soaked cloth, joins seams and presses with hand roller to consolidate bond; inserts sleeve and deflated former into pipe and inflates former by airline to press sleeve firmly against inner surface of pipe; deflates and withdraws former when sleeve is securely bonded to pipe.

May (01) if undertaking repair work, cut away faulty lining or covering and replace as described above

(02) prepare paper patterns for lining or covering pieces

(03) perforate covered moulds, after vulcanising, for use in moulding by vacuum process

(04) make trial product using vulcanised mould.

Other titles include Mould coverer, Pipe liner, Plant liner.

681.04 Rubber mould maker

Presses and vulcanises rubber disc round model to form rubber mould(s) for use in centrifugal casting

Selects metal frame (top and bottom plates) and a pair of uncured rubber discs; positions model between rubber discs, matching discs by location studs; encloses assembly between frame plates; compresses frame plates to specified pressure in vulcanising unit; operates control to heat framed assembly to required temperature; removes assembly from vulcanising unit after specified period and removes rubber mould; splits mould and removes model; cuts channels in mould sections with knife to permit filling of mould during casting; trims surplus rubber from mould with knife.

681.06 Tyre builder

Builds up rubberised fabric, rubber strips and component parts round core to form pneumatic tyres

Starts core (former) rotating and winds several layers of rubber-impregnated cord or rubberised fabric round former; cuts fabric with heated knife; applies roller to rotating former to consolidate and expel air from layered fabric; repeats winding and rolling operations according to specifications; fixes circlet of wire-reinforced rubber (beading) to each edge of layered fabric and manually pulls (pleats) edges of fabric over beading; winds further layers of rubberised fabric round former to build up tyre casing to specification; positions strip or preformed hoop of tread rubber fabric on layered fabric; similarly fixes rubber strip to form sidewalls of tyre; consolidates fabrication as described above; operates control to collapse former and removes built-up tyre.

Other titles include Cover builder (rubber tyres).

681.08 Industrial belting builder

Builds up layers of rubber, rubberised fabric or plastic material by hand to form industrial belting

Arranges layers of material from feed rolls along work table, ensuring that upper layers are placed centrally upon wider bottom layer and are in alignment; checks with ruler that each layer is of specified width; presses layers together with hand roller or fuses layers of plastic material using hot iron; repeats positioning and pressing or fusing of upper layers to form belting of specified thickness; fixes edging strips along belting where specified; wipes exposed margins of bottom layer with solvent-soaked cloth or applies solution to margins and folds margins up and around upper layers to enclose upper layers within bottom layer; fastens end of belting to take-off winder and operates winder to coil belting; pulls additional material from feed rolls and repeats making-up operation as necessary to extend belting to specified length.

May (01) feed made-up belting through chalk bath or through calendering rollers before coiling

(02) repair cured belting by cutting away faulty area and replacing with new material

(03) join lengths of material to cured belting, layer by layer, to lengthen belt

(04) fit or repair belting on operational site

(05) performs tasks of BELT PRESSMAN (591.70)

(06) join ends of rubber belting layer by layer to form endless belt and be known as Belt splicer.

681.10 Roller caster (printing rollers)

Operates machine to cast covering of plastic, rubber or other compound round metal cores to form press rollers

Performs a combination of the following tasks: strips worn or damaged covering from used roller using hand knife or sands or scrubs new metal cores (stocks) and paints with adhesive solution; cleans and lubricates or waxes interior surfaces of moulding tubes; fits bushes to stock ends as necessary, positions and secures stocks in moulding tubes and clamps on bottom-plate to close tube; adjusts controls to heat moulding tubes to specified temperature; charges, or directs charging of, moulding tubes with plastic or other compound; where appropriate operates control to cool moulding tubes after specified curing period; removes bottom plate from tube, withdraws roller and removes bushes from stock where appropriate; trims roller ends with knife or grinds roller to specified size on grinding machine; cleans finished roller.

May (01) mix plastic or other covering compound

(02) operates stripping machine to assist in removal of worn or damaged covering

(03) coil string round stock before covering.

681.12 Artificial eye maker (plastic)

Makes plastic artificial eyes to individual prescription or to stock size

If making eyes to individual prescription ascertains job requirements from prescription and eye model(s); prepares plaster mould of eye model and fills with plastic material to form eyeball (sclerotic); heats sclerotic for specified period; marks position of iris on sclerotic using dividers; drills and grinds cavity in sclerotic for iris; simulates veining with cotton fibres and where necessary stains sclerotic to specified shade with oil paint; cements prepared iris in cavity; covers eye with plastic lens material and heats to deposit transparent film on eye; cleans and polishes surface of eye on buffing machine.
If making eyes to stock size fills selected steel mould with plastic material to form half-spheres; fits iris to half-sphere and performs colouring and finishing tasks to standard designs as described above.

May (01) embed miniature magnet or other implants in sclerotic.

681 .14 Orthopaedic appliance maker (specialised) (plastic)

Makes and repairs plastic parts of artificial limbs, body supports and other orthopaedic appliances

Ascertains job requirements from prescription and plaster cast; selects sheet of plastic and marks out with guide lines using rule, templates, scribers and pencils; cuts out plastic parts using hand knife, shears or powered hand saw; prepares plaster model from plaster cast; heats plastic until pliable and moulds over plaster model; when set removes plastic part from model, drills or punches holes as necessary, inserts eyelets and laces and attaches buckles and straps by stitching or riveting; grinds edges of appliance or part to obtain required finish; repairs or adjusts appliances as required.

May (01) cover plastic part with padding and fabric.

See Orthopaedic appliance maker (general) (692 .10)

681 .16 Spectacle frame maker (plastic), Spectacle frame repairer (plastic)

Makes and repairs plastic spectacle frames to prescription

Ascertains job requirements from prescription; selects plastic material and template(s) according to prescription; marks lens frame on plastic using template and scriber, and cuts out using fret-saw or routing machine; similarly marks and cuts out side pieces or selects preformed side pieces; cuts grooves for lenses in frame using milling cutter; heats lens frame and side pieces and shapes on former using hand press; where appropriate fixes nose pads to bridge with adhesive; finishes shaping of lens frame and side pieces by filing or grinding, or by rubbing with abrasive cloth; rivets hinges to lens frame and side pieces; checks measurements against prescription throughout assembly; polishes frame on buffing machine; if undertaking repair work makes up and fits replacement parts as described above.

May (01) repair metal spectacle frames

(02) perform tasks of LENS FIXER (OPHTHALMIC PRESCRIPTION) (699 .08).

Other titles include Jobbing repairer, Spectacle frame maker-repairer.

681 .50 Dipper (rubber)

Immerses formers or partially made articles in liquid rubber to form rubber products or coat products with rubber

Fills bath with liquid rubber (latex) to specified level and skims surface with sieve to remove skin; makes regular visual and measured checks on latex level if using automated equipment; where necessary mounts formers or part-made product on frame; if dipping by machine fits frame on machine and operates control to position frame above latex bath; lowers frame and immerses formers in latex to specified depth; lifts formers or awaits automatic lifting of formers after specified period; allows coated formers or articles to drain; transfers coated formers or articles to drying oven, curing pan or conveyor leading to drying plant; cleans baths and equipment as required.

May (01) dip former in acid bath prior to immersion in latex

(02) repeat dipping process to increase thickness of coating

(03) dip coated former or article in acid bath between immersions in latex

(04) rinse coated formers or articles in water

(05) operate controls to regulate temperature of latex or water bath

(06) vulcanise product in curing pan (591 .92)

(07) strip formed product from former.

Other titles include Dipper (latex), Glove dipper.

681 .52 Rubber moulder

Prepares plaster or composition mould of specified product or design and presses sheet rubber on mould to reproduce product or design

If making plaster mould mixes appropriate ingredients to form paste; spreads paste on metal moulding plate and covers with linen or paper sheet; reverses covered plate over product or design and presses assembly in hand press; repeats press operation to make clear impression in paste; removes assembly from press, removes paper or linen and heats moulding plate until paste has set and dried.
If making composition rubber mould covers product or design with sheet of composition rubber; inserts covered product or design in heated press and operates press to mould sheet round product or design; withdraws assembly from press and removes formed mould.
Covers plaster or composition rubber mould with sheet of uncured rubber and presses in heated press to form and vulcanise product; withdraws assembly from press and removes vulcanised product; trims formed product with hand knife.

681.54 Glass fibre laminator (hand)

Coats moulds or articles with resin and glass fibre to form glass-reinforced-plastic products, linings or coverings

Cleans or otherwise prepares surface to be covered; applies preparatory coat (gel coat) to prepared surface using brush, roller or spray; positions glass fibre mat on solutioned surface and presses with roller, spatula or by hand to expel air and ensure close contact of mat with surface; applies coating of resin solution and works solution into glass mat; adds layers of glass fibre and resin until specified thickness or number of layers is reached; trims surplus glass fibre with hand knife or shears; allows coating to dry and harden naturally or places covered item in drying oven; removes formed product from mould.

May (01) cut glass fibre to shape
(02) incorporate wood or metal reinforcing pieces or fitting between layers of glass fibre
(03) prepare liquid resin mix
(04) apply powdered glass fibre by compressed air gun to areas of difficult accessibility
(05) apply layers of resin and glass fibre to join preformed glass fibre components.

Other titles include Glass fibre moulder, Tank liner.

681.56 Cutting machine operator (rubber, plastics)

Operates machine(s) to cut rubber and/or plastic material or product to shape or size

Mounts material or product on machine or feeds material or product to machine; where necessary feeds material through guides to take-off core; starts machine to cut material or product to requirements; removes product and waste from machine or watches discharge of product and waste.

May (01) set cutter(s) in position on machine
(02) set machine controls to regulate speed of cutter or thickness of cut
(03) regulate flow of coolant to cutter(s)
(04) warm material prior to cutting
(05) mark material or use template to indicate cutting line
(06) sharpen cutter(s).

Additional factor: number and type(s) of cutting machines to which accustomed.

Other titles include Foam cutter, Guillotine machinist, Latex cutter, Press cutting machinist, Ring cutting machine operator, Skiving machinist, Slitting machine operator, Thread cutting machine operator.

Excluded are workers who cut out parts for rubber footwear (662)

681.58 Extruded covering machine operator

Sets and operates extrusion machine to cover cables or wire with rubber or plastics

Positions appropriate die on machine; loads or directs loading of rubber or plastic material into feed hopper; sets temperature controls; threads cable or wire through extrusion die and where appropriate through vulcanising chamber, water bath or cooling jacket to take-off mechanism; starts machine and watches operation; examines covering as cable or wire is wound on take-off drum; checks dimension of covered wire with micrometer and adjusts die setting, take-off speed and tension, and temperature controls as necessary.

May (01) join ends of cable or wire.

See 594.62 for workers extruding rubber or plastics stock materials.

681.60 Press moulding machine operator

Operates power press(es) to mould plastic material or rubber to specified shape

Secures selected mould sections to head and bed of press where appropriate; fills lower section of mould with material(s); closes mould sections and places closed mould on press bed or operates control to position mould; where appropriate operates control to heat press or regulates press temperatures; operates control to compress material to shape for specified period; separates mould sections and removes formed product from mould.

May (01) brush or spray releasing agent on mould surfaces
(02) set controls to regulate pressure, depth of press stroke or duration of pressing
(03) position metal reinforcing pieces in mould
(04) weigh material for charging mould
(05) mix ingredients for glass fibre product
(06) operate press to fuse plastic backing to product
(07) trim moulded product using hand tools.

Additional factor: number of power presses operated.

Other titles include Gramophone record presser.

681.62 Finisher (rubber, plastic, glass fibre products)

Performs trimming, grinding or polishing tasks in the finishing of rubber, plastic or glass fibre products

Performs a combination of the following tasks: trims edges of rubber, plastic or glass fibre product using hand or powered knife or saw; operates sandblasting equipment, manipulates product against abrasive wheel, applies powered grinding tool to product, files product by hand or rubs down product with abrasive paper or cloth to smooth edges and/or surfaces of product; operates linishing machine, manipulates product against buffing wheel or polishing mop, or brushes, scrubs or polishes product by hand to impart specified finish.

May (01) apply resin and/or glass fibre mat to glass fibre products to rectify defects.

Other titles include Sander and polisher (plastic sheet), Trimmer.

681.64 Inspector-rectifier

Examines rubber or plastic products such as hoses or belting and remedies minor defects

Examines rubber or plastic product visually and marks defects such as blistered or uneven surfaces, cuts, punctures or foreign matter embedded in surface; pricks blisters and applies solution to restick rubber; fills small holes with rubber cement; strips off layers of defective material using knife and pliers; cuts patch and fixes in position with solution or applies heat to fuse plastic materials; trims edges with hand knife or seals edges with solution; re-examines rubber products after repair has been vulcanised; coils length of hose or belting.

May (01) use lifting equipment to position product for examination
(02) check measurements of product to ensure conformity with specifications
(03) grind and/or buff repaired surface.

Other titles include Examiner-rectifier.

Excluded are Tyre repairers (681.96)

681.66 Repairer (electric cable sheathing)

Repairs faulty rubber or plastic sheathing on electric cables

Pares sheathing at ends of faulty cable to expose conductor core; threads cable through test machine and connects conductor core to electric current; starts machine to wind cable on to take-up reel and to locate fault; stops machine when testing device indicates faulty area and switches off current; examines sheathing visually for punctures, blistering or other weakness and cuts away faulty area with knife; selects and cuts strip of matching rubber or plastic; wraps strip round conductor core to required thickness, applying bonding paste between layers of plastic strip; vulcanises rubber repair in mould or welds plastic repair; cleans repaired surface; reconnects cable to current supply and tests repair; restarts winding mechanism and tests for further faults.

May (01) join broken conductor cores by welding.

681.68 Contact lens presser (plastics)

Presses plastic discs between dies to impart curvature in the manufacture of contact lenses

Ascertains job requirements from prescription and written instructions; positions plastic disc (billet) in lens cavity of bottom die; closes and secures dies, pressing top die on billet; places assembly in heating unit at specified temperature; after specified time transfers assembly to cooling unit; separates dies and removes curved lens after specified cooling period; checks lens using focimeter, radiuscope and dial gauge.

681.70 Belt winder

Operates machine to wind rubber strip with cord or rubberised fabric round drum or rollers to form endless belts

Performs some or all of the following tasks: mounts drum of appropriate size on machine or adjusts distance between machine rollers according to size of belt required; positions rolls of rubber strip and reinforcing cord or rubberised fabric on machine; operates control to rotate drum or rollers and feeds material on to drum or round set of rollers until specified thickness has been formed, wiping sheet rubber with solvent-soaked cloth; presses material against drum with hand roller or metal block, or operates control to press material as winding proceeds; cuts material with knife when specified thickness has been wound; removes formed product from drum or rollers.

May (01) affix edging strip to formed belt
(02) slice formed belt by hand or machine to produce belts of narrower width or of V-shaped cross section
(03) blow French chalk between belt and drum and remove cured product from drum using compressed air tool
(04) perform tasks of VULCANISER (591.92).

Other titles include Rubber belt maker (drum), Vee belt maker (rubber).

681.72 Hose builder (rubber)

Performs hand and/or machine tasks in the manufacture of hosepipes from rubber and rubberised fabric

Performs a combination of the following tasks: selects mandrel of appropriate diameter and length and mounts on bearings using lifting equipment where necessary; covers mandrel with rubber tube using compressed air tool; or winds rubber strip spirally round mandrel to form hose lining; applies solution to hose lining or wipes with solvent-soaked cloth; starts mandrel rotating and winds strip of rubberised fabric spirally to cover hose lining, or lays fabric strip round lining and joins edges to form sleeve; presses seam of sleeve with hand roller; repeats process with additional strips of rubber and fabric to build up hose to specified thickness; removes built-up hose from mandrel using compressed air tool or operates machine to withdraw mandrel from hose.

May (01) cut rubber or fabric material to size
(02) brush French chalk, lubricant or other solution on mandrel before fitting rubber tube
(03) operate machine to press calender roller on covered mandrel
(04) vulcanise hose (591.92)
(05) embed wire reinforcement between layers of fabric
(06) affix collars and couplings to hose ends with wire binding (821.30)
(07) solder metal strips to wire bindings
(08) performs tasks of ARMOURING MACHINE OPERATOR (699.56).

Other titles include Embedded hose maker, Petrolic hose maker.

681.74 Winder (pneumatic tyre components)

Operates machine to wind rubber strip, rubberised fabric or rubber coated wire round core to form components for pneumatic tyres

Loads coil of rubber coated wire on machine and fixes end to core (former), or secures end of rubber or rubberised fabric strip to former; where appropriate sets mechanism to regulate the number of revolutions of former; starts machine to rotate former and where appropriate guides and presses rubber or rubberised fabric round former by hand or using hand roller; stops machine as necessary when winding operation is complete and cuts wire or fabric; collapses former and withdraws formed component.

May (01) select and fit former of specified size to machine
(02) wrap formed component in rubberised fabric by hand or machine.

Other titles include Bead builder (rubber tyre), Bead maker (rubber tyre), Pocket builder (rubber tyre), Pocket maker (rubber tyre)

681.76 Pneumatic tyre moulder

Operates or attends moulding press(es) to shape and vulcanise pneumatic tyres

Performs some or all of the following tasks: inserts inflatable tube (curing bag) of appropriate size in built-up tyre; positions tyre and curing bag in lower section of mould; closes mould and secures in clamps or operates control to close and secure mould sections; operates controls to inflate curing bag to specified pressure and to admit steam at specified temperature to moulds; shuts off flow of steam after specified curing period or sets timing device to shut off steam; separates mould sections or watches automatic opening of mould; deflates and extracts curing bag from vulcanised tyre and removes tyre from mould.

May (01) fit metal hoop (curing ring) round external circumference of tyre and/or fit metal rim to internal circumference of tyre
(02) brush or spray releasing agent to surfaces of mould and curing ring
(03) use lifting device to fit and remove curing ring or to position and remove tyre
(04) insert metal plate or stencil in mould to impress markings on tyre
(05) operate mechanical device to extract curing bag from shaped tyre.

Additional factor: number of moulding presses attended.

681.78 Tyre restorer

Restores tread and sidewalls of worn or damaged rubber tyres

(01) **Tread renewer**

Positions and secures stripped (buffed) tyre on machine; operates control to inflate pneumatic tyre; cuts to size rubber strip moulded to tread formation, or selects solutioned strip; where appropriate brushes or sprays tyre surface and rubber strip with solution; rotates tyre and fixes tread strip in position on tyre surface ensuring visually or by operation of guiding device that tread is correctly aligned; presses join of strip with hand roller or operates machine to consolidate bonding; deflates tyre and removes from machine.

Other titles include Tread builder, Tyre retreader.

(02) **Wall veneerer**

Cleans tyre casing with solvent-soaked cloth; cuts uncured rubber sheeting into strips of suitable size;

brushes or sprays walls of buffed tyre and strips with solution; positions strip on tyre wall by hand and presses edge of strip with roller to consolidate bonding; repeats tasks on other wall of tyre.

May (03) warm rubber strip to improve pliability and bonding

(04) fix plain rubber strip to solid tyres and cut tread pattern with heated cutting tool

(05) trim re-treaded tyre, after vulcanising, to specified dimensions.

Other titles include Remould builder, Tyre remoulder.

681.80 Rubber goods builder (not elsewhere classified)

Cuts and assembles materials to make rubber goods other than tyres, belting or hosepipes

Ascertains job requirement from drawing or other specification; measures materials such as sheet rubber, foam rubber or rubberised fabric and cuts to size with knife or scissors; brushes solution on component parts or wipes with solvent-soaked cloth; joins prepared parts by hand and presses joint with hand roller or operates jointing machine to build up product; trims formed product with hand knife.

May (01) use template as cutting guide

(02) operate guillotine or press cutting machine (681.56) to cut components of rubber goods

(03) warm material to improve pliability

(04) build up material on former

(05) operate drilling machine to pierce holes in product for attaching fittings

(06) perform tasks of VULCANISER (591.92).

Other titles include Curing bag maker, Surgical bulb maker.

See Bench hand (rubber footwear) (663.55)

681.90 Vacuum moulding machine operator

Operates machine to mould plastic or rubber sheet to specified shape by vacuum action

Fits selected mould in frame; presses rubber sheet manually on mould or stretches plastic sheet in frame above mould; positions heater or operates machine control to warm plastic and make it pliable; inserts rubber covered mould in curing oven; operates control to press mould against plastic or rubber sheet and to withdraw air between mould and sheet; releases vacuum or awaits automatic release of vacuum after specified period; withdraws mould and removes product.

May (01) dust rubber with French chalk or wash in releasing agent to prevent adhesion to mould

(02) trim or cut apertures in moulded product using hand knife.

681.92 Moulding machine attendant

Attends machine(s) in which rubber or plastic material is moulded to specified shape

Performs a combination of the following tasks: secures specified mould(s) in machine as appropriate; loads machine or fills mould with material to be worked; closes mould(s) or mould sections; places filled mould on bed of press machine as appropriate; operates controls to heat mould; starts machine and watches operation or operates controls to lower and raise press head; removes mould from machine where appropriate; removes formed product from mould or watches automatic ejection of product; trims surplus material (flash) from moulded product; cleans and lubricates machine as required.

May (01) brush or spray mould with releasing agent

(02) operate machine to mix material(s) or blend materials with colouring pigment (592.75)

(03) preheat material in oven or on hot plate

(04) position metal inserts in mould cavity

(05) weigh material for charging moulds

(06) adjust controls to regulate heating of material or cooling of moulds

(07) remove flash from mould or assist removal of product from mould using compressed air hose.

Additional factor: number of machines attended.

Other titles include Blow moulding machine attendant, Compression moulding machine attendant, Injection moulding machine attendant, Press moulding machine attendant, Rotational moulding machine attendant.

681.94 Extruded covering machine attendant

Attends plant or machine in which rubber or plastics materials are extruded to cover wire or metal goods

Performs a combination of the following tasks: loads goods to be coated into machine or positions on intake mechanism; loads machine with plastic or rubber material and where appropriate adhesive; secures end of wire or cable to take-off drum or bobbin; operates controls to start and stop plant or machine; watches operation and checks visually the quality of coating; removes coated product from machine.

Other titles include Extrusion assistant.

See 594.92 for attendants of machines extruding rubber or plastics stock materials.

681.96 Tyre repairer

Repairs defective or damaged rubber tyres

Performs a combination of the following tasks: cuts away rubber in defective or damaged area of tyre with knife and brushes out cavity; applies solution to defective area using brush or spatula; cuts sheet rubber into strips and sticks strips over exposed cord of tyre; kneads rubber strips into cavity or fills cavity with plasticised rubber compound to build up rubber to required thickness; fixes nylon or canvas patch to interior of tyre casing with adhesive; makes cast of tread pattern and presses repaired area of tyre against cast in heated mould to impress tread pattern and to vulcanise repair.

681.98 Trainee

Performs, under instruction or guidance, various tasks including training exercises and as appropriate pursues studies in order to acquire the basic skills and knowledge required to perform the tasks of workers in rubber and plastics working occupations.

681.99 Other rubber and plastics working occupations

Workers in this group perform miscellaneous tasks in the forming of rubber or plastic products and are not elsewhere classified, for example:

(01) **Bead flippers (rubber tyre)** (operate machines to attach flanging to tyre beads); (02) **Breaker strip builders (rubber tyre),** Chafer strip builders (rubber tyre) (build up rubber strips to specified thickness by hand and operate machines to coil built up strips round bobbins); (03) **Buffers (remould tyres),** Raspers (remould tyres) (set and operate machines to strip rubber from worn or damaged tyres ready for remoulding); (04) **Coilers (rubber hose)** (feed rubber hosing or hose components to circular trays and rotate trays manually to coil hose or hose components); (05) **Joiners (rubber strip)** (cut, chamfer and join ends of strips of rubber or rubberised fabric by hand to make up strips or hoops of specified size); (06) **Plastic mould makers (hand)** (make plastic moulds by hand); (07) **Rubber cutters (hand)**; (08) **Rubber wrappers (hand)** (wind strips of rubber or rubberised fabric spirally round rubber products by hand to sheathe product); (09) **Rubber wrappers (machine),** Bead wrappers (machine) (operate machines to wrap sheathing of rubber or rubberised fabric around component parts in the making of products); (10) **Thread block waxers** (set rubber thread blocks in wax ready for thread cutting).

Minor Group 69 MAKING AND REPAIRING OCCUPATIONS NOT ELSEWHERE CLASSIFIED

Workers in this minor group make, repair, adjust, string and tune musical instruments, make and repair orthopaedic appliances, dentures, orthodontic appliances and artificial facial features and perform other miscellaneous fabricating, repairing and related tasks and are not elsewhere classified.

The occupations are arranged in the following unit groups:

690 Foremen (Making and Repairing Occupations Not Elsewhere Classified)

691 Musical Instrument Making and Repairing Occupations Not Elsewhere Classified

692 Surgical Appliance Makers

699 Other Making and Repairing Occupations

Unit Group 690 Foremen (Making and Repairing Occupations Not Elsewhere Classified)

Workers in this unit group directly supervise and co-ordinate the activities of workers in making and repairing occupations not elsewhere classified.

690 .10 Foreman (musical instrument making and repairing occupations not elsewhere classified)

Directly supervises and co-ordinates the activities of workers in musical instrument making and repairing occupations and is not elsewhere classified

Performs appropriate tasks as described under SUPERVISOR/FOREMAN (UNSPECIFIED) (990 .00).

May (01) prepare estimates of cost of repairs
(02) give advice on siting of organs
(03) supervise wood or metal workers.

Additional factor: number of workers supervised.

690 .20 Foreman (surgical appliance makers)

Directly supervises and co-ordinates the activities of surgical appliance makers

Performs appropriate tasks as described under SUPERVISOR/FOREMAN (UNSPECIFIED) (990 .00).

Additional factor: number of workers supervised.

690 .98 Trainee

Performs, under instruction or guidance, various tasks including training exercises and as appropriate pursues studies in order to acquire the basic skills and knowledge required to perform the tasks of foremen (making and repairing occupations not elsewhere classified).

690 .99 Other foremen (making and repairing occupations not elsewhere classified)

Workers in this group directly supervise and co-ordinate the activities of workers in making and repairing occupations and are not separately classified.

Unit Group 691 Musical Instrument Making and Repairing Occupations Not Elsewhere Classified

Workers in this unit group make, repair, adjust, string and tune musical instruments, fit, assemble, install and regulate piano action parts and make bows for instruments and are not elsewhere classified.

691 .05 Musical instrument maker (stringed) (bowed)

Makes throughout or repairs violins, cellos or similar bowed string instruments

Ascertains job requirements from drawings or other specifications; selects wood such as pine, plane, sycamore or willow according to requirements; marks off and cuts, drills, planes, carves or otherwise shapes wood to form required parts using hand and machine tools; joins prepared parts with adhesive, using jigs, clamps and vices; fits pegs, bridge and finger-board and attaches strings to instruments; if undertaking repair work removes defective parts and fits replacements.

May (01) stain and polish prepared instrument
(02) make bows (691 .99).

Other titles include Cello maker, Viola maker, Violin maker.

See Neckfitters (stringed instruments) (673 .99)

691 .10 Musical instrument maker (wood-wind)

Fits and assembles prepared parts to make or repair wood-wind instruments

Ascertains job requirements from drawings or other specifications; selects prepared parts such as keys, pillars, springs, pads and body sections according to instrument to be made; assembles and joins prepared parts making any necessary adjustments using hand tools such as files, planes, pliers, hammers and screwdrivers to ensure accurate fit; checks alignment of keys and makes necessary adjustments; if undertaking repair work removes defective parts and fits replacements.

691.15 Musical instrument maker (drums)

Fits and assembles prepared parts to make drums

Ascertains job requirements from drawings or other specifications; selects prepared parts such as metal, plywood or glass fibre shells, hoops, screws and pedals according to type of drum being made; soaks and stretches vellum or selects prestretched plastic material and covers hoops to form drumheads; fits drumheads to drum shell and secures with screws or other fittings; if undertaking repair work removes defective parts and fits replacements.

May (01) specialise in making or repairing a particular type of drum, eg military drum, kettledrum

(02) prepare component parts from metal or plywood using hand and machine tools.

Other titles include Drum maker.

691.20 Organ builder

Constructs or repairs pipe organs

Performs a combination of the following tasks: ascertains job requirements from drawings or other specifications; selects wood and marks out, cuts, drills and otherwise shapes wood to form required parts using hand and machine tools, or selects prepared wood parts; assembles wood parts by screwing, pegging and gluing to form organ sections such as frame, case, sound-boards and keyboard; fits leather to wood frame to join bellows; assembles wood organ sections and other prepared parts such as keys, stops, bellows, metal pipes, motors and switches by screwing or gluing and installs and solders wiring to form complete organ; if installing organ dismantles after testing and re-assembles on operational site; if rebuilding or undertaking repair work removes unwanted or defective parts and fits replacements.

May (01) make metal pipes and ducts

(02) voice (691.25) and tune (691.30) organ.

Other titles include Organ fitter, Organ repairer, Organ serviceman.

691.25 Voicer (organ pipe)

Adjusts set of organ pipes to obtain required tonal quality, volume and pitch

Selects set of unvoiced pipes and inserts pipe(s) in voicing equipment; depresses equipment key to blow air through one unvoiced pipe and voiced master pipe; compares tone of pipes and determines adjustments required; on metal flue pipe adjusts aperture of lips and adjusts position of and cuts notches into the languid using files and knives; on wooden flue pipes cuts, files and smoothes the mouth edges using hand tools; on reed pipes adjusts position of reed and reed spring using hand tools; adjusts volume of sound by increasing or reducing the aperture in the foot of the pipe using closing cups or taper cutting tools; fits metal tuning slide into metal pipe or tuning stopper into wooden pipe and adjusts position to regulate pitch; repeats the operation with each pipe in the set; sets tone and power of a rank of pipes (stop) in proper balance to other stops.

May (01) cut mouths in pipes and trim pipes to appropriate length

(02) tune organ (691.30)

(03) regulate final tone balance of organ on site.

691.30 Organ tuner

Tunes pipe organ to correct pitch using tuning fork and hand tools

Directs assistant to depress middle 'C' key on organ console; strikes 'C' tuning fork and compares pitch; adjusts position of tuning slide or stopper, languid or reed spring in organ pipe to regulate the pitch using hand tools; using the middle 'C' pipe for reference, tunes the other pipes in turn, judging pitch aurally.

691.35 Piano tuner

Tunes piano to correct pitch and temperament using tuning fork and hand tools

Removes covering panels from piano to expose strings; inserts felt wedges to mute the strings adjacent to middle 'C' string; depresses middle 'C' key on the piano keyboard and compares pitch with that of a middle 'C' tuning fork; turns wrest-pin with tuning hammer or crank to adjust the tension of the string until correct pitch is obtained; using the middle 'C' string for reference, tunes the other strings, judging pitch aurally.

May (01) repair or replace damaged action parts

(02) replace broken strings

(03) adjust lay of keys.

691.40 Piano repairer

Repairs and refinishes pianos

Removes covering panels from piano; examines and checks operation of working parts such as action, keyboard and pedals; removes defective action parts such as hammers and dampers, and replaces with new parts; renews felt coverings on action parts and key frame; replaces worn or broken strings; cleans and polishes keys; adjusts level and depth of depression of keys; regulates action movement.

May (01) tune pianos (691.35)

(02) remove dust from pianos using vacuum cleaning equipment.

691.45 Stringer (piano)

Attaches wire strings to piano frame

Selects piano wire and cuts to required size using hand clippers or selects prepared strings; screws wrest-pins into position in frame plank; secures appropriate string to wrest-pin and threads string across bridge against bridge pins and on to hitch pin on frame, or leads string around hitch pin and back over bridge to next wrest-pin; draws string taut and secures end around pin; repeats stringing for all notes according to specification.

May (01) drill holes for wrest-pins in frame plank.

691.50 Action assembler (piano)

Fits and assembles prepared parts to form piano action assemblies

Selects prepared parts such as action beams, dampers, hammers and keys; fits prepared parts together using hand tools and joins with adhesive and by screwing to form a complete action assembly; makes necessary adjustments to parts to ensure correct assembly.

May (01) perform tasks of ACTION REGULATOR (691.99).

691.55 Piano finisher and regulator

Fits prepared action assemblies and pedal movements into piano cases and regulates completed action

Selects prepared action assembly and pedal movement according to type of piano, for example upright, grand; positions and secures action assembly and pedal movement in piano case using hand tools; adjusts alignment and balance of keys and position of hammers and dampers in relation to strings, checking accuracy with measuring instruments; operates pedals and adjusts action assembly and pedal movement as necessary.

691.98 Trainee

Performs, under instruction or guidance, various tasks including training exercises and as appropriate pursues studies in order to acquire the basic skills and knowledge required to perform the tasks of workers in musical instrument making and repairing occupations not elsewhere classified.

691.99 Other musical instrument making and repairing occupations not elsewhere classified

Workers in this group make, repair, adjust, string and tune musical instruments, fit, assemble, install and regulate piano action parts and make bows and are not separately classified, for example:

(01) **Action regulators (piano),** Action part finishers (piano) (adjust and regulate action parts of completed action assemblies for pianos); (02) **Bow makers** (make bows for stringed instruments); (03) **Clavichord makers;** (04) **Harp makers;** (05) **Harpsichord makers;** (06) **Spinet makers;** (07) **Tester-rectifiers** (test mass produced musical instruments and make adjustments as necessary).

Unit Group 692 Surgical Appliance Makers

Workers in this unit group make and repair orthopaedic appliances, dentures, orthodontic appliances and artificial facial features.

See Orthopaedic appliance maker (specialised) (669.18, 673.55, 681.14 and 734.35) for workers who specialise in making leather, wooden, plastic or metal parts of orthopaedic appliances.

Excluded are Surgical corset makers (652.20) and Surgical footwear makers (661.10)

692.10 Orthopaedic appliance maker (general)

Makes and repairs artificial limbs, body supports and other orthopaedic appliances according to individual prescription using a variety of materials

Performs a combination of the tasks as described under ORTHOPAEDIC APPLIANCE MAKER (SPECIALISED) (LEATHER) (669.18), ORTHOPAEDIC APPLIANCE MAKER (SPECIALISED) (WOOD) (673.55), ORTHOPAEDIC APPLIANCE MAKER (SPECIALISED) (PLASTIC) (681.14) and ORTHOPAEDIC APPLIANCE MAKER (SPECIALISED) (METAL) (734.35) to make appliances such as artificial limbs, callipers, support braces and splints.

May (01) specialise in making appliances for particular deformities or disabilities.

Excluded are Surgical corset makers (652.20) and Surgical footwear makers (661.10)

692.20 Dental technician

Makes and repairs dentures according to individual prescription

Ascertains job requirements from prescription or other specifications; prepares plaster moulds using impressions in wax, hydrocolloid or similar substance taken by dental practitioner; casts plastic or metal plate using plaster mould; sets selected artificial teeth into plate during casting or cements or spot welds teeth on to cast plate; checks that teeth are correctly set for biting using an articulator and adjusts and finishes denture using hand tools or machines such as grinders and polishers; carries out repair work such as replacing broken artificial teeth in plate.

May (01) make crowns and inlays for teeth using stainless steel, gold, plastic or porcelain compound

(02) make and repair orthodontic appliances (692.30).

Other titles include Dental mechanic.

692.30 Orthodontic technician

Makes and repairs appliances used to correct irregular formation of teeth

Ascertains job requirements from prescription or other specifications; prepares plaster model using impressions in wax, hydrocolloid or similar substance taken by dental practitioner; using model as pattern makes orthodontic appliances such as springs, clasps or cribs from stainless steel wire and screws using pliers, clippers, soldering irons and grinding, polishing and spot welding machines; carries out repairs to appliances as required.

May (01) secure appliance to plastic plate.

692.40 Maxillo-facial technician

Makes appliances and artificial features used in the restoration of jaws or other facial features following illness or injury

Ascertains job requirements from prescription or other specifications; prepares plaster model using impression in wax, hydrocolloid or similar substance taken by dental consultant or neurosurgeon; using model as pattern makes appliances such as silver cap splints and obturators, or facial features such as artificial ears, cheeks and noses, from hard and soft plastics and various metals using hand and machine tools and casting equipment; carries out adjustments as necessary following fittings.

692.98 Trainee

Performs, under instruction or guidance, various tasks including training exercises and as appropriate pursues studies in order to acquire the basic skills and knowledge required to perform the tasks of surgical appliance makers.

692.99 Other surgical appliance makers

Workers in this group make and repair orthopaedic appliances, dentures, orthodontic appliances and artificial facial features and are not elsewhere classified.

Unit Group 699 Other Making and Repairing Occupations

Workers in this unit group perform miscellaneous fabricating, repairing and related tasks including candle, nightlight, crayon and chalk moulding, blind making, wig making, wicker products making, battery repairing, racket stringing, cartridge, detonator and fireworks filling and cable covering and armouring and are not elsewhere classified.

699 .02 Battery repairer

Services and/or repairs electric storage batteries

Examines battery visually for defects such as cracked case or damaged terminal posts and tests for faults using electrical testing equipment; removes terminal posts and connecting bars and applies heat to battery top to melt sealing compound; withdraws and dismantles faulty cells, replaces defective plates and separators, and rebuilds cells, welding or brazing parts as necessary; replaces battery case where necessary; re-assembles cells in battery case, refixes top and fits new bars and posts; refills battery cells with appropriate electrolyte; attaches leads from charging equipment to battery terminals and starts charger; tests charged battery for correct functioning using electrical test equipment.

May (01) specialise in repairing acid or alkaline electric storage batteries.

Other titles include Accumulator repairer, Accumulator serviceman.

699 .04 Billiard table fitter

Erects, services and repairs billiard tables

Marks out position of table on floor; assembles and fits together prefabricated parts of wooden frame on marked position, using dowel pins, bolts and screws; positions, levels and secures preshaped pieces of slate or other material on frame to form table bed and fills in joints with sealing compound; smoothes surface of bed using abrasive paper and/or hand tool; stretches length of fabric over table bed and secures to battens; irons fabric to remove wrinkles; fixes table fittings such as cushions, cue rest hooks and pockets; determines position of lines and spots on table and marks lines and affixes adhesive spots; checks level of table with spirit level and corrects variations by adjusting levelling devices or by placing packing material under legs; services table by brushing and ironing fabric surface and taking up any slackness in fabric; mends tears in fabric by hand sewing or using adhesive backing material; repairs or replaces table fittings, billiard cue tips and other billiard room furniture as required.

May (01) make prefabricated parts using hand and machine tools

(02) drill fixing holes in preshaped pieces of slate or other table bed material

(03) dismantle billiard table to repair or replace worn or damaged parts

(04) repair damaged slate with filling compound

(05) strip and repolish table woodwork.

Other titles include Billiard table fixer.

699 .06 Candle maker (hand)

Makes wax candles of specified shapes and sizes by hand

Measures and cuts off required lengths of wick and attaches to frame; pours wax over wicks suspended from frame or dips suspended wicks into vat of molten wax; repeats pouring or dipping operation until sufficient wax has been built up around each wick to form candle of required thickness; removes candles from frame and rolls to required shape on flat surface using flat piece of wood; checks circumference of candles at intervals during shaping using measuring aid; shapes top of each candle using special tool; measures length of candles and removes surplus from bottom using cutting tool; places finished candles in rack or on a slab to harden.

May (01) add prescribed quantity of dyestuffs to molten wax to make coloured candles

(02) thread wick to frame and cut wick using hand-operated machine

(03) operate electric hoist to raise and position frame over dipping vat and to assist in dipping wicks.

699 .08 Lens fixer (ophthalmic prescription)

Secures lenses in spectacle frames and adjusts frames according to individual prescription

Ascertains job requirements from prescription; warms plastic or tortoise-shell spectacle frames until pliable and presses prepared lenses into position in frames by hand; secures grooved lenses to mounts of semi-rimless spectacle frames, by positioning, tightening and securing nylon holding cords; bends sides and earpieces of frames to requirements by hand manipulation, applying heat where required; checks hinges and adjusts as necessary; checks alignment of spectacle frames using measuring aids and makes final adjustments; trims off surplus material using hand file.

May (01) drill holes in semi-rimless spectacle frame mounts and fix nylon holding cords to mounts

(02) operate machine to groove edges of lenses before securing to mounts of semi-rimless spectacle frames.

Other titles include Framer.

699 .10 Musical instrument string maker

Operates lathe-type winding machine to wind wire or other material over cores of gut, nylon, or wire to make musical instrument strings

Places looped end of core over fitting at one end of machine; stretches core and secures it to other end of machine; places reel of winding wire, silk or nylon on feed spindle and threads end through loop on core; starts machine and guides covering material on to rotating core by hand; stops machine and severs covering material when required length has been covered; repeats process for further layers of covering as required; removes covered wire from machine.

May (01) cut core into required lengths
(02) test core for uniform thickness using micrometer
(03) polish wire clad strings by rubbing down with fine abrasive paper.

699 .12 Racket stringer

Strings tennis, badminton or squash rackets with man-made fibre or animal gut

Secures racket in bench vice or holding clamp of stringing machine; threads length of fibre or gut string through hole in racket head and through corresponding hole in neck; tensions string by hand or secures in machine grips and operates pedal to tighten string to required tension; secures string in hole with wedge or grip to hold tension; threads string through subsequent holes and repeats tensioning and securing operations till vertical stringing is completed; ties off ends; repeats process for horizontal stringing, weaving string over and under vertical stringing.

Additional factor: whether accustomed to new or repair work.

699 .14 Reed maker (textile accessories)

Makes reeds of specified shapes and sizes for use in textile looms

Ascertains job requirements from specifications; sets controls of reed making machine according to size of reed required, and gauge and spacing of reed wires specified; positions reels of reed wire, and binding material where appropriate, on feed mechanism of machine and threads ends through guides; positions and secures ribs on machine; starts machine; watches operation and makes necessary adjustments to ensure that reed wires are bound to or inserted in ribs at specified distance from each other; removes formed reed from machine and checks it against specification using measuring aids; straightens or replaces faulty reed wires and trims reed ribs; cleans and polishes reed.

May (01) cut wood to required length for use as ribs
(02) fit reinforcing wire to wooden reed ribs
(03) fit end pieces to reeds to strengthen framework
(04) dip wooden ribbed reed into pitch to protect binding.

Other titles include Metal reed maker, Pitch bound reed maker, Plastic baulk reed maker.

699 .16 Roller blind maker, Roller shutter maker

Makes roller blinds and/or shutters

Performs some or all of the following tasks: ascertains job requirements from written or other instructions; measures and marks off wood or metal required for roller and cuts and shapes material to specification using hand and machine tools, or selects prefabricated roller; secures running attachments to or fixes spring in roller; measures and marks out wood or metal for blind or shutter housing box and cuts and shapes material using hand and machine tools; fits together shaped wood or metal parts to make blind or shutter housing box using hand tools and inserts fittings; measures and cuts blind fabric; secures blind fabric round roller by hand stitching, or tacks fabric to roller with nails; cuts required number of wood or metal slats of appropriate length for shutter; makes up shutter by interlocking metal slats or by securing wooden slats to webbing with adhesive and/or nails; attaches handles to bottom of shutter; machine stitches hems of blinds and inserts precut wooden weighting bars in bottom hem; prepares other fittings such as shutter guides for installation on site.

May (01) fix blinds (869 .16)
(02) repair worn or damaged blinds
(03) make venetian blinds (699 .91) and/or canopies.

Other titles include Bench hand.

699 .18 Styling modeller (motor vehicles)

Constructs reduced scale and full-size styling models of motor vehicles, vehicle components and accessories in a variety of materials

Ascertains job requirements from orthographic drawings, sketches and verbal instructions; moulds or cuts parts of models from materials such as clay, plastics, wood or metal using hand and machine tools; assembles completed parts to form model of required component, accessory or complete vehicle; checks accuracy of work using measuring instruments.

May (01) paint finished model.

699 .20 Wicker products maker

Makes baskets and/or furniture by interlacing cane, willow and similar materials by hand

Performs a combination of the following tasks: selects willow or other rods for framework; cuts rods to required length by hand and splices ends where appropriate; secures framework rods in clamp or shaping device; bends rods to required shape applying heat as necessary; joins rods together to form framework using adhesive and/or nails or screws; winds cane or other material round framework joints to strengthen and/or conceal joints; weaves lengths of cane or other material round framework rods by hand to form articles or parts of articles such as furniture, basket bottoms or basket lids; inserts rods into or glues or staples rods on to woven or preformed solid basket bottoms and weaves cane or other material around rods to form sides of baskets; cuts off and conceals or weaves together loose ends to finish edges using hand tools; attaches lids to baskets and fixes runners, handles, straps, legs or other fittings according to requirements.

May (01) soak lengths of cane and willow to facilitate bending
(02) cut and shape wood or other materials to form solid bottoms or handles for baskets using hand and machine tools
(03) impart decorative finish to baskets or furniture by incorporating strips of dyed raffia or plastic
(04) paint finished articles by brush or spray
(05) repair worn or damaged baskets or furniture.

Other titles include Basket furniture maker, Wicker basket maker, Wicker worker.

699 .22 Wig maker (general)

Makes bespoke and/or stock size wigs and hair-pieces throughout

Ascertains colour, style and method of fixing required; measures customer's head and prepares paper pattern from measurements obtained if making bespoke wig or hair-piece, or selects stock pattern; dampens and secures paper pattern over head-shaped work block; makes mount for wig or hair-piece as described under WIG MOUNT MAKER (659 .35); fits bespoke wig or hair-piece mount on customer and adjusts as necessary to ensure correct fit; holds bunch of hair between brushes, withdraws one or more hairs at a time and knots into mount using fine hooked needle, or prepares warp of silk, nylon or other thread, weaves strands of hair through warp to form continuous fringes (wefts) and hand sews wefts to mount; makes parting, if required, by positioning piece of flesh coloured fabric on mount, drawing individual hairs through fabric and knotting hairs using fine hooked needle, or makes parting piece separately and hand sews it on to mount; brushes and trims formed wig or hair-piece to neaten finish; dresses wig or hair-piece as described under WIG DRESSER (471 .50); fits bespoke wig or hair-piece on customer and advises customer on its care.

May (01) prepare and mix hair for knotting or weaving
(02) repair wigs or hair-pieces.

Other titles include Posticheur.

699 .50 Wig maker (specialised)

Specialises in one or more of the operations in wig and hair-piece making

Performs a combination of the tasks as described under WIG MAKER (GENERAL) (699 .22).

May (01) dress wigs (471 .50).

Other titles include Hair roller and weaver, Hair weaver, Knotter, Parting hand.

Excluded are Wig dressers (471 .50), Wig mount makers (659 .35) and Hair preparers (699 .99)

699 .52 Brush maker (hand)

Sets bristles, hair or other filling material into metal ferrules or brush head blanks by hand

Makes up appropriate filling material into bundle or knot of required size; secures bundle or knot with wire, cord, hemp, rubber band or metal clip; secures bundle or knot in metal ferrule or in or over prepared brush head by fixing in hole or cavity with pitch or resin compound, by binding with wire or by looping wire through holes and drawing in lengths of filling material to form tuft.

May (01) prepare fixing compound
(02) drill holes in brush head blanks
(03) comb or trim completed brush head
(04) fix handles to brush heads.

Additional factors: type of filling materials to which accustomed, eg bristle, hair, nylon, plastic, split bamboo cane, wire; type of brushes to which accustomed, eg hairbrushes, household brushes, industrial brushes.

Other titles include Broom maker, Brush filler, Drawer, Paint brush maker, Pan hand, Shaving brush maker.

699 .54 Brush maker (machine)

Sets bristles, hair or other filling material into brush head blanks by machine

Loads appropriate filling material into feed hopper of machine; fixes brush head blanks on machine; threads wire from holding drum through guides and into filling head as required; starts machine which sets filling material into drilled blanks or which drills blanks and subsequently sets in filling material; transfers drilled blanks manually to filling section of machine between operations as required.

Other titles include Broom maker.

699 .56 Covering machine operator (cable, hose, metal wire, metal strip)

Operates one or more machines to wind insulating, reinforcing or protective material round cables, hoses or metal wire or strip

Ascertains job requirements from written or other specifications; changes dies or guides in winding or braiding heads as required; loads or directs loading of cable, hose or metal wire or strip and appropriate covering materials, such as steel tape, wire, specially treated paper, hessian, rubber, silk, nylon or cotton, on machine; ensures that coating baths are prepared as required; leads ends of covering materials through appropriate winding or braiding heads according to specified lay or sequence of winding; leads cable, hose or metal wire or strip through winding or braiding heads and attaches ends of covering materials; leads cable, hose, or metal wire or strip round capstans or over pulleys and secures to take-off drum or drawing mechanism; starts machine to take cable, hose, or metal wire or strip through winding or braiding and, if appropriate, coating operations; adjusts travelling and rotational speed of cable, hose, or metal wire or strip through machine as necessary; rejoins broken ends; replenishes supplies of covering materials as required, joining metallic materials by soldering or brazing; removes or directs removal of cable, hose, or metal wire or strip from machine on completion of covering operations.

May (01) mark faults as cable or hose passes through machine

(02) operate lathe-type machine with travelling headstock to wind a single wire round pressure hose.

Additional factor: number and type(s) of machines operated.

Other titles include Armouring machine operator (cable, hose), Braiding machine operator (cable, hose), Hose armourer, Lapping machine operator (cable, hose), Taping machine operator.

Excluded are Lead press workers (712 .60) and Extruded covering machine operators (681 .58)

699 .58 Cork cutting machine setter-operator

Sets up and operates one or more machines to cut cork stock or articles to specified requirements

Ascertains job requirements from specifications; selects and fixes appropriate cutting tools as required; positions workpiece(s) on feed mechanism or secures on machine using jigs, clamps and/or other positioning aids or fixing devices; positions and clamps guides or stops as required to set length, width, depth and/or angle of cut; starts machine by automatic or manual control to level, trim and/or cut cork to requirements; checks accuracy of cutting using measuring aids; repositions workpiece(s), changes cutters and re-sets machine as necessary.

May (01) mark off workpiece before cutting

(02) sharpen cutting tools.

Additional factor: number of machines operated.

699 .60 Extrusion press setter (electrode coating)

Sets up extrusion press to coat wire electrode cores with flux paste

Loads lengths of cut wire on to machine; checks that adequate supply of coating material (flux paste) is loaded on to machine; sets machine controls for type and gauge of electrode required and for correct speed; adjusts controls of drying ovens to maintain required temperatures; adjusts settings during production run as required.

699 .62 Extrusion press operator (electrode coating)

Operates extrusion press to coat wire electrode cores with flux paste

Switches on extrusion press; operates machine controls to regulate feed of wire into machine; checks progress of coating visually and makes sample tests for concentricity using meter.

May (01) set up machine (699 .60).

699 .64 Filler (cartridges, detonators, fireworks)

Fills cartridge, detonator, firework or similar cases with explosive materials by hand or machine

If hand filling, places required number of empty cartridge or other cases in holding frame or on work bench; positions feed tray over cases in frame and brushes explosive material into feed apertures or pours or otherwise inserts measured amount of filling into cases; ensures that each case contains prescribed amount of filling material; as required compresses filling in cases by hand or machine; applies sealing compound or places lids or caps on filled cases and seals by crimping using press or crimping tool.
If machine filling, fixes nozzles of appropriate size on feed mechanism of machinery as required; loads explosive material into feed hopper or pan of machine, using hoist as required; loads empty cartridge or other cases on machine conveyor or places under feed mechanism; starts machine and watches filling, compressing and sealing processes, or operates controls to fill cases with explosive material and compresses filling and seals cases by hand or machine.

May (01) fix safety fuses in firework cases before filling
(02) fix sticks, touchpapers, etc to filled firework cases
(03) operate machine to wax filled cartridge cases.

699 .66 Vacuum drying and impregnating tank attendant

Attends one or more steam-heated vessels in which items such as paper-insulated cables or electrical equipment are impregnated with oil or insulating compound

Loads or directs loading of vessel with items such as paper-insulated cables, stator cores or transformers; positions and secures cover on vessel; starts pump or sets controls to create vacuum in vessel and remove moisture from items; operates controls to regulate steam heating and maintain specified temperature in vessel and to admit prescribed impregnating medium; watches instruments and gauges and records variations in temperature and pressure during impregnation; gradually reduces pressure and temperature of vessel after specified time to control cooling process; pumps residue of impregnating medium from vessel; removes vessel cover and removes or directs removal of impregnated item(s); cleans equipment as required.

Additional factor: items to which accustomed, eg paper-insulated cables, stator cores, transformers.

Other titles include Vacuum man (cable impregnating).

699 .68 Lead paster

Operates machine to apply lead paste to grids to make battery plates

Performs a combination of the following tasks; loads grids into feed hopper or on to feed conveyor of machine; adjusts machine controls to produce pasted grids of required thickness and quality; operates controls to carry grids through trimming, pasting, and if appropriate drying units of machine; regulates flow of paste from paste hopper; unloads coated grids from machine; stacks grids and removes to final drying area.

Other titles include Lead pasting machine operator.

699 .70 Felter (printing rollers)

Packs designs outlined in metal on printing rollers with felt or plastic felt composition

Mounts wooden or composition roller bearing design outlined in metal on blocks or spindle holders.
If using felt, cuts felt to shape of design; applies adhesive and places felt over design area on roller; beats felt into position with hammer and presses firmly into all crevices and angles; removes surplus felt and adhesive.
If using plastic felt composition, mixes composition ingredients to a putty consistency; presses composition into design area with a knife, ensuring that all crevices and angles are filled and that surface is smooth and even.

699 .72 Lampshade maker

Makes lampshades from materials such as fabric, parchment, vellum and plastic

Performs a combination of the following tasks: binds wire frames with tape; sews, glues or welds edges of material together to form lampshade cover or lining; fits complete cover or sections of cover over frame, pleating or gathering material as required, and pins in position or fits frame rings to top and bottom of cover; fixes cover to frame by sewing or gluing or with adhesive binding tape; fits and sews or glues lining to frame; cuts surplus material from shade; sews or glues on trimmings such as braid, fringes, tassels or bows.

May (01) cut out lampshades (656)
(02) fix fabric backing to parchment with adhesive
(03) punch lace holes in parchment or plastic cover and fix cover to frame with thonging or other lacing.

Other titles include Lampshade coverer.

699 .74 Match making machine operator

Operates machine to dip prepared match sticks in wax and composition to form matches and to box finished matches

Checks that machine hopper contains an adequate supply of match sticks (splints); checks level and temperature of paraffin wax and dipping composition in storage unit and replenishes composition as required; adjusts ejectors to ensure that correct number of matches are deposited in each box; starts machine and operates controls to regulate supply of splints, wax and match box outers and inners to relevant parts of machine; ensures that heads of splints are correctly dipped in wax and composition and adjusts controls as necessary; checks that drying fans are functioning properly and adjusts as necessary; cleans and oils machine.

699 .76 Machine setter (not elsewhere classified)

Sets up one or more types of machines (making or repairing) operated or attended by other workers and is not elsewhere classified

Ascertains job requirements from drawings or other specifications; decides sequence and method of required operations; selects and fixes appropriate moulds, dies, cutters or other tools on machine; sets pressure, speed, timing and other machine controls and adjusts machine table, stops and guides; operates machine for trial run to check accuracy of setting and adjusts as necessary; adjusts settings as necessary during production runs.

May (01) load or direct loading of raw materials, components, etc on to machine for production run.

Additional factors: number and type(s) of machines to which accustomed.

699 .78 Exhauster (lamp, valve manufacture)

Operates equipment to exhaust glass lamp, valve or tube assemblies, charge with specified gas or vapour and seal

Positions glass stem of assembly in holding device and connects to pumping apparatus; opens exhaust valves, starts vacuum pump and tests connection for leaks; heats assembly in portable oven as appropriate while pumping progresses; connects electric cables to wires protruding from assembly; switches on electricity and bombards assembly with high voltage electric current to eliminate gaseous impurities; watches vacuum gauge and allows exhausting process to continue until specified vacuum reading is obtained; connects supply lines and opens valves to charge assembly with specified volume of inert gas or vapour; melts glass stem with hand gas torch to seal assembly and release sealed assembly from holding device.

May (01) fuse glass stem of lamp valve assembly to glass protrusions on pumping apparatus using hand gas torch

(02) carry out prescribed tests after completion of process to check that assembly is free from impurities and working efficiently

(03) operate hydraulic press to seal copper tube stems of large assemblies.

Other titles include Bench pumper, Neon sign pumper.

699 .90 Exhausting machine attendant (lamp, valve manufacture)

Attends automatic machine in which glass lamp or valve assemblies are exhausted, filled with gas or vapour and sealed

Examines assemblies for defects such as broken glass or wires and rejects faulty ones; positions exhaust tubes of lamp or valve assemblies in machine to fit tightly; connects gas or vapour supply lines to machine and opens feed valves; starts machine which automatically replaces air in lamp or valve with gas or vapour, seals, cuts off exhaust tube and ejects lamp or valve; stops machine in the event of leakages or vacuum pump failure or to clear blockages.

Other titles include Pumper.

699 .91 Venetian blind maker

Makes venetian blinds

Ascertains job requirements from written or other instructions; cuts slats, lowering, raising and turning cord(s) and preformed ladder tape or cord to required lengths by hand and machine; fits together cut parts to make housing box and inserts fittings using hand tools; sets and operates machine to cut fixing slots in slats in required positions; fixes ends of ladder tape or cord to bottom of blind and to housing box, and positions slats on rungs of ladder tapes or cord; threads lowering, raising and turning cord(s) through housing box fittings and fixing slots in slats, and secures ends to bottom of blind.

May (01) pack finished blind for storage or dispatch.

Other titles include Bench hand.

699 .92 Machine operator (not elsewhere classified), Machine attendant (not elsewhere classified)

Operates or attends one or more machines to drill, grind, cut, shape or otherwise prepare, make or finish miscellaneous products or parts of products and is not elsewhere classified

Performs a combination of the following tasks: adjusts machine stops, guides and controls; secures workpiece on machine or feeds raw materials, parts, products, etc into machine; operates machine by manual or automatic control, guiding tool or workpiece as required; removes finished work from machine.

May (01) undertake minor maintenance tasks such as cleaning and oiling machine

(02) check finished work for defects.

Additional factors: type of machine to which accustomed; type of product to which accustomed; number of machines operated or attended.

Other titles include Belt grinder (abrasive cloth and paper making), Belt skiver (abrasive cloth and paper making), Bobbin loader (dry battery making machine), Bobbin press operator (dry batteries), Brush trimming machine operator, Cooker operator (dry batteries), Coring press operator (carbon goods), Cork rounding machine operator, Cup feeder (dry battery making machine), Doll's wig stitching machine operator, Finishing machine operator (asbestos composition goods making), Knife machinist (asbestos composition goods making), Machine operator (candle, nightlight, taper making) (not elsewhere classified), Machine operator (crayon and chalk making) (not elsewhere classified), Pearl shell backing machine operator, Pearl shell cutting machine operator, Pearl shell grinding machine operator, Polishing machine operator (not elsewhere classified), Pressman (asbestos composition goods making), Press operator (cork products making), Press operator (asbestos composition goods making), Radius machine man (asbestos composition goods making), Veiner (artificial flower making).

699 .93 Product finisher (not elsewhere classified)

Performs miscellaneous hand or hand and machine tasks to finish products and is not elsewhere classified

Performs one or more of the following or similar tasks: trims excess material from products such as brushes or artificial teeth using scissors or other hand tools; fits handles or shafts on products such as bats or golf clubs, drilling holes for screws as required, winds protective binding round handle or shafts, fits undergrips or grips and smoothes rough edges with sandpaper or buff; fixes attachments, decorative trimmings, transfers, etc to products such as fishing rods and tennis rackets by binding or gluing and applies coatings of lacquer, varnish or similar finish; sets and brushes out dolls' hair in required styles; fits clothes on dolls and combs out hair.

Other titles include Doll dresser, Dolls' hair brusher, Dolls' hair styler, Gripper (golf club), Hand trimmer (brush, broom), Hand trimmer (artificial teeth), Racket finisher, Shafter (golf club), Whipper and varnisher (fishing rod).

See Product Assembling Occupations (Repetitive) (821)

699 .98 Trainee

Performs, under instruction or guidance, various tasks including training exercises and as appropriate pursues studies in order to acquire the basic skills and knowledge required to perform the tasks of workers in other making and repairing occupations.

699 .99 Other making and repairing occupations not elsewhere classified

Workers in this group perform miscellaneous fabricating, repairing and related tasks and are not separately classified, for example:

(01) **Armouring machine assistants (cable)** (assist in the operation of machines to wind insulating, reinforcing or protective material round cables); (02) **Artificial fishing bait makers** (cut bait and attach to hooks); (03) **Artificial flower makers (excluding plastic)** (make artificial flowers by hand, using materials such as heavy crêpe paper, fabric and wire); (04) **Artificial fly dressers,** Artificial fly makers; (05) **Candle moulders,** Nightlight moulders, Taper moulders (fill dies and moulds in frames by hand to form candles, nightlights and tapers); (06) **Corers (hard)** (dip carbon rod cores in solution and insert into core holes of carbon articles by hand); (07) **Cork goods makers (hand)** (make cork components or articles, other than surgical footwear inserts, by hand); (08) **Crayon moulders (not elsewhere classified),** Chalk moulders (not elsewhere classified) (fill moulds in frames by hand to form crayons and chalks); (09) **Hair preparers (wig making)** (separate hair for wig making according to colour, length and texture and mix and wash hair ready for weaving); (10) **Hand tapers (insulation)** (wind insulating materials by hand round cables, or metal wire or strip); (11) **Stamp pad makers** (make inking pads for rubber stamps and fit pads into cases); (12) **Taper makers' assistants;** (13) **Tooth moulders** (fill moulds for artificial teeth with porcelain or plastic compound prior to pressing); (14) **Vacuum men's assistants (cable impregnating).**

MAJOR GROUP XIV

Processing, Making, Repairing and Related Occupations (Metal and Electrical)

Workers in this major group process, form, treat and work metal, set up and operate machine tools and metal working machines, fit parts in the manufacture of metal and electrical products, install, maintain and repair mechanical, electrical and electronic products, equipment and systems, and plumbing, heating and ventilating systems, make, repair and decorate jewellery articles and perform closely related tasks.

The occupations are arranged in the following minor groups:

71 Metal Processing, Forming and Treating Occupations

72 Machining and Related Occupations (Engineering and Metal Goods Making)

73 Production Fitting (Metal) and Related Occupations

74 Installing, Maintaining and Repairing Occupations (Machines, Instruments and Related Mechanical Equipment)

75 Production Fitting and Wiring Occupations (Electrical and Electronic)

76 Installing, Maintaining and Repairing Occupations (Electrical and Electronic)

77 Pipe, Sheet and Structural Metal Working and Related Occupations

79 Processing, Making, Repairing and Related Occupations (Metal and Electrical) Not Elsewhere Classified

Minor Group 71 METAL PROCESSING, FORMING AND TREATING OCCUPATIONS

Workers in this minor group operate metal processing furnaces, heat treatment furnaces and rolling mills, form and shape metal by extruding, drawing and forging, make moulds and cores for metal castings; pour molten metal into moulds and dies, plate and coat metal stock, parts and articles (other than by painting) and perform closely related tasks.

The occupations are arranged in the following unit groups:

710 Foremen (Metal Processing, Forming and Treating Occupations)

711 Furnace Operating Occupations (Metal Processing)

712 Rolling, Extruding and Drawing Occupations (Metal Processing)

713 Moulders, Coremakers and Casters (Metal Processing)

714 Forging Occupations

715 Metal Plating and Coating Occupations

716 Metal Annealing and Tempering Occupations

719 Metal Processing, Forming and Treating Occupations Not Elsewhere Classified

Unit Group 710 Foremen (Metal Processing, Forming and Treating Occupations)

Workers in this unit group directly supervise and co-ordinate the activities of workers in metal processing, forming and treating occupations.

710 .10 Foreman (furnace operating occupations) (metal processing)

Directly supervises and co-ordinates the activities of workers operating and attending furnaces to smelt, refine, melt, reduce, convert and heat metal

Performs appropriate tasks as described under SUPERVISOR/FOREMAN (UNSPECIFIED) (990 .00).

Other titles include Sample passer.

Additional factor: number of workers supervised.

710 .20 Foreman (rolling, extruding and drawing occupations) (metal processing)

Directly supervises and co-ordinates the activities of workers in metal rolling, extruding and drawing occupations

Performs appropriate tasks as described under SUPERVISOR/FOREMAN (UNSPECIFIED) (990 .00).

Additional factor: number of workers supervised.

710 .30 Foreman (moulders, coremakers and casters) (metal processing)

Directly supervises and co-ordinates the activities of moulders, coremakers and casters in metal processing

Performs appropriate tasks as described under SUPERVISOR/FOREMAN (UNSPECIFIED) (990 .00).

Other titles include Teeming observer.

Additional factor: number of workers supervised.

710 .40 Foreman (forging occupations)

Directly supervises and co-ordinates the activities of workers in forging occupations

Performs appropriate tasks as described under SUPERVISOR/FOREMAN (UNSPECIFIED) (990 .00).

Additional factor: number of workers supervised.

710 .50 Foreman (metal plating and coating occupations)

Directly supervises and co-ordinates the activities of workers in metal plating and coating occupations

Performs appropriate tasks as described under SUPERVISOR/FOREMAN (UNSPECIFIED) (990 .00).

Additional factor: number of workers supervised.

710 .60 Foreman (metal annealing and tempering occupations)

Directly supervises and co-ordinates the activities of workers in metal annealing and tempering occupations

Performs appropriate tasks as described under SUPERVISOR/FOREMAN (UNSPECIFIED) (990 .00).

Additional factor: number of workers supervised.

710 .98 Trainee

Performs, under instruction or guidance, various tasks including training exercises and as appropriate pursues studies in order to acquire the basic skills and knowledge required to perform the tasks of foremen (metal processing, forming and treating occupations).

710 .99 Other foremen (metal processing, forming and treating occupations)

Workers in this group directly supervise and co-ordinate the activities of workers in metal processing, forming and treating occupations and are not elsewhere classified.

Unit Group 711 Furnace Operating Occupations (Metal Processing)

Workers in this unit group operate furnaces, retorts and other heating vessels to smelt metalliferous ores, refine metals, melt metals for casting, reheat metal and metal parts and articles for further working, and store molten metal, operate stoves supplying heated air to blast furnaces and tend sherardising furnaces.

See 716 for workers heating metal to anneal, temper or harden.

711 .02 Blast furnace keeper (iron)

Directs the operation of a blast furnace to smelt iron ore

Checks that all runners, dams, spouts, etc are ready for the tapping operation; checks that ladles for slag and molten metal are in position; at specified time, or as directed by foreman, drills into the clay stopper closing the tap hole, using a portable pneumatic drill; burns through last part of clay with an oxygen lance; ensures that the molten metal flows at an even rate during tapping and that any slag is skimmed off; on completion of tapping operates clay gun to reseal the tap hole; supervises the cleaning of runners after each tapping and the preparation of runners, dams, spouts, etc for next tapping; ensures that clay gun is refilled; inspects air pipes and nozzles and supervises repair work; periodically directs slagger to run off slag from furnace.

May (01) perform any of the tasks of SLAGGER (711 .04) or HELPER (711 .52).

Other titles include First operator.

711 .04 Slagger (iron blast furnace)

Taps slag from surface of molten iron and otherwise assists in the operation of a blast furnace, under the direction of blast furnace keeper

Ensures that slag ladles are in position and slag runners are prepared as required for each tapping operation; as directed by blast furnace keeper, cuts through the clay stopper sealing the slag tap hole using hammer and wedge or pneumatic drill, or operates automatic stopper control to open slag hole; reseals tap hole with clay stopper when slag has been run off; assists blast furnace keeper in drilling and resealing tap hole for metal as required.

May (01) perform any of the tasks of HELPER (711 .52).

Other titles include Second operator.

711 .06 Forehand furnaceman (wrought iron manufacture)

Operates a puddling or ball furnace in which pig or scrap iron is refined to produce wrought iron

(01) **Forehand puddler**

Lines furnace bed and sides with layers of refractory materials containing oxide of iron; lights furnace jets and adjusts valves and controls; raises furnace temperature to a welding heat; adds charge of pig iron and increases temperature of furnace to melt the pig iron and oxidise the carbon, silicon and manganese in the metal; stirs the molten metal with long, heavy iron paddles (robbles) until most of the carbon, silicon and manganese have been removed and metal begins to solidify; works the solidifying metal against the sides of the furnace with robbles to form balls of about 100 lbs. weight; withdraws balls of metal from furnace and loads into bogies; breaks tap hole plug with crow-bar and runs off remaining slag; reseals tap hole with clay.

Other titles include Levelhand puddler.

(02) **Forehand ball furnaceman**

Lines furnace bed with appropriate refractory material; lights furnace jets and adjusts valves and controls; directs the loading of pile of scrap iron on to charging shovel (peel); pushes loaded peel into furnace, deposits pile of scrap and withdraws peel; loads further piles of metal till furnace is fully charged; adjusts furnace controls and heats metal to required temperature, causing film of scale to form on iron; from time to time, runs off thin slag formed on furnace floor by scale combining with sand; when metal has been sufficiently heated, supervises withdrawal of piles; reseals tap hole with clay.

711 .08 Furnace operator (steel making)

Operates or directs the operation of a furnace in which iron is refined to produce steel or in which steel ingots are further refined by remelting through electrically conductive molten slag

(01) **First hand melter (open hearth furnace)**

Supervises charging of furnace with materials such as scrap iron, molten iron and lime; sets controls to regulate furnace temperature and flow of air and gas or oil; reverses flow of air and gas at intervals as required; supervises addition to furnace of oxidising agents such as iron ore, mill scale and lime; withdraws or directs the withdrawal of samples of molten metal for laboratory analysis; taps molten metal and slag from furnace as instructed by foreman; supervises the addition during tapping of de-oxidising agents such as ferro-manganese; directs repair (fettling) of furnace lining.

(02) **First vesselman (steel converter)**

Directs the tilting of converter into position for charging; supervises charging of furnace with materials such as scrap iron, molten iron and lime; instructs crew member in control pulpit when to introduce blast of air or oxygen into converter; directs adjustment of air or oxygen pressure during blowing as required; withdraws or directs the withdrawal of samples of molten metal for laboratory analysis; instructs furnace assistant when to tilt converter for tapping of molten metal and slag; supervises the addition of de-oxidising and alloying agents during tapping; directs fettling of converter lining.

Other titles include First hand converter, Steelmaker (converter).

(03) **First hand melter (electric furnace)**

Supervises charging of furnace with materials such as scrap iron, lime and mill scale; if operating electric arc furnace operates controls to lower electrodes; switches on current and, on arc furnace, withdraws electrodes slightly to form arc; supervises addition of de-oxidising and alloying agents; withdraws or directs the withdrawal of samples of molten metal for laboratory analysis; as instructed by sample passer, operates controls to tilt furnace for tapping of molten metal and slag; directs fettling of furnace lining.

(04) **First hand melter (electro-slag remelting furnace)**

Supervises the melting of slag in induction furnace and the charging of molten slag into water-cooled ingot mould; directs the fixing of steel electrode (ingot to be remelted) to furnace hoist; sets controls for appropriate voltage and amperage and switches on current; operates hoist to lower electrode into mould until contact is made with molten slag and melting begins, and switches to automatic operation; adjusts rate of feed and electrical input during melting and re-forming process as required; supervises withdrawal of re-formed ingot from mould.

May (05) perform any of the tasks of FURNACE ASSISTANT (STEEL MAKING) (711 .56).

Additional factor: type of furnace to which accustomed, eg open hearth, converter, electric arc, high frequency induction.

711 .10 Furnaceman (copper) (non-electrolytic)

Operates a reverberatory furnace to refine copper

Charges or directs the charging of furnace with scrap or partly refined copper (blister copper); adjusts furnace controls as necessary to regulate flow of oil and air; operates metal lances to blow air into molten metal to oxidise impurities; skims impurities off surface of metal; covers surface of molten metal with layer of coke; inserts tree trunks (poles) of green hardwood into melt to reduce oxygen content; withdraws samples of metal periodically for laboratory analysis; breaks open tap hole and directs flow of molten copper into ladles for pouring into moulds or holding furnaces.

Other titles include Ladleman (copper refining).

711 .12 Furnaceman (non-ferrous metal alloy manufacture)

Operates a furnace in which specified quantities of metals are melted to form alloys

Feeds furnace with coke or sets controls to regulate electric current or inflow of air, gas or oil; loads specified amounts of metals into furnace; checks temperature during melting and adjusts controls as necessary; adds chemicals or fluxing agents to remove unwanted gases or bring impurities to the surface, forming a layer of slag; skims off slag from surface; withdraws samples of molten metal for laboratory analysis; breaks open furnace tap hole or operates controls to tilt furnace to pour metal into moulds or ladles.

Additional factors: type of furnace to which accustomed, eg reverberatory, rotary, pot; method of heating to which accustomed, eg gas, coke, oil, electric.

Other titles include Melter.

711 .14 Cupola man

Operates a cupola furnace in which metals are melted for casting

Performs a combination of the following tasks: if coke-fired furnace, prepares and lights bed of kindling coke in base of furnace; charges or directs charging of furnace with scrap metal, coke and limestone; if electric, oil or gas-fired furnace, switches on charged furnace from control panel; turns on hot or cold air blast; adds further metal and coke charges during melting as required; drains slag from surface of metal during tapping; when metal is ready for casting, removes clay plug from tap hole or operates controls to tap molten metal into pouring or casting ladles; on completion of melting, opens bottom door to allow remaining metal, slag and coke to drop out or removes manually with rakes, shovels, etc; chips slag from walls of cupola and patches and relines walls as required; cleans trough leading from tap hole; reseals tap hole with clay plug.

Other titles include Cupola attendant, Cupola operator, Tapper.

711 .16 Crucible furnaceman (foundry)

Operates a pot or crucible furnace in which metals are melted for casting

Feeds coke into bed of furnace or turns valves to regulate flow of air, gas or oil; ignites coke or lights fuel burners; charges crucible with specified amounts of metal and places in furnace using hoist or tongs; watches metal colour to determine when melting process is complete; removes crucible containing molten metal from furnace.

May (01) assist with casting.

Other titles include Pot furnaceman.

711 .18 Heater (reheating furnace, soaking pit)

Operates furnace or soaking pit in which metal ingots, blooms, billets, sheets or plates are heated prior to forging, pressing, rolling or tube making

Sets furnace or soaking pit controls to regulate temperatures and heating times; loads, or directs loading of ingots, blooms, billets, sheets or plates into furnace or pit; checks instruments during heating and adjusts controls as necessary to maintain temperature between specified limits; on completion of heating removes or directs removal of ingots, blooms, etc from furnace or pit.

May (01) adjust position of stock in furnace or pit to ensure even heating
(02) carry out repairs to furnace or soaking pit.

Additional factors: type(s) of metal to which accustomed; type of furnace to which accustomed.

Other titles include Furnaceman.

711.50 Stove minder (iron blast furnace)

Operates two or more stoves to supply heated air blast to iron blast furnace

Opens valves to feed gas and air to stove and ignites burners in combustion chamber; checks temperature and pressure gauges and cuts off gas and air supply when lattice brickwork inside stove reaches required temperature; operates controls to blow blast of cold air through stove, absorbing heat from brickwork, then through air duct (bustle main) and water-cooled nozzles (tuyeres) into furnace; adjusts controls to maintain hot air blast at required temperature; uses stoves in turn to provide continuous blast of hot air to furnace.

Other titles include Stoveman.

711.52 Helper (iron blast furnace)

Assists, under the direction of blast furnace keeper, in the operation of a blast furnace to smelt iron ore

Performs a combination of the following tasks: cleans runners on completion of tapping operation; relines runners with clay or sand and dries off lining with gas burner; rebuilds sand dams blocking various branches of runners; cleans and refills tap hole gun with clay; assists in repairing or replacing air pipes and nozzles; sets ladles for slag and molten metal in position for tapping operation; assists slagger in tapping slag from furnace; during tapping skims off slag; knocks down sand dams to divert flow of metal or slag to empty ladles.

711.54 Underhand furnaceman (wrought iron manufacture)

Assists, under the direction of forehand furnaceman, in the operation of a puddling or ball furnace in which pig or scrap iron is refined to produce wrought iron

(01) **Underhand puddler**

Positions bogies to receive molten slag or balls of metal; wheels bogies containing balls of metal to power hammer; removes bogies containing molten slag from furnace area and empties solidified slag after cooling; otherwise assists forehand puddler as required in the preparation and operation of furnace.

(02) **Underhand ball furnaceman**

Positions bogies to receive molten slag; loads prepared piles of scrap iron on to charging shovel (peel); assists forehand ball furnaceman to push peel into furnace; withdraws heated piles of metal using tongs supported by overhead track chain and removes to power hammer; removes bogies containing molten slag; otherwise assists forehand ball furnaceman as required in the preparation and operation of furnace.

711.56 Furnace assistant (steel making)

Assists, under the direction of furnace operator (steel making), in the operation of a furnace in which iron is refined to produce steel

Performs a combination of the following tasks: operates pulpit controls as directed to tilt furnace or converter for charging or tapping of metal or slag, to introduce blast of air or oxygen into converter, etc; opens and closes tap holes as directed; takes samples of molten steel for laboratory analysis; takes furnace temperature as required; collects specified amounts of additional charging materials and ensures that adequate stocks are maintained; adds de-oxidising and alloying materials to furnace, converter or ladles during heating or tapping as directed; maintains furnace tools in good order; keeps furnace area clean and free from spillages; assists in repairing (fettling) furnace lining; cleans and repairs tap holes and hot metal chutes (launders).

Additional factor: type of furnace to which accustomed, eg open hearth, converter, electric arc, high frequency induction.

Other titles include Assistant steelmaker, Controlman (steel converter), Fourth hand melter (steel furnace), Fourth vesselman (steel converter), Second hand converter, Second hand melter (steel furnace), Second vesselman (steel converter), Third hand converter, Third hand melter (steel furnace), Third vesselman (steel converter).

711.58 Furnace assistant (non-ferrous metal alloy manufacture)

Assists under the direction of furnaceman (non-ferrous metal alloy manufacture) in the operation of a furnace in which metals are melted to form alloys

Performs a combination of the following tasks: assists in charging furnace; skims dross from alloys in moulds; cleans furnace and empties ashes; otherwise assists furnaceman as required.

711.60 Fireman (zinc vertical retort)

Controls the heating of vertical retorts in which zinc is produced

Checks temperature of each section of each retort and adjusts gas and air supplies to maintain required temperature; adjusts depth of immersion of water cooler apparatus to obtain correct temperature in mechanical sumps; checks displacement air supply to each retort and adjusts as necessary.

711.62 Blast furnace control room operator (zinc production)

Regulates temperatures, pressures and flow ratios of zinc blast furnace from instrument control panel

Maintains check on instrument readings; adjusts controls as necessary to maintain required furnace temperatures, pressures and flow ratios at each stage of process; notifies slagger if pressure readings indicate that tapping of slag is overdue; undertakes gas analysis as required.

711.64 Condenserman (zinc blast furnace)

Operates condenser unit in which vapourised zinc from blast furnace is condensed in drops of molten lead

Operates controls to maintain required temperatures in condensers, cooling launders and separation bath circuits; adds scrap or partially refined lead to maintain required level of molten lead in condenser; checks operation of condenser rotors which throw up shower of molten lead, dross extractors and pumps which pump lead and zinc solution to separation bath; ensures that lead and zinc are separating correctly in separation bath, the zinc overflowing into holding bath, the heavier lead flowing through trough back into condenser; removes clay from tap hole of zinc holding bath and draws off metal into ladles; adds metallic sodium to zinc flowing into ladles to reduce arsenic content; transfers treated zinc from ladles to casting bath; removes dross and accretions from pump sump and removes dross boxes to dross treatment section.

711.66 Slagger (zinc blast furnace)

Taps molten lead and slag from zinc blast furnace

Ensures that channels from furnace, lead ladles and slag granulation launder are clean and in position; removes restrictor bar or clay from furnace tap hole; clears tap hole, using oxygen lance, to allow lead and slag to flow freely to forehearth; regulates flow as required by partially re-inserting restrictor bar; ensures that lead and slag separate correctly from forehearth, the slag on top overflowing into granulation launder, the heavier lead flowing through an underflow weir and up a channel (riser) to ladles; checks that slag is solidifying (granulating) under water jet in launder; on completion of tapping, cleans tap hole and reblocks with restrictor bar or clay; drains remaining slag from forehearth; removes lead ladles to casting area and pours lead into ingot moulds; cleans any slag from blast intake nozzles (tuyeres) to ensure free flow of air to furnace; cleans forehearth, furnace area and equipment in preparation for next tapping.

711.68 Bullion melter

Melts gold, silver or other precious metal bullion in crucible and pours into moulds

Places charge of refined precious metal pellets in crucible; places crucible in furnace; regulates furnace temperature to melt metal; on completion of melting removes crucible and pours or ladles molten metal into moulds.

711.70 Furnaceman (lead smelting)

Operates furnace in which ores are smelted to produce unrefined lead

Charges, or directs charging of furnace with ore and scrap lead; after specified time taps molten metal and slag into moulds or ladles; inserts lifting hooks into soft metal when set, for removal to refining department.

Other titles include Smelter.

711.72 Furnaceman (aluminium) (electrolytic)

Attends two or more electrolytic furnaces, in continuous operation, in which alumina is reduced to aluminium

Checks voltmeters at regular intervals; if warning light indicates that proportion of alumina in a furnace (cell) has dropped below required level, breaks alumina crust which has formed on surface of electrolyte (molten cryolite) using a steel bar or pneumatic breaker; removes gases which have formed round carbon anode using compressed-air lance and brushes alumina powder, which has been deposited in channel round anode, into furnace; skims soot from surface of molten aluminium which has been deposited on carbon cathode on floor of cell

711.74 Electrolytic refiner (excluding aluminium)

Operates or attends one or more tanks or vats in which metals, other than aluminium, are refined by electrolytic process

(01) **Electrolytic refiner** (copper)

Directs loading of anode sheets of fire-refined copper and cathode sheets of relatively pure copper into tank or vat of electrolyte (sulphuric acid solution) by crane; during refining process ensures that copper does not build up and short circuit anodes and cathodes; periodically drains sludge containing other metals from bottom of tanks or vats; on completion of process, directs removal of cathodes bearing deposit of almost pure copper and used anodes.

(02) **Electolytic refiner** (gold or silver)

Prepares appropriate electrolyte (gold chloride or silver nitrate solution) and fills tank; suspends anode sheets of gold or silver and cathode sheets of gold, silver or stainless steel from silver wires attached to bar over tank; lowers anodes and cathodes into tank and switches on current; during process, checks and records temperature of electrolyte and electric current ratings and adjusts as necessary; replenishes electrolyte as required; if refining silver, removes cathodes at regular intervals and scrapes off deposited silver crystals; if refining gold, removes cathodes bearing gold deposit at end of process; washes crystals or cathodes to remove electrolyte and dries in oven; melts silver crystals or gold cathodes in crucible and pours molten metal into tank of swirling water in which it granulates; after drying withdraws samples of gold or silver grains for laboratory analysis.

(03) **Lead softener**

Operates electric overhead crane to load anode plates of lead containing silver and bismuth and cathode plates of lead into tank of electrolyte; on completion of process operates crane to remove anodes and cathodes; stacks cathodes bearing pure lead deposit on rollers on a gravity conveyor; pulls lever to tilt conveyor rollers so that cathodes slide into pot for re-melting; lowers anodes into automatic scrubbing unit where the covering of slag or slime containing silver and bismuth is scrubbed off; removes anodes from scrubbing unit and unhooks from crane.

May (04) coat silver cathodes with shellac to prevent deposited metal from sticking

(05) prepare anode and/or cathode sheets.

711.76 Lead softener (non-electrolytic)

Operates one or more furnaces in which lead is softened by heating to remove hardening impurities

Charges or directs charging of furnace with unrefined lead, scrap or molten lead; adjusts controls to regulate furnace temperature; stirs molten metal as required with mechanical mixing equipment; adds reagents to mix, causing hardening impurities such as antimony, tin and arsenic to form a dross on surface of melt; skims off dross at intervals; when metal is ready for casting, opens valves or operates pump to run softened lead from furnace to moulds or to casting machine.

Other titles include Lead refiner, Potman.

711.78 Desilveriser (lead)

Operates kettle in which softened lead is heated to remove silver and zinc content

Charges or directs charging of kettle with softened lead and blocks of low grade silver and zinc dross; operates mixing equipment to stir molten charge thoroughly; at intervals skims off silver and zinc crust mixed with liquid lead which forms on surface and transfers to hydraulic presses; operates presses to squeeze out as much as possible of the lead which runs back into kettle; when all silver and zinc crust has been removed, adds specified amounts of zinc to molten metal to complete the desilverisation; skims off resultant crust, which is of low grade, into moulds as metal cools; operates pumps to run cooled metal to automatic vacuum dezincing unit.

Other titles include Kettleman, Potman.

711.80 Retort furnaceman (lead refining)

Operates one or more retort furnaces in which silver and zinc crust is heated to recover zinc

Positions crucible in retort furnace and lights furnace; charges crucible with silver and zinc crust produced by desilverising process; heats crust for specified time till zinc distils from molten charge and condenses to a liquid in condenser attached to furnace; taps zinc from condenser into moulds; pours remaining silver and lead alloy into moulds for cupellation.

711 .90 Cupel man (silver recovery)

Operates cupellation furnace in which silver and lead alloy is heated to remove lead

Directs charging of furnace with blocks of silver and lead alloy (retort metal) produced by retort process; adjusts controls to regulate flow of fuel to furnace; when metal has melted, removes powdery dross formed on surface by oxidation of remaining zinc content; operates furnace controls to blow a blast of air over surface, hastening oxidation of the lead to form lead monoxide (litharge); adds small amounts of zinc dross which fuses with the litharge; runs off the zincy litharge; repeats process over a period of days, adding retort metal and zinc dross and running off litharge till remaining silver is relatively pure; adds small amounts of pure lead to form litharge containing copper oxide; runs off litharge and adds specified amounts of sodium nitrate to remove remaining lead; taps furnace and pours silver into moulds; charges silver into a second furnace for further refining.

711 .92 Mixer (steel manufacture)

Operates mixer furnace in which molten metal is stored in transit from blast furnaces to steel converters or open hearth furnaces

Performs a combination of the following tasks: notes temperature and amount of molten iron received from blast furnaces; supervises pouring of molten iron from furnace ladles into storage vessel (mixer); regulates mixer controls to maintain molten metal at required temperature; adds soda-ash or limestone to molten metal as required; pours, or supervises pouring of molten metal from mixer into charging ladles; notes amount of molten metal charged into each steel converter or open hearth furnace.

Other titles include First hand mixer, Second hand mixer, Third hand mixer.

711 .98 Trainee

Performs, under instruction or guidance, various tasks including training exercises and as appropriate pursues studies in order to acquire the basic skills and knowledge required to perform the tasks of workers in furnace operating occupations (metal processing).

711 .99 Other furnace operating occupations (metal processing)

Workers in this group operate and attend furnaces to smelt, refine, melt, reduce, convert and heat metal and are not elsewhere classified, for example:

(01) **Coker drawers (zinc)** (operate furnaces in which zinc briquettes are coked prior to charging to vertical retorts); (02) **Drosshousemen** (operate furnaces in which residue from galvanizing or tinning plants is refined); (03) **Furnace attendants (sherardising)** (heat iron or steel articles packed in drums with sand, silica and zinc dust to provide a rustproof coating); (04) **Furnace attendants (shipyard)** (attend furnaces used by ship platers, boiler platers, etc in shipyard); (05) **Furnace attendants (vacuum remelting plant)** (watch melting process and monitor instruments on control panel of vacuum arc furnace in which steel ingots are further refined by remelting in a vacuum); (06) **Furnacemen (non-ferrous metals excluding aluminium, lead, copper, zinc)** (operate non-electrolytic furnaces in which non-ferrous ores are smelted or non-ferrous metals are reduced or refined); (07) **Heaters (cutlery)** (heat cutlery blanks in furnace prior to forging); (08) **Heaters (hand and edge tools)** (heat hand and edge tool blanks in furnaces prior to forging and splitting); (09) **Slaggers (reheating furnaces and soaking pits)** (remove slag and cinders from reheating furnaces or soaking pits); (10) **Vacuum degassing plant operators** (operate vacuum degassing plants to remove gaseous impurities from liquid steel in the ladle).

Unit Group 712 Rolling, Extruding and Drawing Occupations (Metal Processing)

Workers in this unit group operate metal rolling mills, straighten metal tubes, bars and sections by rolling, form seamless metal tubes by roller drawing, form metal rods, bars, tubes and sections by extrusion, finish metal tubes, rods and bars by drawing through dies and operate wire drawing machines.

712.05 Roller (primary reduction or hot rolling mill team)

Operates or directs the operation of a primary reduction or hot rolling mill to roll hot metal into slabs, blooms, billets, bars, rods, strip, sheet, plate or sections

From rolling instructions, determines rolling sequence and calculates required space (draught) between rolls for each stand, rolls' tension, rolling speed, number of passes, etc; sets or directs the setting of rolls' draught, speed and tension, and width of guides; gives signal for rolling to start and supervises entire process; adjusts or directs adjustments to settings during rolling, as required, and takes corrective action if irregularities occur; checks that gauge and finish of rolled metal conform to specifications; directs cleaning and changing of rolls.

(01) **Assistant roller (primary reduction or hot rolling mill team)**

Performs any of the tasks of roller, under his direction, and deputises for him as required.

May (02) perform any of the tasks of ROLLING MILL ASSISTANT (712.50).

Additional factor: metals to which accustomed.

Other titles include Blooming mill operator, Cogging mill operator, Screwer (iron and steel rolling), Slabbing mill operator, Strip mill operator.

712.10 Roller (cold rolling or temper mill team)

Operates or directs the operation of a cold rolling or temper mill to reduce rolled metal strip or sheet to final gauge or to give correct temper and finish to rolled strip or sheet after annealing

From rolling instructions, determines rolling sequence and calculates required space (draught) between rolls for each stand, rolls' tension, rolling speed, number of passes, etc; sets or directs the setting of rolls' draught, speed and tension, and width of guides; supervises the loading of coiled strip or sheet on uncoiling mechanism; ensures that strip is threaded correctly through mill and fixed round re-coiling mechanism at delivery end; gives signal for rolling to start and supervises entire process; adjusts or directs adjustments to settings during rolling as required and takes corrective action if irregularities occur; checks that gauge and finish of rolled strip or sheet conform to specifications; directs cleaning and changing of rolls.

(01) **Assistant roller (cold rolling or temper mill team)**

Performs any of the tasks of roller, under his direction, and deputises for him as required.

May (02) perform any of the tasks of ROLLING MILL ASSISTANT (712.55).

Additional factor: metals to which accustomed.

Other titles include Assistant operator, Cold roller (steel sheet or strip), Operator.

712.15 Piercer (seamless tubes)

Operates equipment to pierce heated metal ingots, bars or billets preparatory to forming seamless tubes

If preparing metal for plug mill or rotary forge processes, ensures that heated ingot, bar or billet is correctly positioned on piercing press; operates hydraulic punch to pierce a small hole part way through centre of ingot, bar or billet lengthwise to form a thick walled tube closed at one end (bottle); transfers bottle to rotary piercer or elongator; operates controls to draw the bottle through barrel shaped rolls and over revolving heavy steel mandrel to enlarge the hole and form a rough tube (bloom).
If preparing metal for push bench process, ensures that heated billet is correctly positioned in container of piercing press; operates press to force a punch through a guide in top of container into billet, pushing out metal to fill container and form a bottle.

Other titles include Piercer rollerman.

712.20 Rollerman (seamless tubes)

Operates equipment to roll seamless tubes from pierced or partly pierced metal ingots, bars or billets

(01) **Plug mill operator**

Ensures that pierced billet (bloom) is correctly positioned on bed of plug mill; operates controls to push bloom through a set of grooved rolls and over a plug, drawing the walls of the bloom between the plug and the rolls; returns partly formed tube to front of mill, rotates it through an angle of 90° and repeats the rolling process over a slightly larger plug.

(02) **Pilger operator (rotary forge process)**

Ensures that pierced ingot, bar or billet (bloom) is correctly positioned on bed of mill; operates controls to insert a mandrel through the bloom; starts mill to push bloom gradually through shaped rollers by means of a piston; rotates bloom through an angle of 90° before each forward movement of piston; stops mill when almost entire bloom has been squeezed through rolls to form a long, thin-walled tube; raises top roll by mechanical controls to allow thick unrolled part of bloom to pass through and withdraws mandrel.

(03) **Push bench operator**

Ensures that partly pierced billet (bottle) is correctly positioned on push bench; operates controls to insert a mandrel into bottle and push mandrel and bottle through a series of roller dies to form a thin-walled

continued

tube, closed at front end; passes tube and mandrel through a series of barrel shaped rolls to loosen tube from mandrel; operates controls to withdraw mandrel from tube.

May (04) set up rolls or dies.

712.25 Roller straightener

Sets up and operates machine to straighten metal tubes, bars, sections and other metal stock, by rolling

Sets up rolls in machine; operates hand or automatic controls to set gap between rolls according to diameter and shape of tubes, bars or sections; starts machine and feeds in metal stock; ensures that straightening proceeds correctly and adjusts rolls' setting as necessary; removes straightened tubes, bars or sections from machine.

Other titles include Roller leveller, Rollerman (tube straightening).

712.50 Rolling mill assistant (primary reduction or hot rolling mill team)

Assists, under the direction of roller, in the operation of a primary reduction or hot rolling mill to roll hot metal into slabs, blooms, billets, bars, rods, strip, sheet, plate or sections

Performs a combination of the following tasks: operates hand or automatic controls to set space (draught) between rolls, speed and tension of rolls and width of guides as directed by roller; adjusts rolls' draught, speed and tension during rolling as required; guides metal to and from each set of rolls with tongs or automatic handling device; if working on hand mills, passes metal sheets through rolls manually; if rolling billets or slabs, rotates metal through 90° after first pass through rolls and repositions ingot after each pass through rolls; operates or attends cutters or shears at various stages of rolling to crop uneven ends, to cut up metal if buckling occurs or to cut metal into lengths; operates controls to push rolled billets or bars off roller table to cooling banks and from cooling banks into bins; operates or attends mechanism to coil and weigh rolled strip and records weight of coil; observes metal during rolling and notifies roller of any irregularities; assists in cleaning and changing rolls.

May (01) assist in conveying metal to be rolled from reheating furnace to rolling stands.

Additional factor: metals to which accustomed.

Other titles include Behinder, Coiler operator, Finishing mill operator, Flying shears operator, Fourth hand, Manipulator operator, Roughing mill operator, Slab shears operator, Third hand, Tongsman.

712.55 Rolling mill assistant (cold rolling or temper mill team)

Assists, under the direction of roller, in the operation of a cold rolling or temper mill to reduce rolled metal strip or sheet to final gauge or to give correct temper and finish to rolled strip or sheet after annealing

Performs a combination of the following tasks: operates hand or automatic controls to set space (draught) between rolls, speed and tension of rolls and width of guides as directed by roller; adjusts rolls' draught, speed and tension during rolling as required; loads coil of strip or sheet to be rolled on uncoiling mechanism; removes binding wire or steel band and positions coil for rolling; feeds end of strip through mill by hand; fixes end of strip round re-coiling mechanism at delivery end of mill; operates valves to control flow of coolant to strip or sheet during rolling; observes strip or sheet during rolling and notifies roller of any irregularities; stops mill as directed by roller and cuts faulty pieces from strip with electric hand shears; if working on hand mills, passes metal sheets through rolls manually; binds finished coil with wire or steel band; transfers finished coil from re-coiling mechanism to scales; weighs coil and records weight; assists in cleaning and changing rolls.

Additional factor: metals to which accustomed.

Other titles include Behinder, Coiler, Feeder, Fourth hand, Third hand.

712.60 Lead press worker

Operates or assists in the operation of a press to extrude lead piping or to extrude lead sheathing over cable

Performs a combination of the following tasks: sets up appropriate die and mandrel in press; if coating cable, loads reel of cable core on to press and feeds end through die; loads lead ingots into melting pot or furnace; transfers molten lead to press by ladle or run-off channel; starts press to extrude lead through die and over mandrel or cable core; attaches end of extruded piping to pulling mechanism or end of piping or sheathed cable to coiling mechanism; cuts extruded piping to length; removes reel of cable or reel or lengths of piping from press.

Other titles include Flaker-on, Lead extruder, Lead press driver, Potman.

712.65 Extrusion press operator (excluding lead)

Sets up and operates press to form rods, bars, tubes or sections or to sheath cable by extruding heated metal other than lead through dies

Sets up press with appropriate die(s) and, if extruding tubes or sheathing cable, with central mandrel or core; loads preheated metal billet into press container or loads supply of cold billets into feed magazine of press heating unit, which ejects heated billet into press container; operates controls to bring hydraulic ram into contact with the metal in the container, forcing it through the die(s); removes any metal remaining in container after extrusion.

May (01) cut the extruded rod, bar, tube or section to length.

Additional factor: metal(s) to which accustomed.

Other titles include Aluminium extruder, Metal extruder.

712.70 Drawer (tube, rod, bar)

Sets up and operates draw bench equipment to draw metal tubes, rods or bars through dies to reduce the diameter, obtain closer tolerances and improve the surface

Sets up drawing die according to diameter required; determines drawing speed required for size of tube, rod or bar and quality of finish, and sets machine controls accordingly; if drawing tubes, inserts draw plug in tube; feeds tapered end of tube, rod or bar through die; operates lever to fix tapered end into grips on carriage (dog) which runs along draw bench; starts chain drive to set carriage in motion and draw tube, rod or bar through die and along draw bench; undertakes day-to-day maintenance of equipment.

May (01) taper end of rod or bar on pointing machine or with hand file

(02) operate equipment which draws, cuts, straightens and polishes rods or bars in a continuous process.

712.75 Wire drawing machinist

Sets up and operates a machine to reduce the diameter of metal wire by drawing through a series of graduated dies

Sets up drawing dies according to diameter required; fits wind-up reel on end of machine; tapers end of coil of wire on pointing machine or with hand file; feeds pointed end of wire through first die and winds a length of wire round drawing block manually or by operating machine controls; feeds end through successively smaller dies, looping wire round drawing blocks between dies; attaches wire to wind-up reel at end of machine; operates controls to start machine and ensures that drawing proceeds correctly; joins end of one coil to start of another and any breaks in wire by butt welding to maintain continuous drawing; removes reel of drawn wire from machine on completion of drawing.

May (01) operate more than one machine.

Other titles include Wire drawer.

712.98 Trainee

Performs, under instruction or guidance, various tasks including training exercises and as appropriate pursues studies in order to acquire the basic skills and knowledge required to perform the tasks of workers in rolling, extruding and drawing occupations (metal processing).

712.99 Other rolling, extruding and drawing occupations (metal processing)

Workers in this group form, straighten and finish metal by rolling, extruding and drawing and are not elsewhere classified, for example:

(01) **Fork rollers** (pass heated fork blanks through rollers to draw out prongs to required dimensions and shape); (02) **Plate drawers (wire)** (draw wire to required diameter on a single drawing block through holes in a drawing plate); (03) **Roller bending machine operators (tube manufacture)** (operate roller bending machines to curve hot or cold metal plates to shape prior to welding to form tubes); (04) **Roller corrugating machine operators** (operate machines to corrugate metal sheets or cylinders by rolling).

See Bending press operator (714.75) for workers operating bending presses or machines to shape heated metal and Bending machine operator (729.20) for workers operating bending or rolling machines to shape cold sheet metal.

Unit Group 713 Moulders, Coremakers and Casters (Metal Processing)

Workers in this unit group make moulds and cores for metal castings from sand, loam, plaster and refractory materials and pour molten metal into moulds and dies, around bearings to form linings and into centres of abrasive wheels to form bushings.

713.05 Moulder (general)

Makes sand or loam moulds for metal castings in moulding boxes and moulding pits

Performs tasks as described under FLOOR MOULDER (713.10) and PIT MOULDER (713.15).

May (01) make cores (713.25)
(02) pour molten metal into moulds (713.62)
(03) operate moulding machines using loose patterns to form the moulds
(04) make moulds using plate patterns (713.20).

Other titles include Moulder-coremaker.

713.10 Bench moulder, Floor moulder

Makes sand or loam moulds for metal castings in moulding boxes on bench or foundry floor

Sets lower half of pattern on moulding board on bench or floor and encloses with frame of lower half of moulding box (drag); packs fine sand or loam around pattern face, fills box with coarser sand and compacts it using hand tools; turns drag over and dusts surface of sand with powder; fits and secures upper half of pattern to lower half; fixes frame of top half of moulding box (cope) to drag and repeats sand packing filling and ramming to complete mould; separates drag and cope and withdraws pattern; repairs damaged mould surfaces; cuts casting channels through sand or loam; dries mould halves and applies refractory bonding solution as required; fits cores in place to form hollow parts in casting; rejoins and secures drag and cope.

May (01) make cores (713.25)
(02) pour molten metal into moulds (713.62).

713.15 Pit moulder

Makes sand or loam moulds for large metal castings in a pit or brick casing in or on foundry floor

Prepares floor of casting pit with a layer of fine sand on bed of cinders or coke, with vents to allow escape of gases; positions pattern in pit; rams and levels sand or loam around pattern, reinforcing with metal and brick as necessary; positions and clamps moulding frame (cope) over pit; fills frame with sand or loam and consolidates by ramming; removes filled cope and withdraws pattern from pit; repairs damaged mould surfaces; cuts casting channels through sand or loam in the cope; dries mould halves and applies refractory bonding solution as required; fits cores in place to form hollow parts in casting; replaces cope over pit and secures with clamps and weights.

May (01) carry out 'sweep' moulding by revolving a template (strickle) on central spindle to form circular mould
(02) make cores (713.25).

713.20 Plate moulder

Makes sand or loam moulds for metal castings in mould box using plate patterns

Sets lower half of mould box over plate pattern; brushes surface of pattern with powder; packs fine sand or loam around pattern face and rams into place; fills box with sand and levels off top; removes completed half mould from pattern; repeats process for other half of mould, using reverse side of pattern or separate pattern; dries mould halves and applies refractory bonding solution as required; fits cores in place to form hollow parts in casting; joins and secures mould halves together.

May (01) pour molten metal into moulds (713.62).

Other titles include Plate pattern moulder.

713 .25 Coremaker (hand)

Makes sand or loam cores used in moulds to form hollow parts of metal castings

Cleans shaped moulding surface of core box with brush, scraper or compressed air; dusts moulding surface with powder to assist removal of finished core; fills core box with sand mixture, and rams and levels mixture using hand and power tools; inserts metal wires, rods and strips for reinforcement as required; pierces holes in sand to allow escape of gases; removes core for baking in drying oven or hardens core in box by injecting carbon dioxide into sand or, if using resin-bonded sand, by heating box to fuse the sand mixture.

May (01) prepare sand mixture

(02) make symmetrical cores in halves and join parts using adhesive

(03) coat cores with a refractory solution before baking

(04) operate core-blowing machine to inject sand into core box under pressure.

713 .30 White metaller

Lines bearings with white metal by hand or machine

Heats white metal in pot over furnace; cleans inside of bearing with cleaning fluid or by applying heat to remove old metal or grease; brushes on tinning fluid and applies heat to assist fluid to adhere to metal; sets component in jig and inserts mandrel as a core in centre of bearing; heats bearing and mandrel with oxy-acetylene torch to reach required temperature; pours molten white metal between mandrel and bearing; leaves to cool, lifts out mandrel and removes bearing from jig.

If using rotary lining machine, sets machine to receive cold bearing for trial run to determine centre of bearing; marks centre, removes bearing and places in tin bath for preheating and lining with white metal; adjusts machine to allow for expansion due to heating; removes bearing from tin bath by overhead crane and lines outside edges with asbestos strips and appropriate chemical solution to prevent leakage of white metal between bearing and end plates of machine; places bearing in machine between end plates; starts machine rotating for set period to spread lining evenly and to ensure solidification.

May (01) shot blast cast iron bearings and tin them by immersion in a tinning pot using the direct chloride process

(02) prepare worn bearings for repair using hand and machine tools.

Other titles include Babbitter.

713 .35 Teemer (steel making)

Pours molten steel produced in steel making furnace into moulds to form ingots

Ensures that stoppers are correctly set in hot metal ladles prior to tapping of furnace; checks that required number and type of ingot moulds are correctly prepared and positioned; directs crane driver transferring ladle of molten steel from furnace in positioning ladle over first mould; operates hand lever to release ladle stopper and pour molten steel into mould; operates lever to replace stopper when mould is filled; repeats process for other moulds; when slag begins to run from ladle, signals crane driver to tip slag from ladle into slag tub or pit.

May (01) pour metal into central funnel or trumpet which then fills surrounding moulds from the base through radiating refractory pipes (uphill teeming)

(02) clean and repair ladles (719 .50).

Other titles include Ladleman-teemer, Senior pitman.

713 .50 Shell moulder, Shell coremaker

Operates machine to make moulds or cores for metal castings by coating heated metal plate patterns with resin-bonded sand

Fixes required pattern on base plate of machine; heats pattern in oven attached to machine or by heating element under hinged lid of machine; operates lever to tilt plate and heated pattern, and clamps them over bin containing resin-bonded sand; inverts bin, plate and pattern to deposit sand on pattern, to which a layer of sand adheres; returns bin and plate to original position and releases plate; bakes sand shell formed on pattern in machine oven or by switching on heating element in machine lid; operates pedal to remove finished mould or core from pattern; repeats operation for other half of mould or core; fits cores in place in mould as required; applies adhesive to mould halves and operates press or vacuum pump to join halves together.

May (01) pour molten metal into moulds (713 .62)

(02) pour sand on pattern using hand scoop.

713 .52 Machine moulder

Operates moulding machine using plate patterns to make sand moulds for metal castings

Fixes on machine bed a metal plate to which required pattern is attached; positions and fixes moulding frame over pattern; fills moulding frame with sand; starts machine which consolidates sand by a jolting and/or squeezing action; inverts mould and withdraws pattern or operates controls of machine to lift mould from pattern; coats mould with refractory bonding solution as necessary; repeats process for other half of pattern; secures two halves of mould together.

May (01) operate a sand slinging machine to propel sand into moulding frame under pressure

(02) insert cores in moulds.

Excluded are Shell moulders (713 .50)

713 .54 Moulder and coremaker (plaster cast process) (foundry)

Makes plaster moulds and cores in sections for metal castings

Strips, cleans and lubricates core boxes and patterns; reassembles in correct sequence, positioning chills, risers, vents and reinforcing grids as necessary; mixes plaster material and weighs out water according to specification; mixes plaster and water to the correct consistency; operates vacuum equipment to remove excess air; pours plaster mix into pattern or core box at appropriate rate to ensure even distribution; scrapes off excess plaster; removes and cleans plaster moulds when set.

Other titles include Plaster cast process operator.

See Plaster mould maker (621 .04)

713 .56 Assembler and caster (plaster cast process) (foundry)

Assembles plaster mould sections to form complete moulds and pours in metal to form castings

Cleans mould sections; assembles mould sections in iron die casing and positions steel inserts; attaches rubber vacuum and air pressure pipes to special attachments on casing; assembles runner and riser cups using sealing compounds as specified; closes moulds using guide pins and dowels; pours molten metal by hand ladle into die casing and operates vacuum or air pressure controls.

Other titles include Plaster cast process operator.

713 .58 Pig casting machine operator

Operates or assists in the operation of a machine to cast blocks of metal from pig iron produced in blast furnace

Performs a combination of the following tasks: positions empty wagon at output end of machine; pulls lever to pour molten iron from ladle into trough of machine; skims slag from surface of ladle during pouring; presses button to start conveyor belt carrying moulds; empties lime into water in container on machine and operates pump to spray lime solution on to moving moulds; operates lever to regulate flow of molten iron into moulds; turns on water supply to spray moulds and cool the cast metal; ensures that the cast metal falls from moulds into wagon at end of conveyor; cleans trough and moulds after casting operation; renews and changes trough and moulds as required.

Other titles include Lime man, Pourer, Troughman.

713 .60 Casting bay helper (steel making)

Assists teemer to cast molten metal into ingots

Performs a combination of the following tasks: prepares ingot moulds to receive molten metal; prepares pans or ladles to receive slag; assists teemer to release ladle stopper; adds de-oxidising agents or alloys to mould during pouring; clears cooling metal from ladle nozzle during pouring using oxygen lance; skims slag from metal in moulds after teeming; plays water jets on moulds after teeming to assist in cooling; sets and secures mould covers in place; cleans up spillages; strips ingot from moulds after cooling; cleans out moulds; cleans and repairs ladles; otherwise assists teemer as required.

Other titles include Ingot stripper, Pitman, Slagger.

713 .62 Caster (foundry)

Pours molten metal into moulds to form metal castings

Positions, or directs positioning of ladle, crucible or pot containing molten metal over mould; skims slag or dross off surface of metal; tilts ladle or crucible, opens spout or stopper or operates pump to pour metal into mould.

Other titles include Lead caster, Pourer.

713.64 Casting machine operator

Operates casting machine to pour molten metal into moulds or die to form ingots, slabs, bars, rods, billets or tubes

If operating machine equipped with moulds, sprays moulds with solution to prevent metal from sticking; turns on water cooling system; starts machine to pour molten metal from holding furnace into water-cooled moulds on conveyor belts; regulates speed of conveyor to ensure that metal has set before falling from mould at end of conveyor.

If operating machine equipped with die, starts machine to pour metal from holding furnace into water-cooled die; ensures that metal is being drawn from die at correct speed and adjusts speed of machine as required; adjusts water controls as necessary.

Excluded are Pig casting machine operators (713.58)

713.66 Centrifugal caster

Operates centrifugal casting machine to form hollow cylindrical metal products

Positions die ring on lower table or plate of machine; cleans inside of die ring with wire brush and compressed air line; inserts cores as necessary and places top cover on die ring using hoist; sprays inside surfaces with insulation powder so that molten metal will not fuse to die; places guard in position and starts machine to rotate die; pours molten metal through hole in top cover using hand ladle; allows die to spin until metal has set; removes guard, unfastens top cover and removes castings using tongs or hoist.

713.68 Gravity die caster

Pours molten metal into dies by hand to form metal castings

Heats die using gas jets; cleans die using compressed air line and coats with refractory compound to prevent sticking; sprays moving parts with graphite oil solution; inserts sand cores as required; closes die and adjusts clamps; scoops molten metal from furnace using hand ladle and pours into die; regulates rate of pouring to ensure that metal is filling die correctly; when metal has solidified, opens die and removes casting using tongs; checks casting for defects.

May (01) tend furnace in which metal is melted.

713.70 Pressure die caster

Operates machine to form metal castings by injecting molten metal under pressure into dies

Heats die using gas jets; cleans die using compressed air line and coats with refractory compound to prevent sticking; sprays moving parts with graphite oil solution; scoops molten metal from furnace with hand ladle and pours into machine or operates machine controls to transfer metal from furnace to machine; operates plunger or piston mechanism to inject metal under pressure into die cavity; removes casting, which is ejected from machine automatically, using tongs; checks casting for defects.

May (01) tend furnace in which metal is melted.

713.72 Investment casting operator

Prepares wax patterns and/or builds ceramic shells around patterns and/or melts wax from shells in the making of moulds for metal castings

Performs one or more of the following tasks: operates machine which forces wax into metal die; assembles small wax parts to make complete pattern; coats wax pattern with refractory material to form surface of mould; builds shell round wax pattern by dipping in container of refractory slurry till required thickness of shell is obtained; places mould in autoclave, hot immersion bath or furnace to melt out wax.

May (01) pour molten metal into mould to form casting.

Other titles include Ceramic shell builder, Investment process worker, Mould dewaxing operator, Mould maker, Precision casting operative, Primary coating operator, Wax injection operator.

713.90 Leader (abrasive wheel)

Pours molten lead into centres of abrasive wheels to form bushes

Melts lead in pot; lays wheel flat on cast iron plate on floor or fixed on bench; screws leading pin into hole in centre of plate; centres wheel over leading pin so that pin protrudes through exact centre of wheel; covers space between pin and circumference of centre hole with a metal disc; fills hand ladle with molten lead and pours through slot in metal disc until area around leading pin is filled; presses a metal sleeve on to circle of lead after metal disc has been removed, and spreads lead to adhere to the sides of the centre hole; removes sleeve, unscrews leading pin and lifts wheel off plate; trims rough edges of lead bush using scrapers and files.

May (01) undertake surface grinding of abrasive wheel.

Other titles include Lead busher.

713.92 Core making machine operator

Operates machine to make sand cores used in moulds to form hollow parts of metal castings

If working on core-blowing machine, cleans plate pattern and fits on machine; positions core box on pattern plate; loads prepared sands into machine hopper; operates machine to blow and ram sand into core box; removes filled core box from machine; removes core from box and places on plate for transfer to drying oven.
If working on core-extruding machine, fits appropriate die on machine; loads prepared sands into machine hopper; operates machine to extrude sand to form cores of uniform cross section.

Other titles include Core blower, Core shooter, Coremaker.

713.98 Trainee

Performs, under instruction or guidance, various tasks including training exercises and as appropriate pursues studies in order to acquire the basic skills and knowledge required to perform the tasks of moulders, coremakers and casters (metal processing).

713.99 Other moulders, coremakers and casters (metal processing)

Workers in this group make moulds and cores for metal castings, pour molten metal into moulds and dies, and are not elsewhere classified, for example:

(01) **Bedstead caster (brass, iron)**; (02) **Moulding machine men (lead)** (tend automatic machines which fill moulds with molten lead); (03) **Type casters** (set and operate machines to cast printing type); (04) **Wheelmen (copper refining)** (cast copper bars, billets or cakes by operating turn-table to carry moulds under pouring ladle).

Unit Group 714 Forging Occupations

Workers in this unit group shape heated metal to requirements by hammering, bending, pressing and stamping.

Included are Taggers working on hot or cold metal.

Excluded are metal plate working occupations (773)

714.05 Drop forger

Operates or directs the operation of a power press or drop hammer to shape heated metal to requirements between closed dies

Fixes dies on press or hammer; supervises the heating of metal to be forged in furnace; positions or directs positioning of heated metal on lower die; operates or directs the operation of controls to start press or hammer; supervises the removal of scale from metal and repositioning of workpiece between strokes; removes or directs removal of forging from press or hammer.

Other titles include Drop hammer smith, Slot drop stamper, Press stamper.

714.10 Forge hammerman

Operates or directs the operation of power hammer to shape heated metal to requirements

Supervises the heating of metal in furnace; positions or directs positioning of heated metal on anvil; operates or directs operation of controls to start hammer; supervises the removal of scale from metal and manipulation of metal on anvil between blows; holds special forming tools against workpiece to shape and cut metal as required; removes or directs removal of forging from anvil.

May (01) perform any of the tasks of FORGING ASSISTANT (POWER HAMMER TEAM) (714.55).

Additional factor: weight of hammer to which accustomed.

714.15 Forge pressman

Operates or directs the operation of a forging press to shape heated metal ingots to requirements between a ram and anvil

Supervises heating of ingot in furnace; directs positioning of heated ingot on anvil; operates or directs operation of controls to start press; supervises the removal of scale from ingot and manipulation of metal on anvil between strokes; holds wedge-shaped steel bars (vee blocks) or cutting tools against ingot during forging to cut and shape metal; removes or directs removal of forging from anvil.

May (01) perform any of the tasks of FORGING ASSISTANT (HEAVY PRESS TEAM) (714.60).

714.20 Blacksmith (general)

Makes and/or repairs various types of metal articles or components by heating and hammering or bending to shape mainly by hand forging methods

Ascertains job requirements from drawings or others specifications; heats or supervises the heating of metal in fire or furnace; positions heated metal on anvil, former or other working surface; bends and shapes metal to requirements using hammers, punches, drifts, setts and other hand tools, or manipulates metal while assistant performs hammering operations; checks accuracy of forging visually and using measuring instruments; hardens and tempers finished articles, as required, by heating and quenching in oil or water.

May (01) cut metal to rough shape prior to forging
(02) shape parts of articles using power hammer or press
(03) assemble metal parts and join together by welding, bolting or riveting.

714.25 Smith (specialised) (excluding farrier)

Makes and/or repairs a limited range of metal articles or components by heating and hammering or bending to shape mainly by hand forging methods

Performs tasks as described under BLACKSMITH (GENERAL) (714.20) but specialises in a particular range of metal articles or components and is usually known accordingly, for example, Angle iron smith, Hand forger (cutlery).

Other titles include Agricultural implement smith, Anchor smith, Chain repairer, Ornamental iron smith, Shackle smith, Spring fitter, Spring smith (laminated, leaf spring).

714.30 Farrier

Forges iron or steel horse shoes and fits iron, steel or aluminium shoes on horses

Examines horses' hooves and removes worn or damaged shoes; cleans and trims hooves using rasps and croppers (pincers); heats iron or steel bars, bends and hammers to shape to fit hooves and pierces nail holes or selects ready-made aluminium shoes and bends to fit hooves; fits shoes to hooves and hammers into place using special nails.

May (01) travel to race meetings to replace shoes as required.

Other titles include Shoeing smith.

714.35 Forger (hand tool, edge tool)

Makes hand or edge tools by hand forging or using power forging hammers and presses

Heats metal to be forged in furnace; removes heated metal from furnace using tongs and positions on anvil; manipulates metal on anvil, bending and shaping to requirements using hand tools and/or power hammer or press; reheats metal during forging as required; finishes forging with hand tools.

May (01) cut metal blanks to rough shape prior to forging
(02) shape parts of tools by passing through forging rollers
(03) grind or polish edges of tools (726)
(04) fit handles on tools.

Other titles include Brace bit maker, Pick maker, Scythe maker, Spade and shovel maker.

714.50 Forging assistant (drop forging team)

Assists, under the direction of drop forger, in the operation of a power press or drop hammer to shape heated metal to requirements between closed dies

Performs a combination of the following tasks: assists in fixing dies in position on press or hammer; oils dies to prevent forging from sticking; heats metal to be forged in furnace; conveys heated metal to press or hammer, using tongs; positions heated metal on lower die as directed; operates controls to start press or hammer as directed; removes scale from metal between strokes; repositions workpiece on lower die between strokes; removes forging from press or hammer as directed; operates trimming or clipping press to remove excess metal from forging; otherwise assists drop forger as required.

Other titles include Clipping press operator, Drop hammer driver, Stamper's helper, Stripper, Trimming press operator.

714 .55 Forging assistant (power hammer team)

Assists, under the direction of forge hammerman, in the operation of a power hammer to shape heated metal to requirements

Performs a combination of the following tasks: heats metal to be forged in furnace; conveys heated metal to hammer using tongs or slings; positions heated metal on anvil; operates controls to start hammer as directed; removes scale from metal between blows; manipulates metal on anvil between blows using tongs or steel bars, or levers suspended from chains; holds special forming tools against metal during forging as directed; removes forging from anvil as directed; otherwise assists hammerman as required.

Other titles include Leverman, Power hammer driver.

Excluded are Manipulator drivers (942 .25)

714 .60 Forging assistant (heavy press team)

Assists, under the direction of forge pressman, in the operation of a forging press to shape heated metal ingots to requirements between a ram and anvil

Performs a combination of the following tasks: positions heated ingot on anvil using chain slings; operates controls to start press as directed; removes scale from ingot between strokes; manipulates ingot on anvil between strokes using steel bars or levers suspended from chains; holds wedge-shaped steel bars (vee blocks) or cutting tools against ingot during forging, as directed, to cut and shape metal; removes forging from anvil as directed; otherwise assists forge pressman as required.

Other titles include Leverman, Press driver.

Excluded are Manipulator drivers (942 .25)

714 .65 Smith's striker

Assists blacksmith (general), farrier or smith (specialised) to make and/or repair metal articles or components by hand forging

Performs a combination of the following tasks: tends forge fire or furnace; heats metal to be forged in furnace; removes heated metal from furnace using tongs or lifting gear; positions metal on anvil, former or other working surface; holds metal in position while smith or farrier bends or hammers to shape; hammers or bends metal to shape as directed; temoves finished forging using tongs or lifting gear; otherwise assists smith or farrier as required.

May (01) shape parts of articles using power hammer or press

(02) tend annealing furnace.

Other titles include Angle iron smith's helper, Anchor striker, Smith's helper, Spring viceman (leaf, laminated springs).

714 .70 Forging machine operator

Operates forging machine equipped with press or roller dies to shape heated metal to requirements

Transfers heated metal from furnace to machine using tongs; positions metal on machine; starts machine and guides metal into rollers or between dies at required angle; re-inserts metal between rollers or further dies until required shape is obtained.

714 .75 Bending press operator (hot work)

Operates bending press or machine to shape heated metal to requirements

Heats metal in furnace; removes heated metal from furnace and feeds into press or machine; operates machine to bend metal to requirements; removes finished part or article from press or machine.

May (01) set forming tools in press or machine.

Other titles include Bending machine operator (hot work).

See Roller bending machine operators (712 .99) for workers operating roller bending machines to curve hot or cold metal plates and Bending machine operator (729 .20) for workers operating bending or rolling machines to shape cold sheet metal. See also Frame bender (ship construction) (729 .18)

714 .98 Trainee

Performs, under instruction or guidance, various tasks including training exercises and as appropriate pursues studies in order to acquire the basic skills and knowledge required to perform the tasks of workers in forging occupations.

714 .99 Other forging occupations

Workers in this group shape heated metal to requirements by hammering, bending, pressing and stamping and are not elsewhere classified, for example:

(01) **Chain makers (hand forging)**; (02) **Cutters-out (cutlery)** (operate machines to cut out final shape of knife blades after forging); (03) **Shinglers (wrought iron manufacture)** (manipulate balls of wrought iron under hammer until slag is hammered out and ball is shaped into bloom ready for rolling); (04) **Stavers (tube manufacture)** (operate staving machines to compress ends of tubes prior to drawing); (05) **Taggers (tube manufacture)** (forge 'stems' or 'tags' on the end of tubes prior to drawing).

Unit Group 715 Metal Plating and Coating Occupations

Workers in this unit group coat parts, articles and stock with metal and other materials by electro- and vacuum deposition and by dipping in and spraying with molten metal, spray plastic powder and ceramic insulating material on metal parts and articles and treat metal parts, articles and stock electrolytically and with chemical solutions to produce particular surface finishes and form metal articles by depositing metal on formers electrolytically.

See 813 and 814 for sprayers and dippers of paint and similar materials.

715.05 Electroplater (hand)

Coats metal articles or parts electrolytically in tanks or vats with chromium, copper, nickel or other non-ferrous metals

Cleans articles or parts loaded on jig or rack by immersing in cleaning and rinsing tanks or vats; masks areas not to be plated using wax, wax copper foil or resistant adhesive tape; attaches jig or rack to rod above tank and immerses articles or parts to be plated in solution; suspends piece of plating metal in solution in plating tank to act as anode and switches on current if not using tank containing fixed anodes with electric current flowing through continuously; examines articles or parts at intervals to check progress of plating; checks instruments and adjusts current flow as necessary; adds solution to tank or vat as required; removes articles or parts from tank or vat when required thickness of metal has been deposited; rinses articles or parts in cold water and dries off.

May (01) prepare plating solutions

(02) calculate current and immersion time according to size of articles, type of plating solution and thickness of deposit required

(03) build up worn parts or protect wearing surfaces of engineering components by depositing a thick layer of chromium (hard chrome surface plating)

(04) perform tasks of ANODISER (715.99)

(05) perform tasks of BRONZER (715.99)

(06) perform tasks of OXIDISER (715.99).

Other titles include Cadmium plater, Chromium plater, Copper plater, Gold plater, Nickel plater, Silver plater.

715.10 Electroformer

Forms metal articles by depositing metal electrolytically on preshaped formers

Examines former (master) for flaws and cleans with methylated spirits; if master is of a non-conducting material, coats with silver nitrate; treats metallic master with separating medium, such as potassium dichromate, if high degree of surface finish is required; places plastic shields or frames around master to obtain even deposition of metal; prepares electrolytic solution according to laboratory specifications and fills tank with solution; attaches master by connecting wire to a rod above the tank and immerses master in solution; sets controls to regulate rate of deposition and switches on current; at specified times, checks progress of forming, records thickness of deposit, tops up tank with distilled water, checks acidity and makes any necessary adjustments; removes article when forming process is complete and withdraws former.

715.15 Operator (electrolytic tinning line) (steel strip)

Controls the operation of a continuous plant to coat steel strip with tin electrolytically

Ascertains job requirements from specifications; directs the setting up of coils of steel strip on machine; sets, or directs the setting of, machine controls according to size and gauge of strip and thickness of coating required; directs setting of automatic shears as required; ensures that cleaning, pickling, plating and chemical treatment solutions are at correct strength, temperatures and levels; controls the speed of strip through plant; adjusts controls to regulate flow of electric current through plating solutions; checks gauges and fault-detecting instruments to ensure that plating is proceeding correctly; directs the clearing of faults and the repair of breakages in strip.

715.20 Tinner (hot dip)

Coats metal articles by dipping in molten tin

Checks levels of cleansing solution, flux and molten metal in cleaning, fluxing and tinning baths and replenishes as required; loads small articles into basket; immerses articles in chemical solution to clean surfaces using tongs or lifting equipment; removes and drains off excess solution; immerses articles in flux bath to protect surface from oxidation and facilitate coating; removes and drains off excess flux; immerses articles in vat of molten tin; removes from vat after specified time; places articles in centrifuge and operates machine to remove excess tin or, if tinning tubes, draws fibre mop along outside and through insides of tubes to remove excess tin; immerses coated articles in quenching bath; checks gauges to ensure that molten tin is kept at required temperature; removes dross from bottom of tinning vat at regular intervals.

Other titles include Tube tinner.

715.25 Hot dip operator (continuous tinning plant)

Operates continuous plant to coat metal sheets, strip or wire by dipping in molten tin

If coating sheets, loads supply of sheets on hydraulic platform and operates controls to raise platform to correct level for feeding into machine; if coating strip or wire, mounts coil of strip or wire on machine, using lifting equipment as required, threads ends of strip or wire through plant and secures to re-coiling mechanism; starts machine to feed sheets, strip or wire through cleaning and rinsing baths, tinning pot and drying chamber; replenishes supply of tin, acids, flux, etc to plant as required; checks progress of coating and adjusts controls as necessary.

Other titles include Wire tinner.

715.30 Flame plating equipment operator

Sets up and operates detonation gun or plasma flame plating equipment to deposit a coating of hard wearing and abrasive-resistant material on workpieces such as tools or machine parts

Ascertains job requirements from drawings and other specifications; determines, from standard charts, amount of coating and time required for different materials and, if operating detonation gun equipment, type of gas to be used (oxygen, acetylene, nitrogen); masks areas of workpiece not requiring coating; secures workpiece in holding fixture on equipment if using plasma plating torch, or in soundproof chamber if using detonation gun; loads appropriate coating material (oxides, carbides, alloys, refractories, pure metals, in powder form) into equipment; sets controls to regulate temperature, gas flow and pressure; operates controls to melt powder particles and force melted powder at extremely high speed on to surface of workpiece to produce required coating.

715.35 Mirror silverer (excluding vacuum metallisation)

Coats flat glass with silver nitrate, copper and paint to form mirror

Cleans surface of glass with chemical solution and water; coats glass surface to be silvered with stannous chloride by hand or machine; places glass on sloping frame in spraying booth; fills spray gun with silver nitrate solution and sprays coating on glass; washes off surplus solution with distilled water; sprays coating of copper on silvering or immerses glass in bath of copper sulphate where a layer of copper is deposited electrolytically; dries coated glass; sprays on coating of paint with spray gun or by passing through spraying machine; when backing paint has dried, cleans backing solutions and paint from edges of mirror; strips off backing on old mirrors with paint remover and chemical solution before resilvering.

May (01) prepare chemical solutions

(02) apply further backing of lead foil as protection against condensation.

715.50 Optical silverer (excluding vacuum metallisation)

Coats backs of optical elements such as mirrors, flats, prisms with silver nitrate, aluminium or other metal

Brushes masking paint on glass surfaces not to be silvered and cleans other surfaces; immerses items for coating alternately in baths of distilled water and silvering solutions until desired thickness of coating is obtained; immerses coated items in bath of copper sulphate where a layer of copper is deposited electrolytically on silvering; brushes varnish and a final coat of paint over copper backing.

715 .55 Vacuum metallisation plant operator

Operates high vacuum equipment to deposit a coating of metal on articles of metal, glass or other material

Cleans surface of article(s) to be coated; loads article(s) on jig as required; positions article(s) on base of vacuum chamber; fixes coiled heating filament in chamber and hangs strip of coating metal such as aluminium, gold, copper or zinc on coils; connects filament to electricity terminals; closes door of vacuum chamber or lowers cover on to base; operates controls to create vacuum in chamber; switches on electricity to filament, causing coating metal to turn to vapour which condenses on article(s); removes coated article(s) from chamber.

Additional factor: type of articles to which accustomed, eg optical elements, lamp reflectors, costume jewellery.

Other titles include Illuminiser.

715 .60 Hot dip assistant (continuous tinning plant)

Assists, under the direction of hot dip operator, in the operation of a continuous plant to coat metal sheets, strip or wire by dipping in molten tin

Performs a combination of the following tasks: assists in feeding sheets, strip or wire into or through plant; collects supplies of solutions from stores; replenishes water tanks; stacks scrap material for removal; unloads coated sheets, strip or wire from plant; keeps work area clean and tidy; otherwise assists operator as required.

715 .65 Galvanizer (hot dip)

Coats metal articles, fabrications, sheets, strip or wire by dipping in molten zinc

Performs a combination of the following tasks: attaches metal articles, baskets of articles, fabrications or sheets to lifting equipment, loads coils of strip or wire on to spindles or feeds sheets to plant manually; if coating strip or wire, feeds ends through cleaning, fluxing and coating baths and attaches to re-coiling mechanism; operates or directs operation of lifting equipment to immerse articles, fabrications or sheets in cleaning, fluxing and coating baths, or starts re-coiling mechanism or rollers to take strip, wire or sheets through plant; skims off scum formed by flux on surface of molten zinc in coating bath; adjusts heating controls to regulate temperature of molten zinc; adds flux, chemical solutions and fresh zinc ingots to baths as required; removes excess zinc from coated articles by tapping with ladles or by spinning in centrifuge; cools coated articles by immersing in quenching tank; removes dross from bottom of zinc bath at regular intervals.

715 .70 Galvanizer (continuous electrolytic plant)

Operates continuous plant to coat metal sheets, strip or wire with zinc electrolytically

Directs loading of metal sheets or coils of strip or wire on to machine; threads ends of strip of wire through plant and fixes to re-coiling mechanism; starts machine to feed sheets, strip or wire through cleaning, electro-galvanizing and rinsing baths; adjusts controls to regulate temperatures of solutions, immersion times and flow of electric current through galvanizing bath; checks levels of solutions in baths and replenishes as required; replaces worn zinc anodes; operates automatic welding equipment to join beginning of new coil to strip or wire on machine; examines sheets, strip or wire visually to ensure that coating is proceeding correctly; directs removal of coated sheets, strip or wire from machine.

Other titles include Cell minder (wire galvanizing).

715 .75 Electrolytic tinning line assistant

Assists, under the direction of operator, in the operation of a continuous plant to coat steel strip with tin electrolytically

Performs a combination of the following tasks: loads coil of strip on mandrel at feed end of line; cuts off length from beginning of coil to remove faulty areas; adjusts guides and gauges according to size and thickness of strip; sets up instruments to detect faults; controls speed of feed end of line as directed to ensure that there is sufficient strip in looping pit to allow feed end of line to be stopped whilst end of strip in plant is joined to beginning of new coil without stopping coating operation; operates automatic welding equipment to join new coil to strip in plant; removes used anodes when instruments indicate replacement is required or as directed by operator; fixes new anodes in place; replenishes solutions in tanks as directed; assists in clearing faults and repairing breakages in strip; collects and stocks scrap metal cut from strip; removes coils of plated strip from re-coiling mechanism at output end of line; otherwise assists as required.

Other titles include Anode attendant, Electrolyte attendant, Feeder.

715.80 Electroplating machine operator

Operates a machine or plant to coat metal articles or parts electrolytically with tin, zinc, chromium or other non-ferrous metals

Fixes rack of articles or parts on machine or puts articles or parts in plating barrel; fixes barrel on hoist if plant is not automatic; switches on water supply and current to machine or plant; operates switches to take articles or parts on rack or in rotating barrel through cleaning, plating and rinsing tanks or operates electric hoist to immerse barrel in various tanks in turn.

May (01) prepare solutions.

Other titles include Barrel plater, Electroplater.

715.85 Metal sprayer

Sprays molten metal on metal parts or articles to form a protective coating or to build up worn or damaged surfaces

Masks areas of part or article not requiring coating; fixes appropriate nozzle on spray gun; inserts powder or wire of zinc, aluminium, copper, bronze or other coating metal in gun; connects feed pipes from gun to gas and air cylinders and turns on supply; ignites gas and air mixture in gun to melt metal powder or wire; admits jet of compressed air to gun to force molten metal from nozzle in spray form; directs spray on to part or article ensuring that coating is applied evenly; checks thickness of coating with measuring instruments.

May (01) prepare surfaces for coating by shot blasting
(02) rotate parts or articles on lathe and spray with gun fixed on mobile trolley
(03) use spray gun in which wire or powder is melted by electric arc
(04) use blow torch to deposit layer of stellite on articles and be known as Stellite depositor.

Excluded are Flame plating equipment operators (715.30)

715.98 Trainee

Performs, under instruction or guidance, various tasks including training exercises and as appropriate pursues studies in order to acquire the basic skills and knowledge required to perform the tasks of workers in metal plating and coating occupations.

715.99 Other metal plating and coating occupations

Workers in this group coat parts, articles and stock with metal, treat metal parts, articles and stock electrolytically and with chemical solutions to produce particular surface finishes and are not elsewhere classified, for example:

(01) **Anodisers** (treat aluminium and aluminium alloys electrolytically to produce oxidised finish); (02) **Bronzers** (dip metal articles in chemical solutions to produce a bronze finish); (03) **Ceramic insulation spraying equipment attendants** (attend equipment which sprays ceramic insulating materials on metal core plates for electrical equipment); (04) **Electroless nickel platers** (coat metal articles or stock by hot dipping in nickel solution); (05) **Oxidisers** (treat metal articles in acid baths to produce oxidised finish); (06) **Phosphaters** (immerse metal articles in phosphating solutions to provide corrosion-resistant finish and to increase wear resistance); (07) **Plastic coating operators** (apply protective coating to pipes and other metal articles by heating then fusing on plastic powder by means of vacuum deposition, spraying or immersion); (08) **Wire platers (excluding galvanizing or tinning)**.

Unit Group 716 Metal Annealing and Tempering Occupations

Workers in this unit group heat treat metal stock and articles to relieve stresses, restore ductility, reduce brittleness, harden throughout and harden outer surfaces.

716.10 Heat treatment operator (general)

Performs any combination of the heat treatment processes of annealing, tempering and hardening

Performs tasks as described under ANNEALER (716.20), HARDENER (716.30) and TEMPERER (716.40) as appropriate.

716.20 Annealer

Heats metal stock or articles to a given temperature and cools them at a predetermined rate to relieve internal stresses and restore ductility

Ascertain, from job instructions and charts, temperature and heating time required; sets equipment controls for required temperature and period of heating and if appropriate sets speed of conveyor or rollers; turns on fuel supply to equipment and lights or adjusts burners, or switches on electric current.
If annealing metal stock or articles other than steel sheet or strip or tinplate, loads stock or articles into equipment or on to mandrel, conveyor or rollers using tongs or lifting equipment; if appropriate, feeds end of wire through equipment and quenching bath and attaches to re-coiling mechanism; if heating in controlled atmosphere, operates controls to admit supply of gas such as split ammonia gas; during heating, checks temperatures, gas flow, pressures, etc and adjusts controls as necessary; after specified time removes metal or articles and allows to cool in atmosphere, or cools by degrees in furnace or oven.
If annealing steel sheet or strip or tinplate, loads or directs loading of coils or sheets on to annealing base; lowers or directs lowering of furnace on to base; fixes furnace covers and seals covers and base with sand; regulates fuel supply to furnace and lights burners; operates valves to inject nitrogen or inert gas into furnace; sets and adjusts heating controls; after heating, removes or directs removal of furnace; lowers or directs lowering of cooling chamber on to base and seals covers and base with sand; regulates flow of air to cooling chamber; removes or directs removal of coils or sheets after required period of cooling.

May (01) heat metal or articles in sealed furnace container from which the air is drawn by vacuum pump

(02) perform tasks of HARDENER (716.30) and/or TEMPERER (716.40).

Other titles include Heat treatment operator, Normaliser.

716.30 Hardener

Hardens steel articles by heating to a given temperature and cooling in air or quenching

Ascertains, from job instructions and charts, temperature and heating time required; sets equipment controls for required temperature and period of heating and if appropriate sets speed of conveyor or rollers; turns on fuel supply to equipment and lights or adjusts burners, or switches on electric current; places salts or lead in bath in furnace, as required, and heats to melting temperature; loads articles into equipment or on to conveyor or rollers using tongs or lifting equipment; during heating, checks temperatures, pressures, etc and adjusts controls as necessary; after specified time removes articles and cools in blast of air or quenches in water, oil or brine.

May (01) harden small articles or parts of articles using oxy-acetylene flame from blow torch

(02) perform tasks of ANNEALER (716.20) and/or TEMPERER (716.40).

Other titles include Flame hardener, Heat treatment operator, Induction hardener.

716.40 Temperer

Reheats hardened steel articles to a given temperature and cools in air or quenches to reduce brittleness and relieve stresses caused by hardening

Ascertains, from job instructions and charts, temperature (lower than that required for hardening) and heating time required; sets equipment controls for required temperature and period of heating and if appropriate sets speed of conveyor or rollers; turns on fuel supply to equipment and lights or adjusts burners, or switches on electric current; places sodium nitrate in bath in furnace as required and heats to melting temperature; loads articles into equipment or on to conveyor or rollers using tongs or lifting equipment; during heating, checks temperatures, pressures, etc and adjusts controls as necessary; after specified time removes articles and cools in atmosphere or quenches in water, oil or brine.

May (01) perform tasks of ANNEALER (716.20) and/or HARDENER (716.30).

Other titles include Heat treatment operator.

716 .50 Case hardener

Hardens outer surfaces of steel articles by heating and chemically treating in a furnace or retort and cooling in air or quenching

(01) **Case hardener (carbonising)**

Packs steel articles into a box containing carbonaceous substances such as charcoal granules or bones and loads box into furnace; sets furnace controls for required temperature and period of heating; after specified time removes box from furnace; removes articles from box and quenches in water, brine, oil or other medium.

Other titles include Carboniser.

(02) **Case hardener (cyanide hardening)**

Prepares bath of potassium or sodium cyanide in pot furnace; immerses steel articles in cyanide bath using tongs or wire basket; sets furnace controls for required temperature and period of heating; after specified time removes articles from furnace and quenches in water, brine, oil or other medium.

Other titles include Cyanide hardener.

(03) **Case hardener (nitriding)**

Places steel articles in wire basket and places basket in retort; sets controls for required temperature and period of heating; regulates flow of ammonia gas into retort; after specified time, turns off heat, reduces flow of ammonia gas and allows articles to cool.

Other titles include Nitrider.

716 .98 Trainee

Performs, under instruction or guidance, various tasks including training exercises and as appropriate pursues studies in order to acquire the basic skills and knowledge required to perform the tasks of workers in metal annealing and tempering occupations.

716 .99 Other metal annealing and tempering occupations

Workers in this group heat treat metal stock and articles and are not elsewhere classified.

Unit Group 719 Metal Processing, Forming and Treating Occupations Not Elsewhere Classified

Workers in this unit group operate plant to sinter ores, operate hot and cold presses in the manufacture of sintered components, clean metal stock and articles before and after processing and perform other miscellaneous tasks in metal processing, forming and treating and are not elsewhere classified.

719 .10 Continuous cleaning plant operator

Operates continuous plant to remove dirt, scale and other surface impurities from metal strip by immersion in chemical solutions

Loads or directs loading of coil of metal strip on machine and ensures that end is correctly fed through plant and attached to re-coiling mechanism; sets controls to regulate running speed of line, flow of hot water and air in rinsing and drying processes and to heat washing tanks to required temperature; ensures that chemical solutions in washing tanks are maintained at required levels; starts machine to take strip through various washing, rinsing and drying processes; if working on electrolytic line, controls flow of electric current through strip to remove oxidation deposit; adjusts speed of drag rolls to maintain correct winding tension.

Other titles include Descaling operator.

719 .50 Ladleman

Cleans and repairs ladles into which molten metal is poured from furnaces

Removes stoppers from empty ladle after teeming; cleans inlet nozzles; cleans slag and other waste material from ladle; inserts new stoppers and fits firmly in place; patches lining of ladle with fireclay mix; otherwise ensures that ladle is ready for next tapping.

719 .60 Hot press operator (sintered components)

Operates electrically heated press to compact and sinter metal powder to form blocks, pellets or component blanks

Weighs out required amount of prepared metal powder; packs powder into graphite mould or die; places mould or die in press; packs insulating material around mould or die as required; operates press to obtain required pressure and current to compact and sinter powder to shape of mould or die; removes mould or die from press on completion of process; cuts or breaks mould or die when cool and removes block, pellet or component blank.

See Roaster (not elsewhere classified) (591 .56) and Press operator (ceramics) (621 .58)

719 .80 Cold press operator (sintered components)

Operates press to compact metal powder to form briquettes, pellets or component blanks prior to heating in sintering furnace

Weighs out required amount of prepared metal powder; packs powder into mould or die lined with steel or carbide; positions mould or die on bed of press; operates press to compact powder to shape of mould; removes shaped briquette, pellet or component blank and places on tray.

See Roaster (591 .56) and Press operator (ceramics) (621 .58)

719 .81 Sinter plant worker (metal processing)

Operates or assists in the operation of plant to fuse metal ores, coke and other materials to form sinter for charging to iron or zinc blast furnaces or zinc vertical retorts

(01) **Sinter machine operator**
Regulates speed of grid conveyor (strand) which carries ore and coke under or over furnace or under ignition hood of heating unit; operates controls to adjust temperature of furnace or hood; regulates supply of coke to strand; ensures that sinter contains correct amount of moisture and operates controls to add water as required; directs feeding to sinter plant of raw materials such as metal ores, scrap metal, limestone and flue dust.

(02) **Sinter plant assistant**
Lights coke, oil or gas-fired furnace or hood of heating unit; operates plant to cool sinter coming from strand; operates valves to feed water, as required, to sinter after cooling to maintain moisture content; clears blockages in feed chutes to strand and in cooling plant.

See Heat Treating Occupations Not Elsewhere Classified (591)

Excluded are Press operators (sintered components) (719 .60 and 719 .80)

719 .82 Continuous cleaning plant assistant

Assists, under the direction of cleaning plant operator, in the operation of continuous plant to remove dirt, scale and other surface impurities from metal strip by immersion in chemical solutions

Performs a combination of the following tasks: loads coil of metal strip on machine; feeds end of strip through plant; attaches end of strip to re-coiling mechanism; controls speed of feed end of line to ensure that sufficient strip is in looping pit to allow feed end of line to be stopped whilst end of strip in plant is joined to beginning of new coil without stopping cleaning operation; operates automatic welding equipment to join new coil to strip in plant; removes coils of cleaned strip from plant; stacks waste material for removal; otherwise assists operator as required.

Other titles include Assistant operator, Feeder.

719 .83 Pickler (excluding continuous cleaning plant)

Removes dirt, scale or other surface impurities from metal parts, articles or stock by immersing in chemical solutions

Loads parts, articles or metal into tank of chemical solutions, using lifting equipment as required; removes after specified time and rinses off acid by immersing in water or by spraying or hosing with water; immerses in further chemical solutions as required; dries parts, articles or stock over hot air grid or in drying oven.

May (01) prepare chemical solutions to specifications.

Other titles include Degreaser.

719 .84 Labourer (blast furnace)

Performs manual tasks in blast furnace area and assists blast furnace crew generally

Performs a combination of the following tasks: refills sand and clay boxes and stacks boxes on furnace deck, using overhead crane as required; fetches oxygen lance from stores; removes scrap and generally keeps furnace area clean; assists in cleaning runners on completion of tapping; assists in rebuilding sand dams blocking various branches of runners; cleans furnace tools and ensures they are ready for use; otherwise assists blast furnace crew as required.

719 .85 Labourer (steel, non-ferrous metal manufacture)

Assists furnace or teeming crew generally in the manufacture of steel or of non-ferrous metals or alloys

Performs a combination of the following tasks: assists in charging of furnaces; weighs manganese or other additives and conveys to furnace area; sprays moulds and pallets on which moulds stand with liquid lime to prevent hot metal sticking; adds chemicals to metal in moulds during teeming, as directed; assists in stripping ingots, etc from moulds after cooling; cleans moulds after use; assists in cleaning pouring ladles; keeps furnace area or casting bay clean; otherwise assists furnace or teeming crew as required.

719 .86 Rolling mill labourer

Performs manual tasks in rolling mill area and assists rolling mill team generally

Performs a combination of the following tasks: removes scrap metal from mill stands; inserts lengths of scrap metal between hot bars, blooms, billets, etc on cooling banks to prevent distortion and removes scrap metal after cooling; cleans scale from shears, rolls and water channels; removes scale and scrap metal from work area; assists in cleaning and changing rolls; keeps work area clean and tidy; otherwise assists rolling mill team as required.

Other titles include Scrapman.

719 .87 Production helper (metal tube manufacture)

Assists metal tube making operators generally

Performs a combination of the following tasks: assists in setting up mandrels, dies, etc on tube making plant such as piercing and extrusion presses and draw benches; assists in loading metal billets or partly formed tubes on presses and draw benches; operates saws, shears or other equipment to cut tubes to length; operates equipment to spray canvas with tar and wind tarred canvas around tubes; cleans machinery and equipment; removes scale from tubes; keeps work area clean and tidy; otherwise assists tube making operators as required.

Other titles include Production labourer.

719 .88 Foundry labourer

Assists moulders, coremakers or casters generally

Performs a combination of the following tasks: operates sand mixing or sand slinging machine; supplies moulders with sand and/or molten metal; charges core stove; assists in pouring molten metal into moulds; removes castings from moulds, using overhead crane as required; conveys castings to dressers, etc; keeps work areas clean; otherwise assists moulders, coremakers or casters as required.

Other titles include Core stove attendant, Sand mixer.

719 .89 Labourer (galvanizing, tinning)

Assists galvanizer or tinner generally

Performs a combination of the following tasks: dries articles in drying machine after coating; loads wire for galvanizing on coil holder (swift); feeds end of wire through galvanizing plant; attaches end of wire to re-coiling mechanism; feeds sheets for coating on to conveyor at intake end of plant; takes coated sheets from conveyor at discharge end of plant and stacks for removal; otherwise assists galvanizer or tinner as required.

Other titles include Blockman (galvanizing), Block minder (galvanizing), Swiftman (galvanizing), Swift minder (galvanizing).

719.98 Trainee

Performs, under instruction or guidance, various tasks including training exercises and as appropriate pursues studies in order to acquire the basic skills and knowledge required to perform the tasks of workers in metal processing, forming and treating occupations not elsewhere classified.

719.99 Other metal processing, forming and treating occupations not elsewhere classified

Workers in this group perform miscellaneous tasks in metal processing, forming and treating and are not separately classified, for example:

(01) **Cutters (nut, bolt, rivet making)** (heat metal bars in furnaces and operate machines equipped with dies to cut nut, bolt or rivet blanks from heated bars); (02) **Doggers** (attach metal tubes to grips on trolleys (dogs) prior to cold drawing); (03) **Labourers (wrought iron manufacture)** (perform manual tasks in furnace areas and assist furnace crews generally); (04) **Operators (continuous cleaning and annealing plant)**; (05) **Operators (continuous normalising, shot blasting and pickling plant)**; (06) **Setters (continuous casting machines)**; (07) **Stampers (metal manufacture)** (stamp cast numbers on ingots, blooms, billets, plates, etc using metal stamps and hammers); (08) **Straighteners' helpers** (assist roller straighteners generally); (09) **Wirers-up,** Jig loaders, Jiggers (attach or wire articles to be plated or heat treated to jigs or metal bars).

Minor Group 72 MACHINING AND RELATED OCCUPATIONS (ENGINEERING AND METAL GOODS MAKING)

Workers in this minor group set up, operate and tend press, machine tool and other metal working machines to cut, shape, abrade, polish and finish metal workpieces, and perform closely related tasks.

The occupations are arranged in the following unit groups:

720 Foremen (Machining and Related Occupations (Engineering and Metal Goods Making))

721 Press, Machine Tool and Other Metal Working Machine Setters

722 Machine Tool Setter-Operators (Metal Working)

723 Machine Tool Operators (Metal Working)

724 Press and Stamping Machine Operators (Metal Working)

725 Automatic Machine Attendants (Metal Working)

726 Fettling, Grinding (Excluding Machine Tool) and Polishing Occupations (Metal)

729 Machining and Related Occupations (Engineering and Metal Goods Making) Not Elsewhere Classified

Excluded are Forging Occupations (714), Sheet Metal Working Occupations (*772*)

Unit Group 720 Foremen (Machining and Related Occupations (Engineering and Metal Goods Making))

Workers in this unit group directly supervise and co-ordinate the activities of workers in machining and related occupations in engineering and metal goods making.

720.10 Foreman (machine shop)

Directly supervises and co-ordinates the activities of machine tool setters, setter-operators and operators

Performs appropriate tasks as described under SUPERVISOR/FOREMAN (UNSPECIFIED) (990.00).

Additional factor: number of workers supervised.

720.20 Foreman (press shop)

Directly supervises and co-ordinates the activities of press tool setters and press and stamping machine operators

Performs appropriate tasks as described under SUPERVISOR/FOREMAN (UNSPECIFIED) (990.00).

Additional factor: number of workers supervised.

720.30 Foreman (automatic machine attendants) (metal working)

Directly supervises and co-ordinates the activities of automatic metal working machine attendants

Performs appropriate tasks as described under SUPERVISOR/FOREMAN (UNSPECIFIED) (990.00).

Additional factor: number of workers supervised.

720.40 Foreman (fettlers, grinders (excluding machine tool) and polishers)

Directly supervises and co-ordinates the activities of fettlers, grinders (excluding machine tool) and polishers

Performs appropriate tasks as described under SUPERVISOR/FOREMAN (UNSPECIFIED) (990.00).

Additional factor: number of workers supervised.

720.98 Trainee

Performs, under instruction or guidance, various tasks including training exercises and as appropriate pursues studies in order to acquire the basic skills and knowledge required to perform the tasks of foremen (machining and related occupations (engineering and metal goods making)).

720.99 Other foremen (machining and related occupations (engineering and metal goods making))

Workers in this group directly supervise and co-ordinate the activities of workers in machining and related occupations in engineering and metal goods making and are not elsewhere classified.

Unit Group 721 Press, Machine Tool and Other Metal Working Machine Setters

Workers in this unit group set up press and machine tools and metal working machines operated and attended by other workers to cut, shape and otherwise form metal workpieces.

721.10 Machine tool setter (excluding electrochemical machine tools)

Sets up one or more types of machine tools, such as lathes, milling, boring, drilling and grinding machines operated or attended by other workers

Ascertains job requirements from drawings and/or other specifications; determines sequence and method of required operations; selects and fixes appropriate cutting or grinding tools; positions and secures test workpiece on machine; sets machine controls for rotation speeds, depth of stroke and cut, etc and adjusts machine table, stops and guides; makes measurements during setting as required, using precision and other measuring instruments; operates machine to check accuracy of setting and adjusts as necessary; changes tools and resets machine as necessary during production runs.

May (01) design cams for automatic machine tools (253.28).

Additional factor: type(s) of machine to which accustomed.

Other titles include Broaching machine setter, Capstan setter.

721.20 Electrochemical machine tool setter

Sets up machine tools which shape workpieces by electrolytic erosion and are operated or attended by other workers

Ascertains job requirements from drawings and/or other specifications; determines sequences of operations; selects and fixes purpose-made electrode tool in ram of machine; positions and secures test workpiece in machine; sets machine controls for depth of cut, duration of eroding action, amperage, voltage, pressure and flow of electrolyte; closes leak-proof cover and operates machine from control console to check accuracy of setting; adjusts settings as necessary; resets machine as necessary during production runs.

721.30 Press tool setter

Sets up hand or power presses operated or attended by other workers

Ascertains job requirements from drawings and/or other specifications; calculates length of ram stroke and pressures involved; positions and fixes press tools and dies on press; positions and secures test workpiece on press; sets machine controls for length of stroke and adjusts machine table, stops and guides; operates press to check accuracy of setting and adjusts as necessary; changes press tools and dies and resets machine as necessary during production runs.

May (01) operate press for production run (724.50).

Additional factors: type(s) and size of press(es) to which accustomed.

Other titles include Die setter, Hand (fly) press setter, Power press setter.

721.40 Tool presetter

Positions and loads cutting tools into detached tool-holders or magazines for use in a numerically controlled machine tool

Sets tools in position in tool-holders in accordance with tooling plan, programmed instruction sketches or similar data using either presetting fixtures such as cross-slides and turret to reproduce machine tool features, or a simulator machine with a workpiece master to control and verify the settings; collects auxiliary tooling (for example, chuck-jaws, collet-packs, work-holding fixtures, locators) punched tape and setting and fixing data in respect of machining program; places preset tools, fixing equipment, tape and job information on trolley for delivery to machine operator; adjusts settings on machine tool as necessary; dismantles tools after machining program has been completed.

May (01) manually cycle the machine tool to check tool clearances

(02) carry out trial run without workpiece then repeat operation with master of workpiece in the machine

(03) machine first workpiece

(04) preprogramme interchangeable plug-boards

(05) pre-assemble fixtures

(06) use optical device to assist in aligning tool in holder.

721.50 Tackler (wire weaving)

Sets up one or more wire weaving looms

Sets up warp beam in wire weaving loom(s); adjusts loom mechanisms to obtain required weave; adjusts loom settings as necessary during weaving; removes empty beams from loom on completion of weaving.

May (01) perform tasks of BEAMER (729.60)

(02) perform tasks of AUTOMATIC MACHINE ATTENDANT (WIRE WEAVING) (725.10)

(03) supervise a number of automatic machine attendants (wire weaving).

Other titles include Overlooker, Tenter.

721.98 Trainee

Performs, under instruction or guidance, various tasks including training exercises and as appropriate pursues studies in order to acquire the basic skills and knowledge required to perform the tasks of press, machine tool and other metal working machine setters.

721.99 Other press, machine tool and metal working machine setters

Workers in this group set up press and machine tools and metal working machines operated and attended by other workers to cut, shape and otherwise form metal workpieces and are not elsewhere classified, for example:

(01) **Setters (automatic latch needle making machines)**; (02) **Setters (file cutting machines)**.

Unit Group 722 Machine Tool Setter-Operators (Metal Working)

Workers in this unit group set up and operate machine tools to cut, shape and otherwise form metal workpieces.

See 799 .06 for workers who set and operate both metal working and woodworking machine tools.

722 .02 Machine tool setter-operator (general)

Sets up and operates two or more types of machine tools such as lathes, milling machines, boring machines, grinding machines and drilling machines or a machining centre to cut, grind or otherwise shape workpieces

Ascertains job requirements from drawings and/or other specifications; determines sequence and method of required operations; selects and fixes appropriate cutting or grinding tools; positions and secures workpiece on machine using jigs, shims, bolts, clamps and other positioning aids and fixing devices; sets machine controls for rotation speed, depth of stroke and cut, etc and adjusts machine table, stops and guides; operates automatic or manual control to feed cutting or grinding tool to workpiece or workpiece to cutting or grinding tool; checks accuracy of machining using measuring instruments; repositions workpiece, changes tools and resets machine as necessary. Performs these tasks in relation to the setting up and operating of two or more types of machine tool or a machining centre.

May (01) mark off workpiece prior to machining
(02) sharpen cutting tools
(03) set up and operate numerically controlled machine tools (722 .36).

Additional factor: types of machine to which accustomed.

722 .04 Centre lathe turner

Sets up and operates centre lathe to shape or otherwise machine workpieces

Performs appropriate tasks as described under MACHINE TOOL SETTER-OPERATOR (GENERAL) (722 .02) but in relation to the setting up and operating of centre lathes.

May (01) mark off workpiece prior to machining
(02) copy a machined workpiece or model using tracer attachment
(03) specialise on particular type of centre lathe such as standard, sliding-bed or hollow-spindle
(04) sharpen cutting tools
(05) set up and operate numerically controlled centre lathe (722 .36).

Other titles include Axle turner, Centre lathe setter-operator, Crankshaft turner, Tool turner, Tool room turner.

Excluded are Roll turners (722 .08)

722 .06 Setter-operator (capstan, turret lathe)

Sets up and operates capstan or turret lathe to shape or otherwise machine workpieces

Performs appropriate tasks as described under MACHINE TOOL SETTER-OPERATOR (GENERAL) (722 .02) but in relation to the setting up and operating of capstan or turret lathes.

May (01) mark off workpiece prior to machining
(02) copy a machined workpiece or model using tracer attachment
(03) sharpen cutting tools
(04) set up and operate a numerically controlled capstan or turret lathe (722 .36).

722 .08 Roll turner

Sets up and operates roll turning lathe to shape metal rolls

Performs appropriate tasks as described under MACHINE TOOL SETTER-OPERATOR (GENERAL) (722 .02) but in relation to the setting up and operating of roll turning lathes.

Other titles include Setter-operator (roll turning lathe).

722.10 Drilling machine setter-operator

Sets up and operates drilling machine to drill, ream, tap, countersink or counterbore holes in a workpiece

Performs appropriate tasks as described under MACHINE TOOL SETTER-OPERATOR (GENERAL) (722.02) but in relation to the setting up and operating of drilling machines.

May (01) mark off workpiece prior to machining
(02) sharpen drills or other cutting tools
(03) specialise in a particular type of drilling machine such as single spindle or radial arm and be known accordingly
(04) harden and temper workpiece after machining
(05) set up and operate a numerically controlled drilling machine (722.36).

Other titles include Multi-spindle driller, Radial arm driller, Scissors borer and hardener, Vertical driller.

Excluded are Circle, faller or hackle drillers (722.38)

722.12 Boring machine setter-operator

Sets up and operates boring machine to make, align or enlarge cylindrical holes in workpieces by means of a rotating cutting tool or fixed tool and rotating table

Performs appropriate tasks as described under MACHINE TOOL SETTER-OPERATOR (GENERAL) (722.02) but in relation to the setting up and operating of boring machines.

May (01) sharpen cutting tools
(02) set up and operate a numerically controlled boring machine (722.36).

Other titles include Horizontal borer, Universal borer, Vertical borer.

Excluded are Jig borers (722.14)

722.14 Jig borer

Sets up and operates a jig boring machine to drill and bore holes in workpieces to extra fine limits of accuracy

Ascertains job requirements from drawings and/or other specifications; determines sequence and method of operations; positions and secures workpiece on machine table and verifies exactness of positioning by means of dial indicators or gauges; turns hand-wheels to position spindle-head in relation to workpiece and verifies accuracy of positioning using built-in instruments such as micrometer heads or locating microscopes; selects and fixes appropriate cutting tool; sets machine controls for cutting and rotation speeds and depth of cut; operates manual controls to lower cutting tool into workpiece; starts machine to rotate cutting tool and perform required boring operation; checks accuracy of machining using measuring instruments; repositions workpiece, change tools and resets machine as necessary.

May (01) make cutting tools
(02) set up and operate a numerically controlled jig boring machine (722.36).

Additional factor: experience of circular dividing table or tilting rotary table.

722.16 Milling machine setter-operator

Sets up and operates milling machine to machine workpieces by means of one or more multi-toothed rotary cutting tools

Performs appropriate tasks as described under MACHINE TOOL SETTER-OPERATOR (GENERAL) (722.02) but in relation to the setting up and operating of milling machines; in addition, fits dividing head on machine if work is to be machined with a specified angle between faces or grooves.

May (01) mark off workpiece prior to machining
(02) perform other machining operations such as drilling and boring, using appropriate cutting tools fixed on milling machine
(03) copy a machined workpiece or model using tracer attachment
(04) sharpen cutting tools
(05) set up and operate a numerically controlled milling machine (722.36).

Other titles include Horizontal miller, Plain miller, Plano-miller, Universal miller, Vertical miller.

Excluded are Gear cutting machine setter-operators (722.28)

722.18 Grinding machine setter-operator

Sets up and operates grinding machine to shape or otherwise machine the surfaces of workpieces by means of a rotating grinding wheel

Performs appropriate tasks as described under MACHINE TOOL SETTER-OPERATOR (GENERAL) (722.02) but in relation to the setting up and operating of grinding machines; in addition, trues cutting surface of grinding wheel using diamond studded block or preset dressing device; in centreless grinding, operates control to rotate workpiece between grinding wheel and regulating wheel.

May (01) copy a machined workpiece or model using tracer attachment
(02) specialise in particular type of grinding such as gear, thread, plunge or crush grinding
(03) set up and operate a numerically controlled grinding machine (722.36).

Other titles include Camshaft grinder, Crankshaft grinder, Cylindrical grinder, External grinder Internal grinder, Plain grinder, Precision grinder, Rotary grinder, Surface grinder, Tool and cutter grinder, Tool room grinder, Universal grinder.

Excluded are Roll grinders (722.20)

722.20 Roll grinder

Sets up and operates roll grinding machine to grind metal rolls to required size and standard of finish

Performs appropriate tasks as described under MACHINE TOOL SETTER-OPERATOR (GENERAL) (722.02) but in relation to the setting up and operating of roll grinding machines.

Other titles include Roll grinding machine setter-operator.

722.22 Setter-operator (lapping, honing machine)

Sets up and operates lapping or honing machine to machine workpiece surfaces to fine limits of finish

Performs appropriate tasks as described under MACHINE TOOL SETTER-OPERATOR (GENERAL) (722.02) but in relation to the setting up and operating of lapping or honing machines; in addition, applies abrasive compound to workpiece or tool as required.

May (01) set up and operate a numerically controlled lapping or honing machine (722.36).

722.24 Planing machine setter-operator

Sets up and operates planing machine to plane or groove workpiece surfaces by reciprocating workpiece against a cutting tool

Performs appropriate tasks as described under MACHINE TOOL SETTER-OPERATOR (GENERAL) (722.02) but in relation to the setting up and operating of planing machines on which the workpiece reciprocates under the cutting tool.

May (01) mark off workpiece prior to machining
(02) sharpen cutting tools
(03) set up and operate a numerically controlled planing machine (722.36).

Excluded are Plano-mill setter-operators (722.16)

722.26 Setter-operator (shaping, slotting, broaching machine)

Sets up and operates a shaping, slotting or broaching machine to plane, shape, slot or groove workpieces by means of a reciprocating cutting tool

Performs appropriate tasks as described under MACHINE TOOL SETTER-OPERATOR (GENERAL) (722.02) but in relation to the setting up and operating of shaping, slotting or broaching machines in which the cutting tool reciprocates against the workpiece.

May (01) mark off workpiece prior to machining
(02) sharpen cutting tools
(03) set up and operate a numerically controlled shaping, slotting or broaching machine (722.36).

722.28 Gear cutting machine setter-operator

Sets up and operates gear cutting machine to cut gear teeth by means of rotary or reciprocating cutting tools

Performs appropriate tasks as described under MACHINE TOOL SETTER-OPERATOR (GENERAL) (722.02) but in relation to the setting up and operating of gear cutting machines.

May (01) sharpen cutting tools
(02) specialise in cutting a particular type of gear such as spline, spiral, hypoid, worm, angle or helical
(03) set up and operate a numerically controlled gear cutting machine (722.36).

Other titles include Hobbing machinist.

722.30 Die-sinking machine setter-operator

Sets up and operates a die-sinking machine to shape workpieces by means of rotary cutting tools guided by a linked tracer head

Ascertains job requirements from drawings and/or other specifications; determines sequence and method of required operations; positions and secures workpiece and model or template on machine; selects cutting tool and tracer point and positions and secures in appropriate spindles; sets machine controls for cutting speed, tool feed and tool pressure; operates manual controls to position tracer point over model or template and linked cutting tool over workpiece; starts machine and operates automatic or manual controls to guide tracer point over model or template while the linked cutting tool shapes workpiece to exact contours followed by tracer point; checks accuracy of machining using measuring instruments; changes tools and resets machine as necessary.

May (01) mark off workpiece prior to machining
(02) sharpen cutting tools.

722.32 Spark erosion machine setter-operator

Sets up and operates machine to shape metal workpieces by means of electrical spark erosion

Ascertains job requirements from drawings and/or other specifications; mounts appropriate electrode die tool(s) on travelling carriage; positions and secures workpiece on machine table; positions tool using mechanical and/or optical measuring aids to line up tool-head on locating point marked on workpiece; sets controls to regulate depth of tool penetration and speed of cut; secures front panel of work tank or raises retractable tank to enclose machine table, workpiece and electrode die tool; switches on pump to circulate dielectric fluid through work tank and sets rate of flow; operates machine controls to start electrical discharge of sparks from electrode die to workpiece, eroding metal to shape workpiece to required form; adjusts controls as necessary during machining; checks workpiece for accuracy of machining using measuring instruments.

May (01) specialise in machining particular components such as dies or gears.

722.34 Metal spinner, Flow turning machine operator

Shapes metal discs or plates over formers on spinning lathe or flow turning machine to make hollow components or articles

Ascertains job requirements from drawings and/or other specifications; on plug-board controlled machine, inserts plugs in accordance with program on punched card; fixes former and if appropriate forming roller on machine; secures metal disc or plate in position against former; operates machine controls to rotate metal at required speed and if appropriate to start forming roller; applies pressure with blunt hand tools or operates roller controls as required to bend metal around shape of former; removes rough edges from finished article with hand files; checks accuracy of work using measuring instruments.

May (01) cut out discs from sheet metal with cutting machine
(02) make formers.

Other titles include Aluminium spinner, Spinner (precious metals).

722.36 Numerically controlled machine tool operator

Sets up and operates a machine tool controlled by plug-board, console switches or tape to mill, drill, grind, bore or otherwise shape metal workpieces automatically

Ascertains job requirements from programmer's written instructions; selects appropriate cutting tools or receives tools preset and arranged in sequence; positions and secures workpiece on machine table, using jigs, bolts and clamps; presets machining sequence by inserting plugs in plug-board or by setting console switches, or loads preset plug-board or inserts prepared tape in machine; fixes preset tools in position on machine or sets tools on machine spindle or on tooling stations; sets machine controls for cutting speed, depth of cut, etc; sets starting co-ordinates on control console and starts operation of machine to complete machining automatically or until a stop-point, indicating a tool change, is reached.

May (01) set up and operate a variety of numerically controlled machine tools
(02) operate console manually for "one-off" jobs
(03) read engineering drawings
(04) sharpen cutting tools
(05) prepare programs (259.20).

722.38 Driller (**circle, faller, hackle**)

Sets up drilling machine and drills holes in circles, fallers or hackles used in fibre preparing machines

Positions circle, faller or hackle on machine; fits appropriate drill or cutter on machine; adjusts machine settings to drill holes at required intervals; starts machine which performs drilling automatically; makes own drills and cutters.

722.98 Trainee

Performs, under instruction or guidance, various tasks including training exercises and as appropriate pursues studies in order to acquire the basic skills and knowledge required to perform the tasks of machine tool setter-operators (metal working).

722.99 Other machine tool setter-operators (**metal working**)

Workers in this group set up and operate machine tools to cut, shape and otherwise form metal workpieces and are not elsewhere classified, for example:

(01) **Routing machine setter-operators**; (02) **Key makers** (**machine**).

Unit Group 723 Machine Tool Operators (Metal Working)

Workers in this unit group operate previously set up machine tools to cut, shape and otherwise machine metal workpieces.

723.10 Machine tool operator (**general**)

Operates two or more types of previously set up machine tools such as lathes, drilling, grinding, boring, milling, planing, honing, and lapping machines

Secures workpiece in chuck, fixture or on machine table according to type of machine and machining process; starts machine to rotate or reciprocate cutting tool or workpiece; operates automatic or manual controls to feed tool to workpiece or workpiece to tool; on multi-tool machines such as turret or capstan lathes brings cutting tools into use in specified sequence; repositions workpiece during machining as required; checks workpiece for accuracy of machining using measuring instruments. Performs these tasks in relation to the operation of two or more types of machine tool.

May (01) change cutting tools according to setter's instructions

(02) sharpen cutting tools.

Additional factor: types of machine to which accustomed.

723.20 Machine operator (**shaping, slotting, broaching machine**)

Operates previously set up machine tool to shape, slot or groove workpieces by means of reciprocating cutting tool

Performs appropriate tasks as described under MACHINE TOOL OPERATOR (GENERAL) (723.10) but in relation to the operating of shaping, slotting or broaching machines.

723.50 Semi-automatic lathe operator

Operates previously set up semi-automatic capstan or turret lathe to machine rotating workpieces

Performs appropriate tasks as described under MACHINE TOOL OPERATOR (GENERAL) (723.10) but in relation to the operating of semi-automatic capstan or turret lathes.

Other titles include Capstan lathe operator, Turret lathe operator.

723 .52 Drilling machine operator

Operates previously set up drilling machine to drill, ream, tap, countersink or counterbore holes in workpieces

Performs appropriate tasks as described under MACHINE TOOL OPERATOR (GENERAL) (723 .10) but in relation to the operating of drilling machines.

May (01) operate two or more drilling machines
(02) harden and temper workpiece after machining.

Other titles include Multi-spindle drilling machine operator, Scissors borer and hardener, Vertical drilling machine operator.

Excluded are Drillers (constructional metal work) (773 .14)

723 .54 Boring machine operator

Operates previously set up boring machine to make, align and enlarge cylindrical holes in workpieces

Performs appropriate tasks as described under MACHINE TOOL OPERATOR (GENERAL) (723 .10) but in relation to the operating of boring machines.

May (01) operate multi-spindle machine.

Other titles include Barrel rifler (small arms), Boring mill operator, Horizontal boring machine operator, Universal boring machine operator, Vertical boring machine operator.

723 .56 Milling machine operator

Operates previously set up milling machine to machine workpieces by means of multi-toothed rotary cutting tool

Performs appropriate tasks as described under MACHINE TOOL OPERATOR (GENERAL) (723 .10) but in relation to the operating of milling machines.

May (01) operate machine with two or more cutters (gang milling).

723 .58 Grinding machine operator

Operates previously set up machine to shape or otherwise machine surfaces of workpieces by means of a rotating grinding wheel

Performs appropriate tasks as described under MACHINE TOOL OPERATOR (GENERAL) (723 .10) but in relation to the operating of grinding machines; in addition, in centreless grinding, operates controls to rotate metal between grinding wheel and regulating wheel.

Other titles include Centreless grinding machine operator, Cutlery grinder, Edge tool grinder, File grinder, Saw grinder.

723 .60 Lapping machine operator, Honing machine operator

Operates previously set up lapping or honing machine to machine surfaces of workpieces to fine limits of finish

Performs appropriate tasks as described under MACHINE TOOL OPERATOR (GENERAL) (723 .10) but in relation to the operating of lapping or honing machines; in addition, applies abrasive compounds to workpiece or tool as required.

May (01) adjust lapping speed or tool pressure.

Other titles include Barrel lapper (small arms).

723 .62 Planing machine operator

Operates previously set up planing machine to plane or groove surfaces of workpiece by reciprocating workpiece against cutting tool

Performs appropriate tasks as described under MACHINE TOOL OPERATOR (GENERAL) (723 .10) but in relation to the operating of planing machines.

723 .64 Electrochemical machine operator

Operates previously set up machine to shape a workpiece to specification by electrolytic erosion

Checks preset machine settings on control console dials to verify that voltage, amperage, duration of eroding action, depth of cut and pressure of electrolyte relating to a specific job are as recorded by the setter in machine control book; opens transparent cover, secures workpiece in prepositioned locating fixture using clamps; closes cover and starts machine causing electrode tool to advance to workpiece or workpiece to tool; stops machine and advises setter if fault is indicated by warning light; when cutting process is completed, opens cover, releases clamps and withdraws workpiece.

Other titles include Anocut machine operator.

723 .98 Trainee

Performs, under instruction or guidance, various tasks including training exercises and as appropriate pursues studies in order to acquire the basic skills and knowledge required to perform the tasks of machine tool operators (metal working).

723 .99 Other machine tool operators (metal working)

Workers in this group operate previously set up machine tools to cut, shape and otherwise machine metal workpieces and are not elsewhere classified, for example:

(01) **Die piercers** (pierce composition dies on multi-spindle or ultrasonic drilling machines); (02) **Routing machine operators.**

Unit Group 724 Press and Stamping Machine Operators (Metal Working)

Workers in this unit group operate presses and drop hammers equipped with dies or formers to shape metal parts and articles and form hollow shapes and relief impressions in metal.

Excluded are Forging Occupations (714)

724 .10 Flat spring maker

Makes flat springs using hand or power press

Selects and fixes tools in hand or power press; cuts metal strip to required length on guillotine; positions metal on press bed; operates press by foot or hand control to form spring.

May (01) anneal, harden or temper finished springs (716)

(02) carry out finishing processes such as grinding or sanding.

724 .50 Hand press operator, Power press operator

Operates previously set up hand or power presses equipped with dies, formers or punches to shape or cut metal parts or articles

Loads metal stock on to press manually or using lifting gear; positions on press bed, or, if in wire or strip form, feeds through press; starts machine by hand, foot or automatic control to shape or cut workpiece to requirements; removes finished workpiece from press and checks visually or with measuring instruments.

May (01) assist setter in setting up press

(02) carry out minor repairs or adjustments to press.

Other titles include Corrugating press operator, Draw press operator, Fly press operator, Metal shoe tree maker, Pin flattener, Punching press operator.

See Press stamper (drop forging) (714 .05) and Automatic press machine attendant (725 .10)

724 .98 Trainee

Performs, under instruction or guidance, various tasks including training exercises and as appropriate pursues studies in order to acquire the basic skills and knowledge required to perform the tasks of press and stamping machine operators (metal working).

724 .99 Other press and stamping machine operators (metal working)

Workers in this group operate presses and drop hammers to shape metal parts and articles and form hollow shapes and relief impressions in metal and are not elsewhere classified, for example:

(01) **Drop stampers,** Cold stampers (set and operate drop hammers to form hollow shapes and relief impressions in cold metal between shaped dies); (02) **Press bending machine operators (metal plate)** (operate bending presses to curve metal plates to shape).

See 714 .05 for workers operating a drop hammer to shape heated metal.

Unit Group 725 Automatic Machine Attendants (Metal Working)

Workers in this unit group tend preset machines which automatically cut, shape, abrade and otherwise machine metal stock, components and articles.

725 .10 Automatic metal working machine attendant

Tends one or more preset machines which automatically cut, shape or otherwise machine metal stock, components or articles

Loads metal stock, components or articles on to, or into, machine manually or using lifting gear; secures in position as required; starts machine which carries out the required operations automatically; removes finished work.

May (01) feed metal stock, components or articles to machine manually during production run

(02) check accuracy of finished work visually or with measuring instruments.

Other titles include Automatic machine attendant (cold extrusion), Automatic machine attendant (fish hook making), Automatic machine attendant (miscellaneous metal goods), Automatic machine attendant (needle making), Automatic machine attendant (nut and bolt making), Automatic machine attendant (pin making), Automatic machine attendant (saw making), Automatic machine attendant (screw making), Automatic machine attendant (small link chain manufacture), Automatic machine attendant (spring making), Automatic machine attendant (tin box manufacture), Automatic machine attendant (wire weaving), Automatic machine minder (engineering), Automatic press machine attendant, Automatic stamping machine attendant.

725 .98 Trainee

Performs, under instruction or guidance, various tasks including training exercises and as appropriate pursues studies in order to acquire the basic skills and knowledge required to perform the tasks of automatic machine attendants (metal working).

725 .99 Other automatic machine attendants (metal working)

Workers in this group tend preset machines which automatically cut, shape, abrade and otherwise machine metal stock, components and articles and are not elsewhere classified, for example:

(01) **Automatic sandblasting machine attendants;** (02) **Automatic shot blasting machine attendants.**

Unit Group 726 Fettling, Grinding (Excluding Machine Tool) and Polishing Occupations (Metal)

Workers in this unit group smooth, polish and sharpen parts and articles of metal, and material worked as metal, by abrading processes, remove surface defects from metal during manufacture by chipping and grinding and remove surplus metal from castings, forgings and machined parts.

Excluded are Automatic Machine Attendants (725) and Wire finishing machinists (729.65)

726.05 Hand grinder

Shapes and/or sharpens and/or removes rough surfaces from metal workpieces by manipulation against grinding wheels or continuous abrasive belts

Applies abrasive compound to wheel or belt as required; sets wheel or belt in motion; manipulates workpiece against wheel or belt by hand or using holding device and applies pressure as necessary with free hand or using wooden lever; checks accuracy of finish visually and by touch.

May (01) use hand tools such as files
(02) sharpen cutlery by rubbing on close grained stones (whetting)
(03) rough or part polish surfaces after grinding (726.20)
(04) true and dress surface of grinding wheels using diamond tipped tools or other dressing devices
(05) fix grinding wheel or abrasive belt in position
(06) undertake machine grinding (723.58).

Additional factor: whether accustomed to working with wheel wet or dry.

Other titles include Cutlery grinder, Edge tool grinder, Scissors grinder, Serrater (cutlery), Swager (cutlery).

Excluded are Fettlers (726.90)

726.10 Card grinder (textile machinery)

Sharpens and levels wire teeth of card clothing for textile machinery using grinding machine(s)

Fixes card clothing over cylinder or on frame of grinding machine(s); adjusts machine control to set angle and pressure of grinding wheels, rollers or discs; starts machine(s) to sharpen and level points and smooth sides of card teeth; checks progress of grinding visually and with measuring instruments.

May (01) carry out minor maintenance of machine.

See Stripper and grinder (textile machinery) (749.25)

726.15 Mill setter-out (sawmilling)

Sharpens and/or shapes edges of cutting blades of woodcutting machines on automatic grinding machines or by manipulation against grindstones

If sharpening standard cutting blade, secures blade in position on automatic grinding machine; adjusts machine controls to set blade at correct angle; switches on machine which sharpens blade automatically.
If shaping and sharpening special purpose cutting blade, ascertains job requirements from drawings; selects appropriate standard blade; sets small grindstone in motion; manipulates blade against grindstone to shape to requirements; passes blade to woodcutting machinist to make trial cuts; continues grinding process as necessary until shape of blade meets specifications.

Excluded are Saw sharpeners (726.99)

726.20 Metal polisher (general)

Performs two or more polishing processes such as emery buffing, grease mopping, burnishing and scratchbrushing to impart a smooth, reflective or other specified finish to surfaces of parts or articles by manipulation against rotating polishing heads

Selects appropriate continuous abrasive band or polishing head, for example, wire brush, wheel or bob of felt, leather or fibre, or polishing mop of calico, cotton or chamois; positions and fixes polishing head on machine; sets controls to regulate speed and angle of polishing head and where appropriate feed rate of lubricant; dresses polishing head as required with abrasive or finishing material such as emery, grease or rouge; operates controls to rotate polishing head; manipulates workpiece against polishing head or applies polishing head and hand tools to rotating or fixed workpiece; applies further dressing compound during polishing as required.

May (01) make polishing heads.

Other titles include Jewellery polisher, Lapper (gold, silver), Polisher (gold, silver).

726 .25 Lithographic plate preparer

Prepares and grains lithographic plates prior to reproduction of printing image

Places plate on bench under polishing machine (levigator), covers with acetate solution and abrasive powder and operates machine to clean and polish plate; removes cleaned plate and places in graining machine; loads machine with glass, porcelain or steel marbles, water and abrasive; operates machine to grain surface of plate, repeating process with smaller marbles and finer abrasive until required finish is obtained; washes grained plate with water and dries off in oven; rinses plate in solution of nitric acid and alum and again dries off.

Other titles include Lithographic plate grainer.

726 .50 Metal polisher (specialised)

Carries out a single polishing process to impart a smooth, reflective or other specified finish to surfaces of parts or articles by manipulation against rotating polishing heads

Performs basic tasks as described under METAL POLISHER (GENERAL) (726 .20) but in relation to one polishing process.

(01) **Emery buffer**

Manipulates metal parts or articles against rotating wheels, bobs and/or continuous bands dressed with emery or similar abrasive to polish surface.

Other titles include Emery band polisher, Emery bobber, Emery glazer.

(02) **Grease mopper**

Manipulates metal parts or articles against rotating mops impregnated with a grease or similar finishing compound to polish surface.

(03) **Scratchbrusher**

Manipulates metal parts or articles against rotating wire brush to impart a rough polished or patterned surface.

(04) **Burnisher**

Applies felt bob dressed with abrasive compound and/or hand tools to metal workpiece mounted on lathe or fixed in holding device to impart a close-grained surface.

May (05) make polishing heads.

Other titles include Linisher, Mirror polisher (cutlery).

726 .55 Die polisher

Manipulates abrasive materials and tools against the interior surfaces of rotating dies to obtain specified final shape, size and reflective finish

Ascertains job requirements from drawings and/or other specifications; mounts die in chuck of lathe-type machine and starts machine to rotate chuck; applies industrial diamond, steel or diamond laps and ground needles to interior surface of die until semi-smooth finish is obtained; applies diamond abrasive paste to cloth over end of wooden dowel; inserts dowel into die and manipulates against interior surface to obtain mirror finish; checks die for accuracy of work with measuring instruments and/or from drawings using an optical enlarger to magnify die for comparison.

May (01) specialise in polishing particular types of dies, eg wire drawing dies, tube drawing dies.

726 .60 Barrel polishing machine operator

Operates machine which cleans and/or polishes small articles in a rotating barrel with abrasive materials and liquids or electrolytically

If polishing with abrasive materials and liquids, loads barrel with specified amount of abrasive materials such as steel balls, stone chips, aluminous oxide, sand or sawdust and liquids such as water or paraffin, or solutions of potassium cyanide or caustic soda; loads barrel with articles to be polished; sets timing controls and starts machine to rotate barrel; on completion of cleaning and/or polishing unloads metal articles, abrasive materials and liquids.
If polishing electrolytically, loads barrel with articles to be polished; sets timing controls and starts machine to lower barrel into tank of electrolyte and to rotate barrel; on completion of polishing, unloads articles from barrel.

See Drum operator (hides, skins, pelts) (531 .65) and Tumbler operator (ceramic components) (622 .65)

726 .65 Chipper (steel dressing), Grinder (steel dressing)

Operates chipping or grinding equipment to remove defects from steel bars, blooms, ingots, billets or slabs during manufacture

(01) **Chipper**

Gouges out deep depressions around defects in, and/or removes surplus metal from, steel bars, blooms, etc with chipping machine which has chisel shaped cutter or pneumatic hammer with chisel attachment.

(02) **Grinder**

Grinds shallow depressions around defects in steel bars, blooms, etc with portable hand grinder or suspended (swing) grinder; if fault is very deep, uses fixed plough grinder and smoothes edges of cut with hand grinder.

May (03) sharpen cutters.

726 .90 Fettler

Removes surplus metal and rough surfaces from castings, forgings or components with hand and power tools

Removes sand from castings using wire brush; files, chisels, grinds or burns off projections or ragged metal; smoothes rough surfaces with hand tools, abrasive wheels or belts.

May (01) remove surplus metal and rough surfaces by shot blasting (726 .92).

Other titles include Dresser (foundry), Fine fettler (metal machining), Machine shop fettler.

Excluded are Chippers (steel dressing) (726 .65)

726 .92 Shot blaster

Cleans and/or smoothes surface of metal workpieces or articles using a jet of vapour or compressed air and abrasive material

Charges blasting equipment with steel grit, shot or other abrasive material; positions workpiece or articles to be cleaned or smoothed in blasting cabinet or compartment; enters cabinet or compartment or places arms through openings in side of cabinet; directs jet of vapour or compressed air and abrasive material against workpiece or article, or manipulates workpiece or articles in jet until required surfaces are evenly abraded; examines finished work visually.

Additional factor: whether accustomed to working on site using portable equipment.

Other titles include Sandblaster, Vapour blasting machine operator.

See Sandblasting machine operator (glass decorating) (614 .91) and Sandblaster (pottery and porcelain) (622 .20)

726 .98 Trainee

Performs, under instruction or guidance, various tasks including training exercises and as appropriate pursues studies in order to acquire the basic skills and knowledge required to perform the tasks of workers in fettling, grinding (excluding machine tool) and polishing occupations (metal).

726 .99 Other fettling, grinding (excluding machine tool) and polishing occupations (metal)

Workers in this group smooth, polish and sharpen parts and articles of metal by abrading processes, remove surface defects from metal during manufacture by chipping and grinding and remove surplus metal from castings, forgings and machined parts and are not elsewhere classified, for example:

(01) **Compo men (metal bedsteads)** (polish brass tubes by machine); (02) **Engravers' polishers** (polish printing rollers from which engraved design has been removed); (03) **Kerners (type founding)** (trim type faced with overhanging letters); (04) **Needle grinders;** (05) **Polishers (needles, textile machinery pins),** Scourers (needles, textile machinery pins) (polish needles and textile machinery pins with abrasive materials between rollers or between reciprocating plates); (06) **Saw sharpeners** (operate machines to sharpen teeth of saw blades); (07) **Surgical needle polishers and finishers;** (08) **Tube and rod polishing machine operators;** (09) **Weld dressers** (smooth welding seams using portable buffs or grinders).

See 749 .10 for workers who repair and sharpen hand, band- or circular saws

Unit Group 729 Machining and Related Occupations (Engineering and Metal Goods Making) Not Elsewhere Classified

Workers in this unit group perform miscellaneous engineering and metal goods making machining and related tasks such as setting and operating machines to make small link chains, operating metal working machines other than press and machine tools, making cutting tips and dies from cemented carbide and are not elsewhere classified.

729 .02 Chain making machine setter-operator (small links)

Sets and operates a machine to cut, twist and link metal wire to form chains of small links

Secures holding devices and forming tools in machine and sets machine controls according to type and size of chain required; mounts coil of wire of appropriate type on holding device and threads into machine; starts machine and makes test length of chain; checks chain for tensile strength, weight, thickness and appearance; adjusts machine until chain of required standard is obtained; starts production run and adjusts controls during run as necessary; if using precious metals, records details of materials used in production and details of waste; makes own holding devices and forming tools; attends a number of machines during production run.

Other titles include Chain maker.

729 .04 Metal working machine operator

Operates metal working machines to drill, punch, bend, shape or form metal components or articles

Positions and secures appropriate jigs, holding fixtures and tools in machine; adjusts machine controls as necessary; secures workpiece on machine or feeds metal through machine guides; operates machine by manual or automatic controls, guiding tool or workpiece as required; removes finished workpiece from machine; checks accuracy of machining visually or with measuring instruments.

May (01) undertake minor maintenance of machine.

Other titles include Barbed wire maker, Cut nail feeder, Machine operator (needle making), Machine operator (nut and bolt making), Saw toothing machine operator, Wire mattress weaving machine operator.

Excluded are Machine Tool Operators (723), press tool operators (724) and Bevelling machinist (tubes, plates) (729 .92)

729 .06 Tip and die cutter (cemented carbide goods)

Cuts and shapes cemented carbide blanks to make cutting tips and dies for metal working machines

Ascertains job requirements from drawings or other specifications; selects appropriate cemented carbide blank; operates drills, grinders, abrasive wheels or other cutting tools to cut blank to shape; smoothes or shapes edges or surfaces of blank by manipulation against abrasive wheels or with grinding machine; checks accuracy of machining with measuring instruments.

729 .08 File cutter

Sets up and operates machine(s) to make metal files

Fits appropriate chisel cutter in machine; sets machine controls for depth of stroke and number of cuts; positions workpiece on machine bed; operates machine to cut file blank to requirements.

May (01) cut teeth missed on machine using hammer and chisel

(02) sharpen tools.

729 .10 Closing machine operator (wire ropes), Laying up machine operator (wire cable)

Sets up and operates machine to twist strands of wire rope or cable core together

Loads on to machine or directs the loading of bobbins of stranded wire and if appropriate wire rope core or cable filling material such as hemp, jute or plastic; fits appropriate forming heads, dies and rollers on machine; threads wire strands, core and filling material through machine and attaches to take-off reel or drum; sets controls to regulate speed of machine, angle of twist and tension of bobbins; operates machine to twist strands together; during operation checks work visually and, if working on wire rope, by feel; makes repairs to cable or rope as necessary; adjusts machine controls as necessary; unloads or directs the unloading of filled take-off reel or drum.

Other titles include Closer driver (wire ropes).

729.12 Wire heald maker

Operates one or more machines to make wire healds

Fits coil of wire on machine; threads wire through machine rollers; fills containers on machine with solder and soldering flux and lights gas jets; starts machine to cut, shape and solder wire to form healds; adjusts running speed of machine during operation as required; rinses formed healds in water and dries off in oven; polishes healds with steel wool; makes finished healds up into bundles.

729.14 Coiled spring maker

Makes coiled springs on hand formers, coiling lathes or machines

If working on hand formers, coiling lathes or semi-automatic machines, fits mandrel of appropriate size on former, lathe or machine; makes any necessary adjustments to machine settings; bends end of metal strip and pierces hole in end of strip as required on press; fits end of strip or wire on to mandrel or holds against mandrel with metal bar; winds strip or wire round mandrel by hand, turning hand wheel or by operating machine controls; cuts off surplus metal from coiled spring; grinds, hardens or polishes spring as required.

If working on automatic machine(s), fits forming tools in machine; sets running speed; guides end of metal strip or wire into machine; starts machine for trial run; adjusts settings as necessary.

May (01) cut metal strip to length before winding
(02) fit coiled spring in binding ring or case
(03) form springs throughout using hand tools.

Additional factor: number of automatic machines attended.

Other titles include Spring coiling machine operator.

729.16 Tube bender

Bends metal tubes to requirements on bending press or machine or against pegs set in special table or template

Fixes forming tools in press or machine, or positions pegs in holes on table or template according to bend required; heats or supervises heating of tube in furnace or oven prior to bending, as required; positions or directs positioning of tube on table or template against pegs, fixing one end in place with clamps and placing steel ropes attached to powered winch or capstan round the other end, or on bed of press or machine against forming tools; operates press or machine controls to bend tube against formers, or operates or directs operation of winch or capstan to bend tube round pegs; reheats small areas of tube during bending, as required, using oxy-propane equipment.

May (01) pack tube with damp sand, resin or pitch, or plug with metal spring to support metal during bending
(02) check angle of bend against full scale drawing.

See Frame bender (ship construction) (729 .18)

729.18 Frame bender (ship construction)

Bends metal girders to form framework of ship

Ascertains job requirements from drawings or other specifications; adjusts machine controls according to angle or curve required; inserts pegs in perforated iron floor to check accuracy of shaping; operates hydraulic machine to bend cold metal girder to required curvature; checks shaped girder against pegs in floor and reshapes as necessary.

May (01) operate tape controlled bending machine.

Other titles include Ship frame bender.

729.20 Bending machine operator (sheet metal), Rolling machine operator (sheet metal)

Shapes cold sheet metal to specified angle or curve using bending or rolling machines

Ascertains job requirements from drawings or other specifications; marks sheet metal with guide lines as required; positions sheet metal in machine manually or using hoisting equipment; operates machine by hand or starts powered machine to bend or roll the metal to specified angle or curve; checks shaped metal with measuring instruments, template or sample and reshapes as necessary.

May (01) adjust roller settings.

See 712 .99 for workers operating roller bending machines to curve hot or cold metal plates in tube manufacture and 714 .75 for workers operating bending presses or machines to shape heated metal.

729.22 Router and mounter (process engraving)

Removes unwanted metal from surface and edges of process engraving printing plates and mounts plates on wooden blocks

Clamps etched printing plate on bed of routing machine, fits rotary cutter (router) and sets machine for required depth of cut; starts machine and removes unwanted metal from surface of plate or cuts out parts of plate completely; files edges to remove roughness; cuts plate to shape on circular or band-saw, using etcher's scribe lines as a guide; fixes plate on wooden block with metal pins or special adhesive; squares off straight edges of block and plate on bevelling machine.

729 .50 Strander (wire rope, cable)

Sets up and operates machine to twist single wires together to form strands for ropes or cores for cables

Loads or directs the loading of bobbins of wire on machine; fits appropriate die heads or forming plate on machine; threads wires through forming plate or dies and over rollers and attaches to take-up bobbin; operates machine to twist wires together; joins breaks in wire by welding, brazing or splicing; unloads or directs the unloading of filled take-up bobbin.

Other titles include Stranding machine driver.

729 .55 Metal straightener (metal stock)

Operates press or straightening machine to straighten metal stock such as tubes, bars, sections or billets

Positions metal tube, bar, section, etc on bed of press or machine; operates press or machine to straighten metal at required point; repositions metal and repeats process as required.

Excluded are Roller straighteners (712 .25)

729 .60 Beamer (wire weaving)

Winds wire on to warp beam preparatory to weaving

Places required number of spools of wire on creeling frame; draws strands of wire from spools through guides and spacing devices and attaches to take-up beam; starts machine to wind wire strands round beam.

729 .65 Wire finishing machinist

Operates machine to flatten and/or straighten and/or polish wire and cut specified lengths as required

Loads coil of wire on machine; threads end of wire through machine guides, wheels, plates, pulleys, rollers or cutters and attaches to wind-off drum or spool; adjusts guides and stops, and sets tension of wheels, pulleys, rollers, etc according to gauge of wire; starts machine to carry out required flattening, straightening, polishing or cutting operations; adjusts machine settings as necessary during operation; unloads coils of finished wire.

Additional factor: number of machines operated.

Other titles include Wire flattener, Wire roller, Wire straightener.

729 .70 Twisted-in wire brush maker

Operates machine to make brushes by twisting wire around brush filling material

Selects required length of U-shaped wire or two separate lengths of wire; fixes closed end of shaped wire or ends of separate lengths of wire in vice on machine and inserts and secures other ends in machine chuck; spreads brush filling material such as bristle, nylon or wire evenly between the strands of wire; starts machine to revolve chuck and twist wires round the filling; removes finished brush from machine.

729 .75 Pen nib maker (general)

Cuts, shapes, grinds and polishes metal to make pen nibs

Performs a combination of the following tasks: converts metal ingot to strip of required thickness on roller press; stamps out nib blanks from strip on hand press; curves nib blanks to shape on hand press; anneals writing tip of nib over gas flame; cuts slit in nib by machine; finishes off nib by grinding; stamps identifying information such as maker's name and carat designation on nib; imparts final polish to nibs in barrel polishing machine.

729 .80 Continuous cut-up line operator

Operates continuous plant to cut metal strip into sheets or to slit strip to required widths

Loads or directs loading of coil of metal strip on machine; sets cutters to cut strip at required intervals to form sheets or to slit strip to required widths and, if required, to trim edges; threads ends of strip through levelling rollers; if slitting strip into widths, passes end under cutters and attaches slit ends to take-up drums; sets controls for speed and tension of strip through machine; starts machine and maintains check on strip for defects; adjusts controls as necessary.

729 .90 Continuous cut-up line assistant

Assists, under the direction of continuous cut-up line operator, in the operation of continuous plant to cut metal strip into sheets or to slit strip to required widths

Performs a combination of the following tasks: assists in loading coil of metal strip on machine; removes scrap metal from machine and bundles for removal; ensures that cut sheets are piling correctly at take-off end of machine and removes sheets with defects; stacks cut sheets ready for removal; removes drums of slit strip from machine; otherwise assists as required.

Other titles include Piler, Scrapman.

729.91 Metal cutting machine operator (excluding continuous cut-up lines)

Operates guillotine, shearing machine, power saw or other cutting machine to cut metal stock to size

Loads or directs loading of metal sheets, bars, ingots or other stock on to machine, using lifting equipment as required; positions and clamps guides or stops as required to set length, width and/or angle of cut; starts machine by foot pedal, or manual or automatic controls to level, trim and/or cut metal to length and width; repositions metal, as required, for further cutting; removes or directs removal of cut metal.

May (01) set up shears or other cutters in machine
(02) mark cutting lines on metal from drawings or using template
(03) specialise in cutting particular types of metal, eg precious metals, stainless steel, nickel.

Other titles include Cropper, Guillotine operator, Metal sawyer, Metal shearer, Saw parer, Shearing machine operator, Tube cutter.

729.92 Bevelling machinist (tubes, plates)

Operates machine to trim and shape edges of plates or ends of tubes ready for welding or riveting

Fixes appropriate cutting tool in machine and sets to required angle for straight or tapered edge; positions plate or tube on machine table using lifting tackle as required; operates controls to bring cutting tool into contact with edge of plate or end of tube; starts machine to cut required amount of metal from edge; repeats process for other edges as required.

May (01) sharpen cutting tools.

Other titles include Plate edge planer.

729.93 Frame bender's helper (ship construction)

Assists frame bender to bend metal girders to form framework of ship

Performs some or all of the following tasks: attaches slings to girders and directs movement by crane driver or moves girders by hand; assists frame bender to feed girders into hydraulic bending machine and unload curved girders from machine; performs other tasks as directed by the frame bender.

Other titles include Frame helper, Ship frame bender's mate.

729.94 Garment pattern grader (machine)

Operates machine to cut patterns for garment parts in various sizes, increasing or decreasing dimensions (grading) of master pattern

Adjusts machine controls to obtain graded pattern of required size; secures master pattern of garment part in position on machine; clamps plastic or metal sheet below machine cutters; places profiling pin against edge of master pattern and starts machine; guides pin round edge of master pattern causing connected cutters to cut pattern of required size from plastic or metal sheet; removes master pattern and graded pattern from machines; smoothes rough edges of graded metal pattern with hand file; marks graded pattern with style number, size and pattern piece number.

See Pattern grader (footwear) (642.30)

729.98 Trainee

Performs, under instruction or guidance, various tasks including training exercises and as appropriate pursues studies in order to acquire the basic skills and knowledge required to perform the tasks of workers in machining and related occupations (engineering and metal goods making) not elsewhere classified.

729.99 Other machining and related occupations (engineering and metal goods making) not elsewhere classified

Workers in this group perform miscellaneous engineering and metal goods making machining and related tasks and are not separately classified, for example:

(01) **Bar benders** (operate machines to bend cold steel bars for reinforcing concrete); (02) **Bar coverers (metal)** (operate machines to impose a surface of metal on a basic material, for example, brass on iron); (03) **Centreless bar turning machine operators** (operate machines to remove skin of metal from round hot-rolled bars to improve surface finish and/or reduce to required size); (04) **Pattern binders (footwear)** (bind edges of paperboard patterns with brass strip); (05) **Rod pointers** (operate machines to point ends of wire rods prior to drawing); (06) **Saw setters** (operate machines to set teeth of saw blades at correct angle for cutting); (07) **Socket machinists (tube manufacture)** (operate machines to expand ends of tubes to form sockets for jointing); (08) **Steel straighteners (colliery)** (straighten steel roof supports by machine); (09) **Straighteners' helpers (excluding roller straightening)** (assist metal straighteners generally); (10) **Worksetters** (position and fix workpieces on detached base plates for subsequent fitting into machining bed of numerically controlled machine tools).

Minor Group 73 PRODUCTION FITTING (METAL) AND RELATED OCCUPATIONS

Workers in this minor group mark out metal for machine tool working, make and repair machine cutting and press tools, dies, moulds, gauges, jigs, fixtures and templates, make precision and optical instruments, watches and clocks, fit and assemble parts in the manufacture of metal products, test and adjust tools, instruments and engines and perform closely related tasks.

The occupations are arranged in the following unit groups:

730 Foremen (Production Fitting (Metal) and Related Occupations)

731 Tool Makers, Tool Fitters and Markers-out

732 Precision Instrument Making Occupations

733 Other Engineering Production Fitters (Excluding Electrical)

734 Other Metal Working Production Fitters

739 Production Fitting (Metal) and Related Occupations Not Elsewhere Classified

Excluded are Repetitive assemblers (metal goods) (821·35 and 821·40)

Unit Group 730 Foremen (Production Fitting (Metal) and Related Occupations)

Workers in this unit group directly supervise and co-ordinate the activities of workers in production fitting (metal) and related occupations.

730 .10 Foreman (tool makers, tool fitters and markers-out)

Directly supervises and co-ordinates the activities of tool makers, tool fitters and markers-out

Performs appropriate tasks as described under SUPERVISOR/FOREMAN (UNSPECIFIED) (990 .00).

Additional factor: number of workers supervised.

730 .20 Foreman (precision instrument making occupations)

Directly supervises and co-ordinates the activities of workers in precision instrument making occupations

Performs appropriate tasks as described under SUPERVISOR/FOREMAN (UNSPECIFIED) (990 .00).

May (01) supervise workers repairing or inspecting precision instruments.

Additional factor: number of workers supervised.

730 .30 Foreman fitter-assembler (engines)

Directly supervises and co-ordinates the activities of fitter-assemblers engaged in the manufacture of engines

Performs appropriate tasks as described under SUPERVISOR/FOREMAN (UNSPECIFIED) (990 .00).

Additional factor: number of workers supervised.

730 .40 Foreman fitter-assembler (machine tools)

Directly supervises and co-ordinates the activities of fitter-assemblers engaged in the manufacture of machine tools

Performs appropriate tasks as described under SUPERVISOR/FOREMAN (UNSPECIFIED) (990 .00).

Additional factor: number of workers supervised.

730 .50 Foreman fitter-assembler (other machinery)

Directly supervises and co-ordinates the activities of fitter-assemblers engaged in the manufacture of machinery other than engines or machine tools

Performs appropriate tasks as described under SUPERVISOR/FOREMAN (UNSPECIFIED) (990 .00).

Additional factor: number of workers supervised.

730 .98 Trainee

Performs, under instruction or guidance, various tasks including training exercises and as appropriate pursues studies in order to acquire the basic skills and knowledge required to perform the tasks of foremen (production fitting (metal) and related occupations).

730 .99 Other foremen (production fitting (metal) and related occupations)

Workers in this group directly supervise and co-ordinate the activities of workers in production fitting (metal) and related occupations and are not elsewhere classified.

Unit Group 731 Tool Makers, Tool Fitters and Markers-Out

Workers in this unit group mark out metal for machine tool working, fit, assemble and repair machine cutting and press tools, dies, moulds, gauges, jigs, fixtures and templates and inspect and rectify tools.

Excluded are Industrial diamond setters (791 .34)

731 .05 Engineering marker-out

Marks out metal castings, forgings, machine blocks and similar metal stock ready for machine tool working

Ascertains job requirements from drawings or other specifications; plans layout; positions metal workpiece on level surface or between centres of holding device using height gauges, jigs, protractors, rules, squares and surface blocks as required; marks out reference points and layout lines on metal workpiece using measuring instruments and tools such as callipers, height gauges, punches, rules, scribers, squares and verniers.

May (01) coat metal with dye or paint prior to marking out

(02) operate co-ordinate measuring machine.

Other titles include Engineering marker-off, Engineering setter-out, Liner-off, Liner-out, Scriber, Surface tableman.

See Marker-out (772 .05) and Marker-off (metal plate, structural metal) (773 .02). See also 739 .05 for workers who mark out and shape metal stock.

731 .10 Tool maker (hand and machine)

Marks out and machines metal stock and fits and assembles prepared metal parts to make or repair machine cutting tools, gauges, jigs or fixtures

Ascertains job requirements from drawings or other specifications; determines sequence and method of required operations; marks out workpiece as described under ENGINEERING MARKER-OUT (731 .05); sets and operates machine tools such as grinders, lathes and shapers to machine workpiece to specification; fits and assembles prepared parts as described under TOOL FITTER (731 .35); if undertaking repair work, dismantles tool, gauge, jig or fixture, removes defective part(s), prepares new part(s) and rebuilds tool, etc.

May (01) anneal, harden or temper tools

(02) machine workpiece using spark erosion machine

(03) join parts by brazing, soldering or welding

(04) make press tools, dies or moulds (731 .20) or templates (731 .25).

Other titles include Jig and gauge maker.

731 .15 Tool maker (hand)

Marks out and hand finishes machine shaped metal stock and fits and assembles prepared metal parts to make or repair cutting tools, gauges, jigs or fixtures

Ascertains job requirements from drawings or other specifications; determines sequence and method of required operations; marks out workpiece as described under ENGINEERING MARKER-OUT (731 .05); shapes workpiece to specification using hand tools such as files, laps, saws and scrapers; fits and assembles prepared parts as described under TOOL FITTER (731 .35); if undertaking repair work, dismantles tool, gauge, jig or fixture, removes defective part(s), prepares new part(s) and rebuilds tool, etc.

See 739 .05 for workers who mark out and shape metal stock, using hand tools.

731 .20 Press tool maker

Marks out and machines metal stock and fits and assembles prepared metal parts to make or repair press tools, dies or moulds

Performs tasks as described under TOOL MAKER (HAND AND MACHINE) (731 .10) but in relation to making press tools, dies and moulds.

May (01) set tools in presses, test operation and rectify faults.

Other titles include Die maker (engineering), Die sinker, Mould maker (press tool).

731 .25 Template maker

Marks out and machines metal stock and fits and assembles prepared metal parts to make or repair engineering templates

Performs tasks as described under TOOL MAKER (HAND AND MACHINE) (731 .10) but in relation to making engineering templates.

731 .30 Forme maker

Constructs formes from strip metal and wood for use in paperboard cutting and creasing machines

Ascertains job requirements from drawings or other specifications; selects suitable block of wood and marks out for machining; cuts wooden block into sections of required size and shape or cuts slots in block using woodworking tools such as circular saws, jigsaws, fret-saws and drills; selects lengths of metal strip and cuts to required size to form creasers or cutting knives; bends cut strip as required using formers and bending machine; assembles wooden block sections inserting prepared strip between sections or inserts strips into slots in wooden block; places prepared forme in metal frame (chase) and secures in position with wooden wedges.

May (01) glue rubber ejector strip to forme
(02) set formes in machines
(03) make test impression from finished forme to test accuracy of work.

Other titles include Die maker (paperboard cutting and creasing machine).

731 .35 Tool fitter

Fits and assembles prepared metal parts to make or repair cutting tools, gauges, jigs or fixtures

Ascertains job requirements from drawings or other specifications; determines sequence and method of required operations; checks prepared metal parts for accuracy of machining using measuring instruments; assembles prepared parts and adjusts as necessary using hand tools such as files, laps and scrapers to obtain accurate fit; checks alignment during assembly using micrometers, optical projectors, slip gauges or other measuring instruments; if undertaking repair work, dismantles tool, gauge, jig or fixture, replaces defective parts and rebuilds tool, etc.

May (01) join parts by brazing, soldering or welding.

Other titles include Tool room fitter.

731 .40 Press tool fitter

Fits and assembles prepared metal parts to make or repair press tools, dies or moulds

Performs tasks as described under TOOL FITTER (731 .35) but in relation to the fitting and assembly of press tools, dies or moulds.

May (01) set tools in press, test operation and rectify faults.

731.98 Trainee

Performs, under instruction or guidance, various tasks including training exercises and as appropriate pursues studies in order to acquire the basic skills and knowledge required to perform the tasks of tool makers, tool fitters and markers-out.

731.99 Other tool makers, tool fitters and markers-out

Workers in this group mark out metal for machine tool working, fit, assemble and repair machine cutting and press tools, dies, moulds, gauges, jigs, fixtures and templates and inspect and rectify tools and are not elsewhere classified, for example:

(01) **Tool inspector-rectifiers** (perform tasks as described under INSPECTOR (TOOL ROOM) (831.15) and adjust tools as necessary).

Unit Group 732 Precision Instrument Making Occupations

Workers in this unit group make precision and optical instruments, fit and assemble watches and clocks, and calibrate, test and rectify instruments.

See 739.99 for dental and surgical instrument makers.

732.05 Precision instrument maker (excluding optical instruments)

Marks out and machines materials and fits and assembles prepared parts to make precision instruments other than optical instruments

Ascertains job requirements from drawings or other specifications; determines sequence and method of required operations; marks cutting and shaping lines on material such as aluminium, brass, steel and plastics; sets and operates machine tools such as grinders, lathes and shapers, to machine material to specifications; fits and assembles prepared parts as described under PRECISION INSTRUMENT FITTER (732.20). Performs these tasks in relation to the manufacture of precision instruments other than optical instruments.

May (01) test and/or calibrate instruments
(02) install, service and repair instruments
(03) harden and temper metal parts.

Other titles include Aircraft instrument maker, Barometer maker, Compass maker, Electrical instrument maker.

732.10 Optical instrument maker

Marks out and machines materials and fits and assembles prepared parts and optical components to make optical instruments

Performs appropriate tasks as described under PRECISION INSTRUMENT MAKER (732.05) but in relation to the manufacture of optical instruments such as binoculars, cameras, periscopes, range-finders and theodolites; in addition positions and aligns optical lenses and secures in mounts by screwing or by bending rim of mount over edge of lens to hold lens in position.

May (01) test and/or calibrate assembled instruments
(02) service and repair optical instruments.

Other titles include Camera maker.

732 .15 Watch maker, Clock maker

Fits and assembles prepared parts to make watches or clocks

Ascertains job requirements from drawings or other specifications; checks prepared mechanical parts for accuracy using measuring instruments; assembles prepared mechanical and other parts such as electrical units or jewels; adjusts as necessary using lathes and hand tools such as files, pliers and screwdrivers to obtain accurate fit; checks alignment during assembly using measuring instruments and gauges; tests completed assembly for accuracy of operation using electronic or other test equipment and adjusts as necessary; mounts watch or clock mechanism in prepared case.

May (01) service and repair watches and/or clocks

(02) make parts from stock metal

(03) carry out shock tests on watch mechanisms

(04) carry out underwater pressure tests on watertight watches.

732 .20 Precision instrument fitter (excluding optical instruments)

Fits and assembles prepared parts in the manufacture of precision instruments other than optical instruments

Ascertains job requirements from drawings or other specifications; determines sequence and method of required operations; checks prepared parts for accuracy using measuring instruments; assembles prepared parts and adjusts as necessary using machine tools and hand tools such as files, laps and scrapers to obtain accurate fit; joins parts by brazing, cementing, riveting, screwing, soldering or welding as required; checks alignment during assembly using micrometers, slip gauges or other measuring instruments. Performs these tasks in relation to the fitting and assembly of precision instruments other than optical instruments.

May (01) test and/or calibrate instruments

(02) install, service and repair instruments.

732 .25 Optical instrument fitter

Fits and assembles prepared parts in the manufacture of optical instruments

Performs appropriate tasks as described under PRECISION INSTRUMENT FITTER (732 .20) but in relation to the fitting and assembly of optical instruments such as binoculars, periscopes, range-finders and theodolites; in addition positions and aligns optical lenses and secures in mounts by screwing or by bending rim of mount over edge of lens.

May (01) test and/or calibrate assembled optical instruments

(02) service and repair optical instruments.

732 .98 Trainee

Performs, under instruction or guidance, various tasks including training exercises and as appropriate pursues studies in order to acquire the basic skills and knowledge required to perform the tasks of workers in precision instrument making occupations.

732 .99 Other precision instrument making occupations

Workers in this group make precision and optical instruments, fit and assemble watches and clocks, and calibrate, test and rectify instruments and are not elsewhere classified, for example:

(01) **Calibrators,** Dividers, Graduators (calibrate instruments by comparison with standard equipment or by calculation); (02) **Tester-rectifiers (precision instruments)** (test correct functioning of instruments and adjust as necessary).

Unit Group 733 Other Engineering Production Fitters (Excluding Electrical)

Workers in this unit group fit and assemble, to close tolerances, parts and sub-assemblies in the manufacture of metal products, test and rectify engines and are not elsewhere classified.

Note: in this context close tolerances are permissible variations in measurements defined in thousandths of an inch.

733 .05 Engineering fitter-assembler (general)

Fits and assembles, to close tolerances, prepared parts and/or sub-assemblies to make various types of metal products or secondary sub-assemblies of such products

Ascertains job requirements from drawings or other specifications; determines sequence and method of required operations; checks prepared metal parts for accuracy of machining or sub-assemblies for accuracy of fit using measuring instruments; working to fine limits assembles prepared parts and/or sub-assemblies and adjusts as necessary using hand tools such as files, laps, reamers, scrapers, spanners and taps to ensure accurate fit; checks alignment during assembly using clock and height gauges, micrometers, rules, verniers or other measuring instruments. Performs these tasks in relation to the manufacture of various types of metal products or secondary sub-assemblies of such products.

May (01) join parts by brazing, riveting, soldering or welding

(02) operate powered hand tools

(03) undertake repair work.

Other titles include Engineering fitter-erector (general)

Excluded are Engineering fitter-assemblers (prototype, experimental) (733 .10)

733 .10 Engineering fitter-assembler (prototype, experimental)

Fits and assembles, to close tolerances, prepared parts and/or sub-assemblies to make prototype or experimental metal products or secondary sub-assemblies of such products

Performs appropriate tasks as described under ENGINEERING FITTER-ASSEMBLER (GENERAL) (733 .05) but in relation to the manufacture of prototype or experimental metal products.

May (01) join parts by brazing, riveting, soldering or welding

(02) undertake repair work.

733 .15 Engineering fitter-assembler (aircraft engines)

Fits and assembles, to close tolerances, prepared parts and/or sub-assemblies to make aircraft engines or secondary sub-assemblies of aircraft engines

Performs appropriate tasks as described under ENGINEERING FITTER-ASSEMBLER (GENERAL) (733 .05) but in relation to the manufacture of aircraft engines.

May (01) join parts by brazing, riveting, soldering or welding

(02) undertake repair work

(03) specialise on piston engines

(04) specialise on gas turbine engines.

Other titles include Aircraft engine fitter-erector.

733 .20 Engineering fitter-assembler (marine engines)

Fits and assembles, to close tolerances, prepared parts and/or sub-assemblies to make marine engines or secondary sub-assemblies of marine engines

Performs appropriate tasks as described under ENGINEERING FITTER-ASSEMBLER (GENERAL) (733 .05) but in relation to the manufacture of marine engines and ships' machinery.

May (01) join parts by brazing, riveting, soldering or welding

(02) undertake repair work

(03) install engines in vessels.

Other titles include Marine engine assembler, Marine engine fitter-erector, Marine engine fitter.

733 .25 Engineering fitter-assembler (agricultural machinery)

Fits and assembles, to close tolerances, prepared parts and/or sub-assemblies to make agricultural machinery or secondary sub-assemblies of agricultural machinery

Performs appropriate tasks as described under ENGINEERING FITTER-ASSEMBLER (GENERAL) (733 .05) but in relation to the manufacture of agricultural machinery.

May (01) join parts by brazing, riveting, soldering or welding

(02) undertake repair work

(03) specialise on a particular type of agricultural machinery, eg combine harvester, hedge cutter.

Other titles include Agricultural machinery fitter-erector.

733 .30 Engineering fitter-assembler (machine tools)

Fits and assembles, to close tolerances, prepared parts and/or sub-assemblies to make machine tools or secondary sub-assemblies of machine tools

Performs appropriate tasks as described under ENGINEERING FITTER-ASSEMBLER (GENERAL) (733 .05) but in relation to the manufacture of machine tools.

May (01) join parts by brazing, riveting, soldering or welding

(02) undertake repair work

(03) specialise on a particular type of machine tool, eg lathe, milling machine, drilling machine.

Other titles include Machine tool fitter-erector.

733 .35 Engineering fitter-assembler (other engines and machinery)

Fits and assembles, to close tolerances, prepared parts and/or sub-assemblies to make engines and machinery or secondary sub-assemblies of such products other than aircraft and marine engines, agricultural machinery and machine tools

Performs appropriate tasks as described under ENGINEERING FITTER-ASSEMBLER (GENERAL) (733 .05) but in relation to the manufacture of engines and machinery such as diesel locomotives, gas engines, motor vehicle engines, printing machinery or textile machinery.

May (01) join parts by brazing, riveting, soldering or welding

(02) undertake repair work

(03) install machinery on operational site

(04) time and/or tune engines.

Other titles include Diesel engine fitter-erector, Diesel locomotive fitter, Gas engine fitter-erector, Hosiery machine fitter, Internal-combustion engine fitter, Lace machine fitter, Loom fitter, Printing machinery fitter, Steam engine fitter, Textile machinery fitter, Textile machinery fitter-erector, Turbine fitter, Turbine fitter-erector.

733 .40 Engineering fitter-assembler (excluding engines and machinery)

Fits and assembles, to close tolerances, prepared parts and/or sub-assemblies to make a particular engineering product or secondary sub-assemblies of a particular product other than engines and machinery

Performs appropriate tasks as described under ENGINEERING FITTER-ASSEMBLER (GENERAL) (733 .05) but in relation to the manufacture of particular products such as aircraft, bespoke guns, grates, ranges, stoves or weighing machines.

May (01) join parts by brazing, riveting, soldering or welding

(02) undertake repair work.

Other titles include Aircraft fitter-erector, Finisher (bespoke guns).

733 .45 Engineering detail fitter

Fits and assembles, to close tolerances, prepared parts to make primary sub-assemblies of metal products

Performs appropriate tasks as described under ENGINEERING FITTER-ASSEMBLER (GENERAL) (733 .05) but in relation to the manufacture of primary sub-assemblies of metal products.

May (01) join parts by brazing, riveting, soldering or welding

(02) drill holes in component parts using powered hand drills

(03) apply anti-corrosive sealing compound to metal parts before assembly.

Other titles include Agricultural machinery detail fitter, Aircraft engine detail fitter, Aircraft detail fitter, Air-frame detail fitter, Beam fitter (scales), Beam maker (textile machinery), Bench fitter (engineering), Carriage maker (textile machinery), Carriage straightener (textile machinery), Dobby maker, Gun fitter (bespoke), Gun-sight gear maker, Internal-combustion engine detail fitter, Jacquard maker, Lever and beam fitter (scales), Ordnance fitter, Precision fitter, Steam engine detail fitter, Stove detail fitter, Temple assembler, Textile machinery detail fitter, Turbine blade fitter, Turbine blader.

733 .50 Engineering fitter-machinist

Operates machines to cut or otherwise shape component parts from metal and fits and assembles parts to close tolerances in the manufacture of metal products

Ascertains job requirements from drawings or other specifications; determines sequence and method of required operations; sets up and operates machine tools such as lathes and milling machines and/or other metal working machines such as bending machines, guillotines, presses and saws to cut or otherwise shape metal to form component parts; fits and assembles prepared parts as described under ENGINEERING FITTER-ASSEMBLER (GENERAL) (733 .05).

May (01) mark out metal prior to machining (731 .05)
(02) join parts by brazing, riveting, soldering or welding
(03) make wooden or rubber rollers for textile temples.

Other titles inlude Fitter-turner, Fitter-borer, Brass finisher, Temple maker, Fitter-machinist (weighing machines), Gun fitter-machinist (bespoke).

733 .55 Systems fitter (aircraft)

Fits, assembles and installs prepared parts and components to close tolerances to build hydraulic or similar systems in aircraft construction

Ascertains job requirements from drawings or other specifications; determines sequence and method of required operations; working to close tolerances fits and installs components such as actuators, filters, pumps and valves in position in fuselage, tailplane or wing of aircraft using hand tools such as files and scrapers, and powered tools such as drills and riveting tools; checks alignment during installation using measuring instruments; connects lengths of cables, piping or rods to components to form systems such as flying control, air conditioning, fuel supply, de-icing and wheel braking; tests completed system for correct functioning and adjusts as necessary.

733 .60 Engine tester-rectifier (internal-combustion engine)

Examines the operation of internal-combustion engine on test bed using test equipment and adjusts as necessary

Positions engine on test bed using hoisting equipment and secures with bolts; connects to engine oil, fuel, water, exhaust and electrical systems, and loading and metering equipment; starts engine and records meter readings such as oil pressure, temperature and revolutions per minute; checks engine visually and aurally for malfunction and adjusts fuel injectors, carburettors, tappets, timing gear, etc as necessary; varies loading on engine and records meter readings; prepares report on performance of engine. Performs these tasks in relation to the test tunning and adjusting of internal-combustion engines.

May (01) run diesel engines using electric motors before testing as described above
(02) dismantle engine and test parts for wear.

See Engine tester (internal-combustion engine) (831 .35)

733 .65 Engine tester-rectifier (jet engine)

Examines operation of jet engines on test bed using test equipment and adjusts as necessary

Performs appropriate tasks as described under INTERNAL-COMBUSTION ENGINE TESTER-RECTIFIER (733 .60) but in relation to the test running and adjusting of jet engines and, on selected engines, examines the effect of the addition of ice to air intakes, the introduction of hot gases into the engine and the prolonged running of the engine.

See Engine tester (jet engine) (831 .40)

733 .98 Trainee

Performs, under instruction or guidance, various tasks including training exercises and as appropriate pursues studies in order to acquire the basic skills and knowledge required to perform the tasks of other engineering production fitters (excluding electrical).

733 .99 Other engineering production fitters (excluding electrical) not elsewhere classified

Workers in this group fit and assemble, to close tolerances, parts and sub-assemblies in the manufacture of metal products, test and rectify engines and are not separately classified.

Unit Group 734 Other Metal Working Production Fitters

Workers in this unit group fit and assemble, other than to close tolerances, parts and sub-assemblies in the manufacture of metal products and test and adjust new motor vehicles.

Note: in this context close tolerances are permissible variations in measurements defined in thousandths of an inch.

Included are workers making and repairing metal parts of orthopaedic appliances.

Excluded are Repetitive assemblers (metal goods) (821 .35 and *821 .40)*

734 .05 Metal working fitter-assembler (general)

Fits and assembles, other than to close tolerances, prepared parts and/or sub-assemblies to make various types of metal products or secondary sub-assemblies of such products

Ascertains job requirements from drawings or other specifications; determines sequence and method of required operations; checks prepared metal parts for accuracy of machining or sub-assemblies for accuracy of fit using measuring instruments; assembles prepared parts and/or sub-assemblies and adjusts as necessary using hand tools such as files, scrapers and spanners; checks alignment during assembly using gauges, rules or other measuring instruments. Performs these tasks in relation to the manufacture of various types of metal products or secondary sub-assemblies of such products.

May (01) join parts by brazing, riveting, soldering or welding

(02) undertake repair work.

734 .10 Metal working fitter-assembler (motor vehicles)

Fits and assembles, other than to close tolerances, prepared parts and/or sub-assemblies to make motor vehicles or secondary sub-assemblies of motor vehicles

Performs appropriate tasks as described under METAL WORKING FITTER-ASSEMBLER (GENERAL) (734 .05) but in relation to the manufacture of motor vehicles such as cars, invalid carriages, lorries and omnibuses.

May (01) join parts by brazing, riveting, soldering or welding

(02) undertake repair work.

Other titles include Chassis fitter-assembler.

Excluded are Vehicle body builders (793 .10)

734 .15 Metal working fitter-assembler (machinery)

Fits and assembles, other than to close tolerances, prepared parts and/or sub-assemblies to make machinery or secondary sub-assemblies of machinery

Performs appropriate tasks as described under METAL WORKING FITTER-ASSEMBLER (GENERAL) (734 .05) but in relation to the manufacture of machinery such as agricultural machinery and printing machinery.

May (01) join parts by brazing, riveting, soldering or welding

(02) undertake repair work.

Other titles include Metal working fitter-assembler (agricultural machinery), Printing machinery fitter-assembler.

734 .20 Metal working fitter-assembler (excluding motor vehicles and machinery)

Fits and assembles, other than to close tolerances, prepared parts and/or sub-assemblies to make specialised metal products or secondary sub-assemblies of such products other than motor vehicles and machinery

Performs appropriate tasks as described under METAL WORKING FITTER-ASSEMBLER (GENERAL) (734 .05) but in relation to the manufacture of metal products such as aluminium ladders, anchors, boilers, brass musical instruments, locks, metal windows, railway wagons, safes, scissors and spring knives.

May (01) join parts by brazing, riveting, soldering or welding

(02) undertake repair work.

Other titles include Anchor fitter, Boiler fitter, Brass musical instrument maker, Casement fitter-assembler, Metal working fitter-assembler (locks), lock fitter-assembler, Railway wagon fitter-assembler, Safe fitter-assembler, Scissors putter-together, Spring knife cutler, Window fitter-assembler.

734.25 Metal working detail fitter

Fits and assembles, other than to close tolerances, prepared parts to make primary sub-assemblies of metal products

Performs appropriate tasks as described under METAL WORKING FITTER-ASSEMBLER (GENERAL) (734.05) but in relation to the manufacture of primary sub-assemblies of metal products.

May (01) join parts by brazing, riveting, soldering or welding
(02) drill holes in component parts using powered hand drills.

Other titles include Bench fitter (metal working), Metal working detail fitter (motor).

734.30 Metal working fitter-machinist

Operates machines to cut or otherwise shape metal component parts and fits and assembles those parts, other than to close tolerances, in the manufacture of metal products

Ascertains job requirements from drawings or other specifications; determines sequence and method of required operations; sets up and operates machine tools such as lathes, milling machines and/or other metal working machines such as bending machines, guillotines, presses and saws to cut or otherwise shape metal to form component parts; fits and assembles the prepared parts as described under METAL WORKING FITTER-ASSEMBLER (GENERAL) (734.05).

May (01) mark out metal prior to machining (731.05)
(02) join parts by brazing, riveting, soldering or welding
(03) cut metal using flame cutter
(04) erect constructional ironwork on site.

Other titles include Brass bedstead maker, Cycle fork builder, Cycle frame builder, Cycle frame maker, Casement fitter-machinist, Constructional ironwork fitter-machinist, Constructional steelwork fitter-machinist, Door frame fitter-machinist, Finisher (cock work), Lock fitter-machinist, Safe fitter-machinist, Safe maker, Staircase fitter-machinist.

734.35 Orthopaedic appliance maker (specialised) (metal)

Makes and repairs metal parts of artificial limbs, body supports and other orthopaedic appliances

Ascertains job requirements from prescription, plaster cast or other specifications; selects suitable steel, aluminium or other metal plate, wire or bar and marks out with guide lines using rules, templates and scribers; cuts and shapes metal parts using hand and machine tools; assembles prepared metal parts and secures by bolting, brazing, riveting, soldering or welding and polishes completed metal work by hand or using buffing machines; repairs or adjusts appliances as required.

May (01) anneal metal parts.

See Orthopaedic appliance maker (general) (692.10)

734.40 Road tester (new motor vehicles)

Checks performance of new motor vehicles by road testing and makes minor adjustments

Examines test instructions; checks vehicle for roadworthiness before commencing road test; drives vehicle on test run and carries out specified tests to check its performance; makes minor adjustments to vehicle during test using feeler gauges, spanners and screwdrivers; reports major faults in performance to foreman.

Additional factor: type(s) of vehicles to which accustomed.

Other titles include Vehicle tester (new vehicles).

See Road tester (used motor vehicles) (742.10)

734.98 Trainee

Performs, under instruction or guidance, various tasks including training exercises and as appropriate pursues studies in order to acquire the basic skills and knowledge required to perform the tasks of other metal working production fitters.

734.99 Other metal working production fitters not elsewhere classified

Workers in this group fit and assemble, other than to close tolerances, parts and sub-assemblies in the manufacture of metal products, test and adjust new motor vehicles and are not elsewhere classified.

Unit Group 739 Production Fitting (Metal) and Related Occupations Not Elsewhere Classified

Workers in this unit group perform miscellaneous production fitting and related tasks, including hand shaping of metal parts, saw making throughout, saw handle fitting and assisting constructional ironwork fitter-machinists and are not elsewhere classified.

739 .05 Bench hand (engineering)

Marks out and shapes metal stock to close tolerances using hand tools

Ascertains job requirements from drawings or other specifications; determines sequence and method of required operations; marks out workpiece using measuring instruments, punches and scribers; shapes workpiece to specification using hand tools such as files, laps, saws and scrapers; checks accuracy of shaping using clock and height gauges, micrometers, verniers and other measuring instruments.

Note: in this context tolerances are permissible variations in measurements defined in thousandths of an inch.

739 .10 Saw maker (circular saws, band-saws)

Makes throughout, by hand and machine, blades for circular and/or band-saws from metal blanks

Selects saw blank and cuts teeth in blank using press, milling or grinding machine.

If making circular saws, hammers blank on anvil to tension blade and remove distortions; grinds surfaces of blade between abrasive wheels; removes any further distortions by hammering; sets teeth to correct cutting angle by hammering or using machine.

If making band-saws, shapes overlapping ends of blade to obtain smooth joint; sets ends of blade in vice, applies flux compound and directs heat along joint to braze ends together or joins by welding; grinds joint smooth; sets teeth to correct cutting angle; passes saw through rolling machine to tension blade.

Operates machine to sharpen teeth.

Other titles include Band-saw maker, Circular saw maker.

739 .50 Constructional ironworks labourer

Assists constructional ironwork fitter-machinist

Performs a combination of the following tasks: assists constructional ironwork fitter-machinist to measure up work; holds metal steady for fitter-machinist during cutting or drilling; assists fitter-machinist to convey metal workpiece from one machine to another; fetches materials and tools to work area; assists in loading parts of construction or installation on to lorry; keeps work area clean; otherwise assists fitter-machinist as required.

May (01) assist with the erection of constructional ironwork on site.

739 .98 Trainee

Performs, under instruction or guidance, various tasks including training exercises and as appropriate pursues studies in order to acquire the basic skills and knowledge required to perform the tasks of workers in production fitting (metal) and related occupations not elsewhere classified.

739 .99 Other production fitting (metal) and related occupations not elsewhere classified

Workers in this group perform miscellaneous production fitting and related tasks and are not separately classified, for example:

(01) **Dental instrument makers;** (02) **Key makers (hand)**; (03) **Saw handle fitters** (examine and true saw blades, fit backs as required and handles); (04) **Surgical instrument makers.**

Minor Group 74 INSTALLING, MAINTAINING AND REPAIRING OCCUPATIONS (MACHINES, INSTRUMENTS AND RELATED MECHANICAL EQUIPMENT)

Workers in this minor group erect plant and machinery on site, install aircraft engines and ship machinery, set up, repair and service plant and machinery, repair and service mechanical parts of motor vehicles, aircraft engines, precision instruments, air-frames, railway carriages, cycles and other plant, machinery and mechanical equipment, lubricate motor vehicles, engines and machinery and perform closely related tasks.

The occupations are arranged in the following unit groups:

740 Foremen (Installing, Maintaining and Repairing Occupations (Machines, Instruments and Related Mechanical Equipment))

741 Installation and Maintenance Fitters and Fitter-Mechanics (Plant, Industrial Engines and Machinery and other Mechanical Equipment)

742 Fitter-Mechanics (Motor Vehicles)

743 Maintenance Fitters and Fitter-Mechanics (Aircraft Engines)

744 Precision Instrument Maintaining and Repairing Occupations

745 Office Machinery Maintaining and Repairing Occupations (Mechanical)

746 Servicing, Oiling, Greasing and Related Occupations (Mechanical)

749 Installing, Maintaining and Repairing Occupations (Machines, Instruments and Related Mechanical Equipment) Not Elsewhere Classified

Unit Group 740 Foremen (Installing, Maintaining and Repairing Occupations (Machines, Instruments and Related Mechanical Equipment))

Workers in this unit group directly supervise and co-ordinate the activities of workers in installing, maintaining and repairing occupations (machines, instruments and related mechanical equipment).

740.10 Foreman (installation and maintenance fitters and fitter-mechanics (plant, industrial engines and machinery and other mechanical equipment))

Directly supervises and co-ordinates the activities of installation and maintenance fitters and fitter-mechanics (plant, industrial engines and machinery and other mechanical equipment)

Performs appropriate tasks as described under SUPERVISOR/FOREMAN (UNSPECIFIED) (990.00).

Additional factor: number of workers supervised.

740.20 Foreman (fitter-mechanics (motor vehicles))

Directly supervises and co-ordinates the activities of fitter-mechanics (motor vehicles)

Performs appropriate tasks as described under SUPERVISOR/FOREMAN (UNSPECIFIED) (990.00).

Additional factor: number of workers supervised.

740 .30 Foreman (maintenance fitters and fitter-mechanics (aircraft engines))

Directly supervises and co-ordinates the activities of maintenance fitters and fitter-mechanics (aircraft engines)

Performs appropriate tasks as described under SUPERVISOR/FOREMAN (UNSPECIFIED) (990 .00).

Additional factor: number of workers supervised.

Note: must possess appropriate maintenance licence.

740 .40 Foreman (precision instrument maintaining and repairing occupations)

Directly supervises and co-ordinates the activities of workers in precision instrument maintaining and repairing occupations

Performs appropriate tasks as described under SUPERVISOR/FOREMAN (UNSPECIFIED) (990 .00).

Additional factor: number of workers supervised.

740 .50 Foreman (office machinery mechanics)

Directly supervises and co-ordinates the activities of office machinery mechanics

Performs appropriate tasks as described under SUPERVISOR/FOREMAN (UNSPECIFIED) (990 .00).

Additional factor: number of workers supervised.

740 .98 Trainee

Performs, under instruction or guidance, various tasks including training exercises and as appropriate pursues studies in order to acquire the basic skills and knowledge required to perform the tasks of foremen (installing, maintaining and repairing occupations (machines, instruments and related mechanical equipment)).

740 .99 Other foremen (installing, maintaining and repairing occupations (machines, instruments and related mechanical equipment))

Workers in this group directly supervise and co-ordinate the activities of workers engaged in installing, maintaining and repairing occupations (machines, instruments and related mechanical equipment) and are not elsewhere classified.

Unit Group 741 Installation and Maintenance Fitters and Fitter-Mechanics (Plant, Industrial Engines and Machinery and Other Mechanical Equipment)

Workers in this unit group erect plant and industrial machinery on operational site, install aircraft engines, ship machinery and related fittings, set up, repair and service plant and industrial machinery and repair and service air-frames, locks, coin-operated machines and other plant, machinery and mechanical equipment.

See 799 .02 and 799 .04 *for workers who install, maintain and repair both mechanical and electrical plant and machinery and* 911 *for workers maintaining ships' engines, plant and mechanical equipment at sea.*

741.02 Machinery erector (mechanical) (installation)

Erects mechanical plant or industrial machinery on operational site

Ascertains job requirements from drawings, technical manuals or other specifications; determines sequence and method of required operations; positions or directs positioning of prepared parts or sub-assemblies using hoisting equipment as necessary; builds up plant or machinery using hand tools such as chisels, drills, files, hammers, screwdrivers, spanners and wrenches; checks alignment during erection using micrometer, vernier or other measuring instruments and spirit level; tests erected plant or machinery for correct functioning and adjusts as necessary.

May (01) prepare foundation for machinery
(02) incorporate electrical components in plant or machinery
(03) join parts by welding (775)
(04) demonstrate operation of plant or machinery.

Additional factor: type(s) of machinery in which specialised.

Other titles include Boot machinery erector, Crane erector, Outfitter (plant, machinery), Outdoor fitter, Printing machinery erector, Refrigeration plant erector, Site fitter, Textile machinery erector, Tobacco machinery erector, Woodworking machinery erector.

See 733 for workers erecting machinery during course of manufacture.

741.04 Aircraft engine installation fitter

Installs engines and auxiliary equipment in aircraft

Ascertains job requirements from drawings, technical manuals or other specifications; positions and aligns or directs positioning and aligning of engine in airframe using hoisting equipment; secures engine in frame with bolts using torque spanners; installs and connects engine controls and auxiliary equipment such as alternators, compressors, auxiliary engines and hydraulic, de-icing fuel and exhaust systems; checks accuracy of installation using measuring instruments; secures engine cowling in position.

May (01) assist in testing installed engines (733.60 and 733.65).

741.06 Marine installation fitter

Installs machinery and related fittings in ships under construction or repair

Ascertains job requirements from drawings or other specifications; selects required machinery and fittings such as generators, propeller shafts, propellers, pumps, steering gear, stern tubes, valves and winches; positions, using hoisting equipment as necessary, and fits machinery and fittings in ship using hand tools such as chisels, files, hammers, scrapers, spanners and powered hand tools such as drills and grinders; checks accuracy of work with measuring instruments such as callipers, gauges and rules.

May (01) join parts by welding (775)
(02) install main engines (741.99)
(03) install pipe systems (771.10) or ventilating ducts (771.25).

Other titles include Marine fitter, Ship fitter.

741.08 Maintenance fitter (mechanical) (general)

Repairs and services various types of mechanical plant and industrial machinery

Examines faulty plant or machinery to ascertain nature and location of defects; studies plant or machinery drawings, technical manuals or other specifications; determines sequence and method of required operations; dismantles plant or machinery and removes damaged or worn parts; repairs defective parts, obtains replacement parts or prepares new parts using hand and machine tools; fits and assembles parts to rebuild plant or machinery; tests plant or machinery for correct functioning and makes necessary adjustments; carries out service tasks such as cleaning, oiling and greasing, according to schedule. Performs these tasks in relation to the repair and servicing of various types of mechanical plant and industrial machinery.

May (01) join parts by welding (775)
(02) prepare foundations for plant or machinery
(03) install or reposition plant or machinery
(04) modify standard machinery for special purposes.

Other titles include Millwright.

741.10 Maintenance fitter (civil engineering plant and machinery)

Repairs and services civil engineering plant and machinery

Performs tasks as described under MAINTENANCE FITTER (MECHANICAL) (GENERAL) (741.08) but in relation to the repair and servicing of civil engineering plant and machinery such as bulldozers, excavators and mechanical shovels.

May (01) join parts by welding (775)
(02) repair and service motor vehicles (742.20).

Other titles include Contractor's plant fitter, Contractor's plant mechanic.

741.12 Maintenance fitter (mechanical) (locomotives)

Specialises in one or more of the operations in the overhaul and major repair of mechanical parts of railway locomotives

Performs tasks as described under MAINTENANCE FITTER (MECHANICAL) (GENERAL) (741.08) but in relation to particular operations in the overhaul and major repair of mechanical parts of railway locomotives for example, stripping down, check of component parts or re-erection.

May (01) run diesel engine on test beds (733.60)
(02) specialise on a particular type of locomotive, eg diesel, diesel electric, diesel multiple unit.

741.14 Maintenance fitter (railway carriages, railway wagons)

Specialises in one or more of the operations in the overhaul and repair of the mechanical parts of railway carriages and/or wagons

Performs one or more of the following tasks: dismantles carriage or wagon assemblies such as brakes, draw gear and buffers; checks mechanical parts for wear or damage using gauges and crack detecting equipment; arranges for repair or replacement of defective parts; fits repaired or replacement parts and rebuilds assembly; tests assembly for correct functioning and adjusts as necessary.

May (01) repair and service valves and pipework on pressure vessels
(02) repair superstructure of wooden wagons.

Other titles include Carriage fitter, Coach and wagon fitter.

741.16 Maintenance fitter (air-frame)

Specialises in one or more of the operations in the overhaul and major repair of mechanical parts of aircraft frames or control systems

Performs one or more of the following tasks: examines air-frame section such as fuselage or wings, or control system such as landing gear assembly for damaged or worn parts; studies work sheets, technical manuals or other specifications; dismantles sections and removes defective parts; fits replacement parts and rebuilds section; checks control system section for correct functioning and adjusts as necessary; carries out service tasks such as oiling and greasing according to schedule.

Additional factor: whether in possession of appropriate maintenance licence.

741.18 Maintenance fitter (other plant and industrial engines and machinery)

Repairs and services plant and industrial machinery, other than civil engineering plant and machinery, locomotives, railway carriages and wagons and air-frames

Performs tasks as described under MAINTENANCE FITTER (MECHANICAL) (GENERAL) (741.08) but in relation to the repair and servicing of plant and industrial machinery such as agricultural machinery, boilers, blast furnaces, colliery machinery, dock plant, laundry machinery, marine engines, machine tools, refrigeration plant, steam engines, steam turbines or textile machinery.

May (01) join parts by welding (775)
(02) install or reposition plant or machinery.

Other titles include Agricultural machinery fitter-mechanic, Boiler maintenance fitter, Colliery fitter, Dock fitter, Iron and steel works maintenance fitter, Laundry maintenance fitter, Machine tool maintenance fitter, Marine engine maintenance fitter, Refrigeration plant maintenance fitter, Shore maintenance fitter, Steam engine maintenance fitter, Steam turbine maintenance fitter, Textile machinery maintenance fitter.

Note: a colliery fitter must have a knowledge of mine safety regulations.

Excluded are Setter fitter-mechanics (741.24, 741.26 and 741.28)

741.20 Service fitter (mechanical) (locomotives)

Carries out running repairs to and routine servicing of mechanical parts of railway locomotives

Examines faulty locomotive to ascertain nature and location of defects in mechanical parts; studies technical manual or other specifications; if fault appears to be of a minor nature dismantles section of locomotive and removes damaged or worn parts; obtains replacements parts and fits and assembles parts to rebuild locomotive section; if major repair is necessary arranges for work to be undertaken by maintenance fitter; carries out service tasks such as cleaning, oiling and greasing, and checks locomotive components according to schedule.

May (01) repair damaged or worn parts using hand and machine tools.

741.22 Service fitter (air-frame)

Carries out running repairs to and routine servicing of aircraft frames or control systems

Examines fuselage, wings, ailerons, rudders, elevators, landing gear, door operating mechanism, etc for damage and fluid leakages and removes any foreign objects; checks condition of brakes and tyres; if fault appears to be of a minor nature removes defective parts and fits replacement parts; if major repair is necessary arranges for aircraft to be grounded; carries out service tasks such as lubrication of elevators and undercarriage bearings, inflation of tyres to correct pressure, de-icing of fuselage, wings, ailerons, rudders and elevators, according to schedule.

Additional factor: whether in possession of appropriate maintenance licence.

741.24 Setter fitter-mechanic (textile machinery excluding knitting machines)

Sets up, repairs and services textile machinery, other than knitting machines, to be operated or attended by other workers

Ascertains job requirements from technical manuals, pattern charts or other specifications; determines sequence and method of required operations; selects and fits machinery components such as belts, cams, cards, chains, cylinders, flats, gearwheels, healds, pulleys, reeds, rollers, shafts and spindles, checking alignment with measuring instruments; sets operational speed or other machine controls; operates or supervises trial run of machine, checks accuracy of machine control settings and adjusts as necessary; carries out repair and servicing of machinery as described under MAINTENANCE FITTER (MECHANICAL) (GENERAL) (741.08).

May (01) join parts by welding (775)

(02) repair worn or broken components.

Additional factor: number of machines set up and maintained.

Other titles include Braiding machine mechanic, Carding engineer, Comb jobber, Comber setter, Combing jobber, Frame overlooker, Loom overlooker, Loom tenter, Loom tuner, Mechanic (industrial sewing machines), Pattern setter (lace), Ring jobber, Spinning jobber, Tackler, Twisting jobber, Undercarder, Winding machine mechanic.

741.26 Setter fitter-mechanic (industrial knitting machines)

Sets up, repairs and services industrial knitting machines to be operated or attended by other workers

Performs appropriate tasks as described under SETTER FITTER-MECHANIC (TEXTILE MACHINERY EXCLUDING KNITTING MACHINES) (741.24) but in relation to the setting up, repair and servicing of industrial knitting machines.

May (01) join parts by welding (775)

(02) repair worn or broken components.

Additional factor: number of machines set up and maintained.

Other titles include Hosiery mechanic (industrial), Mechanic (industrial knitting machines).

741.28 Setter fitter-mechanic (other industrial machinery)

Sets up, repairs and services machinery, other than textile machinery, to be operated or attended by other workers

Ascertains job requirements from technical manuals or other specifications; determines sequence and method of required operations; selects and fits machinery components such as coils, dies, guides, nozzles and stops, checking alignment with measuring instruments; sets pressure, heat, speed or other machine controls; operates or supervises trial run of machine, checks accuracy of machine control settings and adjusts as necessary; carries out repair and servicing of machinery as described under MAINTENANCE FITTER (MECHANICAL) (GENERAL) (741.08).

May (01) join parts by welding (775)

(02) repair worn or broken components.

Other titles include Cigar making machine mechanic, Exhaust machine mechanic, Line mechanic, Sealing machine mechanic.

741.30 Fitter-mechanic (locks)

Repairs and services locks

Examines faulty lock such as mortice, cylinder or combination to ascertain nature of fault; studies drawings or other specifications; dismantles lock and removes damaged or worn parts; repairs defective parts; obtains replacement parts or prepares new parts using hand and machine tools; fits repaired or replacement parts and rebuilds lock; tests lock for correct functioning and adjusts as necessary; carries out service tasks such as cleaning, oiling and greasing.

May (01) change combination of locks
(02) make keys to fit locks.

Other titles include Locksmith (repair).

741.32 Fitter-mechanic (weighing machines)

Repairs and services weighing machines

Performs appropriate tasks as described under MAINTENANCE FITTER (MECHANICAL) (GENERAL) (741.08) but in relation to the repair and servicing of weighing machines such as counter scales, dead weight scales, platform machines and weighbridges.

May (01) replace electrical components
(02) install machines on operational sites
(03) resharpen pivots.

Other titles include Service fitter (weighing machine), Service mechanic (weighing machine).

741.34 Fitter-mechanic (coin-operated machines excluding weighing machines)

Repairs and services coin-operated machines other than weighing machines

Performs appropriate tasks as described under MAINTENANCE FITTER (MECHANICAL) (GENERAL) (741.08) but in relation to the repair and servicing of coin-operated machines such as vending machines, slot machines and ticket issuing machines.

May (01) replace electrical components
(02) repair or replace plumbing or refrigeration systems
(03) install machines on operational sites
(04) restock vending machines.

Other titles include Slot machine mechanic, Ticket machine fitter, Vending machine mechanic.

741.36 Mechanic (domestic sewing, knitting machines)

Repairs and services domestic sewing or knitting machines

Performs appropriate tasks as described under MAINTENANCE FITTER (MECHANICAL) (GENERAL) (741.08) but in relation to the repair and servicing of domestic sewing or knitting machines.

May (01) replace electrical components.

See 741.24 and 741.26 for workers repairing and servicing industrial sewing and knitting machines.

741.38 Cycle mechanic

Repairs and services pedal cycles

Performs appropriate tasks as described under MAINTENANCE FITTER (MECHANICAL) (GENERAL) (741.08) but in relation to the repair and servicing of bicycles and tricycles and in addition: repairs punctures in tyres; trues cycle wheels; renews brake blocks, linings, control cables and rods.

May (01) repair dynamo lighting systems
(02) repair perambulator wheels.

Other titles include Cycle repairer.

741.50 Gas appliance mechanic

Carries out running repairs to and routine servicing of gas appliances

Examines faulty gas appliances such as water heater, boiler, refrigerator, fire or cooker to ascertain nature and location of fault; if fault appears to be of a minor nature dismantles appliance and removes defective parts; fits replacement parts and rebuilds appliance; if major repair is necessary arranges for work to be carried out by gas fitter; tests appliance for correct functioning and adjusts as necessary; carries out service tasks such as cleaning jets.

Other titles include Gas appliance service man.

See Gas fitter (771.20)

741.60 Oil burner mechanic

Repairs and services oil heating equipment or appliances

Performs appropriate tasks as described under GAS APPLIANCE MECHANIC (741.50) but in relation to the repair and servicing of oil heating equipment or appliances and in addition checks and adjusts electrical controls.

Other titles include Oil burner service engineer, Oil burner service man.

741.70 Jobber (waste preparing machinery)

Repairs and services rag and textile waste preparing machines

Starts machines and carries out service tasks such as oiling and greasing and clearing accumulated waste material from mechanism using wire tool; cleans work area between machines; if fault arises, stops machine and locates fault; if fault appears to be of a minor nature removes defective parts and fits replacement parts or carries out simple repairs such as hand sewing broken belt drive; if major repair is necessary arranges for work to be undertaken by overlooker.

741.98 Trainee

Performs, under instruction or guidance, various tasks including training exercises and as appropriate pursues studies in order to acquire the basic skills and knowledge required to perform the tasks of installation and maintenance fitters and fitter-mechanics (plant, industrial engines and machinery and other mechanical equipment).

741.99 Other installation and maintenance fitters and fitter-mechanics (plant, industrial engines and machinery and other mechanical equipment)

Workers in this group erect mechanical plant and industrial machinery on operational site, install aircraft engines, ship machinery and related fittings, set up, repair and service plant, machinery and mechanical equipment and are not elsewhere classified, for example:

(01) **Carriage examiners** (examine railway carriages for defects and undertake minor repairs); (02) **Marine engine installers** (install main engines in ships); (03) **Ordnance maintenance fitters** (repair and service ordnance); (04) **Railway signal locking fitters** (repair and service mechanically operated railway signalling equipment); (05) **Wagon lifters** (remove railway wagons or carriages from bogies and assist with repair and servicing of bogies).

Unit Group 742 Fitter-Mechanics (Motor Vehicles)

Workers in this unit group diagnose faults in vehicles and repair and service mechanical parts of automobiles, motor cycles and other motor vehicles.

Excluded are Motor cycle rectifiers (799.12)

742.10 Reception mechanic, Road tester (used motor vehicles)

Diagnoses faults or evaluates performance of used road vehicles

Ascertains job requirements from customer or from written instructions; examines stationary vehicle or drives vehicle on test run to diagnose mechanical or electrical faults or check performance; prepares report on findings; where appropriate gives customer provisional estimate of cost and length of time required to carry out repair; obtains customer's agreement and arranges for work to be carried out.

May (01) carry out minor adjustments to vehicle during road rest

(02) arrange for vehicles to undergo official roadworthiness test

(03) specialise in testing a particular range of vehicles such as private cars, goods vehicles or fire fighting vehicles.

Other titles include Garage receptionist (mechanic), Service adviser (garage), Service receptionist (garage).

See Road tester (new motor vehicles) (734.40)

742.20 Motor mechanic

Repairs and services mechanical parts of motor cars, lorries, buses and other motor vehicles

Ascertains job requirements from work sheet, technical manuals or other specifications; examines and tests vehicle, diagnoses faults in mechanical parts and obtains customer's agreement where necessary to repair of defects not listed on work sheet; determines sequence and method of required operations; raises vehicle on hydraulic ramp or uses jacking equipment as necessary; removes unit such as engine, transmission, carburettor, gearbox, clutch and brake drums; dismantles units and removes damaged or worn parts; repairs defective parts, obtains replacement parts or units, or prepares new parts using hand and machine tools; makes report on condition of units such as brake linings and exhaust system not requiring immediate attention; cleans, fits and assembles parts and replaces units in vehicle; tests vehicle for correct functioning and adjusts as necessary; carries out routine servicing of vehicle as described under SERVICE MAN (MOTOR VEHICLES) (746.10).

May (01) repair or replace electrical units and wiring (761.60)
(02) repair bodywork
(03) join parts by brazing, soldering or welding
(04) operate electronic equipment such as engine tester-tuner and wheel aligner
(05) repair tyres
(06) examine and prepare report on condition of vehicles for official roadworthiness tests
(07) estimate cost of repairs
(08) recover damaged or defective vehicles or undertake repairs at roadside
(09) specialise on a particular type of vehicle or on a range of vehicles made by one manufacturer
(10) specialise on vehicles with petrol engines
(11) specialise on vehicles with diesel engines
(12) repair and service trailers.

Other titles include Motor fitter (garage), Service motor mechanic.

742.30 Motor cycle mechanic

Repairs and services mechanical parts of motor cycles, scooters and other motorised cycles

Performs appropriate tasks as described under MOTOR MECHANIC (742.20) but in relation to the repair and servicing of motor cycles, scooters, mopeds and similar motorised cycles.

May (01) repair or replace electrical units and wiring
(02) join parts by brazing, soldering or welding
(03) repair tyres
(04) operate electronic equipment such as engine tester-tuner
(05) specialise on two stroke engines
(06) specialise on four stroke engines.

Other titles include Moped repairer, Motor cycle repairer, Scooter mechanic.

See Motor cycle rectifier (799.12)

742.98 Trainee

Performs, under instruction or guidance, various tasks including training exercises and as appropriate pursues studies in order to acquire the basic skills and knowledge required to perform the tasks of fitter-mechanics (motor vehicles).

742.99 Other fitter-mechanics (motor vehicles)

Workers in this group diagnose faults in vehicles and repair and service mechanical parts of motor vehicles and are not elsewhere classified.

Unit Group 743 Maintenance Fitters and Fitter-Mechanics (Aircraft Engines)

Workers in this unit group repair, service and overhaul aircraft engines and ancilliary mechanical equipment.

743.10 Maintenance fitter (aircraft engines) (general)

Overhauls and carries out major repairs to aircraft engines and ancillary mechanical equipment

Ascertains job requirements from work sheets, technical manuals or other specifications; dismantles engine into component parts; degreases and cleans parts, inspects for wear or other defects and obtains replacement parts as necessary; fits and assembles parts to rebuild engine using hand tools such as screwdrivers, torque spanners and wrenches; checks alignment during assembly using clock and height gauges, micrometers, verniers and other measuring instruments; cleans and examines fuel and air intakes, exhaust system propellers, compressors and similar fittings and replaces defective items.

May (01) remove engine from aircraft

(02) install and test repaired engines in aircraft

(03) joins parts by riveting

(04) specialise on piston engines

(05) specialise on jet engines.

Additional factor: whether in possession of appropriate maintenance licence.

743.20 Maintenance fitter (aircraft engine) (specialised)

Specialises in one or more of the operations in the overhaul and major repair of aircraft engines and ancillary mechanical equipment

Performs appropriate tasks as described under MAINTENANCE FITTER (AIRCRAFT ENGINE) (GENERAL) (743.10) but in relation to particular operations in the overhaul and major repair of aircraft engines, for example dismantling, check of component parts, re-erection.

May (01) test repaired engines in aircraft

(02) join parts by riveting.

Additional factor: whether in possession of appropriate maintenance licence.

Other titles include Aircraft engine dismantler.

743.30 Service fitter (aircraft engine)

Carries out running repairs to and routine servicing of engines in aircraft

Examines engine cowlings and inlet and exhaust vents for damage; removes any foreign objects; examines engine and ancillary mechanical equipment for defects such as oil and leaks; if faults appear to be of a minor nature removes defective parts and fits and assembles replacement parts; if major repair is necessary removes or arranges for removal of engine from aircraft and installs or arranges for the installation of replacement engine; carries out servicing tasks such as the check of water content in fuel tanks, the check of position of thrust reversers in jet engine, and the cleaning and adjusting of carburettors and plugs in piston engines according to schedule.

Additional factor: whether in possession of appropriate maintenance licence.

743.98 Trainee

Performs, under instruction or guidance, various tasks including training exercises and as appropriate pursues studies in order to acquire the basic skills and knowledge required to perform the tasks of maintenance fitters and fitter-mechanics (aircraft engines).

743.99 Other maintenance fitters and fitter-mechanics (aircraft engines)

Workers in this group repair, service and overhaul aircraft engines and ancillary mechanical equipment and are not elsewhere classified.

Unit Group 744 Precision Instrument Maintaining and Repairing Occupations

Workers in this unit group adjust, repair and service precision and optical instruments, watches and clocks.

See 749.99 for dental and surgical instrument repairers.

744.10 Optical instrument mechanic

Repairs and services optical instruments

Examines faulty instrument such as binoculars, microscope or theodolite to ascertain nature and location of defects; studies instrument drawings, technical manuals or other specifications; determines sequence and method of required operations; dismantles instrument; removes damaged or worn parts; either repairs defective parts, obtains replacement parts or prepares new parts using hand and machine tools; cleans component parts; fits and assembles parts to rebuild instrument; tests instrument for correct functioning and adjusts as necessary; carries out service tasks such as cleaning, lubricating and re-aligning.

May (01) recalibrate instruments.

Other titles include Optical instrument repairer, Camera repairer, Projector repairer.

744.20 Precision instrument mechanic (excluding optical instruments)

Repairs and services precision instruments other than optical instruments

Performs appropriate tasks as described under OPTICAL INSTRUMENT MECHANIC (744.10) but in relation to the repair and servicing of precision instruments such as ammeters, barometers, flowmeters, pressure gauges, aircraft compasses and air position indicators.

May (01) recalibrate instruments
(02) service and repair electronic and electro-mechanical equipment and instruments.

Additional facror: whether in possession of appropriate aircraft maintenance licence.

Other titles include Aircraft instrument mechanic, Barometer repairer, Electrical instrument mechanic, Electrical instrument repairer.

744.30 Watch and clock repairer

Repairs and services watches and/or clocks

Removes watch or clock mechanism from casing; examines mechanism to ascertain nature and location of defects; dismantles mechanism, removes damaged or worn parts and obtains replacement parts; cleans component parts; fits and assembles parts to rebuild watch or clock and replaces in casing; tests watch or clock for correct functioning using electronic or other test equipment and adjusts as necessary; carries out service tasks such as cleaning, oiling and regulating.

May (01) repair defective parts or prepare new parts using hand tools and lathes
(02) estimate cost of repairs.

Other titles include Clock repairer, Watch repairer.

744.40 Compass adjuster (marine)

Adjusts, repairs and services ships' compasses

Removes compass from mounting on ship (binnacle) and tests for error caused by inclination of ship (heeling error) using special purpose measuring instrument; adjusts compass by adding or withdrawing small magnets and replaces in binnacle; when ship is at sea takes bearings from sun, stars or known landmarks; adjusts compass by inserting magnets to obtain most accurate readings; makes allowances for ship's degaussing equipment when carrying out adjustments; prepares record of deviations; carries out repair and servicing of compasses on board ship or in workshop on land as described under OPTICAL INSTRUMENT MECHANIC (744.10).

Note: must possess certificate of competency as compass adjuster.

744.98 Trainee

Performs, under instruction or guidance, various tasks including training exercises and as appropriate pursues studies in order to acquire the basic skills and knowledge required to perform the tasks of workers in precision instrument maintaining and repairing occupations.

744.99 Other precision instrument maintaining and repairing occupations

Workers in this group adjust, repair and service precision and optical instruments, watches and clocks and are not elsewhere classified.

Unit Group 745 Office Machinery Maintaining and Repairing Occupations (Mechanical)

Workers in this unit group repair and service mechanical office machinery and cash tills and registers.

745.10 Office machinery mechanic (general)

Repairs and services various types of mechanical office machines

Examines faulty machine to ascertain nature and location of defects; studies drawings, technical manuals or other specifications; determines sequence and method of required operations; dismantles machine, removes damaged or worn parts and obtains replacement parts; fits and assembles parts to rebuild machine; tests machine for correct functioning and adjusts as necessary; carries out service tasks such as cleaning, oiling and greasing, according to schedule. Performs these tasks in relation to various types of mechanical office machines.

May (01) replace electrical or electronic components
(02) estimate cost of repairs
(03) sell office machines and office requisites.

Other titles include Service representative (office machines).

745.20 Office machinery mechanic (mechanical adding, accounting, calculating machines)

Repairs and services mechanical adding, accounting or calculating machines

Performs appropriate tasks as described under OFFICE MACHINERY MECHANIC (GENERAL) (745.10) but in relation to the repair and servicing of mechanical adding, accounting or calculating machines.

May (01) replace electrical or electronic components
(02) estimate cost of repairs.

Other titles include Accounting machine mechanic, Accounting and calculating machine mechanic, Adding machine mechanic, Calculating machine mechanic.

See Service mechanic (office electrical machines) (761.80) and Service mechanic (electronic office equipment) (763.40)

745.30 Typewriter mechanic

Repairs and services typewriters

Performs appropriate tasks as described under OFFICE MACHINERY MECHANIC (GENERAL) (745.10) but in relation to the repair and servicing of typewriters.

May (01) replace electrical components.

745.40 Mechanic (cash till, cash register)

Repairs and services cash tills or registers

Performs appropriate tasks as described under OFFICE MACHINERY MECHANIC (GENERAL) (745.10) but in relation to the repair and servicing of cash tills or registers.

May (01) replace electrical components
(02) repair component parts
(03) install cash tills on operational site and demonstrate working of machines.

745.98 Trainee

Performs, under instruction or guidance, various tasks including training exercises and as appropriate pursues studies in order to acquire the basic skills and knowledge required to perform the tasks of workers in office machinery maintaining and repairing occupations (mechanical).

745.99 Other office machinery maintaining and repairing occupations (mechanical)

Workers in this group repair and service mechanical office machinery and are not elsewhere classified.

Unit Group 746 Servicing, Oiling, Greasing and Related Occupations (Mechanical)

Workers in this unit group carry out minor servicing tasks including topping up batteries and water cooling systems, checking tyre pressures and lubricating motor vehicles, stationary engines, rolling stock and other machinery and mechanical equipment and cleaning mechanical parts of machinery and equipment.

746 .10 Motor vehicle service man

Performs minor tasks in the servicing of motor vehicles

Performs some or all of the following tasks: injects grease into greasing points of vehicle using hand or compressed air-powered grease gun; checks level of oil in gearbox, rear axle, steering box and engine and replenishes as required; checks levels of fluid in clutch, brake and power steering reservoirs, of electrolyte in battery and of coolant in radiator and replenishes as required; re-charges battery as necessary; drains oil from engine sump, renews oil filter and fills sump with new oil; renews or cleans and adjusts sparking plugs; oils carburettor dampers, dynamo bearings, water pump and door locks and hinges; checks and reports on condition of tyres; changes position of wheels; checks balance of wheels and tyre pressures and adjusts as necessary; checks lighting system and replaces faulty bulbs.

May (01) repair punctured tyres

(02) fit repaired or replacement tyres (749 .55)

(03) clean and polish vehicles (452 .99 or 979 .60)

(04) service trailers.

Other titles include Oiler and greaser, Greasing bay attendant, Lubricating bay attendant.

746 .50 Oiler and greaser

Lubricates moving parts of stationary engines, rolling stock, machinery and similar mechanical equipment

Ascertains job requirements from lubrication charts or other instructions; fills grease gun with grease of appropriate grade; injects grease into grease points of machinery or equipment using hand or compressed air-powered grease gun; fills oil can with oil of appropriate grade and applies oil to lubrication holes in machinery or equipment; packs grease by hand into lubrication cups or boxes on machinery or equipment; spreads grease by hand over surface of bearings, axles and similar parts; inspects machines or equipment visually and reports faults to foreman.

May (01) clean equipment

(02) operate automatic lubrication system.

Additional factor: whether specialised on a particular type of machinery or equipment, eg gasholder, kiln, stationary engine.

Other titles include Gasholder attendant, Greaser, Kiln greaser, Lift machinery attendant, Oiler, Pulleyman, Rigger (gasworks), Speed frame cleaner.

Excluded are Oilers and greasers (motor vehicles) (746 .10), Greasers (911 .50) and Oilers (911 .50)

746 .55 Oiler and bander

Replaces tapes on spinning frames and lubricates textile machinery

Removes broken tape from spinning frames; selects lengths of cotton, nylon or nylon-edged cotton tape and cuts to required size; threads tape through spinning frame and around drive rollers; overlaps tape ends and sews together or fuses ends together using electrically heated bonding machine; stretches joined tape around spindles and where appropriate round guide pulleys; oils and greases machinery as described under OILER AND GREASER (746 .50).

Other titles include Oiler and tape sewer.

746 .60 Woollen fettler

Removes accumulated woollen fibres, dirt and grease from wire teeth of card clothing using a fettling comb

Unscrews guard plates from carding machine and removes drive belt or chain; rotates rollers by hand and removes accumulated fibres, dirt, grease, etc from wire teeth of card clothing using steel fettling combs of appropriate grades; removes top rollers to clean interior rollers; replaces rollers, drive belt or chain and guard plates.

May (01) clean, oil and grease carding machine (746 .50).

Other titles include Card fettler, Wool textile carding fettler.

746 .65 Rollerman (rope haulage)

Ensures that rollers in rope haulage system run freely

Checks that each roller in rope haulage track will rotate; lifts jammed roller out of its seating, clears the obstruction and replaces roller; replaces any rollers which have been displaced by rope vibration; applies grease to ends of rollers; replaces worn rollers with new ones; reports any faults in haulage ropes to the deputy (coalmining) or foreman.

746.98 Trainee

Performs, under instruction or guidance, various tasks including training exercises and as appropriate pursues studies in order to acquire the basic skills and knowledge required to perform the tasks of workers in servicing, oiling, greasing and related occupations (mechanical).

746.99 Other servicing, oiling, greasing and related occupations (mechanical)

Workers in this group service, lubricate and clean machinery and mechanical equipment and carry out related tasks and are not elsewhere classified, for example:

(01) **Filter cleaners** (strip down filter frames and replace filter cloths); (02) **Oil attendants** (clean and service oil burners in sheet glass manufacture).

Unit Group 749 Installing, Maintaining and Repairing Occupations (Machines, Instruments and Related Mechanical Equipment) Not Elsewhere Classified

Workers in this unit group repair and sharpen saws, maintain mine shafts, fix card clothing and pins in textile machinery, replace tyres on motor vehicles and carry out other miscellaneous tasks in the installation, maintenance and repair of plant, machines, instruments and related mechanical equipment and are not elsewhere classified.

749.05 Service fitter (aircraft engine and air-frame)

Carries out running repairs to and routine servicing of aircraft engines, air-frames and control systems

Performs appropriate tasks as described under SERVICE FITTER (AIRCRAFT ENGINE) (743.30) and SERVICE FITTER (AIR-FRAME) (741.22).

Additional factor: whether in possession of appropriate maintenance licence.

749.10 Saw repairer and sharpener

Repairs and sharpens hand, band- or circular saws

Examines blades for cracks or other defects; brazes or welds cracks in blades; hammers blades to remove dents and twists; tensions band-saw blades using rolling machine, and tensions hand and circular saws by hammering; re-sets teeth to correct cutting angle using swage setting tool; sharpens teeth using special purpose machine; joins broken ends of band-saws by brazing or welding and smoothes joint by filing.

May (01) sharpen saws by hand using files

(02) weld or braze special tips of materials such as stellite or tungsten carbide on to saw blades

(03) repair and sharpen cutters for woodworking machines.

Other titles include Saw doctor.

See 726.99 (06) for workers who sharpen saw blades by machine and 799.14 for workers who tension circular saw blades.

749.15 Shaftsman

Inspects and maintains mine shafts, cages and shaft fittings

Carries out daily inspections of shafts; examines rock or coal shaft facings or concrete, brick or wood shaft linings for cracks and carries out or arranges for repairs; checks water, air and drainage pipes and gutters for defects or blockages, tightens connections, seals leaks and clears blockages; checks condition of guide rails, ropes and supports and carries out repairs or installs replacements parts; examines cages and cage fittings for wear; replaces defective woodwork and small metal fittings such as catches and brackets, and arranges for repairs to other metal work as required; controls the loading and unloading of bulky or heavy equipment into and out of cages.

Note: must have knowledge of mine safety regulations.

749.20 Card nailer

Fixes card clothing on to cylinders of carding machines

Strips worn card clothing from carding machine cylinder; fixes mounting unit on carding machine along surface of cylinder or, if cylinder has been removed from machine, positions cylinder on nailing machine; renews wooden plugs set in surface of cylinder as required; tapers end of strip of card clothing (fillet); threads end of fillet through mounting unit or over and around tension bars along front of nailing machine; nails end of fillet to wooden plugs in cylinder; operates control to rotate cylinder and winds fillet spirally round the cylinder; when cylinder is covered, cuts fillet, tapers end and nails to wooden plugs; nails fillet to plugs at intervals along cylinder.

749.25 Stripper and grinder (textile machinery)

Removes accumulated cotton waste from wire teeth of card clothing and sharpens teeth

Operates suction equipment and hand or machine operated wire brush to clear accumulated cotton waste from wire teeth on carding rollers and flats; sharpens worn wire teeth on carding rollers and flats by grinding on mechanically driven carborundum or emery wheels or rollers.

May (01) oil and grease carding machine (746.50).

See Card grinder (textile machinery) (726.10)

749.30 Pin setter (textile machinery)

Replaces defective steel pins in textile fibre preparing machinery

Removes worn and damaged steel pins from base of comb circles, comb cylinder half laps, top combs, fallers or blades using pliers, or knocks out pins from soldered base after melting solder; selects new steel pins of correct size and shape and knocks into holes in base using hammer and punch, or places pins in grooves in base, clamps in position with wood strip and solders or secures with plastic adhesive; when set removes wood strip and surplus solder or adhesive; straightens and aligns the set pins using steel tubes.

May (01) insert pins in new machinery.

Other titles include Circle comb setter, Faller setter, Needle setter (textile machinery), Repinner (textile machinery).

749.50 Heald mender

Cleans and repairs healds

Removes fluff, dirt, grease and loose threads from healds using wire brush; inspects cotton, worsted or nylon threads or steel wires for defects; straightens bent wires with pliers; cuts off broken or worn threads or wires; inserts fresh thread or wire through eyelet in heald and secures to top or base bar, ensuring that threads or wires are correctly aligned and tensioned.

May (01) arrange sets of healds in readiness for fixing in loom
(02) clean and repair reeds.

Other titles include Gear maintenance man (weaving), Heald dresser.

749.55 Tyre fitter

Removes worn or defective tyres from vehicle wheels and fits repaired or replacement tyres

Raises vehicle using jacking equipment; where appropriate removes hub cap from wheel; unbolts wheel from vehicle using hand or powered hand tools, removes valve core and deflates tyre, removes tyre from wheel using hand tools and/or mechanical equipment; where appropriate removes inner tube; fits new, remoulded or repaired tyre to wheel and inserts inner tube; fits valve core and inflates tyre to correct pressure; checks tyre for leaks and rectifies as necessary; bolts wheel to vehicle, replaces hub cap and lowers vehicle.

May (01) repair tyres and inner tubes
(02) balance wheels
(03) change position of wheels on vehicle to prevent uneven tyre wear
(04) pump water into tractor tyres to act as ballast
(05) check daily the condition of tyres fitted to vehicles.

Other titles include Tyre maintenance fitter.

749.60 Powered supports maintenance man

Tests and carries out minor repairs to powered supports in mine

Carries out daily check of all power supports; tests hydraulic action by operating prop control valve; replaces faulty control valves; checks level of hydraulic fluid and tops up if necessary; replaces cut or worn hose with new length of hose; arranges for damaged supports requiring major repair to be removed to mine surface; keeps records of supports checked and supports removed to surface.

Note: must have knowledge of mine safety regulations.

749.65 Cleaner (boiler, pipe)

Removes deposits from boilers or pipe systems

Closes valves to isolate boiler or pipe system and opens inspection or other access panel.

Removes deposits by one or more of the following methods: directs steam jets on to deposit; burns off deposit; pumps solvent fluid into pipe system; scrapes off deposit using hand or powered hand tools such as chisels, scrapers, wire brushes and flails. Loads extracted deposit into containers for disposal; closes inspection or other access panels, renewing gaskets as necessary and opens connecting valves.

May (01) replace defective boiler tubes.

Other titles include Ascension pipe cleaner, Boiler scaler, Hydraulic main cleaner.

749.70 Conveyor mover

Erects, extends, dismantles and repositions underground conveyors in coal-mine

Clears obstructions from path of conveyor and ensures that ground is level; erects conveyor at coal face or in roadway; as face advances, dismantles sections of conveyor and re-assembles in new position; when face is exhausted, dismantles conveyor and re-erects at new face.

See 873.20 for workers moving conveyors at a mechanised face as part of a cutting-loading team.

749.98 Trainee

Performs, under instruction or guidance, various tasks including training exercises and as appropriate pursues studies in order to acquire the basic skills and knowledge required to perform the tasks of workers in installing, maintaining and repairing occupations (machines, instruments, and related mechanical equipment) not elsewhere classified.

749.99 Other installing, maintaining and repairing occupations (machines, instruments and related mechanical equipment) not elsewhere classified

Workers in this group carry out miscellaneous tasks in the installation, maintenance and repair of plant, machines, instruments and mechanical equipment and are not separately classified, for example:

(01) **Cylinder tester-rectifiers** (test empty acetylene cylinder valve mechanisms and rectify faults prior to refilling); (02) **Dental instrument repairers;** (03) **Fume attendants** (inspect fume extraction and conditioning system and carry out minor repairs in oxygen steel plant); (04) **Surgical instrument repairers.**

Minor Group 75 PRODUCTION FITTING AND WIRING OCCUPATIONS (ELECTRICAL AND ELECTRONIC)

Workers in this minor group fit and assemble parts in the manufacture of electrical and electronic equipment, install wiring and electrical equipment in road and rail vehicles, aircraft and other products and perform miscellaneous production wiring tasks.

The occupations are arranged in the following unit groups:

750 Foremen (Production Fitting and Wiring Occupations (Electrical and Electronic))

751 Production Fitters (Electrical and Electronic)

752 Electricians (Production)

759 Production Fitting and Wiring Occupations (Electrical and Electronic) Not Elsewhere Classified

Excluded are Precision Instrument Making Occupations (732) and Repetitive assemblers (electrical, electronic goods) (821·45)

Unit Group 750 Foremen (Production Fitting and Wiring Occupations (Electrical and Electronic))

Workers in this unit group directly supervise and co-ordinate the activities of workers in production fitting and wiring occupations (electrical and electronic).

750 .10 Foreman fitter (electrical) (production)

Directly supervises and co-ordinates the activities of electrical fitters (production)

Performs appropriate tasks as described under SUPERVISOR/FOREMAN (UNSPECIFIED) (990 .00).

May (01) supervise maintenance fitters.

Additional factor: number of workers supervised.

750 .20 Foreman fitter (electronics) (production)

Directly supervises and co-ordinates the activities of electronics fitters (production)

Performs appropriate tasks as described under SUPERVISOR/FOREMAN (UNSPECIFIED) (990 .00).

Additional factor: number of workers supervised.

750 .30 Foreman electrician (production)

Directly supervises and co-ordinates the activities of electricians (production)

Performs appropriate tasks as described under SUPERVISOR/FOREMAN (UNSPECIFIED) (990 .00).

Additional factor: number of workers supervised.

750 .98 Trainee

Performs, under instruction or guidance, various tasks including training exercises and as appropriate pursues studies in order to acquire the basic skills and knowledge required to perform the tasks of foremen (production fitting and wiring occupations (electrical and electronic)).

750 .99 Other foremen (production fitting and wiring occupations (electrical and electronic))

Workers in this group directly supervise and co-ordinate the activities of workers in production fitting and wiring occupations (electrical and electronic) and are not elsewhere classified.

Unit Group 751 Production Fitters (Electrical and Electronic)

Workers in this unit group fit and assemble parts and sub-assemblies in the manufacture of electrical and electronic equipment.

751 .05 Electrical fitter (general)

Fits and assembles parts and/or sub-assemblies in the manufacture of various types of electrical equipment

Ascertains job requirements from drawings, wiring diagrams or other specifications; determines sequence and method of required operations; checks metal and other parts for accuracy of machining or sub-assemblies for accuracy of fit using measuring instruments; assembles parts and sub-assemblies making any necessary adjustments using hand tools such as files, reamers, scrapers and spanners to ensure accurate fit; checks alignment during assembly using measuring instruments; selects wire or cable, cuts to required length and strips insulation from ends; connects prepared wire or cable to appropriate terminals or connectors by crimping, brazing, soldering or bolting to complete equipment circuit. Performs these tasks in relation to the manufacture of various types of electrical equipment.

May (01) make and machine metal parts
(02) carry out functional tests of equipment
(03) install equipment on site.

Other titles include Electrical fitter-erector (production).

Excluded are Electrical fitters (prototype, experimental) (751 .10)

751 .10 Electrical fitter (prototype, experimental)

Fits and assembles parts and/or sub-assemblies in the manufacture of prototype or experimental electrical equipment

Performs tasks as described under ELECTRICAL FITTER (GENERAL) (751 .05) but in relation to the manufacture of prototype or experimental electrical equipment.

May (01) make and machine metal parts
(02) carry out functional tests of equipment.

751 .15 Electrical fitter (switchgear and control equipment)

Fits and assembles parts and/or sub-assemblies in the manufacture of electrical switchgear and control equipment

Performs tasks as described under ELECTRICAL FITTER (GENERAL) (751 .05) but in relation to the manufacture of electrical switchgear and control equipment.

May (01) make and machine metal parts
(02) carry out functional tests of equipment.

Other titles include Controller maker, Switchgear maker.

751 .20 Electrical fitter (switchboards)

Fits and assembles parts and/or sub-assemblies in the manufacture of switchboards

Performs tasks as described under ELECTRICAL FITTER (GENERAL) (751 .05) but in relation to the manufacture of switchboards.

May (01) drill parts using powered hand drills
(02) joint cables (764 .30)
(03) make connecting bars from copper strip using hand and machine tools
(04) install equipment on site.

Other titles include Switchboard erector.

751 .25 Electrical fitter (transformers)

Fits and assembles parts and/or sub-assemblies in the manufacture of transformers

Performs tasks as described under ELECTRICAL FITTER (GENERAL) (751 .05) but in relation to the manufacture of transformers.

May (01) fit and assemble parts to make tap changers
(02) fill transformer tanks with oil
(03) install equipment on site.

Other titles include Transformer builder.

751.30 Electrical fitter (motors, generators, alternators)

Fits and assembles parts and/or sub-assemblies in the manufacture of electric motors, generators or alternators

Performs tasks as described under ELECTRICAL FITTER (GENERAL) (751.05) but in relation to the manufacture of electric motors, generators, alternators, commutators or armatures.

May (01) adjust balance of armatures by pouring liquid lead into drilled holes or by brazing on weights
(02) fit retaining rings to alternator windings
(03) fit slip rings
(04) install equipment on site.

Other titles include Armature builder, Commutator builder.

751.35 Electrical fitter (other equipment)

Fits and assembles parts and/or sub-assemblies in the manufacture of specific electrical equipment not separately identified

Performs tasks as described under ELECTRICAL FITTER (GENERAL) (751.05) but in relation to the manufacture of specific electrical equipment, not separately identified, such as rectifiers.

May (01) make and machine metal parts
(02) carry out functional tests of equipment
(03) install equipment on site.

Other titles include Segment builder (rectifiers).

751.40 Electronics fitter (general)

Fits and assembles parts and/or sub-assemblies in the manufacture of various types of electronic equipment

Ascertains job requirements from drawings, wiring diagrams or other specifications; determines sequence and method of required operations; marks out and cuts, drills bends or otherwise shapes metal to form component parts of chassis, rack or other unit using hand and machine tools; fits and assembles parts and joins by brazing, riveting or welding; wires up electronic equipment as described under ELECTRONICS WIREMAN (GENERAL) (759.05); tests completed circuit using equipment such as multi-range meter, valve voltmeter and oscilloscope; undertakes repair work as required. Performs these tasks in relation to the manufacture of various types of electronic equipment.

May (01) attach identification tags to circuit wiring.

Other titles include Electronics technician (fitter).

Excluded are Electronics fitters (prototype, experimental) (751.45)

751.45 Electronics fitter (prototype, experimental)

Fits and assembles parts and/or sub-assemblies in the manufacture of prototype or experimental electronic equipment

Performs tasks as described under ELECTRONICS FITTER (GENERAL) (751.40) but in relation to the manufacture of prototype or experimental electronic equipment.

Other titles include Electronics technician (fitter).

751.50 Electronics fitter (telecommunication equipment)

Fits and assembles parts and/or sub-assemblies in the manufacture of electronic telecommunication equipment

Performs tasks as described under ELECTRONICS FITTER (GENERAL) (751.40) but in relation to the manufacture of electronic communication equipment such as radio transmitters and receivers and telephonic equipment.

May (01) attach identification tags to circuit wiring.

Other titles include Electronics technician (fitter).

751.55 Electronics fitter (computer equipment)

Fits and assembles parts and/or sub-assemblies in the manufacture of electronic computer equipment

Performs tasks as described under ELECTRONICS FITTER (GENERAL) (751.40) but in relation to the manufacture of electronic computer equipment.

May (01) attach identification tags to circuit wiring.

Other titles include Electronics technician (fitter).

751.60 Electronics fitter (medical equipment)

Fits and assembles parts and/or sub-assemblies in the manufacture of electronic medical equipment

Performs tasks as described under ELECTRONICS FITTER (GENERAL) (751.40) but in relation to the manufacture of electronic medical equipment such as cardiac monitoring apparatus and electro-encephalographs.

May (01) attach identification tags to circuit wiring.

Other titles include Electronics technician (fitter).

751 .65 Electronics fitter (other equipment)

Fits and assembles parts and/or sub-assemblies in the manufacture of specific electronic equipment not separately identified

Performs tasks as described under ELECTRONICS FITTER (GENERAL) (751 .40) but in relation to the manufacture of specific electronic equipment, not separately identified, such as machine control equipment, office machines and radar equipment.

May (01) attach identification tags to circuit wiring.

Other titles include Electronics technician (fitter).

751 .98 Trainee

Performs, under instruction or guidance, various tasks including training exercises and as appropriate pursues studies in order to acquire the basic skills and knowledge required to perform the tasks of production fitters (electrical and electronic).

751 .99 Other production fitters (electrical and electronic)

Workers in this group fit and assemble parts and sub-assemblies in the manufacture of electrical and electronic equipment and are not elsewhere classified.

Unit Group 752 Electricians (Production)

Workers in this unit group install electrical wiring, fittings and equipment in road and rail vehicles, aircraft and other manufactured products.

752 .10 Aircraft electrician

Prepares electrical wiring sub-assemblies and harnesses for aircraft and installs electrical wiring, fittings and equipment in aircraft

Ascertains job requirements from drawings or other specifications; cuts wires to required length and strips insulation from ends; assembles required number of wires and crimps or solders one end of each wire to socket or plug; lays wires with socket or plug round prepared channels in jig board and secures wires with cord or other binding material to form wiring harness and crimps or solders tags on free ends of wires; removes prepared harness from board ready for inspection; assembles components on instrument panel; installs wiring harness, instrument panels, lighting and other electrical fittings and equipment in aircraft; connects wiring to fittings and equipment.

May (01) test wiring and equipment for faults using equipment such as voltmeters and meggers.

752 .20 Vehicle electrician

Installs electrical wiring, fittings and equipment in road or rail vehicles

Ascertains job requirements from drawings, wiring diagrams or other specifications; fits and secures wiring, including prepared wiring harnesses to vehicle body and chassis; installs electrical fittings and equipment such as lights, starters, generators, alternators, voltage and charging regulators, radio and intercommunication equipment, protective devices, dashboard instruments and wiper and blower motors; connects wiring to fittings and equipment; tests electrical circuits for defects and rectifies as necessary.

May (01) cut openings and drill holes for wiring, light fixtures and fuse holders.

752 .30 Electrical wireman

Wires up prepared parts and/or sub-assemblies in the manufacture of electrical equipment

Ascertains job requirements from drawings, wiring diagrams or other specifications; determines sequence and method of required operations; selects wire, cuts to required length and strips insulation from ends; installs wiring and connects to appropriate terminal tags by crimping or soldering.

May (01) test completed circuit using equipment such as megger or watt-meter

(02) attach identification tags to circuit wiring

(03) undertake repair work.

See Electronics wireman (general) (759 .05)

752.98 Trainee

Performs, under instruction or guidance, various tasks including training exercises and as appropriate pursues studies in order to acquire the basic skills and knowledge required to perform the tasks of electricians (production).

752.99 Other electricians (production)

Workers in this group install electrical wiring, fittings and equipment in manufactured products and are not elsewhere classified.

Unit Group 759 Production Fitting and Wiring Occupations (Electrical and Electronic) Not Elsewhere Classified

Workers in this unit group wire up electronic equipment, make coils and wiring harnesses for electrical and electronic equipment and perform miscellaneous tasks in electrical and electronic production fitting and wiring and are not elsewhere classified.

759.05 Electronics wireman (general)

Wires up prepared parts and/or sub-assemblies in the manufacture of various types of electronic equipment

Ascertains job requirements from drawings, wiring diagrams or other specifications; determines sequence and method of required operations; positions and secures parts such as switches, tags, transformers and valve holders to chassis, rack or other unit, using hand tools; selects electronic parts such as capacitors, resistors, transistors or sub-assemblies and connects to appropriate terminal tags on units or printed circuit panels by soldering; selects wire, cuts to required length and strips insulation from ends; connects wire to appropriate terminal tags by crimping or soldering. Performs these tasks in relation to the manufacture of various types of electronic equipment.

May (01) test completed circuit using equipment such as oscilloscope

(02) attach identification tags to circuit wiring

(03) undertake repair work.

Other titles include Electronics technician (wireman).

See Electrical wireman (752.30)

Excluded are Electronics wiremen (prototype, experimental) (759.10)

759.10 Electronics wireman (prototype, experimental)

Wires up prepared parts and/or sub-assemblies in the manufacture of prototype or experimental electronic equipment

Performs tasks as described under ELECTRONICS WIREMAN (GENERAL) (759.05) but in relation to the manufacture of prototype or experimental electronic equipment.

Other titles include Electronics technician (wireman).

759.15 Electronics wireman (specialised equipment excluding prototype or experimental)

Wires up prepared parts and/or sub-assemblies in the manufacture of specific electronic equipment other than prototype or experimental equipment

Performs tasks as described under ELECTRONICS WIREMAN (GENERAL) (759.05) but in relation to the manufacture of specific electronic equipment (other than prototype or experimental equipment) such as electronic computers or electro-encephalographs.

May (01) test completed circuit using equipment such as oscilloscope

(02) attach identification tags to circuit wiring

(03) undertake repair work.

Other titles include Electronics technician (wireman).

759.20 Armature winder

Fits coils into armatures, rotors or stators

Positions coils in armature, rotor or stator, inserts insulation material as required and secures with wedges; joins (makes off) ends of coils to terminals by brazing or soldering; if undertaking repair work removes defective coils and fits new coils.

May (01) perform tasks of COIL WINDER (HEAVY) (759.50).

Other titles include Rotor winder, Stator winder.

759.50 Coil winder (heavy)

Winds heavy continuous coils for transformers, armatures, rotors or stators from copper wire or strip

Ascertains job requirements from job instruction card, diagrams or other specifications; sets up appropriate former on winding machine; sets drum(s) of copper wire or strip on spindle(s); threads ends of wire or strip through tension clamp and secures to former; operates machine to wind wire or strip round former; winds insulation material round wire or strip between turns and inserts wedges as required; as winding progresses, flattens and tightens coil using soft-headed mallet; removes or directs removal of finished coil from machine.

759.55 Coil former

Forms single and half-turn coils for large armatures and stators from copper strip

Ascertains job requirements from job instruction card, diagrams or other specifications; selects copper strip of appropriate gauge and cuts to required length(s); bends strip to rough shape, using bending press as required; positions partly shaped strip on wooden former and completes shaping using clamps and soft-headed mallet.

759.60 Coil winder (light)

Winds wire on to formers to make coils for light electrical equipment

Secures bobbin or other former and reel of wire of required gauge on machine; threads end of wire through eyelet on former or attaches to tag on former by twisting or soldering; operates machine to wind wire on to former for required number of turns; wraps insulating material round coil; repeats winding and insulating operations as specified to form complete coil; cuts wire, removes coil from machine and secures end of wire to former or tag as described above.

May (01) wind special types of coil by hand.

Other titles include Bobbin winder, Resistance winder.

759.65 Cable former

Lays out and secures lengths of wire following pattern on pegboard or bench to make harnesses for use in electrical or electronic circuits

Positions wiring diagram on pegboard or bench and inserts pegs or nails at marked points, or obtains prepared board; selects wire according to specification; lays wire between specific pegs or nails and cuts to length, or cuts wire to length and lays in position; repeats operation with further wire according to specification; secures the lengths of wire with twine or other binding material to form harness; lifts completed harness from pegboard or bench.

May (01) attach identification tags to wires
(02) remove insulation from ends of wire and solder ends.

Other titles include Cable form maker, Harness maker, Loom former.

759.98 Trainee

Performs, under instruction or guidance, various tasks including training exercises and as appropriate pursues studies in order to acquire the basic skills and knowledge required to perform the tasks of workers in production fitting and wiring occupations (electrical and electronic) not elsewhere classified.

759.99 Other production fitting and wiring occupations (electrical and electronic) not elsewhere classified

Workers in this group perform miscellaneous tasks in electrical and electronic production fitting and wiring and are not separately classified, for example:

(01) **Neon sign assemblers;** (02) **Tester-rectifiers (electrical equipment)**; (03) **Tester-rectifiers (electronic equipment)**.

Minor Group 76 INSTALLING, MAINTAINING AND REPAIRING OCCUPATIONS (ELECTRICAL AND ELECTRONIC)

Workers in this minor group install, maintain and repair electrical, electronic and related plant, machinery and equipment, electrical wiring in buildings and on board ships, lighting for theatre, film and television productions, overhead electricity and telecommunications lines, repair and service radio and television equipment, signalling and telecommunications systems and electrical equipment in aircraft and vehicles, and joint electric and telecommunications cables and perform closely related tasks.

The occupations are arranged in the following unit groups:

760 Foremen (Installing, Maintaining and Repairing Occupations (Electrical and Electronic))

761 Electricians (Installation, Maintenance and Repair) (Plant, Machinery and Other Equipment)

762 Electricians (Installation, Maintenance and Repair) (Premises and Ships)

763 Installing, Maintaining and Repairing Occupations (Electronic and Related Equipment)

764 Linesmen and Cable Jointers

769 Installing, Maintaining and Repairing Occupations (Electrical and Electronic) Not Elsewhere Classified

Excluded are Precision Instrument Maintaining and Repairing Occupations (744)

Unit Group 760 Foremen (Installing, Maintaining and Repairing Occupations (Electrical and Electronic))

Workers in this unit group directly supervise and co-ordinate the activities of workers in installing, maintaining and repairing occupations (electrical and electronic).

760 .10 Foreman installation electrician (plant, machinery and other equipment)

Directly supervises and co-ordinates the activities of installation electricians (plant, machinery and other equipment)

Performs appropriate tasks as described under SUPERVISOR/FOREMAN (UNSPECIFIED) (990 .00).

May (01) supervise maintenance electricians.

Additional factor: number of workers supervised.

760 .20 Foreman electrician (maintenance and repair) (plant, machinery and other equipment)

Directly supervises and co-ordinates the activities of electricians (maintenance and repair) (plant, machinery and other equipment)

Performs appropriate tasks as described under SUPERVISOR/FOREMAN (UNSPECIFIED) (990 .00).

Additional factor: number of workers supervised.

760 .30 Foreman electrician (installation, maintenance and repair) (premises and ships)

Directly supervises and co-ordinates the activities of electricians (installation, maintenance and repair) (premises and ships)

Performs appropriate tasks as described under SUPERVISOR/FOREMAN (UNSPECIFIED) (990 .00).

Additional factor: number of workers supervised.

760 .40 Foreman installation fitter (electronic and related equipment)

Directly supervises and co-ordinates the activities of installers (electronic and related equipment)

Performs appropriate tasks as described under SUPERVISOR/ FOREMAN (UNSPECIFIED) (990 .00).

May (01) supervise maintenance fitters.

Additional factor: number of workers supervised.

760 .50 Foreman fitter (maintenance and repair) (electronic and related equipment)

Directly supervises and co-ordinates the activities of fitters (maintenance and repair) (electronic and related equipment)

Performs appropriate tasks as described under SUPERVISOR/FOREMAN (UNSPECIFIED) (990 .00).

Additional factor: number of workers supervised.

760 .60 Foreman (linesmen and cable jointers)

Directly supervises and co-ordinates the activities of linesmen and cable jointers

Performs appropriate tasks as described under SUPERVISOR/FOREMAN (UNSPECIFIED) (990 .00).

Additional factor: number of workers supervised.

760 .98 Trainee

Performs, under instruction or guidance, various tasks including training exercises and as appropriate pursues studies in order to acquire the basic skills and knowledge required to perform the tasks of foremen (installing, maintaining and repairing occupations (electrical and electronic)).

760 .99 Other foremen (installing, maintaining and repairing occupations (electrical and electronic))

Workers in this group directly supervise and co-ordinate the activities of workers in installing, maintaining and repairing occupations (electrical and electronic) and are not elsewhere classified.

Unit Group 761 Electricians (Installation, Maintenance and Repair) (Plant, Machinery and other Equipment)

Workers in this unit group install, maintain and repair electrical plant, machinery and other equipment.

See 799 .02 and 799 .04 for workers who install, maintain and repair both electrical and mechanical plant and machinery.

761 .10 Installation electrician (plant, machinery)

Erects electrical plant or machinery on operational site

Ascertains job requirements from drawings, wiring diagrams or other specifications; determines sequence and method of required operations; places prepared parts and sub-assemblies in position using hoisting equipment or directs crane driver as necessary; builds up plant or machinery using hand tools such as chisels, drills, files, hammers, screwdrivers, spanners and wrenches; checks alignment during erection using measuring instruments; connects prepared wire or cable to specified terminals or connectors by crimping, brazing, soldering or bolting to complete equipment circuit; connects plant or machinery to electric power supply.

May (01) carry out functional tests on plant or machinery.

Other titles include Generator erector, Installer (electrical), Machinery erector, Transformer erector.

761.20 Maintenance electrician (general) (plant and machinery)

Repairs and services various types of electrical plant and machinery

Examines plant or machinery for defects; studies drawings, wiring diagrams or other specifications; locates and identifies faults using test equipment such as ammeters, voltmeters, meggers, tachometers and neon lamps; dismantles plant or machinery and repairs or replaces damaged or worn parts; replaces faulty wiring; fits and assembles parts to rebuild plant or machinery; tests for correct functioning and adjusts as necessary; carries out service tasks such as cleaning and insulation testing according to schedule. Performs these tasks in relation to various types of electrical plant and machinery.

May (01) install or reposition plant or machinery

(02) perform tasks as described under ELECTRICIAN (INSTALLATION AND MAINTENANCE) (PREMISES) (762.10).

Other titles include Colliery electrician, Maintenance fitter (electrical).

761.30 Maintenance electrician (specialised) (plant, machinery)

Repairs and services specific electrical plant or machinery

Performs tasks as described under MAINTENANCE ELECTRICIAN (GENERAL) (PLANT AND MACHINERY) (761.20) but in relation to the repair and servicing of specific electrical plant or machinery such as motors or generators.

May (01) install or reposition plant or machinery.

761.40 Maintenance electrician (aircraft)

Overhauls and carries out major repairs to aircraft electrical equipment

Examines for defects electrical equipment such as generators, and wiring systems such as engine control, de-icing and lighting; studies drawings, wiring diagrams or other specifications; locates and identifies faults using test equipment such as ammeters, voltmeters and meggers; dismantles equipment and replaces damaged or worn parts; replaces faulty wiring; rebuilds equipment, tests for correct functioning and adjusts as necessary.

Additional factor: whether in possession of appropriate maintenance licence.

Other titles include Aircraft electrician (base), Aircraft maintenance fitter (electrical) (base).

761.50 Service electrician (aircraft)

Carries out running repairs to and routine servicing of electrical equipment in aircraft

Examines aircraft electrical equipment and wiring systems, including emergency systems and batteries, for defects; studies drawings, wiring diagrams or other specifications; locates and identifies faults using test equipment; if faults appear to be of a minor nature dismantles equipment and replaces faulty components, wiring and/or batteries; tests for correct functioning and adjusts as necessary; if major repair is necessary arranges for aircraft to be grounded.

Additional factor: whether in possession of appropriate maintenance licence.

Other titles include Aircraft electrician (line), Aircraft maintenance fitter (electrical) (line).

761.60 Maintenance electrician (motor vehicle)

Repairs and services electrical equipment in motor vehicles

Performs tasks as described under MAINTENANCE ELECTRICIAN (AIRCRAFT) (761.40) but in relation to the repair and servicing of electrical equipment such as dynamos, starters, lighting and wiring in motor vehicles.

May (01) install equipment such as radios in vehicles.

Other titles include Auto electrician.

761.70 Service mechanic (domestic electrical appliances)

Repairs and services domestic electrical appliances

Examines domestic electrical appliances such as cookers, washing machines, vacuum cleaners, kettles or percolators for defects; studies drawings, wiring diagrams or other specifications; locates and identifies faults; dismantles equipment and replaces damaged or worn parts; replaces faulty wiring; re-assembles equipment, tests for correct functioning and adjusts as necessary.

Other titles include Domestic appliance repair electrician.

761 .80 Service mechanic (office electrical machines)

Repairs and services office electrical machines

Performs appropriate tasks as described under SERVICE MECHANIC (DOMESTIC ELECTRICAL APPLIANCES) (761 .70) but in relation to the repair and servicing of office electrical machines such as electrical calculating machines, copying machines and duplicating machines.

See Office Machinery Maintaining and Repairing Occupations (Mechanical) (745) and Service mechanic (electronic office equipment) (763 .40)

761 .98 Trainee

Performs, under instruction or guidance, various tasks including training exercises and as appropriate pursues studies in order to acquire the basic skills and knowledge required to perform the tasks of electricians (installation, maintenance and repair) (plant, machinery and other equipment).

761 .99 Other electricians (installation, maintenance and repair) (plant, machinery and other equipment)

Workers in this group install, maintain and repair electrical plant, machinery and other equipment and are not elsewhere classified, for example:

(01) **Multishot exploder cleaners and testers** (overhaul, clean and test electrical devices used for setting off a number of detonators in shotfiring).

Unit Group 762 Electricians (Installation, Maintenance and Repair) (Premises and Ships)

Workers in this unit group install and repair electrical wiring, fixtures and appliances in buildings, on board ships under construction and repair, install and maintain electrical services in theatres and lighting for film and television productions and perform closely related tasks.

762 .10 Electrician (installation and maintenance) (premises)

Installs, maintains and repairs electrical wiring, fixtures and appliances in buildings

Ascertains job requirements from drawings or other specifications; installs power and lighting wiring and cable systems; positions and fixes distribution boards, fuse boxes, switches, light sockets, power points and connects to wiring; measures and cuts protective channelling material and fits over installed wiring or measures, cuts, bends, threads, assembles and installs electrical conduit and pulls wiring through conduit; erects cable trunking systems; tests for insulation and continuity; installs electrical fixtures and equipment such as water heaters, underfloor heating, electrical storage heater systems, time switches, illuminated signs and domestic appliances; traces faults in electrical wiring systems, fixtures and appliances and makes necessary repairs.

May (01) specialise on a particular type of installation, eg shop fitting and exhibition work, neon sign erection.

Additional factors: type of cabling to which accustomed, eg polyvinyl chloride (PVC), mineral insulated copper covered (MICC), conduit systems or heavy cables; voltages to which accustomed.

Excluded are Electricians (theatre, film, television studio) (762 .30)

762 .20 Electrician (ship)

Installs and repairs electrical wiring, fixtures and appliances on board ships under construction or repair

Ascertains job requirements from drawings or other specifications; fits cables for power, lighting and communications in wire-ways and tray-plates and secures with clips, or threads cables through conduits; fits bulkhead glands and deck tubes, threads cable through and packs glands or tubes to make pressure- or gas-tight; installs electrical equipment such as cooking and refrigeration appliances; connects up wiring for equipment such as motors, generators, pumps and winches; traces faults in wiring systems and makes necessary repairs.

May (01) repair navigation lights

(02) prepare cable-carrying equipment such as wire-ways, tray-plates and conduits by cutting, bending and threading

(03) install cable-carrying equipment on ships

(04) position and fix distribution boards, fuse boxes, junction boxes, switches, sockets, power points, etc.

Additional factors: type of cable to which accustomed, eg polyvinyl chloride (PVC), lead-sheathed, screened, armoured, solid-filled; voltages to which accustomed.

762.30 Electrician (theatre, film, television studio)

Installs and maintains electrical services in a theatre, or lighting for film or television productions

Ascertains job requirements from prepared lighting plots, drawings and other specifications; fits appropriate wiring and cable systems and sets up equipment such as limelights, flood-lights, spotlights, arc-lights, dimmers, lighting battens and lighting dollies; sets up lighting designs, including special effects, for productions.
If working in theatre, operates sound recording equipment to record spoken passages, music and sound effects and operates equipment to relay recorded material during performances; operates stage lighting equipment and controls house lighting during performances; installs and maintains house lighting and electrical services generally.
If working on film or television productions, lays out and connects up lighting equipment on site for outside broadcasts; sets up, maintains and operates generating sets for location work and outside broadcasts; operates and adjusts lighting equipment during productions as required.

May (01) formulate lighting and effects plots for theatre productions
(02) install and maintain general wiring of film or television studio buildings.

762.40 Electrical marker-off

Plans and marks position of electrical cable runs in ships

Ascertains from drawings and specifications position of power and lighting points, ventilators, etc and calculates shortest and most practicable routes for cable runs; examines proposed routes on site and adjusts as necessary to take account of safety regulations and obstructions; prepares working diagrams for use by electricians; marks position of cable runs and holes for cable runs on decks and bulkheads and arranges for holes to be cut; marks position of power points, light fittings, etc on decks, bulkheads and deckheads; calculates length and size of trays or ducts and number of angle brackets, clips, etc required for cable runs and prepares requisition list.

May (01) assist with installation of cable runs (762.20).

762.98 Trainee

Performs, under instruction or guidance, various tasks including training exercises and as appropriate pursues studies in order to acquire the basic skills and knowledge required to perform the tasks of electricians (installation, maintenance and repair) (premises and ships).

762.99 Other electricians (installation, maintenance and repair) (premises and ships)

Workers in this group install and repair electrical wiring, fixtures and appliances in buildings, and on board ships, install and maintain electrical services in theatres and lighting for film and television productions and perform closely related tasks and are not elsewhere classified.

Unit Group 763 Installing, Maintaining and Repairing Occupations (Electronic and Related Equipment)

Workers in this unit group install, maintain and repair electronic and related equipment, including telecommunications equipment.

763.05 Installer (electronic and related equipment)

Erects electronic and/or related equipment on operational site

Performs tasks as described under INSTALLATION ELECTRICIAN (PLANT, MACHINERY) (761.10) but in relation to the erection of electronic and/or related equipment.

May (01) carry out functional tests on equipment
(02) maintain electronic and/or related equipment.

Other titles include Computer system installer, Control equipment installer, Installation fitter (telecommunications equipment), Installation technician (fitter) (electronics), X-ray equipment installer.

Excluded are Telephone fitters (763.10)

763 .10 Telephone fitter

Installs and maintains public and private telephone systems

Installs internal wiring and cabling for telephone systems and fits and wires junction and distribution boxes; fixes connecting wires from outside lines to premises and connects cable terminals to inside wiring; installs telephones, switchboards and coin boxes; tests installation and makes adjustments as required; traces faults in telephone systems and makes necessary repairs.

May (01) install and maintain intercommunications systems.

Other titles include Telephone installer, Telephone repairer.

763 .15 Maintenance fitter (electronic and related equipment) (general)

Repairs and services various types of electronic and related equipment

Examines equipment for defects; studies drawings, wiring diagrams or other specifications; locates and identifies faults using test equipment such as oscilloscopes, signal and pulse generators, ammeters and voltmeters; dismantles equipment and repairs or replaces faulty components; replaces faulty wiring; rebuilds or re-assembles equipment, tests for correct functioning, checks calibration and adjusts as necessary; carries out service tasks such as cleaning and insulation testing according to schedule. Performs these tasks in relation to various types of electronic and related equipment.

May (01) repair and service electrical equipment and be known as Electrical and electronic maintenance fitter.

Excluded are Telephone fitters (763 .10)

763 .20 Maintenance fitter (aircraft electronic and related equipment)

Overhauls and carries out major repairs to various types of aircraft electronic and related equipment

Examines aircraft electronic and related equipment such as radio transmitters, radio receivers, radar systems, intercommunication and passenger address equipment for defects; studies wiring diagrams or other specifications; locates and identifies faults using test equipment such as ammeters, voltmeters, oscilloscopes, signal generators and valve meters; dismantles equipment and replaces faulty components such as condensers, valves, transistors and transformers; replaces faulty wiring; rebuilds equipment, tests for correct functioning, checks calibration and adjusts as necessary.

May (01) carry out running repairs to electronic and related equipment in aircraft (763 .25)
(02) install electronic and related equipment in aircraft
(03) modify standard equipment for special purposes
(04) repair and overhaul airport electronic ground control equipment (763 .30).

Additional factor: whether in possession of appropriate maintenance licence.

Other titles include Aircraft instrument fitter (maintenance), Aircraft radio maintenance engineer (fitter) (base).

Excluded are workers engaged solely on repair of portable communications equipment (763 .75)

763 .25 Service fitter (aircraft electronic and related equipment)

Carries out running repairs to and servicing of electronic and related equipment in aircraft

Examines aircraft electronic and related equipment for defects; studies wiring diagrams or other specifications; locates and identifies faults using test equipment such as ammeters and voltmeters; if faults appear to be of a minor nature dismantles equipment and replaces faulty components or wiring and resolders loose connections; rebuilds equipment, tests for correct functioning, checks calibration and adjusts as necessary; if major repair is necessary arranges for work to be undertaken by maintenance fitter, aircraft electronic equipment.

May (01) install electronic and related equipment in aircraft.

Additional factor: whether in possession of appropriate maintenance licence.

Other titles include Aircraft instrument fitter (servicing), Aircraft radio maintenance engineer (fitter) (line).

763 .30 Service mechanic (airport electronic and related ground control equipment)

Repairs and services various types of airport electronic and related ground control equipment

Performs tasks as described under MAINTENANCE FITTER (ELECTRONIC AND RELATED EQUIPMENT) (GENERAL) (763 .15) but in relation to the repair and servicing of a variety of airport electronic and related ground control equipment such as radio transmitters, radio receivers, precision approach radar, surveillance radar, radio beacons and multi-channel tape recorders.

(May 01) install equipment on operational site (763 .05).

Other titles include Radio technician (fitter) (airport)

763 .35 Maintenance fitter (electronic) (computer equipment)

Repairs and services electronic computer equipment

Performs tasks as described under MAINTENANCE FITTER (ELECTRONIC AND RELATED EQUIPMENT) (GENERAL) (763 .15) but in relation to the repair and servicing of computer equipment.

May (01) feed diagnostic programmed tape or other input material into computer to assist with fault finding

(02) repair and service ancillary equipment such as card punching machines and scanners.

763 .40 Service mechanic (electronic office equipment)

Repairs and services electronic office equipment

Performs tasks as described under MAINTENANCE FITTER (ELECTRONIC AND RELATED EQUIPMENT) (GENERAL) (763 .15) but in relation to the repair and servicing of electronic office equipment such as electronic accounting machines, calculating machines, dictating machines and teleprinters.

See Office Machinery Maintaining and Repairing Occupations (Mechanical) (745) and Service mechanic (office electrical machines) (761 .80)

763 .45 Service mechanic (electronic test equipment)

Repairs and services electronic test equipment

Performs tasks as described under MAINTENANCE FITTER (ELECTRONIC AND RELATED EQUIPMENT) (GENERAL) (763 .15) but in relation to the repair and servicing of electronic test equipment such as oscilloscopes, pulse generators, signal generators, spectrophotometers and contamination testers.

May (01) modify standard equipment for special purposes

(02) recalibrate equipment

(03) install equipment on operational site (763 .05).

Other titles include Electronic instrument mechanic, Electronic instrument service engineer (fitter).

763 .50 Maintenance fitter (railway signalling and telecommunications equipment)

Repairs and services railway electrical signalling and telecommunications equipment

Performs tasks as described under MAINTENANCE FITTER (ELECTRONIC AND RELATED EQUIPMENT) (GENERAL) (763 .15) but in relation to the repair and servicing of railway electrical signalling equipment such as signal lights, pictorial display panels and points motors, and telecommunications equipment such as telephones and teleprinters.

May (01) install or reposition equipment (763 .05)

(02) repair and service mechanically operated signalling equipment (741 .99)

(03) keep emergency power accumulators in working condition.

Other titles include Signal and telecommunications technician (fitter).

763 .55 Maintenance fitter (sound and television transmission equipment)

Repairs and services electronic equipment used in sound and television transmission

Performs tasks as described under MAINTENANCE FITTER (ELECTRONIC AND RELATED EQUIPMENT) (GENERAL) (763 .15) but in relation to the repair and servicing of sound and television transmission equipment and ancillary equipment such as disc and tape recorders, film recorders and television cameras.

May (01) install equipment on operational site (763 .05)

(02) operate network switching equipment at transmitter station.

763.60 Service mechanic (radar equipment)

Repairs and services radar equipment

Performs tasks as described under MAINTENANCE FITTER (ELECTRONIC AND RELATED EQUIPMENT) (GENERAL) (763.15) but in relation to the repair and servicing of radar equipment such as navigational radar, gunnery control and missile control.

May (01) install equipment on operational site (763.05).

Other titles include Radar mechanic.

763.65 Service mechanic (workshop) (domestic radio, television receivers)

Overhauls and carries out major repairs to domestic radio and/or television receivers

Performs tasks as described under MAINTENANCE FITTER (ELECTRONIC AND RELATED EQUIPMENT) (GENERAL) (763.15) but in relation to the overhaul and major repair of domestic radio and television receivers.

May (01) repair tape recorders, record players and/or radiograms
(02) install receivers in customers' premises
(03) carry out running repairs at customers' premises (763.70).

Other titles include Radio and television bench engineer, Radio and television repairer, Radio and television workshop engineer.

763.70 Service mechanic (field) (domestic radio, television receivers)

Carries out running repairs to domestic radio and/or television receivers

Performs tasks as described under MAINTENANCE FITTER (ELECTRONIC AND RELATED EQUIPMENT) (GENERAL) (763.15) but in relation to the repair of domestic radio and television receivers in customers' premises.

May (01) install receivers in customers' premises.

Other titles include Radio and television field engineer, Radio and television service technician, Television serviceman.

763.75 Maintenance fitter (other electronic or related equipment)

Repairs and services specific electronic or related equipment not separately identified

Performs tasks as described under MAINTENANCE FITTER (ELECTRONIC AND RELATED EQUIPMENT) (GENERAL) (763.15) but in relation to the repair and servicing of specific electronic or related equipment not separately identified, such as automatic control equipment, X-ray equipment, medical equipment, metal detecting equipment, microwave ovens, portable communications equipment and hearing aids.

763.98 Trainee

Performs, under instruction or guidance, various tasks including training exercises and as appropriate pursues studies in order to acquire the basic skills and knowledge required to perform the tasks of workers in installing, maintaining and repairing occupations (electronic and related equipment).

763.99 Other installing, maintaining and repairing occupations (electronic and related equipment)

Workers in this group install, maintain and repair electronic and related equipment and are not elsewhere classified, for example:

(01) **Cable engineers** (maintain and repair equipment at overseas cable stations)

Unit Group 764 Linesmen and Cable Jointers

Workers in this unit group install, maintain and repair overhead lines for electricity supply, electric traction and telecommunications services, joint and connect underground, submarine and surface electric cables and test telecommunications cables on site after installation.

764.10 Overhead linesman (electricity supply, electric traction)

Installs, maintains and repairs overhead lines for electricity supply or electric traction

Assists with the erection of wood poles or steel towers to carry overhead lines; connects and anchors stay wires and braces; fits insulators to stays and braces; strings wires or cables to carry current (conductors) from one pole or tower to another and to service intakes; adjusts tension of conductors to allow for changes due to climatic variations; connects and installs equipment such as transformers, fuse gear, lightning arrestors, cable boxes and aircraft warning lights; installs and tests bonding and earthing systems; checks that lines give adequate clearance for trees, television aerials, construction of haystacks, etc; patrols lines and inspects poles, conductors, associated fittings and ancillary equipment; locates faults and makes necessary repairs to lines, ancillary equipment, stays and braces. Performs these tasks in relation to overhead electricity supply and electric traction lines.

Additional factors: type of work to which accustomed, eg power, lighting, electric traction; whether accustomed to working on "dead" or "live" cables; voltages to which accustomed eg up to 30,000 volts, over 30,000 volts; whether accustomed to wood pole or steel tower work.

Other titles include Overhead lineman.

764.20 Overhead linesman (telecommunications services)

Installs, maintains and repairs overhead lines for telecommunications services

Performs appropriate tasks as described under OVERHEAD LINESMAN (ELECTRICITY SUPPLY, ELECTRIC TRACTION) (764.10) but in relation to overhead telephone lines.

764.30 Cable jointer

Joints and connects underground, submarine and surface electric and telecommunications cables

Removes outer protective sheath from cables; separates conductor cores and applies protective insulation; tests conductors for safety and defects; selects corresponding conductor wires at junction of cable and joints them by brazing, soldering or crimping; dries out moisture and applies final conductor insulation to joints; fits metal sleeve around cable joint and wipes molten lead into joint between sleeve and cable sheath to produce moisture-proof joint, or fits mechanical joint and tightens screws to seal joint; fits outer protection box around jointed cable; pours pitch or other insulating compound into box as required to prevent seepage of moisture and seals box; connects cables to distribution boxes on consumers' premises or electricity sub-stations; traces faults in cables and makes necessary repairs.

Additional factors: type of cable work to which accustomed, eg electricity supply, telecommunications; whether accustomed to working on "dead" or "live" cables; voltages to which accustomed, eg up to 650 volts, up to 33,000 volts.

764.40 Cable tester (installation)

Tests telecommunications cables on site after installation and jointing

Connects or directs connecting of cables to test equipment such as capacitor bridges, resistance bridges and meggers; operates equipment to test cables for balance, resistance and insulation; listens to sound signals, checks instrument dials and records readings; if readings are outside specified limits, informs cable jointer so that faults may be traced and rectified; prepares reports as required.

See Cable tester (manufacture) (832.65)

764.98 Trainee

Performs, under instruction or guidance, various tasks including training exercises and as appropriate pursues studies in order to acquire the basic skills and knowledge required to perform the tasks of linesmen and cable jointers.

764.99 Other linesmen and cable jointers

Workers in this group install, maintain and repair overhead lines for electricity supply, electric traction and telecommunications services, joint and connect underground, submarine and surface electric cables and test telecommunications cables on site after installation and are not elsewhere classified.

Unit Group 769 Installing, Maintaining and Repairing Occupations (Electrical and Electronic) Not Elsewhere Classified

Workers in this unit group erect domestic radio and television aerials, install electricity supply meters, directly assist electrical and electronics craftsmen and perform miscellaneous tasks in the installation, maintenance and repair of electrical and electronic equipment and are not elsewhere classified.

769 .10 Television aerial erector (domestic receivers)

Positions and secures aerials for domestic television reception

Selects aerial system appropriate to location of receiver; fixes aerial mast in position internally or externally as required; assembles aerial system and joins aerial cable to aerial system junction box; positions aerial system to obtain transmitted signal of maximum strength and secures to mast; cuts cable to appropriate length and secures in position as necessary; fits plug to end of cable; checks quality of reception and adjusts aerial system as necessary.

May (01) test existing aerial system for faults and carry out repairs

(02) install multipoint television systems

(03) erect domestic radio aerials.

769 .20 Meter fixer

Positions and secures electricity supply meters on consumers' premises

Ascertains job requirements from written instructions; positions and secures meter board to wall using hand tools such as drills and screwdrivers; positions and secures supply meters and other equipment such as mains cut-outs and time switches to meter board; connects wiring in premises to equipment on meter boards.

May (01) connect or disconnect service cables on consumers' premises

(02) seal meters

(03) record meter readings and collect cash from prepayment meters (312 .93).

769 .30 Electrical craftsman's labourer, Electronic craftsman's labourer

Transports materials and otherwise assists electrical or electronic craftsman in the performance of his tasks

Performs a combination of the following tasks: conveys materials and equipment to work area; cuts conduit tubing to required lengths using hack-saws: cuts screw threads into ends of conduit tubing using die cutter; joins length of conduit tubing using threaded sleeves; draws wire or cable through conduit piping or ducting; strips insulation from wire or cable using cutters or pliers; heats lead or pitch to molten state in ladles; performs other tasks as directed by craftsman.

May (01) erect ladders or scaffolding to provide access to work areas.

Other titles include Cable jointer's mate, Electrician's labourer, Linesman's mate.

769 .98 Trainee

Performs, under instruction or guidance, various tasks including training exercises and as appropriate pursues studies in order to acquire the basic skills and knowledge required to perform the tasks of workers in installing, maintaining and repairing occupations (electrical and electronic) not elsewhere classified.

769 .99 Other installing, maintaining and repairing occupations (electrical and electronic) not elsewhere classified

Workers in this group perform miscellaneous tasks in the installation, maintenance and repair of electrical and electronic equipment and are not separately classified, for example:

(01) **Stubbers** (replace steel stubs in electrolytic furnaces); (02) **Temporary lightmen (ship work)** (install and maintain temporary lights on board ships under construction or repair).

Minor Group 77 PIPE, SHEET AND STRUCTURAL METAL WORKING AND RELATED OCCUPATIONS

Workers in this minor group install, maintain and repair plumbing, heating and ventilating, pipe and duct systems, lifting equipment and rigging, make and erect products, structures and structural framework from sheet and plate metal, erect and dismantle supporting framework and working platforms, weld metal, cut metal using flame cutters, directly assist workers carrying out these tasks and perform related tasks.

The occupations are arranged in the following unit groups:

770 Foremen (Pipe, Sheet and Structural Metal Working and Related Occupations)

771 Plumbing, Heating and Ventilating and Pipe Fitting Occupations

772 Sheet Metal Working Occupations

773 Metal Plate Working and Riveting Occupations

774 Steel Erecting and Rigging and Cable Splicing Occupations

775 Welding and Flame Cutting Occupations (Metal)

776 Pipe, Sheet and Structural Metal Workers' Mates and Labourers

779 Pipe, Sheet and Structural Metal Working and Related Occupations Not Elsewhere Classified

Unit Group 770 Foremen (Pipe, Sheet and Structural Metal Working and Related Occupations)

Workers in this unit group directly supervise and co-ordinate the activities of workers in pipe, sheet and structural metal working and related occupations.

770 .10 Foreman (plumbing, heating and ventilating and pipe fitting occupations)

Directly supervises and co-ordinates the activities of workers in plumbing, heating and ventilating and pipe fitting occupations

Performs appropriate tasks as described under SUPERVISOR/FOREMAN (UNSPECIFIED) (990 .00) and in addition: arranges for delivery of materials to sites or workshops according to work programme; prepares progress reports.

May (01) prepare estimates
(02) test installations.

Additional factor: number of workers supervised.

770 .20 Foreman (sheet metal working occupations)

Directly supervises and co-ordinates the activities of workers in sheet metal working occupations

Performs appropriate tasks as described under SUPERVISOR/FOREMAN (UNSPECIFIED) (990 .00).

Additional factor: number of workers supervised.

770.30 Foreman (metal plate working and riveting occupations)

Directly supervises and co-ordinates the activities of workers in metal plate working and riveting occupations

Performs appropriate tasks as described under SUPERVISOR/FOREMAN (UNSPECIFIED) (990.00).

May (01) prepare estimates

(02) test completed work

(03) supervise welders and burners.

Additional factor: number of workers supervised.

770.40 Foreman (steel erecting and rigging and cable splicing occupations)

Directly supervises and co-ordinates the activities of workers in steel erecting, rigging and cable splicing occupations

Performs appropriate tasks as described under SUPERVISOR/FOREMAN (UNSPECIFIED) (990.00).

Additional factor: number of workers supervised.

770.50 Foreman (welding and flame cutting occupations)

Directly supervises and co-ordinates the activities of workers in welding and flame cutting occupations

Performs appropriate tasks as described under SUPERVISOR/FOREMAN (UNSPECIFIED) (990.00).

Additional factor: number of workers supervised.

770.98 Trainee

Performs, under instruction or guidance, various tasks including training exercises and as appropriate pursues studies in order to acquire the basic skills and knowledge required to perform the tasks of foremen (pipe, sheet and structural metal working and related occupations).

770.99 Other foremen (pipe, sheet and structural metal working and related occupations)

Workers in this group directly supervise and co-ordinate the activities of workers in pipe, sheet and structural metal working and related occupations and are not elsewhere classified.

Unit Group 771 Plumbing, Heating and Ventilating and Pipe Fitting Occupations

Workers in this unit group install, maintain and repair plumbing fixtures, heating and ventilating systems, pipe and duct systems, and lead, lead lined and lead covered plant.

771.05 Plumber (construction)

Installs and repairs piping and fittings for hot and cold water, sanitary and drainage systems in buildings

Ascertains job requirements from drawings or other specifications; selects lengths of copper, lead, steel, iron or plastic piping and cuts to required size with hacksaw or pipe cutter; either bends piping by machine, heats with blow lamp and bends by hand or uses preshaped piping; installs fittings such as storage tanks, baths, toilets, taps and valves, and fire fighting equipment, fabricating and fixing supports as required; joins piping or attaches fittings to piping by soldering, welding, cementing, thread cutting and screwing or by tightening compression fittings; installs gutters, rain and soil pipes; tests installations for leaks and correct functioning; cuts protective covering from copper, lead, aluminium, zinc or non-metallic sheeting to required size and "dresses" into position on roofs, ledges, etc; repairs burst pipes; replaces faulty washers, taps, valves, etc; clears blocked drains using connecting rods.

May (01) glaze windows (865.10)

(02) install boilers and radiators (771.25)

(03) install gas appliances (771.20)

(04) install electrical appliances (762.10).

771.10 Ship plumber

Installs, maintains and repairs piping and fittings for water, fuel, heating, sanitary, ventilating and refrigerating systems on ships

Ascertains job requirements from drawings or other specifications; installs piping and fittings as described under PLUMBER (CONSTRUCTION) (771.05) and HEATING AND VENTILATING ENGINEERING FITTER (771.25); tests installations for leaks and correct functioning; carries out regular inspections of installations and undertakes repairs. Performs these tasks in relation to ships' fittings.

May (01) lay piping to carry electric cables

(02) form metal ducting from sheet metal.

771 .15 Chemical plumber

Makes up, installs and repairs lead, lead lined or lead covered plant and piping used in chemical processing

Ascertains job requirements from drawings or other specifications; cuts sheet lead, lead linings or lead coverings to size with knife; welds lead sections together to form plant or piping, using oxy-acetylene or oxy-hydrogen burner; bolts lead covered iron straps through the lead on to an external supporting framework or welds iron support bands around piping as required; positions lead linings in or lead coverings on piping or on other plant, beats to fit using wooden hand tool (dresser) and welds together; supports lead lining in piping by bolting iron straps through the lead on to the pipe; installs and secures fabricated plant and piping in position by welding or bolting; tests installations for leaks; repairs plant and piping.

May (01) line plant and pipes with plastic materials.

771 .20 Gas fitter

Installs, maintains and repairs gas piping and gas appliances in consumers' premises

Ascertains job requirements from drawings or other specifications; installs piping as described under PLUMBER (CONSTRUCTION) (771 .05); trims lengths of metal or plastic ducting to size and joins sections by welding or riveting; installs fittings such as cookers, refrigerators, water heaters, fires and radiators and connects to piping or ducting; tests installations for leaks and correct functioning; carries out regular servicing of installations, traces combustion or mechanical faults and undertakes repairs.

May (01) test installations for electrical faults.

See Gas appliance mechanic (741 .50)

771 .25 Heating and ventilating engineering fitter

Installs, maintains and repairs heating, ventilating and air conditioning systems

Ascertains job requirements from drawings or other specifications; installs piping as described under PLUMBER (CONSTRUCTION) (771 .05); trims lengths of metal or plastic ducting to size using cutters and joins metal sections by riveting and plastic by fusing; installs ducting and fittings such as boilers, flues, tanks, radiators, refrigeration units, pumps, and connects to pipe or duct system; tests installations for leaks and correct functioning; carries out regular servicing of installations, traces combustion or mechanical faults and undertakes repairs.

May (01) test installations for electrical faults

(02) join metal ducting by gas or arc welding and be known as Heating and ventilating fitter-welder.

Other titles include Heating and ventilating fitter.

771 .30 Pipe fitter (fabrication)

Makes up sections of high and/or low pressure piping systems ready for installation

Ascertains job requirements from drawings or other specifications; selects lengths of stainless steel, steel alloy, iron, copper, aluminium or plastic piping and cuts to required size with hacksaw or pipe cutter; bends piping by machine or heats with blow lamp and bends by hand; joints metal piping by soldering or thread cutting and screwing; joints plastic piping by cementing or fusing by hot air welding.

May (01) form piping from sheet metal

(02) weld metal piping

(03) install prefabricated sections on site (771 .05 or 771 .35)

(04) perform tasks of DRILLER (CONSTRUCTIONAL METAL WORK) (773 .14).

Other titles include Pipe fabricator.

771 .35 Pipe fitter (installation, maintenance)

Installs and/or maintains and repairs high and low pressure piping systems

Performs a combination of the following tasks: ascertains job requirements from drawings or other specifications; sets prefabricated piping systems of stainless steel, steel alloy, iron, copper, aluminium or plastic and metal fittings in position and secures to supporting framework; joints piping sections and fittings by soldering, screwing, cementing or fusing; tests completed installation under pressure for leaks and correct functioning; carries out maintenance checks on industrial piping systems; repairs piping and fittings.

May (01) weld sections

(02) erect supporting framework

(03) perform tasks of DRILLER (CONSTRUCTIONAL METAL WORK) (773 .14).

771.40 Ductwork erector

Installs prefabricated sheet metal ducting for heating, ventilating and air conditioning systems

Ascertains job requirements from drawings or other specifications; sets out line and position of duct run using rule and spirit level; cuts holes in walls and ceilings and fixes holding brackets or bolt anchorages using hand tools and powered hand drills and hammers; positions duct sections, using hoisting equipment as necessary, and holds in position with scaffolding or other temporary supports; bolts duct sections to brackets or anchorages; joins sections of ducting using nuts and bolts or pop rivets; inserts sealing material such as asbestos string, mastic composition or rubber strip into ducting joints.

May (01) cut ducting using hacksaws or metal cutters
(02) erect and fix roof ventilators
(03) erect polyvinyl chloride (PVC), asbestos-cement or glass fibre ducting.

Other titles include Duct erector.

771.98 Trainee

Performs, under instruction or guidance, various tasks including training exercises and as appropriate pursues studies in order to acquire the basic skills and knowledge required to perform the tasks of workers in plumbing, heating and ventilating and pipe fitting occupations.

771.99 Other plumbing, heating and ventilating and pipe fitting occupations

Workers in this group install, maintain and repair plumbing fixtures, heating and ventilating systems, pipe and duct systems, and lead, lead lined and lead covered plant and are not elsewhere classified.

Unit Group 772 Sheet Metal Working Occupations

Workers in this unit group mark out, cut, shape and fit sheet metal to make and repair products and components.

Excluded are Metal spinners (722.34), Press and Stamping Machine Operators (724) and Bending and rolling machine operators (729.20)

772.05 Marker-out

Marks out sheet metal ready for cutting and shaping

Ascertains job requirements from drawings or other specifications; plans layout allowing for overlap, joints, metal flow (in beating), etc; marks reference points and layout lines on sheet metal, using templates and measuring instruments such as rules, squares and verniers, and tools such as punches and scribers.

May (01) coat sheet metal with dye or paint prior to marking out
(02) make templates.

See Engineering marker-out (731.05) and Marker-off (metal plate, structural metal) (773.02)

772.10 Sheet metal worker

Makes products or components of sheet metal, other than copper, such as vehicle body panels, ducting and storage cabinets using hand and machine tools

Ascertains job requirements from drawings and other specifications; marks sheet metal with guide lines and reference points using templates as required or uses ready marked sheet metal; cuts metal to markings using hand or machine shears, guillotines, burners or saws; drills or stamps holes and rolls, folds, bends or otherwise shapes sheet metal using hand tools or machines or passes to bending or rolling machine operator; assembles prepared parts and joins by riveting, bolting, welding, brazing, soldering or beating or with adhesives; finishes product or component by grinding and polishing.

May (01) make templates
(02) carry out repair work
(03) cast metal sheet.

Other titles include Organ pipe maker, Sheet iron worker, Tinsmith.

772.15 Coppersmith

Makes and/or repairs products or components of copper sheet or tube such as tanks, vats, coils or ducting using hand and machine tools

Performs tasks as described under SHEET METAL WORKER (772.10) but in relation to working in copper sheet or tube and in addition: cuts piping to required length, packs to prevent flattening and bends to required shape; fits flanges and valves to piping as required.

May (01) make templates
(02) install made-up copper work
(03) work in other materials such as stainless steel, alloy or plastic.

772.20 Panel beater (vehicle body repair)

Repairs or replaces metal parts of vehicle bodies using hand and machine tools

Examines vehicle body to determine type of repair or ascertains job requirements from drawings or other specifications; removes upholstery, trim or other accessories to gain access to vehicle body as necessary; beats out dents using hammers and blocks or sandbags; fills depressions with solder, plastic or other filler compounds; removes excessively damaged panels; selects stock replacement panel or prepares replacement from sheet metal as described under PANEL BEATER (EXCLUDING VEHICLE BODY REPAIR) (772.25); rivets or welds replacement panel in position; smoothes repaired surfaces using hand or powered tools; straightens distorted chassis or engine mountings using hydraulic rams or jacks and jigs.

May (01) paint repaired bodywork
(02) fit fibre glass panels
(03) make jigs.

Other titles include Vehicle body repairer.

772.25 Panel beater (excluding vehicle body repair)

Cuts, beats and curves sheet metal to form shaped panels, other than for vehicles, using hand and machine tools

Ascertains job requirements from drawings or other specifications; marks sheet metal with guide lines and reference points; cuts metal to markings using shears or guillotine; beats metal to rough shape over leather sandbag or wood block using hand hammers; curves metal using wheeling machine; places panel on former and beats to final shape.

May (01) joint panels by welding
(02) make jigs.

772.30 Engine radiator repairer

Repairs engine radiators of vehicles or plant

Receives disconnected radiator or removes radiator from vehicle or plant by unscrewing connections or cutting with burning equipment; separates top, bottom and sides from radiator core where necessary; degreases each piece in solvent and flushes with chemical solution to remove rust or mineral deposits; repairs by beating, soldering or welding, or fits replacement parts; rebuilds dismantled radiator parts by soldering or welding; pumps air into repaired radiator and immerses in water to test for leaks.

May (01) refit repaired radiators in vehicles or plant
(02) cut and make replacement parts from sheet metal (772.10)
(03) paint repaired radiators using spray gun
(04) repair water and fuel tanks.

772.35 Stencil plate maker (hand)

Cuts stencils of lettering and designs from sheet metal using hand tools

Cuts sheet metal such as zinc or brass to size required for stencil using guillotine or hand cutters; draws freehand or marks outline of lettering or design from prepared pattern on sheet metal using scriber; cuts stencil following scribed outline using hand tools such as gouges, gravers or piercing saws; hammers out any rough edges on stencil.

May (01) trace lettering or design using pantograph.

772.40 Metal pattern maker (footwear)

Makes master footwear patterns from sheet metal for use in the production of paperboard working patterns

Cuts sheet metal such as tin or zinc to size required for pattern using guillotine or hand cutters; places prepared paper pattern on sheet metal; marks outline of paper pattern and pattern markings on sheet metal using scriber; cuts pattern following scribed outline using guillotine or hand cutters; smoothes rough edges using hand files and emery paper.

May (01) punch or cut out pattern markings
(02) copy instructions from paper pattern on to metal pattern using pen and ink
(03) perform tasks of PATTERN GRADER (FOOTWEAR) (642.30) or PATTERN BINDER (729.99)
(04) repair damaged patterns.

772.98 Trainee

Performs, under instruction or guidance, various tasks including training exercises and as appropriate pursues studies in order to acquire the basic skills and knowledge required to perform the tasks of workers in sheet metal working occupations.

772.99 Other sheet metal working occupations

Workers in this group mark out, cut, shape and fit sheet metal to make and repair products and components and are not elsewhere classified, for example:

(01) **Former makers (ophthalmic prescription)** (make sheet metal patterns from spectacle frames for use by hand glazers); (02) **Metal sign makers;** (03) **Metal snaggers,** Dingmen (examine mass produced sheet metal components and correct minor faults).

Unit Group 773 Metal Plate Working and Riveting Occupations

Workers in this unit group mark off, drill, bend, position and rivet metal plates and girders, and seal joints in metal plate.

Excluded are Press bending machine operators (724.99) and Frame benders (ship construction) (729.18)

773.02 Marker-off (metal plate, structural metal)

Marks out metal plate or girders ready for cutting and shaping

Performs tasks as described under MARKER-OUT (772.05) but in relation to marking metal plate.

See Engineering marker-out (731.05)

773.04 Plater (unspecified)

Prepares and positions metal platework ready for welding, riveting or bolting and is not separately identified

Ascertains job requirements from drawings or other specifications; marks out metal plate with guide lines and reference points using rules, scribers, punches and templates, or uses ready marked plate; cuts metal plate to markings using hand burners or cutting machines, or passes to cutting department; operates machines to straighten, bend, curve, punch, drill or chamfer edges of metal plate as required; positions and secures prepared metal plate ready for welding or riveting; if undertaking repair work cuts away defective plates and replaces as described above.

May (01) make templates
(02) weld or rivet metal plate.

Additional factor: type of work to which accustomed.

773.06 Ship's plater

Prepares and positions ships' plating ready for welding or riveting

Performs appropriate tasks as described under PLATER (UNSPECIFIED) (773.04) but in relation to ships' plating.

May (01) make templates
(02) weld or rivet metal plate
(03) operate tape controlled burning machines
(04) bend girders to form framework (729.18).

Other titles include Shell plater.

773.08 Boiler plater

Prepares and positions boiler plating ready for welding or riveting

Performs appropriate tasks as described under PLATER (UNSPECIFIED) (773.04) but in relation to the construction and repair of boilers and similar pressure vessels.

May (01) chip and buff edges of plate using powered hand tools
(02) expand ends of tubing to fit tightly into flange plates of boiler
(03) test boiler under pressure for leaks.

773.10 Constructional plater

Prepares and positions constructional metal platework ready for welding, riveting or bolting

Performs appropriate tasks as described under PLATER (UNSPECIFIED) (773.04) but in relation to the construction and repair of metal work such as bridges, storage tanks and gasholders.

May (01) weld metal platework.

773.12 Shipwright (metal)

Erects and fairs ship framework or prefabricated hull sections

Directs crane driver to hoist frame members or prefabricated ship sections into position; aligns sections using hydraulic jacks; secures frame or sections ready for welding or riveting; installs fittings such as davits, hatch covers, winches and pumps.

May (01) perform tasks of MARKER-OFF (773.02)
(02) performs tasks of SHIP'S PLATER (773.06)
(03) perform tasks of SHIPWRIGHT (WOOD) (671.45).

Other titles include Shipwright (iron), Steelwork shipwright.

773.14 Driller (constructional metal work)

Operates portable drilling machine to drill, ream or countersink holes in constructional metal work on site

Sets up pneumatic or electric portable drilling machine in marked position on metal work; selects and fixes cutting tool in machine; operates machine to carry out tasks such as drilling, boring, tapping, countersinking, reaming, chamfering and hole cutting; grinds cutting tools as necessary.

May (01) operate hand drills or stud welding gun
(02) set and operate drilling machine in workshop (722.10).

See Drilling machine operator (723.52)

773.16 Riveter

Rivets together metal parts such as plates and girders using machine and hand tools

Selects rivets of suitable size and type and if heating is required, passes to rivet heater; selects dies according to rivet finish specified, for example, countersunk, cup, flush, snap or pan; directs holder-up to insert and support hot or cold metal rivet into drilled holes of aligned metal parts; fits dies into head of pneumatic or hydraulic riveting machine; places machine head on exposed end of rivet and operates machine to spread rivet in the hole and form the rivet head, or spreads and forms rivet using hand hammers and dies; smoothes off rivet head using hand and powered tools.

May (01) expand ends of tubing to fit tightly into flange plates of boiler
(02) knock out and replace old rivets
(03) test riveted joint using hammer and feeler gauge.

773.18 Caulker

Seals seams, smoothes welds, fixes metal doors and collars and performs other metal plate finishing tasks

Performs some or all of the following tasks: seals seams between metal plates using pneumatic hammers and caulking tools; forces caulking compound into seams using knife, trowel or powered injector; smoothes welds and rivets using hand tools or powered grinders or chippers; removes lugs used for staging or lifting and rivets from metal plates using burning equipment or chipping machines; sets up and bolts in position steel doors, portholes, windows, tank and hatch covers, and packs joints as necessary with rubber sealing strip; fits locks and handles to steel doors; secures prepared metal collars in position ready for welding or riveting; tests tanks and airtight compartments for leaks using compressed air, gas or water.

May (01) grind cutting tools.

Other titles include Caulker burner, Chipper, Gouger.

773.20 Steelworker (general) (ship construction, repair)

Performs a variety of metal plate working tasks in the construction or repair of ships

Performs a combination of tasks as described under FRAME BENDER (SHIP CONSTRUCTION) (729.18), SHIP'S PLATER (773.06), SHIPWRIGHT (METAL) (773.12), RIVETER (773.16), CAULKER (773.18) and DRILLER (CONSTRUCTIONAL METAL WORK) (773.14).

May (01) perform tasks of TACK WELDER (775.99)

(02) perform tasks of HAND BURNER (775.30)

(03) perform tasks of MACHINE BURNER (775.50)

(04) specialise in the construction and/or repair of barges, performing woodworking tasks as required, and be known as Barge builder (metal).

773.50 Holder-up

Inserts and holds metal rivets in position ready for riveting

Operates pneumatic or hydraulic machine to insert hot or cold rivet into drilled holes of aligned metal parts and to hold the rivet firmly in position whilst the riveter spreads and heads the rivet.
OR
Inserts hot or cold rivet into drilled holes of aligned metal parts using tongs and hammer; holds rivet firmly in position with hammer or shaped metal tool (dolly) whilst the riveter spreads and heads the rivet.

May (01) heat rivets (779.50).

Other titles include Holder-on.

773.98 Trainee

Performs, under instruction or guidance, various tasks including training exercises and as appropriate pursues studies in order to acquire the basic skills and knowledge required to perform the tasks of workers in metal plate working and riveting occupations.

773.99 Other metal plate working and riveting occupations

Workers in this group mark off, drill, bend, position and rivet metal plates and girders, and seal joints in metal plate and are not elsewhere classified, for example:

(01) **Mine car repairers,** Tub repairers (repair metal cars used for haulage in mines and quarries).

See Bevelling machinist (729.92)

Unit Group 774 Steel Erecting and Rigging and Cable Splicing Occupations

Workers in this unit group erect metal structures and framework, erect and dismantle scaffolding and working platforms, install and maintain lifting equipment and ships' rigging, make up metal reinforcements for concrete casting and join and fit attachments to wire ropes.

Excluded are Metal Plate Working and Riveting Occupations (773)

774.05 Rigger (engineering plant and machinery)

Sets up lifting equipment and erects working platform for use in construction, maintenance and repair of engineering plant and machinery

Ascertains job requirements from drawings or other specifications; inspects item to be moved, determines weight and decides on type of equipment to be used; erects jib, derrick or similar hoisting equipment using winches as necessary, and instals lifting tackle such as ropes and pulleys; attaches slings, chains or other grappling equipment to the item to be moved and connects to hoisting equipment; directs equipment operator to move object to required position; erects tubular metal scaffolding and wooden working platform as described under SCAFFOLDER (774.25).

May (01) splice wire and fibre ropes (774.35) and (549.59)

(02) operate hydraulic jacking equipment and move objects on rollers.

Additional factor: knowledge of safety regulations.

Other titles include Maintenance rigger.

774.10 Rigger (dock)

Sets up lifting equipment for the loading and unlcading of ships' cargo

Erects jib, derrick or similar hoisting equipment using winches as necessary and installs lifting tackle such as ropes and pulleys; splices wire and fibre ropes as described under SPLICER (WIRE ROPE) (GENERAL) (774.35) and SPLICER (FIBRE ROPE) (549.59); lubricates hoisting equipment and carries out running repairs; dismantles and secures hoisting equipment on completion of loading or unloading.

May (01) secure and release hatch covers
(02) secure cargo to prevent movement at sea
(03) assist with the movement of ship in dock.

Additional factor: knowledge of safety regulations.

774.15 Rigger (ship)

Prepares, installs and repairs ropes, wires and cables on ships

Ascertains job requirements from drawings or other specifications; lays out wire or fibre rope and cuts to required length; forms rope slings, rope ladders, netting, and other rigging and attaches hooks, eyes, blocks and pulleys, splicing ropes by hand or securing ends by machine as described under SPLICER (WIRE ROPE) (GENERAL) (774.35) and SPLICER (FIBRE ROPE) (549.59); installs or replaces rigging for masts, derricks, davits, etc, working at heights as required; tests rigging for correct functioning and adjusts as necessary.

May (01) test chains and ropes and mark with stress rating
(02) make and test chain slings
(03) assist with erection of masts
(04) arrange drag chains on slipways ready for launchings
(05) assist with the movement and mooring of ship in dock.

Additional factor: knowledge of safety regulations.

774.20 Steel erector

Fits together girders and other metal work to form structures such as chimneys or framework for buildings, bridges and other structures

Ascertains job requirements from drawings or other specifications; erects ladders, scaffolding or working cage, and rigs hoisting equipment or erects jib crane for raising and placing metal work; directs hoist operator or crane driver to raise and position girders and other metal parts; checks alignment of metal parts using spirit level and plumb-rule and repositions as necessary; bolts, rivets or welds metal parts together or arranges for riveting or welding.

May (01) drill fixing holes in metal parts
(02) fix cladding or apply protective coating to metal chimneys.

Additional factor: knowledge of safety regulations.

Other titles include Metal chimney erector.

Excluded are Shipwrights (metal) (773.12)

774.25 Scaffolder (metal scaffolding)

Erects and dismantles temporary tubular metal scaffolding for use in the construction and repair of bridges, buildings and similar structures

Ascertains job requirements from drawings or other specifications; examines scaffold tubing and metal couplings for cracks, bends or other defects and oils couplings; erects lengths of tubing in an upright position on metal base plates; supports vertical tubes with tubes positioned horizontally and diagonally and secured to uprights by couplings; checks alignment of scaffolding using spirit level and adjusts position of tubing as necessary; positions and secures additional lengths of tubing in similar manner to extend scaffolding as required; lays and secures wooden planking or scaffolding to form working platforms; fixes guard rails, ladders, cradles and awnings in position; dismantles scaffolding on completion of structural work.

May (01) erect and operate hoisting equipment to transfer materials
(02) erect wooden scaffolding.

Additional factor: knowledge of safety regulations.

Excluded are Stagers (shipbuilding and repairing) (774.30)

774.30 Stager (shipbuilding and repairing)

Erects and dismantles temporary external and internal working platforms for use in the construction and repair of ships

Bolts metal brackets on to metal lugs tack welded on ship's structure, suspends metal brackets from ship's structure using chains or wire, or erects tubular metal or wooden scaffolding; lays and secures planking scaffolding to form working platforms; fixes guard rails, ladders and awnings as required; dismantles working platforms and supports on completion of structural work.

May (01) erect and operate hoisting equipment to transfer materials

(02) work from floating bridge or pontoon.

Additional factor: knowledge of safety regulations.

774.35 Splicer (wire rope) (general)

Joins, repairs and fits attachments to wire ropes using a variety of splicing methods

Cuts out damaged sections of rope using hammer and chisel; joins ropes by opening up rope ends and tucking and interlacing the rope strands to specification to form a joint using spikes and other hand tools (long splicing); forms end of rope into a loop or eye, opens up the end of the rope and tucks and interlaces the rope strands back into the rope (loop or soft eye splicing); fits end of rope around metal eye or thimble, opens up the end of the rope and tucks and interlaces the rope strands back into the rope (thimble or hard eye splicing).

May (01) bind joints or rope ends with hessian strip, wire or yarn

(02) use mechanical hammer to round off splicing

(03) fit rope end into metal socket and secure with solder or by clamping in hydraulic press

(04) splice fibre ropes (549.59).

774.50 Steel bender and fixer

Makes up metal framework by hand to form reinforcing core for concrete structures or products

Ascertains job requirements from drawings or other specifications; selects steel bars, rods, wire or wire mesh and cuts to required length using hand tools or cutting machine, or uses precut lengths; bends lengths as required manually or using bending machine; fixes reinforcing bars, rods, etc in position on construction site, in mould or through prepared channels in concrete units, linking together with metal clips, wire or tension rods as required; tensions reinforcing wire as required using hydraulic jacks (prestressing).

May (01) make and fit metal loops for lifting precast products

(02) operate welding equipment (775)

(03) build up framework prior to erection on site or insertion in mould.

Other titles include Bar bender and reinforcement fixer, Reinforcement fabricator.

774.55 Ropeman

Installs, maintains and repairs wire haulage ropes

Installs new wire ropes in position in haulage systems; splices ropes as described under SPLICER (WIRE ROPE) (GENERAL) (774.35) to form a continuous rope, or fits conical metal caps to rope ends for attachment to shackles using spikes, hammers, chisels and other hand tools; examines ropes for damage or wear, cuts out damaged or worn sections of rope, splices in new lengths and re-caps ends or replaces complete length of rope.

Additional factor: knowledge of safety regulations.

774.60 Splicer (wire rope) (specialised)

Joins, repairs and fits attachments to wire ropes using a particular method of splicing

Performs appropriate tasks as described under SPLICER (WIRE ROPE) (GENERAL) (774.35) but specialises in a particular method of splicing such as thimble or hard eye splicing.

774 .90 Metal shuttering erector

Erects temporary prefabricated metal formwork used in the casting of concrete structures on site

Places selected metal bars in position manually or directs crane driver to position bars and bolts together to form frame; positions sheet metal panels on frame and secures by bolting or clamping; dismantles formwork when concrete has set.

774 .98 Trainee

Performs, under instruction or guidance, various tasks including training exercises and as appropriate pursues studies in order to acquire the basic skills and knowledge required to perform the tasks of workers in steel erecting and rigging and cable splicing occupations.

774 .99 Other steel erecting and rigging and cable splicing occupations

Workers in this group erect metal structures and framework, erect and dismantle scaffolding and working platforms, install and maintain lifting equipment and ships' rigging, make up metal reinforcements for concrete casting and join and fit attachments to wire ropes and are not elsewhere classified, for example:

(01) **Riggers (television)** (erect platforms and supports used in television broadcasting).

Unit Group 775 Welding and Flame Cutting Occupations (Metal)

Workers in this unit group join metal parts and fabrications by welding, brazing and soldering, and cut metal to specifications and remove defects from steel stock during manufacture by means of gas flame and oxygen jet or electric arc.

Excluded are Repetitive assemblers (metal goods) (hand) (821 .35) and Repetitive assemblers (metal goods) (machine) (821 .40) engaged in batch or mass production.

775 .05 Welder (general)

Carries out two or more welding processes to join metal parts or fabrications

Ascertains job requirements from drawings and/or other specifications; positions and secures parts to be welded, using jigs and fixtures as necessary; selects appropriate welding equipment such as gas torch, portable arc equipment, semi-automatic or automatic machine; fits appropriate torch tips, electrodes, etc to equipment; connects hoses to gas tanks or wires from power supply to electrode and workpiece; adjusts controls to regulate gas pressure, voltage or amperage; opens valves or switches on power supply; lights torch, strikes arc or starts machine; guides torch or electrode along line of weld manually or by operating machine controls; cleans and smoothes weld and examines visually.

May (01) preheat parts to be welded
(02) perform the tasks of HAND BURNER (775 .30) or MACHINE BURNER (775 .50).

Additional factors: welding processes to which accustomed, eg gas welding, arc welding, resistance welding, vacuum diffusion welding, explosive welding, electro-slag welding, stellite welding; standards to which accustomed, eg Lloyd's, Aeronautical Inspection Directorate (AID) approved, American Petroleum Institute (API), American Society of Mechanical Engineers (ASME).

775 .10 Gas welder

Joins metal parts together by melting edges with a gas flame and fusing a molten filler metal into the joint

Ascertains job requirements from drawings and/or other specifications; positions and secures parts to be welded using jigs and fixtures as necessary; selects appropriate torch, torch nozzle, filler rod and flux; connects torch hoses to tanks of oxygen and acetylene, propane, butane or other fuel gas; opens valves, lights torch and adjusts gas mixture to obtain flame of desired intensity; guides torch along line of weld, depositing metal from filler rod or wire to fuse edges of parts together; cleans and smoothes weld and examines visually.

May (01) preheat parts to be welded.

Additional factors: types of metal to which accustomed; whether experienced in horizontal, vertical or overhead work; standards to which accustomed, eg Lloyd's, Aeronautical Inspection Directorate (AID) approved, American Petroleum Institute (API), American Society of Mechanical Engineers (ASME).

Other titles include Oxy-acetylene welder.

775.15 Electric arc welder

Joins metal parts together by melting the edges with an electric arc and fusing a molten filler metal into the joint

Ascertains job requirements from drawings and/or other specifications; positions and secures parts to be welded, using jigs and fixtures as necessary or directs positioning of large fabrications; selects suitable electrode and inserts in holder; connects wires from power supply to electrode and workpiece; if using gas shielded arc equipment, fixes gas nozzle to torch, connects hose from tanks of argon, carbon dioxide or other inert or non-combustible gas and adjusts controls to regulate gas pressure and rate of flow; if using submerged arc equipment, fills hopper on welding head with powdered flux; if operating portable, self-propelling welding machine, adjusts electrode feed and machine speed; switches on electrical power supply and sets amperage and voltage controls as required; forms electric arc by touching workpiece with electrode and withdrawing it to appropriate distance; if appropriate, starts flow of gas or flux powder which shields arc and prevents oxidation of metal being welded; maintaining arc, guides electrode along line of weld, depositing metal from filler rod or wire or from electrode, to fuse edges of parts together; regulates power supply as necessary; cleans and smoothes weld and examines visually.

May (01) preheat parts or fabrications to be welded
(02) use equipment which melts the metal to be welded by means of a jet of superheated ionised gas (plasma arc welding)
(03) cut metal tubes, angles and channels to size and weld together to form vehicle chassis and be known as Chassis builder.

Additional factors: types of metal to which accustomed; whether experienced in horizontal, vertical or overhead work; standards to which accustomed, eg Lloyd's, Aeronautical Inspection Directorate (AID) approved, American Petroleum Institute (API), American Society of Mechanical Engineers (ASME).

Other titles include Argon arc welder, CO_2 welder, Inert gas arc welder, Metal arc welder.

775.20 Electron beam welder

Sets and operates machine to join metal parts together by the melting action of a stream of electrons accelerated in a vacuum and focussed to a fine point

Secures workpiece, at atmospheric pressure, in vacuum chamber in a fixed jig on a rotary table and/or travelling carriage; positions electron gun over workpiece, or workpiece under gun, and sets travel speed of gun or workpiece; adjusts controls to set beam voltage, current and focus; closes vacuum chamber and switches on pump to exhaust air; switches on electron beam to start welding process; checks accuracy of beam placing using optical device; as necessary, adjusts electron gun, workpiece and/or deflection coils which make fine adjustments to the beam; on completion of welding, restores atmospheric pressure in vacuum chamber and removes workpiece.

May (01) set and operate tape or computer controlled machine.

775.25 Thermit welder

Joins metal parts or repairs fractures in heavy forgings, castings or metal fabrications by welding with molten metal produced from thermit mixture by chemical reaction

Cleans weld area of parts to be fused; builds mould round weld area, using mould box and moulding sand; if required, fits reinforcing collar round welding area; makes pouring gate and risers in the moulding sand; fills a crucible with thermit mixture such as aluminium and iron oxide and primes with an ignition powder; positions crucible over pouring gate; preheats weld area; lights ignition powder to start reaction in which heat is released and thermit mixture is converted to molten metal; pours molten metal into mould when chemical reaction is complete; removes mould and chips or grinds away excess metal when weld has solidified.

775.30 Hand burner

Cuts, trims and shapes metal by manually applying a gas flame and oxygen jet or an electric arc

Ascertains job requirements from drawings and/or other specifications; positions and secures metal to be cut on table or in fixture as required.

(01) **Flame cutter**

Connects torch hoses to containers of oxygen and fuel gas such as acetylene or propane; selects and fixes appropriate torch tips; turns on gas flow and lights torch; adjusts gas mixture to obtain flame of desired intensity; directs flame on to metal at start of cutting line; when sufficiently heated, operates lever on torch to release additional jet of oxygen to cut through metal; guides flame and oxygen jet along cutting lines.

(02) **Arc cutter**

Inserts suitable electrode in holder; if appropriate, inserts air nozzle in holder and connects hose to compressed air supply; if using plasma torch, connects hose from holder to tank of gas such as argon or nitrogen; connects wires from power supply to electrode and workpiece; switches on power supply and strikes arc; turns on jet of air to blow away molten metal as required; guides electrode along cutting lines. Checks finished work and cleans edges of cuts as required.

May (03) mark out metal to be cut (773.02)
(04) gouge grooves in metal
(05) operate cutting machine (775.50).

Other titles include Oxy-acetylene cutter.

775.35 Flame dresser (rolling mills)

Operates burning equipment to remove defects from steel bars, blooms, ingots, billets or slabs during manufacture

(01) **Deseamer (steel dressing)**

Directs flame from portable flame cutter (deseaming gun or arcair torch) or portable or fixed burning machine on to defective areas of steel bars, blooms, etc; burns away a thin film of metal to form a shallow depression around the defective area or burns away whole surfaces or sections of the metal; removes projections and ragged pieces of waste metal as required.

Other titles include Machine burner.

(02) **Scarfer operator (steel dressing)**

Sets controls on flame-scarfing machine to regulate speed of metal through machine and adjusts oxygen and propane pressures according to type of steel and width and thickness of bars, blooms, etc; starts water pump, air purge blower and smoke removal fans; operates controls to start machine and remove a thin skin of metal (descarfing) from surface of steel as it passes through the burners on roller table.

775.50 Machine burner

Operates machine to cut, trim and shape metal by the melting action of a gas flame and oxygen jet or an electric arc

Ascertains job requirements from drawings and/or other specifications; positions and secures metal to be cut on machine or sets portable machine in position; lights and adjusts burner(s) according to thickness of metal and number of cuts, or inserts electrode(s) in holder(s); sets controls to regulate flow of gas, gas pressure or voltage and amperage as required; if using profile machine, sets tracing or scanning head in position over template or outline drawing; operates automatic or manual controls to guide burner(s) or electrode(s) over cutting lines or, on profile machine, to guide tracing or scanning head round outline of template or drawing while linked burner(s) or electrode(s) cut the metal.

May (01) mark out metal to be cut (773.02).

Other titles include Arc cutter, Flame cutter, Flame cutting machine operator, Profile gas cutter.

775.90 Welding machine operator (non-repetitive)

Operates semi-automatic or automatic electric arc, electric resistance or other welding machine or plant to join metal parts

Positions and secures metal parts on machine, using jigs and fixtures as necessary or tends mechanism which feeds work into continuous welding plant; operates manual or automatic controls to start machine to weld metal parts or, on continuous plant, ensures that welding proceeds correctly; checks weld visually and removes finished work as required; cleans and smoothes weld.

May (01) regulate amperage and voltage if operating electric machine
(02) control movement of workpiece manually during welding.

Other titles include Flash butt welder, Friction welder, Seam welder, Spot welder, Stitch welder, Stud welder, Ultrasonic welder, Welding plant operator.

775.92 Brazer, Solderer (non-repetitive)

Bonds metal parts by applying heat to melt brazing alloy or solder into joint(s)

Assembles and secures parts to be brazed or soldered in jig or other holding fixture on work-bench or machine; places ring or strip of brazing alloy or solder in, over or round joint(s) or loads brazing or soldering wire into machine holder; applies flux compound along joint(s) as required; directs flame from hand torch, applies soldering iron or operates manual or automatic machine controls to heat workpiece and melt brazing alloy or solder into the joint(s); removes finished workpiece and cleans in water or chemical solution as required.

May (01) clean parts to be brazed or soldered

(02) adjust machine controls to set time cycle

(03) apply solder from manually held solder rod

(04) bond metal parts by applying filler metal to joints and heating in furnace.

Other titles include Brazing machine operator, Soldering machine operator.

775.98 Trainee

Performs, under instruction or guidance, various tasks including training exercises and as appropriate pursues studies in order to acquire the basic skills and knowledge required to perform the tasks of workers in welding and flame cutting occupations (metal).

775.99 Other welding and flame cutting occupations (metal)

Workers in this group join metal parts and fabrications by welding, brazing and soldering and cut metal to specification and remove defects from steel stock, during manufacture by flame or arc cutting and are not elsewhere classified, for example:

(01) **Brazers (dip)**, Solderers (dip) (braze or solder metal parts by immersing in baths of molten salts or solder); (02) **Lead burners** (join metal parts using lead solder and oxy-acetylene flame); (03) **Tack welders** (make series of short welds to hold metal parts together temporarily, ready for full welding operation); (04) **Tube making machine minders** (tend automatic machines which form and weld metal tubes from strip).

Unit Group 776 Pipe, Sheet and Structural Metal Workers' Mates and Labourers

Workers in this unit group directly assist pipe, sheet and structural metal workers in the performance of their tasks, for example, Plumber's mate, Shipwright's labourer, Steel erector's mate.

776.10 Mate (plumber's, pipe fitter's, heating and ventilating engineering fitter's)

Assists plumber, pipe fitter or heating and ventilating engineering fitter to make up, install, maintain and repair piping, heating, ventilating and air conditioning systems

Performs some or all of the following tasks: assists with the erection of ladders and scaffolding; assists in rigging suspended cradles or hoisting equipment; conveys tools and materials to work area; cuts or drills holes in walls, floors or ceilings for piping, ducting and fixing brackets; assists in positioning and securing pipework, ducting and fittings; assists in testing installations for leaks and correct functioning; performs other tasks as directed by plumber, pipe fitter or heating and ventilating engineering fitter.

May (01) operate hoisting equipment

(02) cut and bend piping or other materials to required size and shape.

Other titles include Chemical plumber's mate, Heating and ventilating fitter's labourer, Plumber's labourer, Pipe fitter's labourer, Ship plumber's mate.

776.20 Gas fitter's mate

Assists gas fitter to install, maintain and repair gas piping and gas appliances in consumers' premises

Performs some or all of the following tasks: assists with the erection of ladders and scaffolding; conveys tools and materials to work area; cuts or drills holes in walls, floors or ceilings for piping and fixing brackets; assists gas fitter to position and secure pipework, fittings and appliances; assists in testing installations for leaks and correct functioning; performs other tasks as directed by gas fitter.

Other titles include Gas fitter's labourer.

776.30 Plater's helper

Assists plater to mark out, prepare and position metal plating

Performs some or all of the following tasks: conveys tools and materials to work area; attaches slings, hooks, guide ropes to metal plate, etc; assists plater to mark out and straighten, bend, punch, drill or otherwise machine metal plate; performs other tasks as directed by plater.

May (01) direct crane or other hoisting equipment operators

(02) assist with the erection of working platforms.

Other titles include Boilermaker's helper, Boilermaker's labourer, Boiler plater's helper, Constructional plater's helper, Ship's plater's helper.

776.40 Shipwright's labourer

Assists shipwright to erect temporary structures, ship framework or prefabricated hull sections

Performs some or all of the following tasks: conveys tools and materials to work area; attaches slings to keel blocks and crane hooks; performs other tasks as directed by shipwright.

May (01) direct crane driver to move and position keel blocks.

776.50 Steel erector's mate

Assists steel erector with the erection of steel structures or structural framework

Performs some or all of the following tasks: assists with the erection of ladders and scaffolding; assists in rigging hoisting equipment or erecting jib cranes; attaches slings, hooks and guide ropes to stanchions, girders, chimney plates, etc; performs other tasks as directed by steel erector.

May (01) assist steel erector to position and secure steel structures

(02) operate hoisting equipment.

Other titles include Steel erector's labourer.

776.60 Rigger's labourer (ship)

Assists rigger to install and repair ropes, wires and cables on ships

Performs some or all of the following tasks: conveys tools and materials to work area; assists rigger to position and erect derricks, davits, etc, working at heights as required; assists rigger to join or fit attachments to wire ropes; performs other tasks as directed by rigger.

May (01) assist with the movement and mooring of ship in dock, and be known as Sailorman.

776.70 Steelworker's labourer (ship construction, repair)

Assists steelworker (general) to perform metal working tasks in ship construction or repair

Performs a combination of tasks as described under FRAME BENDER'S HELPER (729.93), PLATER'S HELPER (776.30) and SHIPWRIGHT'S LABOURER (776.40) and otherwise assists steelworker as required.

May (01) direct crane or other hoisting equipment operators

(02) assist with the erection of working platforms.

776.99 Other pipe, sheet and structural metal workers' mates and labourers

Workers in this group directly assist pipe, sheet and structural metal workers in the performance of their tasks and are not elsewhere classified.

Unit Group 779 Pipe, Sheet and Structural Metal Working and Related Occupations Not Elsewhere Classified

Workers in this unit group make ornamental metal work using cold metal, and perform miscellaneous tasks in pipe, sheet and structural metal working and are not elsewhere classified.

779 .10 Ornamental metal worker

Cuts, shapes and joins cold metal, using hand and machine tools, to make ornamental metal products such as balustrades, cloakroom fittings, hearth furniture and light fittings

Ascertains job requirements from drawings or other specifications; selects appropriate blank, casting, extrusion or sheet of metal such as copper, brass, bronze, aluminium or stainless steel; marks out metal as described under MARKER-OUT (772 .05); cuts and drills metal using hand and machine tools; beats, files and chases metal using hand tools to obtain required shape and design; assembles prepared parts by brazing or soldering; cleans and polishes metal surfaces as required, by hand or using machine tools.

Other titles include Art metal worker.

See Smith (specialised) (714 .25)

Excluded are Goldsmiths and Silversmiths (791 .02)

779 .50 Rivet heater

Heats rivets in furnace ready for riveting

Sets and lights coke or charcoal furnace or switches on electrically heated furnace; places rivets selected by riveter into hot furnace; operates controls to regulate heat in furnace; removes rivets, using tongs, when heated to specified temperature; throws or carries hot rivets to rivet catcher, holder-up or holder-on.

779 .98 Trainee

Performs, under instruction or guidance, various tasks including training exercises and as appropriate pursues studies in order to acquire the basic skills and knowledge required to perform the tasks of workers in pipe, sheet and structural metal working and related occupations not elsewhere classified.

779 .99 Other pipe, sheet and structural metal working and related occupations not elsewhere classified

Workers in this group perform miscellaneous tasks in pipe, sheet and structural metal working and are not separately classified, for example:

(01) **Reinforcing machine operators** (operate machines to form and weld wire to make circular cages for reinforcing concrete); (02) **Rivet catchers.**

Minor Group 79 PROCESSING, MAKING, REPAIRING AND RELATED OCCUPATIONS (METAL AND ELECTRICAL) NOT ELSEWHERE CLASSIFIED

Workers in this minor group make, repair and decorate jewellery and plate articles of precious and other metals, beat metals to form leaf, cut and polish precious and other stones, set stones in jewellery and tools, perform tasks in metal engraving, construct vehicle bodies and fix fittings to vehicle and aircraft bodies and perform miscellaneous metal and electrical processing, making, repairing and related tasks and are not elsewhere classified.

The occupations are arranged in the following unit groups:

790 Foremen (Processing, Making, Repairing and Related Occupations (Metal and Electrical) Not Elsewhere Classified)

791 Goldsmiths, Silversmiths, Precious Stone Working and Related Occupations

792 Metal Engraving Occupations

793 Vehicle Body Builders and Aircraft Finishers

799 Other Processing, Making, Repairing and Related Occupations (Metal and Electrical)

Unit Group 790 Foremen (Processing, Making, Repairing and Related Occupations (Metal and Electrical) Not Elsewhere Classified)

Workers in this unit group directly supervise and co-ordinate the activities of workers in metal and electrical processing, making, repairing and related occupations and are not elsewhere classified.

790.10 Foreman (goldsmiths, silversmiths, precious stone working and related occupations)

Directly supervises and co-ordinates the activities of workers in goldsmithing, silversmithing, precious stone working and related occupations

Performs appropriate tasks as described under SUPERVISOR/FOREMAN (UNSPECIFIED) (990.00).

Additional factor: number of workers supervised.

790.20 Foreman (metal engraving occupations)

Directly supervises and co-ordinates the activities of workers in metal engraving occupations

Performs appropriate tasks as described under SUPERVISOR/FOREMAN (UNSPECIFIED) (990.00).

Additional factor: number of workers supervised.

790.30 Foreman (vehicle body builders, aircraft finishers)

Directly supervises and co-ordinates the activities of vehicle body builders or aircraft finishers

Performs appropriate tasks as described under SUPERVISOR/FOREMAN (UNSPECIFIED) (990.00).

Additional factor: number of workers supervised.

790 .98 Trainee

Performs, under instruction or guidance, various tasks including training exercises and as appropriate pursues studies in order to acquire the basic skills and knowledge required to perform the tasks of foremen (processing, making, repairing and related occupations (metal and electrical) not elsewhere classified).

790 .99 Other foremen (processing, making, repairing and related occupations (metal and electrical) not elsewhere classified)

Workers in this group directly supervise and co-ordinate the activities of workers in metal and electrical processing, making, repairing and related occupations and are not separately classified, for example:

(01) **Foremen (metal bedstead making)**; (02) **Foremen (saw making)**; (03) **Foremen (scrap metal reclamation).**

Additional factor: number of workers supervised.

Unit Group 791 Goldsmiths, Silversmiths, Precious Stone Working and Related Occupations

Workers in this unit group make and repair articles of plate and jewellery of gold, silver and other metals, decorate metal articles by chasing, engine turning and saw piercing, beat gold and other metals to form metal leaf, cut and polish precious and other stones, make master patterns for articles of jewellery, set precious and other stones in articles of jewellery and in tools and perform closely related activities.

Excluded are Metal Engraving Occupations (792)

791 .02 Goldsmith, Silversmith

Makes and repairs articles of precious metal or white metal

Ascertains job requirements from model, design drawings or other specifications; cuts blanks as required from sheet of metal using hand and powered saws, shears, etc; either shapes blanks gradually by beating with special hammers and mallets over shaped anvils, or stakes (raising) or spins blanks to shape on spinning lathe (see 722 .34), or selects appropriate components spun, pressed or cast by other workers; solders together halves of pressed or cast parts such as spouts; fits parts such as spouts, handles, feet and decorative rims to body of article and fixes in place by soldering, brazing or riveting; cleans joints and removes surplus metal; hammers surface of article and seam joints at various stages of making to produce smooth finish free from distortions (planishing); during making anneals articles as required and checks work visually and with measuring instruments; repairs damaged or worn articles and remakes or replaces damaged or worn parts.

May (01) polish finished article

(02) cut pattern on surface of article by turning on a special lathe (791 .10).

Other titles include Hammerman (gold, silver, white metal), Maker-up (gold, silver, white metal).

791 .04 Britannia metal smith

Makes hollow ware such as tea services, tankards and vases from Britannia metal or pewter

Bends and shapes partly formed components to requirements manually, with hand forming tools or by beating with hammers over a curved metal anvil (neck stake), or cuts blank from sheet of pressed or stamped metal and bends to shape round stake; smoothes edges of pressed, stamped or cast parts with hand files; solders together halves of pressed or stamped parts such as spouts; cuts hole for spout in body of article and fits metal gauze over hole as required; joins spout, handles, feet and decorative rims to body of article, by soldering; manipulates handles, etc against emery belt and subsequently against buffing wheel to polish surface.

791.06 Chaser

Decorates articles of precious or white metal by indenting patterns on articles with hammers and punches

Ascertains job requirements from model, drawings or other specifications; dusts article to be chased with powdered chalk and marks out pattern in the chalk or places perforated paper pattern against article and hits with small bag of chalk (pouncing) to mark pattern on article in a series of dots; for certain hollow ware articles, fills articles with melted pitch which, when solidified, provides a resilient base for working; as required mounts and secures article on pad on work-bench; indents design on article by tapping punches of various shapes and sizes with hammer along pattern markings, working from front of article (flat chasing), from back of article (embossing) or from both front and back (repoussé chasing); if embossing hollow article, clamps one end of long iron tool (snarling iron) in vice, positions article over free end and taps iron near vice with hammer, so that end of iron inside article bumps against surface to form pattern; melts pitch from article on completion of chasing.

May (01) make tools.

791.08 Saw piercer

Cuts out monograms, crests and other designs in articles of metal plate and/or jewellery using piercing saw

Positions article bearing marked out design on special peg on work-bench; drills small hole on guide line of design; threads saw blade through hole and secures in saw frame; saws through metal, manipulating article so that blade cuts round guide lines of design; removes waste metal; on completion of cutting each section of design, releases blade from frame and withdraws it from cut aperture; repeats cutting operation until design is completed; finishes cut edges by filing as required.

May (01) mark out design on article
(02) polish article after cutting.

791.10 Engine turner

Operates a turning engine to cut designs on jewellery or metal articles

Ascertains job requirements from drawings, model or other specifications; mounts article to be turned in block of pitch and clamps mounted article on machine or fits cylindrical article securely on machine mandrel; fits appropriate cutting tool on machine, and, if cutting wavy lines, fits metal guide to control oscillating movement of article against cutting tool; operates machine controls to move or rotate article against cutting tool; controls depth of cut by manual pressure on cutting tool; checks progress of cutting using magnifying glass mounted on machine; removes pitch mounting block from article by heating or hammering.

791.12 Chain maker (hand) (gold, silver)

Makes gold or silver chains by hand

Draws gold or silver wire to required gauge by pulling through successively smaller holes in draw-plate, using hand operated capstan; winds drawn wire to form a coil round paper covered spindle (spit) of same diameter as that of required chain link; burns off paper and removes coil from spit; cuts coil lengthwise with pliers or saw to form open links; joins links together using pliers and solders ends of each link; adds links till chain is of required length; twists chain with pliers if spiral effect is required.

791.14 Goldbeater

Beats gold or other metal to form thin leaf

Beats packet of metal squares interleaved with large squares of vellum, using hand and/or mechanical hammers to reduce thickness and spread metal to size of vellum; repeats beating operation after the squares have been cut and interleaved by the cutter and booker to form a packet (cutch for first and second beatings, shoder for third beating and mould for fourth and final beating); checks thickness of leaf after final beating by viewing colour against daylight.

May (01) perform tasks of CUTTER AND BOOKER (791.16).

791.16 Cutter and booker (metal leaf)

Cuts and arranges metal strip and leaf ready for beating and makes up finished leaf into books

Cuts thin metal strip into squares with knife; interleaves metal squares with larger squares of vellum, using boxwood pincers to lift metal; wraps resultant packet (cutch) in parchment and passes to goldbeater; extracts leaves from cutch after beating, cuts into quarters and repeats interleaving operation to form second cutch; repeats cutting and interleaving operations after second and third beatings; after fourth and final beating, cuts the leaf into squares of required size using a shaped cutter of sharpened rattan cane (waggon); makes up squares of beaten leaf into books (25 squares of leaf interleaved with powdered or rouged tissue papers).

791.18 Diamond sawyer, Diamond cleaver

Divides diamonds by sawing or cleaving

(01) Diamond sawyer

Sets diamond with cutting lines marked in Indian ink in plaster of Paris in holder; mounts holder on lathe above bronze cutting disc treated with diamond dust and oil; positions disc to cut stone as required; starts machine and ensures that cutting, which may take several days, proceeds correctly.

(02) Diamond cleaver

Sets diamond with cutting lines marked in Indian ink in plastic compound in holder; secures holder on work-bench; cuts a small groove where stone is to be split, using a diamond fixed in a holder; inserts a chisel into the groove and taps sharply with mallet to divide stone.

Additional factor: number of lathes attended.

791.20 Diamond cutter, Diamond polisher

Cuts cleaved, sawn and undivided diamonds to shape or cuts facets on diamonds

(01) Diamond cutter

Fixes holder containing cleaved, sawn or undivided diamond in chuck of lathe; operates lathe to rotate chuck; holds diamond set in hand tool against stone in chuck to grind off points and defects and shape stone to requirements.

(02) Diamond polisher

Applies mixture of diamond dust and oil to cast iron grinding wheel and operates controls to rotate wheel; presses diamond mounted in holder against rotating wheel to cut facets on stone at required angles; repositions stone in holder to cut each facet.

Other titles include Industrial diamond cutter, Industrial diamond polisher.

791.22 Gem cutter and polisher (excluding diamonds)

Cuts and polishes gemstones, other than diamonds, for jewellery or for industrial use

Ascertains job requirements from written or other specifications; if cutting fashion stones such as agate, quartz crystal or turquoise, cuts block of stone using rotating saw or other cutting tool to obtain pieces of appropriate size, avoiding flaws in block; mounts stone in wax or plastic cement on the end of a stick; manipulates mounted stone against rotating carborundum disc to remove sharp edges and points (roughing); rounds stone or cuts facets by manipulating roughly shaped stone against appropriate grinding wheel or disc of copper, lead, wood or felt, treated with abrasive material as required; remounts stone in wax or cement on stick to cut each facet; polishes stone by holding against rotating polishing head or disc treated with polishing material such as rottenstone or ruby powder.

Other titles include Lapidary.

791.24 Jewellery model maker

Makes master patterns for articles of jewellery

Ascertains job requirements from written or other specifications; makes scale drawing of article to be reproduced; selects suitable material for model; shapes the wood, metal or other material to form master pattern by cutting, drilling, hammering or carving; fits metal parts together by brazing; checks from drawings and specifications that master pattern is correct in every detail.

See Scale model maker (673.29)

791.26 Jeweller (general)

Makes articles of jewellery throughout

Performs appropriate tasks as described under JEWELLERY MOUNTER (791.30) and GEM SETTER (791.32).

791.28 Jobbing jeweller

Repairs and remodels articles of jewellery

Examines article of jewellery to ascertain nature of repair required, or studies remodelling instructions or designs; repairs clasps, pins and other items by soldering; enlarges or reduces size of rings by sawing through band, adding or removing metal and soldering ends together; makes replacement parts by cutting and shaping metal, using hand and powered tools; smoothes soldered joints and trims off surplus metal with hand file; removes gems from settings, where necessary; cleans articles by immersion in chemical solution; finishes metal parts by hand polishing or by holding against rotating buffing mop, polishing wheel or fine wire brush; re-strings necklaces.

May (01) re-set gems.

Other titles include Jewellery repairer.

791.30 Jewellery mounter

Makes mounts for articles of jewellery

Ascertains job requirements from drawings, model or other specifications; selects suitable sheet, tube, rod or wire of gold, silver, platinum or other metal; shapes metal by sawing, cutting, drilling, filing and bending to form parts of mount, such as frame, gem settings, hinges and catch; assembles parts and brazes or solders together to form complete mount; removes rough edges by filing.

May (01) prepare designs.

791.32 Gem setter

Sets precious, semi-precious or other ornamental stones in prepared jewellery mounts

Fixes jewellery mount in wooden clamp or vice, or in bed of wax; cuts, drills and shapes setting in mount to accommodate stone; smoothes edges of setting using file or pointed steel tool; positions stone in setting and secures it by closing claws or by forcing surrounding metal against stone in a decorative manner (graining); examines stone in setting, using magnifying glass and makes any necessary adjustments.

May (01) set stones in position with adhesive
(02) replace worn or damaged stones.

Other titles include Diamond setter.

Excluded are workers setting jewels in watch movements (821.40)

791.34 Industrial diamond setter

Sets diamonds in tools for dressing and forming grinding wheels, for machining metals and for other industrial uses

Fills cavity in end of tool shank with metallic powder or other fusing agent and fits diamond in cavity so that working point is at required angle, or positions diamond in cavity, fits metal mould round diamond and shank and fills with fusing agent; heats tool shank and diamond in furnace or in gas flame until the metal powder or other fusing agent becomes solid; cools tool shank and diamond by quenching in water or cooling in air; removes surplus metal from around diamond point using hand file or lathe.

791.98 Trainee

Performs, under instruction or guidance, various tasks including training exercises and as appropriate pursues studies in order to acquire the basic skills and knowledge required to perform the tasks of goldsmiths, silversmiths and workers in precious stone working and related occupations.

791.99 Other goldsmiths, silversmiths, precious stone working and related occupations

Workers in this group perform miscellaneous tasks in goldsmithing, silversmithing, precious stone working and related occupations and are not elsewhere classified, for example:

(01) **Industrial diamond drillers** (operate special purpose machines to drill or pierce holes in diamonds used for diamond dies); (02) **Quartz crystal workers** (cut and grind quartz crystals used for frequency control in electronic apparatus).

Unit Group 792 Metal Engraving Occupations

Workers in this unit group engrave metal printing rollers, plates and cylinders, metal dies and punches, engrave lettering and designs on jewellery and metal articles, etch printing plates, cylinders and rollers, and perform miscellaneous tasks in making metal type.

See 161.40 for workers who create original designs and engrave them.

79202 Roller engraver (hand)

Engraves metal printing rollers or cylinders by hand

Secures printing roller or cylinder in position on work-bench; coats roller or cylinder with varnish; places transfer of required design face down on roller or cylinder and presses to transfer design on to varnish; marks outlines of design with scribing tool; cuts away design with hand graving tools; for colour printing, cuts separate roller for each colour; repairs and alters rollers or cylinders already engraved or etched by filling in scratches with metal wire, touching up lettering or areas of design, re-etching parts of design, etc.

792041 Printing plate engraver (hand)

Engraves metal printing plates by hand

Positions printing plate on work-bench; if engraving small intricate lettering or design, positions magnifying glass above plate; transfers outline of lettering or design from gelatine sheet to plate or scribes or marks design or guide lines freehand, using T-square for straight lines; cuts out outlined lettering or design with hand graving tools; if engraving plates for printing music, stamps out note heads, standard symbols and wording with punches and adds note stems, tails, ledger lines, etc freehand; finishes plate by rubbing with oil and charcoal stick; inks plate and takes proof impression in hand press.

May (01) prepare transfer on gelatine sheet by tracing design from sketch, photograph, pattern etc, or by scribing or drawing lettering or design freehand

(02) add shading effects by engraving with ruling machine or etching.

Other titles include Copper plate engraver, Music engraver.

79206 Roller engraver (pantograph machine), Printing plate engraver (pantograph machine)

Sets up and operates pantograph machine to engrave lettering and designs on printing rollers or plates

Fixes template bearing required lettering or design on machine under tracing head; positions and secures printing roller or plate under engraving head; fits appropriate cutter in engraving head; adjusts pantograph mechanism to scale engraving to required size and sets cutting depth; lowers engraving head on to roller or plate; starts machine and guides tracer point over lettering or design on template causing the connected engraving head to reproduce lettering or design on roller or plate; smoothes rough edges with hand files.

May (01) cut template.

79208 Clammer (roller engraving)

Impresses and etches designs in relief on steel roller mills used for engraving copper printing rollers

Calculates size of die required; machines cylindrical steel bar on lathe to form die blank of required size; passes blank to die cutter to cut design on die in reverse (intaglio); on return of cut die, hardens by placing in container filled with bone meal, heating for predetermined period in gas oven and quenching in cold water, or by other means; machines cylindrical mild steel bar on lathe to form roller mill of required size, ensuring that circumference of die and mill are exactly proportionate; fixes die on clamming machine next to drive roller and fits mill on machine adjacent to die; coats mill with acid-resistant wax; operates machine controls to apply pressure and bring die and mill into contact; starts machine to rotate die against mill, removing wax from area of mill corresponding to area of die not engraved; removes mill from machine and dips in acid to etch the metal from the uncovered area, leaving the design in relief on the mill; repeats process until the required depth of design is obtained; hardens patterned mill by heating in gas oven and quenching in cold water.

792.10 Roller engraver (mill engraving machine)

Operates machine to impress design from steel roller mill on to copper printing roller

Secures copper printing roller on engraving machine, ensuring that it is centred correctly and rotating evenly; fits patterned roller mill of hardened steel on to machine in contact with copper roller; operates controls to rotate roller and mill so that design on mill is impressed on copper roller; re-sets machine to impress further widths of design until entire surface of copper roller bears pattern; undertakes day-to-day maintenance of machine.

792.12 Die engraver

Cuts lettering or designs on metal dies or punches by hand and/or machine

Secures die blank in holding device on work-bench or engraving machine; if engraving by hand or using milling machine, coats face of blank with varnish, places design transfer face down on blank and presses to transfer design on to blank, or scribes or draws design on blank freehand or using stencil; if using pantograph machine, secures template bearing design in position on machine, adjusts pantograph mechanism to scale engraving to required size and sets depth of cut; cuts design on blank in relief or in reverse (intaglio) with hand graving tools and/or milling or pantograph engraving machine; smoothes edges of cuts with fine emery cloth and hand files, or removes unwanted metal from surface of die with routing machine.

May (01) use patterned counter punches to punch out lettering or parts of design
(02) prepare transfer on translucent paper, gelatine or plastic material by tracing design from sketch, photograph or pattern
(03) prepare template for use on pantograph machine
(04) harden, temper and polish dies after cutting.

Other titles include Brand letter cutter, Die cutter, Die sinker, Mark maker (metal stamp), Punch cutter.

792.14 Etcher

Etches printing plates, cylinders or rollers

If etching plate, cleans surface of prepared plate with chemical solution; sets temperature, speed and time controls on etching machine according to depth of etch required; positions plate in machine and starts machine; adjusts jets of acid during etching as necessary; after etching removes plate and scrubs clean; rubs French chalk over plate to highlight image; paints on acid resist where plate is sufficiently etched and repeats process, using fine etching machine or by immersing in acid bath till required finish is obtained; removes remaining acid resist with paraffin; scribes outline for finished plate.
If etching cylinder, mounts prepared cylinder on power driven rollers in a trough; pours etching solutions of varying strengths over rotating cylinder to penetrate the gelatine coating and etch the metal surface underneath; after etching, washes cylinder in chemical solution.
If etching copper roller, mounts prepared roller on mandrel over first of a series of troughs containing etching acids, rotates roller in each trough for varying periods of time manually or by operating switches to etch design area; reverses the direction of the roller at frequent intervals; checks progress of etching with depth gauge; when etching is completed washes roller in water trough; if further etching is required, covers areas of design which have been sufficiently etched with acid-resistant paint, or passes to roller painter for painting, and repeats process; removes acid-resistant paint from roller by scrubbing with naphtha solution and sawdust.

May (01) etch plates by immersing in acid bath
(02) engrave plates with electronic engraving machine (792.16)
(03) superimpose shading on 'line' plates (ie plates with no gradation of tone) by transferring shading pattern from gelatine sheet with a roller (tint laying)
(04) prepare plate for etching by coating with acid resist and scribing design through acid resist by hand or with pantograph engraving machine.

Other titles include Colour etcher, Etcher (graphic reproduction), Fine etcher, Half tone etcher, Line etcher, Photogravure etcher, Roller etcher.

792.16 Electronic engraver (process engraving)

Sets and operates an electronic machine to engrave printing plates

Ascertains from instructions number of plates required and finished size of plates; measures copy to be reproduced (flat copy, transparencies, screen negatives or positives) and adjusts machine controls to produce an engraving of the required size; mounts copy on glass with adhesive tape; selects suitable metal plate (for letterpress work) or sheet of plastic film coated with special dye (for lithographic work); cuts the plate or sheet to shape on guillotine; places copy on suction plate at one end of machine under an electronic scanning head and metal plate or plastic sheet on suction plate at other end of machine under an engraving head; sets the scanning and engraving heads in position and switches on; when engraving is completed, removes the engraved plate or sheet and washes it with spirit; rubs chalk into the engraved surface; for colour work, repeats process using a separate plate for each colour.

792.18 Decorative engraver (hand)

Engraves lettering and ornamental designs on jewellery and metal articles by hand

Positions article to be engraved, for example, cigarette case, tray, trophy, medal, watch, on support on workbench or fixes in vice, clamp or jig; marks outline of lettering or design on article; cuts out lettering or design with hand graving tools.

May (01) polish articles after engraving
(02) prepare or alter designs
(03) make and sharpen tools.

Additional factor: metals to which accustomed.

Other titles include Jewellery engraver.

792.20 Pantograph engraving machine setter-operator (excluding printing plates and rollers)

Sets up and operates pantograph machine to engrave lettering and designs on articles of metal, plastic or other material

Performs appropriate tasks as described under ROLLER ENGRAVER (PANTOGRAPH MACHINE) (792.06) but in relation to engraving articles of metal, plastic or other material, for example, medals, labels, instruction plates or jewellery.

Additional factor: materials to which accustomed.

Excluded are Die engravers (792.12)

792.50 Pantograph engraving machine operator (excluding printing rollers and plates)

Operates preset pantograph machine to engrave lettering and designs on articles of metal, plastic or other material

Positions and secures article to be engraved for example, medal, label, instruction plate or item of jewellery under engraving head; lowers engraving head on to article; starts machine and guides tracer point over lettering or design on template causing the connected engraving head to reproduce lettering or design on article.

Additional factor: materials to which accustomed.

792.98 Trainee

Performs, under instruction or guidance, various tasks including training exercises and as appropriate pursues studies in order to acquire the basic skills and knowledge required to perform the tasks of workers in metal engraving occupations.

792.99 Other metal engraving occupations

Workers in this group engrave metal printing rollers, plates and cylinders, metal dies and punches, engrave lettering and designs on jewellery and metal articles, etch textile printing rollers, prepare printing rollers and perform miscellaneous tasks in making metal type and are not elsewhere classified, for example:

(01) **Plate cutters (engraving)** (scribe designs or lettering on metal plates for use as templates on pantograph engraving machines); (02) **Roller painters (engraving)** (apply acid-resistant paint to areas of textile printing rollers not requiring etching or re-etching)

Unit Group 793 Vehicle Body Builders and Aircraft Finishers

Workers in this unit group construct vehicle bodies and fix interior and exterior fittings to vehicle and aircraft bodies.

Excluded are Repetitive assemblers (metal goods) (hand) (821 .35)

793 .10 Vehicle body builder

Constructs bodies for road vehicles or railway coaches

Ascertains job requirements from drawings or other specifications; selects prepared parts for framework and body, and alters to fit by cutting, bending and machining, or marks out, cuts and shapes material to form parts of framework and body; builds up structural framework of wood or metal for underframe, sides and roof on shop floor to be fitted on chassis or builds framework directly on to chassis; fits angle irons, brackets, etc and secures framework to chassis by bolting, welding or riveting; assembles flooring and secures over underframe; positions and secures insulation material, piping and ductwork between skins of bodywork as required; fits roof to framework as required and secures in position; fits side and end panels of sheet metal, wood, glass fibre or plastic laminate, and secures to framework by bolting, welding, screwing or riveting or with adhesives.

May (01) carry out some repair work

(02) specialise on particular type of vehicle, eg cars, omnibuses, lorries, ambulances, caravans, railway coaches

(03) performs tasks of VEHICLE BODY FINISHER (793 .20).

Other titles include Coach body maker, Vehicle body fitter.

See Styling modeller (motor vehicles) (699 .18)

793 .20 Vehicle body finisher

Fixes interior or exterior fittings to vehicle bodies

Positions and secures windows and doors in framework; attaches fittings such as mirrors, door handles and catches, and secures by screwing or bolting; installs interior items such as stairs, steps, seats and racks; installs furniture, sink units, stretchers or other special fittings in vehicles such as caravans, mobile shops or ambulances; fits pipework runs to vehicle body.

May (01) specialise on particular type of vehicle, eg cars, omnibuses, lorries, ambulances, caravans, mobile shops.

793 .30 Aircraft finisher

Fixes interior or exterior fittings to aircraft bodies

Ascertains job requirements from specifications; assembles components such as windows and frames, escape hatches and roof fabrications; fixes brackets and fasteners to components as required; positions doors, windows, hatches, and brackets and stays for bulkheads and panelling, and secures to aircraft framework; fits roof and side panels and bulkhead; installs furniture and fittings such as toilet and sink units and fits associated pipework.

793 .98 Trainee

Performs, under instruction or guidance, various tasks including training exercises and as appropriate pursues studies in order to acquire the basic skills and knowledge required to perform the tasks of vehicle body builders and aircraft finishers.

793 .99 Other vehicle body builders and aircraft finishers

Workers in this group construct vehicle bodies and fix interior and exterior fittings to vehicle and aircraft bodies and are not elsewhere classified.

Unit Group 799 Other Processing, Making, Repairing and Related Occupations (Metal and Electrical)

Workers in this unit group perform miscellaneous tasks in metal and electrical processing, making, repairing and related occupations including combined electrical and mechanical fitting (installation and maintenance), making wire goods throughout, forming card clothing for textile carding machines, tensioning saw blades, adjusting cycle wheels, assisting fitters and fitter-mechanics, and are not elsewhere classified.

799 .02 Installation fitter (electrical and mechanical)

Erects electrical and mechanical plant or industrial machinery on operational site

Ascertains job requirements from drawings, wiring diagrams, technical manuals or other specifications; determines sequence and method of required operations; positions or directs positioning of prepared parts, sub-assemblies or completed units, using hoisting equipment as necessary; builds up plant or machinery as required and secures in position, using hand tools such as chisels, drills, files, hammers, screwdrivers, spanners and wrenches; checks alignment during erection using measuring instruments; connects prepared wire or cable as required to specified terminals or connectors by crimping, brazing, soldering or bolting to complete equipment circuit; connects plant or machinery to electric power supply as required.

May (01) join parts by welding

(02) carry out functional tests on plant or machinery.

Other titles include Escalator erector, Lift erector.

799 .04 Maintenance fitter (electrical and mechanical)

Repairs and services electrical and mechanical plant and machinery

Examines plant or machinery for defects using test equipment as necessary; studies plant or machinery drawings, wiring diagrams or other specifications to determine sequence and method of required operations; dismantles plant or machinery and repairs or replaces damaged or worn parts; replaces faulty wiring; fits and assembles parts to rebuild plant or machinery; tests for correct functioning and adjusts as necessary; carries out service tasks such as cleaning, oiling and insulation testing according to schedule.

May (01) perform ancillary tasks such as straightforward welding, pipe fitting or rigging.

Other titles include Service fitter (lifts, escalators).

799 .06 Metal working and woodworking machines setter-operator

Sets up and operates both metal working and woodworking machines to cut or otherwise shape workpieces

Ascertains job requirements from drawings or other specifications; determines sequence and method of required operations; selects and fixes appropriate cutting tools and/or dies; positions workpiece on machine and secures as required; sets machine controls and feeds, and adjusts table stops and guides to requirements; operates machine controls and feeds tool to workpiece or workpiece to tool; checks accuracy of machining using measuring instruments; repositions workpiece, changes cutting tools or dies, and re-sets machines as necessary.

May (01) mark off workpiece prior to machining

(02) sharpen cutting tools

(03) assemble shaped components

(04) specialise in working materials such as bakelised paper, fired ceramics or micanite and be known as Insulation machinist.

Additional factors: machines to which accustomed, eg centre lathes, drilling machines, milling machines, routers, spindle cutters; materials worked.

799 .08 Wireworker (bench hand)

Makes wire goods throughout by hand or by hand and machine

Forms frame of article such as machinery guard, fireguard or sieve, from wire, metal rods or tubes or wood; selects wire of required gauge and cuts to length; bends or weaves wire to shape and ties, twists or welds joints together; cuts formed mesh to required size and fixes to frame; fits or welds brackets or other fixtures to frame.

799 .10 Barrel setter

Corrects distortions in gun barrels

Fixes gun barrel in clamps; rotates barrel and examines visually to locate distortions in barrel; taps with hammer to correct distortions; checks barrel after final grinding, reaming and turning, and re-sets as necessary.

Other titles include Barrel straightener.

799 .12 Motor cycle rectifier

Rectifies mechanical and electrical faults (other than in engine and gearbox) in new motor cycles following road tests

Ascertains job requirements from road test report; carries out adjustments to parts such as brakes, controls, horn, lights, starter and suspension; replaces defective parts using hand tools such as screwdrivers, spanners, soldering irons and powered hand drills.

May (01) rectify faults discovered during manufacture
(02) carry out final general inspection of motor cycle.

See 742 .30 for workers who repair motor cycles.

799 .14 Saw smith

Tensions and imparts or restores rigidity and trueness of surface to circular saw blades

Positions or directs the positioning of circular saw blade on specially shaped anvil; places straight-edge or level on surface of saw blade; checks amount of light showing between straight-edge or level and saw blade to locate distortions; hammers saw blade to remove distortions and to tension blade.

Other titles include Saw hammerer.

See 749 .10 for workers who repair and sharpen hand, band- or circular saws.

799 .16 Design cutter (printing rollers, blocks)

Outlines designs on textile, wallpaper or linoleum printing rollers or blocks with metal strip or pins

Secures wooden or composition roller or block bearing design impression on work-bench; selects brass or gilding metal strip or brass pins of appropriate gauge; measures strip against design contours and cuts required length; bends, files or shapes strip to fit design contours as required; hammers strip or pins into roller or block following design outline; ensures that strip or pins protrude an even height above surface of roller or block; if roller has paper covering, removes paper inside the design outlines; smoothes edges of metal with hand tools.

May (01) cut grooves along design outlines and hammer metal strip into grooves
(02) performs tasks of FELTER (699 .70).

799 .18 Marker maker (footwear)

Makes blocks and templates for marking stitch lines and position of punch holes on footwear uppers

Places paper pattern of footwear upper on plywood board; traces through pattern to mark stitching lines and position of punch holes on the plywood; cuts grooves along marked stitching lines using cutting machine; cuts lengths of metal strip and bends to shape of stitching lines; slots strip into groove and hammers or presses into place, allowing strip to protrude above surface of board; makes punch holes with nails; smoothes nail heads and edge of strip with file and emery paper to finish marker block; fits block on top holder of marking machine and operates machine to mark stitching lines and punch holes on hardboard for use as template on marking machine.

May (01) mark stitching lines on footwear uppers.

799 .20 Card setting machine tenter

Sets up and tends a number of machines which cut and shape wire to form card teeth and insert teeth into a foundation to form clothing for textile carding machines

Sets up coil of wire on wind-off reel and threads end into machine; fixes cam wheels, pricker dies and blades and shaping tools on machine; positions roll of foundation material on machine and threads end over feed rollers or pulleys and through machine; sets controls to regulate speed of machine according to width and thickness of foundation, number of rows of wire teeth to be inserted and the distance between the teeth; starts machine which pierces cloth with pricker blades, cuts and shapes wire to form teeth and presses teeth into pierced holes in cloth; adjusts machine settings during operations as required.

May (01) grind cutters and dies
(02) make pricker dies and blades.

Additional factor: number of machines tended.

799 .50 Card fillet dresser

Trims card fillet to exact size for mounting on textile carding machine and ensures that card teeth are set and finished correctly

Adjusts paring machine to cut required width from edge of strip of card clothing (fillet); feeds end of fillet between guide plates and through machine and winds over rollers at take-off end; starts machine to trim one edge of fillet; repeats operation for other edge; winds fillet on to a cylinder for examination; turns cylinder and checks that fillet edges have been trimmed exactly and that card teeth are set accurately and ground correctly; holds small hand tool (runner) between the rows of teeth as the cylinder turns to correct spacing between rows; stops cylinder to rectify the setting of individual teeth; sharpens cutting blades of paring machine on grinding machine.

Other titles include Card dresser.

799 .52 Card top clipper

Clips spiked metal holding strips along edges of card top fillets or clips fillets to cast iron plates

(01) **First process worker**
Positions two spiked metal strips (clips) for the sides of a short strip of card clothing (card top fillet) in slots on clipping machine; places two more clips over ends of card top fillet and positions fillet on the clips in machine; operates machine to bend top edges of clips over fillet and to press spikes of clips firmly into the fillet foundation cloth; removes fillet from machine.

(02) **Second process worker**
Positions fillet, with clips attached, on cast iron plate (flat); places flat and fillet in clipping machine and operates machine to secure edges of clips round edges of flat; removes flat and attached fillet from machine and checks that surface of fillet is even.

May (03) cut fillet from sheet of card clothing and trim edges.

799 .54 Filler-up (card clothing)

Examines card fillets and sheets, replaces damaged teeth and inserts missing teeth

Positions strip (fillet) or sheet of card clothing on work-bench and examines for malformed or missing teeth; removes malformed teeth, cleans holes or pricks holes where teeth are missing; sets replacement teeth into holes at correct angle using hand tools.
Other titles include Filler-in.

799 .56 Needle straightener

Removes bends and other distortions from needles using hand tools

Examines needles to locate bends, warps or other irregularities caused during machining or heat treating; positions needles on rubber anvil or other working base and corrects distortions using metal plates, hammers, pliers and other hand tools; verifies conformance to specification using micrometer and optical projector.

799 .58 Cycle frame setter

Sets frames or sections of frames of bicycles and motor cycles in alignment

Fixes frame or section of frame in holding jig; checks that the various tubular parts are in alignment and fit properly into jig; bends, levers and hammers the various sections till frame sits correctly in jig and all parts are in alignment.

799 .60 Cycle wheel truer

Adjusts wheels of bicycles and motor cycles to run true

Clamps wheel in truing machine or fixture; spins wheel by hand and checks pointers on scale of instrument on machine or fixture which indicate deviations from the true; tightens or loosens tensioners on spokes to correct deviations; continues to make adjustments till wheel runs absolutely true.

799 .62 Measurer, coiler and cutter (wire rope, wire cable)

Operates machine to wind a measured length of wire rope or cable on to a drum

Loads or directs the loading of drum of wire rope or cable on to input end of measuring and coiling machine, and empty drum on to output end; threads end of rope or cable into machine, through measuring device and attaches to empty drum; starts machine to wind rope or cable on to empty drum; stops machine when required length has been wound and cuts rope or cable; secures end of rope or cable to drum; unloads or directs the unloading of drum.

Other titles include Measuring machine driver (wire rope/wire cable), Reeler (wire cable), Reeler (wire rope).

799.90 Fitter's mate

Assists fitters or fitter-mechanics generally

Performs a combination of the following tasks: cleans and degreases equipment parts or sub-assemblies; conveys tools, materials and equipment parts to and from work areas manually or using trucks or hoisting equipment; assists with the positioning of equipment parts or sub-assemblies; performs other tasks as directed by fitter or fitter-mechanic.

Other titles include Engineering mechanic's mate, Fitter-mechanic's mate, Maintenance fitter's mate, Mechanic's mate.

799.98 Trainee

Performs, under instruction or guidance, various tasks including training exercises and as appropriate pursues studies in order to acquire the basic skills and knowledge required to perform the tasks of workers in other processing, making, repairing and related occupations (metal and electrical).

799.99 Other processing, making, repairing and related occupations (metal and electrical) not elsewhere classified

Workers in this group perform miscellaneous tasks in metal and electrical processing, making, repairing and related occupations and are not separately classified, for example:

(01) **Brass printing rule makers** (make brass rules for printing lines, diamonds, squares, corners or other shapes); (02) **Die casers** (fix composition die blanks into metal casings by shrinking, brazing or forging); (03) **Dressers (type founding)** (cut grooves by hand at base of lines of set-up type); (04) **Filament winders** (operate machines to wind filaments for valves and lamps); (05) **Fish hook benders (hand)**; (06) **Formation hands (battery making)** (charge plates or cells for electric storage batteries); (07) **Frame setters (metal bedsteads)** (fix moulds in position on frames ready for insertion of rails, tubes, etc preparatory to casting of joints); (08) **Heavy core builders** (assemble metal laminations to form heavy cores for electrical equipment); (09) **Lift adjusters,** Lift testers (check lift control systems after installation); (10) **Matrix makers (type founding)** (make and/or mount and correct inaccuracies in metal moulds for casting type); (11) **Metal bobbin makers;** (12) **Razor hafters,** Razor setters-in (fit razor blades to hafts and sharpen edges of blades on whetting stones); (13) **Scrap balers** (operate hydraulic presses to compress scrap metal into bales); (14) **Scrap cutters-up,** Scrap breakers (cut and break up scrap metal, old machinery, etc using a variety of equipment including flame cutters, hydraulic presses and mechanical shears); (15) **Sealing end attendants (electric cables)** (reseal ends of metal-sheathed cables after testing); (16) **Setters-up (type)** (arrange cast type on rule ready for dressing); (17) **Stitchers (wire goods making)** (sew sections of wire mesh goods together by hand or machine); (18) **Weight adjusters (other than fine balance)** (fill holes in brass or iron weights with lead until correct weight is obtained); (19) **Wire benders (textile machinery fittings)**; (20) **Wire winders** (wind wire on to bobbins or drums, or spool wire into coils of required length for dispatch to customers).

MAJOR GROUP XV

Painting, Repetitive Assembling, Product Inspecting, Packaging and Related Occupations

Workers in this major group apply paint and similar decorative and protective coatings to prepared surfaces; perform repetitive tasks in the batch or mass production assembly of prepared parts; inspect, test, examine, sort, grade and measure materials, goods and products; pack, wrap and label products and other articles, fill and seal containers and perform closely related tasks.

The occupations are arranged in the following minor groups:

81 Painting and Related Coating Occupations

82 Product Assembling Occupations (Repetitive)

83 Product Inspecting, Examining, Sorting, Grading and Measuring Occupations (Excluding Laboratory Technicians)

84 Packaging, Labelling and Related Occupations

Minor Group 81 PAINTING AND RELATED COATING OCCUPATIONS

Workers in this minor group prepare surfaces for painting and decorating, apply paint and similar decorative and protective coatings to prepared surfaces and polish coated surfaces.

The occupations are arranged in the following unit groups:

810 Foremen (Painting and Related Coating Occupations)

811 Painting and Decorating Occupations (Structures)

812 Painting and Related Coating Occupations (Brush) (Excluding Structures)

813 Painting and Related Coating Occupations (Spray) (Excluding Structures)

814 Painting and Related Coating Occupations (Dip)

815 Wood Staining, Waxing and French Polishing Occupations (Hand)

819 Painting and Related Coating Occupations Not Elsewhere Classified

Unit Group 810 Foremen (Painting and Related Coating Occupations)

Workers in this unit group directly supervise and co-ordinate the activities of workers in painting and related coating occupations.

810 .10 Foreman (painting and decorating occupations) (structures)

Directly supervises and co-ordinates the activities of workers in painting and decorating occupations (structures)

Performs appropriate tasks as described under SUPERVISOR/FOREMAN (UNSPECIFIED) (990 .00).

May (01) measure up work

(02) prepare estimates.

Additional factor: number of workers supervised.

810 .20 Foreman (painting and related coating occupations) (brush) (excluding structures)

Directly supervises and co-ordinates the activities of workers in painting and related coating occupations (brush) (excluding structures)

Performs appropriate tasks as described under SUPERVISOR/FOREMAN (UNSPECIFIED) (990 .00).

May (01) mix and match colours

(02) determine temperature required for stoving painted articles.

Additional factor: number of workers supervised.

810 .30 Foreman (painting and related coating occupations) (spray) (excluding structures)

Directly supervises and co-ordinates the activities of workers in painting and related coating occupations (spray) (excluding structures)

Performs appropriate tasks as described under SUPERVISOR/FOREMAN (UNSPECIFIED) (990 .00).

May (01) mix and match colours

(02) set controls of automatic and semi-automatic machines

(03) undertake minor repairs to machinery and equipment.

Additional factor: number of workers supervised.

810.40 Foreman (painting and related coating occupations) (dip)

Directly supervises and co-ordinates the activities of workers in painting and related coating occupations (dip)

Performs appropriate tasks as described under SUPERVISOR/FOREMAN (UNSPECIFIED) (990.00).

May (01) mix dipping solutions
(02) set controls of automatic dipping plant.

Additional factor: number of workers supervised.

810.50 Foreman (wood staining, waxing and French polishing occupations) (hand)

Directly supervises and co-ordinates the activities of workers in wood staining, waxing and French polishing occupations (hand)

Performs appropriate tasks as described under SUPERVISOR/FOREMAN (UNSPECIFIED) (990.00).

Additional factor: number of workers supervised.

810.98 Trainee

Performs, under instruction or guidance, various tasks including training exercises and as appropriate pursues studies in order to acquire the basic skills and knowledge required to perform the tasks of foremen in painting and related coating occupations.

810.99 Other foremen (painting and related coating occupations)

Workers in this group directly supervise and co-ordinate the activities of workers in painting and related coating occupations and are not elsewhere classified.

Unit Group 811 Painting and Decorating Occupations (Structures)

Workers in this unit group prepare surfaces of buildings, metal structures, ships, and stage, film and television studio sets for painting and decorating, and apply paint, wallpaper and similar protective and decorative materials to prepared surfaces.

811.10 Painter and decorator

Prepares surfaces, fittings and fixtures of buildings for painting and decorating and applies paint, wallpaper or similar protective and decorative materials

Performs tasks as described under PAINTER (BUILDINGS) (811.20) and PAPERHANGER (811.30).

May (01) apply lining materials to walls or ceilings before decorating
(02) coat surfaces with plastic mixture
(03) comb or otherwise treat plastic-coated surfaces to produce textured finish
(04) affix expanded polystyrene tiles to ceilings
(05) perform graining (811.99), marbling or gilding tasks
(06) perform signwriting tasks (812.05)
(07) perform glazing tasks (865.10).

Additional factors: maximum height at which accustomed to work; whether accustomed to work from suspended scaffolding or cradle.

811.20 Painter (buildings), Ship painter

Prepares interior and exterior surfaces, fittings and fixtures of buildings or ships for painting, and applies coats of paint, varnish or similar protective and decorative materials

Washes down surfaces; removes old paint using blow lamp, gas torch, electric paint remover or paint solvent and scrapers; fills holes and cracks with appropriate filling material; applies sealing solution to knots in wood; smoothes surfaces using abrasive block or paper, or powered sanding tool; removes rust and other deposits from metal surfaces using wire brushes, scrapers, mechanical blasting equipment, etc; selects prepared paint, varnish or other coating material or mixes paint to required shade; where appropriate, applies masking tape to areas not to be coated; applies one or more priming coats, undercoats and finishing coats to surfaces using brush, roller or spray equipment; rubs down coated surfaces with abrasive block or paper between coats, as necessary.

May (01) erect scaffolding

(02) apply paint using electrostatic hand gun

(03) coat surfaces with plastic mixture

(04) comb or otherwise treat plastic-coated surfaces to produce textured finish

(05) affix wallpaper or other coverings in ships' cabins and public rooms

(06) prepare and paint surfaces of metal structures (811.50)

(07) perform graining (811.99), marbling or gilding tasks

(08) perform signwriting tasks (812.05)

(09) perform glazing tasks (865.10).

Additional factors: maximum height at which accustomed to work; whether accustomed to work from suspended scaffolding or cradle.

Other titles include House painter, Spray painter.

811.30 Paperhanger

Prepares ceilings and interior walls of buildings for decorating and covers them with paper or other flexible decorative material

Removes old covering material with scrapers and water or chemical solution; fills in cracks and holes with appropriate filling material; brushes sealing solution on to new walls; measures surfaces to be covered and cuts strips of required lengths from rolls of covering material; mixes adhesive to desired consistency and applies it evenly on back of covering material using brush or pasting machine, or removes protective backing from self-adhesive covering material; marks plumb line on wall; positions covering material on ceiling or wall, matching up pattern where appropriate; smoothes material to remove wrinkles and air bubbles, using soft brush or felt roller; cuts off surplus material; smoothes joins with seam roller.

May (01) apply lining materials to walls or ceilings before decorating

(02) affix expanded polystyrene tiles to ceilings.

811.50 Painter (metal structures), Red leader

Prepares surfaces of bridges or other metal structures or ships' exteriors for coating, and applies paint or similar protective materials

Removes rust, dirt and other deposits from surface of metal using wire brushes, scrapers, pneumatic chisels, mechanical blasting equipment, etc; applies coat of red lead or other primer and where appropriate finishing coat of paint or other protective material using brush, roller or spray equipment.

May (01) erect scaffolding

(02) apply coat of heat-resistant compound to metal structures.

Additional factors: maximum height at which accustomed to work; whether accustomed to work from suspended scaffolding or cradle.

Other titles include Chipper and painter, Industrial painter.

811.98 Trainee

Performs, under instruction or guidance, various tasks including training exercises and as appropriate pursues studies in order to acquire the basic skills and knowledge required to perform the tasks of workers in painting and decorating occupations (structures).

811.99 Other painting and decorating occupations (structures)

Workers in this group prepare surfaces of buildings, ships, studio sets and other structures for painting and decorating, and apply paint, wallpaper and similar protective and decorative materials to prepared surfaces and are not elsewhere classified, for example:

(01) **Grainers** (simulate wood grain, knot markings, veining, on materials such as wood or stone, using brushes, combs, etc); (02) **Scenery painters** (apply paint and where appropriate wallpaper to stage, film or television studio sets).

Unit Group 812 Painting and Related Coating Occupations (Brush) (Excluding Structures)

Workers in this unit group apply paint and similar decorative and protective materials by brush, other than to buildings, ships and other structures.

812.05 Signwriter, Show-card writer

Lays out and paints lettering and designs on surfaces such as wood, glass, plastics and metal, to make signs or on paper or board to make show-cards for display purposes

Ascertains job requirements from sketches and/or other specifications; draws guide lines on surface to be painted according to height of lettering or design required, as necessary; sketches outline of lettering or design freehand in chalk or pencil, or marks outline using pattern; selects prepared paints or mixes colours to desired shade and consistency; selects brushes; paints in lettering or design, steadying painting hand on stick with padded end (maulstick).
If gold or silver lettering or design is required, paints lettering or design on to surface using size or adhesive fluid; presses gold or silver leaf on to lettering or design and trims or brushes off surplus, or cuts out letters or design in gold or silver leaf, places them on adhesive and smoothes them in position using brush; if applying letters to glass, varnishes letters after gilding.

May (01) prime and paint surface or otherwise prepare material on which lettering or design is to be painted

(02) prepare sketches

(03) plan layout on paper and perforate outline using spiked wheel (pounce) for use as pattern

(04) apply paint to show-card using printing pens

(05) affix lettering by means of transfer

(06) cut stencils (639.60)

(07) perform screen printing tasks (635.10)

(08) perform lining (812.99) or graining tasks.

Other titles include Letterer, Ticket writer, Writer.

812.10 Glass painter

Paints decorative designs freehand on glassware or glass workpieces in accordance with design specification using hand brushes

Ascertains job requirements from sketches and/or other specifications; selects prepared paints or mixes colours to desired shade and consistency; selects brushes; applies paint to glass article or workpiece in accordance with design specification; where appropriate, applies further coats of paint over design or part of design to produce required shade or shading effects, allowing time for drying between applications.

May (01) specialise in painting glass for church windows.

Other titles include Glass enameller.

812.15 Ceramics painter (freehand)

Paints decorative designs freehand on ceramic articles in accordance with design specification using hand brushes

Performs basic tasks as described under GLASS PAINTER (812.10) but in relation to ceramic articles.

May (01) execute own designs

(02) perform enamelling (812.20) and banding and lining (812.50) tasks.

Other titles include Decorator, Freehand paintress, Gilder, Pattern gilder, Pottery artist, Pottery painter.

812.20 Ceramics enameller

Colours decorative designs already printed or outlined on ceramic articles using hand brushes

Ascertains colour requirements from sketches and/or other specifications; selects prepared paints or mixes colours to desired shade and consistency; selects brushes; fills in printed or outlined pattern with colours in accordance with specification.

May (01) apply additional colour to parts of design to produce shading effects

(02) inscribe lettering on articles using lettering pen.

812.25 Ceramics toucher-up (decorating)

Touches up ceramic articles by brush to remove decorative defects

Examines article for defects; selects brushes and colouring materials; applies colours to article freehand in appropriate areas to ensure perfection of pattern.

812.50 Ceramics bander, Ceramics liner

Paints bands or lines of specified width on surface or edge of ceramic articles using hand brushes and revolving holding device

Ascertains job requirements from sketches and/or other specifications; selects prepared paints or mixes colours to desired shade and consistency; positions article centrally on hand-rotated table (wheel) or mechanical revolving device; selects brushes, starts wheel or other holding device rotating and applies paint with brush to article to paint band(s) or line(s) in accordance with specification; removes decorated article from holding device.

May (01) apply colour freehand to irregular shapes.

Other titles include Bander and liner, Edge liner, Edger, Wash bander.

812.60 Ceramics coater

Coats surfaces of ceramic articles with slip, glaze, paint or similar decorative and protective material using hand brushes

Ascertains coating requirements; selects prepared coating material or mixes coating material to required shade and/or consistency; brushes one or more coats of material evenly on to surfaces to be coated, as required; removes excess material using sponge, razor blade or chemical solvent.

May (01) sponge surfaces before coating
(02) warm articles to be coated to assist even spreading of coating material.

Other titles include Button glazer, Glaze brusher, Glaze painter, Glazer, Lustrer, Sanitary glaze bodier, Silver painter, Slip decorator, Slip painter (hand).

812.70 Painter (excluding ceramics, glass)

Coats surfaces and/or edges of articles or workpieces of material other than ceramics or glass with paint, lacquer, or similar decorative and protective coating using hand brushes

Ascertains coating requirements; selects prepared coating material or mixes coating material to required shade and/or consistency; brushes one or more coats of appropriate material on to surfaces and/or edges of article or workpiece as required.

May (01) prepare surfaces for painting using scrapers, wire brushes, abrasive paper or block, powered hand sanding tool, or revolving brushes or mops
(02) fill holes, dents, etc in surface using appropriate filling material
(03) hold coated article against revolving brushes or mops to extract excess moisture.

Other titles include Bottom painter, Bottom stainer, Brushhand, Doper, Edge colourer, Edge inker, Lacquerer, Machinery painter, Varnisher.

812.90 Slip painting machine attendant

Attends preset machine which applies bands of coloured liquid clay (slip) to ceramic articles by brush

Places article to be decorated on circular pad on machine bed; starts machine to rotate pad and article and to raise article to brush which automatically applies band of coloured slip of required width round appropriate part of article; stops machine and removes decorated article from pad.

812.98 Trainee

Performs, under instruction or guidance, various tasks including training exercises and as appropriate pursues studies in order to acquire the basic skills and knowledge required to perform the tasks of workers in painting and related coating occupations (brush) (excluding structures).

812.99 Other painting and related coating occupations (brush) (excluding structures)

Workers in this group apply paint and similar decorative and protective materials by brush, other than to buildings, ships and other structures and are not elsewhere classified, for example: (01) **Glass banders** (paint bands or lines of specified width round glass articles using brushes); (02) **Decorators (excluding ceramics),** Paintresses (excluding ceramics) (paint decorative designs or lettering on articles other than ceramics in accordance with specification using brushes); (03) **Liners (coachwork, metal articles)** (paint ornamental lines on coachwork or metal articles using brushes); (04) **Mark painters,** Markers, Stencillers (paint identification or other markings on articles or containers using brushes); (05) **Wallpaper stencillers** (apply colours to wallpaper using brushes and stencils); (06) **Touchers-up (excluding ceramics)** (touch up sprayed articles, other than ceramics, using brushes and appropriate coating material).

Unit Group 813 Painting and Related Coating Occupations (Spray) (Excluding Structures)

Workers in this unit group apply paint and similar decorative and protective materials by spray, other than to ships, buildings and other structures.

Excluded are Metal sprayers (715.85)

813.10 Spray polisher (wood) (hand)

Applies stain, lacquer, cellulose or similar finishes to wood surfaces of articles such as furniture or musical instruments by hand spraying

Ascertains finishing requirements; selects prepared finishes or mixes finishing materials to required colour and/or consistency; fills container attached to spray gun with finishing material as necessary; adjusts nozzle of spray gun and pressure valves; operates spray gun and directs spray to apply required number of coats of finishing materials evenly on to surfaces to be coated; as necessary rubs down coated surfaces lightly by hand between applications, using wet and dry abrasive; cleans equipment.

May (01) fill surface dents or cracks with appropriate filling material by hand or using spray gun
(02) smooth surface to be coated by rubbing down by hand with wet and dry abrasive or by using sanding machine
(03) apply stain, using hand brushes, before spray polishing
(04) polish sprayed surfaces (819.95)
(05) touch up defects in sprayed surfaces using brushes and appropriate finishing material.

Other titles include Cellulose sprayer, Colour sprayer, Polyester sprayer.

Excluded are Electrostatic paint sprayers (hand) (813.60)

813.20 Spray painter (aircraft, vehicles) (hand)

Applies paint, varnish, cellulose or similar decorative and protective materials to air-frames or to the bodywork of motor vehicles, railway coaches or wagons by hand spraying

Ascertains coating requirements; selects prepared coating materials or mixes materials to required colour and/or consistency; applies masking material to areas not to be sprayed; fills container attached to spray gun with coating material, as necessary; adjusts nozzle of spray gun and pressure valves; operates spray gun and directs spray to apply priming and subsequent coats evenly to surfaces to be coated; cleans equipment.

May (01) fill surface dents and holes with appropriate filling materials
(02) smooth surfaces to be coated and/or rub down coated surfaces between applications using abrasive paper or block, hand sanding tool or sanding machine
(03) polish finishing coat with solvent by hand or using mechanical polisher
(04) paint insignia and identification details on surface using stencils.

Other titles include Coach painter.

See 819.20 for workers painting by brush and spray.

Excluded are Electrostatic paint sprayers (hand) (813.60)

813.50 Spray glazer (hand), Spray painter (ceramics) (hand)

Coats or decorates ceramic articles with glaze, paint or similar decorative and protective materials by hand spraying

Ascertains coating or decorating requirements; selects prepared coating or decorating materials or mixes materials to required colour and/or consistency; where appropriate, positions ceramic article in or on fixture or on hand-operated or power-driven wheel or turntable; masks areas not to be sprayed; fills container attached to spray gun or pressure feed tank with coating or decorating material; adjusts nozzle of spray gun and pressure valves or starts pump; starts wheel or turntable rotating or holds or secures article in suitable position for spraying; operates spray gun or lowers article over fixed spray and directs spray evenly on to article or manipulates article in or over spray until surface has been coated or decorated to requirements; removes sprayed article from fixture, wheel or turntable; cleans equipment.

May (01) filter (lawn) coating or decorating material before use
(02) spray designs on to articles using stencils
(03) scrape or otherwise remove surplus material from articles using razor blade, wet sponge or brush
(04) perform machine spraying tasks (813.90).

Other titles include Aerograph glazer, Aerograph sprayer, Aerographer, Aerographing stenciller, Cellulose sprayer, Colour sprayer, Enamel sprayer, Glaze blower, Glaze sprayer, Glazer, Sprayer.

813.55 Spray painter (not elsewhere classified) (hand)

Coats or decorates articles or parts of articles with paint, varnish, cellulose or similar decorative and protective materials by hand spraying and is not elsewhere classified

Carries out tasks as described under SPRAY PAINTER (CERAMICS) (HAND) (813.50) but in relation to articles other than ceramics, air-frames and vehicles.

May (01) remove dust from articles to be coated using air blast from gun
(02) spray designs on to articles using stencils
(03) stove articles after coating (591.92)
(04) if decorating glass articles, apply finely powdered glass to sprayed surface (crinkling).

Other titles include Aerograph sprayer, Aerographer, Bottom painter, Bottom sprayer, Bottom stainer, Edge colourer, Edge inker, Enameller, Lacquerer, Paint sprayer, Stenciller, Stove enameller.

813.60 Electrostatic paint sprayer (hand), Electrostatic polish sprayer (hand)

Applies charged particles of paint or polish to articles or workpieces using electrostatic hand gun

Ascertains coating requirements; mixes coating material to required consistency, where necessary; fills feed tank or powder hopper with coating material; hangs object to be coated on support; sets controls to obtain specified pressure and to regulate flow of paint or polish to gun; starts flow of coating material; switches on current flow and points gun at object to be coated; operates gun to discharge electrically charged particles of paint or polish which are drawn to object by electrostatic attraction; repositions object on support, as necessary, and repeats spraying operation until entire surface has been covered; applies further coats to object, as required; removes coated object from support; cleans equipment.

May (01) finish corners of objects using ordinary spray gun.

Other titles include Cellulose sprayer, Polyester sprayer.

813.65 Spray painting machine operator

Sets and operates machine to spray articles, workpieces or stock material with dye, paint or similar finishing materials

Ascertains coating requirements; tests prepared coating material for viscosity and adjusts composition as necessary, or mixes materials to required colour and/or consistency; fills feed tank with coating material; sets controls to regulate pressure in tank, flow of coating material to spray equipment and movement of spray(s) over objects to be coated, sets conveyor speed and drying unit temperature controls; loads or directs loading of objects on to conveyor; starts machine to convey objects under spray equipment and through drying unit; watches operation and adjusts as necessary; removes or directs removal of coated and dried objects from conveyor; cleans machine.

May (01) check samples of coated objects visually for quality of coating.

Other titles include Spray dyeing machine operator.

Excluded are Electrostatic spray painting plant operators (813.70)

813.70 Electrostatic spray painting plant operator, Electrostatic spray polishing plant operator

Sets and operates electrostatic plant to spray charged particles of paint or polish on to articles or workpieces

Ascertains painting or polishing requirements; mixes paint or polish to required consistency where necessary; fills feed tanks or hoppers with paint or polish; sets controls to obtain specified pressure and to regulate flow of paint or polish to spray equipment; sets conveyor speed controls; starts conveyor and flow of paint or polish to spray equipment; places or directs placing of objects to be sprayed on conveyor; starts current flow at specified voltage and switches on spray equipment; watches spraying operation and adjusts as necessary; cleans plant.

May (01) check samples of sprayed articles or workpieces for thickness of coating using measuring instrument

(02) operate plant in which articles or workpieces are dried and stoved after spraying.

Other titles include Polyester sprayer.

813.75 Spray dyer (hand)

Applies dyes to leather pieces or dressed skins by hand spraying

Ascertains dyeing requirements; selects prepared dye or mixes dye to required consistency; positions leather piece or dressed skin on working surface or suspends it from hooks, or clips or places a number of leather pieces or skins on to conveying equipment or platforms of rotating spraying unit; fills container attached to spray gun or pressure feed tank with dye, as necessary; adjusts nozzle of spray gun and pressure valves; starts conveyor or rotating unit; operates spray gun and directs spray evenly on to leather or skin until it has been dyed to requirements; removes dyed leather or skin; cleans equipment.

May (01) apply coat of resin or cellulose to dyed leather

(02) place dyed leather on rack in drying cabinet.

Other titles include Spray finisher, Sprayer (leather and skin dyeing), Suede dyer.

813.90 Glaze spraying machine attendant, Spray painting machine attendant (ceramics)

Attends preset automatic or semi-automatic machine which sprays glaze, liquid clay (slip) or paint on to ceramic articles

Loads articles to be sprayed on to conveyor or places article on machine head fitted with appropriately shaped shielding mask; starts machine to convey articles through spray chamber and drying unit, or to rotate head and spray exposed surface of article; notifies malfunctioning of machine to foreman; removes glazed or decorated articles from conveyor or machine.

May (01) fill feed tanks with spraying material

(02) place glazed articles in firing cranks.

Other titles include Dipping machine attendant, Machine spray liner, Slip spray banding machine attendant, Spray glazing machine attendant.

813.92 Spray painting machine attendant (excluding ceramics)

Attends preset automatic or semi-automatic machine which sprays paint, dye or similar finishing materials on to articles, workpieces or stock material other than ceramics

Loads articles to be sprayed on to conveyor or positions articles on work spindles; starts machine to convey articles through spray chamber and where appropriate drying unit, or operates control to start spray cycle; notifies malfunctioning of machine to foreman; removes sprayed articles from conveyor or work spindles.

Other titles include Automatic paint sprayer, Bottom painter.

813.98 Trainee

Performs, under instruction or guidance, various tasks including training exercises and as appropriate pursues studies in order to acquire the basic skills and knowledge required to perform the tasks of workers in painting and related coating occupations (spray) (excluding structures).

813.99 Other painting and related coating occupations (spray) (excluding structures)

Workers in this group apply paint and similar decorative and protective materials by spray other than to ships, buildings and other structures and are not elsewhere classified.

Unit Group 814 Painting and Related Coating Occupations (Dip)

Workers in this unit group apply paint, varnish and similar decorative and protective materials to articles by dipping.

Excluded are workers in Metal Plating and Coating Occupations (715)

814.10 Ceramics dipper (hand)

Applies glaze or colour to surfaces of ceramic articles by hand dipping or pouring

Lifts articles to be dipped from tray, trolley or revolving platform, using dipping hook where appropriate, or removes tray of articles from trolley frame using lifting tackle; immerses article or part of article by hand in dipping solution or pours quantity of solution into article and manipulates article as necessary to ensure coverage of area to be coated, or lowers tray of articles into solution using lifting tackle; withdraws article or tray of articles from solution or pours excess solution from article; twists dipped article to ensure even coating and to remove excess solution as necessary; places dipped article on board or revolving rack to drain and dry or on draining appliance for conveyance to automatic drier, or replaces tray of articles in trolley frame.

May (01) mix colours
(02) if glazing inside of hollow ware, wipe round rim with sponge to give even line of glaze.

Other titles include Glazer.

814.20 Dipper (excluding ceramics) (hand)

Applies enamel, varnish, dye or similar decorative and protective materials to surfaces of articles, other than ceramics, by hand dipping

Removes article(s) to be dipped from container or overhead conveyor, where necessary; attaches article to dipping hook or clip, or places articles in wire basket or on rack or frame, where required; immerses article in dipping solution by hand or lowers or operates control to lower basket, rack or frame of articles or tips articles into solution; manipulates article(s) in solution to ensure complete coverage, as necessary; withdraws article(s) or container of articles from solution, using hook where appropriate, and shakes off excess solution; places each dipped article on rack, hook or draining board to dry, or hangs it on conveyor hook for transfer to drying equipment.

May (01) mix or adjust composition of dipping solution
(02) replenish supply of dipping solution
(03) withdraw samples of articles from solution periodically and check colour visually against specimen
(04) remove dipped articles to drying chamber
(05) operate drying equipment.

Other titles include Dyer (pearl button), Enameller, Lacquerer, Stainer, Stick and handle polisher, Swiller.

814.30 Electrophoretic painting plant operator

Assists in the operation of dipping plant to coat articles with paint by electro-deposition

Performs one or a combination of the following tasks: loads articles to be painted on to conveyor bars; starts up plant, where necessary; watches immersion of articles in painting solution; reports malfunctioning of equipment to foreman; tests painting and rinsing solutions at prescribed intervals for acidity and alkalinity and where appropriate for percentage of solids in solution, using measuring instruments; checks clarity and flow of water from cathode boxes at regular intervals, using measuring instruments; checks at set intervals thickness of film of paint deposited on articles using measuring instrument; records readings shown on measuring instruments and notifies foreman of readings outside prescribed limits; adjusts composition of painting and rinsing solutions under direction of foreman as required; unloads painted articles from conveyor bars.

See Metal Plating and Coating Occupations (715)

814.50 Dip painting machine attendant

Attends machine which dips articles in paint, lacquer, cellulose or similar decorative and protective materials

Positions articles in holders, where necessary, and places holders in rack or frame on dipping machine, or attaches clips to articles and hangs them on conveyor chain; starts machine when necessary to lower articles into and remove them from dipping solution or to convey articles through solution; notifies malfunctioning of equipment to foreman.

May (01) mask parts not to be coated
(02) remove surplus material from metal pressings using hand scraper before dipping.

Other titles include Dipping machine attendant, Lacquering plant attendant, Pencil finisher

814.98 Trainee

Performs, under instruction or guidance, various tasks including training exercises and as appropriate pursues studies in order to acquire the basic skills and knowledge required to perform the tasks of workers in painting and related coating occupations (dip).

814.99 Other painting and related coating occupations (dip)

Workers in this group apply paint, varnish and similar decorative and protective materials to articles by dipping and are not elsewhere classified, for example:

(01) **Centrifuge operators (japanning)** (operate machines to immerse articles in japan enamel, and to remove surplus enamel by centrifugal force).

Unit Group 815 Wood Staining, Waxing and French Polishing Occupations (Hand)

Workers in this unit group stain, wax and French polish wood surfaces by hand.

Excluded are Polishers (small wooden articles) (679.94)

815.10 French polisher

Prepares wood surfaces for polishing and stains and polishes prepared surfaces by hand

Rubs down surface to be polished, using abrasive paper; applies stain of appropriate colour to surface by brush or pad; fills dents in porous grain with appropriately coloured filling composition; rubs down surface to remove excess filler; applies first coat of polish to surface (fads-up) using cloth pad (rubber); applies further coats of polish and works it into surface with rubber until required finish is obtained; rubs down polished surface gently between applications using abrasive paper or sprinkles abrasive powder on surface and rubs down powdered surface.

May (01) mix and match stains

(02) apply wax polish to surfaces

(03) apply two pack cold cure finishes to surfaces

(04) strip and repolish damaged or used furniture.

815.98 Trainee

Performs, under instruction or guidance, various tasks including training exercises and as appropriate pursues studies in order to acquire the basic skills and knowledge required to perform the tasks of workers in wood staining, waxing and French polishing occupations (hand).

815.99 Other wood staining, waxing and French polishing occupations (hand)

Workers in this group stain, wax and French polish wood surfaces by hand and are not elsewhere classified, for example:

(01) **Stainers** (apply stain to wooden articles such as tobacco pipes using brushes); (02) **Wax polishers (furniture)**.

Unit Group 819 Painting and Related Coating Occupations Not Elsewhere Classified

Workers in this unit group prepare surfaces for painting, apply paint and similar decorative and protective materials to articles and workpieces by pad, quill, roller and sponge, apply decorative transfers to articles, paint vehicle bodywork, railway coaches and wagons using brushes and sprays, operate and attend curtain-coating machines, polish sprayed surfaces, and perform other miscellaneous tasks in painting and decorating and are not elsewhere classified.

819 .05 Glass decorator (general)

Decorates glass articles by a variety of processes according to type of decoration required

As required, carries out basic tasks as described under GLASS BANDER (812 .99), SPRAY PAINTER (CERAMICS) (HAND) (813 .50), SPRAY PAINTING MACHINE ATTENDANT (EXCLUDING CERAMICS) (813 .92), TRANSFERRER (EXCLUDING CERAMICS) (819 .99); where appropriate, positions sprayed article on holding device, starts device rotating and removes lines or rings of enamel using finger or lining stick to make decorative pattern (clear lining).

819 .10 Groundlayer

Coats ceramic articles or parts of articles with oil and applies powdered colouring medium to the oiled surface in accordance with design specification

Ascertains decorating requirements from patterns and/or other specifications; brushes thin coating of oil over article or part(s) of article to be decorated; removes brush marks from oiled surface using silk pad and allows article to stand until oiled surface is nearly dry; selects appropriate powdered colouring medium; dips pad of cotton wool into medium and applies evenly to oiled surface until article is decorated to requirements.

Other titles include Colour duster, Duster, Oil and dust bander.

819 .15 Ceramics stenciller

Paints decorative designs on ceramic articles using stencils, brushes and sponges

Ascertains decorating requirements from patterns and/or other specifications; selects prepared paints or mixes colours to required shade and consistency; positions stencil accurately on surface of article; selects stencilling brushes or sponges according to type of decoration required; applies paint to surface exposed through stencil until article has been decorated to requirements; removes stencil from article; cleans equipment.

May (01) produce shading or mottled effects on articles by varied manipulation of brushes or sponges against surface.

819 .20 Coach painter

Applies paint, cellulose or similar decorative and protective materials to the bodywork of motor vehicles or railway coaches and wagons by brush and spray

Ascertains coating requirements; selects prepared coating materials or mixes materials to required colour and/or consistency; applies masking material to areas not to be coated; selects brushes or adjusts nozzle of spray gun and pressure valves; applies appropriate coating materials to work surfaces using hand brushes or operates spray gun and directs spray evenly on to surfaces to be coated; as necessary, rubs down coated surfaces between applications by hand, using wet and dry abrasive paper or by using portable sanding machine; cleans equipment.

May (01) prepare bodywork for painting (819 .94)
(02) perform lining tasks (812 .99)
(03) apply transfers to coated surfaces.

See 813 .20 for workers painting coachwork solely by hand spray.

819 .25 Wallpaper grounder

Sets and operates machine to apply background colour to wallpaper

Supervises loading of roll of wallpaper on, and threading of paper through, machine; sets controls to regulate roller speed and tension; adjusts distance between paper and air knife, which directs blast of air on to paper as it leaves paint roller, according to thickness of ground colour required; fills paint box of machine with appropriate coloured paint; starts machine; watches painting operation, checks pressure gauge and makes necessary adjustments; replenishes supply of paint as required; supervises unloading of wallpaper from machine.

819 .30 Jewellery enameller

Applies enamel to articles of jewellery such as badges and brooches, using hand tools, and fires articles in furnace to fuse enamel to surface

Ascertains enamelling requirements; cleans article in baths of acid and water and scrubs surface with brush; grinds block of enamel to powder, using pestle and mortar, and adds water to powdered enamel; pours off water when powdered enamel sinks to bottom of container; applies enamel to designated area(s) of article, using quill or metal spill; places article in furnace to melt and fuse enamel; removes article from furnace after appropriate firing period and allows to cool; repeats enamelling, firing and cooling operations as required; immerses fired article in baths of acid and water to remove scale; rubs enamelled article with abrasive stone to smooth surface and to remove excess enamel; polishes article using polishing compound and revolving buffer.

May (01) perform decorative engraving tasks (792 .18).

819 .50 Sponge mottler

Produces mottled decorative effects on ceramic articles using sponge

Ascertains mottling requirements; selects prepared glazes or paints or mixes decorating materials to required colour and/or consistency; selects sponges and where appropriate brushes of suitable texture; holds article in convenient position for decorating or positions article on hand-rotated table (wheel); dabs glaze or paint on to surface of article with sponge to produce mottled effect, or paints surface or part of surface by brush, rotating article as necessary, and dabs colour lightly with sponge while still wet to impart mottled texture.

May (01) produce stippled effects using sponge.

Other titles include Decorative sponger, Dipper's mottler, Glaze mottler, Powderer.

819 .55 Ceramics lithographer, Printer's transferrer (ceramics)

Applies decorative patterns, outlines of patterns, or painted labels to ceramic articles by hand using transfers

Performs a combination of the following tasks: ascertains decorating requirements and selects transfers; brushes or directs brushing of size on area of article to be decorated; places transfer in water to loosen backing sheet; separates tissue paper or film carrying pattern from backing sheet; applies transfer to surface of article in correct position, ensuring that ends of patterns meet accurately where appropriate; rubs or directs rubbing of tissue or film with fingers, brush, pad, sponge or squeegee to transfer coloured pattern or outline to surface of article and/or to expel air bubbles and excess moisture and adhesive; removes or directs removal of tissue paper from article using wet cloth or sponge; dries decorated article with cloth; stacks decorated articles.

May (01) prepare size mix
(02) immerse articles in water before application or removal of transfer.

Other titles include Transferrer.

819 .60 Toucher-up (glaze)

Touches up ceramic articles to remedy glazing faults using brushes, sponges and spray gun

Examines article for mark indicating fault; determines best method of applying glaze to remedy defect, according to type and location of fault; selects glaze mix and where appropriate fills container attached to spray gun with glaze; selects brushes or sponges or adjusts nozzle of spray gun and pressure valves; applies glaze by brush or sponge, or operates gun and directs spray to faulty area.

Other titles include Glaze painter.

819 .65 Curtain-coating machine operator (excluding ceramics)

Sets up and operates machine to coat workpieces or articles, other than ceramics, by passing them under a cascade (curtain) of paint or similar decorative and protective material

Ascertains coating requirements; tests prepared coating material for viscosity and adjusts composition as necessary, or mixes materials to required colour and/or consistency; fills holding tank with coating material; fits pump into holding tank; adjusts controls to obtain required thickness of curtain; sets conveyor speed and drier unit temperature controls; loads or directs loading of objects to be coated on to conveyor; starts machine to convey objects beneath curtain of coating material and through drying unit; watches coating operation and makes necessary adjustments; removes or directs removal of coated and dried objects from conveyor; cleans machine.

819.70 Polisher's filler-in

Prepares surfaces of wood for staining or polishing

Smoothes surface of wood with sandpaper or wire wool as necessary; fills cracks and blemishes in grain of wood with wood filler or wax and rubs down surface with sandpaper ready for polishing; rubs down surfaces of wood between spraying operations.

May (01) apply wood stain to surfaces by hand (815.99)

(02) spray on colour base coat (813.10).

Other titles include Polisher bench hand.

819.90 Tube liner

Applies raised pattern to surface of ceramic articles by hand extrusion

Ascertains decorating requirements; mixes glaze or clay to required colour, where necessary; fills tube with glaze or clay; squeezes tube to force glaze or clay through nozzle on to article and decorates surface in accordance with pattern requirements.

Other titles include Clay bander.

819.91 Curtain-glazing machine attendant

Attends one or more machines which automatically glaze ceramic articles by passing them under a cascade (curtain) of glaze

Loads articles to be glazed on to conveyor; starts machine which pumps glaze from holding tank to trough over conveyor, automatically carries articles beneath cascade of glaze falling from trough and removes excess glaze from articles by automatic edge cleaning wheels or scrapers; reports malfunctioning of machine to foreman.

May (01) fill holding tank with glaze

(02) clear machine blockages.

Other titles include Dipping machine attendant.

819.92 Painting machine attendant (ceramics) (pad, roller)

Attends machine which paints lines on surfaces or edges of ceramic articles by pad or roller

Places article to be painted on holding fixture on machine, using tweezers where necessary; starts machine to rotate article, bring article and paint applicators together and paint lines of required width round appropriate parts of article; removes painted article from machine.

May (01) fill paint container on machine with appropriate coloured paint.

Other titles include Gilding machine operator.

819.93 Curtain-coating machine attendant (excluding ceramics), Flow-coating machine attendant (excluding ceramics)

Attends machine which automatically coats articles, other than ceramics, by passing them under a cascade (curtain) or flow of paint, cellulose, or similar decorative and protective material

Loads articles to be coated into machine hopper or on to conveyor; starts machine which automatically conveys articles through dies, where appropriate, and beneath pressurised cascade or gravity flow of coating material; notifies malfunctioning of machine to foreman.

May (01) fill machine container with coating material

(02) clear machine blockages

(03) attend machine which dries articles after coating.

Other titles include Lacquering machine attendant (pencil), Pencil finisher, Polishing machine attendant (pencil).

819 .94 Flatter

Prepares vehicle bodywork, railway coaches and wagons or air-frames for painting and/or rubs down painted surfaces between coats

Performs one or a combination of the following tasks: washes down unpainted surfaces with water, cleaning solution or solvent; fills dents and other irregularities by hand with appropriate filling material; masks areas not to be painted using paste, paper or tape; smoothes unpainted surfaces by hand using wet and dry abrasive paper or by using portable sanding machine; rubs down painted surfaces by hand between coats to produce smooth finish using wet and dry abrasive paper; otherwise assists coach painter as required.

Other titles include Coach painter's labourer, Facer, Rubber and flatter, Rubber-down.

819 .95 Polisher finisher

Polishes surfaces sprayed with cellulose, lacquer or similar materials to impart required finish

Performs one or more of the following tasks according to type of finish required: burnishes sprayed surface by hand using rubbing compound; rubs over sprayed surface by hand with pad impregnated with solvent (pulling over); smoothes sprayed surface by hand using wet and dry abrasive paper; rubs over sprayed surface by hand using wax and wire wool; selects appropriate polishing head, dresses polishing head as required with appropriate polishing compound and attaches to fixed or portable polisher, starts polisher and guides tool over sprayed surface, or manipulates article against rotating polishing head.

May (01) prepare surfaces for final spraying by rubbing down with wet and dry abrasive paper

(02) touch up defects in final coat using hand, brushes and appropriate coating material.

Other titles include Buffing machine operator Cellulose polisher, Cellulose polisher finisher, Finish polisher.

819 .98 Trainee

Performs, under instruction or guidance, various tasks including training exercises and as appropriate pursues studies in order to acquire the basic skills and knowledge required to perform the tasks of workers in painting and related coating occupations not elsewhere classified.

819 .99 Other painting and related coating occupations not elsewhere classified

Workers in this group perform miscellaneous painting and related coating tasks and are not separately classified, for example:

(01) **Assistant transferrers** (rub transfers positioned on articles by transferrers and remove tissues when patterns have been transferred to articles); (02) **Brushers-off**, Prickers (remove surplus enamel from components using brush or pricking tool); (03) **Colour labellers,** Vitreous enamellers (label or decorate glassware using transfers); (04) **Colour padders,** Dopers (pad), Stainers (pad) (apply stain to articles or workpieces using pads); (05) **Dial writers** (mark figures on dial-plates using transfers); (06) **Dippers' assistants,** Dippers' attendants, Dippers' takers-off (clean articles ready for glazing, remove surplus glaze and otherwise assist dippers); (07) **French polishers (machine)** (set and operate machines to coat pieces of board or wood with layers of polish); (08) **Fur grounders,** Toppers (apply dye to fur using pads); (09) **Groundlayers' assistants** (apply resist medium to areas of articles to be masked and wash off medium after decoration of articles by groundlayers); (10) **Lithographers' assistants,** Lithographers' cutters, Lithographers' preparers (cut out transfers, prepare and apply size and otherwise assist lithographers); (11) **Polishers (sponge)** (apply coatings of polish to articles using sponges); (12) **Printers' cutters,** Transferrers' cutters (cut out transfers from printed sheets for use in decorating ceramics); (13) **Reeler boys** (load, thread and unload grounding machines under direction of grounders); (14) **Rubbing machine operators,** Transfer pressing machine operators (operate machines to press positioned transfers on to articles); (15) **Tippers** (apply enamel to edges of articles using fingers); (16) **Tracers** (mark outlines of designs on articles as series of dots using perforated patterns (pounces) and charcoal bags); (17) **Transfer printing machine operators** (operate machines to transfer coloured designs from paper to surface of knitwear); (18) **Transferrers (excluding ceramics)** (affix decorations on articles other than ceramics by means of transfers); (19) **Ware cleaners** (remove surplus colour from decorated articles using pointed sticks, cotton wool, rags and chemical solutions).

Minor Group 82 PRODUCT ASSEMBLING OCCUPATIONS (REPETITIVE)

Workers in this minor group perform repetitive tasks such as bolting, riveting, gluing and soldering in the batch or mass production assembly of previously shaped or otherwise prepared component parts.

The occupations are arranged in the following unit groups:

820 Foremen (Product Assembling Occupations (Repetitive))

821 Product Assembling Occupations (Repetitive)

Unit Group 820 Foremen (Product Assembling Occupations (Repetitive))

Workers in this unit group directly supervise and co-ordinate the activities of workers in product assembling occupations (repetitive).

820.10 Foreman (product assembling occupations (repetitive))

Directly supervises and co-ordinates the activities of workers in product assembling occupations (repetitive)

Performs appropriate tasks as described under SUPERVISOR/FOREMAN (UNSPECIFIED) (990.00).

May (01) set up machines.

Additional factor: number of workers supervised.

820.98 Trainee

Performs, under instruction or guidance, various tasks including training exercises and as appropriate pursues studies in order to acquire the basic skills and knowledge required to perform the tasks of foremen (product assembling occupations (repetitive)).

Unit Group 821 Product Assembling Occupations (Repetitive)

Workers in this unit group perform repetitive tasks such as bolting, riveting, gluing and soldering in the batch or mass production assembly of previously shaped or otherwise prepared component parts.

Excluded are workers in sewing occupations (641, 657, 658 and *665) and in fitter-assembling occupations (673, 733 and 734)*

821 .05 Repetitive assembler (mineral products)

Fixes together previously prepared parts in the batch or mass production assembly of mineral products or components

Fastens together prepared parts or positions and fastens parts with dowels, pins or similar fasteners or by applying adhesive or other jointing substance and pressing or clamping together, using hand tools or powered hand tools or by operating or tending an assembly machine.

May (01) clean parts before assembly

(02) use tweezers or other devices for holding small parts

(03) use aid such as magnifying lens when assembling small parts

(04) clean assembled article

(05) examine assembled article.

Other titles include Assembler (asbestos fittings), Assembler (carbon brushes), Bi-focal assembler, Fitter (car window, windscreen), Handler (pottery), Lens cementer (ophthalmic), Lens mounter (optical instruments), Putter-together (ophthalmic lenses), Ring tier (incandescent mantles), Springer-in (spectacles), Sticker-up (hand) (chinaware, porcelain, pottery), Tube assembler (water filters).

821 .10 Repetitive assembler (paper, paperboard products)

Fixes together previously prepared parts in the batch or mass production assembly of paper or paperboard products or components

Positions prepared parts in prescribed order; fastens parts together by bonding, stapling, clipping or similar means by hand, using hand or powered hand tools or by operating or tending an assembly machine.

(01) Paperboard container assembler

Makes up container from flat, previously creased shape; inserts stiffeners and/or partitions; as required applies adhesive to and presses joints together or secures joints with staples or similar fasteners.

May (02) apply adhesive to, position, smooth and trim lining paper

(03) frill ends of crêpe paper by hand

(04) operate machine to wrap cracker, remove metal tube and tie or otherwise secure ends

(05) count, check and stack finished products

(06) pack crackers in boxes (841 .40)

(07) cover exterior of container and be known as Coverer (paperboard containers).

Other titles include Christmas cracker maker, Folder (paperboard containers), Hand finisher (greetings cards), Label tagger, Mounter (printed paper), Wire stitcher (paperboard containers).

821 .15 Repetitive assembler (textile products)

Fixes together previously prepared parts in the batch or mass production assembly of textile products or components

Fastens together prepared parts or positions and fastens parts with pins, staples or similar fasteners, by applying adhesive and pressing together, or by applying pressure or heat and pressure to parts previously coated with adhesive, using hand tools or powered hand tools or by operating or tending an assembly machine.

May (01) examine assembled article.

Other titles include Clipper (garments, textile products), Fuser (interfacing, interlining), Fusing press operator (interfacing, interlining, trimmings), Garterer, Grommeter (light clothing), Hook and bar stamping machinist, Hosepipe coupler, Jointer (soft toys), Lace tagger (textiles), Laminator (light clothing), Lining inserter (hats), Riveter (soft toys), Spot welder (collar linings), Studder (garments, textile products), Swedging machine operator, Tasseller.

821.20 Repetitive assembler (leather goods)

Fixes together previously prepared parts in the batch or mass production assembly of leather goods or components

Fastens together prepared parts or positions and fastens parts with brads, tacks, nails, slugs, rivets, press or similar fasteners, by applying adhesive and pressing together, or by applying pressure or heat and pressure to parts previously coated with adhesive, using hand tools or powered hand tools, or by operating or tending an assembly machine in the assembly of leather goods.

May (01) make holes for fasteners in parts before assembly
(02) set machine for type and size of product
(03) examine assembled article.

Other titles include Backer machine operator (slippers), Bottom attacher (footwear), Channel closer, Fibre fastener (footwear), Framer (handbags, purses), Glove liner, Hand liner, Hand riveter, Heel attacher, Heel builder, Heel coverer, Heel slugger, Ironer (footwear stiffener), Lining press operator (footwear), Loose nailer (footwear), Louis heel maker, Machine liner, Paster, Picker riveter, Rand attacher, Rand cementer, Rand layer, Rand tacker, Rib attacher (footwear), Riveting machinist, Shanker, Socker (footwear), Sole attacher, Sole layer, Sole nailer, Sole preparer, Stapling machine operator (footwear), Stiffener inserter (footwear), Toe puffer, Top piece attacher (footwear), Unifier (footwear), Upper stapler.

821.25 Repetitive assembler (wood products)

Fixes together previously prepared parts in the batch or mass production assembly of wood products and components

Fastens together prepared parts or positions and fastens parts with dowels, rivets, nails, screws, nuts and bolts, staples or similar fasteners, or by applying adhesive and pressing or clamping together, using hand tools or powered hand tools, or by operating or tending an assembly machine.

May (01) make fixing holes in parts before assembly
(02) use jig to ensure correct alignment
(03) fix lining, outer cover, padding or decoration to article
(04) examine assembled article.

Other titles include Brush handle fixer, Brush finisher, Case coverer, Case liner, Case maker's fitter-up, Chair maker, Chip basket assembler, Deck chair assembler, Edge tool handler, Fence assembler, Fishing rod plugger, Gate assembler, Musical instrument assembler (stringed), Nailing machine assembler (packing cases), Packing case assembler, Pencil gluer, Saw handler, Shovel handler, Trellis maker, Umbrella handle mounter, Walking stick mounter.

821.30 Repetitive assembler (rubber, plastics goods)

Fixes together previously prepared parts in the batch or mass production assembly of rubber or plastics goods or components

Performs appropriate tasks as described under REPETITIVE ASSEMBLER (LEATHER GOODS) (821.20) but in relation to rubber or plastics goods or components.

May (01) fasten plastics parts together by welding.

Other titles include Artificial flower maker, Drum assembler (plastic skin), Riveting machinist, Rubber footwear cementer, Rubber stamp assembler, Welding machinist.

821.35 Repetitive assembler (metal goods) (hand)

Fixes together by hand previously prepared parts in the batch or mass production assembly of metal goods or components

Fastens together prepared parts or positions and fastens parts with bolts, clips, rivets, screws or similar fasteners or by soldering or other methods by hand, using tools such as hand riveters, hand or powered screwdrivers, spanners, wrenches and soldering irons.

May (01) use tweezers or other devices for holding small parts
(02) make fixing holes in parts before assembly
(03) use jig to ensure correct alignment
(04) use aid such as magnifying lens when assembling small parts
(05) examine and/or test assembled article (832.50/832.60)
(06) assemble particular products or parts and be known accordingly, eg Axle assembler, Office equipment assembler, Piston assembler, Watch and clock assembler.

Other titles include Assistant temper setter (iron and steel), Detonator crimper, Fitter (butt, cap, ferrule), Frame assembler (textile), Gas meter maker, Mattress stapling machine operator, Motor cycle assembler-erector, Motor engine erector, Perambulator mounter, Pin inserter (textile machinery), Solderer, Spring knife cutler, Wheel builder (cycle, motor cycle), Wire brush finisher.

821.40 Repetitive assembler (metal goods) (machine)

Operates or tends one or more machines which fasten together previously prepared parts in the batch or mass production assembly of metal goods or components

Positions parts on machine or loads machine hoppers, spindles, trays or other devices with prepared parts; depresses pedal or otherwise starts machine to fasten parts together by clamping, riveting, spot welding or similar method; watches operation and reports any malfunctioning to foreman.

May (01) remove assembled parts individually or in batches
(02) examine or test assembled article (832.50/832.60).

Other titles include Jewel setter (watches), Riveting machine attendant, Riveting machine operator, Umbrella frame finisher.

821.45 Repetitive assembler (electrical, electronic goods)

Fixes together previously prepared parts in the batch or mass production assembly of electrical or electronic goods or components

Fastens together prepared parts, or positions and fastens parts, or mounts parts on chassis with nuts and bolts, rivets, screws or similar fasteners, or by soldering or other methods using tools such as hand or powered screwdrivers, pliers, spanners or soldering irons, or by operating or tending an assembly machine.

May (01) tie binding string around grouped wires to form a harness
(02) place plastic sleeves over wires to insulate them from other parts or connectors
(03) use aid such as magnifying lens when assembling small parts
(04) examine or test assembled article (832.55/832.65).

Other titles include Armature assembler, Battery assembler, Bulb finisher, Capper (electric lamp), Cementer (electrical insulators), Commutator assembler, Core builder (excluding heavy), Electric fire assembler, Electric lamp assembler, Electric lamp sealer (automatic), Filament assembler, Filament mounter, Machine operator (electric lamp manufacture), Machine operator (thermionic valve manufacture), Pin inserter (electric lamp filament support), Plate separator (car battery), Plug and socket assembler, Printed circuit assembler, Radio chassis assembler, Rectifier assembler, Switchgear assembler, Thermionic valve assembler.

821.99 Other product assembling occupations (repetitive)

Workers in this group perform repetitive tasks in the batch or mass production assembly of previously shaped or otherwise prepared component parts and are not elsewhere classified, for example:

(01) **Belt makers (abrasive cloth or paper)** (glue ends together to make continuous belts); (02) **Cane gluers**; (03) **Cap checkers**, Cap sorters, Clothing dividers, Fitters-up, Folders-in (gloves) (gather together appropriate component parts ready for making-up); (04) **Channel solutioners,** Solution hands (apply adhesive to component parts); (05) **Corkers (fishing rods)** (slide cork rings along rods to marked position); (06) **Cork frame makers** (glue parts together); (07) **Corset boners,** Corset lacers (insert stiffeners in encasing strips of fabric sewn to corsets or foundation garments, or thread laces through eyelets in corsets or foundation garments and arrange holding knots); (08) **Fireworks finishers** (bend fireworks to shape as required and fix sticks, touch-paper, etc); (09) **Gumming machine operators** (apply adhesive to paper or paperboard parts); (10) **Nightlight wickers** (thread wicks through night-lights and seal to base); (11) **Paper pattern folders** (gather items together and fold for packing); (12) **Perambulator hood assemblers** (fix together the various parts); (13) **Stamp pad assemblers** (secure parts and fix them in containers; may moisten parts).

Minor Group 83 PRODUCT INSPECTING, EXAMINING, SORTING, GRADING AND MEASURING OCCUPATIONS (EXCLUDING LABORATORY TECHNICIANS)

Workers in this minor group inspect, test, examine, view, check, sort, grade and measure materials, goods and products and perform closely related tasks.

The occupations are arranged in the following unit groups:

830 Foremen (Product Inspecting, Examining, Sorting, Grading and Measuring Occupations (Excluding Laboratory Technicians))

831 Inspecting and Testing Occupations (Metal and Electrical Engineering)

832 Examining, Viewing and Checking Occupations (Metal and Electrical Engineering)

833 Examining, Viewing and Checking Occupations (Excluding Metal and Electrical Engineering)

834 Sorting and Grading Occupations

835 Weighing and Measuring Occupations

839 Product Inspecting, Examining, Sorting, Grading and Measuring Occupations (Excluding Laboratory Technicians) Not Elsewhere Classified

Excluded are workers who also undertake rectification and repair (see making and repairing occupations in minor groups 54 and 61 to 79)

Unit Group 830 Foremen (Product Inspecting, Examining, Sorting, Grading and Measuring Occupations (Excluding Laboratory Technicians))

Workers in this unit group directly supervise and co-ordinate the activities of workers in product inspecting, examining, sorting, grading and measuring occupations (excluding laboratory technicians).

830 .10 Foreman (inspecting and testing occupations) (metal and electrical engineering)

Directly supervises and co-ordinates the activities of workers in inspecting and testing occupations (metal and electrical engineering)

Performs appropriate tasks as described under SUPERVISOR/FOREMAN (UNSPECIFIED) (990 .00).

Additional factor: number of workers supervised.

830 .20 Foreman (examining, viewing and checking occupations) (metal and electrical engineering)

Directly supervises and co-ordinates the activities of workers in examining, viewing and checking occupations (metal and electrical engineering)

Performs appropriate tasks as described under SUPERVISOR/FOREMAN (UNSPECIFIED) (990 .00).

Additional factor: number of workers supervised.

830 .30 Foreman (examining, viewing and checking occupations) (excluding metal and electrical engineering)

Directly supervises and co-ordinates the activities of workers in examining, viewing and checking occupations (excluding metal and electrical engineering)

Performs appropriate tasks as described under SUPERVISOR/FOREMAN (UNSPECIFIED) (990 .00).

Additional factor: number of workers supervised.

830 .40 Foreman (sorting and grading occupations)

Directly supervises and co-ordinates the activities of workers in sorting and grading occupations

Performs appropriate tasks as described under SUPERVISOR/FOREMAN (UNSPECIFIED) (990 .00).

May (01) value poor quality or damaged wool.

Additional factor: number of workers supervised.

830 .98 Trainee

Performs, under instruction or guidance, various tasks including training exercises and as appropriate pursues studies in order to acquire the basic skills and knowledge required to perform the tasks of foremen (product inspecting, examining, sorting, grading and measuring occupations (excluding laboratory technicians)).

830 .99 Other foremen (product inspecting, examining, sorting, grading and measuring occupations (excluding laboratory technicians))

Workers in this group directly supervise and co-ordinate the activities of workers in product inspecting, examining, sorting, grading and measuring occupations (excluding laboratory technicians) and are not elsewhere classified.

Unit Group 831 Inspecting and Testing Occupations (Metal and Electrical Engineering)

Workers in this unit group inspect and test metal stock, parts and products, electrical plant and industrial machinery, and electronic systems using knowledge of metal, electrical and electronic characteristics and/or production processes and making judgement based on considerable experience or a lengthy period of training.

Excluded are engineering technicians (256) and Goods vehicle testers (839 .50)

831 .05 Inspector (metal castings)

Inspects metal castings for conformance to specifications using knowledge of metal characteristics and/or casting processes and making judgement based on considerable experience or a lengthy period of training

Inspects castings visually for holes, protrusions or other surface defects; verifies, from drawings or other specifications, dimensions, angles, etc using instruments such as callipers, micrometers or vernier gauges; checks weight of small castings as required; informs foreman of defects and their probable cause; determines appropriate treatment for castings which do not conform to specifications.

May (01) operate checking equipment (832 .60)

(02) mark out castings ready for machining (731 .05).

Additional factor: metals to which accustomed.

831 .10 Inspector (forgings)

Inspects forgings for conformance to specifications using knowledge of metal characteristics and/or forging processes and making judgement based on considerable experience or a lengthy period of training

Performs tasks as described under INSPECTOR (METAL CASTINGS) (831 .05) but in relation to the inspection of forgings.

May (01) operate checking equipment (832 .60).

(02) mark out forgings ready for machining (731 .05).

Additional factor: metals to which accustomed.

831.15 Inspector (tool room)

Inspects tools, gauges, jigs and fixtures used in production and inspection processes for conformance to specifications

Computes angles, radii, etc not given in specifications, using workshop mathematics; marks out centre lines and reference points on item to be inspected; verifies, from drawings or other specifications, dimensions, angles, contours, clearances, etc using instruments such as micrometers, callipers, protractors or gauges; tests item for fit of moving parts, where appropriate; compares projected image of shape of tool, jig or fixture with enlarged drawing of item, using profile projector; determines accuracy of new gauges and other measuring instruments using master gauges or master parts; examines used gauges and other measuring instruments or parts for wear, warping or other defects; directs necessary corrective operations.

May (01) inspect "first-offs"
(02) prepare drawings for use on profile projector
(03) operate checking equipment (832.60).

831.20 Inspector (aircraft assembly)

Inspects aircraft assemblies such as fuselage and wings during construction and completed aircraft to verify correctness of assembly

Checks sequence of assembly operations to ensure that specified procedure is followed; verifies from drawings or other specifications the location and size, shape, etc of bolt or rivet holes, struts, etc using instruments such as callipers, micrometers or vernier gauges; inspects parts before assembly to ensure that they have been treated in the prescribed manner to prevent corrosion; checks accuracy of jigs used in construction from drawings or other specifications; verifies that wing and tail assemblies are correctly fitted and secured to fuselage; prepares reports on defects.

May (01) inspect skin of aircraft using portable X-ray equipment.

Additional factor: whether approved by Aeronautical Inspection Directorate (AID).

831.25 Inspector (metal) (not elsewhere classified)

Inspects metal parts or products for conformance to specifications using knowledge of metal characteristics and/or production processes and making judgement based on considerable experience or a lengthy period of training and is not elsewhere classified

Inspects article for surface flaws such as cracks, dents or scratches; examines article for faulty workmanship such as defective machining, welding, coating or other poor finish; verifies from drawings or other specifications that dimensions, angles, etc are within permitted tolerances, using instruments such as vernier, callipers, dial gauges, micrometers, clinometers, optical flats or profile projectors; checks assemblies and sub-assemblies against parts lists or other specifications for omissions, and inspects item for alignment of parts and correctness of assembly; manipulates moving parts of mechanical assemblies to check true running; marks or notes defects; prepares reports as required on articles which do not conform to specifications; makes recommendations for changes in production processes where appropriate.

May (01) examine and test material before manufacture
(02) operate checking equipment (832.60)
(03) supervise examiners (metal, metal products) (not elsewhere classified).

Additional factor: whether approved by Aeronautical Inspection Directorate (AID).

831.30 Electrical inspector (aircraft)

Inspects and tests aircraft electrical wiring systems for conformance to specifications

Checks that positioning of conduit boxes, switches, wiring, etc conform to drawings or other specifications; inspects wiring for faulty connections and insulation; operates de-icers, heaters, lights, etc to check functioning; tests systems such as engine control, flight control, heating, lighting or pressurising, using appropriate test rigs to determine that circuit continuity, frequency, power, output, etc conform to specifications; watches control and indicator instruments during functional testing of mechanical, fuel and hydraulic systems to detect malfunction; prepares reports on defects.

831.35 Engine tester (internal-combustion engine)

Tests the operation of internal-combustion engines on test bed

Positions internal-combustion engine on test bed, using hoisting equipment, and secures with bolts; connects to engine, oil, fuel, water, exhaust and electrical systems and loading and metering equipment; starts engine and records meter readings such as oil pressure, temperature and revolutions per minute; calculates brake horse-power and rate of fuel consumption; checks engine visually and aurally for malfunction; prepares report on engine's performance.

831 .40 Engine tester (jet engine)

Tests the operation of jet engines on test bed

Performs tasks as described under ENGINE TESTER (INTERNAL-COMBUSTION ENGINE) (831 .35) but in relation to the test running of jet engines; on selected engines, examines the effect of the addition of ice to air intakes, the introduction of hot gases into the engine and the prolonged running of the engine.

831 .45 Tester (electrical plant and industrial machinery)

Tests the operation of electrical plant and industrial machinery

Positions item for testing and connects leads to power source and test equipment; starts item to be tested and runs for specified period, regulating controls to vary speeds, voltages and loading as required; watches and adjusts measuring instruments such as meggers, ammeters, voltmeters or wattmeters to measure insulation and electrical characteristics such as resistance and power output; notes defects such as current leakages and short circuits; records test data; prepares reports as required.

May (01) perform tasks of EXAMINER (ELECTRICAL, ELECTRONIC EQUIPMENT) (832 .55).

Other titles include Inspector.

831 .50 Systems tester (electronics)

Tests the operation of complete electronic systems immediately after production for conformance to specifications

Sets up test equipment according to tests required; connects system to bet ested to equipment such as test circuits, oscilloscopes, signal generators or voltmeters; operates test equipment to verify correct functioning of system; reads dials indicating electrical characteristics of system such as capacitance, output and power; compares dial readings with specifications; traces circuits of defective system from schematic and wiring diagrams or other specifications to locate defects such as wiring errors, short circuits or faulty components; records test data and reports on adjustments or replacements required.

May (01) perform tasks of EXAMINER (ELECTRICAL, ELECTRONIC EQUIPMENT) (832 .55).

Other titles include Systems inspector.

831 .55 Test welder

Tests samples of electrodes using arc welding equipment

Positions and secures workpieces to be welded; inserts sample electrode in holder; connects wires from power supply to electrode and workpiece; switches on power supply and sets amperage and voltage controls as required; guides electrode along weld line to fuse edges of workpieces and produce specimen weld; examines specimen weld visually and compares with standard weld; tests strength of weld using testing equipment or by striking with hammer; records test data; reports defects in electrodes to foreman.

May (01) measure concentricity and length of electrode using micrometer and rule

(02) prepare specimen welds for mechanical tests.

831 .98 Trainee

Performs, under instruction or guidance, various tasks including training exercises and as appropriate pursues studies in order to acquire the basic skills and knowledge required to perform the tasks of workers in inspecting and testing occupations (metal and electrical engineering).

831 .99 Other inspecting and testing occupations (metal and electrical engineering)

Workers in this group inspect and test metal stock, parts and products, electrical industrial plant and machinery and electronic systems using knowledge of metal, electrical or electronic characteristics and/or production processes and making judgement based on considerable experience or a lengthy period of training and are not elsewhere classified.

Unit Group 832 Examining, Viewing and Checking Occupations (Metal and Electrical Engineering)

Workers in this unit group examine, view and check metal stock, parts and products and electrical and electronic components, sub-assemblies and products to detect processing, manufacturing and other defects, making judgement for which knowledge of metal, electrical and electronic characteristics and production processes based on considerable experience or a lengthy period of training is not required.

Note: the titles of occupations included in this unit group vary; in some establishments the workers concerned may be known as Inspectors or Testers.

832 .10 Examiner (vehicle body)

Examines vehicle coachwork and body fittings for conformance to specifications making judgement for which knowledge of body building based on considerable experience or a lengthy period of training is not required

Performs a combination of the following tasks: examines exterior and interior surfaces for chips, scratches or other defects; checks fitting and tests operation of parts such as doors, windows, locks, boot lid and bonnet; examines fittings such as carpets, furniture and seat settings to ensure conformance to specification; checks that furniture and other fittings are properly secured; verifies that rubber grommets are in position in floor bulk-head, etc; examines interior for cleanliness; checks vehicle to ensure that required accessories such as heater and radio have been installed; checks that electrically operated equipment such as lights, wipers and gauges function correctly; operates pressure equipment to spray water over closed body to test weather sealing and examines interior after spraying for water seepage; checks that hydraulically or pneumatically operated fittings such as lifting equipment and folding doors function correctly; connects caravan water supply system to mains supply and tests operation of system; completes defects list according to findings.

May (01) road test vehicle (734 .40).

Other titles include Inspector (light vehicle body) (mass production).

See Goods vehicle tester (839 .50) for checking of vehicles for compliance with statutory regulations.

832 .50 Examiner (metal, metal products) (not elsewhere classified)

Examines metal stock, parts or products for conformance to specifications making judgement for which knowledge of metal characteristics and/or production processes based on considerable experience or a lengthy period of training is not required and is not elsewhere classified

Performs a combination of the following tasks: examines surface by sight and touch to detect flaws such as blisters, burns, burrs, cracks, dents, holes, distortions or defective coating, or faulty brazing, soldering or welding; verifies dimensional accuracy, angles, contours, etc using gauges, rules, protractors or other measuring instruments, or checks items against patterns, templates or samples; checks assemblies or sub-assemblies against parts lists or other specifications to detect missing items and examines them for alignment of parts and correctness of assembly; manipulates moving parts of articles such as gears or bearings to check true running; strikes articles against metal blocks to detect flaws by sound; draws pieces of specially hardened steel (provers) across articles to check hardness; compares colour of articles with colour standards; separates rejected items and marks faults; stamps or otherwise marks accepted items as required.

May (01) operate lifting equipment to position items for examination
(02) use equipment such as inspection lamp, magnifying glass or projector to facilitate examination
(03) operate checking equipment (832 .60)
(04) undertake routine chemical tests (839 .30)
(05) test items for adhesion of plating using special spatula
(06) count, weigh and/or pack examined items.

Other titles include Assorter (steel sheets), Checker, Counter (fish hooks), Cylinder inspector, File prover, Gauger, Inspector (enamelling), Inspector (plating), Inspector (sherardizing), Inspector and counter (fish hooks), Looker-out (pen nibs), Passer, Rough inspector, Viewer.

832 .55 Examiner (electrical, electronic equipment)

Examines electrical or electronic components, sub-assemblies or products for defects making judgement for which knowledge of materials or production processes based on considerable experience or a lengthy period of training is not required

Performs a combination of the following tasks: examines items visually for defects such as scratches, dents, cracks, broken wires, unevenly wound coils, faulty connections or defective sealing or coating; compares sub-assemblies with parts lists or other specifications to detect missing items; traces cable and harness assemblies to verify routeing of wires to specified connections; checks alignment of doors, panels and control dials with adjacent parts; opens doors and sliding compartments to check movement and operation of catches; verifies dimensions of parts using gauges, callipers or other measuring instruments; rejects defective components, sub-assemblies or products.

May (01) use equipment such as magnifying glass or microscope to facilitate examination
(02) undertake functional checking (832 .65).

832 .60 Checking equipment operator (metal)

Operates equipment to check metal stock, parts or products for processing or manufacturing defects

Performs a combination of the following tasks: positions metal item to be checked on or in machine, test rig or other checking equipment, or brings equipment into contact with item to be checked; connects item to pressure outlet; sets equipment controls to obtain specified tension, load, etc; operates controls to start checking operation; observes dial readings, automatic graph or wave-form recordings; measures item after check or indentation in item resulting from check, using micrometer, callipers, vernier, etc; compares readings or measurements with specification to ensure that they are within acceptable limits; checks item for leaks indicated by pressure gauge, cracks, escaping air, bubbles, etc; removes checked item from equipment; rejects and/or marks defective items; reports unusual check results to foreman.

May (01) operate lifting equipment to position item for checking
(02) apply coating material by brush or spray to item to facilitate checking operation
(03) make simple calculations before and/or after checking
(04) pass flame from hand-held torch round joints to detect leaks
(05) weigh items
(06) operate equipment to check items after repair.

Other titles include Cylinder tester, Expanding and testing machine operator (tubes), Fittings tester (water supply), Gas fittings tester, Hydraulic tester, Inspector (spring), Meter tester, Prover (tubes), Spring tester, Tube tester, Ultrasonic testing machine operator, Water tester (castings).

Excluded are Industrial radiographers (256 .99), Checkers (electrical, electronic equipment) (832 .65) and Testers (chemical and physical) (routine) (839 .30)

832 .65 Checker (electrical, electronic equipment)

Checks the operation of electrical or electronic components, sub-assemblies or products to ensure correct functioning making judgement for which knowledge of electrical or electronic characteristics and/or production processes based on considerable experience or a lengthy period of training is not required

Connects item to be checked to power source and/or connects leads from testing equipment such as ammeters, oscilloscopes, potentiometers, voltmeters or watt-meters to item or directs these operations; checks that equipment functions correctly, and where necessary observes dials or signals indicating electrical characteristics such as capacitance, frequency, power, resistance, wave pattern or defects such as current leakage or short circuits; compares dial readings or signals with specification; rejects faulty equipment.

May (01) check operation of equipment under particular conditions such as heat, cold, humidity, wetness or vibration.

Other titles include Cable tester, Cell tester, Inspector (electric lamp), Sparker, Valve tester.

See Cable tester (installation) (764 .40)

Excluded are Testers (electrical plant and industrial machinery) (831 .45) and Systems testers (electronics) (831 .50)

832 .98 Trainee

Performs, under instruction or guidance, various tasks including training exercises and as appropriate pursues studies in order to acquire the basic skills and knowledge required to perform the tasks of workers in examining, viewing and checking occupations (metal and electrical engineering).

832.99 Other examining, viewing and checking occupations (metal and electrical engineering)

Workers in this group examine, view and check metal stock, parts and products and electrical and electronic components, sub-assemblies and products to detect processing, manufacturing and other defects making judgement for which knowledge of metal, electrical and electronic characteristics or production processes based on considerable experience or a lengthy period of training is not required and are not elsewhere classified, for example:

(01) **Examiners (cast type).**

Unit Group 833 Examining, Viewing and Checking Occupations (Excluding Metal and Electrical Engineering)

Workers in this unit group examine, view and check materials, parts and products (excluding metal and electrical engineering) to detect processing, manufacturing and other defects, making judgement for which knowledge of materials or production processes based on considerable experience or a lengthy period of training is not required.

Note: the titles of occupations included in this unit group vary; in some establishments the workers concerned may be known as Inspectors or Testers.

833.05 Examiner (yarn)

Examines yarn packages for defects after reeling or winding

Examines yarn on cones, cops or other packages by sight and touch for defects such as matted fibres (slubs), loose ends, stains, mixed counts, or variations in colour or shade; checks package for winding faults such as incorrect shape, excessively loose or tight winding, or yarn passing beyond winding limit on package; separates defective yarn packages; reports major faults to foreman.

May (01) pack and weigh yarn packages after examination.

Other titles include Yarn inspector.

833.10 Examiner (textile fabric)

Examines textile fabric (piece goods) for manufacturing defects

Positions fabric on table or floor, or pulls end of fabric over rollers and inspection table or frame and passes end round take-up roller or through lapping device; where appropriate, sets yardage counter and starts machine to draw fabric over table or frame; examines fabric visually and by touch for defects such as holes, knots, marks, stains, loose ends, imperfect threads, weaving or knitting faults, missing tufts, colour or pattern variations or uneven dyeing; identifies faults with chalk, tape, thread, etc or prepares fault plan; reports major faults or an excessive number of defects in piece of fabric to foreman.

May (01) cut out defective areas
(02) remove stains using soap and water or chemical solutions
(03) count number of threads per inch using magnifying glass (inch glass)
(04) measure fabric or pattern length using tape or other hand measuring device
(05) count folds to determine yardage
(06) weigh fabric
(07) cut examined fabric to specified lengths using scissors or hand knife.

Other titles include Cloth examiner, Cloth inspector, Cloth looker, Drawer, Examiner (carpet), Inspector (carpet), Passer (carpet), Passer (textile piece goods), Percher, Piece looker, Roll inspector.

See Examiner (garments, textile products) (833.35) and Grader (textile fabric, textile products) (834.55)

833 .15 Examiner (tobacco, tobacco products)

Examines tobacco or tobacco products for processing or manufacturing defects

Performs a combination of the following tasks: examines tobacco leaves for cleanliness and to ensure that stems have been removed; examines stems to ensure that they have been properly stripped; returns badly stripped leaves or stems to stemmer; collects cigarettes discharged from cigarette making machine and examines them for defects such as faulty filling, gluing, cutting or brand name printing; rejects defective cigarettes.

May (01) weigh and record quantity of stems examined.

Other titles include Cigarette machine catcher, Cigarette machine receiver, Leaf inspector, Passer.

833 .20 Examiner (wood, wood products)

Examines wood or wood products for processing or manufacturing defects

Examines wood or wood products by sight or touch for defects such as chips, holes, knots, scratches, splits or rough finish; checks measurements, as necessary, using rules, tapes or gauges; rejects faulty material or products, or marks repairable defects with chalk.

Other titles include Inspector, Inspector and stamper, Plywood inspector.

833 .25 Examiner (paper, paperboard)

Examines paper or paperboard stock material or products for processing or manufacturing defects

Examines material or products for defects such as joins, marks, tears, wrinkles, inaccurate cutting, creasing, perforating or punching, defective coating or gluing, printing or numbering errors, and variations in pattern, colour or shade; rejects faulty material or products, marks repairable faults, or groups or allocates number to materials or products of consistent shade.

May (01) check against charts or other guide that products such as paper patterns have been correctly collated.

Other titles include Checker (paper pattern), Inspector (paperboard box), Overhauler, Ream inspector, Shader, Sorter (paper), Taker-off.

833 .30 Examiner (mineral products)

Examines mineral products for manufacturing defects

Performs a combination of the following tasks: examines product by sight and touch for defects such as chips, cracks, scratches, discolouration, air bubbles, warps, sags or other malformations, incorrect positioning of handles, holes, etc, faulty fusing, annealing or graduating, or imperfections in glazing or other finish; detects cracks by sound using hand tapping tool or coin; verifies dimensions, angles, etc using rules, gauges, measuring arms, protractors, templates, etc; checks levelness of product using level table; checks weight of article against specifications; rejects defective products or marks repairable defects with chalk, etc.

May (01) operate lifting equipment to position products for examination

(02) use equipment such as illuminated table, screen, magnifier, spotlight or strain viewer to facilitate examination

(03) calculate density of product

(04) check capacity of product

(05) remove sample of product using hand tool (grading blade) and compare for hardness against sample from master product.

Other titles include Check inspector, Checker (mica), Examiner (abrasive wheel), Examiner (ceramics), Examiner (glass), Examiner (mica), Greenhouse assistant, Inspector, Inspector (abrasive wheel), Inspector (ceramics), Inspector (glass), Inspector (mica), Looker-over, Overlooker, Sorter (glass), Stilt picker, Thimble picker, Thrower's looker-to-ware.

Excluded are Examiners (optical elements) (839 .10)

833 .35 Examiner (garments, textile products)

Examines garments, made-up textile products or parts for imperfections in cutting out or making-up and for flaws in material

Carries out a combination of the following tasks; lays item to be examined on inspection board or table, or positions it over frame, former or model: examines parts for inaccurate cutting out; checks that colour and style of product conform to specification; measures product at designated places using tape, gauge, template, etc to verify conformance with size specifications; examines product for making-up defects such as misplaced pockets, buttons or buttonholes, seaming, hemming and other stitching faults, imperfectly set collars or sleeves, or inaccurate matching of patterned material; examines material for defects such as holes, ladders, stains, broken or pulled threads or dropped stitches; checks that product has been properly pressed; identifies defects with chalk, thread, labels, etc.

May (01) remove stains
(02) fold and/or pack examined products (841 .35, 841 .50)
(03) distribute work to operatives.

Other titles include Checker, Cutting inspector, Final passer, Garment examiner, Garment inspector, Intermediate passer, Passer, Trank examiner, Viewer.

See Examiner (textile fabric) (833 .10) and Grader (textile fabric, textile products) (834 .55)

833 .40 Examiner (leather products)

Examines leather products or parts other than garments or garment parts for manufacturing defects

Examines product or part by sight and touch for defects such as faulty shape, uneven or broken stitching, loose threads, protruding tacks, scratches, tears or defective fasteners; marks defects with chalk or records details on ticket and attaches to product; reports major or recurrent faults to foreman; where appropriate, checks that paired products are correctly matched for size, style and colour.

May (01) make random leather thickness checks using micrometer
(02) pair products such as shoes.

Other titles include Closing room checker, Passer, Table hand.

833 .45 Examiner (plastics, rubber)

Examines plastic or rubber material or products for processing, manufacturing or other defects

Examines material or product by sight and touch for defects such as blisters, cracks, cuts, holes or foreign matter, faulty shaping, curing or finishing, bead wire breaks or ply separation; checks dimensions of material or products, where required, using gauges, steel tapes, etc; rejects faulty material or products, or marks repairable faults with chalk, crayon or paint; reports major faults to foreman.

May (01) operate lifting or spreading equipment to position material or products for examination
(02) use hand tools such as prickers or operate pressurising equipment to assist in detecting faults
(03) use portable light or electric magnifier to facilitate examination.

Other titles include Checker, Inspector, Viewer.

833 .50 Examiner (materials, products) (not elsewhere classified)

Examines stock material or products for processing or manufacturing defects and is not elsewhere classified

Performs a combination of the following tasks: examines item by sight and touch for defects such as chips, cracks, creases, dents, foreign matter, holes, scratches, tears, faulty forming or shaping, defective soldering, filling, coating or other finishing or over or under-drying; verifies dimensional accuracy using templates, gauges, rules, etc; checks assemblies or sub-assemblies against parts lists or other specifications to detect missing items, and examines them for alignment of parts and correctness of assembly; compares colour with sample or standard; checks weight against specifications; rejects or marks defective items or refers them to foreman.

May (01) use magnifying equipment to facilitate inspection
(02) cut out defective parts
(03) cut examined material to specified lengths
(04) sort examined items according to size or colour
(05) bundle or pack examined items
(06) check sample gramophone records on audio equipment for faults in tone or other recording defects.

Other titles include Checker inspector (cork products), Colour tester (linoleum), Inspector (asbestos composition goods), Inspector (cartridges), Inspector (leathercloth), Inspector (plasterboard), Passer (brush), Tester (artificial teeth), Tester (gramophone records), Viewer.

833.55 Checking equipment operator (excluding metal and electrical and electronic equipment)

Operates equipment to check parts, products or sample materials, other than metal and electrical and electronic equipment, for processing or manufacturing defects

Performs appropriate tasks as described under CHECKING EQUIPMENT OPERATOR (METAL) (832.60) but in relation to the checking of parts, products or materials other than metal and electrical and electronic equipment.

May (01) operate lifting equipment to position item for checking
(02) apply coating material by brush or spray to item to facilitate checking operation
(03) make simple calculations before and/or after checking
(04) weigh items
(05) operate equipment to check items after repair.

Other titles include Cord tester, Rope tester, Tester (abrasive wheel), Tester (asbestos-cement pipe), Yarn tester.

Excluded are Industrial radiographers (256.99) and Testers (chemical and physical) (routine) (839.30)

833.90 Examiner (food products)

Examines food products for processing defects

Performs one or a combination of the following tasks: checks closing temperature of contents of food cans; examines cans or jars of food products for faulty closure; opens cans or other containers, where necessary, and examines contents by sight, taste or smell for colour, appearance or flavour; examines products on conveyor after cooking and removes any that are burnt, discoloured, broken, etc.

Other titles include Can tester, Inspector (canned food), Passer, Potato crisp inspector, Sniffer.

833.98 Trainee

Performs, under instruction or guidance, various tasks including training exercises and as appropriate pursues studies in order to acquire the basic skills and knowledge required to perform the tasks of workers in examining, viewing and checking occupations (excluding metal and electrical engineering).

833.99 Other examining, viewing and checking occupations (excluding metal and electrical engineering)

Workers in this group examine, view and check materials, parts or products (excluding metal and electrical engineering) to detect processing, manufacturing or other defects making judgement for which knowledge of materials or production processes based on considerable experience or a lengthy period of training is not required and are not elsewhere classified, for example:

(01) **Checkers (glass capacity)**, Testers (glass capacity) (insert dip tool in water-filled drinking glasses to check capacity); (02) **Egg candlers** (examine eggs to ascertain quality and fitness for consumption); (03) **Examiners and testers (match)**, Inspectors (match) (examine and test matches and match containers to ensure conformity with British Standards Institute specifications); (04) **Penetrant testers (double glazing)** (paint dye round frames of double glazing units and check that dye does not penetrate between frame and glass); (05) **Raw material samplers (foodstuffs)** (draw samples of foodstuffs from bulk and examine them by sight, touch or smell to check that foodstuffs are up to standards required for processing); (06) **Yarn straighteners** (straighten dyed hanks of yarn and examine for uneven dyeing); (07) **Testers (safety fuse)** (ignite safety fuses and check rate of burning).

Unit Group 834 Sorting and Grading Occupations

Workers in this unit group sort and grade materials, products, and other articles.

See Classifier and marker (farm livestock) (509.10)
Excluded are Mail sorters (343.10)

834.05 Grader-sorter (hides, skins, leather)

Grades and sorts hides, skins or leather pieces before or after processing or cutting

Examines hides, skins or leather pieces visually and by touch to assess their quality and to detect faults such as natural blemishes, fleshing or other processing defects or incorrect cutting; estimates weight and thickness of, or weighs and measures, hides, skins or leather pieces; selects hides, skins or leather pieces for tanning, dyeing or other treating or for making up, as required; grades and sorts hides, skins or leather pieces according to quality, size, colour or other requirements.

May (01) prepare job cards indicating processing requirements

(02) trim off irregular pieces and rough edges to improve shape or quality of hides, skins or leather pieces using hand knife or shears.

Other titles include Grader, Hide and skin classer, Preparer (upper sorting and grading), Sole examiner, Sorter, Sorter assembler (footwear), Suede sorter and matcher, Trank sorter.

834.10 Grader-sorter (pelts)

Grades and sorts fur-bearing or wool-bearing pelts before or after dressing, dyeing or other treatment

Examines pelt visually and by touch to determine its size and the colour, length and quality of hair or wool; inspects skin side of pelt for natural blemishes, fleshing cuts or other processing faults and/or handles dressed pelt to assess its softness and texture; selects pelts for dressing, dyeing or other treating or for making up, as required; grades and sorts pelts according to quality, size, colour or other requirements.

May (01) determine size of pelts using template or electronic measuring equipment

(02) weigh pelts

(03) trim off irregular pieces and rough edges to improve shape or quality of pelts using hand knife or shears.

Other titles include Fur sorter, Pelt grader, Sheepskin classer.

834.15 Grader (raw wool)

Grades whole fleeces or wool separated from fleeces

Places whole fleece or quantity of wool on worktable; examines whole fleece or wool visually and by touch to determine cleanliness and to ascertain length, strength, and texture of wool fibres; notes colour of wool and areas of discolouration; grades fleece or wool fibres according to specified standards of quality and places them into appropriate containers.

May (01) weigh fleeces

(02) cut away unscourable identification markings and rough, badly stained or matted wool ends, using hand shears.

Other titles include Fleece classer, Grader (fleece), Sorter-grader, Wool sorter.

834.20 Grader (metal production)

Grades metal rejected during production processes

Examines rejected metal to determine its suitability for further processing; separates metal which can be reprocessed according to type of treatment required, for example, recutting, levelling, rerolling; grades remainder for sale as 'seconds' or for use as scrap.

Other titles include Sorter.

834.25 Scrap metal sorter

Sorts and grades scrap metal

Examines scrap visually to determine type and quality of metal; runs magnet through pile of scrap, where necessary, to separate ferrous from non-ferrous metals; chips or scratches plated metal using chisel to reveal base metal; separates and groups scrap according to type and quality; places sorted scrap in appropriate containers.

May (01) break up large pieces of metal using hand tools or portable powered tools

(02) feed sorted scrap into hydraulic press for compression into bales

(03) weigh containers of sorted scrap.

834.50 Rag sorter

Sorts and grades rags and material clippings for subsequent blending or shredding or for use as wiping cloths

Lifts quantity of rags or material clippings on to work-bench or spreads them over floor; removes unwanted items such as buttons, fasteners, tapes, elastic, etc using hand shears or bench knife; sorts and grades rags and clippings visually and by touch according to fibre content, colour and quality, and throws them into appropriate containers; cleans work area and removes waste containers when required.

May (01) bag sorted rags

(02) attend waste cutting machine (541.70).

Other titles include Cloth sorter, Flock sorter, Merino sorter, New clip sorter, Cotton sorter, Rag picker, Waste sorter, Wiper sorter, Woollen sorter.

834.55 Grader (textile fabric, textile products)

Grades textile fabric, garments or other textile products after processing, manufacture or repair

Performs tasks as described under EXAMINER (TEXTILE FABRIC) (833.10) or EXAMINER (GARMENTS, TEXTILE PRODUCTS) (833.35), or inspects items for marked or repaired faults; in addition grades examined items within specified standards of quality or finish, rejecting any below minimum standard requirements.

May (01) pair graded products.

Other titles include Selector (textile bags, textile sacks).

834.60 Grader (tobacco pipe)

Grades tobacco pipe bowls during or after manufacture

Examines pipe bowls visually and by touch to detect grub holes, cracks and other natural flaws in the wood, or manufacturing defects such as incorrect shaping or poor finish; grades pipe bowls according to specified standards of quality or finish, rejecting any below minimum standard requirements.

Other titles include Bowl picker.

834.65 Grader-sorter (fish)

Examines, classifies and sorts fish according to species, quality and weight

Examines whole or filleted fish to ascertain its species and quality, and to determine its approximate weight; grades and sorts fish and fish fillets of each species according to quality and weight; groups sorted fish and fish fillets in appropriate containers.

May (01) feed fish fillets into automatic size grading machine

(02) sort fish and fish fillets according to their suitability for freezing or for immediate sale.

834.70 Grader (ceramics)

Grades ceramic products after firing

Performs tasks as described under EXAMINER (MINERAL PRODUCTS) (833.30); in addition grades examined products within specified standards of quality or finish, rejecting any below minimum standard requirements.

May (01) sort articles according to colour before grading.

Other titles include Selector, Sorter (bricks, tiles).

834.90 Fibre sorter

Sorts bass, bristle, coir, hair or similar fibres by hand or machine

Opens bale of fibre bunches (hanks) or unwraps bundle of fibres; measures length of fibre hanks by hand or feeds hanks into hopper of sorting machine or secures fibres in clamp of machine which draws bristles of specified lengths from clamp (dragging); places measured hank, or checks that hanks or fibres are mechanically deposited, in appropriate containers.

May (01) examine measured hanks visually and by touch and sort them according to colour and texture.

Other titles include Bristle dresser, Raw material sorter.

834.92 Sorter (laundering, dry cleaning, dyeing)

Sorts textile fabric or goods before or after laundering, dry cleaning, or dyeing

Performs a combination of the following tasks: examines fabric or articles and sorts them according to identification markings, colour or type of material, or method of processing; removes articles such as keys, money, etc left in garment pockets; passes articles considered unsuitable for processing to supervisor; sorts processed fabric and articles according to identification markings; groups sorted articles in readiness for packing.

May (01) weigh articles and make them into loads of specified weight for processing.

Other titles include Classifier, Dyed assembly man, Dye-house sorter, Racker.

834.94 Sorter (hand) (materials, products) (not elsewhere classified)

Sorts raw or reclaimed materials or manufactured or used products by hand according to requirements and is not elsewhere classified

Examines materials or products to ascertain shape, size, type, colour or other characteristics, identification markings, etc; separates unwanted items and groups remainder according to requirements.

May (01) use measuring and/or visual aids to facilitate sorting

(02) wash or otherwise clean reclaimed materials

(03) pack sorted materials or products.

Other titles include Assembly man (textile piece goods), Bottle sorter, Cullet washer, Picker (sorting), Scrap bundler, Waste paper sorter.

834.98 Trainee

Performs, under instruction or guidance, various tasks including training exercises and as appropriate pursues studies in order to acquire the basic skills and knowledge required to perform the tasks of workers in sorting and grading occupations.

834.99 Other sorting and grading occupations

Workers in this group sort and grade materials, products and other articles and are not elsewhere classified, for example:

(01) **Feather sorters (machine)**; (02) **Graders and bundlers (ferns)** (grade and bundle ferns for mounting for decorative purposes).

Unit Group 835 Weighing and Measuring Occupations

Workers in this unit group weigh and otherwise measure materials, goods and products and perform closely related tasks.

Included are weighing room clerks (horse-racing).

835.10 Weigher (production)

Weighs or measures out prescribed quantities of materials for use in production processes

Ascertains material(s) required from formula, recipe, order card or other specification; weighs selected material(s) on scale pan or in container positioned on weighing machine and adds or removes amount, allowing for weight of container as necessary, to obtain specified quantity, or measures out prescribed amount(s) in graduated vessel, or adjusts flow regulator(s) to obtain required quantity of material(s) in container or on feed table; transfers weighed material(s) from scale pan or vessel to containers or removes or directs removal of container from weighing machine; prepares and places or marks identification data on container(s).

May (01) cut materials before weighing

(02) operate mechanical handling devices

(03) pack and seal containers

(04) deliver, or direct delivery of, weighed materials manually or mechanically to appropriate department

(05) clear spillage and clean equipment.

Other titles include Compounder, Dispenser, Feeder table attendant, Furnace drum packer, Ingredients preparer, Ingredients preparation assistant, Load preparer, Manganese man, Scaleman, Skipman.

Excluded are Weighers (weighbridge) (835 .30)

835.20 Weigher (goods, products)

Weighs or checks weight of goods or products using weighing equipment such as balance, spring, weighing platform or automatic scales

Places or directs placing of goods or products to be weighed on equipment; records net weight, or adds or removes goods or products to obtain specified weight, or checks weight and rejects products or goods which do not conform to weight specification; as necessary, allows for weight of container to calculate net weight; removes or directs removal of weighed goods or products from equipment; prepares label or other form of identification.

May (01) regulate flow of goods from hopper on to weighing equipment
(02) bag goods or products
(03) assist in loading and/or unloading goods
(04) operate mechanical aids, such as lifting, loading or compressing equipment
(05) clean equipment and work area
(06) group weighed items to make sets of specified total weight and be known as Set weigher.

Other titles include Banksman, Check weigher (food products), Coal yard man, Scaleman.

See Packer (chemical, pharmaceutical and allied products) (841.15)

Excluded are Weighers (weighbridge) (835.30)

835.30 Weigher (weighbridge)

Weighs loaded vehicles or other large containers on automatic or manually controlled weighbridge

Signals for loaded container to be moved on to weighbridge platform; reads weight recorded automatically, or adjusts manual controls to obtain correct balance and reads weight; records gross weight and allowance for unladen container (tare), and calculates net weight of contents; checks delivery notes; prepares documents recording identification details and other information such as arrival and departure times of vehicles.

May (01) weigh empty vehicle or container to obtain tare
(02) accept payment for loads removed in customers' vehicles
(03) accept weighing fees at public weighbridge.

Other titles include Check weighman (colliery), Rail dispatcher, Road dispatcher, Truck weighman, Tub weighman, Wagon weighman, Weigh clerk, Weighbridge clerk, Weighbridgeman.

835.40 Measuring machine operator (linear)

Operates machine to measure length of rolls of material such as carpets

Loads roll of material to be measured on to machine; passes end of material through machine and wraps it round take-up roller; sets measuring meter; starts machine; stops machine when material has been fully wound on to take-up roller and records measurement indicated on meter; removes measured roll from machine and attaches label showing identification data and measurement.

May (01) cut off end pieces of material.

Other titles include Measurer, Measuring machine operator (carpet).

835.50 Measuring machine operator (area)

Operates machine to measure area of irregularly shaped materials such as leather or sheepskin

Sets dial to record measurement and starts machine; spreads material flat on feed table and feeds material into machine which carries it under measuring wheels connected to dial; removes measured material from machine; reads dial and records area measurement on material.

Other titles include Measurer, Measuring machine operator (leather, sheepskin).

835.98 Trainee

Performs, under instruction or guidance, various tasks including training exercises and as appropriate pursues studies in order to acquire the basic skills and knowledge required to perform the tasks of workers in weighing and measuring occupations.

835 .99 Other weighing and measuring occupations

Workers in this group weigh and otherwise measure materials, goods and products and perform closely related tasks and are not elsewhere classified, for example:

(01) **Counters (cloth)** (count number of laps in pieces of cloth to determine length of pieces); (02) **Counting machine operators** (operate machines to count articles); (03) **Markers (linear),** Markers off (linear), Measurers (hand), Piece boys (measure or check and/or calculate measurements of materials using hand measuring devices such as rules, measuring tapes or tables, and mark off as necessary;) (04) **Measurers (coating)** (measure thickness of coatings using measuring scales); (05) **Weighing room clerks (horse-racing)** (weigh riders and racing equipment prior to race and riders and equipment of placed horses after race).

Unit Group 839 Product Inspecting, Examining, Sorting, Grading and Measuring Occupations (Excluding Laboratory Technicians) Not Elsewhere Classified

Workers in this unit group, perform routine chemical and chemical and physical tests on materials and products, check goods vehicles for compliance with statutory regulations, and perform other miscellaneous tasks in inspecting, examining, sorting, grading and measuring and are not elsewhere classified.

839 .10 Examiner (optical elements)

Examines smoothed polished optical elements for defects

Holds lens or prism against dark background under light, and examines surface and edges for defects such as chips, scratches or pits, using magnifying glass; checks curvature of lens using spherometer, or places lens in contact with proof plate of required curvature to check that bands of colour (Newton's rings) spread evenly from centre to outward edge of lens; measures angles and faces of prism using protractor, micrometer, etc; passes parallel rays of light through prism and observes light displacement; returns imperfect elements for further machining.

Other titles include Inspector.

839 .20 Prescription checker (ophthalmic)

Checks spectacles for quality of work and for compliance with ophthalmic prescription

Examines finished spectacles to ascertain that type of frame and lenses comply with prescription; examines frame to ensure that it has been properly assembled; checks eye size of frame, length and angle of sidepieces, and distance between lenses, using rules; examines lenses for scratches or other blemishes; checks that lenses are securely fixed and properly aligned in frame; examines each lens using focimeter to ensure that position of optical centre and lens power are in accordance with prescription; returns faulty spectacles for rectification.

839 .30 Tester (chemical, chemical and physical) (routine)

Performs routine checks using standardised test procedures to verify at various stages of production the chemical composition or chemical and physical characteristics or qualities of materials or products

Examines test card or other instruction to ascertain type of test required; sets up appropriate equipment; prepares item for testing, where necessary, using equipment such as grinders, mixers or vibratory screens; carries out prescribed tests to check composition of item or to test characteristics such as absorption, acidity, alkalinity, colour, density, elasticity, melting point, solubility, specific gravity or viscosity, or adhesive, corrosive, drying, etc qualities; records test data.

May (01) make calculations based on results of tests
(02) make up solutions for use in production processes
(03) operate checking equipment to detect processing or manufacturing defects (832 .60).

Other titles include Laboratory assistant.

839 .50 Goods vehicle tester

Checks bodywork, lighting and mechanical condition of goods vehicles for compliance with statutory regulations

Performs a combination of the following tasks: checks identity of vehicle against particulars on test application form; visually inspects condition of bodywork and checks that fixtures and parts such as bumper bars, wings, spare wheel, driver's cab and driving seat are secure; examines tyres for excessive wear and other defects; checks condition of mirrors and windows and operation of windscreen wipers, speedometer, horn, brake pedal and hand lever; tests suspension and steering for wear; examines hydraulic and pneumatic systems for leakages; checks position and condition of all lights and battery; tests direction and degree of dip of headlight beam; tests braking efficiency; runs engine and checks smoke emission; records results of each test on inspection card.

See Examiner (vehicle body) (832 .10)

839 .90 Examiner (laundering, cleaning, dyeing)

Examines articles to ensure they have been satisfactorily laundered, cleaned or dyed

Examines articles for stains, dirt, missing items such as buttons or stiffeners, uneven dyeing, faulty pressing or other poor finish, and repairs not carried out; segregates faulty articles for reprocessing or repair.

Other titles include Inspector.

839 .98 Trainee

Performs, under instruction or guidance, various tasks including training exercises and as appropriate pursues studies in order to acquire the basic skills and knowledge required to perform the tasks of workers in product inspecting, examining, sorting, grading and measuring occupations (excluding laboratory technicians) not elsewhere classified.

839 .99 Other product inspecting, examining, sorting, grading and measuring occupations (excluding laboratory technicians not elsewhere classified

Workers in this group perform miscellaneous tasks in product examining, sorting, grading and measuring occupations (excluding laboratory technicians) and are not separately classified, for example:

(01) **Cable end preparers** (prepare power cable ends for connection to test equipment); (02) **Drug room checkers** (select appropriate recipe cards and check contents of batch cans prepared by weighers (production), or examine bottles or other containers and their contents to detect damage or faults); (03) **Samplers** (collect, mark and where necessary prepare samples of materials or products for laboratory analysis or other checking); (04) **Smellers** (examine exteriors of washed casks for damage and to ensure removal of old brew markings, and check cleanliness of cask interiors by visual examination and smell); (05) **Test end attendants** (connect prepared ends of power cables to test equipment); (06) **Turners-up (metal)** (assist inspectors or examiners during examination of billets, blooms, slabs, etc); (07) **Viewer projectionists** (load and operate film projectors and check projected films for sound, vision or other defects).

Minor Group 84 PACKAGING, LABELLING AND RELATED OCCUPATIONS

Workers in this minor group pack, wrap and label products and other articles, fill and seal containers and perform closely related tasks.

The occupations are arranged in the following unit groups:

840 Foremen (Packaging, Labelling and Related Occupations)

841 Packaging, Labelling and Related Occupations (Hand)

842 Packaging, Labelling and Related Occupations (Machine)

Unit Group 840 Foremen (Packaging, Labelling and Related Occupations)

Workers in this unit group directly supervise and co-ordinate the activities of workers in packaging, labelling and related occupations.

840 .10 Foreman (packaging, labelling and related occupations)

Directly supervises and co-ordinates the activities of workers in packaging, labelling and related occupations

Performs appropriate tasks as described under SUPERVISOR/FOREMAN (UNSPECIFIED) (990 .00).

Additional factor: number of workers supervised.

840 .98 Trainee

Performs, under instruction or guidance, various tasks including training exercises and as appropriate pursues studies in order to acquire the basic skills and knowledge required to perform the tasks of foremen (packaging, labelling and related occupations).

Unit Group 841 Packaging, Labelling and Related Occupations (Hand)

Workers in this unit group pack, wrap and label products and other articles by hand and perform closely related tasks including filling cylinders with gas and folding articles ready for packing.

841 .05 Gas cylinder filler

Fills cylinder with liquefied or compressed gas

Examines cylinder and valve mechanism for corrosion or other damage; ensures that appropriate cylinder is used for type of gas being bottled; rejects faulty cylinders and those due for safety testing; positions cylinder on platform scale or in filling rack; attaches exhaust pipe to cylinder and opens valve to remove residual gas; replaces exhaust pipe with feed pipe and opens valve to fill cylinder with gas under pressure; watches pressure gauge, checks cylinder for leakage or overheating during filling and observes other safety precautions; closes valve when pressure or weight reaches specified level and removes feed pipe; maintains records as required.

May (01) load and unload vehicles
(02) use portable equipment to fill cylinders on vehicles
(03) test gas for moisture content or test mixture of gases in cylinder.

Additional factor: type(s) of gas to which accustomed (eg acetylene, argon, butane, nitrogen, oxygen, propane).

Other titles include Argon filler, Oxygen-free nitrogen (OFN) filler.

See 949 .50 for workers filling road or rail tankers with gases or liquids.

841.10 Packer (heavy goods)

Packs heavy goods such as car engines or components, machinery or castings in crates, boxes or similar containers

Places article in crate or box using hoist, mobile crane or similar lifting equipment as necessary; secures article with wedges or blocks, or cushions it with padding; fixes lid of crate or box with screws, nails, metal strapping or binding wire; weighs filled container and records weight on container, job sheet or label.

May (01) line container with canvas or paper
(02) make up crate.

841.15 Packer (chemical, pharmaceutical and allied products)

Fills containers such as ampoules, tubes, bottles, carboys, drums, cans, barrels, bags or sacks by hand with chemical, pharmaceutical or allied products

Examines containers and rejects any which are defective or otherwise unsuitable; places or pours product into container by hand using weighing or measuring aid, or positions container under feed spout or chute and operates hand controlled mechanism to fill container with a specified quantity of the product; caps or seals containers by hand, machine or by heat application; complies with safety regulations when handling dangerous or poisonous substances.

Other titles include Bagger, Boxer, Cartoner, Drug filler, Drug packer, Filler and sealer (ampoules), Glycerine drummer, Packager, Red lead packer, Sterile filler.

841.20 Packer (food, horticultural products)

Packs food or horticultural products by hand in containers such as bags, sacks, bottles, jars, cans, tubes, cartons or boxes

Examines container and product and rejects any which are defective or otherwise unsuitable; places container on filling platform or conveyor, or positions it under feed spout or chute; places or pours product into container, or operates hand controlled mechanism to release specified quantity from feed spout; where appropriate packs product with cushioning material or preserving agent, or covers product with protective material; checks and adjusts weight of filled containers or quantity of items; closes or seals pack and affixes identification tag or label, or records identifying information on container.

May (01) sort, grade or otherwise prepare products for packing
(02) use mechanical aid to cap or secure closure of container
(03) extract air from plastic bag or pouch after filling and be known as Vacuum packer.

Other titles include Bottler (food products), Egg packer, Fish packer, Flower packer.

841.25 Packer (glass, china)

Packs glass, china or earthenware goods for transport or storage

Examines articles for flaws or cracks and rejects if faulty; wraps articles in protective materials and packs in container using shaped insets or separators as necessary; closes and secures container; affixes label to, or records identifying information on, container.

May (01) clean or polish glass or china before packing
(02) make up container from flat carton
(03) specialise in packing particular types of china or glass, eg medical, surgical or scientific equipment.

841.30 Packer (laundry, dry cleaning, dyeing)

Packs laundered, dry cleaned or dyed articles of clothing or soft furnishings in parcels or containers

Checks identification markings on articles against list or invoice; locates or records details of missing items; folds articles for packing using stiffeners or protective padding where necessary; bags or wraps articles in polythene paper or in other wrapping material or places them in baskets or other containers; prepares price tickets or enters charges in laundry books; affixes destination label on package or container.

May (01) seal polythene bags by hand or operate sealing machine

(02) inspect articles for damage or processing faults.

841.35 Packer (textiles)

Packs yarn, fabric, clothing, made-up textile or similar goods by hand for dispatch or storage

Performs a combination of the following tasks: packs goods into bags, boxes or other containers; seals container or secures container lid; binds goods into bundles or bales; affixes prepared label to packed goods and/or container; records information such as quantity, colour and size of contents, on container.

May (01) perform tasks of FOLDER (TEXTILES) (841.50)

(02) examine, regrade or reject goods below specified standard

(03) remove marks or clean soiled areas with chemical cleaner

(04) operate press to compress material for bundling or baling

(05) remove creases from fabric using hand or rotary iron

(06) pair items such as stockings or group items to form sets

(07) select goods and assemble selection for packaging.

Other titles include Baler (textile goods), Baler (rags), Baler (sacks), Locker (hatter's fur), Parceller (yarn), Wool baler, Wrapper (textile goods), Yarn packer.

841.40 Packer (other goods)

Packs or wraps by hand goods not elsewhere specified

Performs a combination of the following tasks: forms paperboard container from flat, creased blank; examines goods and rejects any which are defective or otherwise unsuitable; places container on packing table, filling platform or conveyor or positions container under feed chute or spout; wraps goods in protective material; places or pours goods into container or operates hand controlled mechanism to release specified quantity from feed outlet; packs goods with cushioning material where appropriate; checks and adjusts weight of filled container or quantity of items; seals container or otherwise secures packed goods; affixes identification label to, or records identifying information on, container.

May (01) sort, grade or otherwise prepare goods for packing

(02) use mechanical aids such as heat sealing, stapling or taping machines to secure containers.

Other titles include Wrapper, Pager (type foundry).

841.50 Folder (textiles)

Folds fabric, clothing or made-up textile goods by hand for packaging or storage

Spreads material or article on work-bench; selects stiffeners as required; folds item by hand round stiffener or in specified manner; secures folds with pins, clips or other fasteners as necessary.

May (01) use template or other guide to position folds

(02) press folded item with steam iron to remove creases

(03) pair items such as stockings or group items to form sets

(04) stack folded items and compress stack in power press.

Other titles include Blouse folder, Dress folder, Folder (laundry), Shirt folder.

841.60 Labeller

Affixes identification labels to products or containers

Performs one or more of the following tasks: moistens and positions label on product or container and secures it to item by hand pressure, or removes protective backing from label or transfer, positions it and secures it by hand pressure or the application of heat; secures identification tag or label to product or container.

May (01) finish and pack articles.

Other titles include Ticketer.

See 639.99 for workers printing or stamping trade marks and similar identification information on articles.

841.98 Trainee

Performs, under instruction or guidance, various tasks including training exercises and as appropriate pursues studies in order to acquire the basic skills and knowledge required to perform the tasks of workers in packaging, labelling and related occupations (hand).

841.99 Other hand packaging, labelling and related occupations

Workers in this group pack, wrap and label products and other articles by hand and perform closely related tasks and are not elsewhere classified, for example:

(01) **Card mounters** (mount articles such as combs and scissors on cards ready for marketing); (02) **Paper cappers,** Paper hatters (cover openings of empty glass containers with paper to keep containers clean during transit); (03) **Paperers (sanitary ware)** (glue strips of paper to edges of sanitary ware for protection).

Unit Group 842 Packaging, Labelling and Related Occupations (Machine)

Workers in this unit group operate machines to fill and seal bottles, jars, cans and other containers and to wrap and label containers, products and other articles and perform closely related tasks.

842.10 Container filler (excluding bottles, jars and cans)

Tends machine which fills and seals containers other than bottles, jars and cans

Performs some or all of the following tasks: loads machine with packaging materials or containers such as cartons, carton blanks, boxes and cups and with cellophane, plastic film, adhesive, adhesive tape and twine; positions container on conveyor or under filling spout or inserts filling spout in container; starts machine and watches filling or operates control to release flow from filling spout; stops machine to clear blockages; adjusts mechanism to regulate package forming, filling or sealing as necessary; places lid on container or operates sealing device; removes filled container.

May (01) load hoppers with product being packed

(02) operate thermo-sealing device

(03) weigh filled container and make good underfilling

(04) clean machine and work area.

Other titles include Box filler, Boxer, Cartoner, Pouch filler, Pouch sealer.

See 561.99 for workers who operate machines to fill formed capsules.

842.20 Wrapping machine attendant

Tends machine which wraps products or other articles in foil, paper, cellophane or similar material

Performs some or all of the following tasks: loads hopper of machine with items to be wrapped, or places items on conveyor or on bed of machine; loads machine with wrapping material and threads leading end through feed and tension rollers; keeps machine supplied with glue or sealing compound; switches on heating device to cut and/or fuse wrapping material; starts machine and watches operation; clears blockages and adjusts mechanism as necessary; examines wrapped products and removes damaged packages.

May (01) remove and stack wrapped products or other articles

(02) tend machine which packages products after wrapping them individually

(03) clean machine and work area.

Other titles include Foil machine operator, Matchbox wrapper, Packager.

842.30 Bottling machine attendant

Tends machine which fills and seals bottles or jars

Performs some or all of the following tasks: examines containers and rejects any which are defective or dirty; feeds bottles to washing or sterilising plant; places containers on filling platform or on conveyor belt and watches positioning at filling nozzle or spout; stops machine if necessary to clear blockages; places caps or stoppers on containers or watches machine capping; removes and stacks or crates filled containers.

May (01) load hoppers with product being bottled

(02) load hoppers with wadding, protective inner covering material, caps or capping material

(03) tend machine which also labels filled bottles.

Other titles include Bottle filling and capping machine attendant, Bottling machine minder, Capper, Corker, Jar filler.

842.40 Canning machine attendant (food, drink)

Tends machine which fills and seals cans with foodstuffs or beverages

Performs some or all of the following tasks: examines cans and rejects any which are defective; places cans on filling platform or conveyor belt; watches filling of cans and as necessary checks level of contents; stops machine to clear blockages; places lids on cans; operates device to seal cans; removes and stacks sealed cans. Performs these tasks in relation to the canning of foodstuffs or beverages.

May (01) load hoppers with product being canned

(02) make good any under-filling.

Other titles include Can clinching machine operator, Can feeder, Can seamer, Canner, Closing machine operator, Filling machine operator, Seaming machine operator.

842.50 Canning machine attendant (excluding food and drink)

Tends machine which fills and seals cans with products other than foodstuffs or beverages

Performs tasks as described under CANNING MACHINE ATTENDANT (FOOD, DRINK) (842.40) but in relation to the canning of products other than food and drink; if filling aerosol cans, fits valve nozzles to cans.

Other titles include Canner (lubricants, chemical products), Can clinching machine operator, Can feeder, Can seamer, Closing machine operator, Filling machine operator, Seaming machine operator.

842.60 Labelling machine attendant

Tends machine which sticks labels to products or containers

Adjusts feed mechanism and guides according to size and type of label and article to be labelled; loads machine with labels and where appropriate fills glue reservoir; starts machine, watches operation and clears blockages and spoiled labels; regulates feed mechanism and pressure of applicator rollers or of smoothing brushes; removes labelled items; cleans machine and work area.

May (01) inspect labelled bottles, jars or cartons

(02) record number of articles labelled.

Other titles include Labeller, Ticketer.

842.98 Trainee

Performs, under instruction or guidance, various tasks including training exercises and as appropriate pursues studies in order to acquire the basic skills and knowledge required to perform the tasks of workers in packaging, labelling and related occupations (machine).

842.99 Other packaging, labelling and related occupations (machine)

Workers in this group operate machines to fill and seal bottles, jars, cans and other containers and to wrap and label containers, products and other articles and perform closely related tasks and are not elsewhere classified, for example:

(01) **Card mounting machine operators** (machine stitch articles to paper or cards); (02) **Needle stickers** (operate machines to mount needles on paper or cloth); (03) **Splint bundling machine operators** (attend machines which bundle sticks for match manufacture); (04) **Tying machine operators** (operate machines to tie cord around packages or bundles).

MAJOR GROUP XVI

Construction, Mining and Related Occupations Not Elsewhere Classified

Workers in this major group lay bricks, stones, tiles, mosaic and terrazzo mixtures, apply plaster to structures, cover roofs, glaze windows, make and repair roads, pavements and railway tracks, erect concrete structures, sink shafts and wells, drive underground tunnels, extract coal and other minerals from underground workings, assist workers carrying out these tasks and perform closely related tasks and are not elsewhere classified.

The occupations are arranged in the following minor groups:

86 Construction and Related Occupations Not Elsewhere Classified
87 Mining, Quarrying, Well Drilling and Related Occupations Not Elsewhere Classified

Minor Group 86 CONSTRUCTION AND RELATED OCCUPATIONS NOT ELSEWHERE CLASSIFIED

Workers in this minor group lay bricks, stones, tiles, mosaic and terrazzo mixtures, apply plaster to structures, cover roofs, fit and set glass in buildings and vehicles, make and repair roads, pavements and railway tracks, erect prefabricated concrete structures, assist workers carrying out these tasks and perform other tasks in construction and related occupations and are not elsewhere classified.

The occupations are arranged in the following unit groups:

860 Foremen (Construction and Related Occupations Not Elsewhere Classified)

861 Bricklaying and Stone Setting Occupations

862 Plastering Occupations

863 Terrazzo Working and Tile Setting Occupations

864 Roofing Occupations

865 Glazing Occupations

866 Road and Railway Track Making and Repairing Occupations (Excluding Machine Operating)

867 Concrete Erecting Occupations

868 Building and Civil Engineering Craftsmen's Mates and Labourers Not Elsewhere Classified

869 Other Construction and Related Occupations

Unit Group 860 Foremen (Construction and Related Occupations Not Elsewhere Classified)

Workers in this unit group directly supervise and co-ordinate the activities of workers in construction and related occupations and are not elsewhere classified.

860 .05 Foreman bricklayer

Directly supervises and co-ordinates the activities of bricklayers

Performs appropriate tasks as described under SUPERVISOR/FOREMAN (UNSPECIFIED) (990 .00) and in addition plans work in conjunction with other trades' foremen and ensures that materials are delivered to site according to construction programme.

May (01) set out brickwork

(02) lay courses of brickwork to indicate system in which bricks are to be laid (bond) and position of openings, recesses, arches, etc

(03) supervise fixer masons.

Additional factor: number of workers supervised.

860 .10 Foreman fixer mason

Directly supervises and co-ordinates the activities of fixer masons

Performs appropriate tasks as described under SUPERVISOR/FOREMAN (UNSPECIFIED) (990 .00) and in addition plans work in conjunction with other trades' foremen and ensures that materials are delivered to site according to construction programme.

Additional factor: number of workers supervised.

860 .15 Foreman plasterer

Directly supervises and co-ordinates the activities of workers in plastering occupations

Performs appropriate tasks as described under SUPERVISOR/FOREMAN (UNSPECIFIED) (990 .00) and in addition plans work in conjunction with other trades' foremen and ensures that materials are delivered to site according to construction programme.

May (01) prepare estimates for repair work.

Additional factor: number of workers supervised.

860 .20 Foreman (terrazzo working, tile setting occupations)

Directly supervises and co-ordinates the activities of workers in terrazzo working or tile setting occupations

Performs appropriate tasks as described under SUPERVISOR/FOREMAN (UNSPECIFIED) (990 .00) and in addition plans work in conjunction with other trades' foremen and ensures that materials are delivered to site according to construction programme.

May (01) measure area to be covered and mark out for laying.

Additional factor: number of workers supervised.

860 .25 Foreman (roofing occupations)

Directly supervises and co-ordinates the activities of workers in roofing occupations

Performs appropriate tasks as described under SUPERVISOR/FOREMAN (UNSPECIFIED) (990 .00) and in addition plans work in conjunction with other trades' foremen and ensures that materials are delivered to site according to construction programme.

May (01) measure site and assist with preparation of estimates.

Additional factor: number of workers supervised.

860 .30 Foreman glazier

Directly supervises and co-ordinates the activities of workers in glazing occupations

Performs appropriate tasks as described under SUPERVISOR/FOREMAN (UNSPECIFIED) (990 .00) and in addition plans work in conjunction with other trades' foremen and co-ordinates preparation of glass in workshop with installation of glass on site.

May (01) measure area to be glazed
(02) prepare templates for curved glass.

Additional factor: number of workers supervised.

860 .35 Foreman (road making and repairing occupations (excluding machine operating))

Directly supervises and co-ordinates the activities of workers in road making and repairing occupations, other than machine operating

Performs appropriate tasks as described under SUPERVISOR/FOREMAN (UNSPECIFIED) (990 .00) and in addition: ensures that adequate supplies of paving and asphalt are delivered to site; checks level of site prior to asphalting and marks instructions for rakers; checks level of laid asphalt.

Additional factor: number of workers supervised.

Other titles include Ganger (road construction).

860 .40 Foreman (trackmen and platelayers)

Directly supervises and co-ordinates the activities of trackmen and platelayers

Performs appropriate tasks as described under SUPERVISOR/FOREMAN (UNSPECIFIED) (990 .00) and in addition orders equipment and materials for railway track maintenance and repair.

Additional factor: number of workers supervised.

Other titles include Track chargeman.

860.45 Area works inspector (railway)

Inspects bridges and other structures to determine maintenance requirements and supervises workers carrying out maintenance

Performs appropriate tasks as described under SUPERVISOR/FOREMAN (UNSPECIFIED) (990.00) and in addition: inspects structures such as culverts, engine sheds and station roofs, foot-bridges, permanent way bridges and signal gantries in accordance with area schedule; examines brick, concrete, metal, stone and woodwork for subsidence, cracks, erosion, fractures, growing vegetation or rot; checks condition of bolts, rivets, joints and paintwork; examines drainage systems for blockages; prepares detailed report on findings; on approval of maintenance proposals, informs appropriate departments of proposed date and type of work to be carried out, arranges for single line working, if necessary, and obtains supplies of materials, equipment, etc; reports completion of work.

May (01) mark location of defects on structures.

See Bridge inspectors (railway) (869.99)

860.50 Permanent way inspector (railway)

Patrols sections of railway track to determine maintenance requirements and supervises workers carrying out maintenance

Performs appropriate tasks as described under SUPERVISOR/FOREMAN (UNSPECIFIED) (990.00) and in addition: examines condition of sections of track; ascertains density, weight and speed of traffic expected to use the track and advises engineering department when maintenance such as track reballasting or relaying will be required; on approval of maintenance proposals informs appropriate departments of the proposed date and type of work to be carried out; arranges for single line working if necessary; obtains supplies of materials, equipment, etc; ensures that new or relaid tracks are set at the correct distance from other tracks; reports completion of work.

860.55 Foreman (concrete erecting occupations)

Directly supervises and co-ordinates the activities of workers in concreting occupations

Performs appropriate tasks as described under SUPERVISOR/FOREMAN (UNSPECIFIED) (990.00) and in addition checks alignment of prefabricated units before they are secured by concrete erectors.

May (01) mark out fixing positions for concrete erectors.

Additional factor: number of workers supervised.

860.98 Trainee

Performs, under instruction or guidance, various tasks including training exercises and as appropriate pursues studies in order to acquire the basic skills and knowledge required to perform the tasks of foremen (construction and related occupations not elsewhere classified).

860.99 Other foremen (construction and related occupations not elsewhere classified)

Workers in this group directly supervise and co-ordinate the activities of workers in construction and related occupations and are not separately classified, for example:

(01) **Foremen sewermen;** (02) **Foremen insulators;** (03) **Foremen waste prevention inspectors (water supply).**

Additional factor: number of workers supervised.

Unit Group 861 Bricklaying and Stone Setting Occupations

Workers in this unit group erect and repair structures of brick, stone and similar materials.

861 .10 Bricklayer (construction)

Erects and repairs walls, piers, arches or other structures with brick or similar building blocks other than stone

Ascertains job requirements from drawings or other specifications; examines instructions regarding type of bond (for example English, Flemish or stretcher) and types of brick or block (for example breeze, clay, concrete, glass insulating) to be used; plans set out of bricks; spreads mortar on foundation and on end of brick with trowel and places brick on mortar bed; levels, aligns and embeds brick in the mortar, allowing specified thickness of mortar joint; lays courses of bricks to specification; checks alignment as work progresses using line, plumb rule and spirit level; where necessary cuts brick to shape using hammer and bolster chisel or trowel; finishes mortar between bricks or blocks with pointing trowel; leaves openings in brickwork for fittings such as door and window frames or builds in door and window frames; lays damp course of polythene, mastic or bitumen felt between layers of brickwork where required; if building cavity walls fixes ties between the two walls; if building arches and similar structures uses full size templates and supports; if undertaking repair work removes damaged brickwork and mortar and replaces with new bricks and mortar as described above.

(01) Colliery bricklayer

Performs bricklaying tasks underground in colliery and in addition prepares and lays concrete.

May (02) fix wall or floor tiles and fireplaces

(03) fix prefabricated concrete units such as stairways

(04) operate mechanical bricklaying machine.

Additional factors: whether accustomed to corbelling or building quoins or manholes; whether accustomed to fairface or rough work; knowledge of mine safety regulations.

Other titles include Colliery mason.

Excluded are bricklayers (industrial chimneys) (861 .30)

861 .20 Refractory bricklayer

Erects, lines or repairs refractory structures and equipment with fire-bricks, refractory blocks or other refractory material

Ascertains job requirements from drawings or other specifications, or determines type of repair required; if undertaking repair work removes burned or damaged bricks or blocks using hammers, chisels and punches; plans set out of bricks or blocks for structures and equipment such as furnaces, kilns, ovens, retorts and ladles; selects suitable refractory bricks or blocks of materials such as fire-clay, magnesites, silicas and aluminas; lays bricks or blocks as described under BRICKLAYER (CONSTRUCTION) (861 .10) using fixing agents such as fire-clay cement or pyrolite powder or lays bricks or blocks sheathed with metal which fuses in furnace heat and binds bricks or blocks together.

May (01) prepare and lay concrete bases for furnaces, etc

(02) repair damaged furnace lining by spraying with slurry of refractory material using pressure gun

(03) cast furnace lining in one piece or in large sections with slurry of refractory material.

Other titles include Brick setter (fire-brick), Furnace bricklayer.

861 .30 Bricklayer (industrial chimneys)

Erects industrial chimneys with bricks

Ascertains job requirements from drawings or other specifications; lays bricks as described under BRICKLAYER (CONSTRUCTION) (861 .10) but sets each course to produce desired taper; erects scaffold platform inside chimney and raises height as work progresses.

May (01) install lightning conductors.

861.40 Fixer mason

Erects and repairs walls, piers, arches or other structures with stone and faces brick, concrete or steel backing with stone

Ascertains job requirements from drawings or other specifications; lays or directs labourer to lay mortar bed; selects cut and dressed stone and places it on mortar bed manually or using lifting equipment; fills joints with mortar using trowel; levels, aligns and embeds stone in mortar; lays courses of stone to specification; checks alignment as work progresses using line, plumb rule and spirit level; faces brick, concrete or steel frame with stone by tying stone to frame with bronze or copper wire cramps or steel bolts; fills space between frame and facing stone with mortar; if undertaking repair work removes damaged stonework and mortar and replaces with new stone and mortar as described above.

May (01) build stone fireplaces on site

(02) strengthen upright joints by drilling dowel holes in adjacent faces of stone and inserting steel pins

(03) cut and dress stones (624)

(04) build brickwork backing for masonry (861.10).

Other titles include Stonemason (walling, fixing), Walling mason.

861.50 Trowel worker (general)

Erects and repairs stone and brick structures, lays paving stones and sewage and drainage pipes

Performs appropriate tasks as described under BRICKLAYER (CONSTRUCTION) (861.10) and FIXER MASON (861.40) and in addition lays paving stones (866.10) and sewage and drainage pipes (869.32).

May (01) rough cast and apply pebble dash to walls (862.10)

(02) construct or repair dry walls (861.99)

(03) erect fencing (869.06).

Other titles include Mason bricklayer.

861.98 Trainee

Performs, under instruction or guidance, various tasks including training exercises and as appropriate pursues studies in order to acquire the basic skills and knowledge required to perform the tasks of workers in bricklaying and stone setting occupations.

861.99 Other bricklaying and stone setting occupations

Workers in this group erect and repair structures of brick, stone and similar materials and are not elsewhere classified, for example:

(01) **Block setters** (lay blocks in basic oxygen supply converters); (02) **Cupola patchers,** Patchers (coke oven) (apply fire-clay and silicious stone mixtures to cupola or coke oven walls); (03) **Dry wallers** (construct or repair dry walls); (04) **Trumpet men** (lay and joint refractory pipe sections in metal casings).

Unit Group 862 Plastering Occupations

Workers in this unit group apply plaster or cement mixtures to walls and ceilings, cast and fix ornamental plaster work and carry out other plastering tasks.

862.10 Plasterer (solid work)

Applies plaster or cement mixtures to walls and ceilings to produce a finished surface

If plastering interior surfaces, removes protuberances from walls and ceilings, fixes angle shapes and otherwise prepares surface to be plastered; informs labourer of plaster or cement mixture required; carries working quantity of mixture on hawk (holding board); spreads a coating of the mixture on wall or ceiling with trowel, filling in any irregularities to produce an even surface; checks surface level using line, spirit level and straight-edge; scratches first coating with nailed float to produce a surface on which subsequent coats of plaster will bond; applies further coats of plaster according to specification.

OR

Cuts plasterboard to required size and nails to walls or ceilings; seals joints between boards with scrim and a thin plaster mixture; coats board with a thin layer of plaster mixture.

If plastering exterior surfaces, covers exterior with coatings of cement mixture using trowel; produces special finishes such as stipple or stone effect using brushes or other hand tools; applies pebble, spar or similar material to wet cement manually or using mechanical spray.

May (01) apply plastic mixture to walls and ceilings

(02) apply plaster mixture using spray equipment

(03) comb or otherwise treat surface sprayed with plastic mixture to produce textured finish

(04) make templates for decorative plasterwork from wood or sheet metal

(05) mould cornices and other decorative plasterwork directly on to walls or ceilings

(06) fix precast plasterwork to walls and ceilings

(07) lay concrete or composition flooring

(08) tile floors and walls (863.30).

Other titles include Solid plasterer.

862.20 Plasterer (fibrous work)

Casts and installs ornamental plasterwork

Ascertains job requirements from drawings or other specifications; cuts templates in zinc sheet.

For simple casting work, mounts template on plywood in a running mould; fills mould with liquid plaster and draws template along surface of plaster to produce the required shape.

For complicated casting work, uses templates to make a model in wood, scrim and plaster or modelling clay; makes a mould from the model using plaster, rubber, gelatine or plastic mixture; places wooden laths and layers of scrim and liquid plaster in the mould and allows to set hard.

Releases casting from mould; fixes castings in position on site using nails or screws; fills in nail or screw heads and joints or blemishes with liquid plaster using hand tools.

May (01) cast plasterwork using prepared models.

Other titles include Fibrous plasterer.

862.98 Trainee

Performs, under instruction or guidance, various tasks including training exercises and as appropriate pursues studies in order to acquire the basic skills and knowledge required to perform the tasks of workers in plastering occupations.

862.99 Other plastering occupations

Workers in this group apply plaster or cement mixtures to walls and ceilings, cast and fix ornamental plasterwork and carry out other plastering tasks and are not elsewhere classified, for example:

(01) **Tapers (plasterboard)** (fill joints between plasterboard panels with gypsum and seal with tape).

Unit Group 863 Terrazzo Working and Tile Setting Occupations

Workers in this unit group lay and finish granolithic and terrazzo mixtures, set mosaic and tiles in floors and walls and set tiles to form fireplaces.

Excluded are Tile casters (terrazzo, mosaic) (623.20)

863.10 Terrazzo layer

Lays terrazzo mixture on cement screed to finish floors or walls

Prepares or directs the preparation of sand and cement screed and spreads mixture over floor or wall using trowel; places metal, ebonite or plastic strips in the screed to form required pattern or to divide a large area into smaller sections; mixes or directs the mixing of marble or other stone chippings with white or coloured cement to form required terrazzo mixture; fills section with terrazzo mixture to top of strip using hand trowel and levels with straight-edge; rolls with heavy roller to consolidate mixture; removes any surplus mixture; repeats operation until all sections have been filled.

May (01) lay precast terrazzo slabs on screed.

863.20 Granolithic layer

Lays a mixture of fine granite chippings and cement on floors, footpaths and similar areas

Cleans surface of concrete base by brushing, washing or using compressed air; divides area into sections and places wooden battens as laying guides; fills alternate sections with mixture of cement and granite chippings, spreads with trowel and levels with traversing rule; obtains smooth finish using steel float or powered hand tool; when set removes battens and lays remaining sections as described above.

May (01) lay granite chippings on to newly laid concrete screed and smooth surface

(02) apply coating of liquid polyurethane to granolithic surface.

863.30 Floor and wall tiler

Sets tiles on surfaces of floors or walls

Checks surface to be covered with plumb rule and spirit level and marks laying points; mixes or directs the mixing of cement screed or other adhesive; if laying floor tiles spreads cement screed or adhesive over floor with trowel, serrated tool or wooden board; if fixing wall tiles spreads screed or adhesive on to wall or on to back of each tile; trims or cuts tiles as necessary using hand tools or cutting machine; presses tiles into position; checks alignment of tiling with spirit level and straight-edge; levels tiles using wooden beater or metal roller; when ceramic tiles are set in position seals joints with grouting compound.

May (01) warm plastic tiles before setting

(02) lay terrazzo or mosaic flooring (863.10).

Other tiles include Tile fixer.

863.40 Mosaic design layer

Sets mosaic chips or panels in cement foundation to decorate floors, walls and other surfaces

Constructs mosaic panels by sticking small squares (chips) of glass, granite, marble, etc to sheets of paper according to specified design or uses prepared paper-covered mosaic panels; sorts panels according to order of laying; spreads fairly dry cement screed over a section of the area to be decorated; presses panel with paper uppermost evenly into cement screed and levels surface with wooden beater or metal roller; when mosaic is completely set, soaks paper covering with water and peels or scrapes it off; fills any gaps between chips with grouting compound of specified colour.

May (01) trim mosaic chips using pincers.

Other titles include Mosaic fixer.

863 .50 Fireplace builder

Arranges tiles or stones in moulds with cement or mortar to build fireplaces

Ascertains job requirements from drawings or other specifications.

If building tiled fireplace, sets up wooden mould of fireplace surround on work-bench; places stainless steel or other frame or template of fire opening in mould; arranges tiles face downwards in mould using packing to adjust position of tiles; checks alignment using rule and square; cuts tiles as necessary with tile saw, cutting machine or by scoring polished surface and breaking by hand; removes rough tile edges on grinding machine; places quick-setting stiff cement mixture or sprinkles sand along joints to prevent conventional cement from seeping through to face of tiles; primes backs of tiles with very thin cement mixture to provide bonding surface; pours in stiffer cement mixture to level of mould; places metal strips in mixture for reinforcement and metal ties for fire opening frame and wall attachments.

If building stone fireplace, positions metal reinforcement such as wire mesh in wooden mould of fireplace surround or section of fireplace surround; shovels or pours mortar into mould; beds prepared pieces of stone in mortar base.

When cement is dry removes mould and template, washes joints and fills with grouting compound; cleans completed fireplace.

May (01) use prepared wooden or plaster moulds.

Other titles include Tile slabber.

863 .60 Terrazzo polisher (hand)

Smoothes and polishes terrazzo floors, walls and similar surfaces by rubbing with abrasives or using powered hand tools

Applies water to terrazzo surface as required; selects rubbing stone or fits grinding disc of rough grade to head of powered hand tool; rubs terrazzo surface with stone by hand or manipulates head of powered hand tool over terrazzo surface; sweeps dust or slurry from terrazzo; examines terrazzo surface, fills holes with cement mixture of appropriate colour using trowel and allows to set; selects stones or grinding discs of finer grades and repeats grinding process until required finish has been obtained.

May (01) apply acid solutions or wax polish to obtain final finish.

See Stone polisher (hand) (624 .55)

863 .70 Terrazzo polisher (machine)

Smoothes and polishes terrazzo floors, walls and similar surfaces by machine

Applies water and sand to terrazzo surface as required; fits carborundum stones of rough grade to machine heads; starts machine heads rotating and guides machine over terrazzo surface; sweeps dust or slurry from terrazzo; examines terrazzo surface, fills holes with cement mixture of appropriate colour using trowel and allows to set; fits stones of finer grades to machine and repeats grinding process until required finish has been obtained.

May (01) apply acid solutions or wax polish to obtain final finish
(02) perform tasks of TERRAZZO POLISHER (HAND) (863 .60) to smooth and polish areas inaccessible to machine.

See Stone polisher (machine) (624 .60) and Polisher (machine) (terrazzo or mosaic tiles or slabs) (624 .65)

863 .98 Trainee

Performs, under instruction or guidance, various tasks including training exercises and as appropriate pursues studies in order to acquire the basic skills and knowledge required to perform the tasks of workers in terrazzo working and tile setting occupations.

863 .99 Other terrazzo working and tile setting occupations

Workers in this group lay and finish granolithic and terrazzo mixtures, set mosaic and tiles in floors and walls and set tiles to form fireplaces and are not elsewhere classified.

Unit Group 864 Roofing Occupations

Workers in this unit group cover roofs and exterior walls with felting, sheeting, slates, tiles and thatch.

See 869.08 for workers covering roofs with asphalt.
Excluded are Sheet Metal Working Occupations (772)

864.10 Roof slater and tiler

Makes roofs weatherproof by covering with underfelt and slates or tiles

Measures roof and calculates amount of underfelt, battens, laths and slates or tiles required; cuts felt to size and secures with clout nails to rafters; saws wooden battens to required lengths and nails horizontally over felt to rafters at measured intervals, according to type of slates or tiles to be fixed; lays slates or tiles so that they overlap or interlock and nails to battens; positions and fixes ridge tiles with mortar; seals edges of roof to adjoining brickwork with mortar; lays and nails or cements strips of lead, zinc or copper along wall or roof intersections to make joints watertight; trims edges and makes holes in slate as necessary using hand or machine tools; if undertaking repair work strips off old slates or tiles and renews as described above.

May (01) perform tasks of ROOFING FELT FIXER (864.30)
(02) hang slates or tiles to wall cladding
(03) apply cement mixtures and pebble dash to walls (862.10)
(04) fit aluminium or lead flashing to roof ridges.

Other titles include Roofer (slates, tiles).

864.20 Thatcher

Makes roofs weatherproof by covering with thatching material

Selects bundles of thatching material such as Devon or Norfolk reed, combed wheat reed or long straw thatch; lays first course of reed bundles with ends projecting over the eaves; secures reed bundles to roof by placing hazel rods (sways) or metal rods across bundles and driving iron hooks over the rods into the roof rafters; lays further courses of reed bundles to overlap the lower course and cover the rods until the roof is covered; prepares ridge rolls from reeds or straw tied with yarn; positions rolls on ridge of roof; lays sedge across the rolls and secures in the reed thatch by hammering in hazel spars; cuts decorative pattern in sedge with a knife; beats thatch with a wooden or alloy beater to even roof surface and to form level edge at eaves.

May (01) carry out maintenance such as resparring ridges
(02) use heather for thatching
(03) soak thatching material in fireproofing solution.

864.30 Roofing felt fixer

Makes roofs weatherproof by covering with layers of felt

Brushes dirt from roof surface; dries damp surfaces with gas torch; measures and cuts strips of underfelt and roofing felt to size and shape required; lays underfelt and insulation media if specified over roof surface and cements or nails it in position; pours hot bitumen or other adhesive compound over the underfelt and spreads using brush or mop; lays roofing felt on coated underfelt, overlapping edges to seal joints; nails felt as required.

May (01) perform tasks of POTMAN (869.66)
(02) cut and erect metal roof decking and cladding
(03) operate lifting equipment
(04) lay hot adhesive and spread reflective stone chippings.

Other titles include Roofing felt layer.

864.40 Sheet fixer (roofs, exterior walls)

Covers roofs and exterior walls with precut sheets of material such as aluminium, asbestos or insulated metal

Positions and overlaps selected sheets on roof or wall framework according to specifications; drills holes in sheets as necessary and secures to framework by screwing, bolting, pop riveting or clipping; fits and secures additional layers of sheets until area is covered; secures ridge covering and eaves and fits barge boards as necessary

May (01) cut, trim and mitre sheets
(02) fit roof lights, using materials such as transparent plastic
(03) position and secure ventilating cowls
(04) tack weld nuts to bolts after tightening
(05) seal edges of bitumastic insulated sheet after cutting to shape
(06) erect scaffolding
(07) rig and operate lifting equipment

Other titles include Roof mechanic, Sheeter.

864.98 Trainee

Performs, under instruction or guidance, various tasks including training exercises and as appropriate pursues studies in order to acquire the basic skills and knowledge required to perform the tasks of workers in roofing occupations.

864.99 Other roofing occupations

Workers in this group cover roofs and exterior walls with felting, sheeting, slates, tiles and thatch and are not elsewhere classified.

Unit Group 865 Glazing Occupations

Workers in this unit group cut, fit and set glass in windows, doors, shop fronts, vehicles and other structural frames.

Excluded are Glass cutters (flat glass) (619.30)

865.10 Glazier

Installs glass in windows, doors, skylights and on interior and exterior surfaces of buildings

Ascertains job requirements from drawings or other specifications; obtains glass of specified type and size or made up leaded light; on wooden frame applies coat of primer as required and spreads layer of putty in rebate; on metal frame coats rebate with mastic compound or putty; trims glass to size as necessary, positions glass or leaded light in frame and inserts plastic or wooden spacers between glass and frame as required; inserts nails in wooden frame or metal clips in metal frame to secure glass or leaded light; applies further mastic or putty between frame edge and glass and levels off using putty knife; nails or screws beading strip on to frame as required; trims off excess putty or mastic with knife and cleans glass; if undertaking repair work removes broken glass and old putty or mastic from the rebate of the frame and replaces as described above; fixes mirror panels to interior and exterior walls using adhesive compounds or screws.

May (01) cut glass to size (619.30)
(02) install leaded lights by wiring to metal frame bars
(03) install patent roof glazing (865.20)
(04) fit hinges, handles and locks to plate glass doors and set doors in position
(05) install moulded glass prisms in iron or concrete framework in floors or pavements
(06) fit glass in rubber moulding (gasket) secured to metal strip on window frame.

Other titles include Lead light fixer.

865.20 Patent roofing glazier

Fixes metal glazing bars on roof frame and fits sheet glass to form patent roofs

Ascertains job requirements from drawings or other specifications; obtains glass of specified type and size from glass cutter; measures and marks out on roof frame positions for metal glazing bars; screws glazing bars to roof timber or bolts bars on to metal framework; cuts fitting cord to required lengths and inserts in channels of glazing bars; trims glass with glass cutter as necessary; slides cut glass into the channels of glazing bars on top of the fitting cord and secures in position with metal strip; fixes aluminium or lead flashing to ridge of roof.

May (01) cut glass to size (619.30).

865.30 Screen glazier (vehicles)

Cuts and fits glass panels in window frames of vehicles

Scores plain or safety glass with hand glass cutter using rule, square or template as guide; breaks off glass by hand or with pliers; cuts nylon panel in laminated glass with knife; smoothes edges of cut glass on abrasive wheel or belt; coats edge of glass with adhesive and fixes moulded rubber beading around edge of glass; fixes rubber-edged glass in windscreen, side or back window frame of vehicle with adhesive, or cements rubber beading to window frame and inserts glass into beading; inserts strip of chrome or stainless steel in rubber beading when specified; fits glass panel on door to winding mechanism.

May (01) fit precut glass panels.

865.40 Leaded light maker

Cuts and assembles glass pieces in a lead framework to specified design to make leaded lights

Ascertains job requirements from drawings or other specifications; scores clear, coloured or ornamental glass with hand cutter following line of drawing, gauge or template; breaks off glass by hand or with pliers; stretches, cuts and fits grooved lead strips (cames) around glass pieces until complete design or section of design is assembled; rubs tallow stick on each came joint to act as flux and solders joints; applies oil cement or putty between glass and cames by hand or with a stiff brush and presses cames against glass; cleans surface of glass with whiting or similar powder; when cement has dried polishes leaded light with a soft cloth.

May (01) install leaded lights (865.10)
(02) fire painted glass
(03) strengthen cames with aluminium bars
(04) solder copper fixing wires to cames.

865.98 Trainee

Performs, under instruction or guidance, various tasks including training exercises and as appropriate pursues studies in order to acquire the basic skills and knowledge required to perform the tasks of workers in glazing occupations.

865.99 Other glazing occupations

Workers in this group cut, fit and set glass in windows, doors, shop fronts, vehicles and other structural frames and are not elsewhere classified.

Unit Group 866 Road and Railway Track Making and Repairing Occupations (Excluding Machine Operating)

Workers in this unit group construct, repair and maintain roads, railway tracks and paving.

Excluded are welding occupations (775), Concreters (site work) (869.54) and Earth Moving and Civil Engineering Equipment Operating Occupations (941)

866.10 Pavior and kerb layer

Lays paving slabs and kerb-stones on prepared foundation to form pavements and street gutters

Marks out work area with guide lines; lays bedding of sand, concrete or mortar on prepared foundation; places paving slabs or kerb-stones on bedding and taps with wooden hammer, maul or beetle to level, align and embed slabs or kerb-stones in the sand, concrete or mortar; checks alignment using spirit level and line; cuts slabs or kerb-stones to required size as necessary using hammer and chisel; fills in joints with mortar; on repair work removes damaged paving slabs or kerb-stones and replaces with new ones as described above.

May (01) prepare foundation
(02) lay asphalt paving (866.60).

Other titles include Flagger, Kerb and slab layer, Pavior, Street mason.

866.20 Trackman

Patrols section of railway track to ascertain condition and carries out routine maintenance

Patrols length of track; visually inspects rails, bolts, fishplates and chairs for distortion or fractures and examines track bed for adequacy of ballast; uses hand tools to check tightness of bolts and wedges; reports major faults immediately to foreman; tightens or replaces bolts and wedges; replaces damaged rail chairs; repacks ballast under sleepers; lubricates points; examines fences, drains, culverts and embankments and carries out any necessary maintenance.

May (01) assist with track laying or relaying (866.30
(02) supervise one other trackman and be known as Leading trackman.

Other titles include Lengthman (rail).

866 .30 Platelayer

Lays, relays and repairs railway track and maintains track area

When working on track laying or relaying levels ground and spreads and builds up ballast as necessary; lays sleepers or metal plates at specified intervals on prepared ground or ballast; positions lengths of rail, sets of points and crossovers on sleepers or plates and secures rail with spikes or bolts or positions rail in chairs affixed to sleepers and secures with wooden wedges or spring clips; fastens together sections of rail by bolting fishplates to rails.

When undertaking maintenance and repair work performs duties as described under TRACKMAN (866 .20); clears fallen debris or overspill from track.

May (01) bend rails to required curvature using mechanical press

(02) excavate underground track bed to increase headroom.

Other titles include Track layer, Road layer (rail), Rail relayer.

866 .50 General roadman

Performs a variety of manual tasks in the construction or repair of roads

Performs some or all of the following tasks: cuts away broken road surface with pick or pneumatic drill; pours and levels concrete, adding reinforcing wire as specified; spreads prepared paving material such as asphalt, bitumen or tar using rake; compacts surface using hand roller; spreads aggregate over road surface using shovel.

May (01) operate concrete mixer

(02) operate tar spraying machine.

866 .60 Raker (asphalt, bitumen, tar paving)

Spreads prepared material such as asphalt, bitumen or tar paving evenly over roads, footpaths, parking areas, runways or similar surfaces using hand tools

Works to instructions regarding depth of paving material to be laid and camber or fall of the surface; uses hand rake or fork to spread asphalt, bitumen, or tar paving to form required surface; checks level of surface using rule and line.

May (01) perform tasks of TAMPERMAN (ASPHALT PAVING) (866 .90).

Other titles include Asphalter, Bitumen layer, Bitumen pavior, Tar pavior, Tarmac layer, Tarmacadam spreader.

866 .90 Tamperman (asphalt paving)

Seals and smoothes joints and edges of newly laid asphalt road or similar surfaces

Heats bitumen in bucket, brushes warm bitumen into joints in newly laid sections of asphalt and around edges of asphalt at kerbs, hydrants, manholes, etc; heats iron head of tamper; beats or draws tamper head on asphalt to close joints, seal edges and obtain smooth finish; reheats tamper head as necessary.

866 .92 Road lengthsman

Performs maintenance tasks, other than repairs, on a section of public roadway

Performs some or all of the following tasks: inspects road surfaces for deterioration and roadside hedges and trees for possible hazards to traffic, and reports findings to foreman; clears mud, weeds, dead leaves and other litter from road surface, verge channels, ditches or open drains using brush, shovel, rake or other hand tools; trims grass verges using scythe or reap hook; gathers rubbish on verge for collection; spreads grit or other material on road surfaces, as required, using shovel.

May (01) trim hedges

(02) fill in damaged parts of road surface with aggregate pending repair

(03) perform tasks of GENERAL ROADMAN (866 .50) during construction or repair of his road section.

Other titles include Road section man.

866 .98 Trainee

Performs, under instruction or guidance, various tasks including training exercises and as appropriate pursues studies in order to acquire the basic skills and knowledge required to perform the tasks of workers in road and railway track making and repairing occupations (excluding machine operating).

866 .99 Other road and railway track making and repairing occupations (excluding machine operating)

Workers in this group construct, repair and maintain roads, railway tracks and paving and are not elsewhere classified, for example:

(01) **Chippers** (spread granite chips on road surfaces using hand shovel); (02) **Road markers** (lay white or yellow lines or similar markings on road surfaces).

Unit Group 867 Concrete Erecting Occupations

Workers in this unit group erect prefabricated concrete structures on site.

867.10 Concrete erector

Positions and joints prefabricated concrete units on site to form structures such as car parks, factories, garages, offices, residential buildings or weather shelters

Selects appropriate units according to drawings or instructions; manipulates units into position manually or directs crane driver to position units; holds units in position using adjustable stays, guides or other temporary supports; checks alignment using spirit level and adjusts supports as necessary; secures supported unit by interlocking or wiring reinforcing rods, or by bolting; fits insulating materials into damp courses and window recesses; inserts packing such as tarred rope into joints; grouts joints with sand and cement mixture; removes temporary supports when jointing has set hard.

May (01) drill holes in concrete units and fit steel window brackets or outer cladding panels
(02) repair surface blemishes on units with cement mixture
(03) fit roofs, windows, doors, etc when erecting small buildings such as domestic garages.

Other titles include Concrete assembler, Erector (industrial building).

867.98 Trainee

Performs, under instruction or guidance, various tasks including training exercises and as appropriate pursues studies in order to acquire the basic skills and knowledge required to perform the tasks of workers in concrete erecting occupations.

867.99 Other concrete erecting occupations

Workers in this group erect prefabricated concrete structures on site and are not elsewhere classified.

Unit Group 868 Building and Civil Engineering Craftsmen's Mates and Labourers Not Elsewhere Classified.

Workers in this unit group directly assist building and civil engineering craftsmen in the performance of their tasks, dig trenches for cables and pipelines, perform other miscellaneous assisting and labouring tasks in building and civil engineering construction and repair work and are not elsewhere classified

868.02 Craftsman's mate (general)

Directly assists a number of craftsmen of different building trades in the performance of their tasks

Performs a combination of the tasks as described under CARPENTER'S MATE (679.90), BRICKLAYER'S MATE (868.04), PLASTERER'S MATE (868.08), FLOOR AND WALL TILER'S MATE (868.12) and ROOF SLATER AND TILER'S MATE (868.14).

868.04 Bricklayer's mate

Mixes mortar, transports materials and otherwise assists bricklayer in the performance of his tasks

Performs some or all of the following tasks: mixes mortar to specified consistency manually or using mixing machine; conveys blocks, bricks and mortar to bricklayer's work area using hod, wheelbarrow or lifting equipment; stacks blocks or bricks and deposits mortar in position for bricklayer's use; cuts holes in brickwork for piping; dresses used bricks; prepares joints for repointing; removes burned or damaged blocks or bricks from refractory-lined furnaces, ovens or ladles using hammers, chisels and mechanical tools; performs other tasks as directed by bricklayer.

May (01) erect scaffolding and working platform for bricklayer.

Other titles include Bricklayer's labourer.

868.06 Fixer mason's mate

Mixes mortar, transports materials and otherwise assists fixer mason in the performance of his tasks

Performs some or all of the following tasks: mixes mortar and/or grouting material manually or using mixing machine; conveys mortar, stone and other materials and equipment to work area using hod or wheelbarrow; assists in moving and setting stone manually or using lifting equipment; cleans facing of finished stonework using chemicals or water; cuts away old or damaged stonework using chisel and hammer; prepares joints for repointing; performs other tasks as directed by fixer mason.

May (01) erect scaffolding
(02) cut stone following chisel lines made by mason
(03) lay mortar bed.

Other titles include Fixer mason's labourer.

868.08 Plasterer's mate

Mixes plaster or cement, transports materials and otherwise assists plasterer in the performance of his tasks

Performs some or all of the following tasks: mixes cement or plaster manually or using mixing machine; conveys cement or plaster and other materials such as castings, laths, plasterboard, nails, screws, scrim and hand tools to work area manually or using lifting equipment; deposits cement or plaster in position for plasterer; erects and moves trestles and working platforms; assists plasterer to position and fix laths and plasterboards; cleans equipment, tools and work area; performs other tasks as directed by plasterer.

May (01) lay protective coverings over floors, etc.

Other titles include Plasterer's labourer.

868.10 Terrazzo layer's mate, Granolithic layer's mate

Mixes cement screed, transports materials and otherwise assists terrazzo or granolithic layer in the performance of his tasks

Performs some or all of the following tasks: mixes cement screed and terrazzo or granolithic mixture manually or using mixing machine; conveys equipment and materials to work area using wheelbarrow or lifting equipment; assists with laying ebonite, metal or plastic strips or wooden battens in cement screed; performs other tasks as directed by terrazzo or granolithic layer.

Other titles include Granolithic layer's labourer. Terrazzo layer's labourer.

868.12 Floor and wall tiler's mate

Mixes cement screed, transports materials and otherwise assists floor and wall tiler in the performance of his tasks

Performs some or all of the following tasks: sorts tiles and soaks them in water; sprays cement surfaces with water; removes old or damaged tiles from floors and walls and roughens surfaces; mixes cement screed and grouting manually or using mixing machine; conveys equipment and materials to work area manually or using lifting equipment; cleans finished surfaces; performs other tasks as directed by floor and wall tiler.

May (01) grout joints between tiles
(02) assist in marking out work areas.

Other titles include Floor and wall tiler's labourer.

868.14 Roof slater and tiler's mate

Mixes mortar, transports materials and otherwise assists roof slater and tiler in the performance of his tasks

Performs some or all of the following tasks: erects ladders to provide access to work area; mixes mortar manually or using mixing machine; removes old or damaged slates and tiles; conveys materials such as battens, laths, mortar, roofing felt, slates and tiles to work area manually or using lifting equipment; performs other tasks as directed by roof slater and tiler.

May (01) punch holes in tiles using hand tools or holing machine.

Other titles include Roof slater and tiler's labourer, Roof slater's labourer, Roof tiler's labourer.

868.16 Roofing felt fixer's mate

Cleans roof surfaces, transports materials and otherwise assists roofing felt fixer in the performance of his tasks

Performs some or all of the following tasks: erects ladders to provide access to work area; brushes dust and dirt from roof surfaces; dries damp surfaces with gas torch; conveys roofing felt, nails and heated bitumen to work area manually or using lifting equipment; performs other tasks as directed by roofing felt fixer.

May (01) perform tasks of POTMAN (869.66).

Other titles include Roofing felt fixer's labourer.

868 .18 Sheet fixer's mate (roofing, walling)

Transports materials and otherwise assists sheet fixer in the performance of his tasks

Performs some or all of the following tasks: erects ladders or scaffolding to provide access to work area; rigs up lifting equipment; conveys bolts, clips, rivets, screws and precut sheets of material such as aluminium or asbestos insulated metal to work area manually or using lifting equipment; performs other tasks as directed by sheet fixer.

Other titles include Sheet fixer's labourer.

868 .20 Steeplejack's mate

Assists steeplejack to maintain and repair high structures such as steeples and industrial chimneys and to install and repair lightning conductors

Performs some or all of the following tasks: attaches ladders to spikes in stone or brickwork; assists with the erection of scaffolding and working platforms; conveys materials to steeplejack's work area using lifting equipment; mixes mortar manually or using mixing machine; holds sections of metal structures in position for welding or bolting; drills holes in brick or stone for explosive charges in demolition work; performs other tasks as directed by steeplejack.

Other titles include Steeplejack's labourer.

868 .50 Builder's labourer (general)

Performs miscellaneous labouring tasks in the erection and repair of buildings

Performs a combination of the following tasks: loads materials, equipment and tools on to and unloads from vehicles; transports materials and equipment to and from work areas using wheelbarrow, driving dumper or hoist, or secures load to be moved by crane driver; digs trenches, foundations and other excavations using pick and shovel or powered hand equipment; lays and levels hard core to form foundation for concrete; mixes concrete to specified consistency manually or operates or assists in operating mixing machines; assists with the erection of ladders, scaffolding and working platforms; cleans equipment and tools; performs other tasks as directed by foreman.

868 .60 Civil engineering labourer (general)

Performs miscellaneous labouring tasks in the construction and repair of roads, bridges, pipelines, gas and water mains and similar civil engineering and public utilities work

Performs appropriate tasks as described under BUILDER'S LABOURER (GENERAL) (868 .50) but in relation to civil engineering and public utilities work.

868 .70 Trenchman

Excavates earth or other surface material for cables or pipelines using hand tools

Digs trenches and similar excavations to specified depth and width using pick and shovel or powered hand equipment, taking care to avoid damaging existing cables or pipe systems; refills trenches with excavated material, using hand shovel; cleans equipment and tools; performs other tasks as directed by foreman.

May (01) erect timber supports in trenches and assist in laying pipes or cables

(02) place and arrange bottoming material in trenches to obtain level foundation for pipes.

868 .98 Trainee

Performs, under instruction or guidance, various tasks including training exercises and as appropriate pursues studies in order to acquire the basic skills and knowledge required to perform the tasks of building and civil engineering craftsmen's mates and labourers not elsewhere classified.

868 .99 Other building and civil engineering craftsmen's mates and labourers not elsewhere classified

Workers in this group directly assist building and civil engineering craftsmen in the performance of their tasks, perform other miscellaneous assisting and labouring tasks in building and civil engineering construction and repair work and are not separately classified, for example:

(01) **Paviors' mates;** (02) **Pipe layers and jointers' mates;** (03) **Property repairers' mates;** (04) **Public lighting fitters and erectors** (dig holes and erect poles and columns and fix brackets for street lighting, replace lamps and perform other public lighting routine maintenance tasks); (05) **Timbermen's mates.**

Unit Group 869 Other Construction and Related Occupations

Workers in this unit group perform general maintenance and repair tasks to buildings, including steeples and other high structures, lay surfaces with mastic asphalt, concrete, composition mixtures and floor coverings, lay and joint main piping systems, carry out construction and other tasks under water and perform other miscellaneous tasks in building and civil engineering and are not elsewhere classified.

869.02 Builder (general)

Undertakes a combination of operations in the construction, alteration, maintenance or repair of buildings and is not elsewhere classified

Performs a combination of appropriate tasks described under separately defined building occupations such as CARPENTER AND JOINER (671.05), ELECTRICIAN (INSTALLATION AND MAINTENANCE) (PREMISES) (762.10), PLUMBER (CONSTRUCTION) (771.05), PAINTER (BUILDINGS) (811.20), BRICKLAYER (CONSTRUCTION) (861.10), PLASTERER (SOLID WORK) (862.10), FLOOR AND WALL TILER (863.30), ROOF SLATER AND TILER (864.10), GLAZIER (865.10), and CONCRETER (SITE WORK) (869.54) and is not elsewhere classified.

Other titles include Jobber (building), Property repairer.

Excluded are Trowel workers (general) (861.50) and Handymen (residential establishments) (869.68)

869.04 Steeplejack

Maintains and repairs steeples, industrial chimneys and other high structures and installs and repairs lightning conductors

Reaches work area by one of the following methods: climbs ladders attached to structure; hammers steel spikes into brick or stone and attaches ladder sections to spikes, or attaches brackets to spikes and fixes working platform to brackets (flying stage); erects scaffolding around the structure; erects block and tackle and rigs boatswain's chair.

Performs appropriate tasks as described under CARPENTER (CONSTRUCTION) (671.10), STEEL ERECTOR (774.20), PAINTER (METAL STRUCTURES) (811.50), BRICKLAYER (INDUSTRIAL CHIMNEY) (861.30), FIXER MASON (861.40), ROOF SLATER AND TILER (864.10). Installs and repairs lightning conductors.

May (01) erect staging for other workers
(02) demolish structures
(03) erect tubular steel chimneys.

Other titles include Lightning conductor fitter.

869.06 Fence erector

Erects and repairs concrete, metal or wood fencing on sites

Measures and marks out fencing line and position of posts; digs holes for support posts using spade, auger or power tools; places precast concrete, metal or wood support post in upright position in the hole; pours in concrete and allows to set.

If erecting concrete fencing, inserts precast sections into slots in concrete support posts and slides into position, securing with bolts as necessary.

If erecting chain link fencing, attaches and tensions wire to metal or concrete support posts and attaches chain link fencing to the tensioned wire.

If erecting tubular metal fencing, inserts tubing through holes drilled in support posts, joining sections of tubing as necessary with metal sleeves.

If erecting metal railing, bolts together sections of metal railing and bolts railing sections to support posts.

If erecting wood strip fencing, nails or bolts horizontal wood rails to support posts; nails wood strips vertically to the wood rails.

If erecting wood panel fencing, nails or bolts prefabricated wood panels directly to support posts.

Replaces worn or damaged sections of fencing as required.

May (01) secure gates to fencing.

Other titles include Fencer.

869.08 Mastic asphalt spreader

Spreads hot mastic asphalt on exterior surfaces such as roofs, walls or floors using hand tools

Measures area to be covered and determines grades and quantities of asphalt required; cleans surface to be covered; fixes metal reinforcements as required; fixes wooden battens as laying guides; spreads hot molten asphalt on to surface and smoothes to required level using metal trowels or wooden floats; when set removes battens and seals joints; applies further layers of mastic asphalt according to specification; smoothes surface; on repair work heats and digs out old asphalt before laying new asphalt as described above.

May (01) cover surface with waxed paper, felt or glass fibre tissue before laying mastic asphalt
(02) sprinkle sand or chippings over top surface.

869 .10 Composition floor layer

Mixes and lays composition mixtures, other than mastic asphalt, to form flooring using hand tools

Cleans prepared floor surface; measures area into sections and fixes wooden battens as laying guides; mixes ingredients to form required composition such as bitumen, cement latex, magnesite or synthetic resin; pours prepared mixture into laying sections; spreads to required level using metal trowels or wooden floats; when set removes battens, seals joints with further mixture and smoothes surface.

May (01) lay rubber or plastic tiles on composition surface
(02) apply additional layers of composition mixture when flooring ships' decks.

Other titles include Cold lay spreader.

869 .12 Linoleum fitter

Lays and fits linoleum or similar covering material on floors

Ascertains job requirements from floor plan or other specifications; smoothes floor surface with sanding machine or lays paper, hardboard or a fine cement screed.

If laying sheet material marks out guide lines on material using rules, squares and pencil; cuts to markings using hand knife; lays covering material in position on floor according to plan ensuring that pattern matches.

If laying tiles marks out guide lines on floor; spreads adhesive on section of floor or on back of tiles; lays tiles on floor starting in the centre or along one wall according to pattern; cuts tiles as required using hand knife.

May (01) plan layout of covering material as described under CARPET PLANNER (656 .26)
(02) stick sheet material to floor with adhesive
(03) trim sheet linoleum if spreading occurs after period of use.

See Carpet layer (659 .40)

869 .14 Ceiling fixer

Fixes framework below a roof, floor or existing ceiling and fits panels or tiles to framework to form a suspended ceiling

Ascertains job requirements from drawings and other specifications; marks position of suspension wires, clips or hangers for main bearers and fixes to roof, underside of floor or existing ceiling by screwing into wood, fastening to metal, drilling and plugging concrete or shooting bolts into concrete; cuts metal section or wood strips into lengths for main bearers, cross bearers and angle edge trim; attaches main bearers to supports and checks that bearers are horizontal using water level; positions cross bearers the width of panel or tile apart and secures to main bearers with spring clips; fixes angle edge trim around wall level with cross bearers; inserts panels or tiles by laying on bearers or slots on to bearers and adjacent panels or tiles by tongue and groove joint leaving spaces as necessary for lights and ventilation; cuts panels or tiles to fit at corners and along wall.

May (01) fix cross bearers direct to wooden joists
(02) staple tiles to wooden battens
(03) fix tiles to smooth dry surface with adhesive
(04) fit special panels or tiles for lighting or ventilation
(05) fit single sheet to form room ceiling.

Other titles include Suspended ceiling erector.

869 .16 Blind fixer

Installs window blinds and roller shutters on windows, doors and shop fronts

Marks out, drills and plugs walls according to type of blind or shutter to be installed, for example, spring roller or venetian blind, metal or wooden roller shutter; positions holding box or brackets and screws into wall; fits blinds or shutters in box or on to brackets; winds springs in spring rollers to required tension; fits metal support arms to blinds as required; tests blind or shutter for correct functioning and adjusts gears, springs or pulleys as necessary.

May (01) repair damaged blind or shutter
(02) install electrically operated blinds
(03) advise client on type of blind to fit, and measure window, door or shop front.

869 .18 Land drainage worker

Excavates, constructs and maintains land drainage systems

Digs ditches and water channels using mechanical equipment as necessary; trims and shores up banks of water courses; repairs concrete retaining walls; builds up flood banks; lays tile or other drains; cuts and clears weeds, working from a boat where necessary, and removes other obstructions; clears silt using hand shovel or mechanical equipment such as dragline or pump.

May (01) erect fencing (869 .06)
(02) trim hedges
(03) operate weed-cutting launch
(04) control gates for pasture flooding and be known as Drowner.

Other titles include Ditcher, Drainer.

869.20 Sewerman

Patrols and maintains main sewerage system and clears blockages

Performs some or all of the following tasks: digs trenches using mechanical excavator or pick and shovel; assists pipe layers and other craftsmen to lay, renew or repair pipes, and renew and repair masonry and brickwork; erects and dismantles timber supports in shafts, trenches or tunnels; mixes and lays concrete; tests for presence of sewer gas using safety lamp; patrols section of sewer wearing protective clothing as necessary and examines for blockages and damage; flushes sewers with water from high pressure hose; draws bucket or scraper through sewer using rope and winch to remove silt; breaks up hardened encrustations using boring rods; replaces broken gully gratings and manhole covers; renews valves as necessary.

May (01) inspect and clear water courses in natural drainage systems
(02) test for leakages using dye.

869.22 Insulator (structures) (hand)

Fastens sheets or slabs of insulation material to ceilings, floors and walls in buildings to prevent loss or absorption of heat, absorb sound or provide protection against fire

Cuts required insulating material such as asbestos, cork or compressed felt to size and shape as necessary using hand or portable power tools; fastens to joists, rafters or fixing strips with adhesives, nails or staples; cuts and fits insulating material round obstructions such as pipes or wiring.

May (01) fasten fixing strips to ceilings and walls.

869.24 Insulator (structures) (machine)

Operates machine to pump insulating mixtures into cavities or spray internal surfaces of buildings to prevent loss or absorption of heat, absorb sound or provide protection against fire

Applies adhesive to surface using hand brush or spray; fills machine container with specified insulating mixture; positions hose and starts machine to fill cavities or coat surfaces with insulating mixture; manipulates hose or spray gun to distribute insulating material evenly until cavities are filled or surface is coated to required thickness; smoothes insulating mixture on surfaces using float.

May (01) drill holes in wall to facilitate filling of cavities and seal holes after filling
(02) impress decorative patterns on insulated surfaces
(03) spray paint on insulated surfaces (813).

869.26 Insulator (boilers, pipes, plant, equipment)

Covers exposed surfaces of boilers, pipes, plant or equipment with insulating materials to prevent loss or absorption of heat or to absorb sound

Mixes ingredients to make specified pastes; fixes wire netting to surface to be covered; applies coats of priming, insulating and finishing pastes to surfaces to specified level; smoothes final coat.
OR
Covers surface with layers of insulating materials such as asbestos, cork, felt, glass, mineral wool or rope; fixes with tie-wire(s) and applies finishing coat of paste.
OR
Fits preformed insulation sections to surfaces, secures with adhesives, tie-wire(s) or metal clips and applies finishing coat of composition paste.

May (01) apply finishing coat of bituminous or other paint
(02) fit final covering of sheet metal
(03) erect ladders and scaffolding.

Other titles include Boiler coverer, Lagger, Pipe coverer.

869.28 Pipe layer

Lays pipe sections in trenches for drainage, gas, water or similar piping systems

Ascertains job requirements from drawings or other specifications; selects appropriate asbestos, clay, concrete, metal or plastic pipe sections; lowers pipes into position in prepared trench using hoisting equipment as necessary or directs crane driver; adds or removes gravel, sand or earth in trench bottom to obtain correct gradient; tests accuracy of gradient using measuring rods and spirit level.

Additional factor: maximum diameter of pipes laid.

869.30 Pipe jointer

Joints pipe sections for drainage, gas, water or similar piping systems

Ascertains job requirements from specifications or other instructions; joints pipes of material such as asbestos, clay, concrete, metal or plastic by one of the following methods: caulks joint with yarn and seals with cement or lead; fits rubber ring and pulls pipe into joint; fits washer or gasket between flanged ends and bolts together to form joint; coats joint with solvent cement. Connects piping to manholes and attaches pipe junctions as required; tests jointing by filling piping with water, smoke or compressed air and makes good any leaking joints.

May (01) remove faulty valves and fit replacements.

Additional factors: maximum diameter of pipes jointed; method of jointing to which accustomed.

869.32 Pipe layer and jointer

Lays and joints pipe sections in trenches for drainage, gas, water or similar piping systems

Performs appropriate tasks as described under PIPE LAYER (869.28) and PIPE JOINTER (869.30).

May (01) remove faulty valves and fit replacements.

Additional factor: maximum diameter of pipes laid.

Other titles include Drain layer, Main layer, Service layer.

869.34 Waste prevention inspector (water supply)

Examines mains supply and consumer water systems for leaks and misuse of water

Detects leaks in supply pipes, hydrants and valves using electronic test equipment, flowmeters and stethoscopes; visits consumers' premises and examines plumbing systems for leaks, contamination or unauthorised use of water; reports findings to foreman; makes return visits to consumers' premises to ensure that necessary work has been carried out as requested or that misuse of water has terminated.

May (01) carry out temporary repairs to burst pipes
(02) replace defective washers
(03) investigate consumer complaints such as inadequate water pressure, pipe noise and excessive meter readings
(04) trace position of underground pipes using electronic equipment.

Other titles include Waterman.

869.36 Diver, Frogman

Works under water in diving or frogman's suit to install, inspect, repair or remove equipment and structures, inspect or repair ships or carry out survey and search operations

Examines and checks diving or frogman's suit, equipment and underwater tools; puts on suit and equipment, and where appropriate calculates air pressure and sets gauge; descends into water from land or boat; communicates with surface staff by signal line or telephone; works under water on ships, oil rigs, harbours, jetties, bridges, reservoir beds, sluice gates, sewers, etc; carries out tasks such as welding, cutting, sawing, drilling, bolting and concreting; fixes ropes or steel hawsers for removal or recovery of heavy objects; sets explosive charges for demolition or excavation work; carries out echo-sounding and seismic underwater surveys; operates underwater photographic equipment; searches for sunken objects.

May (01) work from diving bell
(02) operate recompression chambers for other divers
(03) man communication lines for other divers.

Additional factor: whether in possession of diver's fitness certificate.

869.50 Timberman (surface excavations)

Fixes supports in trenches or similar excavations to prevent sides falling in

Measures and cuts timber to required size or selects cut timber or metal sheeting according to depth of trench or excavation; positions supports of timber or metal vertically against side of trench; places length of timber horizontally along supports and fastens to supports by bolting, clamping or nailing; fixes timber cross-pieces between horizontal lengths on opposite sides of trench using wooden wedges, or fits hydraulic or screw jacks; removes shoring when work in trench has been completed.

See Timberer (mining) (879.20)

869.52 Demolisher

Demolishes buildings using hand or powered hand tools

Performs some or all of the following tasks: strips roof slates or tiles, floor boards and fittings such as cupboards, doors, fireplaces and piping using tools such as cold chisels, crowbars and pick axes; cuts away roof timber using hand or power saws; demolishes brick or stonework using crowbar, pick or sledge hammer, or positions and operates mechanical jacks; breaks up concrete structure using pneumatic drill; cuts steel reinforcement in concrete with mechanical cutters; cuts steel girders with oxy-acetylene equipment; secures steel ropes around section of building to be pulled down by bulldozer, tractor or winch.

May (01) erect hoardings round buildings before starting demolition
(02) cut off and seal gas and water pipes and electricity supply cables
(03) operate winch to pull down sections of building
(04) load vehicles with rubble
(05) burn timber which cannot be re-used.

Other titles include Mattock man, Topman.

869 .54 Concreter (site work)

Pours and levels concrete in the construction of floors, walls, roads, beams and columns on site

Assists in unloading concrete from barrow, skip or chute; spreads layer of mixed concrete between guide boards or in formwork; compacts concrete manually with wooden screed board or using powered agitators or vibrators; spreads and compacts further layers of concrete to obtain required level; levels and smoothes final surface using wooden float.

May (01) mix concrete manually or by machine
(02) place steel reinforcement in concrete
(03) spray plastic coating over concrete
(04) fill in surface blemishes when concrete has set.

Other titles include Concrete leveller, Reinforcement concreter, Screeder.

See Casting hand (concrete, cast stone) (623 .10)

869 .56 Installer (auxiliary track equipment)

Positions and fixes structures to support or house cables and other rail, signal and telecommunication equipment

Digs out foundations using pick and shovel; places support posts in foundations and mixes and pours in concrete to secure posts in position; bolts, clips or screws structures such as brackets, panels, signal bridges and troughs to support posts.

869 .58 Plasterboard fixer, Dry liner

Fixes plasterboard or dry lining to ceilings and walls

Selects plasterboard or dry lining panels according to specifications; cuts panels to required size using saw; positions and nails each panel to wood strips on ceilings or walls to cover the surface.

May (01) seal and tape joints between panels (862 .99).

869 .60 Cleaner (structural stone, brickwork)

Cleans exterior surfaces of buildings, monuments and similar structures

Obtains access to area to be cleaned by means of ladders, cradles or similar devices; cleans surface areas by such methods as brushing on and washing off caustic solutions, by spraying with high pressure steam or water, by abrading with wire brushes, abrasive stones or powered abraders or using sand-blasting equipment; cleans intricate stonework using hammer and steel chisels.

May (01) cut away eroded stone or brickwork and cut out holes for reinforcing clips
(02) resurface eroded stone or brickwork.

869 .62 Restorer (stonework, brickwork)

Resurfaces eroded stonework and brickwork with plastic compound

Mixes ingredients to make plastic or other composition filling material of required consistency and colour; inserts wire reinforcing clips in holes cut in stonework; applies plastic mixture to the prepared surface, filling holes and cracks and building up surfaces as necessary using trowel; repoints joints between bricks or stones with mortar using trowel and jointing tool.

869 .64 Reservoir attendant

Carries out minor repairs and maintenance of reservoir area and adjusts valves and sluices to regulate flow and level of water

Performs a combination of the following tasks: checks condition of banks, fences and foot-bridges and carries out minor repairs or arranges for repairs to be carried out; removes or arranges for the removal of weeds, trees, dead animals or other debris from the water to prevent blockages or pollution; operates valves and sluices to vary rate of water flow; checks rate of flow and depth of water and rainfall at specified periods using measuring or recording instruments and prepares records; cleans or directs the cleaning of filter beds; cleans and lubricates valves and sluice mechanisms.

Other titles include Reservoir caretaker, Reservoir keeper, Reservoir superintendent, Waterworks linesman.

869.66 Potman

Operates portable heating vessel on site to prepare asphalt, bitumen or tar for laying as protective coating

Lights gas, oil, coal or coke boiler or other heating vessel; breaks up blocks of asphalt, bitumen or tar into suitably sized pieces using a heavy hammer; loads correct quantity of material into heating vessel and regulates heat; stirs melting material using a metal rod or operates mechanical paddle; adds specified quantity of aggregate such as granite chips where necessary; when melted material is of required consistency loads it into buckets; turns off heat and cleans vessel and buckets.

May (01) assemble cast iron boiler on site
(02) assist in laying molten asphalt, bitumen or tar.

Other titles include Mixerman.

869.68 Handyman (residential establishments)

Undertakes minor maintenance and repair tasks in residential establishments

Performs some or all of the following tasks in establishments such as hotels, large private houses and service flats: replaces tap washers; repairs leaking pipes; cleans drains; repairs fuses; replaces electric lamps and fluorescent tubes; reglazes windows and renews sash cords; repairs or replaces broken door handles; rehangs doors.

May (01) redecorate property
(02) undertake domestic tasks such as window cleaning
(03) perform gardening tasks such as grass cutting, weeding and pruning (504.20).

869.70 Diver's linesman

Assists diver to dress and maintains communication with him during diving operations

Prepares diving equipment and tools; helps diver into diving suit; fits and secures metal corslet, belt, boots, lead weights, helmet and face piece, and air, life and telephone lines; checks that suit and gear are in order for diving and that air and communication lines have no obstructions; helps diver to submerge; maintains communication with diver by telephone or life line; lowers equipment and tools to diver on weighted ropes; takes emergency action to aid diver if necessary; raises tools and assists diver to ascend; removes diving gear and suit; dries suit, tools and other equipment.

May (01) operate winch or other lifting equipment
(02) maintain and repair diving equipment
(03) perform tasks of AIR PUMP ATTENDANT (DIVING) (979.50).

869.90 Grave digger

Prepares graves for burials

Locates site and marks off area for new grave or re-opening of existing grave for further burial; digs hole to specified dimensions using spade, pick, or pneumatic shovel; shores up sides of grave with timber or metal frame; arranges excavated earth into a neat pile and covers with artificial grass carpet; positions coffin supports on grave; after burial removes shoring, fills in grave with earth and arranges wreaths and flowers.

May (01) erect temporary protective canopy at grave site
(02) maintain burial ground
(03) assist in lowering coffin at burial
(04) blast rock during excavation.

Additional factor: whether in possession of shot-firer's certificate.

869.98 Trainee

Performs, under instruction or guidance, various tasks including training exercises and as appropriate pursues studies in order to acquire the basic skills and knowledge required to perform the tasks of workers in other construction and related occupations.

869.99 Other construction and related occupations not elsewhere classified

Workers in this group perform miscellaneous tasks in construction and related occupations and are not separately classified, for example:

(01) **Bridge inspectors (railway)** (inspect bridges and other railway structures to determine maintenance requirements); (02) **Chainmen** (assist land surveyors); (03) **Leaded light cementers;** (04) **Metal window fixers**; (05) **River maintenance workers,** Canal maintenance workers (maintain river or canal banks).

Minor Group 87 MINING, QUARRYING, WELL DRILLING AND RELATED OCCUPATIONS NOT ELSEWHERE CLASSIFIED

Workers in this minor group drill holes for blasting and for probing extent of mineral deposits, set up and operate well drilling equipment, set and detonate explosive charges, drive underground tunnels, sink vertical shafts and wells, extract coal and other minerals from underground workings, erect supports in underground workings, stow waste materials in worked-out areas and perform other miscellaneous mining, quarrying, well drilling and related tasks and are not elsewhere classified.

The occupations are arranged in the following unit groups:

870 Foremen (Mining, Quarrying, Well Drilling and Related Occupations Not Elsewhere Classified)

871 Drilling and Shotfiring Occupations

872 Tunnelling Occupations

873 Underground Coalmining Occupations Not Elsewhere Classified

879 Other Mining, Quarrying, Well Drilling and Related Occupations

Unit Group 870 Foremen (Mining, Quarrying, Well Drilling and Related Occupations Not Elsewhere Classified)

Workers in this unit group directly supervise and co-ordinate the activities of workers in mining, quarrying, well drilling and related occupations and are not elsewhere classified.

870 .10 Foreman (drilling and shotfiring occupations

Directly supervises and co-ordinates the activities of workers in drilling and shotfiring occupations

Performs appropriate tasks as described under SUPERVISOR/FOREMAN (UNSPECIFIED) (990 .00).

Additional factor: number of workers supervised.

Other titles include Tool pusher.

870 .20 Foreman (tunnelling occupations)

Directly supervises and co-ordinates the activities of workers in tunnelling occupations

Performs appropriate tasks as described under SUPERVISOR/FOREMAN (UNSPECIFIED) (990 .00).

Additional factor: number of workers supervised.

870 .30 Deputy (coalmining)

Directly ensures the safe and efficient working of an underground district of a coal-mine and supervises the activities of workers in that district

Makes regular inspections of floors, roofs and walls in district; tests regularly for gas and checks ventilation; ensures that haulage systems and equipment are working safely and efficiently and in addition performs appropriate tasks as described under SUPERVISOR/FOREMAN (UNSPECIFIED) (990 .00).

May (01) perform tasks of SHOTFIRER (COALMINING) (871 .15).

Additional factors: whether in possession of first aid certificate; number of workers supervised.

Other titles include Fireman (coalmining).

Note: must possess deputy's certificate.

870.98 Trainee

Performs, under instruction or guidance, various tasks including training exercises and as appropriate pursues studies in order to acquire the basic skills and knowledge required to perform the tasks of foremen (mining, quarrying, well drilling and related occupations not elsewhere classified).

870.99 Other foremen (mining, quarrying, well drilling and related occupations not elsewhere classified)

Workers in this group directly supervise and co-ordinate the activities of workers in mining, quarrying, well drilling and related occupations and are not separately classified.

Unit Group 871 Drilling and Shotfiring Occupations

Workers in this unit group drill holes for blasting, for probing depths of seams of mineral deposits, for taking core samples, for infusion of water into strata and to release gas or water from strata, set and detonate explosive charges to break up and loosen coal, rocks and ores, set up and operate equipment to drill wells for oil, gas and water and perform closely related tasks.

871.05 Driller (coalmining)

Drills holes for blasting, for bursting, for water infusion in coal or stone or to release gas or water from strata and/or to probe extent of coal seams

Sets up supports if required for portable drill or positions drilling machine; fits appropriate bit(s) in drill chuck; removes from drilling surface by hand or with pick any loose material likely to be dislodged by drilling; sets drilling head in position against surface at required angle by operating machine controls or holding portable drill manually or on supports; starts drill and bores hole(s) to required depth; adds further drilling rods if drilling deep holes; renews drill bit(s) as required; drills further holes at specified intervals and in specified pattern.

May (01) bleed away outbreaks of gas or water
(02) connect water pipe to drill to flush water through hole while drilling.

Additional factors: type of drill to which accustomed, eg electric, compressed air, rotary, hammer; whether in possession of first aid certificate.

Other titles include Borer, Gas emission borer, Hard ground man.

871.10 Well drilling operative

Sets up and operates equipment to drill wells for oil, gas or water

Performs a combination of the following tasks: assists in erecting derrick and installing hoisting equipment; assembles drilling tools on end of drilling rod or cable; connects sections of drill pipe; assembles tubing and casing sections; operates controls to lower or raise drill pipe, tubing or casing sections; guides lower end of pipe sections to or from well opening; operates controls to start drill and to regulate speed and pressure of drilling; mixes drilling mud; operates pump to circulate water or mud through drill pipe and borehole to cool drill bit and flush out drill cuttings; removes drill cuttings from borehole; changes drilling bits; pumps or pours cement into borehole between casing and sides of borehole.

May (01) probe for and recover lost drill bits or other equipment
(02) if strike is made, operate valves at wellhead to control flow of oil, gas or water.

Additional factors: whether accustomed to land or marine drilling; type of drilling to which accustomed, eg rotary, percussion.

Other titles include Derrickman (drilling rig), Floorman (drilling rig), Well borer, Well driller.

871.15 Shotfirer (coalmining)

Sets and detonates explosive charges to break and loosen coal or rock from solid formations in coal-mine

Determines amount and position of charge required and blasting procedure to be followed; inspects blasting area to ensure that roof, face and sides are safely propped and tests for gas; checks position and direction of drilled shot holes and directs redrilling as required; removes dust from holes; inserts appropriate explosives in holes and compacts by tamping; positions primers in holes and attaches detonator wires; packs charged holes with clay, rock dust, fine sand or other materials and tamps to secure charges; lays out detonator wires to safe distance; ensures that all personnel are cleared from area and erects barriers or posts guards as required; when all necessary precautions have been taken, connects wires to firing device and operates plunger or switch to set off charges; checks that all charges have blown and that blasting area is safe before allowing personnel to return.

May (01) drill holes for blasting (871.05)
(02) attach and lay fuses in place of detonator wires.

Additional factors: type of explosives to which accustomed, eg shells, gelignite; whether in possession of first aid certificate.

Note: must possess shotfirer's certificate and deputy's certificate.

871.20 Shotfirer (excluding coalmining)

Sets and detonates explosive charges to break and loosen rock or ore from solid formations and/or to break up large pieces of rock or ore in quarry or mine (other than coal-mine) or on civil engineering site

Performs appropriate tasks as described under SHOTFIRER (COALMINING) (871.15) but in quarry or mine (other than coal-mine) or on civil engineering site.

May (01) drill holes for blasting (871.05)
(02) mix explosives.

Additional factors: whether accustomed to working underground or on surface; types of explosives to which accustomed, eg gelignite, dynamite, TNT; type of materials worked, eg iron ore, limestone, anhydrite; whether in possession of shotfirer's certificate.

Other titles include Popper, Rock man (quarry), Stone getter.

871.50 Driller (excluding coalmining or well drilling)

Drills holes for blasting, for probing depth of seams or for taking core samples in quarry or mine (other than coal-mine) or on civil engineering site

Performs appropriate tasks as described under DRILLER (COALMINING) (871.05) but in quarry or mine (other than coal-mine) or on civil engineering site.

May (01) connect water pipe to drill to flush water through hole while drilling.

Additional factors: whether accustomed to working underground or on surface; type of drill to which accustomed, eg electric, compressed air, hammer, diamond; type of material worked, eg ironstone, rock salt, limestone, granite.

Other titles include Core borer, Rock driller, Sample driller.

871.98 Trainee

Performs, under instruction or guidance, various tasks including training exercises and as appropriate pursues studies in order to acquire the basic skills and knowledge required to perform the tasks of workers in drilling and shotfiring occupations.

871.99 Other drilling and shotfiring occupations

Workers in this group drill holes in rock and other mineral deposits, set and detonate explosive charges, set up and operate well drilling equipment and perform closely related tasks and are not elsewhere classified.

Unit Group 872 Tunnelling Occupations

Workers in this unit group excavate and enlarge underground roadways and tunnels and sink vertical shafts and wells.

872.10 Ripper (coalmining)

Removes stone, rock or other material to extend and enlarge underground roadways or airways in coal-mine and erects supports

Operates mechanical equipment such as heading or ripping machine to remove material from working face or drills shot holes for blasting and secures roof and sides of road with temporary supports; shovels loose stone, rock, etc from working area or ensures that conveyor carrying loose material from mechanical excavator is kept clear of blockages; packs loose material between roof and floor to form a dry-stone wall support for road sides as required; erects permanent roof and wall supports; makes refuge holes (manholes) in sides of roadway as required; maintains existing roadways and airways, renewing supports as required.

May (01) lay rails to extend haulage track as roadway advances (866.30).

Additional factor: whether in possession of first aid certificate.

872.20 Tunnel miner (excluding coal-mining)

Excavates vertical shafts and underground tunnels other than in coal-mine

Performs a combination of the following tasks: erects timber shoring to support roof at tunnel face or operates hydraulic jacks to move protective shield forward against tunnel face; excavates material from working face using pick and shovel, powered drills, spades, borers or mechanical excavating equipment such as drifting machine or drum digger; erects timber supports, or tunnel or shaft rings or linings; bolts metal lining in position; fills space behind lining with soil or concrete; lays concrete floor in tunnel.

May (01) drill holes for blasting (871.05)
(02) set off explosive charge (871.15)
(03) sink shafts for coal-mines (872.99).

Additional factors: whether accustomed to working in compressed air conditions; whether in possession of shotfirer's certificate.

872.98 Trainee

Performs, under instruction or guidance, various tasks including training exercises and as appropriate pursues studies in order to acquire the basic skills and knowledge required to perform the tasks of workers in tunnelling occupations.

872.99 Other tunnelling occupations

Workers in this group excavate and enlarge underground roadways and tunnels and sink vertical shafts and wells and are not elsewhere classified, for example:

(01) **Manhole makers** (make refuge holes in sides of underground roadways in mines); (02) **Sinkers (coal-mines)** (sink and deepen shafts in coal-mines); (03) **Well sinkers** (dig wells by pick and shovel and line sides with material such as timber, bricks and cement).

Unit Group 873 Underground Coalmining Occupations Not Elsewhere Classified

Workers in this unit group extract coal from underground workings, build dry-stone roof and wall supports in underground coal workings, stow waste materials in areas from which coal has been removed and perform miscellaneous tasks in the extraction of coal from underground workings and are not elsewhere classified.

873.05 Face console operator (remotely operated longwall face (ROLF) installation)

Operates console to control coal getting operations on an automated longwall face

Operates controls to move rail-mounted console equipment forward as coal face advances; operates console controls to start cutting-loading equipment at face and to advance face supports; monitors instruments and gauges indicating pressures, power consumption, methane concentrations and other conditions at face.

Additional factor: whether in possession of first aid certificate.

873.10 Power loader man

Performs, as required, all of the tasks involved in coal getting operations at a coal face operated by a power cutting-loading machine

Performs, as required, all of the tasks described under DRILLER (COALMINING) (871.05), RIPPER (COALMINING) (872.10), COAL CUTTING-LOADING MACHINE OPERATOR (LONGWALL FACE) (873.15), COAL CUTTING-LOADING MACHINE ASSISTANT (LONGWALL FACE) (873.20), COLLIER (873.35), PACKER (873.40), WATER INFUSION MAN (873.99) appropriate to coal getting operations at a coal face operated by a power cutting-loading machine (other than a remotely operated longwall face), and as required, undertakes routine maintenance of, or replacement of components on, face equipment.

873.15 Coal cutting-loading machine operator (longwall face)

Operates and directs the moving of a coal cutting-loading machine on a longwall face

Directs positioning of cutting-loading machine at coal face; supervises setting of supports; ensures that cutting tools are properly fixed and set and that machine is in working order; switches on machine to start cutting and loading operations; clears or directs clearance of obstructions from track of machine and guide channel to conveyor; regulates speed of machine along face as required; stops machine at end of face.

Additional factor: whether in possession of first aid certificate.

Other titles include Power loader operator.

873.20 Coal cutting-loading machine assistant (longwall face)

Assists in the operation and moving of a coal cutting-loading machine on a longwall face

Performs a combination of the following tasks: sets hydraulic and other supports in position ahead of and behind coal cutting-loading machine; positions cutting-loading machine at coal face as directed by coal cutting-loading machine operator; advances conveyor and operates hydraulic ram to push conveyor into position against coal face; clears obstructions from track of machine and guide channel to conveyor as directed; connects water supply to machine and ensures that water sprays are working correctly; checks conveyor supports and inserts wedges as required to ensure that conveyor is level; otherwise assists coal cutting-loading machine operator as required.

Additional factor: whether in possession of first aid certificate.

873.25 Coal cutterman

Operates and directs the moving of a coal cutting machine

Directs the positioning of coal cutting machine at coal face; operates controls to bring cutting tools into contact with face; starts machine to cut under or over coal seam; operates water jets to spray water into cut under pressure; operates controls to move machine along face; changes or directs changing of cutting tools as required; withdraws cutting tools from face at end of cut and supervises moving of machine to safe position while face is blasted; directs repositioning of machine.

Additional factor: whether in possession of first aid certificate.

See Cutting machine operator (879.50)

873.30 Coal cutting machine assistant

Assists in the operation and moving of a coal cutting machine

Performs a combination of the following tasks: positions and secures prop (anchor) for coal cutter, boring floor holes as required; removes any obstructing props and connects machine to anchor with chain or rope; starts propulsion mechanism to draw machine towards anchor until machine is correctly positioned; clears loose coal or stone and projections from roof and floor in path of coal cutter and from coal face; repositions any props which would obstruct machine; clears wet slack (slurry), small coal (gum), stone and fine coal dust from groove cut by machine; inserts wedges in undercut to prevent seam from collapsing; operates hydraulic props to support roof behind machine; moves machine away from face at end of cut as directed by coal cutterman; otherwise assists coal cutterman as required.

Additional factor: whether in possession of first aid certificate.

Other titles include Coal cutter mover, Coal cutterman's assistant, Gummer, Tracker.

873.35 Collier

Hews and/or clears coal, stone and other materials from working faces and headings manually and erects roof supports

Hews coal or stone using hand or powered hand tools; breaks up large lumps of coal with pick; shovels or lifts on to conveyor or into trams coal got by hand, machine or by blasting; shovels stone and other debris into area from which coal has been removed (waste, gob, goaf); erects temporary or permanent roof supports, cutting timber props to required size with saw.

Additional factor: whether in possession of first aid certificate.

873.40 Packer

Builds dry-stone packs to support underground roofs and walls in coal-mine

Erects temporary timber or metal supports in area behind working face from which coal has been removed (waste, gob, goaf); builds dry-stone pillars (packs) to support roof of waste, using large stones for outside of pack and filling centre with small stones and rubble; withdraws temporary and as required other timber or metal supports; builds wall packs in roadways to strengthen walls and support roof.

Additional factor: whether in possession of first aid certificate.

873.45 Power stower

Fills area from which coal has been removed with waste materials using compressed air equipment

Performs a combination of the following tasks: withdraws timber and metal supports from area to be stowed; erects temporary wooden supports along sides of area; fixes screen to supports to prevent dust from spreading along working face; loads crushed stone, slurry or other waste material into feed hopper of stowing machine; starts machine and ensures continuous flow of material through pipe; directs flow of material from pipe into spaces between dry-stone packs until area is filled.

Additional factor: whether in possession of first aid certificate.

Other titles include Stowing machine operator.

873.98 Trainee

Performs, under instruction or guidance, various tasks including training exercises and as appropriate pursues studies in order to acquire the basic skills and knowledge required to perform the tasks of workers in underground coalmining occupations not elsewhere classified.

873.99 Other underground coalmining occupations not elsewhere classified

Workers in this group perform miscellaneous tasks in the extraction of coal from underground workings and are not separately classified, for example:

(01) **Bursters** (operate hydraulic equipment to break coal away from face by air pressure); (02) **Water infusion men** (operate equipment to inject water into coal seams under pressure to suppress dust).

Unit Group 879 Other Mining, Quarrying, Well Drilling and Related Occupations

Workers in this unit group extract minerals, other than coal, from underground workings, erect supports, withdraw supports and equipment from abandoned underground workings, assist miners generally and perform related tasks and are not elsewhere classified.

879.10 Miner (excluding coalmining)

Extracts minerals, other than coal, from underground workings

Performs a combination of the following tasks: drills holes for blasting as described under DRILLER (COALMINING) (871.05); sets and detonates explosive charges as described under SHOTFIRER (COALMINING) (871.15); breaks material from working face using powered drill or spade, or hand tools; breaks up large slabs of material by drilling or blasting or with hand tools; shovels or lifts materials brought down from face into tubs or wagons; pushes loaded tubs or wagons to tipping or haulage point; erects timber or metal supports to shore up tunnels; lays rails to extend haulage track as workings advance.

Additional factors: type of material worked, eg ironstone, limestone, anhydrite; whether in possession of shotfirer's certificate.

879.20 Timberer (mining)

Erects and replaces timber or metal supports in mines or other underground workings

Performs some or all of the following tasks: examines working area to determine type of support required and arranges for supply of materials; cuts timber supports to size; sets timber or metal supports in position and secures in place by wedging, bolting or nailing; lays timber on tunnel floors; fills spaces between wall supports with timbers or cladding material; removes faulty or damaged supports and sets new supports in place.

Additional factors: whether in possession of first aid certificate.

Other titles include Airway repairer, Timberman.

See Timberman (surface excavations) (869.50)

879.30 Wasteman (mining)

Withdraws roof supports and serviceable materials and equipment from worked-out faces and abandoned roadways in underground mine

Withdraws roof supports from workings where packs have been built or from abandoned roadways using chains where necessary to keep clear of roof falls; recovers serviceable materials and equipment from abandoned roadways, dismantling large items such as conveyors; loads recovered materials and equipment into trolleys or tubs to be transported to other areas of mine for re-use.

May (01) assist PACKER (873.40) to build packs in waste or roadways.

Additional factor: whether in possession of first aid certificate.

Other titles include Prop withdrawer, Salvage man.

879.50 Cutting machine operator (mining excluding coal)

Operates a machine to cut a horizontal groove in a working face in a mine, other than coal-mine, prior to blasting

Positions cutting machine at working face; operates controls to bring cutting tools into contact with faces starts machine to cut under or over seam; operate; water jets to spray water into cut under pressure; operates controls to move machine along face; changes cutting tools as required ; withdraws cutting tools from face at end of cut and moves machine to safe position while face is blasted; repositions machine.

See Coal cutterman (873.25)

879 .90 Tunnel miner's labourer

Assists tunnel miner with the excavation of vertical shafts and underground tunnels

Performs a combination of the following tasks: saws timbers to required lengths for shoring; assists in erecting timber shoring; operates hydraulic jacks to move protective shield as directed by tunnel miner; shovels mined materials into tubs and pushes tubs from working area; assists in erecting sections of tunnel lining; fills space behind lining with soil or concrete as directed by tunnel miner; otherwise assists tunnel miner as required.

Additional factor: whether accustomed to working in compressed air conditions.

879 .98 Trainee

Performs, under instruction or guidance, various tasks including training exercises and as appropriate pursues studies in order to acquire the basic skills and knowledge required to perform the tasks of workers in other mining, quarrying, well drilling and related occupations.

879 .99 Other mining, quarrying, well drilling and related occupations not elsewhere classified

Workers in this group perform miscellaneous mining, quarrying, well drilling and related tasks and are not separately classified, for example:

(01) **Clay getters** (dig clay from open pits using hand tools and pneumatic spades); (02) **Hosemen (open pit)** (operate high pressure water hoses to wash china clay from face of open pit); (03) **Linesmen-measurers** (place and maintain direction lines in mines and/or make regular measurements of rippings, packs, face advance, etc); (04) **Miner's helpers** (generally assist miners other than in coalmining); (05) **Roof bolters** (drill holes in roofs of underground roadways and fix bolts or steel rods to bind loose or split strata).

MAJOR GROUP XVII

Transport Operating, Materials Moving and Storing and Related Occupations

Workers in this major group carry out tasks to transport passengers and freight by sea, road and rail, operate and drive civil engineering machinery and equipment, move loads manually and using mechanical equipment, store and issue goods, equipment and materials, and perform closely related tasks.

The occupations are arranged in the following minor groups:

91 Water Transport Operating Occupations

92 Rail Transport Operating Occupations

93 Road Transport Operating Occupations

94 Civil Engineering and Materials Handling Equipment Operating Occupations

95 Transport Operating, Materials Moving and Storing and Related Occupations Not Elsewhere Classified

Excluded are Ships' officers (243 and 244)

Minor Group 91 WATER TRANSPORT OPERATING OCCUPATIONS

Workers in this minor group carry out deck duties, operate and maintain engines and other mechanical equipment on ships and small craft and perform shore duties concerned with the movement and berthing of ships and small craft.

The occupations are arranged in the following unit groups:

910 Foremen (Water Transport Operating Occupations)

911 Deck and Engine Room Ratings

919 Water Transport Operating Occupations Not Elsewhere Classified

See unit groups 940 and 941 for workers engaged in operating dredging equipment.

Excluded are the masters, deck officers, pilots, engineers and radio officers of ships (243, 244)

Unit Group 910 Foremen (Water Transport Operating Occupations)

Workers in this unit group directly supervise and co-ordinate the activities of workers in water transport operating occupations.

Excluded are mates of fishing vessels (510.10) and mates of inland waterways craft (911.15)

910.10 Boatswain (excluding fishing vessel)

Directly supervises and co-ordinates the activities of workers engaged on deck duties on board seagoing or coastal ships

Performs appropriate tasks as described under SUPERVISOR/FOREMAN (UNSPECIFIED) (990.00) and in addition: inspects and supervises maintenance of deck gear, winches and derricks, hatch covers, anchor cables, rigging, mooring ropes, fire fighting equipment and boats, in accordance with instructions issued by deck officers; instructs deck hands lowering and raising the anchor, lowering and securing gangways and accommodation ladders, and erecting staging; arranges watch-keeping and special duties on a rota system; maintains lifeboat stores and equipment.

(01) **Boatswain's mate**

Assists boatswain on large vessels or deputises for him.

May (02) supervise seamen securing cargo in holds or on deck, or re-stowing cargo at sea.

Additional factor: number of workers supervised.

Note: a boatswain on a seagoing or coastal ship must possess a valid certificate of competency as Able seaman.

910.20 Donkeyman

Directly supervises and co-ordinates the activities of engine room ratings tending boilers and operating auxiliary plant on board seagoing or coastal ships and carries out minor repairs to boilers and plant

Performs appropriate tasks as described under SUPERVISOR/FOREMAN (UNSPECIFIED) (990.00) in respect of engine room ratings tending boilers and operating auxiliary plant and in addition carries out minor repairs to and maintenance work on boilers, auxiliary plant and other engine room equipment.

May (01) carry out repairs to mechanical equipment unconnected with the engine room such as catering or laundry equipment or equipment in passenger quarters

(02) perform duties of ENGINE ROOM STOREKEEPER (910.30)

(03) maintain cargo pumps, deck valves and cargo pipelines on tanker at sea and tend cargo valves, etc during their loading and unloading in port and be known as Pumpman.

Additional factor: number of workers supervised.

Other titles include Winchman.

910.30 Engine room storekeeper

Directly supervises and co-ordinates the activities of engine room ratings performing lubricating, cleaning and similar duties on board seagoing or coastal ships and takes charge of ship's engineering stores

Performs appropriate tasks as described under SUPERVISOR/FOREMAN (UNSPECIFIED) (990.00) in respect of engine room ratings lubricating machinery and cleaning and tidying engine room, and in addition: takes charge of engineering stores; issues items to engineer officers and other users as required and maintains records of issues.

Additional factor: number of workers supervised.

910.40 Foreman lighterman

Directly supervises and co-ordinates the activities of workers employed on lighters operating on rivers and other inland waters

Performs appropriate tasks as described under SUPERVISOR/FOREMAN (UNSPECIFIED) (990.00) and in addition: receives details of cargoes and tonnage from dock office; inspects cargoes to determine number and types of lighters required; directs movement of lighters; charters tugs as required.

Additional factor: number of workers supervised.

910.50 Dock foreman

Directly supervises and co-ordinates the activities of workers engaged in mooring craft at quays, dock-sides, lock-sides and piers

Performs appropriate tasks as described under SUPERVISOR/FOREMAN (UNSPECIFIED) (990.00) and in addition: checks serviceability of ropes and fixings to bollards; directs positioning of ship's gangways and link-spans on vehicle ferries.

Additional factor: number of workers supervised.

Other titles include Berthing foreman, Dock overseer, Head gateman (lock).

910.98 Trainee

Performs, under instruction or guidance, various tasks including training exercises and as appropriate pursues studies in order to acquire the basic skills and knowledge required to perform the tasks of foremen (water transport operating occupations).

910.99 Other foremen (water transport operating occupations)

Workers in this group directly supervise and co-ordinate the activities of workers in water transport operating occupations and are not elsewhere classified.

Unit Group 911 Deck and Engine Room Ratings

Workers in this unit group carry out a variety of deck duties and operate and maintain engines, boilers and mechanical equipment on board ships operating at sea and in coastal and inland waters.

Excluded are fishermen and related occupations (511 and 519) and workers engaged in operating dredging equipment (940 and 941)

911 .05 Quartermaster

Steers ship under instructions of duty deck officer of the watch and controls the admission of passengers and visitors to the ship

Receives instructions from the duty deck officer of the watch; operates steering wheel (helm) to keep vessel on course, watching compass; keeps bridge, chartroom and wheelhouse clean and orderly; in port, controls use of gangway; checks credentials of passengers and visitors to the ship.

May (01) assist with navigation

(02) scan radar screen as a directional aid

(03) perform duties of BOATSWAIN or BOATSWAIN'S MATE (910 .10) in their absence.

911 .10 Seaman

Performs a variety of tasks on deck of seagoing or coastal ship

Performs some or all of the following tasks: services and maintains deck gear and rigging; splices wire or fibre ropes; greases winches and derricks; repairs canvas hatch covers, winch covers and awnings; chips and scales rust and paint and repaints hull and superstructure; opens up and battens down hatches; restows cargo as necessary during voyage; steers vessel under supervision, watching compass; keeps lookout for aids and hazards to navigation; makes mooring ropes fast; secures gangways and ladders; lowers and raises lifeboats and ship's boats; mans ship's boats to and from shore.

May (01) take depth sounding using weighted line

(02) lower and raise anchor

(03) assist with general duties in engine room or catering department

(04) in port, control use of gangway of hovercraft and be known as Coxswain.

Other titles include Able seaman (AB), Deck hand, Deck rating, Efficient deck hand (EDH), Junior ordinary seaman, Senior ordinary seaman.

Note: an able seaman or efficient deck hand on a seagoing or coastal ship must possess a certificate of competency of the appropriate class.

911 .15 Boatman

Performs deck duties and other related tasks on board craft operating on rivers, canals or other inland waterways and in docks or harbour

Performs some or all of the following tasks: casts off mooring ropes and pushes boat off with boathook; steers boat by wheel or tiller, making use of navigational aids as necessary; watches for hazards; opens and closes lock gates where necessary; stows cargo; assists passengers to embark and disembark; moors boat to bollards with ropes; cleans and paints boat as necessary.

May (01) steer "dumb" unpowered barge drawn by horse or tractor

(02) assist with mooring of ships to buoys

(03) operate machine or hand winch crane

(04) clean and grease engines

(05) hire out pleasure boats and collect fares

(06) operate engines under supervision of engineer mechanic

(07) directly assist captain or skipper and be known as Mate.

Other titles include Bargeman, Deck hand, Ferryman, Launch driver, Lighterman, Motor boatman, Steerer (barge), Tugboatman, Tugman, Waterman.

Note: the boatman in control of a river, harbour, canal or other inland waterways craft must possess a licence if carrying 12 or more passengers; in addition he must pass the British Waterways Board test, if operating on the river Severn.

911.20 Senior mechanic

Performs day-to-day servicing and maintenance tasks on main engine, boilers, auxiliary plant and other mechanical equipment on board seagoing or coastal ships

Works under instructions of engineer officer; inspects main engine, boilers and other mechanisms for correct functioning; dismantles plant, machinery or equipment and removes damaged or worn parts; repairs defective parts, uses replacement parts or prepares new parts using hand and machine tools; fits and assembles parts to rebuild plant, machinery or equipment, tests plant, etc for correct functioning and makes necessary adjustments.

May (01) when ship reaches terminal port, prepare engines, boilers and auxiliary plant for maintenance work and overhaul by land-based marine engineers

(02) perform tasks of JUNIOR ENGINEER (244.20), including watch duties, and be known as Operator.

See Installation and Maintenance Fitters and Fitter-Mechanics (Plant, Industrial Engines and Machinery and Other Mechanical Equipment) (741)

911.50 Engine room rating

Lubricates engines and plant mechanisms, and cleans and tends main engine, auxiliary plant and other mechanical equipment on board seagoing or coastal ship

Performs some or all of the following tasks as member of the watch or on day duties: adjusts automatic flow of lubricant to engine and plant mechanism; replenishes oil feed wells; applies oil or grease manually to engine and plant mechanism using oil-can or grease gun; wipes excess oil or grease from bearings or mechanism; turns valves to regulate flow of fuel oil and air to boilers or plant; watches gauges to ensure that water supply, steam pressure and boiler temperature remain at required levels; cleans oil burning equipment and cleans and tidies engine room.

May (01) assist with general duties in deck or catering department

(02) specialise on certain duties or on a particular type of equipment and be known accordingly, eg Engine-wiper, Fireman, Fireman-trimmer, Greaser, Oiler, Refrigeration greaser, Stoker

(03) assist engine room storekeeper and be known as Leading hand

(04) assist donkeyman and be known as Mechanic.

Other titles include Engine room attendant, Fireman-greaser.

See Oiler and greaser (746.50) and Boiler operator (steam generating) (971.15)

911.60 Engineer mechanic (fishing or coastal ship, or craft on inland waters)

Operates main and auxiliary engines and other plant and machinery of fishing or coastal ship or craft on inland waters

Checks that adequate supplies of fuel are on board before the voyage begins or takes on additional supplies during voyage; starts engines and checks that they are adequately fuelled, lubricated and maintained; maintains ship's auxiliary engines such as winches, capstans and pumps, and other plant and machinery, such as electricity generators and operates them as required; maintains engine room log.

May (01) assist with fishing operations

(02) work on a floating crane, grain elevator, dredger or hopper and maintain and repair its mechanism

(03) supervise crew undertaking engine room tasks and delegate some of his manual tasks.

911.98 Trainee

Performs, under instruction or guidance, various tasks including training exercises and as appropriate pursues studies in order to acquire the basic skills and knowledge required to perform the tasks of deck and engine room ratings.

Other titles include Deck boy.

911.99 Other deck and engine room ratings

Workers in this group carry out miscellaneous tasks on deck and in the engine room of ships operating at sea and in coastal and inland waters and are not elsewhere classified, for example:

(01) **Lifeboatmen**; (02) **Lightshipmen** (attend to lights and other warning apparatus and perform general duties); (03) **Seamen (cable hands)** (lay deep-sea cables); (04) **Watchmen (barge)** (steer towed barges and perform deck duties).

Unit Group 919 Water Transport Operating Occupations Not Elsewhere Classified

Workers in this unit group perform miscellaneous water transport operating and related tasks, such as lighthouse keeping, and survey sounding and mooring craft and are not elsewhere classified.

919 .10 Lighthouse keeper

Operates lighting system and signal warning apparatus in lighthouse to guide ships at sea

Performs some or all of the following tasks as member of a 24 hour watch: switches lamp on at dusk and off at dawn; winds up clock mechanism to rotate lens reflecting and projecting the light beam; cleans lamp and lenses; in fog, switches on diesel engine which operates fog alarm system; communicates with vessels using rockets, morse lamp or semaphore flags as necessary; keeps lighthouse and equipment, including emergency generator, clean; reports defective equipment to mechanics, electricians, radio mechanics, etc; keeps daily record (log) of weather and visibility conditions; reports unusual occurrences by radio telephone to coastguards, other lighthouses and other authorities.

May (01) operate radio beacon
(02) be in charge of lighthouse and be known as Principal lighthouse keeper.

919 .20 Survey sounder

Measures depth of water in canals, rivers, docks and harbours to determine sites for dredging or dumping or to ascertain navigational channels

Takes soundings from a boat at fixed distances along a designated course by lowering a hand lead line into the water or by observing an echo-sounder.
OR
Calculates position of boat, using sextant or other instrument from the boat or the shore; informs boat crew either by flag signals or verbally when and where to make soundings.

May (01) record tidal heights at specified intervals using tide gauge
(02) perform some or all of the duties of BOAT-MAN (911 .15).

Other titles include Hydrographic survey assistant, Leadsman.

919 .50 Berthing man

Assists in mooring craft at quay, dock-side, lock-side or pier

Receives berthing instructions from dock foreman, harbourmaster or dockmaster; shouts instructions to ship's captain or member of crew from quay, dock-side, lock-side or pier; catches heaving lines attached to heavy ropes from ship's bow and stern; hauls ropes ashore and secures around bollards; moves ropes to convenient bollards to assist ship's manoeuvres in confined space; when ship is in position secures ropes to shore bollards at fore and aft; adjusts ropes to control movement of ship while tide or level of water in lock is rising or falling.

May (01) row boat and carry mooring ropes from ship to shore
(02) maintain record of ships' identification particulars.

Other titles include Pier man, Rope tenderman.

919 .60 Bridge man

Opens and closes moving bridge across inland waterways and docks

Watches waterway for approaching vessels; listens for signal from vessel indicating that she is ready to proceed; shuts gates and operates signals to close bridge to land-borne traffic; as appropriate co-ordinates action with other members of the team by visible or audible signals; opens bridge by pressing a button or signals to valveman (moving bridge) to operate hydraulic mechanism; signals to vessel to proceed; closes bridge and opens gates to land-borne traffic when vessel has passed; maintains log of vessels passing; reports any damage to bridge to dock or waterway authority.

May (01) collect tolls from road users of bridge
(02) clean, lubricate and undertake minor maintenance work on bridge and its mechanism
(03) direct work of other members of team and be known as Bridgemaster
(04) co-ordinate activities with signalmen on railway bridge and be known as Steersman.

Other titles include Swingbridge man.

See Crane and Hoist Operating Occupations (942)

919.70 Lock gateman (inland waterways and docks)

Opens and closes lock gates and sluices on inland waterways or in docks

Operates levers or electrical switches to open or close sluices or activate pumps to vary water level in lock or dock and to open or close lock gates to permit passage of vessels along river or canal or through docks; fastens and unfastens ropes between vessel and bollard or capstan, and operates capstan to move vessel if necessary; opens gate when water level on both sides is equal; signals to gateman at next section or opposite end of lock or dock and to vessels using lock or dock.

(01) **Lock keeper**

Operates both sets of gates and sluices at a small lock; communicates with neighbouring lock keepers and other waterway operatives by telephone about movement of traffic; maintains record of vessels using lock.

May (02) open sluice gates after heavy rainfall or high tide to clear surplus water

(03) perform minor maintenance duties, such as oiling gates and removing floating debris with boathook

(04) collect fees and dues from lock or dock users

(05) lay keel blocks in a dry dock before operating sluices and be known as Dry dock attendant, Graving dock attendant.

Other titles include **Dock gateman, Lockman.**

See Turncock (972 .60)

919.98 Trainee

Performs, under instruction or guidance, various tasks including training exercises and as appropriate pursues studies in order to acquire the basic skills and knowledge required to perform the tasks of workers in water transport operating occupations not elsewhere classified.

919.99 Other water transport operating occupations not elsewhere classified

Workers in this group perform miscellaneous water transport operating and related tasks and are not separately classified, for example:

(01) **Lightkeepers** (maintain navigational lights in docks and harbours); (02) **Lloyd's signalmen** (signal by loud hailer and identify passing vessels); (03) **Lockmasters** (regulate and record movement and berthing of traffic on inland waterways).

Minor Group 92 RAIL TRANSPORT OPERATING OCCUPATIONS

Workers in this minor group supervise and inspect rail transport operations, drive locomotives on surface and underground railways, manoeuvre railway coaches and wagons, operate railway signals and perform other tasks closely related to the transport of passengers, goods and animals by rail.

The occupations are arranged in the following unit groups:

920 Foremen and Inspectors (Rail Transport Operating Occupations)

921 Drivers and Secondmen (Rail Transport)

922 Guards (Rail Transport)

923 Traffic Controlling Occupations (Rail Transport)

Unit Group 920 Foremen and Inspectors (Rail Transport Operating Occupations)

Workers in this unit group directly supervise the activities and examine the working methods of train drivers, guards, signalmen and other workers concerned with the operation of rail transport and test workers' knowledge of railway procedure.

See Station foreman (450 .20)

920 .10 Train crew inspector

Directly supervises and co-ordinates the activities of train crews

Performs appropriate tasks as described under SUPERVISOR/FOREMAN (UNSPECIFIED) (990 .00) and in addition: decides whether crews are fit for duty and allocates replacements and relief crews where necessary; provides crews for breakdown trains, specials, etc; keeps crews informed of any irregularities on route such as speed restrictions, single line working, bridge repairs; examines crews on their knowledge of routes and railway operating rules and regulations.

Additional factor: number of workers supervised.

920 .20 Foreman (marshalling yard)

Directly supervises and co-ordinates the activities of workers in marshalling yard

Performs appropriate tasks as described under SUPERVISOR/FOREMAN (UNSPECIFIED) (990 .00) and in addition: records train arrivals and departures; ensures that wagon numbers are recorded for assessment of demurrage charges; prepares train control sheet; arranges for the maximum number of wagons destined for the same location to be marshalled into one train, subject to safety limits; maintains liaison with signalmen to allocate sidings for and regulate movement of coaches and wagons; ensures that safety rules are observed; arranges for the removal of damaged wagons.

Additional factor: number of workers supervised.

920 .30 Inspector regulator

Directly supervises and co-ordinates the activities of signalmen

Performs appropriate tasks as described under SUPERVISOR/FOREMAN (UNSPECIFIED) (990 .00) and in addition: assists with the routine operation of a power signal box; records all train movements and reports any signals and/or points failures; adheres to trains' plan laid down by traffic controllers and liaises with them regarding alterations to time schedules and routes; advises signalmen of irregular movements of trains caused by diversions and delays.

Additional factor: number of workers supervised.

920 .40 Movements inspector

Tests staff on their knowledge of signalling regulations, examines signalling procedure and supervises the transportation of abnormally sized loads

Examines signalmen, supervisors and chargemen on their knowledge of signalling rules and regulations; visits signal boxes, checks procedure and investigates complaints of faulty signalling; examines firms' records of wagon movements for demurrage charges; discusses irregularities with firms' officials; supervises the loading and transportation of abnormally sized loads; checks train running times for punctuality.

920 .98 Trainee

Performs, under instruction or guidance, various tasks including training exercises and as appropriate pursues studies in order to acquire the basic skills and knowledge required to perform the tasks of foremen and inspectors (rail transport operating occupations).

920 .99 Other foremen and inspectors (rail transport operating occupations)

Workers in this group carry out tasks in the supervision and inspection of workers in rail transport operating occupations and are not elsewhere classified.

Unit Group 921 Drivers and Secondmen (Rail Transport)

Workers in this unit group drive and assist in the driving of diesel, diesel-electric, electric and steam locomotives and multiple unit passenger trains on surface and underground railways.

921 .10 Locomotive driver (standard gauge)

Drives diesel, diesel-electric, electric or steam locomotive or multiple unit passenger train on standard gauge rail

Inspects controls, gauges and brakes before start of journey; receives and studies route schedule, track conditions and time table; starts train when signalled by guard or other authorised person; manipulates controls, handles, brakes and accelerators as necessary to regulate speed; observes signals and watches for track hazards; if hauling passenger or freight train stops as directed to allow passengers to enter and alight, freight to be loaded or unloaded or wagons and carriages to be coupled or uncoupled; reports engine defects or unusual incidents on journey and completes daily record of driving time. Performs these tasks in relation to driving on standard gauge rail track.

May (01) lubricate engine and do minor repairs.

Other titles include Engine driver, Ferryman (rail), Motorman (standard gauge rail).

Excluded are Locomotive drivers (mine) (921 .60)

921 .20 Secondman (rail)

Assists driver of locomotive or multiple unit train

Accompanies driver of electric, diesel-electric, diesel or steam locomotive, or multiple unit train; observes signals and watches for track hazards; establishes contact with signalmen as necessary, watches temperature, pressure and other gauges and warns driver of any irregularities; regulates steam generating system for heating passenger compartments; checks safety equipment; undertakes minor adjustments and repairs to engine under supervision of driver.

May (01) operate hand points when shunting
(02) couple and uncouple locomotives or train units
(03) feed fuel to steam locomotive and be known as Locomotive fireman.

Additional factor: whether qualified as driver (senior secondman).

921 .50 Locomotive driver (narrow gauge)

Drives diesel, diesel-electric or steam locomotive to haul passenger and freight trains on narrow gauge surface rail

Performs appropriate tasks as described under LOCOMOTIVE DRIVER (STANDARD GAUGE) (921 .10) but in relation to driving on narrow gauge surface rail track.

May (01) operate hand points when shunting
(02) couple and uncouple carriages and wagons
(03) fire boiler when driving one-man operated steam locomotive
(04) assist with maintenance of track and rolling stock.

921 .60 Locomotive driver (mine)

Drives diesel or electric locomotive in underground mine, adit or drift to transport men and materials between shaft or mine entry and working area

Inspects controls, gauges, brakes, batteries, front and rear lights and couplings at start of shift; starts locomotive and operates levers and brakes to control speed; shunts locomotive into position to collect tubs (about 30 tubs make up a "train" or "journey") for loading or unloading; receives signals from guard or other authorised person; sounds warning of train's approach; watches track for hazards.

May (01) change points when shunting
(02) couple and uncouple tubs
(03) help to load and unload tubs.

921 .98 Trainee

Performs, under instruction or guidance, various tasks including training exercises and as appropriate pursues studies in order to acquire the basic skills and knowledge required to perform the tasks of drivers and secondmen (rail transport).

Other titles include Traction trainee.

921 .99 Other drivers and secondmen (rail transport)

Workers in this group drive and assist in the driving of locomotives and trains and are not elsewhere classified, for example:

(01) **Automatic train attendants** (operate starting control and emergency brake of automatic trains).

Unit Group 922 Guards (Rail Transport)

Workers in this unit group take charge of and safeguard passenger and goods trains operating on surface and underground railways.

922.10 Conductor guard

Takes charge of and safeguards passenger train and collects tickets during journey on surface railway

Performs tasks as described under GUARD (SURFACE RAILWAY) (922.20) and in addition: inspects or collects tickets of passengers; on train or at unmanned stations issues tickets or collects excess fares where appropriate; deals with passengers' inquiries; checks that washbasins and toilets are properly equipped; replaces unserviceable light bulbs; operates public address system on train.

May (01) perform some of the tasks of RAILMAN (453.10).

922.20 Guard (surface railway)

Takes charge of and safeguards passenger or freight train during journey on surface railway

Makes a survey of train before start of journey to check length, loading of wagons and security of couplings; notes position of wagons or coaches to be detached on the journey; informs driver of load distribution and any special features on the route such as speed restrictions and gradients; signals driver when to start train; operates guard's brake on difficult gradients to facilitate balanced movement of wagons; applies brakes in emergency; takes charge of goods such as parcels, livestock, passengers' luggage, being carried in guard's van and ensures that they are unloaded at the correct destination; completes daily record of running times.

May (01) perform some of the tasks of RAILMAN (453.10).

922.30 Guard (underground railway excluding mine)

Takes charge of and safeguards passenger train during journey on underground railway other than in mine

Tests operation of switches on control panel before start of journey; travels on train throughout journey and at each station operates push button switch to open doors; when passengers have boarded or left train pushes button to close doors; signals to motorman to start train; watches indicators on control panel; completes record of running schedules; assists motorman in the event of a breakdown.

922.40 Loco guard (mine)

Makes up, takes charge of and safeguards passenger or freight train on underground railway in mine

Couples tubs or carriages together and to locomotive to make up train; makes survey of train before start of journey to check loading of tubs or carriages and security of couplings; ensures that passengers observe mine safety regulations; informs driver by whistle or light signal when to start or stop train; rides at rear of train or walks in front to ensure that track is clear; changes points and transfers tubs from locomotive to rope at junction with rope haulage system.

May (01) load tubs
(02) act as relief driver.

922.98 Trainee

Performs, under instruction or guidance, various tasks including training exercises and as appropriate pursues studies in order to acquire the basic skills and knowledge required to perform the tasks of guards (rail transport).

922.99 Other guards (rail transport)

Workers in this group take charge of and safeguard passenger and goods trains and are not elsewhere classified.

Unit Group 923 Traffic Controlling Occupations (Rail Transport)

Workers in this unit group guide wagons and coaches in marshalling yards and railway sidings to make up trains, operate signals to control the movement of rail traffic and perform tasks closely related to the movement of rail traffic

923.10 Head shunter

Directs shunters and drivers to move wagons and coaches along designated railway lines in marshalling yard to make up trains

Works from written instructions giving destination of train; indicates to driver by hand signal the lines to which train should be shunted; indicates to shunters which wagons and coaches should be uncoupled and where they should be moved; keeps in touch with signalman by bell signal or telephone during shunting operations; assists with training of shunters.

923.50 Shunter

Changes points to allow movement of wagons and coaches along designated railway lines in marshalling yard to make up trains

Receives verbal or other instructions from head shunter; disconnects vacuum brake system and steam-heating pipes, uncouples wagons and coaches in marshalling yard and guides them on to different lines as directed; operates manual points and wagon hand-brakes to control their movement; links up wagons and coaches, using coupling stick, to form complete train; connects vacuum brake system and steam-heating pipes.

Other titles include Pointsman.

923.60 Signalman (rail)

Operates signals and points to control the movement of trains over a section of line

Reads instructions and time schedules of trains entering and leaving section of line; decides priority of movement of trains; receives and sends messages of train movements from or to signalmen of neighbouring line sections by telephone or telegraph; records time of trains passing through line section.

(01) **Signalman (power box)**
Moves switches on electrically controlled panel to set signals and points.

(02) **Signalman (lever frame)**
Moves levers on mechanically controlled equipment to set signals and points.

May (03) operate electrical or mechanical controls to open and close gates or barriers at a level crossing

(04) receive hand or whistle signals from shunters or drivers when shunting is in progress.

923.98 Trainee

Performs, under instruction or guidance, various tasks including training exercises and as appropriate pursues studies in order to acquire the basic skills and knowledge required to perform the tasks of workers in traffic controlling occupations (rail transport).

923.99 Other traffic controlling occupations

Workers in this group perform tasks connected with the control of rail traffic and are not elsewhere classified, for example:

(01) **Crossing keepers** (open and close gates and barriers at level crossings on railway); (02) **Transport control operators (mine)** (watch panels which indicate by remote control (mimic diagrams) the functioning of transport systems in mines and notify movement instructions to locomotive drivers).

Minor Group 93 ROAD TRANSPORT OPERATING OCCUPATIONS

Workers in this minor group supervise and inspect road transport service operations, drive motor and horse-drawn vehicles, collect fares from passengers and perform other tasks closely related to the transport of passengers, goods and animals by road.

The occupations are arranged in the following unit groups:

930 Foremen and Inspectors (Road Transport Operating Occupations)

931 Omnibus and Coach Drivers

932 Heavy Goods Vehicle Drivers

933 Other Motor Vehicle Drivers

934 Conductors (Road Transport)

935 Drivers' Mates (Road Transport)

939 Road Transport Operating Occupations Not Elsewhere Classified

Note: drivers of motor vehicles used on public roads are required to hold one or more driving licences depending on the type of vehicle driven.

Unit Group 930 Foremen and Inspectors (Road Transport Operating Occupations)

Workers in this unit group directly supervise the activities of vehicle drivers, conductors, drivers' mates and other road transport depot workers, other than vehicle maintenance workers, and inspect the issue of tickets on bus journeys, the running of buses to schedule and the loading of goods vehicles.

930.10 Inspector (public service vehicles)

Directly supervises and co-ordinates the activities of drivers and conductors and deals with operational difficulties arising on scheduled services

Performs appropriate tasks as described under SUPERVISOR/FOREMAN (UNSPECIFIED) (990.00) and in addition: boards vehicle on route and checks that passengers hold valid tickets and that tickets issued agree with conductor's way-bill; checks that vehicle is keeping to time schedule and that company's regulations regarding the carrying of passengers and luggage are being observed; deals with irregularities in service by redirecting or withdrawing vehicles or arranging crew replacements; organises supplementary services for sports fixtures, etc; answers passengers' inquiries; takes census of passengers travelling over various routes; submits reports of time schedule irregularities and passengers' complaints to traffic superintendent; makes recommendations for improvement of services; attends breakdowns and accidents.

May (01) deal directly with passengers' complaints

(02) drive omnibus in emergency

(03) call at passengers' homes to collect unpaid fares.

Additional factors: whether in possession of public service vehicle driver's licence or conductor's licence; number of workers supervised.

Other titles include Road inspector, Ticket inspector, Traffic regulator.

930 .20 Depot foreman (motor vehicles)

Directly supervises and co-ordinates the activities of motor vehicle drivers and road transport depot workers, other than vehicle maintenance workers

Performs appropriate tasks as described under SUPERVISOR/FOREMAN (UNSPECIFIED) (990 .00) and in addition: arranges for the servicing, refuelling, cleaning and repair of vehicles in depot; ensures that drivers carry out checks on vehicles before leaving depot; checks that goods have been correctly loaded on vehicle.

May (01) check drivers' log sheets and subsistence claims

(02) prepare wages sheets

(03) conduct road tests of applicants for employment as drivers.

Additional factors: whether in possession of driving licence of appropriate class; number of workers supervised.

Other titles include Traffic foreman, Vehicle foreman, Yard foreman.

930 .30 Depot foreman (horse-drawn vehicles)

Directly supervises and co-ordinates the activities of horse-drawn vehicle drivers and road transport depot workers, other than vehicle maintenance workers

Performs appropriate tasks as described under SUPERVISOR/FOREMAN (UNSPECIFIED) (990 .00) and in addition: arranges for the feeding, grooming, bedding down and general care of the horses; inspects the cleaning of harnesses and vehicles; checks the harnessing of horses to vehicles.

Additional factor: number of workers supervised.

Other titles include Carting foreman.

930 .98 Trainee

Performs, under instruction or guidance, various tasks including training exercises and as appropriate pursues studies in order to acquire the basic skills and knowledge required to perform the tasks of foremen and inspectors (road transport operating occupations).

930 .99 Other foremen and inspectors (road transport operating occupations)

Workers in this group supervise the activities of workers in road transport operating occupations and perform inspecting tasks in road transport operating and are not elsewhere classified.

Unit Group 931 Omnibus and Coach Drivers

Workers in this unit group drive road passenger-carrying vehicles such as omnibuses, motor coaches, minibuses, trolley buses and tramcars.

See 933 for drivers of taxis and similar vehicles.

931 .10 Omnibus driver, Coach driver

Drives omnibus or motor coach to transport passengers by road

Checks tyres, lights, brakes and fuel and water levels before journey commences; drives single- or double-decked vehicle over predetermined route with due regard to other traffic and traffic regulations; stops at pre-arranged places or when signalled by conductor or passengers to allow passengers to board or alight; keeps to time schedules.

May (01) undertake emergency repairs

(02) operate automatic doors

(03) load and unload passengers' luggage

(04) comment to tourists on places of interest on route

(05) on tours liaise with hotel and catering establishments.

Additional factor: whether accustomed to driving over Continental routes.

Note: must possess public service vehicle driver's licence of appropriate class if carrying passengers for hire or reward in addition to ordinary driving licence—see Note following minor group definition.

Excluded are fare-collecting drivers (931 .20)

931.20 Driver (one-man-operated omnibus)

Drives omnibus, motor coach or minibus, collects fares and controls passengers

Performs appropriate tasks as described under OMNIBUS DRIVER (931.10) and in addition: controls passengers entering and leaving vehicle; observes regulations concerning number of passengers carried and carriage of animals or parcels; collects fares from passengers and issues or checks tickets as necessary using machine, or ensures that passengers insert fare in machine to release turnstile or insert ticket in machine for cancelling; completes way-bill; balances cash with way-bill at end of duty and hands cash and way-bill to cashier; changes destination indicators as necessary.

May (01) undertake emergency repairs

(02) give passengers change for use in machine

(03) deliver newspapers and parcels on country routes

(04) operate automatic doors.

Other titles include Minibus driver.

Note: must possess public service vehicle driver's licence of appropriate class if carrying passengers for hire or reward, in addition to ordinary driving licence—see Note following minor group definition.

931.98 Trainee

Performs, under instruction or guidance, various tasks including training exercises and as appropriate pursues studies in order to acquire the basic skills and knowledge required to perform the tasks of omnibus and coach drivers.

931.99 Other omnibus and coach drivers

Workers in this group drive road passenger-carrying vehicles and are not elsewhere classified, for example:

(01) **Tramcar drivers** (drive electrically powered tramcars along rail tracks on roads); (02) **Trolley bus drivers** (drive omnibuses obtaining power from overhead electric cables).

Unit Group 932 Heavy Goods Vehicle Drivers

Workers in this unit group drive vehicles with rigid chassis with an unladen weight of more than three tons and articulated vehicles to transport goods and animals by road.

932.10 Heavy goods vehicle driver (excluding articulated vehicle)

Drives motor vehicle with rigid chassis and exceeding three tons unladen weight to transport goods or animals by road

Checks tyres, lights, brakes, fuel and oil and water levels before journey commences; drives vehicle between depot and loading and unloading points with due regard to other traffic, traffic regulations and time schedules; assists with loading and unloading of vehicle using lifting or tipping equipment as necessary; checks that load is evenly distributed, properly secured by ropes, chains or other securing devices and where necessary protected by waterproof covers; maintains record of journey times, mileage and hours worked; keeps vehicle clean and undertakes minor running repairs. Performs these duties in relation to a heavy goods vehicle.

May (01) drive a heavy goods vehicle with automatic transmission

(02) drive a heavy goods vehicle with more than four wheels

(03) drive vehicle drawing a trailer

(04) check load against invoice or delivery note

(05) use automatic weighing equipment when delivering coal

(06) as Tanker driver, fill container with acid, beer, milk, oil, petrol or other liquid or powder, or discharge contents of container, where necessary connecting earth wire to chassis of vehicle to discharge static electricity as a precaution against fire or explosion.

Other titles include Cattle wagon driver, Coal delivery driver, Furniture van driver, Tipper driver.

Note: must possess heavy goods vehicle driver's licence of appropriate class in addition to ordinary driving licence—see Note following minor group definition.

Excluded are Roundsmen (362)

932 .20 Articulated vehicle driver

Drives articulated motor vehicle to transport goods or animals by road

Performs appropriate tasks as described under HEAVY GOODS VEHICLE DRIVER (932 .10) but in relation to driving an articulated motor vehicle (motor tractive unit with trailer, part of the weight of the latter being taken by the chassis of the tractive unit); couples and/or uncouples trailer to or from tractive unit; connects brake, lighting and other control cables between units; changes trailer registration plates as necessary; drives with special skill while negotiating narrow passages, turning or reversing.

May (01) drive an articulated vehicle with automatic transmission

(02) drive an articulated vehicle with tractive unit which exceeds two tons unladen weight

(03) check load against invoice or delivery note

(04) tow trailer with abnormal load and be assisted by steersman or brakeman operating a steering unit or braking equipment behind the trailer.

(05) as Tanker driver, fill container with acid, beer, milk, oil, petrol or other liquid or powder, or discharge contents of container, where necessary connecting earth wire to chassis of vehicle to discharge static electricity as a precaution against fire or explosion

(06) drive tractive unit to tow trailer connected by draw bar and be known as Tractor driver.

Note: must possess heavy goods vehicle driver's licence of appropriate class in addition to ordinary driving licence—see Note following minor group definition.

932 .98 Trainee

Performs, under instruction or guidance, various tasks including training exercises and as appropriate pursues studies in order to acquire the basic skills and knowledge required to perform the tasks of heavy goods vehicle drivers.

932 .99 Other heavy goods vehicle drivers

Workers in this group drive rigid vehicles with an unladen weight of more than three tons and articulated vehicles and are not elsewhere classified, for example:

(01) **Brakemen** (travel on unit behind the load and operate braking equipment operating on wheels on that unit); (02) **Steersmen** (travel on unit behind the load and operate steering equipment controlling wheels on that unit).

Unit Group 933 Other Motor Vehicle Drivers

Workers in this unit group drive motor vehicles of three tons or less unladen weight (excluding articulated vehicles) to transport goods, drive motor cars for private individuals, government departments and industrial organisations and for private hire, drive taxis for public hire, drive new cars to delivery and shipping points, drive motor cycles and other motor vehicles and are not elsewhere classified.

See 443 .20 for Ambulance driver-attendants.

933 .10 Light goods vehicle driver

Drives motor vehicle of three tons or less unladen weight (excluding articulated vehicle) to transport goods or animals by road

Performs tasks as described under HEAVY GOODS VEHICLE DRIVER (932 .10) but in respect of vehicle of three tons or less unladen weight (excluding articulated vehicle).

May (01) drive vehicle with automatic transmission

(02) collect payment for goods delivered

(03) check load against invoice or delivery note

(04) drive armoured vehicle for transport of cash or valuables and report details of movements by radio to controlling office.

Other titles include Van driver.

Note: must possess driving licence of appropriate class.

Excluded are Roundsmen (362)

933 .20 Taxi driver

Plies for hire and drives taxi to transport passengers by road

Drives passenger-carrying taxi with due regard to other traffic and traffic regulations; collects passengers in response to hand signals, telephone or radio telephone messages; conveys passengers to required destination by most direct route; collects fares based on fixed tariff; assists with loading and unloading of luggage; cleans cab and carries out running repairs.

May (01) drive vehicle with automatic transmission.

Additional factor: whether in possession of certificate of Institute of Advanced Motorists.

Notes (i) must possess driving licence of appropriate class

(ii) must possess hackney carriage licence.

933 .30 Motor car driver

Drives motor car for private individual, government department or industrial organisation or for private hire, to transport passengers by road, or drives new car to delivery or shipping point

Drives motor car with due regard to other traffic and traffic regulations; where appropriate collects passengers and assists them to enter car, loads and unloads luggage, conveys passengers to their destination as instructed and assists them to leave car; cleans car and carries out running repairs.

May (01) drive vehicle with automatic transmission
(02) collect payment from passengers
(03) act as coffin bearer if driver of car for funeral
(04) undertake gardening duties and be known as Chauffeur-gardener
(05) undertake household duties and be known as Chauffeur-handyman.

Additional factor: whether in possession of certificate of Institute of Advanced Motorists.

Other titles include Chauffeur, Car delivery driver.

Note: must possess driving licence of appropriate class.

933 .40 Mechanical road sweeper driver

Drives vehicle with left-hand drive along kerbside to spray road with water and sweep and collect refuse from roadside

Inspects vehicle before leaving depot and fills water tank at supply point; drives to starting point of route; operates levers to rotate brushes and release water on to road and to start suction equipment; drives slowly along road, close to kerb-side, sweeping and collecting refuse; returns to depot and disposes of refuse.

May (01) operate equipment to clean gullies and drains.

Note: must possess driving licence of appropriate class.

933 .50 Road patrolman

Drives a mini-van to patrol roads in a defined area and renders assistance to members of his organisation in difficulties

Accepts calls for help in response to hand signals or radio telephone messages; diagnoses fault in vehicle and carries out minor mechanical repairs; supplies or arranges for the supply of petrol, oil, water and spare parts; where necessary arranges for conveyance of vehicle to a garage; renders first aid in cases of sickness or accident; gives advice to motorists on matters such as routes, road conditions, places of interest and accommodation; erects directional notices to special events, alternative routes or warning notices of road hazards; assists police to direct traffic and organise parking at special events; notifies his headquarters of motoring hazards such as adverse weather conditions and items of interest noticed on patrol; keeps record of accident reports; recruits new members to his motoring association.

May (01) drive vehicle with automatic transmission
(02) assist motorists who are non-members.

Note: must possess driving licence of appropriate class.

933 .98 Trainee

Performs, under instruction or guidance, various tasks including training exercises and as appropriate pursues studies in order to acquire the basic skills and knowledge required to perform the tasks of other motor vehicle drivers.

933 .99 Other motor vehicle drivers not elsewhere classified

Workers in this group drive motor vehicles and are not separately classified.

Unit Group 934 Conductors (Road Transport)

Workers in this unit group collect fares, issue tickets and control passengers on public service vehicles.

934 .10 Conductor (public service vehicle)

Collects fares, issues tickets and controls passengers on public service vehicle

Controls passengers entering and leaving vehicle; observes regulations concerning number of passengers carried and carriage of animals or parcels; gives driver starting and stopping signals; guides driver when reversing; collects fares from passengers and issues or checks tickets; completes way-bill at scheduled points on route to show the time and number of tickets issued; balances cash with way-bill at end of duty and hands cash and way-bill to cashier; changes destination indicators as necessary; takes charge of property found on vehicle.

May (01) deliver newspapers and parcels on country routes
(02) engage trolley with overhead power wires if employed on tram or trolley bus.

Other titles include Bus conductor.

Note: must possess public service vehicle conductor's licence.

934 .98 Trainee

Performs, under instruction or guidance, various tasks including training exercises and as appropriate pursues studies in order to acquire the basic skills and knowledge required to perform the tasks of conductors (road transport).

Unit Group 935 Drivers' Mates (Road Transport)

Workers in this unit group accompany drivers of motorised and other road vehicles and assist with the loading and unloading of vehicles.

935 .10 Driver's mate

Accompanies driver of motorised or other road vehicle and assists with the loading and unloading of vehicle

Accompanies driver of motorised or horse-drawn vehicle on journey; assists driver to load and unload vehicle; where necessary secures goods to prevent movement or damage during journey; guides driver when reversing or manoeuvring; assists driver to clean vehicle and undertake running repairs; carries out other tasks as directed by driver.

May (01) act as relief driver
(02) assist with filling and weighing of sacks of coal for delivery using automatic weighing equipment
(03) perform stable duties and be known as Drayman's mate.

Additional factor: whether in possession of driving licence.

Other titles include Motor attendant, Second man, Van boy.

See Loader (vehicle) (959 .65)

935 .98 Trainee

Performs, under instruction or guidance, various tasks including training exercises and as appropriate pursues studies in order to acquire the basic skills and knowledge required to perform the tasks of drivers' mates (road transport).

Unit Group 939 Road Transport Operating Occupations Not Elsewhere Classified

Workers in this unit group drive horses and horse-drawn vehicles and perform miscellaneous road transport operating tasks and are not elsewhere classified.

939.10 Driver (horse-drawn vehicle)

Drives vehicle drawn by one or more horses to transport goods or passengers by road

Grooms horse, and harnesses and hitches to vehicle; drives to depot and, where appropriate, loads vehicle with goods manually or using mechanical equipment, chute, etc; ensures that goods are evenly distributed and properly secured or that passengers are protected from the weather; drives to delivery point and assists with unloading of goods, or helps passengers to alight; cleans vehicle and harness.

May (01) feed and water horses
(02) clean stables
(03) shoe horses
(04) collect payment for goods delivered or passengers carried
(05) prepare horse and equipment and attend horse shows and parades.

Additional factor: possession of hackney carriage licence for conveyance of passengers.

Other titles include Cabman (horse-drawn vehicle), Carter, Coachman, Drayman.

939.98 Trainee

Performs, under instruction or guidance, various tasks including training exercises and as appropriate pursues studies in order to acquire the basic skills and knowledge required to perform the tasks of workers in road transport operating occupations not elsewhere classified.

939.99 Other road transport operating occupations not elsewhere classified

Workers in this group perform miscellaneous tasks in road transport operating and are not separately classified, for example:

(01) **Horsemen (timber haulage)** (drive horses to drag felled timber); (02) **Pony drivers (mine)** (drive horses or ponies to haul trams or tubs along railed tracks in mine).

Minor Group 94 CIVIL ENGINEERING AND MATERIALS HANDLING EQUIPMENT OPERATING OCCUPATIONS

Workers in this minor group operate earth moving, pile driving and road surfacing equipment, operate cranes, hoists, winches, conveyor systems, loading machines and other equipment to move loads, drive trucks in factories, warehouses and on sites and perform closely related tasks including the operation of machinery and equipment to charge and empty blast furnaces and load and unload road and rail containers.

The occupations are arranged in the following unit groups:

940 Foremen (Civil Engineering and Materials Handling Equipment Operating Occupations)

941 Earth Moving and Civil Engineering Equipment Operating Occupations

942 Crane, Hoist and Other Materials Handling Equipment Operating Occupations

949 Civil Engineering and Materials Handling Equipment Operating Occupations Not Elsewhere Classified

Unit Group 940 Foremen (Civil Engineering and Materials Handling Equipment Operating Occupations)

Workers in this unit group directly supervise and co-ordinate the activities of workers operating civil engineering and materials handling equipment.

940.10 Foreman (earth moving and civil engineering equipment operating occupations)

Directly supervises and co-ordinates the activities of workers operating earth moving and civil engineering equipment

Performs appropriate tasks as described under SUPERVISOR/FOREMAN (UNSPECIFIED) (990.00).

Additional factor: number of workers supervised.

Other titles include Dredgermaster.

940.20 Foreman (crane, hoist and other materials handling equipment operating occupations)

Directly supervises and co-ordinates the activities of workers operating cranes, hoists and other materials handling equipment

Performs appropriate tasks as described under SUPERVISOR/FOREMAN (UNSPECIFIED) (990.00).

Additional factor: number of workers supervised.

940.98 Trainee

Performs, under instruction or guidance, various tasks including training exercises and as appropriate pursues studies in order to acquire the basic skills and knowledge required to perform the tasks of foremen (civil engineering and materials handling equipment operating occupations).

940.99 Other foremen (civil engineering and materials handling equipment operating occupations)

Workers in this group directly supervise and co-ordinate the activities of workers operating civil engineering and materials handling equipment and are not elsewhere classified.

Unit Group 941 Earth Moving and Civil Engineering Equipment Operating Occupations

Workers in this unit group operate machines to excavate, grade, level and compact earth, gravel, sand and similar materials, drive piles into the ground and lay surfaces of asphalt and concrete.

Note: drivers of mechanically propelled vehicles which traverse public roads must possess driving licence of appropriate class.

Excluded are Concrete mixer drivers (592.92) and Dumper drivers (942.64)

941.10 Pile driver

Sets up and operates as member of a team, pile driving equipment to hammer piles into the ground as foundations for structures such as buildings, bridges, dams and docks

Performs some or all of the following tasks: ascertains job requirements from site plans; marks starting point of piling with pick or hammers wooden peg into ground; signals to crane driver to lift piling rig or frame and guides it into position; bolts metal parts, nails wooden supports or fixes ropes to secure frame or directs the performance of these tasks; checks distances and angles between frame supports and ground using rule and plumb-line; measures and marks wooden, concrete or steel piles at intervals, as guide to progress of pile driving; signals to crane driver to lift and position pile in frame; positions sleeve or helmet over top of pile; signals crane driver to lift and guide hammer into sleeve; manipulates controls to start engine and regulate power to raise and drop hammer and force pile into ground; watches progress and adjusts engine and hammer as necessary; repeats operation until piles have been driven to required depth; cleans and greases grooves on steel sheet piles; climbs ladder or rides in safety chair to top of sheet piles to guide piles into position and ensure that edges of adjacent piles interlock.

May (01) extract piling using a vibration unit.

Other titles include Hammerman, Topman.

941.20 Driver (asphalt spreading machine)

Drives tracked or wheeled machine to spread and level hot asphalt on road surfaces

Fixes extensions or cut-offs to screed plates, screw spreader and tamper according to width of surface to be covered; lights burners to heat screed plate; signals to lorry driver to tip asphalt into machine hopper; pulls levers to start conveyor system and watches progress of material from hopper to conveyor; starts engine and drives machine slowly forward following contour of road or guide line; directs re-filling of machine hopper, as necessary; cleans, oils and greases machine and carries out minor repairs.

May (01) fix or dismantle automatic levelling device assisted by leveller

(02) specialise in driving a particular type or make of machine and be known accordingly.

Other titles include Driver (road surface laying machine).

941.30 Leveller (asphalt spreading machine)

Operates controls of spreading machine to regulate depth of asphalt being laid

Assists driver to fix or remove extensions or cut-offs to screed plates, screw spreader and tamper; stands at rear of machine and operates hand wheels to raise or lower screed plate to give specified depth of material to be laid; watches flow of material from conveyor to spreader screw; measures depth of layer with metal dipstick and adjusts height of screed plate as necessary; cleans, oils and greases machine.

May (01) set automatic levelling device and check its operation

(02) specialise in operating a particular type or make of machine and be known accordingly.

Other titles include Plateman, Screwman.

941.50 Road roller driver

Drives motor road roller to compact, level and smooth layers of surfacing material on roads, pavements, runways and similar surfaces

Fills rollers with water or sand to specified weight; adjusts steering chain and scrapers (iron bars fitted near rollers to remove material adhering to rollers); moves levers and hand wheels to control and guide machine; drives machine backwards and forwards to compact rubble and waste material on to existing surface or to compact and smooth asphalt; operates mechanism to spray water on to rollers to prevent adhesion of asphalt; pulls levers to lower attachments such as scarifiers (iron spikes which break or roughen road surface to provide a key for new material) and cutters (a wheel used to cut a straight edge on newly laid surface to eliminate overlap with next section to be laid); cleans, greases and oils machine.

May (01) drive vibratory roller.

Additional factor: maximum weight of roller to which accustomed.

Other titles include Diesel roller driver, Motor roller driver, Steam roller driver.

Note: must possess driving licence of appropriate class.

941.55 Dredger driver

Operates excavating equipment mounted on a floating vessel to remove gravel, sand and sludge from the bottom of a stretch of water

Receives instructions from dredger foreman regarding area and depth to be dredged; manipulates levers, pedals and switches to lower arms or jib supporting suction pipes, grab-bucket or bucket chain to bottom of river, canal, dock or harbour; starts or directs the starting of motors to activate suction pumps or bucket chain or operates levers to close jaws of grab-bucket and raises load; watches operations and removes objects liable to obstruct mechanism; directs flow of sludge to hopper on or alongside dredging vessel; deposits sand or gravel on shore or on lorries; stops mechanism when hopper is filled; takes periodic soundings of depth of water using plumb-line or rod.

May (01) direct sailing dredger to working position

(02) moor vessel to buoys or to river or canal bank

(03) deposit sludge on shore to reclaim land

(04) grease and oil machinery.

Other titles include Dredgerman.

Note: ship's officers and seamen engaged in deck and engine room duties on dredgers are classified in minor groups 24 and 91.

941 .60 Grader driver

Drives wheeled machine with scraper or scoop mounted underneath to level ground for the construction of roads, airport runways, buildings and similar purposes

Operates levers to regulate height and angle of blade according to nature of surface; manoeuvres vehicle to scrape loose earth or stone from surface of high ground or to transfer earth or stone from high ground to low ground, thereby levelling surface; repeats operations and traverses ground until specified level or incline is obtained; undertakes day-to-day maintenance of machine.

Additional factor: maximum size (eg horse power) of vehicle to which accustomed.

941 .65 Mechanical excavator driver

Drives and operates tracked or wheeled machine with moveable bucket to excavate and move earth, gravel, rock, sand, or other material, or dig ditches, shafts or trenches

Positions machine at working area on building site, in quarry, etc and lowers hydraulic jacks as necessary to support and steady machine, or operates levers and pedals to drive machine along line of ditch or trench; moves levers to lower arm or jib and push bucket into material; raises bucket upright and rotates arm; tilts bucket or operates bucket-opening mechanism to deposit material into lorry or conveyor or at side of trench; repeats operations as necessary; undertakes day-to-day maintenance of machine.

May (01) operate machine to dig above level of excavator and be known as Face shovel operator

(02) operate excavator fitted with special-purpose equipment and be known accordingly, eg Back acter operator, Back hoe operator, Drag line operator, Grab-bucket operator, Trench digging machine operator.

Additional factors: maximum bucket capacity to which accustomed; maximum length of jib to which accustomed.

Other titles include Digger driver, Navvy driver.

941 .70 Mechanical shovel driver

Drives and operates tracked or wheeled vehicle with shovel or bucket to load and transport earth, rock or other materials

Drives vehicle to working area; operates levers to lower shovel at front of vehicle and force shovel into pile of material; operates levers to move loaded shovel to upright position and raise shovel; drives to lorry or stockpile; operates levers to tilt shovel and drop contents into lorry or on to stockpile; repeats operations and advances machine into pile as removal progresses; oils and greases machine.

May (01) drive mechanical shovel equipped with additional bucket at rear for digging trenches.

Additional factor: maximum shovel capacity to which accustomed.

Other titles include Front end loader operator, Loader operator.

941 .90 Bulldozer driver

Drives tracked or wheeled machine with concave steel blade across front to move, distribute or level earth, or to move rocks, trees or other obstacles

Drives vehicle forward and operates levers to regulate height of blade from ground; estimates depth of cut by feel of lever and stalling action of engine; drives in successive passes over ground to level earth to specification and remove all obstacles; undertakes day-to-day maintenance of machine.

May (01) drive vehicle equipped with an angled blade to push material to one side, eg angledozer or snowplough

(02) level site following demolition of buildings.

Additional factor: maximum size (eg horse power) of vehicle to which accustomed.

Other titles include Angledozer driver.

941.92 Operator (concrete paving machine)

Drives and operates a paving machine to spread, tamp and level concrete on surfaces such as roadways and runways

Starts machine and manipulates levers to control movement of machine along railed tracks at sides of work area until machine is positioned over section to be concreted; turns wheels to set height of hopper and spreader and to control thickness of concrete; signals to lorry driver to tip ready-mixed concrete into hopper; manipulates levers to control wheeled hopper moving slowly along bridging beams spanning work area; watches flow of concrete through hopper and assists flow with hand shovel; switches panel controls to operate vibrator which tamps concrete to expel trapped air; repeats traverse with appropriate attachment to produce required surface, eg smooth or striated.

941.94 Sprayer (tar, bitumen)

Operates equipment mounted on motor vehicle to spray tar or bitumen on road surfaces

Fills tank with tar or bitumen; on site, starts engine to operate pumps; lights oil burner and regulates heat to maintain tar or bitumen at specified temperature; visually checks temperature and pressure gauges; stands on platform at rear of vehicle and opens and closes valves regulating flow of tar or bitumen to jets in spray bar at rear of vehicle; regulates flow to obtain even distribution of tar or bitumen on road surface; closes a number of jets at end of spray bar when a narrow strip of road is to be tarred; signals to driver when to start and stop vehicle.

May (01) use hand-operated lance spray for small areas

(02) clean jets in spray bar.

941.98 Trainee

Performs, under instruction or guidance, various tasks including training exercises and as appropriate pursues studies in order to acquire the basic skills and knowledge required to perform the tasks of workers in earth moving and civil engineering equipment operating occupations.

941.99 Other earth moving and civil engineering equipment operating occupations

Workers in this group operate machines to excavate, grade, level and compact earth, gravel, sand and similar materials, drive piles into the ground and lay surfaces of asphalt and concrete and are not elsewhere classified, for example:

(01) **Ballast cleaning machine operators** (operate machines to clean ballast); (02) **Chipping machine operators (road surfacing)** (operate machines to spread stone chippings on freshly tarred or asphalted road surface); (03) **Pedestrian-controlled roller operators** (walk beside and drive roller to compact surfacing material on pavements, roads, etc); (04) **Pneumatic drill operators** (operate portable pneumatic machines with attachments to break, cut or tamp road surfaces); (05) **Scraper drivers** (operate machines with steel blade mounted beneath to scrape earth, stone, etc into container on machine); (06) **Slipform paver drivers** (drive and operate self-propelled tracked machines to lay continuous strip of concrete); (07) **Tamping, levelling and/or lining machine operators** (operate machines to tamp and level ballast and/or align tracks); (08) **Track laying machine operators** (operate machines to lay railway lines).

Unit Group 942 Crane, Hoist and Other Materials Handling Equipment Operating Occupations

Workers in this unit group operate cranes, hoists, winches, conveyor systems, aerial ropeways and other equipment to move loads, drive and operate multi-purpose trucks in factories, warehouses and on sites to transfer material, drive and operate machines to charge and empty blast furnaces, coke ovens and similar industrial equipment and perform closely related tasks.

Note: drivers of vehicles which traverse public roads must possess driving licence of appropriate class.

See Bridge man (919.60)

942.05 Winding engineman (mine)

Operates power-driven hoisting machinery to raise and lower mine cages carrying workers, tubs or other equipment or materials

Starts motor from control cabin in engine-house and manipulates levers and switches to raise, lower, stop or control speed of cage; raises or lowers cage on receipt of bell or light signals from banksman (mine) at top of shaft and onsetter (mine) at bottom of shaft; watches control panel for warning lights and indicators recording brake pressure, rate of winding and depth of cage in shaft; stops motor when indicator shows that cage has reached required level; reports faults to maintenance workers and makes test run with empty cage when faults have been rectified.

May (01) communicate with banksman and onsetter by telephone

(02) operate two counterbalanced cages travelling in opposite directions.

Other titles include Engine winder.

942.10 Cageman

Gives signals for movement of cage used to raise and lower men, materials or equipment between surface and underground levels and loads and unloads cage

(01) **Banksman (mine)**

Opens cage and shaft gates at top of shaft manually or by remote control and lowers bridge across gap between surface, and cage floor; marshals passengers travelling in cage and searches for cigarettes, matches and other prohibited articles; prevents overloading of cage; operates levers to change rail track points and releases brakes or sprags from wheels of tubs; pushes tubs into cage manually or operates hydraulic or pneumatic rams; secures tubs to prevent movement in cage; raises bridge and closes cage and shaft gates; signals to onsetter and winding engineman, using approved signalling code, when upper cage is ready for moving; where necessary communicates by telephone to supplement signals and relay messages; reports faulty equipment, delays or accidents to maintenance workers or to haulage foreman.

Other titles include Shaft top attendant.

(02) **Onsetter (mine)**

Performs appropriate tasks as described under Banksman (mine) but in relation to the loading and unloading of cages at shaft bottom or at underground landing levels; organises escape procedure in emergency.

Other titles include Shaft bottom attendant.

May (03) collect identity tokens from passengers

(04) grease and oil gate hinges and closing mechanism

(05) clean work area and remove spillage.

942.15 Bunker control man (underground)

Controls the operation of automated equipment in mine to transfer materials from underground conveyors to bunkers and tubs

Confirms by telephone that each conveyor section is ready to start operating; switches on television cameras and receivers and starts conveyors; watches television screen which shows each transfer point in rotation and watches for damaged conveyors, excessive spillage or obstructions; where necessary, tunes second screen manually to show any part of conveyor system requiring closer scrutiny; asks belt patrol man by telephone to investigate irregularities; as necessary stops appropriate conveyors to regulate feed to main bunker.

942.20 Bunker control man (surface)

Controls the operation of automated equipment to transfer material from surface bunkers to rail trucks

Starts conveyor to fill main bunker with material, for example coal; watches filling operations on screen and switches off when bunker is full; sets dials and switches on control panel to number and capacity of trucks to be loaded; sets main switch to automatic control to start sequence of operations to fill loading hoppers with specified weight of material from main bunker and to signal locomotive driver to position empty trucks beneath loading hoppers; watches progress of operations on screen and control panel; when trucks are in position, operates control to open hopper doors to release material into trucks; repeats cycle of operations until train is fully loaded; sets main switch to manual control when breakdown occurs and operations are performed manually by other workers.

May (01) clear spillage from work area and track switching devices.

942.25 Manipulator driver

Drives and operates mobile machine equipped with arms or jaws to lift and position billets of metal in furnace, and to remove, transport and place hot billets on forging anvil

Starts machine and drives to stockpile or receives billets of metal from crane or truck; manipulates controls to open hydraulic arms or jaws and to grip sides of billet; raises arms holding billet clear of obstructions and drives to position in front of furnace; places billet in furnace, lowers arms, releases grip and reverses machine leaving billet in furnace; returns to furnace when billet has reached required temperature; grips billet with arms, raises and carries it to anvil; positions billet on anvil by lowering, tilting or rotating arms; carries completed forging to crane or truck for disposal.

May (01) hold billet in position or re-position billet on anvil
(02) drive manipulator on railed tracks
(03) grease, oil and clean machine.

Additional factor: maximum weight of billet lifted.

942.30 Straddle carrier driver

Drives equipment which straddles, lifts and moves containers and long bulky loads

Drives mobile carrier into position astride container or other load; manipulates controls to secure container with grappling device or to lower hooks or other holding equipment for ground workers to attach load; lifts loads and drives carrier to specified position; lowers container and releases grappling device or lowers load for ground workers to detach hook or other holding equipment.

May (01) stack containers.

Additional factors: maximum loading capacity to which accustomed; maximum height to which accustomed to lift.

942.50 Jib crane driver

Operates crane with lifting equipment suspended from end of mobile jib to lift, mvoe and lower equipment, machinery or materials

Starts motor from control cabin of crane and checks that cables run freely; manipulates levers, pedals and switches to raise or lower jib and to rotate jib so that hook, bucket, grab or other holding equipment is above load; lowers lifting equipment for ground workers to attach load or operates grab or bucket mechanism; lifts load and watches indicators showing angle of jib and safe load carrying capacity of crane; rotates jib to move load to specified position and lowers load for ground workers to detach, or releases load from grab or bucket; greases and oils crane and inspects ropes.

May (01) operate crane in response to signals from other workers
(02) drive crane along rails or fixed track
(03) operate crane carrying heavy weight which is dropped from a height to break up stone or scrap metal and be known as Drop ball operator.

Additional factors: maximum loading capacity to which accustomed; maximum length of jib to which accustomed.

Other titles include Derrick crane driver.

Excluded are Tower crane drivers (942.52) and Mobile crane drivers (942.54)

942 .52 Tower crane driver

Operates crane with lifting equipment mounted on horizontally rotating jib on tower to lift, move and lower equipment, machinery or materials

Starts motor from control cabin of crane and checks that cables run freely; manipulates levers, pedals and switches to rotate jib, move lifting equipment along jib and raise and lower hook, bucket or other holding equipment; positions holding equipment above load and lowers for ground workers to attach load; lifts load and watches indicators showing safe load carrying capacity of crane; swings jib and/or moves bogie to move load to specified position; lowers load for ground workers to detach; watches instruments showing wind speed and direction, and takes safety precautions as necessary by repositioning jib, reducing load or ceasing operations; greases and oils crane and inspects ropes.

May (01) operate crane in response to signals from other workers
(02) drive tower crane mounted on wheels or crawler tracks
(03) assist in erecting and dismantling crane on site.

Additional factors: maximum loading capacity to which accustomed; maximum length of jib to which accustomed.

942 .54 Mobile crane driver

Drives and operates jib crane mounted on wheeled or tracked motor vehicle to lift, move and lower machinery, equipment or materials

Performs appropriate tasks as described under JIB CRANE DRIVER (942 .50) and in addition: positions vehicle within easy access of load; checks that vehicle is standing on level surface or operates screw or hydraulic jacks fitted to vehicle or to retractable beams to take weight of crane from vehicle wheels and make crane turntable level.

May (01) with assistance, erect jib on site by bolting sections together
(02) estimate weight of load to be lifted
(03) move load to required position by driving vehicle, taking care to keep load steady
(04) demolish wall or building by swinging heavy weight suspended from jib against wall or building.

Additional factors: maximum loading capacity to which accustomed; maximum length of jib to which accustomed.

942 .56 Overhead crane driver

Operates crane with lifting equipment mounted on overhead bridge which runs on rails to lift, move and lower equipment, machinery or materials

Starts crane motor and checks that cables run freely; manipulates levers, pedals or switches to move bridge along rails and lifting equipment along bridge to loading point; lowers hook, magnet, suction plate or other holding equipment for ground workers to attach load, or operates device to grip load; visually checks that fixing is secure and checks by raising load a short distance; raises and moves load to required position; releases grip on load or lowers load for ground workers to detach.

May (01) help to attach load (942 .76)
(02) oil and grease equipment
(03) operate crane in response to signals from other workers
(04) signal warning to other workers of approach of crane
(05) operate crane to pour molten metal into moulds and be known as Ladle engineman
(06) operate dock-side crane to load containers on to ships and be known as Portainer driver
(07) operate motor driving light car and lifting equipment suspended from and running on girder or aerial cable and be known as Telpher driver.

Additional factor: maximum loading capacity to which accustomed.

Other titles include Billet crane driver, Discharger crane driver, Gantry crane driver, Ladle crane driver, Vacuum rack operator (asbestos-cement).

942.58 Hoist driver

Operates power-driven stationary engine which winds cable round drum to raise or lower cage (other than mine cage), container, platform or sling carrying materials or workers

Operates controls at ground level, at top of hoist or in hoist cage to start motor and checks that cables and hoisting equipment run freely; manipulates switches, levers or ropes to raise, lower, stop or control speed of cage, container, platform or sling; loads or directs the loading of cage, container, platform or sling; opens and closes gates as appropriate.

May (01) operate hoist in response to signals from other workers

(02) operate hoist to raise tubs and feed materials into blast furnace and be known as Hoistman (blast furnace)

(03) perform general labouring tasks.

Additional factor: maximum loading capacity to which accustomed.

Excluded are Lift attendants (459.30)

942.60 Winch driver

Operates power-driven stationary engine which winds cable round drum(s) to haul objects, tubs or trams carrying materials or workers on horizontal or inclined roads or rail tracks

Checks that cables, winch drum and brake are working freely; connects or directs connecting of end of cable to object or load to be moved; starts engine and manipulates handle to turn winding drum and pull or raise object or load into position; moves handles to control speed and applies brake to stop engine; watches rope to prevent overwinding; oils and greases ropes and bearings.

May (01) control engine on signals from other workers

(02) operate engine to haul tubs or trams in mine and be known as Haulage engineman (mine).

Other titles include Shore donkeyman.

942.62 Trolley driver, Lifting truck driver

Drives light motorised truck with platform, fork lift or pole to transport goods or materials in a factory, storeroom, warehouse or other establishment

(01) **Trolley driver**

Drives truck to location of load; loads or assists with loading of goods or materials on to truck using crane or other lifting equipment as necessary; drives to unloading position and unloads; oils and greases truck.

(02) **Lifting truck driver**

Performs tasks as described above and in addition: operates controls to position fork lift in baseboard or pallet and raise load; where necessary raises fork lift to desired height for stacking load in piles, on to shelves or road or rail vehicles, or to position materials for further processing.

May (03) couple and uncouple trailers

(04) recharge battery of electrically operated trucks

(05) drive truck with special attachments such as grips, clamps, push and pull devices.

Additional factors: maximum loading capacity to which accustomed; maximum height to which accustomed to lift.

Other titles include Fork lift truck driver, Stacker truck driver.

942.64 Dumper driver

Drives and operates motorised tipping truck to transfer bulk materials from one location to another on construction site, dumping site, mining area or storage yard

Positions dumper ready for filling from chute, excavator buckets, mechanical shovel or by other means; drives to unloading point; operates tipping mechanism to discharge load into chute, storage bin or on to dumping site; restores empty container to normal position and returns to loading point; cleans container.

May (01) load or unload dumper manually.

Additional factor: maximum loading capacity to which accustomed.

See Earth Moving and Civil Engineering Equipment Operating Occupations (941)

942.66 Charger car driver

Drives car with hopper(s) along railed track to transfer raw materials from stockyard or storage bins to furnace, mixing machine or other container

Ascertains job requirements from loading specification chart; manipulates controls to drive car along rails or moves car by remote control to stockyard or storage bins; positions car hopper under appropriate bin; operates mechanism to open bin door and deposit material in car hopper; closes bin door when specified amount has been transferred to hopper; repeats operations at other bins as specified; drives car to unloading position at mixing machine, furnace, skip or other container; pulls lever to open hopper doors or tilt hopper to discharge contents; cleans hoppers.

May (01) operate hoist to raise materials to top of furnace (942.58)

(02) direct the loading of materials manually into car hoppers

(03) weigh materials using weighbridge or scale fixed to car.

Other titles include Charger carman (coal-gas oven, coke oven), Coal charger (coal-gas oven, coke oven), Scale car driver, Transfer carman, Weigh car driver.

942.68 Charger driver (iron and steel)

Drives and operates machine to charge materials such as pig-iron and scrap metal into open hearth or electric furnace

Manipulates levers to control movement of machine and loading arm; engages arm of charging machine in slot of pan containing material and lifts pan; positions charging machine in front of furnace and signals to furnaceman to open furnace doors; operates ram to push pan into furnace and rotates pan to deposit material in required position; withdraws pan and disengages loading arm.

May (01) position brick-lined chute to direct flow of molten metal from ladle into furnace.

942.70 Cupola charger (foundry)

Transports prescribed quantities of coke, limestone, pig-iron, scrap iron, or other materials and charges cupola in which iron is melted

Shovels or directs shovelling of prescribed quantities of coke, limestone, pig-iron, scrap iron, or other materials into buckets or skips; operates controls to lift bucket, or run skip along rails, to charging platform and discharges contents into cupola; inspects level of materials in cupola periodically and re-charges as necessary.

May (01) operate hoist with electro-magnet to transport scrap iron or ignots.

Other titles include Charge weighman, Cupola back tenter.

942.72 Pusherman (coal-gas oven, coke oven)

Drives and operates mechanical ram to discharge hot coke from oven

Drives machine along rails to required position in front of oven; operates mechanism to remove top oven door; receives signals that bottom door and door in discharge side of oven have been removed and that guide and coke car are in position; manipulates controls to insert ram into oven and push coke out opposite side; withdraws ram and replaces door; signals to charger carman that oven is ready for re-charging; inserts leveller in top door and levels fresh charge of coal; secures door when oven is fully charged; records time oven is emptied.

Other titles include Ram driver, Ram man.

942.74 Coke carman (coal-gas oven, coke oven)

Drives coke car to carry hot coke from ovens to quenching station

Drives coke car along rails to specified oven; receives hot coke discharged from oven; drives car with coke to quenching station; operates equipment to spray measured amount of water over hot coke; drives car to coke wharf and deposits coke on wharf to cool; reverses car and repeats operation.

942.76 Crane slinger

Attaches chain, hook, rope, sling or other grappling attachment to load and/or to lifting equipment and signals to crane driver to lift, move and lower load

Selects and visually inspects chain, hooks, magnet, net, pallet, rope, sling or other grappling attachment according to weight and type of load to be moved; attaches chains, net, rope, slings to or round load and secures to crane hook or places electro-magnet or vacuum lifting device at approximate centre of load; signals by hand or whistle to crane driver to lift, move and lower load to required position; checks visually that load is correctly balanced; walks beside load being moved near ground level to ensure that route is clear and to warn other workers of approach; releases grappling attachment when load has been lowered.

May (01) assist driver to assemble parts of crane and/or lifting equipment

(02) ensure that slings and chains are maintained in serviceable condition.

Additional factor: maximum loading capacity to which accustomed.

Other titles include Banksman (crane).

See Docker (*952.10*)

942.78 Loader (bulk materials)

Operates semi-automatic or non-automatic equipment to fill road and/or rail trucks or containers with dry materials such as cement, coal, flour, gravel, sand or sugar

Performs some or all of the following tasks: checks that supply hoppers or bunkers are filled and that conveyor belt is operating; signals to driver to drive into loading position; removes or opens loading hatch on container; inserts chute or pipe from feed hopper into container or truck; operates switches to open hopper valve or door to allow material to flow by chute or conveyor into container or truck; watches instrument dials recording amount of material loaded; clears blockages from chute or conveyor belt; operates switches to close hopper valves or doors and stop flow of materials; withdraws chute or pipe and closes loading hatch.

May (01) weigh empty and loaded trucks on weighbridge

(02) clear spillage from work area

(03) load specified mixtures of materials.

Other titles include Batch mill attendant, Bunker control man (sand, gravel).

942.80 Operator (gathering arm loader)

Operates power loading tracked machine with gathering arms and conveyor to load coal, rock or similar materials into lorry or tub, or on to conveyor

Manipulates controls to start conveyor and operate gathering arms of loader; drives machine forward until gathering arms are in position at base of pile of material to be moved; signals to driver of lorry or tub to take up position under discharge end of conveyor; starts conveyor and operates gathering arms to sweep material on to moving conveyor; drives machine into pile of material as removal progresses and maintains steady flow of material into lorry or tub, or on to conveyor; stops machine when container is full; clears spillage.

Other titles include Power loader operator.

942.82 Conveyor operator

Controls conveyor(s) to load or unload vehicles or ships, or move materials or products between departments, processes or stockpiles

Starts conveyor or section of conveyor system; where appropriate loads or directs others to load conveyor; adjusts chute or gate or positions pipe into bin, hopper or stockpile to permit material to flow on to or from conveyor; operates controls to regulate rate of movement and routeing of materials or products according to control panel lights, signals from other workers or knowledge of process; clears or directs clearance of blockages using pole or bar; clears spillage; oils and greases equipment.

May (01) collect samples of materials for analysis

(02) operate conveyor by remote control

(03) operate bucket conveyor loader to load material on to conveyor in coal-mine and be known as Slusher operator.

Other titles include Belt attendant.

942.98 Trainee

Performs, under instruction or guidance, various tasks including training exercises and as appropriate pursues studies in order to acquire the basic skills and knowledge required to perform the tasks of workers in crane, hoist and other materials handling equipment operating occupations.

942.99 Other crane, hoist and materials handling equipment operating occupations

Workers in this group operate cranes, hoists, winches, conveyor systems, aerial ropeways and other equipment to move loads, drive and operate trucks in factories, warehouses and on sites to transfer material, drive and operate machines to charge and empty blast furnaces, coke ovens and similar industrial equipment and perform closely related tasks and are not elsewhere classified, for example:

(01) **Aerial ropeway operators;** (02) **Brakesmen (mine)** (control haulage ropes on self-acting inclines); (03) **Conveyor transfer point attendants** (control conveyor systems at intersections and clear blockages); (04) **Drivers (motorised hand trucks)** (walk beside and drive motorised trucks to transport goods and materials); (05) **Ingot car operators** (transport hot ingots from soaking pits to rolling mills); (06) **Turntable operators** (control rotation of turntables at junctions of roller conveyor systems to direct loads to appropriate conveyor lines); (07) **Wagon traverser operators** (control rail mounted platforms moving across ends of railway tracks and carrying filled coal wagons to designated tracks).

Unit Group 949 Civil Engineering and Materials Handling Equipment Operating Occupations Not Elsewhere Classified

Workers in this unit group perform miscellaneous tasks in the operation of civil engineering and materials handling equipment including refuelling aircraft, filling tankers with liquids and gases, and changing ropes on rope haulage systems and are not elsewhere classified.

949.10 Aircraft refueller

Refuels aircraft from mobile tanker

Ascertains from written or verbal instructions aircraft to be refuelled and type and quantity of fuel required; loads fuel into tanker at airport fuel depot as described under TANKER FILLER (949.50); drives loaded tanker to aircraft and positions in accordance with safety regulations; connects bonding wire (earth) from tanker to aircraft; unreels fuelling hose and connects nozzle to aircraft fuel intake point on wing or fuselage; operates controls on tanker to start fuel pump and opens valves to start flow of fuel to aircraft tanks; checks instruments on tanker indicating pressure, flow and quantity of fuel being discharged; closes valves on completion of fuelling and disconnects hose and bonding wire; records amount of fuel delivered; drives empty tanker back to depot for reloading.

949.50 Tanker filler (liquids, gases)

Operates equipment to fill road and/or rail tankers with liquids or gases

Performs some or all of the following tasks: checks that supply tanks contain sufficient liquid or gas; signals to tanker driver to drive to loading position; opens tanker inlet hatch and checks visually that tanker is empty and clean; checks that tanker outlet valves are closed; connects earth wire to tanker to discharge static electricity as precaution against explosion when filling with inflammable products; secures feed pipe to inlet valve; opens feed valve to allow product to flow into tanker; checks volume of load in tanker with dip-stick, by noting calibration markings inside tank, by flowmeter or pressure gauge readings, or presets automatic feed control; closes valves when tanker is filled; disconnects feed pipe and earth wire.

May (01) weigh empty and loaded tankers on weighbridge

(02) record temperature and specific gravity of liquids

(03) specialise in filling tanker with a particular product such as diesel oil, liquid oxygen or petrol.

Other titles include Liquid dispenser, Rail tanker filler, Road tanker filler.

See 841.05 for workers filling cylinders with gas and 952.30 for workers loading and discharging bulk liquid cargoes.

949 .55 Tippler operator

Operates mechanism to invert loaded containers and tip out contents

Sets rail track points to direct container to specified tippler; uncouples or directs assistant to uncouple container; adjusts brake or controls chain drive to guide container on to tippler; manipulates controls to secure container to tippler, to revolve tippler and invert container and tip out contents; restores tippler to original position and releases container; pushes container by hand or uses hydraulic or pneumatic ram, or restarts chain drive to move container from tippler.

May (01) keep records of receipt and dispatch of wagons
(02) visually check quality of materials received.

Other titles include Tub tippler operator, Wagon tippler operator.

949 .60 Coke guide man (coal-gas oven, coke oven)

Drives and operates equipment to remove and replace oven doors and position guide to direct flow of discharged coke into coke car

Drives machine along rails till door-removing mechanism is opposite oven and operates mechanism to remove oven door; moves guide into position over door opening to channel discharged coke from oven into coke car; signals to pusherman when coke car is in position alongside guide ready to receive coke; operates mechanism to replace oven door when oven has been emptied.

May (01) clear spillage
(02) assist in cleaning oven door.

949 .65 Rope runner

Accompanies sets of trams or tubs on rope haulage and changes ropes at junctions or at end of run

Couples trams or tubs together at sidings to form set or journey; secures end of haulage rope to end tram or tub; moves lever to set rail points to appropriate position; releases brakes or removes sprags from wheels of trams or tubs; signals to haulage engineman when trams or tubs are ready to move; walks alongside or rides on tram or tub to next junction or to end of run; applies brakes, inserts sprags in wheels, attaches chain to fixed post or otherwise secures trams or tubs while rope changing proceeds; detaches haulage rope and/or tail rope and attaches new rope(s); alters rail points to divert trams or tubs to appropriate rails; reports faulty equipment to foreman.

May (01) operate portable compressed air winch or other mechanical aid to draw rope ends together
(02) accompany trams carrying workers and be known as Train guard (ropes).

949 .98 Trainee

Performs, under instruction or guidance, various tasks including training exercises and as appropriate pursues studies in order to acquire the basic skills and knowledge required to perform the tasks of workers in civil engineering and materials handling equipment operating occupations not elsewhere classified.

949 .99 Other civil engineering and materials handling equipment operating occupations not elsewhere classified

Workers in this group perform miscellaneous tasks in the operation of civil engineering and materials handling equipment and are not separately classified, for example:

(01) **Banksmen's assistants (mine)** (assist banksmen (mine) to load and unload cages at top of mine shafts); (02) **Belt patrol men** (patrol stretch of conveyor system and clear blockages) (*see 664 .70 for Belt patrol men who undertake repair work*); (03) **Clippers (rope haulage)**, Shacklers (rope haulage) (couple or uncouple tubs to or from endless rope); (04) **Dredger drivers' mates** (assist dredger drivers generally); (05) **Onsetters' assistants** (assist onsetters (mine) to load and unload cages at bottom of mine shafts); (06) **Rope changers** (change ropes at junctions or sidings of rope haulage system).

Minor Group 95 TRANSPORT OPERATING, MATERIALS MOVING AND STORING AND RELATED OCCUPATIONS NOT ELSEWHERE CLASSIFIED

Workers in this minor group perform miscellaneous tasks in transport operating, store, select and issue, load, unload and convey materials, goods, equipment, baggage and other items, load and discharge cargoes and perform related tasks and are not elsewhere classified.

The occupations are arranged in the following unit groups:

950 Foremen (Transport Operating, Materials Moving and Storing and Related Occupations Not Elsewhere Classified)

951 Storekeepers, Warehousemen

952 Stevedores, Dockers and Related Occupations

959 Other Transport Operating, Materials Moving and Storing and Related Occupations

Unit Group 950 Foremen (Transport Operating, Materials Moving and Storing and Related Occupations Not Elsewhere Classified)

Workers in this unit group directly supervise and co-ordinate the activities of workers in transport operating, materials moving and storing and related occupations not elsewhere classified.

950.10 Foreman storekeeper

Directly supervises and co-ordinates the activities of storekeepers and warehousemen

Performs appropriate tasks as described under SUPERVISOR/FOREMAN (UNSPECIFIED) (990.00).

Additional factor: number of workers supervised.

Other titles include Warehouse keeper.

950.20 Foreman (stevedores, dockers and related occupations)

Directly supervises and co-ordinates the activities of stevedores, dockers and workers in related occupations

Performs appropriate tasks as described under SUPERVISOR/FOREMAN (UNSPECIFIED) (990.00).

Additional factor: number of workers supervised.

950.98 Trainee

Performs, under instruction or guidance, various tasks including training exercises and as appropriate pursues studies in order to acquire the basic skills and knowledge required to perform the tasks of foremen (transport operating, materials moving and storing and related occupations not elsewhere classified).

950.99 Other foremen (transport operating, materials moving and storing and related occupations not elsewhere classified)

Workers in this group directly supervise and co-ordinate the activities of workers in transport operating, materials moving and storing and related occupations and are not separately classified, for example:

(01) **Coal yard foremen;** (02) **Foremen (refuse collection)**; (03) **Reception foremen (dairy, milk products manufacture.**

Additional factor: number of workers supervised.

Unit Group 951 Storekeepers, Warehousemen

Workers in this unit group store, select and issue materials, goods, equipment, furniture, freight, baggage and other items and maintain stock records.

Excluded are Stock records clerks (314.15), Attendants of personal property (459.35) and Property masters (479.10)

951.05 Storekeeper (industrial)

Checks materials, goods, equipment and other items into and/or out of stockyard, stockroom or warehouse of industrial establishment and maintains stock and stock records

Performs a combination of the following tasks: checks receipt of incoming raw materials, semi-manufactured items and general stores from outside suppliers and/or finished parts or articles from production departments; records receipt of all items; stores or directs storage of items in appropriate section of stockyard, stockroom or warehouse; issues materials, parts, tools, equipment, drawings, etc to departments against requisitions; selects appropriate items of finished stock to make up customers' orders and arranges for dispatch; maintains stock records of all items in store.

May (01) assist with loading and unloading of materials, goods, equipment and other items
(02) specialise on a particular section of stores, eg goods inward, finished goods, goods outward, tools
(03) use mechanical aids such as fork lift trucks, hoists or conveyors.

Additional factor: industry in which employed, eg engineering, building, chemicals, textiles.

Other titles include Storeman, Warehouseman.

951.10 Warehouseman (furniture depository)

Checks furniture and household articles into and out of furniture depository and ensures proper storage

Supervises unloading of furniture and household articles from vans; checks items against inventories provided or prepares inventories; notes any losses or damage; prepares articles for storage, dismantling furniture as required and wrapping mirrors, glassware, carpets and soft furnishings to prevent damage; allots storage space and supervises storage of articles, ensuring that space is used as economically as possible; checks condition of stored furniture periodically and ensures that warehouse temperature is maintained at required level; when articles are to be withdrawn from storage, removes wrappings and re-assembles dismantled articles; packs articles for transit by road, rail or sea as required.

May (01) assist with loading, unloading and stowing of articles
(02) prepare catalogue of items for auction.

951.15 Baggage master

Arranges stowage and discharge of seagoing or air passengers' baggage and storage of baggage in ship's or aircraft's hold or baggage room

Supervises the sorting of passengers' baggage for hold, baggage room or cabins; directs segregation of baggage for hold or baggage room by destination; checks baggage for damage caused by handling; supervises stowage of baggage in hold or baggage room.

On board ship, supervises distribution of baggage to passengers' cabins by stewards; investigates losses of baggage reported by passengers; collects any charges from passengers relating to carriage or insurance of baggage; arranges for care of animals during voyage and prepares relevant documents required by authorities at foreign ports; advises passengers on customs formalities and on completion of declaration forms; ensures that appropriate baggage is assembled at each port of disembarkation; maintains records of baggage and livestock carried.

On board aircraft, ensures that baggage, mail and cargo are stowed in accordance with load distribution form; records weight of baggage, mail and cargo loaded in each hold; covers and secures loads.

Supervises discharge of baggage.

951.20 Cellarman

Stores and maintains stocks of alcoholic and non-alcoholic beverages in catering and other establishments

Checks and stores new deliveries of alcoholic and non-alcoholic beverages; records and arranges return of chargeable empty containers; ensures that wines, beers and other stock are kept at required temperatures; issues stocks to bars according to requisitions, ensuring that beer stocks are used in order of delivery, and records issues; orders or prepares estimates of new stocks required; connects pipes from beer machines in bar to barrels in cellar and changes over to other barrels as required; cleans pipes from beer machines at regular intervals; ensures that cellar is kept clean and tidy and at all times secure.

May (01) maintain stocks of dry stores such as tinned goods, cigarettes and drinking glasses.

See 433.10 for cellarmen who also undertake the duties of barmen.

951 .25 Timber tallyman

Checks timber into and out of timber yard and maintains stock records

Checks receipt and verifies measurements of incoming timber; calculates amount of timber required for stacks of specified size; stacks or directs stacking of timber according to size and quality; selects and measures timber for machining or to make up customers' orders; loads or directs loading of timber on to vehicles for dispatch; maintains stock records.

951 .50 Warehouseman (wholesale, retail distribution)

Checks goods into and/or out of warehouse or stockroom of wholesale or retail distributive establishment and maintains stock and stock records

Performs a combination of the following tasks: unloads or directs unloading of goods from vehicles; checks goods against invoices; stores or directs storage of goods in appropriate section of warehouse or stockroom; records receipt of goods; makes up orders against requisitions from customers, branches or departments; loads or directs loading of orders on to lorries or internal transport; arranges for goods to be taken to internal departments; records issue and dispatch of goods; maintains stock records of all items in store.

May (01) store and issue general items such as cleaning materials, staff overalls or office requisites
(02) specialise in a particular type of goods, eg foodstuffs, clothing, hardware
(03) specialise in a particular section of warehouse or stockroom, eg goods inward, dispatch
(04) use mechanical aids such as fork lift trucks, hoists or conveyors.

Additional factor: experience of cold storage work.

951 .55 Storekeeper (excluding industrial)

Checks materials, goods, equipment and other items into and out of stores department, other than in industry or distribution, and maintains stock and stock records

Checks receipt of incoming materials, goods, equipment, etc; records receipt of all items and stores or directs storage of items in appropriate section of storeroom; issues materials, equipment or other items to individuals or departments against requisitions and records issue; maintains stock records of all items in store.

May (01) assist with loading and unloading of goods
(02) use mechanical aids such as fork lift trucks, hoists or conveyors.

Additional factor: type of goods to which accustomed, eg foodstuffs, stationery, medical and surgical supplies.

Other titles include Catering storeman, Shore steward, Storekeeper (hospital), Storekeeper (ship) (excluding engine room).

Excluded are Engine room storekeepers (seagoing) (910 .30) and Linen keepers (951 .60)

951 .60 Linen keeper

Stores and maintains domestic linen in hotel, hospital or similar establishment

Issues clean linen such as table linen, bed linen, towels and staff overalls to replace soiled linen brought to linen room; records items of linen received and issued; packs soiled linen for laundry collection and prepares laundry lists; checks returned laundry for cleanliness, shortages and damage and resolves complaints with laundry; stores laundered articles on racks or in cupboards; repairs or supervises repair of linen; examines stock periodically and discards unusable items; orders or prepares estimates of new linen required; stamps or sews identification marks on articles.

May (01) repair or supervise repair of soft furnishings such as loose covers or curtains
(02) make dish towels, table-cloths or staff overalls.

Other titles include Linen maid, Linen storeman.

951 .65 Lampman (mining)

Stores, maintains and issues electric and safety lamps used in mines

Fills oil lamps used for detecting gas and charges electric lamps; cleans and tests lamps and makes, or arranges for, any necessary repairs; tops up battery cells with distilled water; issues numbered lamps to persons going underground to correspond with numbered identity tokens; retains tokens while lamps are in use and re-issues tokens when lamps are returned; maintains records of issue and return of lamps; notifies management where tokens are still held at end of shift and reason for persons remaining underground is unknown.

Other titles include Lamp room attendant.

951.90 Warehouseman (freight)

Checks freight into and out of warehouse at transport depot, airport or docks

Checks freight off-loaded from vehicles, aircraft or ships against consignment notes, air way-bills, etc; opens consignments of freight for customs examination as required and secures after examination; stows or directs stowage of freight in appropriate section of warehouse according to type and destination; stows freight such as precious metals, watches, cameras or spirits in strong room; assembles freight for dispatch against delivery notes, cargo manifests, etc; loads or directs loading of assembled freight on to vehicles for dispatch or for carriage to aircraft or ships; maintains records of receipt and dispatch of freight.

May (01) operate automatic or semi-automatic control systems to perform warehousing operations

(02) use mechanical aids such as fork lift trucks, hoists, conveyors, stacker cranes or pallet and container transporters.

Additional factor: whether accustomed to utilising a computer for information on storage and movement of freight.

Other titles include Warehouseman (cargo).

951.92 Intakeman (grain, sugar and similar materials)

Checks supplies of grain, sugar and similar materials into storage silos, transfers materials to processing departments and maintains stock records

Operates suction plant, conveyors or elevators to transfer bulk grain, sugar, etc from transport to storage silos or checks the tipping of bulk materials or the unloading of materials in sacks from transport; ensures that materials are dry enough for storage; records amounts of materials received; operates suction plant, conveyors or elevators to transfer required amounts of materials from storage to processing departments; records amounts of materials transferred; clears blockages and spillages and keeps work area clean.

May (01) undertake day-to-day maintenance of machinery.

Other titles include Siloman.

951.94 Fuel issuer (transport depot)

Refuels company motor vehicles in garage or transport depot and maintains records

Checks level of fuel in vehicle tank and fills up tank with required quantity of petrol or diesel fuel; checks level of oil in engine sump and tops up as required; records quantities of fuel and oil issued; checks and records amounts of incoming supplies.

Other titles include Petrol pumpman.

See Petrol service station attendant (361.92)

951.98 Trainee

Performs, under instruction or guidance, various tasks including training exercises and as appropriate pursues studies in order to acquire the basic skills and knowledge required to perform the tasks of storekeepers and warehousemen.

951.99 Other storekeepers, warehousemen

Workers in this group store, select and issue materials, goods, equipment, furniture, freight, baggage and other items and maintain stock records and are not elsewhere classified, for example:

(01) **Countermen (wet, dry)** (weigh and issue bulk quantities of liquid or solid drugs and medicines for packing); (02) **Customs attendants** (select samples of goods from cases, crates or other containers in warehouse for customs examination and repack goods after examination as required); (03) **Lookers-out (ophthalmic lenses)** (select appropriate lenses from stock according to prescription requirements); (04) **Supports checkers (coalmining)**, Supports recovery checkers (coalmining) (check supplies of supports to coal face and recovery of supports from coal face).

Unit Group 952 Stevedores, Dockers and Related Occupations

Workers in this unit group load cargoes on to and discharge cargoes from ships, boats and barges, supply berthed ships with water and perform related tasks.

952.10 Docker

Loads and unloads ships' cargoes

Performs a combination of the following tasks: arranges cargo on quayside or in hold for loading or unloading using small mobile cranes, mechanical bogies and fork lift trucks as required; fixes slings, hooks, clamps or ropes to cargo ready for lifting; signals crane driver when load is ready for lifting or operates winch or derrick to lift cargo from or into hold; guides cargo being moved; removes slings, hooks, clamps or ropes from cargo after loading or unloading; stows cargo in hold; loads items of cargo on to lorries or railway wagons or stacks in warehouses.

If handling bulk cargoes such as grain, sugar or cement, connects suction hoses to ship's flow connections; starts pump to load or discharge cargo; uncouples hose system when loading or discharging has been completed.

Additional factors: type(s) of cargo to which accustomed; mechanical handling equipment to which accustomed.

Other titles include Dock labourer, Stevedore.

Note: in some ports the title Stevedore relates to workers on board ship only.

See Crane slinger (942.76)

Excluded are Goods porters (canal) (952.20)

952.20 Goods porter (canal)

Loads and unloads barge and boat cargoes at canal wharves

Performs a combination of tasks as described under DOCKER (952.10) but in relation to barge and boat cargoes at canal wharves.

952.30 Jetty operator (bulk liquids, gases)

Loads and discharges oil, petroleum, liquefied gases or other bulk liquid cargoes

Performs a combination of the following tasks: prepares hose couplings; operates crane to lift hoses; connects hoses to ship's flow connections; adjusts hoses to allow for ship's rise and fall with tide; starts pump to transfer oil or petroleum to or from ship; checks pressure gauges and records readings; checks hoses and valves for leaks and failures during pumping operation; uncouples hose system when loading or discharging has been completed.

Other titles include Jetty hand.

See Tanker filler (liquids, gases) (949.50) and Valveman (972.50)

952.40 Fish lumper

Unloads fish from fishing vessels

Performs a combination of the following tasks: removes hatch covers from holds containing fish (fishrooms); loads fish into baskets; attaches winch hook or rope to loaded baskets; operates winch to hoist loaded baskets from hold; transfers baskets from ship to quayside; transports baskets of fish to fish market or auction area; sorts fish by species and size; loads fish from baskets to metal containers (kits); attaches hook or rope to empty baskets; lowers empty baskets into hold.

Other titles include Bobber.

952.50 Dock waterman

Supplies berthed ships with water

Connects hoses to shore water supply outlets and to ship's intake fittings; opens valves to start flow of water to ship; operates stopcock to regulate flow of water; checks hoses, pipes and valves for leaks during watering; turns off supply on completion of watering and disconnects hoses and pipes; records amount of water supplied to ship; assists with repair of canvas hose pipes.

See Turncock (972.60)

952.98 Trainee

Performs, under instruction or guidance, various tasks including training exercises and as appropriate pursues studies in order to acquire the basic skills and knowledge required to perform the tasks of stevedores, dockers and related occupations.

952.99 Other stevedores, dockers and related occupations

Workers in this group load and unload waterborne cargoes and perform related tasks and are not elsewhere classified, for example:

(01) **Car lashers** (guide vehicles on and off car ferries, including hovercraft, and make secure); (02) **Coal trimmers** (distribute coal evenly in ships' holds or bunkers); (03) **Rafters** (rope together floated timber to form rafts).

Unit Group 959 Other Transport Operating, Materials Moving and Storing and Related Occupations

Workers in this unit group convey materials, goods and equipment about work areas, move furniture from and to premises, direct the movement of aircraft by visual signals, carry passengers' baggage at docks and air terminals, load and unload vehicles, unload ceramic goods from kilns and ovens, collect refuse from premises and perform other miscellaneous transport operating, materials storing and moving tasks and are not elsewhere classified.

959 .10 Furniture remover

Moves household and office furniture and effects to, from or about premises or furniture depository

Packs china, glassware and small articles into tea chests or cartons as required; dismantles articles of furniture too unwieldy or heavy to move in one piece; removes any structural fittings such as doors, which would obstruct the passage of large objects; lifts floor coverings, conveys articles to internal transport or removal van using trolleys, rollers or lifting tackle as required; stows articles on transport compactly, distributing weight evenly and covers with protective wrappings as required; makes good any structural dismantling; accompanies transport to destination and unloads contents, placing furniture, etc in rooms or storage areas as required; re-assembles dismantled articles and unpacks chests and cartons.

959 .50 Porter (warehouse, store, shop, market, slaughterhouse)

Loads, unloads and/or conveys materials, goods or equipment within or near warehouse, store, goods depot, shop, market or slaughterhouse

Performs one or more of the following tasks: loads goods, materials, or equipment on to, and unloads goods, etc from, road or rail transport; conveys goods about storage areas, stalls, counters, etc manually or using hand trucks; stacks goods in storage areas.

May (01) checks goods against invoices
(02) use mechanical aids such as powered trucks, hoists or conveyors
(03) weigh carcasses and record weight.

Additional factors: type of establishment in which accustomed, eg market, retail store, goods depot, furniture depository, slaughterhouse; type of goods or produce to which accustomed, eg meat, fruit, flowers, textiles, engineering products.

Other titles include Fish porter, Flower porter, Fruit porter, Furniture porter, Meat humper, Meat porter, Stores labourer.

Excluded are workers operating crane, hoist and other materials handling equipment (942)

959 .55 Materials handler (works)

Conveys materials, goods or equipment to, from or about work areas in an industrial establishment

Performs one or more of the following tasks: conveys materials, goods and equipment from stores to work areas manually or using hand trucks; conveys materials, goods and equipment from one machine to another or from one work area to another; stacks materials or goods; collects scrap and waste materials and removes from work areas.

May (01) use mechanical aids such as powered trucks, hoists or conveyors.

Other titles include Bobbin carrier, Glass carrier, Lap carrier, Smudger, Supplies transporter (coal-mine), Timber stacker, Ware carrier (pottery manufacture), Waste collector Works porter.

Excluded are workers operating crane, hoist and other materials handling equipment (942)

959 .60 Aircraft marshaller

Directs by visual signals the movement of aircraft arriving at, moving across or departing from an aerodrome

Receives from ground movement controller (aerodrome) information and instructions concerning the movement of aircraft using aerodrome; conveys movement instructions to pilot-in-command by approved visual signals using fluorescent bats or battery illuminated rods; ensures that ample space is left between parked aircraft and between aircraft and aerodrome buildings.

May (01) precede moving aircraft in motor vehicle in radio contact with ground movement controller (aerodrome).

959 .65 Loader (vehicle, aircraft)

Loads goods, materials, equipment on to or into vehicles (including container units) or aircraft and/or unloads goods, materials or equipment from vehicles or aircraft

continued

Performs a combination of the following tasks: loads goods, materials or equipment on to or into vehicles (including container units) or aircraft manually or using lifting equipment; stows goods, etc compactly, distributing weight evenly; covers load and/or secures with ropes as required; unloads goods, etc from vehicles or aircraft manually or using lifting equipment; stacks unloaded goods, etc for removal to storage area or transfers goods, etc to storage area manually, by loading on conveyor or using hand or powered trucks; checks goods, etc against invoices or consignment notes.

959.70 Baggage porter (docks, air terminal)

Carries baggage for passengers at docks or air terminal

Collects passengers' baggage at docks or air terminal; conveys baggage manually or by hand truck to check-in-area, to customs department, to freight department for weighing and labelling as required, to outside transport such as coach or private car or to loading point for ship or plane; assists handicapped passengers, for example, by pushing wheelchairs.

May (01) weigh and label baggage.

959.75 Loader (wagon, mine car or similar container), Tub manipulator

Fills and/or empties wagons, tubs, mine cars or similar containers manually and/or manually controls movement of wagons, tubs or mine cars

Performs one or more of the following tasks: shovels mined, quarried or similar raw materials into wagons, tubs, mine cars, hoppers or similar containers; manually releases trap door, wagon side or similar barrier to allow materials to flow from holding containers into other containers for storage or transportation; pushes full or empty containers between work areas; controls movement of containers by operating brake levers or by inserting pieces of wood or metal (sprags, scotches) between wheel spokes.

Other titles include Emptier, Filler (mining, quarrying), Spragger, Trammer (mining, quarrying), Wagon tipper (manual).

Excluded are Shunters (923.50)

959.80 Kiln unloader (ceramics goods)

Removes fired pottery, bricks, tiles or refractory goods from kilns or kiln cars and conveys fired articles to appropriate departments

Performs a combination of the following tasks: removes items of pottery, bricks, tiles or refractory goods from kilns after firing; removes fired articles and kiln furniture from kiln cars; loads fired articles on to barrows, trucks or conveyor belt; conveys articles on barrows or trucks to storage area or to other departments for inspection or further processing.

May (01) remove fired articles from kilns using fork lift truck (942.62).

Other titles include Kiln drawer, Kiln emptier, Oven emptier, Ware emptier.

959.85 Refuse collector

Collects refuse from business and private premises and loads it into refuse vehicle

Conveys rubbish and waste material in dustbins or other containers from premises to refuse vehicle manually or using trolley; empties rubbish and waste material into vehicle manually or secures bin to mechanical tipping device and operates controls to tip contents into vehicle; returns bins to premises.

May (01) undertake general labouring tasks at refuse tip
(02) drive refuse vehicle.

Other titles include Dustman.

959.98 Trainee

Performs, under instruction or guidance, various tasks including training exercises and as appropriate pursues studies in order to acquire the basic skills and knowledge required to perform the tasks of workers in transport operating, materials moving and storing and related occupations.

959.99 Other transport operating, materials moving and storing and related occupations not elsewhere classified

Workers in this group perform miscellaneous transport operating, materials storing and moving tasks and are not separately classified, for example:

(01) **Apron controllers** (control the movement of aircraft on aerodrome apron and allot stands); (02) **Coke wharfmen** (manually operate gates to release supplies of coke from coke cooling bunker (wharf) on to conveyor belts for feeding to screening plants or blast furnaces); (03) **Linen porters.**

MAJOR GROUP XVIII

Miscellaneous Occupations

Workers in this major group operate machinery, plant and equipment to generate power and to control the movement of gases, liquids and materials through pipes, operate and attend other electrical and electronic machinery and equipment, and perform labouring and other routine tasks of a general nature and other miscellaneous tasks and are not elsewhere classified.

The occupations are arranged in the following minor groups:

97 Machinery, Plant and Equipment Operating Occupations Not Elsewhere Classified

99 Miscellaneous Occupations Not Elsewhere Classified

Minor Group 97 MACHINERY, PLANT AND EQUIPMENT OPERATING OCCUPATIONS NOT ELSEWHERE CLASSIFIED

Workers in this minor group operate equipment to produce electricity and control its distribution, operate boilers to produce steam power and hot water, operate valves to control the movement of gases, liquids, powders and granulated materials through pipes, and operate and attend stationary engines, turbines, compressors, pumps, vehicle and container washing machines and attend electricity switchboards and other equipment and are not elsewhere classified.

The occupations are arranged in the following unit groups:

970 Foremen (Machinery, Plant and Equipment Operating Occupations Not Elsewhere Classified)

971 Boiler and Power Generating Machinery Operating Occupations

972 Valvemen, Turncocks and Related Occupations

973 Electricity Switchboard Attending Occupations

979 Other Machinery, Plant and Equipment Operating Occupations

See materials handling equipment operating occupations (949)

Unit Group 970 Foremen (Machinery, Plant and Equipment Operating Occupations Not Elsewhere Classified)

Workers in this unit group directly supervise and co-ordinate the activities of workers operating machinery, plant and equipment and are not elsewhere classified.

970.10 Foreman (boiler and power generating machinery operating occupations)

Directly supervises and co-ordinates the activities of workers in boiler and power generating machinery operating occupations

Performs appropriate tasks as described under SUPERVISOR/FOREMAN (UNSPECIFIED) (990.00).

Additional factor: number of workers supervised.

970.20 Foreman (valvemen, turncocks and related occupations)

Directly supervises and co-ordinates the activities of valvemen, turncocks and workers in related occupations

Performs appropriate tasks as described under SUPERVISOR/FOREMAN (UNSPECIFIED) (990.00).

Additional factor: number of workers supervised.

970.30 Foreman (electrical switchboard attending occupations)

Directly supervises and co-ordinates the activities of workers in electrical switchboard attending occupations

Performs appropriate tasks as described under SUPERVISOR/FOREMAN (UNSPECIFIED) (990.00).

Additional factor: number of workers supervised.

970.98 Trainee

Performs, under instruction or guidance, various tasks including training exercises and as appropriate pursues studies in order to acquire the basic skills and knowledge required to perform the tasks of foremen (machinery, plant and equipment operating occupations not elsewhere classified).

970.99 Other foremen (machinery, plant and equipment operating occupations not elsewhere classified)

Workers in this group directly supervise and co-ordinate the activities of workers operating machinery, plant and equipment and are not separately classified.

Unit Group 971 Boiler and Power Generating Machinery Operating Occupations

Workers in this unit group operate boilers, compressors, turbines and other machinery to produce hot water and steam, to fuel nuclear reactors and to drive blowers, pumps, electricity generators and other equipment.

Included are incinerator operating occupations.

971.05 Plant operator (nuclear generating station)

Operates machinery to load fuel into nuclear reactors and transfer fuel to storage, and controls or directs the control of auxiliary plant such as pumps and blowers

Performs some or all of the following tasks: operates machine by remote control to load fuel elements into reactor; removes discharged fuel elements by remote control from reactor and transfers to cooling storage pond; seals fuel elements into metal containers under water by remote control; operates machine to move containers around cooling pond and into shielded boxes (flasks); removes flasks from pond using lifting equipment; decontaminates exterior surfaces of flasks and prepares for loading and dispatch; operates pneumatic and hydraulic equipment to clean turbo-alternators, condensers and coolers; watches instruments recording temperatures, pressures and tank levels and records readings periodically; operates controls regulating pumps and blowers supplying cooling liquids and gases to reactor, boilers and auxiliary equipment; reports faulty equipment to foreman; directs the activities of plant attendants.

May (01) perform tasks of TURBINE OPERATOR (971.20)

(02) oil and grease mechanical parts of machinery and equipment.

Additional factor: size (in kilowatts) of generating unit.

971 .10 Unit operator (power station)

Controls the operation of electricity generating unit(s) comprising boiler, turbo-generator and auxiliary plant

Ascertains job requirements from operating instructions or from switchboard attendant; operates or directs the operation of valves and controls to start generating unit or takes over unit in operation; watches instruments and gauges indicating conditions affecting the operation and output of boilers, turbines and auxiliary plant; adjusts or directs adjustment of control mechanisms manually or by remote control; takes appropriate action to correct minor faults or to effect shut down of equipment; records instrument readings periodically; prepares reports as required.

Additional factors: size (in kilowatts) of generating unit; number of units controlled.

971 .15 Boiler operator (steam generating)

Operates one or more boiler(s) to produce steam for central heating systems and industrial use

If operating solid fuel boilers, opens feed gate from fuel bunker, starts mechanical stoking device and operates controls to adjust speed of stoking; if operating gas or oil fired boilers, adjusts valves and pumps to control flow of fuel; checks water level in boiler and adjusts valves and pumps to control water feed; switches on forced draught blowers and ignites fuel; opens output valve when steam pressure has reached specified level; watches meters and gauges recording temperature, pressure and other conditions affecting the operation of boiler plant and adjusts controls to maintain required output; regulates smoke emission to comply with clean air regulations; shuts down boiler(s) as directed; records instrument readings periodically.

May (01) oil and grease mechanical parts of boiler(s) and carry out minor repairs

(02) clean oil burners

(03) operate stand-by equipment in emergency or carry out stoking or pumping operations manually.

Additional factor: type, size and number of boilers operated.

Other titles include Boiler fireman, Stoker.

See Boiler operator (hot water supply) (971 .92)

Excluded are Firemen (seagoing) (911 .50), Stokers (seagoing) (911 .50) and Locomotive firemen (921 .20)

971 .20 Turbine operator

Operates one or more steam, gas or water driven turbine(s) to drive equipment such as electricity generators, forced draught blowers or compressors

Ascertains job requirements from operating instructions or from switchboard attendant; opens valves to admit steam, fuel or flow of water to start turbine(s) or takes over turbine in operation; adjusts valves to maintain correct running speed of turbine or checks automatic speed control equipment to ensure that power output is consistent with requirements; watches meters and gauges recording temperatures, pressures and other conditions affecting the operation of the equipment; records instrument readings periodically; closes valves to shut off steam, fuel or water supply and decrease power output or to cut out faulty generating units; cleans and lubricates equipment and carries out minor running repairs such as repacking valve glands and repairing air pumps; reports faults to foreman.

May (01) maintain emergency turbo-generator in operational condition.

Additional factors: size (in kilowatts) of generating unit; number of turbines operated.

Other titles include Turbo-blower operator.

971 .50 Stationary engine driver

Operates stationary engine to drive industrial or other plant or equipment

Starts engine and adjusts controls to maintain specified operating conditions; watches instruments and gauges indicating engine's performance and adjusts controls as necessary; records instrument readings periodically; reports marked variations in readings and faults on equipment to foreman; cleans, oils and greases engine as required and carries out minor adjustments and running repairs.

971 .55 Assistant unit operator (power station)

Assists unit operator to control the operation of electricity generating unit(s) comprising boiler, turbo-generator and auxiliary plant

Performs as directed some or all of the tasks described under UNIT OPERATOR (971 .10); cleans and lubricates equipment; reverts to manual operation of equipment during emergency; directs the activities of auxiliary plant attendants.

Additional factor: size (in kilowatts) of generating unit.

971 .60 Gas compressor operator

Operates one or more compressor(s) to compress, recover or move atmospheric or other gases

Starts compressor power unit as directed, watches instruments and gauges, and adjusts controls to regulate flow rate, pressure and temperature of gas; reports marked variations, leaks or blockages in feed pipes or faults in equipment to foreman; cleans, oils and greases power unit(s) as required and carries out minor adjustments and running repairs.

May (01) assist chemical processing plant operator to produce gases from the atmosphere

(02) operate pump(s) to assist the transfer of gases to processing plant, storage tanks or container filling equipment

(03) open valve(s) to release excess moisture from pipelines

(04) fill small containers with gas from storage tanks (841 .05)

(05) record instrument readings.

Additional factor: number of compressors operated.

Other titles include Booster attendant, Compressor attendant.

971 .90 Air compressor operator

Operates and services compressor unit to generate and supply compressed air for pneumatic tools, hoists or other equipment

Opens air release valve of compressor unit and starts engine; closes air release valve and builds up specified air pressure in compression chamber; sets automatic pressure control mechanism and opens supply valve(s); watches meters and gauges recording pressure, temperature and other conditions affecting the operation of compressor unit and adjusts controls as necessary; connects flexible pipeline(s) from compressor unit to pneumatic equipment as necessary; cleans and oils equipment and carries out running repairs; reports major faults to foreman.

May (01) operate pneumatic tools or other equipment

(02) drive vehicle carrying mobile compressors to operational site.

971 .91 Crematorium furnace attendant

Operates furnace in which human bodies are cremated

Slides coffin containing body into furnace; ignites furnace and regulates fuel and air supplies to raise temperature to prescribed level and to maintain the temperature for required period; removes ashes and cremated remains not fully reduced; crushes the remains to powder in pulverising machine; places all ashes in casket for subsequent disposal and attaches identification details.

May (01) strew ashes in garden of remembrance

(02) clean furnace room and equipment

(03) make minor repairs to furnace and ancillary equipment.

Other titles include Cremator operator.

See Heat Treating Occupations Not Elsewhere Classified (591)

971 .92 Boiler operator (hot water supply)

Operates one or more boiler(s) to produce hot water for central heating systems, hot water supplies or industrial processes

If operating solid fuel boilers, opens feed gate from fuel bunker, starts mechanical stoking device and operates controls to adjust fuel flow or shovels solid fuel manually into fire box; if operating gas or oil fired boilers, adjusts valves and pumps to control flow of fuel; checks water level in boiler; switches on forced draught blower as necessary and ignites fuel; opens output valve when water has reached specified temperature and starts circulating pump; watches meters and gauges recording temperature, pressure and other conditions affecting the operation of the boiler and adjusts controls to maintain specified temperature; cleans boiler and removes clinker and ash as necessary; regulates smoke emission to comply with clean air regulations; shuts down boiler(s) as directed.

May (01) oil and grease mechanical parts of boiler(s) and carry out minor repairs

(02) clean oil burners

(03) descale boilers

(04) attend auxiliary plant such as pumps, blowers, etc.

Additional factor: type, size and number of boilers operated.

Other titles include Boiler fireman, Stoker.

See Boiler operator (steam generating) (971 .15)

971.93 Incinerator operator

Controls equipment to burn waste material in incinerator plant

Feeds or directs feeding of refuse or other waste material into furnace with shovel or using conveyor or mechanical grab; switches on forced draught blower as necessary; ignites waste material and regulates draught to maintain combustion; breaks up material and clinker in furnace using long poker and rake; rakes ash from grate manually or operates levers to transfer ash on to conveyor.

May (01) operate water sprinkler to cool and settle ash

(02) operate hot water boiler using heat from incinerator (971.92).

Other titles include Destructor stoker.

971.98 Trainee

Performs, under instruction or guidance, various tasks including training exercises and as appropriate pursues studies in order to acquire the basic skills and knowledge required to perform the tasks of workers in boiler and power generating machinery operating occupations.

971.99 Other boiler and power generating machinery operating occupations

Workers in this group operate boilers, compressors, turbines and other machinery to produce hot water and steam, to fuel nuclear reactors and to drive equipment and are not elsewhere classified, for example:

(01) **Fixed diesel engine operators** (start and control diesel engines to drive electricity generators);

(02) **Mobile power generating plant operators** (operate mobile generators to supply electricity for equipment such as electric welding units and auxiliary lighting units).

Unit Group 972 Valvemen, Turncocks and Related Occupations

Workers in this unit group operate valves to control the supply and movement of gases, liquids, powders and granulated substances through pipes.

Excluded are Jetty operators (bulk liquids, gases) (952.30)

972.10 Control room operator (gas supply)

Operates valves to control the supply of gas to gas holders and distribution mains

Watches meters and gauges on control panel showing pressure, temperature and volume of gas and whether valves and pumps are functioning correctly; operates controls to adjust valves to vary the rate of flow and pressure of gas according to requirements; reports faults and serious fluctuations in readings to foreman; records instrument readings periodically.

972.50 Valveman (materials flow)

Operates valves to control the supply of gases, liquids, powders and/or granulated materials through pipes

Operates controls to open valve(s) and start flow of material through pipe(s); adjusts valve(s) to vary rate of flow according to requirements; closes valve(s) to stop flow as required; checks valve(s) and pipe(s) for leaks and reports defects to foreman.

May (01) watch meters and gauges recording rate of flow, pressure, quantity, temperature, etc

(02) clean pipe(s) by injecting steam or detergent, or by controlling movement and recovery of mechanical cleaning device

(03) withdraw sample of materials for testing

(04) operate or direct the operation of filtering equipment

(05) perform tasks of PUMPMAN (979.50)

(06) operate valve(s) from central control panel.

Other titles include Condenser attendant, Waterman.

See Jetty operator (bulk liquids, gases) (952.30)

Excluded are Control room operators (gas supply) (972.10) and Turncocks (972.60)

972.60 Turncock

Operates valves to control the water supply in mains and pipelines

Opens and closes valves, using valve key, to regulate quantity and pressure of water in a district or to particular premises; reports to foreman abnormal water pressure, defective valves, leaks, dirty water or any other conditions which might endanger the water supply or cause wastage; attends fire with fire fighting crew to control water mains and produce maximum volume and pressure of water; closes valves to stop the supply of water in an emergency, or during the servicing or repair of mains and pipelines; notifies consumers likely to be affected by interruption of supply; inspects restoration of road surfaces and water apparatus in street; opens valves to flush out rust and dirt and to recharge mains and pipelines on completion of servicing or repair.

May (01) perform tasks as described under WASTE PREVENTION INSPECTOR (WATER SUPPLY) (869.34) and be known as Waterman.

See Dock waterman (952.50)

972.98 Trainee

Performs, under instruction or guidance, various tasks including training exercises and as appropriate pursues studies in order to acquire the basic skills and knowledge required to perform the tasks of valvemen, turncocks and workers in related occupations.

972.99 Other valvemen, turncocks and related occupations

Workers in this group operate valves to control the supply and movement of gases, liquids, powders and granulated substances through pipes and are not elsewhere classified.

Unit Group 973 Electricity Switchboard Attending Occupations

Workers in this unit group operate equipment to control the power output and distribution of electricity from power stations and substations.

973.10 Switchboard attendant (electricity supply)

Operates main and auxiliary switchboards to regulate the output and supply of electricity from generating plant to distribution system

Operates switches to start or notifies unit or turbine operator to start generator and bring to operating speed; watches indicators and synchroscope and operates controls to synchronise speed of generator with units already in operation and to match output voltage and frequency; operates switches to connect electricity supply to distribution system and ensures that output is sufficient to meet demand; disconnects supply generators as demand decreases; carries out prescribed checks on equipment and watches instruments to check that equipment is operating efficiently; records instrument readings periodically; notifies foreman of faults affecting output.

May (01) isolate and earth equipment to be serviced or repaired.

Additional factor: type and size (in kilowatts) of switchboard.

973.50 Substation attendant (electricity supply)

Operates and attends equipment at one or more substations to regulate the supply and distribution of electricity

Operates switches as directed by foreman to regulate, interrupt or divert the supply of electricity to distribution mains; collects data from recording instruments and prepares reports; inspects and carries out prescribed checks on equipment and alarm systems and reports overheating of equipment or other faults to foreman; services or directs minor servicing of equipment and cleaning of substation.

May (01) operate auxiliary power generator during supply failure

(02) control a group of unmanned substations from control room in central substation.

973.98 Trainee

Performs, under instruction or guidance, various tasks including training exercises and as appropriate pursues studies in order to acquire the basic skills and knowledge required to perform the tasks of workers in electricity switchboard attending occupations.

973.99 Other electricity switchboard attending occupations

Workers in this group operate equipment to control the power output and distribution of electricity from power stations and substations and are not separately classified.

Unit Group 979 Other Machinery, Plant and Equipment Operating Occupations

Workers in this unit group operate and attend machinery, plant and equipment such as pumps, vehicle and container washing machines and cleaning machines and perform related tasks and are not elsewhere classified.

979.10 Auxiliary plant attendant (power generating)

Attends, cleans and oils mechanical equipment auxiliary to boilers, turbine plant(s) or nuclear reactors generating power

Starts up or takes over equipment such as coal and ash handling machinery, reactor auxiliaries, pumps, blowers, fans, compressors or condensers in operation, as directed by boiler operator, turbine operator, unit operator or plant operator; watches instruments and gauges to check that equipment is operating correctly; carries out prescribed tests and reports irregularities or faults to operator; oils and greases equipment, cleans pump strainers, flushes pipes, tightens leaking valve glands and carries out other minor maintenance tasks; shuts down equipment in prescribed sequence as directed.

May (01) repack valve glands

(02) record instrument readings.

Other titles include Plant attendant (nuclear generating station).

979.50 Pumpman

Attends one or more pumps to transfer gases, liquids, powders and granulated substances through pipes

Starts up or takes over pump(s) in operation; watches instruments and gauges and adjusts controls to maintain speed of pump(s) and to control pressure and flow rate; cleans, oils and greases pump(s) and carries out minor servicing and repairs; reports major faults to foreman; records instrument readings periodically.

May (01) operate hand pump in emergency

(02) maintain emergency pump(s) in operational condition

(03) perform tasks of VALVEMAN (972.50)

(04) drive mobile pump to remove condensed liquor from gas mains and be known as Syphon attendant.

Additional factor: number of pumps attended.

Other titles include Air pump attendant (diving), Exhauster man (coal-gas, coke oven), Pump attendant, Pumping station attendant, Slurry pump attendant, Still pumpman (distillery), Tankfield pumper.

Excluded are Pumpmen (seagoing) (910.20) and Jetty operators (bulk liquids, gases) (952.30)

979.55 Cylinder preparer

Prepares cylinders for filling with compressed acetylene gas

Performs some or all of the following tasks: places cylinder on machine and operates machine to feed absorbent material into cylinder to pack cylinder tightly; places cylinder in heated container, using lifting equipment as necessary, and bakes for specified time to remove moisture from absorbent material; adds more absorbent material as required and rams tight; renews metal plug in base of cylinder; cleans screw threads in neck of cylinder on valving machine and fits valve; operates machine to exhaust air in cylinder; operates machine to charge a prescribed amount of acetone into cylinder; charges cylinder with prescribed amount of low pressure acetylene gas ready for filling with compressed acetylene gas; fixes metal identification label to cylinder; weighs cylinder before and after each operation.

May (01) report weight of cylinder to control room staff after each operation

(02) paint cylinder.

Other titles include Acetoner.

979.60 Washing plant attendant (vehicles)

Attends plant to clean exteriors of vehicles such as rail carriages, omnibuses, coaches or motor cars

Closes doors, windows and ventilators of vehicle before vehicle enters washing plant; turns on water sprays and starts revolving brushes or other cleaning heads; signals to driver or operates controls to move vehicle slowly through plant where cleaning heads revolve against sides and top of vehicle and remove dirt; replaces worn cleaning heads as necessary; clears blockages in water sprays and drainage pits; cleans work area.

May (01) spray chemical detergent on to vehicle body to remove stubborn dirt

(02) dry surface and windows of vehicles by hand using wash-leather.

Other titles include Carriage washing machine attendant.

979.65 Washing machine attendant (containers)

Attends automatic or semi-automatic machine to clean and rinse containers such as bottles, casks and jars

Places containers on feed belt, in racks or other conveying equipment; ensures that level of water and detergent in tank is adequate or controls supply through taps and jets; adjusts temperature of water in tanks by injecting steam or hot or cold water as necessary; starts machine and conveyor and watches operation; reports faults to foreman.

May (01) mix washing solutions and feed solution into tank

(02) set brushes according to size of casks

(03) remove bungs from casks before washing, using hand tools

(04) adjust speed of conveyor through washing machine

(05) remove unclean and damaged containers after washing

(06) clean machine and remove waste material from sump.

Other titles include Barrel washer, Bottle washer, Bottle washing machine operator, Cask washer, Cask washing machine operator.

979.98 Trainee

Performs, under instruction or guidance, various tasks including training exercises and as appropriate pursues studies in order to acquire the basic skills and knowledge required to perform the tasks of workers in other machinery, plant and equipment operating occupations.

979.99 Other machinery, plant and equipment operating occupations not elsewhere classified

Workers in this group perform miscellaneous tasks in the operation of machinery, plant and equipment and are not separately classified, for example:

(01) **Bag cleaners,** Sack cleaners (hold open end of bags or sacks to mouth of suction cleaners which extract dust and dirt); (02) **Bulb washers** (feed automatic washing machines with glass bulbs or envelopes for electric lamp and electronic valve making); (03) **Duplicators (tape recordings)** (operate electronic equipment to reproduce a number of tape recordings from a master or original tape recording); (04) **Dust separating plant attendants** (attend and clean out electrostatic precipitators which remove dust from flue gases and smoke); (05) **Fanmen** (attend motor driven fans which ventilate underground workings, factories and buildings); (06) **Magnetic tape cleaners,** Sound erasers (feed and attend machines to erase information or sound from magnetic recording tapes); (07) **Mechanical sweeper operators** (operate machines fitted with rotating brushes and vacuum cleaner to remove dirt and refuse from factory floors, paths and similar large areas); (08) **Remote indication system attendants** (watch panels of coloured lights (mimic diagrams) showing state of operations of underground equipment in mine and report faults); (09) **Valvemen (other than materials flow)** (open and close valves to control the movement of equipment (eg moving bridge) on instructions from other workers).

Minor Group 99 MISCELLANEOUS OCCUPATIONS NOT ELSEWHERE CLASSIFIED

Workers in this minor group perform heavy and light manual tasks and other miscellaneous tasks and are not elsewhere classified.

The occupations are arranged in the following unit groups:

990 Supervisors and Foremen Not Elsewhere Classified

991 Labourers and General Hands Not Elsewhere Classified

999 Other Occupations

Unit Group 990 Supervisors and Foremen Not Elsewhere Classified

Workers in this unit group directly supervise and co-ordinate the activities of groups of workers and are not elsewhere classified.

990 .00 Supervisor (unspecified), Foreman (unspecified)

Directly supervises and co-ordinates the activities of a group of workers (unspecified)

Considers the work to be undertaken by the group; determines work priorities and procedures and assigns duties to workers; ensures that the quantity and quality of output of individual workers and the group as a whole is satisfactory and re-allocates workers and duties as necessary; maintains record of output; assists workers who encounter difficulties; keeps workers informed of management policies and ensures that company and other regulations are adhered to; informs manager of problems and suggestions arising from the work and advises on or effects the engagement, transfer, discharge and promotion of workers; liaises with other supervisors; trains workers; estimates, requisitions and inspects materials; confers with shop stewards or other workers' representatives to resolve grievances; ensures that plant or equipment is in good working order; progresses output on production, assists with rate fixing, liaises with, and oversees the work of, specialists and performs tasks similar to those of workers supervised, as required.

Additional factor: number of workers supervised.

Note: this definition is provided as a base definition for all supervisor/foreman occupations and the occupational number is not intended to be used when coding occupations.

990 .10 Supervisor (miscellaneous occupations not elsewhere classified), Foreman (miscellaneous occupations not elsewhere classified)

Directly supervises and co-ordinates the activities of workers in miscellaneous occupations not elsewhere classified

Performs appropriate tasks as described under SUPERVISOR/FOREMAN (UNSPECIFIED) (990 .00).

990 .20 Supervisor (occupations straddling major groups), Foreman (occupations straddling major groups)

Directly supervises and co-ordinates the activities of workers in occupations coded in more than one major group

Performs appropriate tasks as described under SUPERVISOR/FOREMAN (UNSPECIFIED) (990 .00).

Other titles include Ramp supervisor (airport).

990 .98 Trainee

Performs, under instruction or guidance, various tasks including training exercises and as appropriate pursues studies in order to acquire the basic skills and knowledge required to perform the tasks of supervisors and foremen not elsewhere classified.

Unit Group 991 Labourers and General Hands Not Elsewhere Classified

Workers in this unit group perform heavy and light manual tasks requiring a minimum of training and experience and are not elsewhere classified.

Notes: (*i*) *certain of the tasks included under Heavy labourer (not eslewhere classified) (991 .10) and Light labourer (not elsewhere classified) (991 .20) have been identified elsewhere as separate occupations. Workers whose duties are restricted to such tasks should be classified accordingly, for example Materials handler (works) (959 .55), Loader (vehicle, aircraft) (959 .65)*

(*ii*) *separate classifications have also been provided for certain labourers who perform tasks relating to particular areas of work, for example Furnace labourers in metal manufacture (719), Craftsmen's mates (776 and 868) and General labourers in building and civil engineering (868)*

991 .10 Heavy labourer (not elsewhere classified)

Performs one or more manual tasks requiring a minimum of training, little or no previous experience and considerable physical effort and is not elsewhere classified

Performs one or more of the following or similar tasks in relation to work of a heavy nature: conveys materials, equipment, goods, etc about work areas and stacks materials or goods; opens bales, crates or other containers manually; assists in setting up machinery or equipment; assists in loading materials on to or into, and unloading finished or processed materials or products from, machinery or equipment; provides general assistance to craftsmen, operators, machinery minders, etc as required; washes or cleans parts, components or finished articles, or crates or similar containers manually; clears machine blockages and cleans machinery, equipment and tools; loads and unloads vehicles, trucks, trolleys, etc; keeps work areas tidy and clears waste materials and spillages; disposes of waste materials by baling, tipping on waste heap, burning, etc.

Additional factor: whether accustomed to working outdoors or indoors.

Other titles include Bale opener (hand), Cleaner (machines, equipment), Condenser cleaner (zinc vertical retort), Conveyor plough attendant (coalmining), Door man (retort house), Door shutter (retort house), Drainman, General hand (airport), Packman (woollen carding), Poker-in (coke oven), Roughneck (drilling rig), Roustabout (drilling rig), Sheet opener (woollen carding), Topman (coke oven), Wet char man (sugar and glucose manufacture).

991.20 Light labourer (not elsewhere classified), Factory worker (general) (not elsewhere classified)

Performs one or more manual tasks requiring a minimum of training, little or no previous experience and little physical effort and is not elsewhere classified

Performs one or more of the following or similar tasks in relation to work of a light nature: conveys materials, equipment, goods, etc about work areas and stacks materials or goods; opens bales, crates or other containers manually; assists in setting up machinery or equipment; prepares equipment such as tools, laboratory apparatus and lamps for use; assists in loading materials on to or into, and unloading finished or processed materials or products from, machinery or equipment; provides general assistance to craftsmen, operators, machine minders, etc as required; washes or cleans parts, components or finished articles, or crates or similar containers manually; paints or fixes identification markings, labels, etc on products or containers; clears machine blockages and cleans machinery, equipment and tools; loads and unloads vehicles, trucks, trolleys, etc; keeps work areas tidy and clears waste materials and spillages; disposes of waste materials by baling, tipping on waste heap, burning, etc; sweeps and cleans paths, roadways, parking areas, etc; performs routine tasks in the maintenance of premises and grounds such as rough painting, washing windows and cutting grass.

Additional factor: whether accustomed to working indoors or outdoors.

Other titles include Bale opener (hand), Bottle washer (hand), Bulb washer (hand), Cleaner (machines, equipment), Laboratory attendant, Signal lampman, Waterman (coalmining), Wiper (cutlery, scissors making).

991.30 Stage hand

Moves scenery and other stage items required for theatrical productions before, during and after performances

Erects sets on stage for productions; moves scenery, furniture and properties on to and from stage during performances; lowers and raises scenery suspended on pulleys above stage; lowers and raises curtains; assists in operating stage and auditorium lighting as required; dismantles sets and clears stage at end of productions.

Other titles include Flyman, Scene shifter.

Unit Group 999 Other Occupations

Workers in this unit group perform miscellaneous tasks and are not elsewhere classified.

999.99 Other occupations not elsewhere classified

Workers in this group perform miscellaneous tasks and are not separately classified.

Printed in England for Her Majesty's Stationery Office by McCorquodale Printers London
HM 7969 Dd. 586239 K 8 1/78.